The Revelation Record

A Scientific and Devotional Commentary on the Book of Revelation

A Scientific and Devotional Commentary
on the Book of Revelation

Henry M. Morris

Tyndale House Publishers, Inc.
Wheaton, Illinois

Creation-Life Publishers
San Diego, California

Scripture references are from the
King James Version of the Bible.

This book is co-published by
Tyndale House Publishers, Inc., Wheaton, Illinois,
and Creation-Life Publishers, San Diego, California.

First printing, January 1983
Library of Congress Catalog Card Number 82-60016
ISBN 0-8423-5511-1, cloth; Tyndale House Publishers, Inc.
ISBN 0-89501-092-X, cloth; Creation-Life Publishers
Copyright © 1983 by Henry M. Morris
All rights reserved
Printed in the United States of America

Contents

Foreword

Through the years, many scholars have studied and written to show that the Bible is a reliable historical record. At the forefront of the struggle against the man-made philosophy of evolution, Dr. Henry Morris has consistently upheld the Bible as inerrant through unbiased, scientific investigation.

In his earlier work, *The Genesis Record,* Dr. Morris showed himself to be not only a man of great scientific knowledge but also a man of the Word, a scholar of the Scriptures. I am delighted to see him use the same literal approach to this devotional commentary on the Book of Revelation.

I agree with Dr. Morris' comment that *The Revelation Record* might be the most literal approach to this most difficult to understand portion of Scripture. I believe that it will offer the most understandable and valuable insights that you could read on this topic.

Jerry Falwell, Pastor
Thomas Road Baptist Church
Lynchburg, Virginia

Foreword

The book of Revelation never loses its fascination for the Christian. Not only is it a superbly fitting conclusion to the sixty-six-volume library of God's Word, but it provides the exciting dimension of foretelling the events of the future—a future that seems to be coming upon us all too rapidly.

There is no guarantee, of course, that we are the generation which our Lord predicted in Matthew 24, that would see all the end-time events foretold in detail in this book, but as we approach the twenty-first century, closing almost two millennia of the church age, it is likely that interest in the prophecies in this book will become more intense. Such was the case in 990 A.D. as our forefathers of the faith thought the year 1000 would usher in the Kingdom Age.

I predict that interest in our Lord Jesus Christ's coming will again increase as we approach the closing days of this century. Certainly we have more signs fulfilled than any generation before us, particularly those who lived a thousand years ago. In addition, we have experienced a thirty-year soul harvest unprecedented in the Western world. We have witnessed an incredible interest in Bible study as a result of the many new translations of Scripture that have made the Bible so easy to understand. In addition, training in personal witnessing has made it contagious to share one's faith openly, Bible-teaching churches have experienced incredible growth in numbers, and the Holy Spirit has touched the minds, hearts, and lives of millions. The Gallup poll of religious beliefs indicating that "69 million adults" claim to be "born again" suggests the soul harvest of the past few years has exceeded everyone's expectations.

These young Christians and those mature saints of God, like Simeon and Anna who were awaiting our Lord's first coming because of their knowledge of the Old Testament, will find this commentary on Revelation a welcome addition to their biblical library.

Dr. Henry M. Morris is not just a scientist, scholar, Christian apologist, and prolific writer. He is all that and more. To those of us who know him well, he is a meticulously accurate student of the Scriptures. God has endowed him with mental genius. He has added to that thousands of hours of patient Bible study and the meticulous company of Scripture with Scripture which makes him unique. Add to that a genuine humility and deep love for the Christ who is revealed in this book, and you will see why the Holy Spirit has selected him to write such a commentary of this end-time book for such a time as this.

If you are a new Christian you will find it easy to understand, and Dr. Morris's commentary will clarify many troublesome passages. If you are a deep student of Revelation, I guarantee you will find new material in this book you have never read elsewhere. Some of his concepts are unique. They will make you think.

Of all the commentaries on Revelation which I have in my library (and I have more than fifty-five) none treats the interpretation more literally. None were more fascinating to read and none offered me more surprises. As an author of a commentary on Revelation, I found it a little bit disturbing. It made me question some of the things I had said. It made me think! And that is good. You may not agree with everything my friend says in this book but I am sure of one thing. If you are a serious student or even serious about understanding what Revelation teaches, you will find *The Revelation Record* helpful.

It was my privilege to read the manuscript of Dr. Morris' superb commentary, *The Genesis Record,* before it was published. I said then it was the finest commentary on the book of Genesis ever written. Since its publication, many others have echoed my prediction. Now that I have read his commentary on Revelation, I predict the same will be said of it.

Few men of God have written commentaries on both the first and last books of the Bible. But then, there are few men with the capabilities of Henry Morris. This book is well worth reading—and teaching to others.

Tim LaHaye
Author, Educator, Minister

Preface

The Revelation Record was undertaken only after many years of study and teaching in this remarkable and climactic book of the Holy Scriptures, the last book of the Bible. Even as promised in the opening verses of the book (Revelation 1:3), it has proved to be of great personal blessing, and I hope the results of this present study will also be of benefit and blessing to others who may read it.

Scientists do not often write expositions of Revelation, but the book is so full of allusions to natural phenomena that this lack of scientific attention is surprising. Consequently, what might seem at first to be an unlikely background may actually, I hope, be helpful toward filling a real need.

Since so many previous writers have published studies on the Book of Revelation, the reader has a right to know what else, if anything, is different about *this* commentary. In addition to the scientific flavor associated with the many natural phenomena and physical events described in Revelation, I have tried to emphasize the physical *reality* of the great events recounted in the book. The Book of Revelation is not a theological treatise but an actual *record* of the final phases of world history, when the mighty King of Creation undertakes to finish the work He began long ago.

Furthermore, I have tried to follow a strictly literal and sequential approach to the events narrated, on the assumption that the *best* interpretation of a historical record is *no* interpretation but simply letting the divine Author of the record say what He says and assuming He says what He means.

Although many other writers have also tried to follow such an approach, the student may well find this to be the most literal approach he has encountered. Some have felt that scientific considerations preclude a literal exposition of certain portions of Revelation, but I have tried to show the plausibility of all such sections.

The difficult passages have not been avoided. An attempt has been made to explain every verse in detail, yet all in the context of a narrative style which I hope will show it all to be natural and believable in the fullest sense. In addition, since the Book of Revelation presents the most exalted portrait of the Lord Jesus Christ and the most profound epic of His ultimate triumph to be found in all the Bible, I have tried to make this a truly devotional and Christ-honoring exposition.

In a very real sense, the Book of Revelation is the sequel to the Book of Genesis, the two books together bounding all history and bounding all of God's revelations to mankind. They constitute the alpha and omega of God's written Word, the Book of Beginnings and the Book of Unveilings.

Thus this commentary, *The Revelation Record,* is in a peculiar way a sequel to my earlier commentary, *The Genesis Record* (published in 1976). As in *The Genesis Record,* I have used a narrative style of exposition rather than a critical exegetical approach, intending this book for practical use by the busy pastor or teacher as well as for devotional use in personal or home Bible study rather than for critical analysis by seminarians.

For the same reasons, the Authorized King James Version is the basic text followed in this commentary, rather than one of the more recent translations. This is still the most familiar and most widely used Bible in the English-speaking world, as well as unquestionably the most majestic and beautiful. It is also highly accurate and reliable. Whenever its meaning is not clear, I believe the exposition will satisfactorily indicate the proper meaning.

The serious student of the Book of Revelation will note immediately that I am following the literalistic, futuristic, sequential, premillennial, pretribulational interpretation of the book. This approach has been assumed to be the most natural, and therefore the most proper, way to understand the book.

This does not mean, however, that I am unappreciative of the studies and writings of the numerous commentators who have followed different routes of interpretation. Many godly and scholarly men have used a wide variety of approaches (amillennial, postmillennial, preterist, historical, cyclic, posttribulational, midtribulational, etc.). However, this book is quite voluminous even as it stands, so that trying to deal with the wide variety of alternate views in the same volume would make it impractically long. If the reader wants other points of view, he may consult other commentaries, of which a great abundance are available.

I personally am convinced, of course, that the literal and sequential approach is the most natural, most scientific, most Christ-honoring, and most soul-satisfying way to understand Revelation. Therefore, although I respect others who disagree, I have limited my own exposition to that approach, and I would assume the reader will use it with that understanding.

The reader will also note that, in following a narrative style, I have often attempted to read between the lines, as it were. One can use a sanctified imagination to visualize details that are not specifically stated in Scripture as long as it isn't done in a way that contradicts Scripture. These interpolations are not intended dogmatically but to visualize the way in which the brief statements of the inspired text may reasonably be fulfilled when the time comes. The reader can always discern what is specific revelation and what is interpretive interpolation and extrapolation by referring to the actual text which is being expounded. Each verse of the text, for ease of reference, is incorporated in the book just before the commentary on the verse.

I have been thankful for the wide and favorable reception given my "alpha" commentary, *The Genesis Record*. This "omega" commentary, *The Revelation Record,* is based on the same premises, so I trust this also will help many people, if the Lord so wills. These two great books of the Bible comprise the foundation and capstone of God's inspired Word to man, and it is vital that Christians believe and understand them if they would have a truly effective life and witness in today's confused and hurting world. It is my prayer that God may be pleased to use *The Revelation Record* to that end.

Henry M. Morris
San Diego, California

Introduction

The Book That Unveils the Future

Purpose of the Book of Revelation

The last book in the Bible has intrigued and fascinated multitudes of people throughout the centuries. More commentaries have surely been written and a greater variety of interpretations published about this book than any other in the canon of Scripture.

The reason for such absorbing interest is that we are time-bound creatures and, as the days and years flow by, we want to know what future time will bring. Will we become rich or paupers? Will our home life be happy and fruitful, or full of strife and defeat? Will we all be destroyed in a coming war, or will the future be one of peace and prosperity?

And, even more important, what happens when death comes? Is death the end of everything, as the humanists insist, or is it only the beginning of endless ages yet to come? If there is life after death, what will it be like, and what should we do now to prepare for it? What is the meaning and purpose of existence?

Speculations and would-be answers to such questions have been great in number and nature, but who is right? As far as the immediate future is concerned, many competent and well-trained people actually make a good living by predicting the future (weather forecasters, market analysts, and political pundits). Such forecasts are based on sound scientific and statistical techniques but are only partially successful and only on a very short-range basis.

In addition to these, one of the most amazing phenomena of our so-called "age of science" is the burgeoning of occultistic and pseudosupernaturalistic cults and practices, much of their attraction being their supposed ability to predict

17

or even to control the future. The proliferation of astrologers, seers, mediums, and other later-day "prophets" is one direct result of widespread dissatisfaction with present circumstances and the wistful desire of millions throughout the world to know the future. Feeling that "science" and "humanism" have failed, people shift their faith to pseudoscience and superhumanism, still desperately searching for meaningful answers for their future.

But these false prophets are still less reliable. To illustrate this fact, consider the predictions made by the nation's leading seers at the beginning of 1979, concerning the major events which would occur in 1979. Each year the nation's most-read newspaper, the *National Enquirer,* publishes their current predictions at the beginning of the year. Significantly, however, they never publish their success ratios at the end of the year!

As a matter of fact, instead of being supernaturally *inspired* prophets, they would almost have to be supernaturally *uninspired!* Their success ratio is so low that it seems they could have done better just by random guessing. Approximately ninety predictions were published, made by the ten top psychics interviewed by *National Enquirer.* So far as I can determine, not one of these prophecies was fulfilled in 1979 (or even in 1980) as they were supposed to have been.

One prediction was partially fulfilled—namely, that "Ted Kennedy will make a bid for the Presidency" (almost anyone could have guessed this), but the same prediction also said that John Connally would be his running mate. Another said that Ted Kennedy would announce his belief in reincarnation, and still another that Angie Dickinson would tell all about her secret affair with John F. Kennedy.

The most flagrantly unfulfilled prediction was that "inflation would be stopped dead in its tracks," along with others that scientists would announce amazing discoveries that would cure cancer, tooth decay, heart disease, diabetes, kidney disease, arthritis, the common cold, and the aging process itself. Other notoriously unfulfilled prophecies include the following:

President Carter injured in a hang-gliding accident
Debbie Boone appearing in an X-rated movie
Fabulous oil discoveries in East Texas
Pope John Paul II announcing plans to ordain women priests
An Eskimo girl elected as Miss World
Food prices dramatically slashed
A woman football referee in the NFL
Spiro Agnew winning an acting award
Ford Motor Company leaving America to protest taxes
Ronald Reagan deserted by his wife
California coastline reshaped by a fearfully devastating earthquake
Idi Amin assassinated
New planet discovered by the Venus probe
Jackie Onassis appointed ambassador to an African nation

Walter Cronkite appointed a U. S. diplomat in the South Pacific
Genuine Holy Shroud found in Egypt
Muhammad Ali winning a seat in Congress
First human, a red-haired boy, cloned in Kentucky

And on and on. None of the psychics predicted such major 1979 events as the Iranian crisis, the Russian troops in Cuba, the tragic DC-10 crash in Chicago, the Nicaraguan revolution, the tragedies of the Cambodian genocide and Vietnamese boat-people, or any of the other really important events of 1979. A similar record of failure resulted with the *Enquirer's* 1980 prophecies. It is amazing that so many millions of people continue to show any interest in such notoriously unreliable false prophets as these.

Even many Christians are overly impressed by such seers, attributing their psychic abilities to demonic powers. If they were really supernaturally guided, however, even by demons, one would think their predictions would have a better percentage of success.

The fact is that neither angels nor demons are omniscient and therefore they know little more about the future than human beings. It is true that men and women can—through planning and working—influence the future to some degree. Also, through analyses and reasoning they could to some extent predict the future. By virtue of their greater powers and greater knowledge, plus their ability to share such knowledge and abilities with other invisible spirits, it is no doubt true that angels and demons can both foresee and influence the future more than could human beings.

But only God is so omniponent, omnipresent, and omniscient. Since He created time, He stands outside time and thus knows and controls all events everywhere through all time. He may, on occasion, choose to share some of this knowledge with His holy angels, or with chosen men. To this extent—*and only this extent*—can we really know the future, which brings us to the purpose of the Book of Revelation.

This capstone on the wonderful structure of the written Word of God was written specifically to provide knowledge of the future. This is made clear in the very first verse:

The Revelation of Jesus Christ, which God gave unto him, to shew unto his servants things which must shortly come to pass; and he sent and signified it by his angel unto his servant John (Revelation 1:1).

What God desires us to know about the future is written for us in this book. Its scope proceeds from the events of the immediate future (that is, for those who would read the book first, the Christians of about A.D. 100) on through the return of Christ to the establishment of His eternal kingdom in the new earth and new heavens which He would create.

Nor need we fear that these prophecies may go unfulfilled. Unlike the false prophets of both past and present, God's prophecies are sure:

We have also a more sure word of prophecy; whereunto ye do well that ye take heed. ... For the prophecy came not in old time by the will of man: but holy men of God spake as they were moved by the Holy Ghost (2 Peter 1:19-21).

If we should wonder whether these amazing forecasts in Revelation will actually come to pass, we need only look at the record compiled by earlier biblical prophets who were moved by the Holy Ghost. That there have been hundreds of these biblical prophecies literally and meticulously fulfilled is a fact so well known as hardly to need documentation.[1] These commonly were long-range prophecies, scheduled for fulfillment in the distant future, far beyond the ingenuity of either man or angel to derive by analytical reasoning or by guessing. Furthermore, prophecies of this type are unique to the Bible, not found in the *Koran* or the *Analects* or in the writings of other religions or philosophies. They are not even found in the writings of modern self-styled prophets such as Nostradamus, Edgar Cayce, or Joseph Smith.

Biblical prophecies, therefore, are genuine and divinely inspired, sure to be fulfilled. The Book of Revelation is the final and definitive assemblage of God's prophecies of the future, incorporating and explicating all those other prophecies of both Old and New Testaments that are yet to be fulfilled. It is therefore a tremendously important book for every Christian to study and master. It is a book of real history—real events with real people—written ahead of time by the One outside of time. Since every individual who ever lived or will live is to be a participant in at least some of these events, and since they are the most profoundly important events since the resurrection of Christ, it is vital that we understand them and be prepared for them.

Sadly, however, the Book of Revelation has been a book of confusion and mystery to most of its readers, even Christian readers.

The Apocalypse ("unveiling") has become Apocrypha ("hidden"). This should not be. The book was written to *show* those things which were coming to pass, not to obscure them in a maze of symbolism and dark sayings. Great blessing was promised to all who would read (or even hear) the *words* of the book of this prophecy (Revelation 1:3), but how could anyone be blessed by words he could not even understand?

It seems anomalous that so many different exegetes of a book that was written

---

[1]*For those who wish such documentation, however, reference may be made to the writer's book,* Many Infallible Proofs *(San Diego: Creation-Life Publishers, 1974), pp. 181-199. This book contains a summary of the major fulfilled prophecies plus a bibliography of works with more extended treatments.*

as an unveiling of the future would publish such an unending variety of differing interpretations as to leave most seekers after such knowledge altogether confused. Such was certainly not the purpose of its original writer John, nor of Jesus Christ who sent it by John, nor of God who gave it to Christ.

As the Book of Genesis is the *foundation* of God's written Word, so is the Book of Revelation its *capstone*. The whole structure must stand upon its foundation and be displayed in its full perfection by its headstone. All Scripture is inspired by God and profitable to men (2 Timothy 3:16, 17) but these two books are the most essential of all, if one must choose. It is small wonder that the great Enemy of God's truth has directed his most intense attacks against Genesis and Revelation, denying the historicity of the former and the perspicuity of the latter. With neither creation nor consummation—neither beginning nor ending—all that we would have is the existential present, and this unfortunately has become the almost universal emphasis of modern philosophy and religion.

Men and women today urgently need to regain a true perspective on God's creative and redemptive purposes in the world. They need a true sense of history and prophecy, of time and eternity, of meaning and purpose. But, like Little Bo Peep, they don't know where to find them.

The Book of Genesis records the real events of the earth's primeval ages, and Revelation describes the equally real events of the ages to come. Thus the purpose of the Book of Revelation is one of proper orientation and firm preparation for those events yet coming on the earth.

Relation to the Book of Genesis

The inseparable relation of the first and last books of the Bible has already been mentioned in the previous section. In a sense, this commentary is essentially a sequel to the writer's commentary on the book of Genesis.[2] The thrust of both is to emphasize the scientific accuracy and the genuine historicity and perspicuity of these two key books of the Bible.

"Genesis" means "beginnings," being derived from the Greek Septuagint translation of the Hebrew *toledoth* ("generations"). "Revelation" is from the Greek *apokalupsis* and means, literally, an "unveiling" of something previously concealed. Thus Genesis is the "Book of the World's Beginnings," while Revelation is the "Book of Unveilings of the World's Future." The great themes of Scripture commonly have their beginnings in Genesis, then are progressively developed throughout the Bible, and finally come to their climactic consummations in Revelation.

The first chapters of Genesis describe a sinless world, made for man and placed under his dominion. Even though sin and the curse have intruded for a time, God cannot be defeated in His purpose, and all that God intended in the beginning

---

[2]The Genesis Record *(Grand Rapids: Baker Book House, 1976, 716 pp.).*

will ultimately be accomplished. The earth must be restored to its original perfection and then continue forever. Sin and the curse must be removed and death will be no more. The first three chapters of Genesis outline the entrance of sin into God's perfect creation. The last three chapters of Revelation outline the purgation of sin from God's redeemed creation.

Note the following interesting and instructive comparisons between the probationary (and then cursed) world described in Genesis and the eternal (because redeemed) world described in Revelation.

PROBATIONARY WORLD (Genesis)	ETERNAL WORLD (Revelation)
Division of light and darkness (1:4)	No night there (21:25)
Division of land and sea (1:10)	No more sea (21:1)
Rule of sun and moon (1:16)	No need of sun or moon (21:23)
First heavens and earth finished (2:1-3)	New heaven and earth forever (21:1)
Man in a prepared garden (2:8, 9)	Man in a prepared city (21:2)
River flowing out of Eden (2:10)	River flowing from God's throne (22:1)
Tree of life in the midst of the garden (2:9)	Tree of life throughout the city (22:2)
Gold in the land (2:12)	Gold in the city (21:21)
Bdellium and the onyx stone (2:12)	All manner of precious stones (21:19)
God walking in the garden (3:8)	God dwelling with His people (21:3)
The Spirit energizing (1:2)	The Spirit inviting (22:17)
Bride formed from her husband (2:21-23)	Bride adorned for her husband (21:2)
Command to multiply (1:28)	Nations of the saved (21:24)
Garden accessible to the Liar (3:1-5)	City closed to all liars (21:27)
Man in God's image (1:27)	Man in God's presence (21:3)
Man the probationer (2:17)	Man the heir (21:7)

CURSED WORLD (Genesis)	REDEEMED WORLD (Revelation)
Cursed ground (3:17)	No more curse (22:3)
Daily sorrow (3:17)	No more sorrow (21:4)
Sweat on the face (3:19)	No more tears (21:4)
Thorns and thistles (3:18)	No more pain (21:4)
Eating herbs of the field (3:18)	Twelve manner of fruits (22:2)
Returning to the dust (3:19)	No more death (21:4)
Coats of skins (3:21)	Fine linen, white and clean (19:14)
Satan opposing (3:15)	Satan banished (20:10)
Kept from the tree of life (3:24)	Access to the tree of life (22:14)
Banished from the garden (3:23)	Free entry to the city (22:14)
Redeemer promised (3:15)	Redemption accomplished (5:9, 10)
Evil continually (6:5)	Nothing that defileth (21:27)
Seed of the woman (3:15)	Root and offspring of David (22:16)
Cherubim guarding (3:24)	Angels inviting (21:9)

Other similar comparisons could be drawn between the two worlds revealed in Genesis and Revelation. In addition to such comparisons and contrasts, a number of specific themes begun in Genesis are either elaborated in Revelation or else simply mentioned in reference to a particular exhortation.

For example, the original creation of the world is specifically mentioned at least four times in Revelation (4:11; 10:6; 13:8; 14:7). There is an implicit reference to the Noahic flood ("fountains of waters") in Revelation 14:7, and to the rainbow covenant with Noah in Revelation 10:1. Although the two witnesses (Revelation 11:3-12) are not identified by name, there is a good possibility that one is the antediluvian patriarch Enoch.

The age-long conflict between the seed of the serpent and the seed of the woman, first announced in Genesis 3:15, is elaborated at considerable length in Revelation 12:1-17. The old serpent of Eden is clearly identified here as Satan (Revelation 12:9), the deceiver of the whole world.

The post-Flood rebellion which began at Babel under Nimrod is developed and analyzed throughout history until its climax under the coming Antichrist at Babylon the Great in Revelation 17 and 18. There is a reference to the wickedness of Sodom in Revelation 11:8, and to fire and brimstone in Revelation 14:10.

In the letters to the seven churches, mention is made of the tree of life and paradise in Revelation 2:7, as well as a reference to "the beginning of the creation of God" in Revelation 3:14. The cherubim of Genesis 3:24 are probably the creatures mentioned in Revelation 4:6-8 and throughout the book.

In Revelation 5:5, Christ is called the "Lion of the tribe of Juda(h)," a reference to Jacob's prophecy in Genesis 49:9. In the same prophecy the mention of washing garments in blood seems to be picked up in Revelation 1:5 and 7:14. All the children of Israel as named in this prophecy, with the exception of Dan, are named again in Revelation 7:4-8.

Not only the Book of Genesis, but many other books of the Old Testament are referred to in Revelation. The concepts and terminology of the Old Testament, especially the prophets Isaiah and Daniel, permeate the book. Some writers have estimated that more than two-thirds of the verses in Revelation contain quotations or allusions to the Old Testament (no specific citations, however). The writer of Revelation, John the Apostle, clearly presupposed that his readers would already be familiar with the rest of the Bible and thus prepared to accept and understand God's last climactic written revelation as He completed the Bible.

God's Word has been "forever settled in heaven" (Psalm 119:89). Gradually, however, "by the mouth of all his holy prophets since the world began" (Acts 3:21), God has been transmitting His Word from His own heart in heaven to men on earth. Apparently beginning with Adam, with his "book of the generations of Adam" (Genesis 5:1), and on through Moses and David and many others, God "at sundry times and in divers manners spake in time past unto the fathers by the prophets" (Hebrews 1:1). Then Christ came, and the Word of His New Covenant was transmitted to parchment and papyrus through Peter and Paul and others.

Finally, a hundred years after Christ entered the world, the last surviving Apostle, John the Beloved, was chosen to seal the written Word once and forever. All the remaining Scriptures, long settled in heaven, also entered the world. The Book of Revelation was transcribed, and God's Word was complete.

Interpretation of the Apocalypse

The main problem with the book of Revelation—the Apocalypse—has always been the question of how to interpret it. Interpretations of Revelation have been so numerous and varied that many earnest Christians have concluded that the book is simply impossible to understand. Thus they have missed the great blessing promised to those who do read and understand the book.

It may seem presumptuous for one who is not a professional theologian to undertake yet another exposition of a book which has already generated so many differing interpretations. I hope my background in science can provide certain needed insights. If there is anything really *new* in this commentary, however, it is its literal approach to Bible study, one that assumes the best interpretation to be *no* interpretation. That is, it is assumed that John and the other Bible writers, like most other writers, wanted to *communicate* to their readers. So they wrote plainly, saying exactly what they wanted to say and what they believed would be most effective in communicating definite and explicit truth to all the generations who would read their writings.

They wrote for their own generation, of course, but they also realized that they were writing the inspired Word of God and that their words would eventually have to be read and understood, then believed and obeyed, by people in all nations through all time. Or, at least, if *they* did not understand this, the Holy Spirit who was inspiring their writings did, and He would see to it that the inspired words did actually communicate the great truths God desired His people to know.

I am not the only one who has advocated a literal interpretation of the book of Revelation by any means. However, it could possibly be the *most* literal, since even literalist and futurist expositors seem often to resort to doubtful symbolic and figurative interpretations here and there throughout their expositions. Actually, a "literal interpretation" is a contradiction in terms, since one does not *interpret* (that is, "translate" saying "this means that") if he simply accepts a statement as meaning precisely what it says. Furthermore, the terms "more literal" or "most literal" are redundancies. Literal is *literal*.

The exposition in this commentary is based throughout on the premise that the writer (John directly, ultimately the Holy Spirit) was primarily, intensively, carefully concerned to communicate precise truth to the reader. This does not, of course, preclude the use of symbols or figures of speech when these can serve more effectively to that end, but it does mean that the interpretation of such figures is not left up to the reader's imagination or ingenuity. They must be defined and explained, unambiguously, either in the immediate context or in the broader context of the historical and prophetic Scriptures which John could assume his readers should already have mastered.

One will find that this approach to the exegesis of Revelation effectively eliminates most of the difficulty in *understanding* it. But, as someone has said, "The Book of Revelation isn't hard to understand—it's hard to *believe!*" The main reason why so many have resorted to allegorical interpretations is that they have found the literal meaning of its prophecies difficult to accept, scientifically and aesthetically, and have tried to "explain" them on some less offensive basis. This stratagem, however, in the absence of any contextual guidelines for such interpretations, has led to precisely that jumble of variation among the commentaries on Revelation, and this is what we explicitly seek to avoid in this commentary.

At the same time, it is certainly true that many "spiritualizing" commentaries, written by sincere and godly men who loved the Lord and His Word, contain much material of great value. While any given passage of Scripture has only one *interpretation,* the one intended ultimately by the Holy Spirit, it may well lead to many other illustrations and applications, or even to useful analogies and broad principles. This seems to be the case with many of these alternative—sometimes quite fanciful—interpretations of the Apocalypse.

Therefore, even though this present commentary will not follow them in its primary exposition, it is acknowledged that many valuable insights can be obtained using other approaches. God's character and principles never change, and we can see many parallels between His dealings with His people in the Apostolic period, His dealings with His people throughout history, and His dealings with His people in the prophetic future.

The various primary methods that have thus been used in interpreting the Book of Revelation are summarized below:

1. Preterist (Past) Interpretation. This interpretation regards the Book of Revelation as applying specifically to the problems and persecutions of the early church existing at the time of its writing. The many symbolic expressions in the book represent devices to encourage the church throughout its trials under the imperial Roman Empire, and were deliberately intended to prevent the book from being understood by any who were not believers.

2. Historical Interpretation. By this approach, the events symbolically described in Revelation represent the chronological sequence of historical events from the time of its writing until the coming of Christ and the establishment of His eternal kingdom. Much of it, especially the sections dealing with Babylon and the "beast," are identified in particular with the Roman Catholic Church and the pope, with other symbols tied to such events as the rise of Islam and the Napoleonic wars.

3. Futurist Interpretation. Futurist interpreters, though differing among themselves in various details, generally regard all of Revelation from Chapter 4 to

22 as describing events at the very end of the Church Age and thus still future. Many futurists still employ much symbolism, while others take most of these future events in a very literal sense.

4. Cyclic Interpretation. This interpretation seeks to combine the chronological interpretations of the above-described past, present, and futurist schools by noting a cyclic repetition of similar prophetic sequences (seals, trumpets, and bowls), each beginning with the early church, proceeding through history, and culminating in the coming kingdom.

5. Idealist Interpretation. No attempt is made by idealistic or mystical interpreters to relate the events described in Revelation to any historical events at all—past, present, or future. Rather, it is all treated as a series of parables or allegories designed to encourage troubled believers to trust in the ultimate triumph of good over evil and of Christ over Satan.

Since the preterist and idealist interpretations are not committed to predictive prophecy in Revelation, they tend chiefly to be advocated today by liberal or neo-orthodox interpreters. To them, Revelation is merely a statement of faith in sociological progress and the eventual triumph of a more equable world order.

Historical or cyclical interpreters have dominated Protestant thought for centuries, using the Book of Revelation as a sword against Roman Catholicism, which they judged to be symbolized by Babylon the Great. In fact, probably the first preterist interpreters arose among the Catholics as a reaction against this system. The problem, however, with the historical interpretation is that the correlation of events with prophecy is far too ambiguous. None of the symbols which supposedly prophesied certain historical events could ever have been used to anticipate those events. Even in retrospect, the correlation is so vague and uncertain that hardly any two historical interpreters agree. Even with regard to Babylon, Protestants may interpret it as Romanism, while the Catholics may interpret it as Protestantism.

It is inevitable that literalistic expositors of Revelation will be primarily futurists since practically none of the events of Revelation 4—22 have yet taken place in any literal sense. Many futurists do accept a cyclical development in the various sequences, but probably most (including myself) follow a strictly chronological approach. This seems required by the actual sequential terms accompanying the events, except occasionally when the context demands a retrospective view at the beginning of a particular prophecy.

It is also evident that literalistic expositions of Revelation will usually be *premillennial,* rather than *amillennial* or *postmillennial.* The millennium—the thousand-year reign of Christ with His resurrected saints, as outlined in Revelation 20:1-7—can only be future if it is literal. Amillennialists spiritualize the millennium, while postmillennialists spiritualize the resurrection which precedes it.

Thus, since this commentary is based on belief in full verbal inspiration and the straightforward natural meaning of all the verses in Revelation, it is necessarily also both futuristic and premillennial. It does recognize many valuable insights and implications from other schools of interpretation and seeks to incorporate them wherever helpful. Nevertheless, the events described in the Book of Revelation are real events, just as sure to take place in future history as the events in Genesis, and all the other historical books of Scripture, took place in past history. Since each reader of these pages must inevitably participate to at least some degree in some of these great future events, he needs to know about them and to prepare for them. To help him appreciate the absolute reality and importance of these coming events is the purpose of this commentary.

Chronological Framework of Revelation

As indicated in the previous section, the literal view of Revelation accepts the book as truly prophetic, built around a chronology beginning with the time of its writing about A.D. 100, and extending on to eternity, in the new earth. Prior to the establishment of the new heavens and the new earth, which inaugurates the ages of eternity, there is identified a final period of a thousand years on the present earth—the millennium (Revelation 20:1-7).

Prior to the millennium, the world is to be ruled by a satanically-controlled man identified as the "beast." This period of totalitarian world rule under the beast is predicted to be just "forty-two months" before he is defeated and the millennium begins (Revelation 13:4, 5; 19:20). Before that period is still another period of "1260 days," marked by the unrestrained prophesying and miraculous works of "two witnesses" (Revelation 11:3), whose influence is finally overcome by the "beast" as he consolidates his world power (Revelation 11:7).

These two periods—1260 days and forty-two months—are obviously consecutive and each corresponds to a period of three-and-a-half years, each composed of twelve months containing thirty days each. Thus there is to be a final seven-year period of earth history immediately prior to the millennium. The last half of this period apparently contains the events described in Chapters 12—19. Correspondingly, the first half of the period is outlined in Chapters 4—11. The plagues called down on earth during the days of their prophecy by the two witnesses are detailed in Chapters 6—10, then summarized in 11:6. The first gives the scene as viewed from heaven, the second as from earth. Chapters 4 and 5 describe a great scene in heaven immediately preceding this epochal seven-year period on earth. At this grand assemblage are gathered all the redeemed (Revelation 5:8-13), singing the praises of the Lamb of God, the Redeemer.

Since such an assemblage can only take place when Christ returns to gather His own people to Himself in the heavens (John 14:2, 3; 1 Corinthians 15:51-57; 1 Thessalonians 4:16, 17), it becomes clear that the seven years of plagues and judgments on the earth, described in Chapters 6—19, are prophesied to take place only *after* the coming of Christ to raise and receive His redeemed ones.

This leaves only Chapters 2 and 3 to deal with the time from A.D. 100 to the resurrection of the saints. It is appropriate that these chapters consist of letters to seven representative churches, churches whose needs and problems would embrace in essence all the needs and problems of all the churches of the Church Age.

Additional reasons will be developed later to further justify this chronology. Summarizing, the framework of Revelation seems to be as follows:

Chapters 1—3	Church Age	Unknown Duration
Chapters 4—19	Period of Judgment	Seven Years
Chapter 20	Kingdom Age	One Thousand Years
Chapters 21, 22	Eternal Age	Endless Years

The chronology of Revelation thus looks forward to all the future ages. A complete picture, however, must also look back to the past. The close connection of Revelation with Genesis has already been noted, and the events catalogued in Revelation comprise only a part of God's complete chronology of all the ages from creation to consummation.

In this broader framework of chronology, there appear to be five major ages of the cosmos, with each of these separated from the others by a profound convulsion of the whole creation. These are all illustrated in the diagram.

The Seal of the Seven

A unique aspect of the Book of Revelation, a feature which needs to be noted as a whole before we begin studying specific passages, is its remarkable "sevenness." Note, for example, some of the many systems of seven components found in Revelation:

1. Seven churches (Revelation 1:4, 11, 20)
2. Seven Spirits (Revelation 1:4; 3:1; 4:5; 5:6)
3. Seven candlesticks (Revelation 1:12, 13, 20; 2:1)
4. Seven stars (Revelation 1:16, 20; 2:1; 3:1)
5. Seven lamps (Revelation 4:5)
6. Seven seals (Revelation 5:1; 5:5)
7. Seven horns (Revelation 5:6)
8. Seven eyes (Revelation 5:6)
9. Seven angels (Revelation 8:2, 6)
10. Seven trumpets (Revelation 8:2, 6)
11. Seven thunders (Revelation 10:3, 4)
12. Seven thousand (Revelation 11:13)
13. Seven heads (Revelation 12:3; 13:1; 17:3, 7, 9)
14. Seven crowns (Revelation 12:3)
15. Seven angels (Revelation 15:1, 6, 7, 8; 16:1; 17:1; 21:9)
16. Seven plagues (Revelation 15:1, 6, 8; 21:9)

Five Ages of the Cosmos

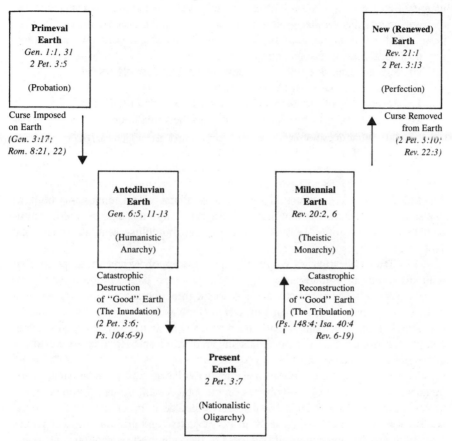

The relationships suggested in the chart will be discussed and amplified later as needed. It is obvious, however, that the chronology of the Book of Revelation deals primarily only with the second "leg" of this cosmic chronology, as the earth is returning from its present state of bondage and decay to its intended state of eternal perfection.

17. Seven vials (Revelation 15:7; 17:1; 21:9)
18. Seven mountains (Revelation 17:9)
19. Seven kings (Revelation 17:10, 11)

This unusual format can hardly be accidental. The word seven appears in Revelation more than in any other book of the Bible and, in fact, more than in all other books of the New Testament put together. It was not just a pedagogical device utilized by John, since John was merely recording what he had seen and heard. The book is "The Revelation of Jesus Christ"—not "the revelation of St. John," as many have called it (note Revelation 1:1, 2).

Furthermore, the above-listed "sevens" are only the ones that are directly identified by their association with the actual word seven (Greek *hepta*). One can discover many other similar groups of seven things in the book, but these have to be searched out by direct study of the various words and associations. For example, note the following fascinating groups:

20. Seven beatitudes (the statements beginning with "Blessed . . ." (Revelation 1:3; 14:13; 16:15; 19:9; 20:6; 22:7; 22:14).
21. Seven years of judgments (Revelation 11:3; 12:6, 14; 13:5).
22. Seven divisions of each of the letters to the seven churches (see commentary on Revelation 2).
23. Seven "I am's" of Christ (Revelation 1:8, 11, 17, 18; 21:6; 22:13, 16).
24. Seven doxologies in heaven (Revelation 4:9-11; 5:8-13; 7:9-12; 11:16-18; 14:2, 3; 15:2-4; 19:1-6).

Many similar associations of seven can be found in this remarkable book as one studies it in depth. For that matter, there are many other numbers also prominent in Revelation (666, 144,000, twelve gates, four horsemen, ten kings, and 1000 years).

An obvious question is, Why? Why is the Book of Revelation so permeated with this emphasis on numbers?

Actually, this same phenomenon is found throughout the Bible, though not usually to the same extent as in Revelation. Perhaps this is not as surprising as some might think. The natural world is constructed in such a way as to be describable in mathematical terms and God's inspired Word and His created world are consistent with each other.

In fact, the numerical phenomena in the Bible are so abundant that many authors have written extensive volumes on the subject. Unfortunately none of these writers have evaluated the numerical features they describe on any kind of sound statistical basis, and they often seem to be subjective and arbitrary in their identification of specific mathematical patterns, so that one must be cautious and selective in making use of them. Although the phenomenon is undoubtedly real and meaningful, the present "state of the art" of the interpretation and application of biblical numerology is still too tentative for much confidence.

In the special case of the book of Revelation, however, the mathematical apparatus is clearly intentional and meaningful, so that to ignore it would be to miss much of the message of the book. Consequently the various numbers and the reasons for their use will be discussed as we encounter them while proceeding with our verse-by-verse study.

But the remarkable "seven-ness" of the book needs special recognition right at the outset. Why are there so many "sevens" in this last book of the Bible?

Although this question is not discussed explicitly in the Book of Revelation itself, almost certainly one of the primary reasons is to emphasize that this *is* the last book of the Bible! In fact, the book closes with a grave warning against anyone who would pretend to add anything further to God's inspired Word (Revelation 22:18).

The number "seven" has always been regarded as representing fullness or completion. This is true not only in the Bible but among almost all peoples throughout history. Seven is the "lucky" number, the "perfect" number.

The emphasis on seven as a number of fullness is understandable, of course, in terms of the weekly calendar by which we order our everyday lives. Again, most nations throughout history have followed the seven-day week.

But this fact does not really answer the question, for it does not explain why nations ever started following a seven-day week in the first place. The seven-day week has no astronomical basis, as do the month and year, nor does the number seven have a physiological basis like the number ten.

The only real explanation why people have always followed a seven-day week and why the number seven has always symbolized fullness and completion is the divine decree of Genesis 2:3: "And God blessed the seventh day, and sanctified it; because that in it he had rested from all his work which God created and made." Once again, to understand Revelation we must return to Genesis.

God completed His mighty work of creating, constructing, and energizing the entire cosmos and all its creatures in the very first seven-day period of history. Because of sin and the curse, He has ever since been accomplishing His mighty work of redeeming and saving the creation.

One day this work also will be completed, though it has taken far longer than seven days. Much of this latter work was preparatory, getting the world ready for the coming of its Redeemer to pay the price for its deliverance and restoration. The Old Testament, beginning with Genesis, describes the history of this preparation, and the New Testament details the coming of the Savior, the payment of the price, and the establishment of a great witnessing community of His redeemed people under the leadership of chosen apostles.

Eventually, this great work of "the redemption of the purchased possession, unto the praise of his glory" (Ephesians 1:14) will also be completed, and God's eternal Rest will begin. The Book of Revelation, inscribed through the last of the apostles at the very end of the Apostolic Age, provides guidance for His people through all the other ages to come, focusing especially on the great climactic events that will bring God's work to completion and fullness. The Apocalypse, therefore, above all else, is designed to assure us that what God has said is true. What He has promised, He will do. The Book of Revelation is real, future history as sure as Genesis is real, primeval history. Its characters are real and the events it prophesies will indeed come to pass. God will finish His work.

1

The Man in the Glory

(Revelation 1)

The Last Apostle

Just before the Lord Jesus Christ went back to heaven after His death and resurrection, He spoke to Peter concerning his fellow apostle, John the beloved: "If I will that he tarry till I come, what is that to thee? follow thou me" (John 21:22).

Jesus did not say that John would remain alive until His second coming, but the disciples interpreted it that way for a time. It was an elliptical way of answering Peter's question about John. As a matter of fact, according to all the available records and traditions, John did outlive every one of the other eleven disciples. All had long since gone to a martyr's death when John, more than sixty years later, wrote the matchless words of the Book of Revelation.

Christ had deliberately left the time of His return uncertain, but He did tell His disciples they must always be watchful and ready (as in Matthew 24:42-44), so that He could actually have returned in that very generation—at least as far as they could know and as far as divine prophecy had revealed. That the apostles did actually believe His coming could have been in their own lifetime is evident in many passages of Scripture (such as 1 John 2:28 and 1 Thessalonians 4:16, 17).

The same is true for every generation since. The Lord wanted all His servants to live in an attitude of expectancy, knowing that He might return at any moment, and that is still true today. And finally, "He that shall come will come, and will not tarry" (Hebrews 10:37).

In one sense, John did indeed tarry until Christ came. On the wonderful "Lord's day" (Revelation 1:10) when John received the Book of Revelation,

Christ did "come" back to John's presence (or perhaps caught John up to heaven), so that John saw his beloved Lord once more. Furthermore, John was allowed to "see" all the events that would be associated with Christ's eventual second coming to the earth, so that he could record them for the instruction and inspiration of all believers between his day and the last day. We today still have the privilege of seeing and hearing, through the eyes and ears of John, all these great future events that will take place when Christ returns.

Revelation 1:1. The Revelation of Jesus Christ, which God gave unto him, to shew unto his servants things which must shortly come to pass; and he sent and signified it by his angel unto his servant John.

The word "revelation" is the Greek *apokalupsis* and means literally "unveiling" or "taking off the cover." Thus this book is not intended to be mysterious or confusing, but illuminating and revealing. In this opening statement, John stresses the wonderful fact that Jesus Christ, even though now glorified in heaven, is still a resurrected *man*. In His continuing humanity (even though also deity), He received from God this prophetic unveiling of the future, with full authority to reveal it to His servants for their guidance and blessing.

The things being revealed would be fulfilled beginning almost immediately. The word *shortly* means literally "in a brief time." Even though many years yet remained in actuality, His coming could have been almost immediate, at least in principle, as far as John's first readers were concerned—or as far as his future readers in any generation would be concerned. Furthermore, even thousands of years constitute only a "brief time" on the eternal time frame within which He was speaking.

The revelation was intended for the guidance of the "servants" (literally "bondslaves") of Jesus Christ, and He chose to use His specially beloved servant to convey it, preserving his life through perils and persecutions without number through sixty long years until the time was ready. The "angel" by whom the revelation was "signified" is not here identified (though later, in chapter 22, verses 6-9, he is said to be a "fellow-servant" of John and other servants of Christ). Whoever he is, he had the ability to "signify" and to "shew" (Revelation 22:6) John the great visions and revelations of this book, by the power and authority of Christ. The word "signify" is closely related to "sign," or "miracle," and may well refer to the miraculous nature of the marvelous prophetic visions which John was enabled to see. On the other hand, the word is also occasionally used merely in the sense of "identify" or "specify" (Acts 25:27).

Revelation 1:2. "Who bare record of the word of God, and of the testimony of Jesus Christ, and of all things that he saw."

The writer of Revelation identifies himself as John, and the uniform testimony of early Christian writers is that this was, indeed, John the Apostle. Nevertheless, liberals have often alleged that it was some other John, largely because the vocabulary of Revelation seemed different from the vocabulary of the Gospel and epistles of John. This verse clearly asserts, however, that the John who wrote the Revelation was the very one "who bare record of the word of God," terminology which clearly identifies him as the author of John's Gospel and epistles. The phrase, "bear record" (Greek *martureo,* also translated "testify" or "bear witness" or "bear testimony"), is highly characteristic of John, occurring forty-four times in his writings and only twenty-five times in all the rest of the New Testament. Here he emphasizes that in Revelation he is bearing witness of the very word of God. Furthermore he is bearing record of the "testimony of Jesus Christ." This word "testimony" (Greek *marturia*) is also characteristic of John, occurring thirty times in his writings and only seven times in all the rest of the New Testament.

Thus there can be no doubt, both from the fact of the assertion and the very words in the assertion, that the same John who was the Lord's beloved disciple was the great apostle chosen by Him to write down the final words of the written Word of God to men.

Note the threefold nature of the record that John wrote: (1) "the word of God," stressing that the entire book was verily inspired by God; (2) the testimony of Jesus Christ, referring to the frequent statements made by Christ Himself to John throughout the book; and (3) the "things that he saw," recording the great future events in heaven and on earth which he was permitted to "see" through the special ministry of the angel who miraculously "signified" them to him.

This verse emphasizes the extremely important fact that the Book of Revelation is an actual eye-witness *record* of real events and real people. Just as Genesis is the record of the people and events of the world's primeval history, so Revelation is the record of the terminal events of history, written by one who was *there.* John was miraculously translated in time and space, by the omnipotent Creator of time and space, to enable him actually to see and hear these momentous events of future history.

John was always careful to emphasize that he wrote only what he saw and heard. In the concluding section of his Gospel he had written: "This is the disciple which testifieth of these things, and wrote these things: and we know that his testimony is true" (John 21:24). Writing of the amazing events on the cross, he had written: "And he that saw it bare record, and his record is true: and he knoweth that he saith true, that ye might believe" (John 19:35). The opening words of his first epistle again stressed that he had heard and seen and touched the very One of whom he was writing, concluding with this testimony: "That which we have seen and heard declare we unto you" (1 John 1:3).

Similarly, John claims over and over in the Book of Revelation that his eyes had seen and his ears had heard all these amazing future scenes of which he was writing. In fact, this claim is even impressed with "the seal of the seven." That is, John makes the claim "I heard" twenty-eight times (that is, four sevens), and he makes the statement "I saw" (or "I looked" or "I beheld," all of which are translations of the same Greek word) no less than forty-nine times, or seven sevens. This phrase is used, in fact, more often than in any other New Testament book. John would have us know, beyond any possible misunderstanding, that he was not writing his own dreams or imaginings. He was writing precisely what he had seen and heard, and nothing more. To us, the Book of Revelation is a prophecy. To John it was actual history, recorded just as he had observed it.

Revelation 1:3.   Blessed is he that readeth, and they that hear the words of this prophecy, and keep those things that are written therein; for the time is at hand.

A special blessing is promised to all who read or even who hear the words (note the emphasis on the very *words,* not just the themes) of *this* book of prophecy, and who "keep" what is written in it. It is obvious that one cannot keep what he does not possess, nor could he be blessed by it, so that this wonderful promise clearly presupposes that those who read or hear these words are well able to understand and appropriate them. And this can only be true if the words are to be taken literally.

The exhortation to recognize the imminence of the "time" is explicitly repeated at the end of the book (22:10). If it was urgent for Christians in John's time to study this book of prophecy: how much more urgent it is for those of us who are 1900 years closer to the time when it will all be actually taking place.

John's Salutation

Revelation 1:4.   John to the seven churches which are in Asia: Grace be unto you, and peace, from him which is, and which was, and which is to come; and from the seven Spirits which are before his throne.

Here is the first of the "sevens" with which Revelation abounds (see discussion in previous chapter), and it is John's salutation to "the seven churches." It is obvious that the message is really to all churches of all the centuries and it is thus very significant that John does not address is message to "the Church"—not even to "the Church of Asia," but to "the *churches.*" Christ's message is to be conveyed to and through local churches, with real, visible members and activities, not to an invisible illusory body called "the church universal." Even though all churches are in mind here, Christ through John selects seven representative churches in Asia Minor to stand for all churches everywhere.

John opens with the salutation of grace and peace, common to the epistles of Paul (Paul also wrote *inspired* epistles to just seven churches: Rome, Corinth, Galatia, Ephesus, Philippi, Colosse, and Thessalonica). Paul, however, always expressed grace and peace as coming from God the Father and the Lord Jesus Christ. John here invokes the entire Trinity!

First, grace and peace are from "him which is, and which was, and which is to come"—God in His eternal omnipotence, "the Father of lights, with whom is no variableness" (James 1:17), the "everlasting Father" (Isaiah 9:6), the "high and lofty one who inhabiteth eternity" (Isaiah 57:15).

Then, they come through the "seven Spirits" before the throne. In view of the placement of this unique name between the names of the eternal one and of Jesus Christ, this is necessarily a reference to the Holy Spirit, rather than to seven great angelic spirits, as might otherwise be thought. Furthermore, grace and peace are not mediated through angels, but through the Holy Spirit.

But why is He called the "seven Spirits?" It has been suggested that the reference in Isaiah 11:2 to "the spirit of the Lord . . . the spirit of wisdom and understanding, the spirit of counsel and might, the spirit of knowledge and of the fear of the Lord" may be the key. The Holy Spirit is sevenfold in His gracious character and imputation of spiritual attributes. The phrase may also, by its symbolic seven-ness, emphasize that, while the Spirit is indeed "before the throne," He is also omnipresent.

Revelation 1:5.   And from Jesus Christ, who is the faithful witness, and the first begotten of the dead, and the prince of the kings of the earth. Unto him that loved us, and washed us from our sins in his own blood.

The salutation also includes an invocation of grace and peace from Jesus Christ, thus incorporating the entire Trinity. John also ascribes to Him three marvelous titles. These titles, respectively, testify to His sinless suffering unto death, His victorious resurrection from the grave, and His imminent triumphant return. The word "witness' (Greek *martus*) is the source of our word "martyr." Jesus Christ, like many other "witnesses" to God's truth before and since, was faithful unto death, a martyr. He, unlike other martyrs, however, had power to lay down His life and power to take it again (John 10:18), and thus became the firstborn from the dead (see also Acts 13:33; Colossians 1:18). Although most kings and other great men of the earth continually try to rebel against Him (Psalm 2:1-3), He is "prince" (Greek *archon* = "chief," "first") and must soon be acknowledged "King of kings and Lord of lords" (Revelation 19:16).

As John rehearses this thrilling testimony *from* the Lord, he is impelled to present a doxology *to* His Lord. He is the one who loved us lost sinners so much as to offer up His sinless blood to free us from our sins.

Revelation 1:6.   And hath made us kings and priests unto God and his Father; to him be glory and dominion for ever and ever. Amen.

Having been cleansed of sin's guilt and power, we are no longer bond slaves of sin (Romans 6:20-22). But to the One who loved us, that is only the beginning. Those who *were* slaves became kings and priests, (or "a kingdom of priests") seated with Him in heavenly places (Ephesians 2:6) and serving as a holy priesthood, offering up spiritual sacrifices to God (1 Peter 2:5). In the coming kingdom, He promises that we shall actually "reign with him" (Revelation 20:6; 2 Timothy 2:12). But though we shall reign *with* Him, we are still His servants (Revelation 22:3) and it will be our joy to acknowledge His glory and dominion forever.

Revelation 1:7.   Behold, he cometh with clouds; and every eye shall see him, and they also which pierced him: and all kindreds of the earth shall wail because of him. Even so, Amen.

John needed no new revelation for this information, since it had previously been recorded in Scripture. That Christ is coming with clouds had already been told the disciples (Matthew 24:30) by the Lord Himself, together with the fact that all men would see Him and mourn (same word as "wail"). John himself had seen Him "pierced" with the Roman's spear (John 19:34), marveling at the mingled blood and water which emerged from His side. It had recalled to him the great prophecy in Zechariah 12:10, where the Lord promised that the inhabitants of Jerusalem who through their ancestors had called for His death, would one day look upon Him whom they had pierced and *mourn* for Him (John 19:37). Here he again recalls the prophecy, as well as those made by the Lord on Olivet, recognizing that he is now about to witness in vision their final accomplishment, and then a great "*Amen*" issues from his heart and pen.

Revelation 1:8.   I am Alpha and Omega, the beginning and the ending, saith the Lord, which is, and which was, and which is to come, the Almighty.

Here are the first words actually heard by John from heaven, calling him to the work at hand. These first words had come from Christ Himself, the Son of man (verse 13), yet John describes Him in the same terms used in verse 4 for the Father ("is . . . was . . . is to come"). Also, these first words constitute the first of the seven great "I am's" of Revelation, and a more glorious and comprehensive claim to self-existing deity cannot be imagined. "Alpha and Omega!" He who is the Word, from the first letter to the last letter of all of language itself, comprises all there is, to know and be. In Him "are hid all the treasures of wisdom and knowledge" (Colossians 2:3).

Further, He is the Almighty. The word is the Greek *pantokrator,* meaning "the One of all power." He is omnipotent, as well as eternal and omniscient. And this is Jesus Christ—the one who loved us and washed us from our sins in His own blood. No wonder the Book of Revelation both begins (verse 4) and ends (Revelation 22:21) with *grace!*

As He Is

Revelation 1:9.   I John, who also am your brother, and companion in tribulation, and in the kingdom and patience of Jesus Christ, was in the isle that is called Patmos, for the word of God, and for the testimony of Jesus Christ.

John thus identifies himself with the members of the churches to which he was going to send his book of prophecy. Though he was the last of Christ's apostles, entitled to all respect and esteem, he considered himself only one of the brethren, sharing in the common persecutions which had already claimed the lives of all the other apostles, as well as countless others among the brethren. This was in the time of Domitian, among the cruelest of the Roman emperors. John himself was in prison, banished because of his preaching to a small barren island in the Aegean.

His offense, he says, was exactly that of which he had been "guilty" for over sixty years, bearing witness of the Word of God and the testimony of Jesus Christ (compare verse 2).

Revelation 1:10.   I was in the Spirit on the Lord's day, and heard behind me a great voice, as of a trumpet.

There has been much argument as to whether "the Lord's day" here refers to Sunday or "the day of the Lord." If the latter, John was translated in the Holy Spirit forward to the great future day of the Lord, the subject of much prophecy in both Old and New Testaments. His experience may have been similar to that of Paul (2 Corinthians 12:1-4).

However, there are serious problems with this interpretation. If John meant "the day of the Lord," he should have said so. "The Lord's day" is a quite different construction, meaning "the day belonging to the Lord." The construction is used only one other time ("the Lord's supper" in 1 Corinthians 11:20). Secondly, the assumption that he was translated in the Spirit forward to the day of the Lord is inconsistent with the fact that the first two chapters of his book deal with current situations in existing churches. The assumed translation should not have taken place until *after* his messages to the churches.

The main objection to the "Sunday" interpretation, on the other hand, is that the day after the Sabbath is nowhere else in Scripture called the Lord's day. The oldest known use of that term is 100 years after John.

This, however, is an argument from silence. It could well be, in fact, that this expression was applied here by John for the first time to the day elsewhere known in Scripture as "the first day of the week." In such a case the later use of the term, extending to modern times, could even have originated from John's use of it here. There certainly was ample justification for identifying the day of Christ's resurrection with the Lord, and in two recorded instances at least the early Christians had begun to have services on this day long before this occasion (Acts 20:7; 1 Corinthians 16:2).

Thus, although there is some uncertainty, it does seem that the weight of evidence shows that John was in a time of meditation and prayer—"in the Spirit"—on a certain day, a first day of the week, in his barren prison land, remembering his beloved Lord when he heard the great voice behind him, loud and clear as a trumpet, and he suddenly was aware that the Lord Himself had come from heaven to be with him on that great Lord's day, to show him things to come.

Revelation 1:11.   Saying, I am Alpha and Omega, the first and the last, and, What thou seest, write in a book, and send it unto the seven churches which are in Asia; unto Ephesus, and unto Smyrna, and unto Pergamos, and unto Thyatira, and unto Sardis, and unto Philadelphia, and unto Laodicea.

The voice repeats the "I am." Alpha and Omega are the first and last letters of the Greek alphabet, so that this incomparable claim incorporates all existence, all knowledge, all reality. Furthermore, it is the same claim made by God Himself three times through Isaiah (Isaiah 41:4; 44:6; 48:12).

Then came the command: "Write what you see in a book." Just as there was a book of the generations of Adam (Genesis 5:1), so there is to be a book of the last generations, both serving to anchor and guide all other generations. Initially this book (Greek *biblion,* from which we get our word "Bible") was to be sent to seven churches among whom John had evidently ministered. The churches were all in southwest Asia Minor, more or less facing the Isle of Patmos on which John was imprisoned. They are enumerated in clockwise order, beginning at Ephesus on the coast, then northward to Smyrna and Pergamum, east to Thyatira, and southeast to Sardis, Philadelphia, and Laodicea, the latter due east and inland from Ephesus.

Revelation 1:12.   And I turned to see the voice that spake with me. And being turned, I saw seven golden candlesticks.

The great voice, like a trumpet, was behind John so he turned and saw the most glorious sight ever beheld by mortal eyes—none other than the glorified

Christ there in the midst of seven golden candlesticks. These "candlestands" probably called to John's mind the Menorah, the lampstands in the tabernacle, each of which had one main and six side branches (Exodus 25:31). The lampstands seen by John, however, had seven equal branches.

Revelation 1:13. And in the midst of the seven candlesticks one like unto the Son of man, clothed with a garment down to the foot, and girt about the paps with a golden girdle.

The one who spoke was "in the midst" of the candlesticks. John long ago had heard the Lord say concerning the Church He would build: "For where two or three are gathered together in my name, there am I in the midst of them." The candlesticks represented the churches, all of whom were enduring great tribulation for the testimony of Jesus Christ, but the Lord would remind them that He was still in their midst (Matthew 18:20).

And despite the glory of His appearance, John recognized Him to be a man—indeed the very Son of man, the representative man, true man, man as God intended man to be. This term, "Son of man," was Christ's favorite term for Himself; he used it more than eighty times in the four Gospels. The term is used first in Psalm 3:4, prophesying His first coming in humility, and last in Revelation 14:14, prophesying His second coming in power.

But though he is a true man, He is only *like unto* the *son* of man. Adam also was a man, but was not a son of man. Jesus Christ was "made in the likeness of men" (Philippians 2:7); He was "made like unto his brethren" (Hebrews 2:17); He was sent "in the likeness of sinful flesh" (Romans 8:3). He was not born of the union of a sinful man and a sinful woman (terms which apply to *all* human beings save Jesus, even to Joseph and Mary), but was divinely conceived and virgin born. Nevertheless He is to be forever *like unto* the Son of man.

Note also the fullness of His garments. There is no nudity or seminudity among the inhabitants of heaven. Jesus was stripped of His garments when made *sin* on the cross, but in heaven, and in the new earth, He is always appropriately arrayed, and so are all His servants.

Revelation 1:14. His head and his hairs were white like wool, as white as snow; and his eyes were as a flame of fire.

No one living today knows what Jesus looked like during His days on earth, though imaginative portrayals of Him adorn innumerable homes and churches. The New Testament writers speak not one word concerning His physical appearance—whether He was short or tall, dark or light, lean or stout. This omission is significant—He is the *representative* man. Furthermore, whatever His appearance may have been then, His present appearance is far more important, for this is the way we shall see Him, and this will be His appearance through all future ages. John describes Him as He *is* and *will be.*

The most striking feature is His snow-white hair. The same appearance was seen by Daniel: "The Ancient of days did sit, whose garment was white as snow, and the hair of his head like the pure wool" (Daniel 7:9). Isaiah 9:6 speaks of Him as the "everlasting Father." The white hair crowning His head (beards are never mentioned at all in the New Testament) clearly speaks of His great age. This contrasts with the wistful desire of modern men to retain the appearance of youth, even using dyes to mask their gray hair. The Bible says: "The glory of young men is their strength: and the beauty of old men is the grey head" (Proverbs 20:29). "The hoary head is a crown of glory, if it be found in the way of righteousness" (Proverbs 16:31). The Scripture promises that "we shall be like him; for we shall see him as he is" (1 John 3:2). Note we shall see Him as He *is,* not as He *was.*

His eyes were, as it were, burning with anger. This aspect was to be seen especially by the immoral church at Thyatira (Revelation 2:18). Yet these were the same eyes that could weep over human need (John 11:35; Luke 19:41). His eyes are all-seeing as He is all-knowing. "All things are naked and opened unto the eyes of him with whom we have to do" (Hebrews 4:13).

Revelation 1:15.   And his feet like unto fine brass, as if they burned in a furnace; and his voice as the sound of many waters.

His feet once had rough spikes driven through them and, even in this glorified body, the wounds are still there (Luke 24:39, 40). But these same feet shall trample His enemies (Psalm 110:1; Isaiah 63:3). This aspect of judgment is dominant here, as though the feet had been shod in brazen boots, heated to white heat in the great furnace of judgment where they were treading.

"The voice of his words like the voice of a multitude" (Daniel 10:6). Clear and strong like the trumpet, broad and deep like the sea—so the voice seemed to John. This is the voice that one day will raise the dead (John 5:28, 29) and the same voice that called the world into being (Psalm 33:6).

Revelation 1:16.   And he had in his right hand seven stars: and out of his mouth went a sharp two-edged sword: and his countenance was as the sun shineth in his strength.

Christ was in the midst of the churches, but He held the angels of the churches, represented by the seven stars, in His own right hand. The word "star" (Greek *aster*) can mean any heavenly "light"—meteorites, planets, etc., as well as stars in the modern scientific sense. Evidently the majesty of the Son of man was such that His face gave the appearance of the shining sun and the objects in His hand that of shining stars, both as set against the background of the heavens over Patmos.

The two-edged sword is, in other Scriptures, compared to the power of the Word of God (Hebrews 4:12; Ephesians 6:17). Here it clearly speaks of judgment (compare Revelation 19:15). The very appearance of the glorified Christ and the sound of the majestic voice flowing from the blinding light of His countenance gave every word a swordlike brilliance and sharpness that was almost visible.

The Keys of Hell

Revelation 1:17.   And when I saw him, I fell at his feet as dead. And he laid his right hand upon me, saying unto me, Fear not; I am the first and the last.

The first "Fear not" of the Bible occurs just before the first "I am" of the Bible. "Fear not, Abram: I am thy shield, and thy exceeding great reward" (Genesis 15:1). For mortal, sinful man to come into the presence of the living God is death, and this would have been John's experience were he not "in the Spirit." The hand in which the seven stars were held was laid upon John and the double-edged sword from His mouth spoke peace instead of judgment. John need not fear, for the One who spoke was not only his Creator ("the first and the last") but also His Savior, who died for him and rose again.

Revelation 1:18.   I am he that liveth, and was dead; and, behold, I am alive for evermore, Amen; and have the keys of hell and of death.

This is one of the mountain-peak verses of Scripture, and one of the most amazing of the great claims of Christ. Multitudes of religious philosophers as well as scientists have searched for the key to life and death, but Christ claims to *have* the key. Further He claims to possess the keys to hell (Greek *Hades*). Hades is the New Testament equivalent of the Hebrew *sheol*, both terms describing the abode of departed human spirits.

The position of the scientific establishment, of course, is that neither Hades nor heaven has any real existence. The popular lay view, on the other hand, is that both do exist but in some kind of different state of existence, completely outside the framework of our present physical universe. The fact is, however, the Bible clearly teaches that both heaven and hell literally exist in the present cosmos, and this teaching has not been refuted in any way by modern science.

When the Lord Jesus died on the cross and His body was placed in the tomb, His spirit "descended first into the lower parts of the earth" (Ephesians 4:9). These lower parts of the earth are also called "the deep" (literally "the abyss" from the Greek word *abussos* as in Romans 10:7), and are apparently the same as Hades. But in fulfillment of the prophecy of Psalm 16:10, "He seeing this before spake of the resurrection of Christ, that his soul was not left in [Hades], neither his flesh did see corruption" (Acts 2:31).

Until Christ descended into Hades, It had housed all the souls and spirits of all people who had lived and died before that time. Those who died in faith were "comforted" in one compartment of Hades; all others were separated from these by "a great gulf" and were "in torments" (see Luke 16:23-26). Pre-Calvary believers were safe in God's keeping, trusting His Word that someday the redemption price would be paid and they would be freed. "Forasmuch then as the children are partakers of flesh and blood, he also himself likewise took part of the same; that through death he might destroy him that had the power of death, that is the devil; and deliver them who through fear of death were all their lifetime subject to bondage" (Hebrews 2:14, 15).

Therefore, after He went and proclaimed His victory to the evil spirits still incarcerated in prison (see 1 Peter 3:18-20), "When he ascended up on high, He led captivity captive. . . . He that descended is the same also that ascended up far above all heavens, that he might fill all things" (Ephesians 4:8-10).

All of this is implied in the great assertion by Christ that He now possessed the very keys to Hades and death. "Knowing that Christ being raised from the dead dieth no more; death hath no more dominion over him" (Romans 6:9). "Wherefore he is able also to save them to the uttermost that come unto God by him, seeing he ever liveth to make intercession for them" (Hebrews 7:25).

Ever since, those who die in Christ are translated to "be with Christ" (Philippians 1:23) in heaven. The unsaved dead remain in Hades, whence they will later be brought forth for eternal judgment (Revelation 20:13). In the meantime, the great abyss in the heart of the earth continues to "enlarge herself" (Isaiah 5:14) with multitudes dying in their sins.

Angels of the Churches

Revelation 1:19.   Write the things which thou hast seen, and the things which are, and the things which shall be hereafter.

The conclusion of these wonderful revelations is: "Therefore, *write!*" The threefold division here has been noted by almost every commentator on Revelation: (1) "the things thou hast seen" (perhaps including not only the immediate vision but all the great events of the Apostolic Age in which John himself had been a leading participant); (2) "the things which are" (specifically the existing situation in the church of John's day, representing the needs of all churches throughout the Church Age); (3) "the things which shall be hereafter," clearly identified by use of the same phrase in Revelation 4:1 to be those events described from Revelation 4 onward—the Ages of Judgment and the Kingdom and the New Earth. The last phrase is, literally, "the things which shall be after these things," that is, after the things described in Revelation 2—3. Since at least three of these church exhortations include specific references to the second coming of Christ (Revelation 2:25; 3:3, 11), there is strong indication that the third division relates to events taking place after the initial phases, at least, of the second coming.

Revelation 1:20.   The mystery of the seven stars which thou sawest in my right hand, and the seven golden candlesticks. The seven stars are the angels of the seven churches: and the seven candlesticks which thou sawest are the seven churches.

This verse points up the fact that, when symbols are used in the Book of Revelation, they are explained internally, not subject to imaginative suggestions by allegorizing expositors. The great lampstands symbolize light-bearing churches, and the stars represent the angels of the churches.

But who are these angels? By far the greater number of modern expositors say they represent the pastors of the churches. The Greek word is *aggelos* and apparently has the basic meaning of "messenger." However, the word is used 188 times in the New Testament, practically always (with at most a half-dozen exceptions) to denote real angels rather than human messengers. It would seem that the context must clearly demand it if any messengers other than true angels are meant.

If "angel" means "pastor" here, it is used with this meaning here and nowhere else. If the Lord Jesus meant the pastors of the churches, why did He not *say* "pastors?" Or why did He not say "elders," a term which is used in the New Testament as essentially synonymous with "pastors," and which is later used twelve times in Revelation.

Instead, He spoke of the *angels* of the churches, and this term is used sixty-seven other times in Revelation, in none of which could the meaning possibly be that of "pastors." The principle of natural, literal interpretation seems to require us to understand here that true churches of the Lord have individual angels assigned for their guidance and watch-care.

This fact is hardly surprising in view of the innumerable company of angels (Hebrews 12:22) and their assigned function as ministering spirits to those who are heirs of salvation (Hebrews 1:14). Individual believers have angels assigned to them (Matthew 18:10; Acts 12:15). Angels are present in the assemblies during their services (1 Corinthians 11:10) and are intensely interested in their progress (1 Corinthians 4:9; Ephesians 3:10; 1 Timothy 3:16; 5:21; Hebrews 13:2; 1 Peter 1:12).

Admittedly, the concept of an angel of God assigned to each church and, in some degree, responsible for the effectiveness of its ministry is one which is largely unrecognized among Christians. Nevertheless this seems to be the teaching of the Lord's words here. The symbolism is also appropriate to angels. Stars are frequently identified with angels in Scripture, especially here in Revelation 9:1, 11; 12:3-9).

Thus the letters to the churches were indeed addressed to the churches and to their members and ministers, but they were somehow to be transmitted through their angels. Pastors, elders, deacons, teachers—all may change from time to time as the membership changes. But the individual church itself goes on, sometimes continuing over many generations, and its angel continues with it. Though its members may not be able to see him or communicate with him, he is *there,* and the very knowledge of his protecting and ministering presence should be a source of encouragement and purification in all its activities.

2

Spots and Wrinkles
and Such Things

(Revelation 2)

The Sevenfold Message to the Sevenfold Church

When Christ first promised to build His Church, He also promised that the gates of hell would not prevail against it (Matthew 16:18). When He returned from the dead, He Himself had the keys of hell (Revelation 1:18), the gates had been opened, and those of its captives who had died in faith had been set free to ascend with Him to Paradise. He still retains the keys, and the gates of hell can never close again on those who die in faith, as members of His Church. When they become absent from the body they are immediately present with the Lord (2 Corinthians 5:8).

While still in the flesh, those who are a part of His Church are by no means yet made perfect. But they have been placed into His Body by the Holy Spirit (1 Corinthians 12:13) and can no longer be imprisoned behind the gates of hell. "Christ is the head of the church. . . . Christ also loved the church, and gave himself for it; that he might sanctify and cleanse it with the washing of water by the word, that he might present it to himself a glorious church, not having spot, or wrinkle, or any such thing; but that it should be holy and without blemish" (Ephesians 5:23, 25-27).

Someday, the "spirits of just men" will be "made perfect," as we all gather "to the general assembly and church of the firstborn, which are written in heaven" (Hebrews 12:23). For the time now present, however, we are yet imperfect, and the individual churches in which we now assemble are therefore likewise full of spots and wrinkles. Nevertheless, we belong to Christ, and He is "in our midst," through the Holy Spirit (John 16:7), comforting and leading, convicting and chastening, building His Church.

The picture we see in Revelation 2 and 3 is amazing. Seven churches—the perfect number representing *all* churches—and *all* are most unpromising churches. The churches, outwardly strong, are full of compromise and moral decay. The spiritually strong churches are physically weak. All are highly fallible, persecuted, subject to imminent disintegration and scattering, and none are destined to survive very long. Yet Christ is in their midst, and the Holy Spirit is speaking to them, promising great blessings to those who overcome.

These seven churches were real churches, and visitors by the thousands today include a visit to the ruins of the seven churches of Asia on their chartered tours to the Bible lands. They were real churches, but they are also chosen as representative churches and they still represent our churches today. There is some of Ephesus and Smyrna and all of the others in each of our own churches today. Their problems are *our* problems, and Christ's exhortations to them apply with equal force to us.

Although it is by no means the dominant theme, there is a sense also in which the seven churches seem to depict the respective stages of development and change of Christ's churches during the ensuing centuries. History has, indeed, shown such a general development through the years, and it is reasonable that the sequential development of the respective exhortations in these messages should be arranged by the Lord in the same sequence. He is not capricious in His selection. There is bound to be some significance in the *sequence* of the seven, as well as in the total. The Book of Revelation—*all* of it—is said to be prophecy, and if there is any prophecy in it concerning the Church Age, it must be here in these two chapters. Further, in one way or another, the last four of the churches are to survive until the return of Christ (note verses 2:25; 3:3, 11, 20), and this can only now be fulfilled if these four churches specifically represent stages of church development which persist until the end of the age.

The same format describes each of the seven messages, a fact which further confirms the all-encompassing theme of the messages. Each letter is composed of seven parts, as follows:

1. Salutation. "Unto the angel of the church at . . . write: . . ." As shown in the previous chapter, the "angel" can only have been the *angel*—not a pastor or other human messenger. No church epistle in the New Testament is ever addressed to the pastor, or bishop, or elders of the church. They are always addressed to the *church,* to the people. The context in these indicates the same, with the angel merely representing the church and guarding the transmission of its epistle.

2. Identification of Christ as Sender. "These things saith He that . . ." In each case, He is identified by some characteristic of His appearance that was appropriate to the individual message to the particular church.

3. Assertion of Knowledge. "I know thy works . . ." Christ is in their midst, and so has intimate knowledge of all the works and circumstances and attitudes of each church.

4. Comment and Exhortation. Here is the core of the message to each assembly, sometimes commendatory, sometimes critical, adapted perfectly to the particular situation in each. Always there is an exhortation. None can simply relax as having attained all that Christ desires of them.

5. Promised (or Threatened) Coming. To some, He threatens a coming in judgment for faithlessness, to others, a coming to receive them in death, and to others, His coming at the end of the age. In each case there is a promise or warning that He will come personally to terminate their present circumstances.

6. Admonition to Heed. "He that hath an ear, let him hear what the Spirit saith unto the churches." Though each church has its own particular message, it is vital that each church hear and heed what Christ, through the Spirit, says to all the churches.

7. Promised Blessing. "To him that overcometh. . . ." A special blessing is promised to all those faithful ones in every church who, through their faith (note 1 John 5:4, 5), overcome the world and all its temptations and persecutions.

The Zealous Church

Revelation 2:1.   Unto the angel of the church of Ephesus write; These things saith he that holdeth the seven stars in his right hand, who walketh in the midst of the seven golden candlesticks.

Ephesus was the capital and largest city of the province of Asia (modern southwest Turkey), and a great seaport. It was also a very immoral city, dominated by the worship of the fertility goddess, Diana (Artemis). The Apostle Paul established the church there (Acts 19) and spent more time there than at any of his other churches (Acts 20:31). According to extrabiblical sources, the Apostle John later ministered there for many years and Mary the mother of Jesus died there. Between Paul and John, Timothy was said to have been in charge of the churches in the area.

He who is "better than the angels" (Hebrews 1:4) and who, in fact, holds them all in His hand, and who walks in the midst of every church, reminds all the churches of His position and power as He begins His messages to them by way of the largest and strongest of the churches, the one from which apparently the others had been founded (Acts 19:10).

Revelation 2:2.   "I know thy works, and thy labour, and thy patience, and how thou canst not bear them which are evil: and thou hast tried them which say they are apostles, and are not, and hast found them liars.

The Ephesian Christians, forty years after their church was started by Paul, were still zealous in "works and labour and patience," but they can be contrasted with the first Thessalonian believers, who Paul said exhibited a "work of faith, and labour of love, and patience of hope" (1 Thessalonians 1:3). Faith, love, and hope —these three (1 Corinthians 13:13)—should "abide" in a church, or it will eventually die, no matter how great its zeal. It was good and necessary, however, that the church had indeed been careful to reject those who falsely claimed to be apostles or successors of the apostles. Innumerable people have been led away from God through the centuries by such false leaders. There are *no* successors to the apostles, since one prime requirement of the Apostleship was that he must be one who had seen Christ (1 Corinthians 9:1, 2).

Revelation 2:3.   And hast borne, and hast patience, and for my name's sake hast laboured, and hast not fainted.

Again the Lord emphasizes the zeal and steadfastness of the Ephesian church, all done in the name of Christ. Such characteristics were typical of the churches of the first century—the Apostolic Age. As a result, the gospel had spread all over the known world (Colossians 1:5, 6, 24).

Revelation 2:4.   Nevertheless I have somewhat against thee, because thou hast left thy first love.

This also was typical of the churches of the late Apostolic period; their zeal and faithfulness were still strong, but the warmth of their original love—for one another, for the lost, for the Lord—was beginning to cool. But this sad testimony can be applied to multitudes of churches in every age, and every church needs continually to search its heart and test its love.

It was to the Ephesians, in fact, that Paul had written as he closed his epistle: "Grace be with all them that love our Lord Jesus Christ in sincerity" (Ephesians 6:24). A "first love" (or "chief love," or "best love") is a *sincere* love. Do we love our Lord Jesus Christ *in sincerity,* or have we lost our first love? That is the great question.

Revelation 2:5.   Remember therefore from whence thou art fallen, and repent, and do the first works; or else I will come unto thee quickly, and will remove thy candlestick out of his place, except thou repent.

To the church at Ephesus, zealous and steadfast as it was, it was necessary for Christ to give a call to repentance (literally, a "changing of the mind"). They must return to their first love, go back to their first works, rise up to their first level of spirituality. If not, the day would inevitably come when its angel would be withdrawn and Christ would no longer remain in their midst. A group of people would continue to assemble in Ephesus for many years, calling themselves a church, but it would no longer belong to Christ. It would still be a "candlestick," but it would be "out of his place"—that place being where Christ is. Eventually, even the very city of Ephesus became a ruin.

Ephesus, of course, represents every other church whose love for Christ and His Word and His people has cooled, and the Ephesian warning still applies.

Revelation 2:6.   But this thou hast, that thou hatest the deeds of the Nicolaitanes, which I also hate.

Does it come as a surprise that Christ can *hate* and that He approves of hating on the part of His followers? Strange paradox—coming from the One who said: "Love your enemies." But it was the deeds, not the doers, which were hated. An object of hatred on the part of the One who is Love must indeed be hateful, and it is vital that we know what it is so that we also can hate it—these deeds of the Nicolaitanes!

If the Nicolaitanes were indeed some unknown sect, as most commentators assume, then the reason why Christ included this strange comment in an inspired epistle is also unknown. There was, indeed, a sect of Gnostics later called Nicolaitanes but this was much later than the time of the Book of Revelation. These Gnostics were bitter opponents of the writings of John, and probably adopted the name of Nicolaitanes as a direct affront to those who did accept John's authority.

But who were the Nicolaitanes at the time of John? There is no reliable record of any such cult, although some have speculated that it could have been a group named after the early deacon, Nicolas of Antioch (Acts 6:5). Furthermore there is no other biblical reference to any such sect or teaching.

Yet we must believe that the reference here is important, understandable in its context, and profitable instruction for all churches everywhere. The only clue in the Ephesian letter itself is the previous reference—quite parallel, in fact—to those who falsely claimed to be apostles and who had therefore been rejected by the church.

The Apostle Paul spoke of such pseudo-apostles: "For such are false apostles, deceitful workers, transforming themselves into the apostles of Christ. And no marvel, for Satan himself is transformed into an angel of light. Therefore it is no great thing if his ministers also be transformed as the ministers of righteousness; whose end shall be according to their works" (2 Corinthians 11:13-15). Christ also warned against false Christs and false prophets (Matthew 7:15; 24:5, 24). John himself had warned: "Beloved, believe not every spirit, but try the spirits whether they are of God" (1 John 4:1). John certainly must have taught these Ephesians to do this during his ministry there, and they had indeed "tried them which say they are apostles—and hast found them liars." John also had warned that "every spirit that confesseth not that Jesus Christ is come in the flesh is not of God: and this is that spirit of antichrist" (1 John 4:3).

If there are any deeds that the Lord Jesus Christ must hate, it must be the attempts by men to claim divine authority for themselves—as apostles or as prophets or even as Christ Himself—and thus to deny His own nature and authority. It is very probable that the term "Nicolaitanes" was thus a name originally applied to that considerable group of men who plagued the first-century church by their pretensions to divine authority. The name itself comes from the Greek words *nikao* ("overcome"—used also several places in Chapters 2 and 3 to refer to those who "overcome" in the Christian life) and *laos* ("people"). It is also possible that some prominent false apostle was named Nicolaus, and the Nicolaitan name thus became associated also with him, but probably the primary reason for adopting the name was its meaning—"Those who conquer the people." This, at least, must be the reason why Christ, through John, used it here without any other identification or explanation.

Thus, the Nicolaitanes, whose deeds Christ *hates,* were men who came into these early churches with the purpose of usurping the authority of the true apostles, such as John, and even of Christ Himself. To accomplish, this, they claimed to have divine unction or powers, even working pseudo-miracles. They were eloquent and persuasive men. Peter described them as "false teachers" bringing in "damnable heresies, even denying the Lord that bought them," able to succeed in this by using "feigned words" and "great swelling words of vanity" (2 Peter 2:1, 3, 18). By such means, these false apostles, these "conquerors of the people," sought to turn "the grace of our God into lasciviousness" (Jude 4) and to "allure through the lusts of the flesh, through much wantonness" (2 Peter 2:18) the young believers in these struggling churches. John had warned his converts, no doubt including those at Ephesus, about such deceivers in very strong language: "For many deceivers are entered into the world, who confess not that Jesus Christ is come in the flesh. This is a deceiver and an antichrist. . . . If there come any [such] unto you, . . . receive him not into your house, neither bid him God speed" (2 John 7, 10). The Ephesians were well taught in doctrine—by Paul, by Timothy, and then by John—so they were able to recognize these lying "apostles," and they "hated" their deeds, and the Lord commended them because of it.

This danger was not unique to the early church, and Christ desires all churches to watch for, and repudiate, Nicolaitanism. The dangers are as real today. False prophets, false apostles, pseudo-miracles, people-conquerors, false teachers who deny the true divine/human nature of Christ, antinomian teachers who teach that God's grace excuses deliberately licentious behavior, men who take authority and power to themselves that Christ never intended, are at least as great a problem in the modern church as in the early church. Christ hates the deeds of such as these, and so should we. We should not hate the men or women who practice such things, but we must hate and repudiate their deeds and doctrines.

Revelation 2:7.   He that hath an ear, let him hear what the Spirit saith unto the churches; To him that overcometh will I give to eat of the tree of life, which is in the midst of the paradise of God.

It is a divine principle that only those who *desire* to do God's will can know God's will (John 7:17). So, only those who have spiritual ears can hear the Spirit's word. Note that Christ and the Holy Spirit are so much *one* that what one says, the other says. Also note that the message to the church at Ephesus was also the message to all the churches.

John occasionally had used the word "overcome" (*nikao* in the Greek, same as in the prefix in *Nicolaites*) in his epistles (as in 1 John 2:13) and in his Gospel (John 16:33), but in these it always has an object (such as "wicked one" or "world"). Here in these epistles, however, the picture is one of overcoming all things in Christ—"overcoming" in general. This is the first of these seven gracious promises to the "overcomer," and it looks back to the primeval creation, with the life-giving tree in the midst of the garden (Genesis 2:9; 3:22, 24). But it also looks forward to the new creation, where the tree of life will again be planted —not one tree only, but in the midst of the streets and along the banks of the river of water of life in the New Jerusalem. Adam was barred from the tree of life but the overcomer will have free access to it eternally.

The Church in Tribulation

In recent decades, there has been much theological disputation as to whether or not the Church will go through the tribulation. The fact is that every real church must endure some degree of tribulation. "We must through much tribulation enter into the kingdom of God" (Acts 14:22). "All that will live godly in Christ Jesus shall suffer persecution" (2 Timothy 3:12). The church at Smyrna is the Lord's choice to illustrate the suffering church and its needs.

Revelation 2:8.   And unto the angel of the church in Smyrna write; These things saith the first and the last, which was dead, and is alive.

Smyrna was also a port city, about thirty-five miles north of Ephesus. It survives today as Ismir, in Turkey. One of John's converts, Polycarp, served as a minister there until his martyrdom about A.D. 155.

No greater comfort could be addressed to a persecuted church than to be reminded that the Lord was still in their midst and that He Himself, as the Creator and Heir of all things, had already conquered death. In Him, they were certain to gain the ultimate victory.

Revelation 2:9.   I know thy works, and tribulation, and poverty (but thou art rich) and I know the blasphemy of them which say they are Jews, and are not, but are the synagogue of Satan.

The Smyrna Christians were not only persecuted but impoverished as a result of their stand for Christ. Nevertheless they were wealthy because they were laying up treasures in heaven (Matthew 6:20) and possessed "the true riches" (Luke 16:11). Paul also noted that true "ministers of God" would be "as sorrowful, yet alway rejoicing; as poor, yet making many rich; as having nothing; and yet possessing all things" (2 Corinthians 6:10).

There was another problem. As Ephesus was plagued with men who said they were apostles but were not, so Smyrna was beset by men who said they were Jews but were not. As false apostles are "ministers of Satan" (2 Corinthians 11:15), so false Jews constitute a "synagogue of Satan." Their very claim to be Jews (and therefore God's chosen people) is blasphemy, Christ says.

There was, indeed, a very large community of Jews in Smyrna, and these strongly opposed the church and the gospel. They were directly instrumental in persuading the Roman officials of the city to execute Polycarp. The records say they even carried logs to the pyre on which he was burned.

But these were real Jews, in the physical sense at least. It is possible that the Lord is here referring to the fact that, in God's sight, those who are truly Jews are Jews who are spiritually in tune with God's will and thus have received the Lord Jesus as their Messiah (Romans 2:28, 29; John 8:39; Romans 9:6-8). This is a doubtful interpretation, however, for the New Testament everywhere continues to call those who were born of Jewish stock Jews regardless of whether they were Jews spiritually. It would hardly be surprising, let alone blasphemous, for the Jewish colony in Smyrna to call themselves Jews, since everyone else did too.

The probability is that this reference denotes a group who were claiming to be Jews spiritually, but were not Jews, either physically or spiritually. The church had been burdened almost from its inception with Jewish converts who did not want to separate themselves from the synagogue fellowship and from their lifelong customs, and so were trying to impose circumcision and other aspects of the Old Testament ritual and national ordinances upon the church—not only the Jews in the church but the Gentiles as well (Acts 15:2; Galatians 2:14; Colossians 2:16). These "Judaizers" influenced many Gentiles, and soon many of these came to believe that conversion to Christianity meant, in effect, conversion also to Judaism and that the latter was to be perpetuated, with some modifications, in the church.

Eventually this would lead to a monstrous system of works-salvation and almost a complete disappearance of the doctrines of salvation by grace and justification by faith. As one group of false teachers, in Ephesus, wanted to continue the Apostleship, so the other, in Smyrna, wanted to continue the priesthood. Eventually the two merged in a vast worldly system, with an imaginary apostolic succession and an elaborate visible priesthood, both having (as Nicolaitanes) conquered the laity and placed them again in legalistic bondage under a complex system of ritualistic ordinances, sacrifices, and penances. This system was experiencing its embryonic development among cliques in such churches as that in Smyrna, where the heavy outward pressure of the large colony of ethnic Jews was encouraging such compromise.

Revelation 2:10.   Fear none of those things which thou shalt suffer: behold, the devil shall cast some of you into prison, that ye may be tried; and ye shall have tribulation ten days; be thou faithful unto death, and I will give thee a crown of life.

Although suffering, including imprisonment and even martyrdom, would be the lot of many in Smyrna, as well as in countless other churches through the centuries, the gracious word from Christ is: "Fear not!" Not even death can separate us from the love of God in Christ (Romans 8:38, 39) and the martyr's promised "crown of life" (see also James 1:12) will far overbalance the testing he is called to endure in this life.

The phrase "ten days of tribulation" has been variously interpreted. Some have taken it to mean ten years of special persecution which was coming to the church in Smyrna, perhaps being climaxed in the burning of Polycarp, their pastor. But, if that were so, why did Christ not say "ten years?" Further, how could this be applied to all other churches?

Many, assuming that Smyrna specifically represents the period of the great Roman persecutions of the church in the second and third centuries, have tried to enumerate ten waves of persecution, the last under Diocletian just before the conversion of Constantine. But such a list is forced and very arbitrary at best. And again, why would not Christ have predicted such a situation plainly if that were His meaning?

The intent of the passage is obviously to prepare the church for intense suffering and yet to assure them it would be very brief and ephemeral in contrast to the endless ages of glory beyond it. As Paul had said; "For our light affliction, which is but for a moment, worketh for us a far more exceeding and eternal weight of glory" (2 Corinthians 4:17).

If we assume the "ten days" to be a symbolic expression designed to contrast the brevity of the suffering with its benefits, is there any reason for mentioning "ten days" instead of, say, "seven days" or some other small number? The most likely parallel reference is in the Book of Daniel, which of course is a book quite intimately related to Revelation. There, right at the beginning of his ministry (just as Smyrna is at the beginning of the Church Age and the beginning of the Book of Revelation), Daniel and his three Jewish friends offered to undergo "ten days" of what might seem to outsiders to be sacrifice and deprivation (Daniel 1:12, 14, 15) on a diet of only pulse and water. Instead of hurting them, however, this ten days of "proving" or "testing" (Daniel 1:14), produced most salutary results. "And in all matters of wisdom and understanding, that the king inquired of them, he found them ten times better than all . . . in all his realm" (Daniel 1:20). Ten days of testing, in Daniel's case, then yielded over seventy years of uniquely effective service for God.

Just so, Christ's assures Christians in Smyrna and all other suffering churches that a brief "ten days" of testing will, if accepted with a resolve to be "faithful unto death," yield a crown of life and glory that will be ten times greater when Jesus comes. Furthermore, "the blood of the martyrs is the seed of the church," and a patient endurance of unjust persecution has always been one of the church's most potent tools of evangelism.

Revelation 2:11.   He that hath an ear, let him hear what the Spirit saith unto the churches; He that overcometh shall not be hurt of the second death.

What Christ says "unto the angel of the church" is the same as "what the Spirit saith unto the churches." The glorified Lord gives the message, John writes the message, the angel guards and assures the arrival of the message, then the Spirit speaks the message to listening ears and open hearts.

And the wonderful promise to those who overcome fear and, in their work for Christ, remain steadfast unto death is that death in this world is entrance to life in a better world where they will never face a second death. Those who die without Christ, however, will also die again (Revelation 20:12-14).

The Church Infiltrated

Though Ephesus had left its first love, and Smyrna was suffering from attacks both internal and external, both churches had maintained sound doctrine and practice despite all the efforts of false teachers to subvert them and gain control over them. But Pergamos is another story. Despite much good in the church, evil influences had gained a real foothold in the church, and they needed to be rebuked.

Revelation 2:12.   And to the angel of the church in Pergamos write; These things saith he which hath the sharp sword with two edges.

Pergamos was at the center of the province of Asia, sixty miles north of Smyrna. It was a great religious center, with the cult of the emperor as well as the Greek pagan mysteries, flourishing there. The great altar of Zeus, one of the Seven Wonders of the World, was located here—the largest altar in the world. It was also an intellectual center, with a 200,000 volume library—the word "parchment" is derived from its name—as well as a medical center, with the deity of medicine, Aesculapius (whence our word "scalpel") being worshiped, commonly under the sign of a coiled snake on a pole (note Numbers 21:8-9).

The twin heresies of Nicolaitanism and Balaamism had made sharp inroads in the Pergamos church, so Christ emphasized He must come to them cutting these out, as it were, with the double-edged sword proceeding from His mouth.

Revelation 2:13.   I know thy works, and where thou dwellest, even where Satan's seat is: and thou holdest fast my name, and hast not denied my faith, even in those days wherein Antipas was my faithful martyr, who was slain among you, where Satan dwelleth.

The Lord Jesus commends the Pergamites because they had maintained the true faith and preached it in the name of the true Christ under extremely trying circumstances and against much temptation to compromise. One member had been a witness faithful even to death (the words "witness" and "martyr' are the same). The man Antipas is not mentioned elsewhere in Scripture. Although he was undoubtedly a real martyr at Pergamos, the fact that his name can mean "Against All" may suggest he also represents any believer who has been willing to stand for the true faith in the name of Christ against all opposition, even if it costs his life.

Satan's seat (literally "throne") may have been an expression used to refer to the gigantic temple of Zeus at Pergamos, set on a high hill with its altar towering 800 feet over the plain. More likely, however, it refers to the fact that Pergamos had become probably the greatest center of pagan religion in the world at that time. In fact, Alexander Hislop, in his famous book *Two Babylons,* gave much documentation to show that Pergamos had inherited the religious mantle of ancient Babylon when Babylon fell in the days of Belshazzar. The priests, who had kept the secrets of the ancient mystery religions centered at Babylon ever since the days of Nimrod, were forced to migrate at that time, transferring what amounted to the headquarters of Satan's religious system away from Babylon north and west to Pergamos where it endured for several centuries in that great center of evolutionary pantheistic paganism. Still later, it moved to Rome. If Hislop's analysis is correct, "Satan's throne" becomes a very literal description of the invisible principalities and powers centered at Pergamos.

Revelation 2:14.   But I have a few things against thee, because thou hast there them that hold the doctrine of Balaam, who taught Balac to cast a stumblingblock before the children of Israel, to eat things sacrificed unto idols, and to commit fornication.

The Pergamites had not kept out the false teachers, as had the churches at Ephesus and Smyrna. Even though they had not yet embraced their teachings, they had allowed them in the church, and the leaven was beginning to work.

The meaning of Balaam (Hebrew meaning "not of the people") is similar to that of the Nicolaitanes (Greek meaning "conquering the people"). The doctrine of Balaam (who, like the Nicolaitanes, had also been a false prophet) was to gain control over God's people by seducing them to compromise with the world, especially in sexual sins (Numbers 31:15, 16; Jude 11; 2 Peter 2:15), and in going along with those who worshiped false gods. This spirit of compromise has surely been one of the greatest evils in the Christian church ever since the days of the church at Pergamos.

Revelation 2:15.   So hast thou also them that hold the doctrine of the Nicolaitanes, which thing I hate.

The church at Ephesus had encountered the Nicolaitanes, but had not countenanced them (for the identity and teaching of these false apostles see the comments above on Revelation 2:6). The difference here was twofold: (1) the Pergamites were allowing the Nicolaitanes to be members of their church and to begin to propagandize their heresies; (2) the *doctrine* of the Nicolaitanes (or their "teaching") was a problem at Pergamos, rather than only their "deeds," as at Ephesus. Christ, of course, makes it plain that He hates both their deeds and their doctrines.

Revelation 2:16.   Repent; or else I will come unto thee quickly, and will fight against them with the sword of my mouth.

For the sin of harboring and listening to Balaamites and Nicolaitanes in their assembly, Christ must call the church at Pergamos to repentance. Their minds must be changed (which is the meaning of "repent") from an attitude of compromise to one of insistence on doctrinal and moral purity. Otherwise they would face the fearful prospect of judgment by the same verbal sword which will one day smite the nations (Revelation 19:15).

Revelation 2:17.   He that hath an ear, let him hear what the Spirit saith unto the churches; To him that overcometh will I give to eat of the hidden manna, and will give him a white stone, and in the stone a new name written, which no man knoweth saving he that receiveth it.

The promise to the overcomers in Pergamos is striking and unique. The "hidden manna" alludes to the manna that was hidden in the ark of the covenant (Exodus 16:33; Hebrews 9:4) as a reminder to future generations how God had fed His people in the wilderness. The Lord Jesus had already made it clear that this hidden manna represented Himself. "I am the living bread which came down from heaven: if any man eat of this bread, he shall live for ever" (John 6:51). The "white stone" also refers to the wilderness experience. In the breastplate of the high priest were woven twelve different precious stones, each inscribed with the name of one of the twelve tribes (Exodus 28:15-21). None of these were white stones, however. The white stone presumably is a sparkling diamond, perhaps answering to the *Urim* ("lights") also worn in Aaron's breastplate (Leviticus 8:8). In any case, all were worn by the high priest when he would enter into the holy place into the presence of the Lord. He alone could then have access to the ark of the covenant wherein reposed the hidden manna.

This promise to those who overcome—particularly those who are unwaveringly faithful to God's truth in an environment of religious compromise, as at Pergamos—is thus of assured access to God's presence and faithful provision of all needs. The most precious promise, however, is that the Lord will give each such faithful one a new name chosen by Himself, a name of special communication and fellowship known only to the Giver and receiver, a name reflecting our service for Him in this world and the world to come. The names we bear now were chosen by our parents, and may or may not be appropriate. In the Scriptures, names were chosen (especially *new* names—Abraham, Israel, etc.) to accord with the character and calling of the one so named. When we all appear before the judgment seat of Christ, those who are overcomers will have accumulated to their heavenly accounts "gold, silver, precious stones" (1 Corinthians 3:12), and the Lord will "make up [His] jewels" in that day for "them that feared the Lord, and that thought upon his name" (Malachi 3:16, 17). Then that new name, inscribed in a beautiful pure white gem, will be worn and borne by us in His name, forever.

The Adulterous Church

The letter to the church at Thyatira is the central and longest of the seven letters. There was much to commend in this church, but also a more serious and flagrant sin to be rebuked. Thyatira was about forty miles east of Pergamos, perhaps the least important of the seven cities politically. Its main importance was as a trade center, with many trade guilds. Paul's convert, Lydia, was a "seller of purple" from Thyatira (Acts 16:14) and possibly could have assisted in the formation of this church.

Revelation 2:18.   And unto the angel of the church in Thyatira write; These things saith the Son of God, who hath his eyes like unto a flame of fire, and his feet are like fine brass.

The salutation to Thyatira identifies the speaker as the Son of God—the only place in Revelation where He is so called. He was described initially as "one like unto the Son of man" (Revelation 1:13). The aspect is awesome—one of offended and angry deity, with burning eyes searching "the reins and hearts" (verse 23) and with trampling feet in burnished brass breaking men like potsherds (verse 27).

Revelation 2:19.   I know thy works, and charity, and service, and faith, and thy patience, and thy works; and the last to be more than the first.

Unlike Ephesus, which had left its first love and ceased its first works (verses 4, 5), the later works of Thyatira were more impressive than in its beginning. A church manifesting much "love and service and faith and patience and good works," and with these increasing all the time, would seem to be almost an ideal church. It may be that Lydia of Thyatira (Acts 16:13-15, 40) had left a lasting mark on the church and its members. But such attributes, vital as they are, cannot substitute for sound doctrine and godly living, and these were rapidly failing at Thyatira.

Revelation 2:20.   Notwithstanding I have a few things against thee, because thou sufferest that woman Jezebel, which calleth herself a prophetess, to teach and to seduce my servants to commit fornication, and to eat things sacrificed unto idols.

Ephesus had not been duped by those who falsely called themselves apostles, but Thyatira had actually entrusted a position of teaching leadership to an immoral woman calling herself a prophetess. Paul had specifically forbidden women to speak in the church (1 Corinthians 14:34, referring especially to the use of supposed supernatural gifts, such as tongues and prophecy) or to teach in such a way as to exercise authority over men (1 Timothy 2:11, 12), and ignoring such instruction had led to a tragic situation at Thyatira.

Whether Jezebel was the actual or assumed name of this false prophetess or merely a graphic appellation given her by Christ, the spiritual kinship with the Jezebel of old is clearly recognized. *That* Jezebel ws the cause of a vast turning to "whoredoms and witchcrafts" in Israel in the days of Elijah (2 Kings 9:22) as well as Baal-worshiping idolatry (1 Kings 16:30-33). *This* Jezebel had, under the guise of promoting spirituality in the soul, promoted carnality in the life, no doubt stressing "love" while degrading "doctrine" and "separation" (as multitudes of churches do today), and justifying this teaching by asserting she had received it by supernatural revelation. She had persuaded them there was no need to create an unnecessary antagonism with those around them by refusing to participate in the approved practices of the state system (including even religious prostitution and orgiastic feasting with friends in the temples), since salvation was free and the important matters were love and faith and good works. Even those in the church who still had not followed her teachings were guilty of "suffering that woman Jezebel."

Revelation 2:21.   And I gave her space to repent of her fornication; and she repented not.

The Thyatiran "prophetess" had, in some way not stated, actually been made aware of the serious nature of her sin; it was not merely a case of a misguided but sincere woman who thought she was divinely inspired and sharing God's revelations with the church. Rather, she knew she was in the wrong, but had deliberately rejected God's Word and refused to change her mind. Evidently this was also true of those who had become her followers in the church. The only remedy was judgment.

Revelation 2:22.   Behold, I will cast her into a bed, and them that commit adultery with her into great tribulation, except they repent of their deeds.

The pagan rites of the trade guilds at Thyatira involved immoral feasts along with idol worship, under the aegis of the "priestess" or "oracle" of their temple, and her bevy of temple prostitutes. Jezebel had seemingly led the Thyatiran church into a pseudo-Christian imitation of this system, perhaps ostensibly as a means of more easily winning converts to Christianity. But this was not only physical adultery but religious adultery and could no longer be tolerated by the true Head of the church. It is remarkable that similar wicked sophistries have been practiced in one way or another in the name of Christ in many churches and Christian movements over the centuries and are still cropping up frequently today.

The bed into which Jezebel and her disciples will fall, however, will not be one of orgiastic abandon, but one of *great tribulation*. The same words had been used by Christ long before on the Mount of Olives: "For then shall be great tribulation, such as was not since the beginning of the world to this time, no, nor ever shall be" (Matthew 24:21). The same words are also used in the Book of Revelation to describe a coming time in which great numbers of Christian martyrs will be slain. "These are they which came out of great tribulation, and have washed their robes, and made them white in the blood of the Lamb" (Revelation 7:14). This "great tribulation" will be discussed more fully later, but it should be noted that this particular church, and others like it (or more precisely those people in such churches who are, in effect, followers of the false prophetesses and false prophets —the Nicolaitanes and Balaamites—who have deceived them and led them to deny the truth of Christ and His Word) will indeed experience great tribulation, whether (as will be true of many adulterous churches at the end of the Church Age) they will go through *the* great tribulation or will experience great tribulation in other ways and times.

Revelation 2:23.   And I will kill her children with death; and all the churches shall know that I am he which searcheth the reins and hearts: and I will give unto every one of you according to your works.

The children of Jezebel possibly included actual illegitimate children of her promiscuity, but the term more definitely refers to her converts. As Timothy was a "son" of Paul (1 Timothy 1:2) "in the faith," so Jezebel had won many to her hedonistic brand of pseudo-Christianity, and they would share with her in the coming tribulation. To "kill with death" is an idiom denoting sure death by execution.

The Lord Jesus Christ searches and understands the hearts and secret thoughts of men. He had said: "Out of the heart proceed evil thoughts, murders, adulteries, fornications, thefts, false witness, blasphemies" (Matthew 15:19). All of the churches (not just Thyatira) must know that Christ will judge such behavior appropriately, when repentance is not forthcoming.

Revelation 2:24.   But unto you I say, and unto the rest in Thyatira, as many as have not this doctrine, and which have not known the depths of Satan as they speak; I will put upon you none other burden.

This letter is actually being addressed to the faithful remnant in Thyatira. Jezebel and her followers are *"they,"* not *"you"*; even though they dominate the church, they are not really in the church, as Christ views it, and are destined for destruction in a fast-approaching time of great tribulation. The Lord now directs his remaining exhortation to those in the church who are faithful to His Word and manifesting so beautifully His will in other ways (verse 19).

The depths (or "deep things") of Satan may be contrasted with "the deep things of God" (1 Corinthians 2:10). Nicolaitanism had been rejected in Ephesus, countenanced in Pergamos, and indulged in Thyatira. The pagan mystery religions surrounding the churches did indeed instruct their own "adepts" in many of the deepest secrets of the great satanic conspiracy against God, and the same has been—and still is—true in the various occult religions of the world. Satan is a bitter enemy of any true church and accomplishes a victory whenever he can corrupt a church in any degree. But his most satisfying triumphs are when he introduces his own "deep things" into the church instead of the deep things of God. This he had done so successfully at Thyatira that the godly remnant there was helpless to combat it. It must be expunged by Christ Himself. In the meantime, the true church there must simply wait for Him.

Revelation 2:25.   But that which ye have already, hold fast till I come.

This is the first explicit reference in the seven epistles to the return of Christ. Although the existing church at Thyatira would not be existing when He returned, as far as they knew at the time. However, they were certainly expected to be watching for Him—as is true for all churches through the centuries. Christ's admoition is directly applicable to all churches with similar problems to those at Thyatira. And since Christ knows all churches (He is Alpha and Omega), He clearly anticipates here that some Thyatira-like churches will actually be functioning in the world when He finally does return. Certainly there are many such today.

Revelation 2:26.   And he that overcometh, and keepeth my works unto the end, to him will I give power over the nations.

Immediately after this mention of Christ's return comes mention of the millennial kingdom which follows His return. These "overcoming" believers in Thyatira, as in other churches, will thus share Christ's reign over the nations with those future believers who will be martyred during the reign of the beast which precedes it (Revelation 20:4).

Revelation 2:27.   And he shall rule them with a rod of iron; as the vessels of a potter shall they be broken to shivers: even as I received of my Father.

The introduction to this letter marks Revelation's only reference to Christ as the Son of God. However, there are three references to God as His Father (2:27; 3:5, 21). The terminology here is clearly taken from Psalm 2:7-9. There, however, the specific promise is to the Son. Here the same promise is shared by the Son with his faithful servants. "The *saints* shall judge the world" (1 Corinthians 6:2; see also Daniel 7:18, 27). The "rule" which is to be exercised is actually "tend," or "feed," like a shepherd or pastor. The "rod" with which he rules is the same as the word for "sceptre" (Hebrews 1:8).

Revelation 2:28.   And I will give him the morning star.

Jesus Christ Himself is "the bright and morning star" (Rev. 22:16) so that this promise assures His own presence as a gift to His people. Perhaps it also refers again to His second coming—this time in its very first aspect, when He comes to catch up into His presence those who believe on Him (1 Thessalonians 4:16, 17).

Revelation 2:29.   He that hath an ear, let him hear what the Spirit saith unto the churches.

This regular exhortation has appeared previously before the promise to the overcomers; in the last four epistles, however, it comes after the promise and concludes the epistle. There is no obvious reason for this change, but it is also true that each of the last four epistles also contains exhortations concerning the imminent return of Christ. Thus they seem to represent four types of churches that will be active when Christ comes, perhaps more in need of a final exhortation from the Holy Spirit to be ready than of a promised blessing in the world to come.

3

The Hour of Temptation

(Revelation 3)

The History of the Church

As noted earlier, there is indication of a certain parallel between church history and the seven church epistles of Revelation 2 and 3. This prophetic interpretation, in fact, has often been taken as the primary meaning of these chapters, covering the history of the period between John's time and the "rapture" of the church. Entire books have been written developing this one theme.

The problem with this interpretation, however, is that there is no suggestion in the Scriptures themselves that the intention of these letters was to outline seven periods of church history. At best, therefore, this could only have been an incidental and secondary purpose. The format is not one of prophecy, as is true of the rest of Revelation, but simply of exhortation. The churches addressed were all real churches, active at the time John was writing. The symbolic significance of the seven-part messages to seven selected churches, as pointed out earlier, is simply that these churches do represent all true churches, in all nations and all times. The message to each church is profitable for every church. "He that hath an ear, let him hear what the Spirit saith unto the *churches*," is the admonition to each church and each reader.

It is possible, on the other hand, that there may be a secondary prophetic application, even though it is not the primary interpretation. Although the prophetic aspects are not so specific that they would have enabled the reader to predict the events before they happened, one can indeed discern some historical parallels in retrospect, some correspondence as the following rough correlation suggests:

Letter to the Church	Period in Church History	
1. Ephesus	Apostolic Age	Before A.D. 100
2. Smyrna	Age of Persecution	A.D. 100-A.D. 313
3. Pergamos	Imperial Church Age	A.D. 313-A.D. 590
4. Thyatira	Age of Papacy	A.D. 590-A.D. 1517
5. Sardis	Reformation Age	A.D. 1517-A.D. 1730
6. Philadelphia	Missionary Age	A.D. 1730-A.D. 1900
7. Laodicea	Age of Apostasy	A.D. 1900-?

There is no doubt that many parallels can be drawn between the conditions described in each church and the corresponding developments in ecclesiastical history. At the same time, writers have often seriously strained their exegesis in seeking to make the parallels more convincing than they actually are.

It is not unreasonable to think that the Lord Jesus Christ should arrange His seven messages in some logical order, since He is "not the author of confusion" (1 Corinthians 14:33) and, therefore, does nothing capriciously. For that matter, they *are* arranged in a logical geographical order, proceeding clockwise around the seven, beginning with the one closest to Patmos, where John first heard the messages. But it is certainly possible that the order was also selected to correlate with Christ's prescient awareness of how various movements and problems would later develop among churches worldwide.

Since such a prophetic application of these seven messages is at least equivocal, however, and since there is nothing directly said by Christ to require—or even to suggest—such an application, a literalistic approach to the study of Revelation cannot place much emphasis on it. This reservation, however, in no way suggests that the messages are applicable only to the specific churches to whom they were originally addressed. The vision of Christ walking in the midst of seven representative churches is more than sufficient reason to conclude that the messages apply to all churches in all ages, some to some churches more than others, and perhaps some to some periods more than others.

That the messages were intended to apply to the very end of the church age is evident from the fact that, in some cases at least, the imminent return of Christ is mentioned in the epistles. This is especially true of the last four churches—Thyatira, Sardis, Philadelphia and Laodicea. Chapter 3 of Revelation concludes the seven letters with the last three of these, all written, so to speak, in the shadow of the coming period of judgment, the great tribulation, "the hour of temptation, which shall come upon all the world, to try them that dwell upon the earth" (Revelation 3:10).

The Church of Dead Orthodoxy

Revelation 3:1.   And unto the angel of the church in Sardis write; These things saith he that hath the seven Spirits of God, and the seven stars; I know thy works, that thou hast a name that thou livest, and art dead.

Sardis was a wealthy and wicked city, famed as the capital of ancient Lydia, the home of King Croesus and of Aesop. It was located about thirty miles southeast of Thyatira. A small remnant of the city still exists, but most has been in ruins for over 500 years.

The Sardis letter contains no specific commendation whatever of the church at Sardis. Whatever the church had once been, it now retained only a remnant of its original zeal and spirituality. The deadness of the church perhaps is the reason why the Lord identified Himself as the one with the seven Spirits of God (that is, the omnipresent and all-seeing Holy Spirit) and with the seven stars, or seven angels. The church was in dire need of the quickening power of the Holy Spirit, as well as the protection of its ministering angels.

The church had once been known as a strong, Christ-honoring church. They still used the name of Christ, and were outwardly a church of Christ, but the life was gone. Evidently most of the members were professing Christians, but not truly regenerate, and thus only going through the motions of religion. This situation is sadly true also of multitudes of churches today.

Revelation 3:2.   Be watchful, and strengthen the things which remain that are ready to die: for I have not found thy works perfect before God.

Each of the four previous churches had been commended by Christ for certain good works. Sardis, however, had none that were sufficient to warrant any approbation at all. Some of its works might have been outwardly impressive toward man, but not "before God," for the motivation was wrong even when the works were good.

There were some in Sardis, however, who were genuine believers and were halfheartedly trying to maintain a testimony. Evidently they were discouraged and about to give up; the ungodly environment in which they lived and the lethargic church in which they served were altogether deadening.

Note also that these in the remnant at Sardis were admonished to "be watchful." The implication is to *become* watchful. The remedy for lethargy and routine religiosity is an awakening to the imminence of Christ's return. Long before, Christ had told His disciples: "Watch therefore: for ye know not what hour your Lord doth come" (Matthew 24:42).

Revelation 3:3.   Remember therefore how thou hast received and heard, and hold fast, and repent. If therefore thou shalt not watch, I will come on thee as a thief, and thou shalt not know what hour I will come upon thee.

The promised return of Christ is sure; the time of that return is unknown. It could have taken place in the lifetime of those living in Sardis at the time it was written. As time goes on, the probability of Christ's return at the time of the then living generation becomes ever greater, and thus the more urgent it becomes for believers to watch for Him. "For yourselves know perfectly that the day of the Lord so cometh as a thief in the night. But ye, brethren, are not in darkness, that that day should overtake you as a thief" (1 Thessalonians 5:2, 4). One of the saddest things a Christian could contemplate is the prospect of being engaged in some Christ-dishonoring activity at the moment of Christ's return, thus to "be ashamed before him at his coming" (1 John 2:28).

Christians in such all-but-dead churches must not only awaken to the truth of Christ's second coming but must also look back to their own conversions, when they received Christ and heard His voice. To these great truths they must hold fast, repenting of their spiritual indifference.

Revelation 3:4.   Thou hast a few names even in Sardis which have not defiled their garments; and they shall walk with me in white: for they are worthy.

The gracious Lord, as at Sodom, was glad to acknowledge even the very few whose garments of salvation (Isaiah 61:10) were genuine. Their names were still in the book of life (see next verse) and their robes had been washed and made "white in the blood of the Lamb" (Revelation 7:14). Their worthiness was not in their own good works, which had been pronounced imperfect before God (verse 2), but in the Lord, who alone is truly worthy (Revelation 4:11; 5:9, 12). These would be included at the marriage of the Lamb, when to the true bride of Christ it will be "granted" (not bartered) that she should be "arrayed in fine linen, clean and white: for the fine linen is the righteousness of saints" (Revelation 19:8). Those who truly have eternal life through faith in the atoning blood of the Lamb will, of course, also demonstrate in their redeemed lives the evidence of good works, the "righteous acts of the saints."

Revelation 3:5.   He that overcometh, the same shall be clothed in white raiment; and I will not blot out his name out of the book of life, but I will confess his name before my Father, and before his angels.

It is infinitely important that one's name be in the book of life, for at the last judgment, "whosoever was not found written in the book of life was cast into the lake of fire" (Revelation 20:15). Thus the term "he that overcometh" applies to all who are not finally cast into the lake of fire, for it is only these whose names will remain "in the book of life of the Lamb slain from the foundation of the world" (Revelation 13:8). During the coming reign of the beast, those believers living at that time will demonstrate their overcoming faith by not worshiping the beast, even at the cost of their lives (Revelation 13:15). In any age, the overcomers are those not afraid to confess Christ (Luke 12:8). The "fearful," however, will have their part in the lake of fire (Revelation 21:8).

But what is the meaning of "blotting out" these names from the book of life? Are certain people saved for a while only to be lost forever when the judgment comes? This seems to be the most obvious meaning of these words, but such an interpretation would contradict many other Scriptures (such as John 10:28, 29 and Romans 8:35-39) which teach clearly that anyone who is *genuinely* saved is eternally saved.

This is a controversial passage, but a possible harmonization can be made by noting the special circumstances of infants who die before the age of "accountability." The book of life, as its very name implies, probably contains the names of all those for whom Christ died—in other words, all who have ever been conceived in the womb, and who thus have received God's created spirit of life. Since Christ died for the sin inherent in every person conceived, a child who dies before becoming a deliberate and conscious sinner does not need to be "saved" from sin, since he has never sinned, and since Christ has made propitiation for his innate sin. When a child does become a conscious sinner, however, he thenceforth is lost and needs to be saved; he needs to be "born again." His name is still inscribed in the book of life, because he is still living and may, before he dies, trust Christ to save him and give him everlasting life. If he continues in his sin and his unrepentant, unforgiven state until death, however, then his name will finally and irrevocably be blotted out of the book of life, and he will experience a *second* death (Revelation 20:14) as well as physical death.

Those who believe on the Lord Jesus Christ unto salvation and everlasting life (John 10:28), however, will indeed "overcome" in whatever test the Lord may allow them to experience. Their names are not blotted out, and therefore the Lord will be able to confess their names before His Father.

Revelation 3:6.   He that hath an ear, let him hear what the Spirit saith unto the churches.

Even in such a church as Sardis, where both belief and practice have deteriorated to mere form and only a handful of its professing members really possess eternal life through trust in the name of Christ, the Spirit still calls men to repentance and revival. "He that heareth my word," saith the Lord (stressing genuine hearing in obedient faith) "is passed from death unto life" (John 5:24).

The Church of the Open Door

Only two of the seven churches were living and serving in such a way as to receive no explicit rebuke from the Lord, and both of these were small and weak churches in the eyes of the world. The first was Smyrna, a church undergoing terrible persecutions for its testimony; the last was Philadelphia, a church which is maintaining a faithful witness in the midst of general apostasy and unbelief.

Revelation 3:7.   And to the angel of the church in Philadelphia write; These things saith he that is holy, he that is true, he that hath the key of David, he that openeth, and no man shutteth; and shutteth, and no man openeth.

As is well known, the name Philadelphia means "brotherly love," and the word is used (in slightly different form) seven other times in the New Testament to refer to this beautiful Christian attribute (as in Romans 12:10). The city was so named by its founder (King Attalus of Pergamum) in honor of his brother, and was located about twenty-eight miles southeast of Sardis. It still survives today as the town of Alasehir.

For the first time, the salutation of Christ to the church does not refer back to the introductory description in Revelation 1. This suggests a distinctively new message to this particular church on the basis of distinctively appropriate attributes of the Head of the church. First, He emphasizes His own unique attributes of absolute holiness and truth. What He does is right, and what He says is true—by definition! "For the word of the Lord is right; and all his works are done in truth" (Psalm 33:4). This doctrine of the sovereign God is the basis of all genuine witness for Christ, and the Philadelphia church had acknowledged this.

With such a concept of the nature of Christ, the church was well prepared to have an effective testimony, since truth and holiness must go together. Sound doctrine always generates godly practice; conversely, "evil communications corrupt good manners" (1 Corinthians 15:33). Therefore, Christ also assures them that it is He alone who can open and shut doors of witness and service.

The reference is to Isaiah 22:22: "And the key of the house of David will I lay upon his shoulder; so he shall open, and none shall shut; and he shall shut, and none shall open." In the Old Testament, this promise was given specifically to Eliakim, who was a high official and faithful servant under King Hezekiah. His predecessor, Shebna, had proved unfaithful in his service, so God was promising to give his position to Eliakim. The "key of the house of David" specifically referred to the keys to the treasuries of the kings of Judah, but figuratively it also refers to all the great responsibilities of government which would thereby be resting upon him in an office essentially equivalent to that of prime minister. Eliakim alone, under the king, would be responsible—the government, like the heavy key-chain hanging from his shoulder, was to be upon him. The same prophetic promise had been made to the coming Savior in Isaiah 9:6, 7. The government was to be upon His shoulder and He would occupy the throne of the house of David forever.

Thus, Eliakim was presented to the people in Hezekiah's Jerusalem as an actual visible type of the coming Messiah upon whose shoulders someday God would place eternally the kingdoms of all the world. To the church at Philadelphia, Christ now claims to be the antitype, the fulfillment of the typological promise made over 800 years before through Eliakim (whose very name means "God raising up"). He already has the keys of death and Hades (Revelation 1:18) and here claims the keys to the kingdoms of the earth as well. He possesses *all* the keys, and so He alone has the ability and prerogative of opening and shutting doors.

Revelation 3:8.   I know thy works: behold, I have set before thee an open door, and no man can shut it: for thou hast a little strength, and hast kept my word, and hast not denied my name.

The Lord Jesus Christ, who holds the key to every door, has chosen to maintain an open door for those in the Philadelphia church, one that cannot be shut by men however hard they try. The church doors cannot be shut, prison doors cannot hold them, the gates of hell can't prevail against them, and God's treasure-house itself is open to them. Certainly a door of witness and ministry is open to them as long as they are faithful.

The reason for this expansive promise is: "I know thy works." In this epistle alone, the works are not described in any way; it is evident that, whatever they are, they please the Lord. And the reason they please the Lord is that they proceed from an attitude of heart and life that finds its strength only in Christ, its faith only in His Word, and its very basis for existence only in His name.

"A little strength" actually conveys the thought in the original of "*but* little strength." It is not that the church still has a little strength and thus can still function to some degree. Rather, the very fact that it has *but* little strength is itself the source of its power for this means it must depend wholly on the Lord. "My strength is made perfect in weakness," says the Lord (2 Corinthians 12:9). Neither wealth nor influence, neither promotional schemes nor the eloquence of its pulpit, nor the harmonies of its musicians can give it an effective ministry. The Lord alone has opened the door; the Lord alone "giveth the increase" (1 Corinthians 3:7).

A Philadelphia-like church, furthermore, *keeps* God's Word! The pressures to repudiate His Word, to distort the Word, to dilute the Word, to allegorize the

Word, or just to ignore God's Word, have always been great, and multitudes of believers have compromised their witness throughout the centuries by yielding to these pressures. The modern scene is saturated with innumerable compromise-generating pressures, and most churches today have yielded in one way or another. The Scriptures are filled with warnings: "Keep that which is committed to thy trust" (1 Timothy 6:20); "Hold fast the form of sound words" (2 Timothy 1:13); "Earnestly contend for the faith" (Jude 3). "Continue in the faith grounded and settled" (Colossians 1:23).

When a church begins to deal loosely with the *word* of Christ, it will sooner or later deny the *name* of Christ. The name of a person stands for his character, his position, his work—all that he is and does. The concept of the name of Christ is, therefore, vital. There are at least 125 references to His name, as such, in the New Testament alone.

His formal name could be said to be "the Lord Jesus Christ" (note Acts 2:36). The name "Jesus" means "salvation," and one who honors this name accepts the great salvation provided by His substitutionary atonement and justifying resurrection (Acts 4:12). One who honors the name "Christ" (that is, "the anointed one") acknowledges His person—His threefold eminence as God's anointed prophet, priest, and king. One who honors Him as "Lord" believes and obeys His Word.

To these who have little strength, but keep His Word and acknowledge His name, Christ gives the marvelous assurance of the open door, which no man can close. Conversely, to those who rely on their own power, their own intelligence, their own influence—thereby denying His strength, His Word and His name—the doors which they manage to force open will soon be shut, for there are always other men with greater power and wit and importance than theirs.

Revelation 3:9.   Behold, I will make them of the synagogue of Satan, which say they are Jews, and are not, but do lie; behold, I will make them to come and worship before thy feet, and to know that I have loved thee.

Another common experience to the two faithful churches, Smyrna and Philadelphia, was opposition from the false Jews of the so-called synagogue of Satan (see comments on Revelation 2:9). Apparently the false apostles and other false prophets who plagued the other churches had been unable to get any hearing in these two churches, but the Judaizers and would-be priests and ritualists were a problem. The true believers would be vindicated, however, when these legalists, who desired spiritual worship for themselves (when not even angels would allow men to worship before their feet—note Revelation 22:8, 9) would be forced to bow down in their presence—certainly not to worship *them,* but rather to worship

Christ in His redeeming grace. Since this promise is not one of salvation to such pseudo-Jews, but of condemnation, its fulfillment probably is the great judgment assembly as expounded in Philippians 2:10, 11.

Revelation 3:10.   Because thou hast kept the word of my patience, I also will keep thee from the hour of temptation, which shall come upon all the world, to try them that dwell upon the earth.

This is an important and somewhat controversial verse, one of the key verses supporting the doctrine of the pretribulation rapture of the believing church, as exemplified at Philadelphia. It is somewhat parallel to the promise to Smyrna: "Ye shall have tribulation ten days; be thou faithful unto death, and I will give thee a crown of life" (Revelation 2:10). Both speak of a coming time of trouble, and both stress its brevity compared to the glory that follows. The one, however, is caused by the devil, and is suffered by the church; the other is sent by the Lord and suffered by men who dwell on the earth.

Both churches represent all those churches who are true to the Lord, keeping His Word, patient in tribulation. All their members will be called to endure suffering in some degree, many even to death. "For unto you it is given in the behalf of Christ, not only to believe on him, but also to suffer for his sake" (Philippians 1:29). This is because of the age-long opposition of the world and the devil to Christ and His followers (John 15:20; 16:33).

But there is also a time of judgmental suffering coming on the earth whose purpose is not to try the church but to try them that dwell on the earth. This is nothing less than the seven-year period described here in Revelation, whose judgments come when the Lamb opens the seals (Revelation 6:1) and His angels sound the trumpets (Revelation 8:2) and pour out the vials of God's wrath upon the earth (Revelation 16:1). The purpose of these judgments is neither to allow Satan to test the church nor for Christ to judge the church (the latter will be done at His judgment seat, not on earth).

Therefore, this promise seems clearly to promise a deliverance of the Philadelphians from this coming time of judgment. There is no suggestion that this promised deliverance will be by death, as at Smyrna, and it would be redundant to say that they would be delivered "through" it.

There will be multitudes of men and women who will become believers during this great tribulation (Revelation 7:14), as a result of this last great "trial" of those who dwell on the earth. However, great numbers of these will be martyred as a result (Revelation 13:15), so that it could hardly be said that they would be delivered "out of" the tribulation.

The only legitimate conclusion from this verse, therefore, is that genuine believers will be delivered from this coming hour of judgment of the earth by Christ Himself, as He returns to take them by resurrection and rapture to be with Him, in fulfillment of His age-long promise (John 14:2, 3; 1 Corinthians 15:51-53; Philippians 3:20, 21; 1 Thessalonians 4:16, 17; etc.).

Posttribulationists reject this conclusion, contending there is no reason why Christians in the last generation deserve to escape the great tribulation. The fact is, however, that Christians in every other generation have escaped the great tribulation, so there is no reason why the last should be singled out for participation in it. No generation of the Christian church has ever escaped satanic tribulation, including the last, but none will be judged with the world in Christ's coming purging of the earth. Even those who are saved during the tribulation, while they will suffer persecution and, in some cases, death because of Satan and his followers, will not be the objects of the wrath of God as will others during this time.

Revelation 3:11.   Behold, I come quickly: hold that fast which thou hast, that no man take thy crown.

The Lord promises to return while Philadelphia-type churches are still functioning, just as He had in the cases of Thyatira and Sardis. The Thyatira profligates, however, would be cast into the great tribulation (Revelation 2:22) and Sardis would be caught unawares (3:3), while Philadelphia, faithfully watching and serving, would be kept from the coming hour of temptation.

Although the Philadelphians were faithful, there is always the danger of backsliding, especially in the face of sustained opposition: hence, the admonition to hold fast. The "crown of life" had been promised to those who are faithful unto death (2:10), but there is always the possibility of losing one's reward (1 Corinthians 3:14, 15), though not of losing one's salvation (John 10:28, 29).

Revelation 3:12.   Him that overcometh will I make a pillar in the temple of my God, and he shall go no more out: and I will write upon him the name of my God, and the name of the city of my God, which is new Jerusalem, which cometh down out of heaven from my God: and I will write upon him my new name.

In the spiritual temple now being erected, each new believer is a living stone (Ephesians 2:19-22; 1 Peter 2:5). In the new Jerusalem, however, "the Lord God Almighty and the Lamb are the temple of it" (Revelation 21:22), and overcoming Christians will be the eternal pillars of it. Upon their apparel will be emblazoned three marks of glorious identification: (1) the name of his Savior God; (2) his heavenly citizenship; (3) his own distinctive new name, selected and awarded him by Christ Himself (Revelation 2:17).

Revelation 3:13.   He that hath an ear, let him hear what the Spirit saith unto the churches.

Note the remarkable sequence of revelation to each of the churches. The Lord speaks to John, John writes to the church's angel, and the angel somehow communicates it to the church (note the implications in the phrase "tongues of angels" in 1 Corinthians 13:1, and in the phrase 'the spirits of the prophets" in 1 Corinthians 14:32). And all of this information was incorporated in John's all-inclusive letter to the seven churches (Revelation 1:4; 22:16, 21). But, however the information finally reached the churches, it was none other than the Holy Spirit Himself speaking to the churches.

The Neutral Church

The last of the seven letters was to the church at Laodicea, a city forty-five miles southeast of Philadelphia and almost one hundred miles east of Ephesus. It was a very wealthy trade center, and the church members at Laodicea shared in that wealth. Outwardly, the church at Laodicea was the most impressive of the seven, but spiritually it was the most distressing of all.

Revelation 3:14.   And unto the angel of the church of the Laodiceans write: These things saith the Amen, the faithful and true witness, the beginning of the creation of God.

As at Philadelphia, the opening salutation to Laodicea goes beyond the description of Christ in the first chapter, calling attention to those attributes especially needing recognition at Laodicea. Because of its worldly success, the church had become indifferent to its real spiritual need. Doubting the absolute and unique authority of the Word of God, it had imbibed much of the humanistic philosophy of the intellectual world of that day. The neighboring church at Colosse, to whom Paul had written thirty years before, had even in his day been influenced by such speculations, and Paul had urgently warned them against all philosophies of men (Colossians 2:8-10). Furthermore, all false philosophies of past and present have been based on evolutionism, the denial of an ultimate Creator transcendent to His creation. The Lord Jesus Christ, therefore, in His message to the Laodiceans (as Paul did to the Colossians) reminded them of the basic distinctives of the true biblical theism in which they once had expressed belief. He was the beginning of the Creation, none other than the Creator of all things in heaven and earth. (See also Colossians 1:16-19). Not only was He the Alpha but also the Omega—the Amen. Of Him and for Him are all things, and His word is true and faithful.

The compromising neutrality and self-centeredness of Laodicea is characteristic of great numbers of so-called evangelical churches today and they, like the church at Laodicea, need to be called back to belief in true creationism and true biblical authority, and to belief in Jesus Christ as the true Creator and the faithful witness.

Revelation 3:15.   I know thy works, that thou art neither cold nor hot: I would thou wert cold or hot.

In one sense, Laodicea was a better church than Sardis; it was at least tepid, but Sardis seemed cold and dead. Yet the Lord says He would rather it be cold like Sardis. In modern terminology, a church of dead orthodoxy is better than one of prosperous but neutral evangelicalism.

The Laodicean church was not one of complete apostasy; its candlestick had not been removed, and the Lord was still in the midst of the candlesticks. Neither was it barren and cold, as many doctrinally sound churches had become, such as Sardis. It was apparently receiving many new members. It had a large and prosperous congregation, impressive facilities, and an active program. But it sought to be neutral on controversial matters, to maintain open dialogue with both left and right, to have recognition from the mighty and the wealthy and the intelligentsia. It was not cold to the vital truths of God, His Creation, His Word—but neither would it take a firm stand and proclaim a true witness. And Christ amazingly said, if they could not be "hot," He would rather see them "cold."

Revelation 3:16.   So then because thou art lukewarm, and neither cold nor hot, I will spue thee out of my mouth.

The Lord Jesus Christ, the same as any other man, could enjoy either a hot drink or a cold drink, but no one wants a tepid drink. He uses graphic language to describe His reaction: "I will [literally, 'am about to'] spue thee out of my mouth." His determination to cast out such a church was not final; there was still room for repentance and revival, but the situation was grave.

The number of such churches today is legion, and they are a greater hindrance to the cause of Christ than if they were cold and dead. The latter reach no one, so they harm no one. The neutral churches, however,—the middle-of-the-road churches, the mediating churches, the compromising churches—reach many whose temperaments favor accommodationism anyhow and, with eloquent dissimulation, persuade them that, while a little religion is good, they must avoid fanaticism. Furthermore, they bitterly resent "hot" churches and do all they can to cool their enthusiasm and dilute their convictions. They cannot abide churches which, by their very existence, constitute a rebuke to their own lack of doctrinal conviction and missionary zeal.

Revelation 3:17.   Because thou sayest, I am rich, and increased with goods, and have need of nothing; and knowest not that thou art wretched, and miserable, and poor, and blind, and naked.

Such words as these bite and burn. Yet many commentators on these verses have come from just such neutralist churches—as well as other compromising Christian institutions and organizations. Such commentaries apply the passage to modernistic and apostate churches, churches where the inspiration of the Scriptures, the virgin birth of Christ, the substitutionary atonement and other basic doctrines are openly denied and repudiated. Neutralist writers find it easy enough to reject such blasphemies as these, and it soothes their conscience to do so, yet all the while—as Christ says—they know not it is *"thou"* (the Greek here is emphatic) to whom He speaks. Blatantly liberal churches are not churches at all in the biblical sense. They have no candlestick, and Christ is not in their midst. It is the neutral churches of which He here speaks.

Such churches, commonly calling themselves conservative, or evangelical, or charismatic, or even fundamentalist, may have big church buildings and ostentatious programs and be very much impressed with themselves, but if they do not stand solidly and fervently for true creationism and full biblical inerrancy and authority in all things, He who *is* the Creator and the Word finds them intolerably distasteful and threatens to spue them out.

Revelation 3:18.   I counsel thee to buy of me gold tried in the fire, that thou mayest be rich; and white raiment, that thou mayest be clothed, and that the shame of thy nakedness do not appear; and anoint thine eyes with eyesalve, that thou mayest see.

He who is the "Wonderful Counsellor" (Isaiah 9:6) still loves this church (verse 19) in spite of its tepid accommodationism. He therefore lovingly gives His counsel concerning their desperate, but unrecognized, need. "Buy from me!" He says. But all their wealth cannot buy what they need. Buy "without money and without price" (Isaiah 55:1). The purchase price is merely to recognize their wretched condition and come to Him in repentance, forsaking their riches and prestige for the true riches (faith tried in the fire—1 Peter 1:7) and their worldly wisdom for true wisdom (Colossians 2:3) in Christ. They must receive the pure white garments of His righteousness to replace the filthy rags of their own righteousnesses (Isaiah 64:6). As eyesalve is needed for physical blindness, so their spiritual blindness must be assuaged by "the spirit of wisdom and revelation in the knowledge of him: The eyes of your understanding being enlightened; that ye may know what is the hope of his calling, and what the riches of the glory of his inheritance in the saints" (Ephesians 1:17, 18).

Revelation 3:19.   As many as I love, I rebuke and chasten: be zealous therefore, and repent.

It is obvious that these lukewarm, compromising Christians in Laodicea are, indeed, Christians. Otherwise Christ would not rebuke and chasten them. "For whom the Lord loveth he chasteneth, and scourgeth every son whom he receiveth" (Hebrews 12:6). The Lord does not indicate what the chastening would be, but it would certainly include exposure of their spiritual poverty and nakedness to the worldly crowd whom they had been so anxious to impress. "That the shame of thy nakedness do appear" would certainly be among the worst chastisements for such a proud and intellectual church. But Christ loves them, and desires their repentance.

Revelation 3:20.   Behold, I stand at the door, and knock: if any man hear my voice, and open the door, I will come in to him, and will sup with him, and he with me.

Here the Lord uses a different figure, but to the same purpose. His rebuke and chastening are like a knock at one's door. If that person hears His knock and also hears His voice—both through his experience of chastisement and through Christ's written Word—then he ought to respond, though Christ does not compel him to do so. He does not force the door. The occupant must open the door. That is, he must repent of his pride and his self-sufficiency, his human wisdom, and his cowardly neutrality. Then—but not until then—will he know the real joy of true fellowship with his Lord.

Clearly, this exhortation is directed to compromising worldly believers in the church at Laodicea, and in all other such churches, of which there are multitudes today. It is not a gospel verse addressed to the unsaved, though it is so used widely today. The verse contains nothing of the gospel message as such—no mention of substitutionary atonement, of Christ's resurrection, of repentance, of faith in the person and work of Christ. Neither is there anything in the adjacent context about these vital matters. Yet evangelists and personal workers everywhere commonly employ this verse as a gospel invitation. God, in His grace, does occasionally use it to help bring an unsaved person to Christ, since it does enjoin a proper attitude of openness to God's call, but that is not its intent. It was addressed only to compromising, lukewarm Christians in compromising, lukewarm churches, and it is they whom Christ is seeking to draw back to Himself.

There is a further important truth here. In the three previous letters, He had urged His people to expect and prepare for His imminent return, either in judgment or blessing. In that context, the lukewarm Laodiceans should certainly be expected likewise to prepare for the Lord's coming. His knocking also takes the form of prophetic fulfillments and world events in the light of His word ("hear my voice"). As these are observed, even a lukewarm compromising brother might well be stirred up, to look for the Lord, and to believe His Word.

So, when He says, "I stand at the door, knocking," He is also referring to His imminent personal coming back to earth again, where one day, indeed, He will literally "sup" with His people, at the great marriage supper of the Lamb (Revelation 19:9). "So likewise ye, when ye shall see all these things, know that it is near, even at the doors" (Matthew 24:33).

Revelation 3:21.   To him that overcometh will I grant to sit with me in my throne, even as I also overcame, and am set down with my Father in his throne.

This is an amazing manifestation of grace. One who was about to be spewed out of His mouth is invited to sit with Him on His throne. When the Lord was faithful unto death, He was raised from the dead and "is set down at the right hand of the throne of God" (Hebrews 12:2). In like manner, those who are His will reign with Him when His own throne is set up, first His millennial throne (Revelation 20:4) and finally His eternal throne (Revelation 22:3, 4).

Notice again that all seven of the promises to the overcomers involve features that are mentioned again in the description of the ages to come, where all will be fulfilled. Thus, the tree of life was promised at Ephesus (Revelation 22:2), deliverance from the second death at Smyrna (20:6), the new name written at Pergamos (22:4), the morning star to the Thyatirans (22:16), white raiment to the church at Sardis (19:8), the new Jerusalem to the Philadelphians (22:2) and a sharing of His throne at Laodicea (20:4).

Revelation 3:22.   He that hath an ear, let him hear what the Spirit saith unto the churches.

The seven epistles close with the seventh rehearsal of this exhortation. Such a seven-fold repetition of an identical commandment stresses its extreme importance. It is *vital* that we read and heed these messages to the churches. The same problems that faced *their* churches, confront *our* churches, and the same warnings and promises apply to us as well as them.

In this verse is the last mention of the church in the Book of Revelation until the last chapter, where John is reminded that the entire book is to be sent to the churches (Revelation 22:16). There are no churches as such on earth during the climactic events of judgment described from Revelation 4 onwards, and so no reference to the churches appears in these chapters. The message of all the chapters (Revelation 1:4) is for all of Christ's churches, however, and it is that message to which we now proceed.

4

Round About the Throne

(Revelation 4)

The Promise of His Coming

The final messages from Christ to His churches had been completed, insofar as their activities and attitudes in this present age are concerned. The Apostle Paul had also left divinely-inspired instructions for seven representative churches (at Rome, Corinth, Galatia, Ephesus, Philippi, Colosse, and Thessalonica) and four other apostles (James, Peter, Jude, and John) had written seven epistles, in addition to the special epistle to the Hebrews, of unknown authorship, and Paul's four pastoral letters (to Timothy, Titus, and Philemon). The churches had received ample direction for every need they might encounter until Christ's return. They did not know how long this might be, of course, and had been urged by Christ to be watchful and ready always.

However, until this point, they knew very little about what would take place after Christ's return. They did have the prophecies of the Old Testament, of course, and there was much information in them.

But there were two problems. In the Old Testament, the church and the Church Age constituted a mystery "which in other ages was not made known unto the sons of men, as it is now revealed unto his holy apostles and prophets by the Spirit" (Ephesians 3:5). Consequently, the prophecies of Isaiah, Daniel, and others largely focused on the nation Israel, and on other nations in their relation to Israel. But there was little that the early Christians could derive from them about the future of the church.

Second, the Old Testament prophecies had the peculiar characteristic of mingling events which were to be fulfilled very soon with events which would be fulfilled near the end of the age. God, of course, is outside of "time," since He created time as well as space and matter, and to Him all events of all time are seen in all their aspects—future, present, and past—simultaneously. Two events separated in time by thousands of years may be viewed by God as essentially a single event, with the first a precursor of the second, and the latter a causal effect and continuation of the former.

By the time of the early church, many Old Testament prophecies had already been fulfilled—such as the Babylonian captivity, the judgments on various nations, the first coming of the Messiah—so Christians were much better able to distinguish between the fulfilled and unfulfilled aspects of these prophecies than earlier believers had been. Nevertheless, there was still much that was uncertain.

The Lord Jesus Christ Himself had clarified many of these questions, especially in His great prophetic discourse on the Mount of Olives (Matthew 24; Mark 13; Luke 21), but even these contained many minglings of near fulfillments (such as the destruction of Jerusalem in A.D. 70) with end-of-the-age fulfillments. The Church Age itself was only partially explained by Christ during His pre-Calvary ministry, and that largely in the form of parables which they could not fully comprehend until after His resurrection and ascension, along with the subsequent teaching ministry of the Holy Spirit (note Matthew 13:9-17; 34, 35; John 14:25, 26; 16:12-15, 25), who would "shew you things to come" (John 16:13).

Indeed the Holy Spirit, through the epistles of the apostles, did reveal some of the things that were to come. These, however, largely had to do with general trends in the world as they would affect the church, especially in the latter days (1 Timothy 4:1-3; 2 Timothy 3:1-13; James 5:1-8; 2 Peter 3:3-13; 1 John 2:18-20, 28). None of these had to do with specific events, and the trends were already evident in many places, so these early days of the church could well have also been the last days of the church, so far as they could tell at the time (or, for that matter, so far as we can tell at *this* time).

Furthermore, there was much revealed in these epistles concerning the actual return of Christ for His Church—especially the great resurrection and rapture passages of 1 Thessalonians 4:13—5:10, and 1 Corinthians 15:49-43. There are numerous other less extensive sections also (Philippians 3:20, 21: Colossians 3:4, Titus 2:11-13; Hebrews 9:27, 28; 10:25, 37; 1 Peter 1:3-7; 1 John 3:2, 3; Jude 14-18). Again, however, these had little to do with any events other than the one great truth that Christ was coming back for His Church—His bride. Furthermore, even these still contained certain confusing elements which suggested the same old mingling of near and far fulfillments. For example, one prophecy might say He was coming to the air where His followers, both dead and living, would be caught up to meet Him (1 Thessalonians 4:16, 17). Another would say He was coming out of Zion to deliver Israel (Romans 11:25, 26). Christ Himself had said He would return to the earth in power and glory immediately after the coming great tribulation (Matthew 24:21, 29) and that the tribulation would not begin until after the "abomination of desolation, spoken of by Daniel the prophet" would "stand in the holy place" (Matthew 24:15, 21). Yet, in the same discourse, He had urged His hearers to "watch therefore: for ye know not what hour your Lord doth come" (Matthew 24:42), a warning which would seem pointless during any generation prior to the establishment of the abomination of desolation in the temple at Jerusalem.

Thus the sequence of events associated with Christ's second coming was still almost as obscure to His followers after Calvary as it was to those before. It was at least discernible that His second coming, just as His first coming, would involve a considerable period of time and many different events. But there was still a great need for another final prophecy, which would enable the church to sort out and harmonize all the remaining unfulfilled prophecies of the Old Testament, those given by Christ while He was on earth, and those given through the apostles to equip them with real assurance and understanding concerning God's great purposes for His creation in the ages to come.

This is the primary purpose of the book of the "unveiling" (Revelation 1:1-3). After the final instructions to His churches, provided at the very end of the Apostolic Age and covering all their remaining needs until the end of the Church Age, the Lord then proceeded, beginning at Revelation 4, to show unto His servants all the great events associated with His second coming and eternal reign.

The Emerald Rainbow

Revelation 4:1.   After this I looked, and, behold, a door was opened in heaven: and the first voice which I heard was as it were of a trumpet talking with me; which said, Come up hither, and I will shew thee things which must be hereafter.

This is a critically important verse in Revelation. It begins and ends with the same words in the original, "after these things," which ties it back rigidly to the third component in the prophetic outline set out by the Lord in Revelation 1:19. "Write the things which thou hast seen, and the things which are, and the things which shall be hereafter" (i.e., "after these things"). At this point, the Lord proceeds to *show* John the things which shall be after these things, that is, after the things associated with the churches, as described in Chapters 2 and 3—"the things which are." It would seem obvious that the events beginning at this point must occur after Christ's dealings with His churches on earth have been completed, and He is now turning His attention to other urgent matters as far as the earth is concerned. Correspondingly, there is no mention at all made of churches in all the great happenings outlined in the next eighteen chapters.

What, then, has happened to the churches? The answer is evident. Some, like Ephesus, have had their candlestick removed (Revelation 2:5), and are no longer true churches, if they exist at all. Some, like Thyatira, will have been "cast into . . . great tribulation" (Revelation 2:22) because of their wickedness, which demonstrated that they had never known Christ at all and had knowingly followed false teaching. But others, like Philadelphia, had been graciously kept by their Lord "from the hour of temptation, which shall come upon all the world, to try them that dwell on the earth" (Revelation 3:10).

But how could this be accomplished? The answer is clearly given in John's experience at this point. The purpose of the Book of Revelation was to show (not merely to tell) these great events of the future, and this was to be done through *signifying* (that is, miraculously demonstrating) it through John (Revelation 1:1), who actually *saw* (Revelation 1:2) all these events first hand. He was *there!* This was not a dream, or even a vision, but the real thing.

The Lord had promised the Philadelphians an open door, and had warned the Laodiceans He was knocking on their closed door. Now He shows John the door opened in heaven and invites him to enter. The voice was the same he had heard at first "as of a trumpet" (Revelation 1:10).

Other references relate the future coming of the Lord to the trumpet. "The Lord himself shall descend from heaven with a shout, with the voice of the archangel, and with the trump of God" (1 Thessalonians 4:16). "For the trumpet shall sound, and the dead shall be raised incorruptible, and we shall be changed" (1 Corinthians 15:52).

The invitation accompanying the trumpet was to come up. The door was in heaven and John was on earth, but the Lord had preceded him into heaven, and now he was to go up to meet Him there. John had become, to all intents and purposes, one of those who would be alive when the Lord returns. "Then we which are alive and remain shall be caught up together with them in the clouds to meet the Lord in the air" (1 Thessalonians 4:17). "I will come again, and receive you unto myself; that where I am, there ye may be also" (John 14:3).

Revelation 4:2.   And immediately I was in the spirit: and behold, a throne was set in heaven, and one sat on the throne.

After the trumpet-like voice cried out the invitation, "in a moment, in the twinkling of an eye" (1 Corinthians 15:52), John was at the scene in heaven where all the great events to come would be taking place before his eyes. Paul had similarly once been translated, "whether in the body, or out of the body, I cannot tell" (2 Corinthians 12:3) to the "third heaven," to "paradise," but the things he saw were not permitted him to utter.

Paul had been translated far out in space, but now John was translated in both space and time, to the throne of God and the end of the age, and what he saw he was commanded to utter. Our present physical bodies are creatures of space and time, but God is the Creator of space and time as well as matter and can therefore control them all. John was miraculously "in the spirit" for such a mighty miracle. To all intents and purposes, he was a participant in the great "rapture" that will occur to the saints when Christ returns, and found himself instantaneously translated, as will they, up to the heavens.

As a matter of fact, the particular heaven will be that of earth's high atmosphere. When Jesus ascended from earth, angels told His disciples that He would return "in like manner" (Acts 1:11). At the end of this present age, He "will descend from heaven" (1 Thessalonians 4:16), but not at first all the way back to earth. Both living and dead believers will be resurrected and glorified as they are caught up "to meet the Lord in the air" (1 Thessalonians 4:17). It seems that it was to this very scene that John was called.

He saw, as shall we in that day, a beautiful throne "being set," as the Greek implies, in the heavens near the earth. The heavenly throne "far above all heavens" (Ephesians 4:10) had been itself translated swiftly through the cosmos to earth's environs, for the time had finally come to "judge the world in righteousness" (Acts 17:31).

The throne John saw is quite possibly the same as "the judgment seat of Christ," before which all Christians must appear (Romans 14:10; 2 Corinthians 5:10). Although the question of salvation is already settled for the believer, there are many Scriptures indicating that believers must be judged according to their works, either to receive rewards or suffer loss of rewards (Matthew 12:36; 1 Corinthians 3:11-15; Galatians 6:7; Colossians 3:24, 25; 2 Timothy 4:1-8; Revelation 22:12; etc.). This judgment must have been completed prior to the millennium, because the believers will by then have been arrayed in white garments representing the "righteous acts" of the saints and given thrones of judgment reserved for "overcomers" during the millennium (Revelation 19:8; 20:4). The judgments described in Revelation chapters 6-19 have to do with the earth and its Christ-rejecting inhabitants, and nothing is said concerning the judgment of believers in heaven for rewards. Consequently, the latter can only have occurred immediately after the rapture and prior to the unleashing of the plagues on earth.

The promises to the overcomers at the end of each of the seven letters to the churches are some of the rewards to be dispensed at the judgment seat of Christ, when "the fire shall try every man's work of what sort it is" (1 Corinthians 3:13). Billions of believers will assemble before Him in the air, and the fiery eyes and flaming face of the glorified Son of man will instantly purge all dross from their lives and hearts. Like John, we shall fall "at his feet as dead" (Revelation 1:13-17). Then "we shall be like him; for we shall see him as he is" (1 John 3:2). That in itself will be abundant reward.

Revelation 4:3.   And he that sat was to look upon like a jasper and a sardine stone: and there was a rainbow round about the throne, in sight like unto an emerald.

Whether or not this throne is the same as the "judgment seat of Christ," it does appear that the scene at this point is subsequent to the purging of sins and dispensation of rewards that will take place at the judgment seat. The prospect now is one of preparation for the judgments on the earth. The triune God is on His throne, incapable of being seen or described in His fullness even by resurrected saints, "dwelling in the light which no man can approach unto; whom no man hath seen, nor can see" (1 Timothy 6:16). The light emanating therefrom, however, can be seen, and John saw and described its ineffable beauty, with all the colors of the rainbow.

In fact a beautiful rainbow, with the emerald green color dominating, completely encircled the throne. The light from the divine presence on the throne, however, featured the two colors at the ends of the rainbow spectrum, red and violet. The red, speaking to John perhaps of judgment and sacrifice, reminded John of the blood-red sardine stone (after which the city of Sardis had been named). The purple, speaking possibly of divine royalty, was as the crystal-clear purple jasper stone (note Revelation 22:11). The green of the rainbow was like the verdure clothing God's terrestrial creation. The whole panorama glorified God as Creator, as Sovereign, as Redeemer.

The rainbow is very significant. The Bible refers to it only on four occasions. The first is in Genesis 9 (verses 13, 14, 16) when it was first established by God after the Flood and acknowledged by Him as a sign of the Noahic covenant made between God and "all flesh." This "everlasting covenant," and the rainbow which betokens it, assures the world that God will never again send a world-destroying deluge. Thus the rainbow speaks of God's mercy toward mankind even in the midst of judgment.

The second notice of the rainbow is found in Ezekiel 1:28, in Ezekiel's vision of the glory of God. In a scene much like that which John saw "in the spirit," Ezekiel saw in a "vision" (Ezekiel 1:1) the throne of God, with the cherubim, and the rainbow. "As the appearance of the bow that is in the cloud in the day of rain, so was the appearance of the brightness round about."

The third occasion is in the Book of Revelation, here at 4:3 and again at 10:1. Again it is associated with the very presence and character of God. Evidently the rainbow perpetually surrounds the throne of God, or at least at such times (as in Ezekiel's day, as in Noah's day, and in John's day) when God's judgments are being visited on the earth. The rainbow, as it were, continually "reminds" God that there is a remnant of believers even in the midst of an ungodly culture ripe for judgment, and that He, as the "God of all grace" (1 Peter 5:10) will "in wrath remember mercy" (Habakkuk 3:2).

The Elders of the Redeemed

Revelation 4:4.   And round about the throne were four and twenty seats: and upon the seats I saw four and twenty elders sitting, clothed in white raiment; and they had on their heads crowns of gold.

The word "seats" is the Greek *thronos,* the same word as used for "throne." The elders were seen by John seated on thrones exactly as he had seen the divine presence seated on the throne (4:2). The identity of these elders, sometimes mistakenly interpreted as angels, is very important.

The elders are undoubtedly redeemed and glorified men, or, at the least, representative of such men, in view of the following considerations: (1) although there are principalities and powers in the angelic hierarchy, there can be no "elders," since all angels are of the same age, created probably on the first day of creation; (2) the term "elder" is always used elsewhere in the Bible only of men; (3) elders are always chosen representatives and leaders of the people, both in Israel and in the church; (4) there are no elders in the visions of God's throne in Isaiah 6 and Ezekiel 1—10, in consequence of the fact that prior to the cross the spirits of all the redeemed were still confined to Hades; (5) the elders were wearing white raiment (as promised to overcoming believers in Revelation 3:5) and victors' crowns (Greek *stephanos,* "wreath," as also promised to overcomers in Revelation 2:10 and 3:11); angels, being "ministering spirits" (Hebrews 1:14) are never described in the Bible as wearing crowns of any kind; (6) in Revelation 5:8, 9, these elders sing a song of praise to the Lamb who had redeemed them by His blood.

But why twenty-four elders? The Israelites used seventy elders (Exodus 24:1) and no indication is given as to the number of elders in the early church. There were twenty-four orders of priests in Israel (1 Chronicles 24:7-19), but these were not the elders and, even though believers are to be kings and priests (Revelation 1:6), there seems no reason why the office of the priest should be commingled with that of the elder in heaven. The number twenty-four has often been held to be symbolic of the twelve patriarchs plus the twelve apostles. The latter, however, are specifically assigned to the job of judging the twelve tribes of Israel on twelve thrones in the millennial kingdom (Revelation 19:28), whereas the twenty-four elders are at the throne in heaven. If twelve of these are the twelve apostles, assigned to judging the twelve tribes, then the identity and function of the other twelve are left up in the air. It is barely possible that they are the twelve sons of Jacob.

There is one other interesting possiblity as to their identity. The term "elder" has both an administrative and a chronological connotation (note 1 Peter 1:1, 5). That the elders in Revelation are individual men, and not just symbolic of all believers, is indicated by the individual conversations reported of individual elders (Revelation 5:5; 7:13). They *do* represent all believers of all the ages, but they are also individual men, the *elders* of all redeemed humanity. It is interesting, and possibly the answer to this question, that in the Book of Genesis there are twenty-four patriarchs listed in the line of the promised seed (Adam, Seth, Enos, Cainan, Mahalaleel, Jared, Enoch, Methuselah, Lamech, Noah, Shem, Arphaxad, Salah, Eber, Peleg, Reu, Serug, Nahor, Terah, Abraham, Isaac, Jacob, Judah, Pharez). These men could more properly be denoted the "elders" of God's elect than anyone else. Finally, another possibility is that, since the Lord did not choose to specify their identity, His method of selecting them is on the basis of merit, and thus He cannot reveal their identity until after the assignment of rewards at the judgment seat of Christ.

Revelation 4:5. And out of the throne proceeded lightnings and thunderings and voices; and there were seven lamps of fire burning before the throne, which are the seven spirits of God.

Although the throne was encircled by the emerald rainbow, denoting grace overseeing judgment, as it were, from the throne itself came forth sounds of judgment. Before the great Flood (following which the rainbow was established) there had been no rain on the earth (Genesis 2:5), a condition resulting from a worldwide canopy of invisible water vapor—the "waters above the firmament"—established by God on the second day of creation. The greenhouse effect maintained by this thermal vapor blanket supported a pleasant and permanent universal subtropical climate in the antediluvian world, with no great winds and therefore no rains and snows. The breaking up of the "fountains of the great deep" (Genesis 7:11) induced the condensation and participation of the canopy and resulted in the global cataclysm of the deluge. Psalm 29 describes this great flood in words of poetic grandeur centered around events following the seven-times uttered "voice of the Lord." The first utterance released the waters, the second introduced the great thunderings from heaven, as the vapors condensed and began to move, generating the first and most violent atmospheric electrical storm in history. These "lightnings and thunderings and voices" emanating from God's throne mirror that great time of judgment in the past and betoken another great time of judgment about to break on the earth once more (though, in accordance with God's promise to Noah, it would not "destroy the earth").

The sevenfold Holy Spirit (see comments on 1:4) now appears, in conformity with the scene of judgment, as seven lamps of fire. Although the Holy Spirit is invisible and omnipresent, He does on occasion appear in visible manifestation—for example, as a dove at the baptism of Jesus (Matthew 3:16; Mark 1:10; Luke 3:22). He had appeared on the day of Pentecost as "cloven tongues like as of fire"

(Acts 2:3). One of His ministries is to "reprove the world of sin, and of righteousness, and of judgment" (John 16:8). Although He is at the throne, with the elders, He will continue to exercise this convicting ministry on earth.

Cherubim and Seraphim

Revelation 4:6.   And before the throne there was a sea of glass like unto crystal: and in the midst of the throne, and round about the throne, were four beasts full of eyes before and behind.

The sea of glass before the throne (no doubt "before" it on all four sides, separating the unmovable throne of majesty from all His creatures surrounding it), is obviously the antitype of the laver in the tabernacle (Exodus 30:18-21) and the sea in the temple (2 Chronicles 4:2-6), both used for the cleansing of the priests before they could minister in the work of the Lord. In the heavenly temple, however, the sea was not moving water but still as crystal. The priests had already been cleansed and thus could already walk on the sea as it were, entering directly into the presence of the Lord. The crystal sea may also be in view in the two visions of God as noted in Exodus 24:10 and Ezekiel 1:22.

The four beasts (Greek *zoon,* "living creatures") have been the subject of inordinate speculation. The introductory statement concerning them is that they are round about the throne—one on each side, but also in the midst of the throne, closer to God than any other of His creatures. Thus these are the highest of the angelic hierarchy, in immediate access to the throne of God. Furthermore, they are full of eyes, able to see in all directions at once so that nothing escapes their observation. Their very name, "living ones," denotes the fact that they are vibrant with life, imparted to them by God their Creator.

These, like the elders, are real beings—not symbols. They also speak, both as a unit (Revelation 4:9; 5:14) and individually (Revelation 6:1, 3, 5, 7). They are not men, however, like the elders, but are specially created beings—angels—for a very special set of ministries related to the immediate presence of God.

Revelation 4:7.   And the first beast was like a lion, and the second beast like a calf, and the third beast had a face as a man, and the fourth beast was like a flying eagle.

Because the Greek word is *zoon,* from which is derived our English words "zoo" and "zoology," the King James translators used the word "beast," but it means simply "living creature." The appearance of these living ones immediately is seen to resemble that of the four cherubim described in Ezekiel 1:10. "As for the likeness of their faces, they four had the face of a man, and the face of a lion, on the right side: and they four had the face of an ox on the left side; they four also had the face of an eagle.'' Ezekiel also says, however, that ''this was their appearance; they had the likeness of a man. And every one had four faces, and every one had four wings'' (Ezekiel 1:5, 6).

The picture seems to be one of four mighty angelic cherubs, each of whom has four faces. The four faces represent the lion (greatest of the wild animals), the ox (greatest of the domestic animals), the eagle (greatest of the flying animals) and the man (greatest of all creatures). The different order as described by John and by Ezekiel evidently resulted simply from the different points from which they viewed them. That these were the cherubim (Hebrew plural of ''cherub'') is stated in Ezekiel 10:20-22. They all have ''the likeness of a man'' in their general mien even though three of their four faces depict other creatures. The manlike face of each may be always directed toward the presence of God, judging from the representations of the two cherubim over the ark of the covenant (Exodus 20:17-22). They can proceed in any direction without turning (Ezekiel 1:12).

Cherubim had been placed at the entrance to the garden of Eden after the expulsion of Adam and Eve. Wherever the cherubim are mentioned, they are represented as in the presence of God, either symbolically (as in the tabernacle and temple) or actually (as in the descriptions of John and Ezekiel).

Isaiah also was granted a glorious vision of the heavenly temple, where he saw certain angelic beings which he called ''seraphim'' (Isaiah 6:1-7). The word means ''fiery ones'' and they are probably the same—or at least of the same order —as the cherubim (the root meaning of which is not known). Ezekiel describes the cherubim thus: ''As for the likeness of the living creatures, their appearance was like burning coals of fire, and like the appearance of lamps: it went up and down among the living creatures; and the fire was bright, and out of the fire went forth lightning'' (Ezekiel 1:13). Both the seraphim (Isaiah 6:2) and the living creatures in Revelation (4:8) are said to have six wings, whereas the cherubim in Ezekiel 1:6 are said to have four wings. The latter, however, are presumably the wings for flying, two to move backward and forward, two to move left and right. An additional two wings on each face were said in Isaiah's vision to be for covering the face and two for covering the feet.

Revelation 4:8. **And the four beasts had each of them six wings about him; and they were full of eyes within: and they rest not day and night, saying, Holy, holy, holy, Lord God Almighty, which was, and is, and is to come.**

Further identification of these living ones with the seraphim is indicated by their occupation—the unending ascription of threefold holiness to the Lord of hosts (Isaiah 6:3). Though these cherubim/seraphim are no doubt the most gloriously beautiful of all God's creatures (the fallen cherub, evidently Satan, of Ezekiel 28:11-19 was said to have been originally ''full of wisdom and perfect in beauty''), they give all glory to God. The connection of the three-times repeated "Holy!" to the past, present, and future work of the triune God is evident. God is perfectly holy in His work of creation, His work of redemption, and His work of consummation.

In Praise of Creation

Revelation 4:9.   And when those beasts give glory and honour and thanks to him that sat on the throne, who liveth for ever and ever.

The amazing scene before John's eyes now begins to move to a new activity. The glorious resurrection and rapture of the saints has been consummated, their sins have been purged and rewards given, and their elders have assumed the thrones prepared for them. The four living ones now change their perpetual refrain of holiness to the Lord and take up a new theme, ascribing glory and honor to Him as well as holiness. The term "honor" is a word meaning "value." He is all-worthy!

But they also *thank* Him! They are not among the redeemed ones, since they were never lost, so their doxology of thanksgiving must center on the fact of their creation, as is evident from verse 11, and their preservation through all the ages of satanic and human rebellion.

It is noteworthy that the last three references in the Bible to thanksgiving all apply to this throne-room in heaven. The first, as noted above, focused on God's work of creation. The second (Revelation 7:12), is primarily in relation to God's work of salvation. The last (Revelation 11:17), anticipates the great work of consummation. Only the "elders" are participants in all three (Revelation 4:10; 7:11; 11—16). Only the redeemed know the full meaning of thanksgiving.

Revelation 4:10.   The four and twenty elders fall down before him that sat on the throne, and worship him that liveth for ever and ever, and cast their crowns before the throne, saying, . . .

When the four living ones give the signal, as it were, by their action of glorifying, honoring, and thanking the eternal one, then the twenty-four elders likewise join in the chorus of praise. It is probable also that this action in turn is followed by the millions of redeemed men and women whom the elders represent, who also will fall down in adoration before the One on the throne.

Before they can prostrate themselves before *His* throne, they must descend from their own kingly thrones. Furthermore, the beautiful crowns with which they have been rewarded for faithful service as overcoming believers will somehow suddenly seem unseemly. They will realize that even *their* faithfulness has been made possible by *His* faithfulness. They have nothing which they were not given; they accomplished only what He willed and enable. All is of God. Consequently their crowns are not really their own, and they must return them to Him.

And then how wonderful it will be to accompany their Redeemer back to earth in triumph, observing Him leading them, viewing Him in His majesty, for "on his head were *many* crowns" (Revelation 19:12). Though they have indeed been made kings and priests, and rewarded according to their works, the greatest joy of every redeemed saint will be simply to "enjoy him forever," as the old creed puts it, and to fulfill His purpose in each life.

"His servants shall serve him: And they shall see his face; and his name shall be in their foreheads" (Revelation 22:3, 4).

Revelation 4:11. Thou art worthy, O Lord, to receive glory and honour and power: for thou hast created all things, and for thy pleasure they are and were created.

Before God can be truly known as Redeemer, He must first be believed and acknowledged as Creator. It is significant that this great doxology of creation is offered up by the twenty-four elders, no doubt accompanied by all the saints, as their first response after the resurrection and rewards at Christ's judgment seat. This in sharp contrast to the attitude of most living "evangelicals," who consider the doctrine of creation to be of only incidental importance. Many even compromise with atheism to the extent of trying to say that evolution was God's method of creation.

Not so the redeemed in glory! To them all things "are" (that is, "have existence") solely because of God's creative will. They "were created" (not "are being created," as evolutionary theory must postulate). The system known as "theistic evolution" is contrary to both science and Scripture and is dishonoring to God's grace and power.

The word "pleasure" is the Greek *thelema,* normally translated "will," and this is its last occurrence in the Bible. Its first occurrence in the New Testament is in the prayer which the Lord taught the disciples: "Thy will be done in earth, as it is in heaven" (Matthew 6:10). The final answer to that prayer is foreseen in Revelation, and this first occurrence of "will" looks forward to the consummation, just as the last occurrence looks back to the creation. God's will is eternal, with beginning and ending all of one to Him.

This doxology also answers the question as to *why* God created all things. It was simply God's will to do so! Since our very minds were created by Him, it is presumptuous to question His will in so doing. "The Lord hath made all things for himself: yea, even the wicked for the day of evil" (Proverbs 16:4). "Even every one that is called by my name: for I have created him for my glory, I have formed him; yea, I have made him" (Isaiah 43:7). "For who hath known the mind of the Lord? or who hath been his counsellor?" (Romans 11:34). "Nay but, O man, who art thou that repliest against God? Shall the thing formed say to him that formed it, Why hast thou made me thus? . . . What if God, willing to shew his wrath, and to make his power known, endured with much longsuffering the vessels of wrath fitted to destruction: And that he might make known the riches of his glory on the vessels of mercy, which he had afore prepared unto glory" (Romans 9:20-23).

The evidence that God has created all things, when rightly and openly examined, is overwhelming. That being the case, we can be sure that such an omnipotent God is also omniscient. He is not capricious, and we can be absolutely confident that His will is good and right. That is all the reason needed by us to explain and justify His creation.

Therefore He alone is worthy to receive "*the* glory and *the* honor and *the* power" (the definite article is present in the Greek original). Neither men nor angels can create anything, and certainly random matter cannot create or organize itself. Only God *can* create and *has created!* All that exists can find its meaning and explanation for existence *only* in the fact of special creation by the eternal, transcendent, personal Creator God.

5

Worthy Is the Lamb

(Revelation 5)

The Book of Destiny

The fifth chapter of Revelation is certainly one of the most glorious chapters ever penned. The grandeur of the setting is incomparable and the theme is nothing less than the very destiny of the world. Its Creator is seated on the glorious throne established high in earth's atmosphere, encircled by the emerald rainbow and surrounded by the elders of redeemed humanity.

But the earth itself, depleted of its "salt" by the resurrection and rapture of all its saints, is more corrupt than ever, rapidly degenerating into a morass of wickedness and violence. The price for earth's redemption was paid long ago on Calvary's cross, but it is still bound tight in the power of the wicked one (1 John 5:19), so that its *actual* redemption must still be accomplished. It is as though a man had purchased a tract of land, and had clear title to it legally but was barred from occupying it by unlawful usurpers who had settled on it.

Just so, earth's final redemption is yet to come. "And when these things begin to come to pass," Jesus said, "then look up, and lift up your heads; for your redemption draweth nigh" (Luke 21:28). "Ye were sealed with that holy Spirit of promise, which is the earnest of our inheritance until the redemption of the purchased possession, unto the praise of his glory" (Ephesians 1:13, 14). In this glorious fifth chapter of Revelation, earth's great Redeemer is preparing to finish the task of purging the purchased world.

95

Revelation 5:1.   And I saw in the right hand of him that sat on the throne a book written within and on the backside, sealed with seven seals.

The majestic presence of God on the throne was hidden in the rainbow-hued light, but now it seemed as though a man's right hand were there, clasping a most remarkable scroll. The scroll had writings on it, on both front and back. Then it was rolled tight and sealed with seven strong seals.

But what is this remarkable scroll? It is nothing less than the title deed to the earth itself. This is not explained in the immediate context, but it is clearly the antitype of all the rich typological teaching associated with the divinely specified procedures for land redemption in the Old Testament.

In the first place, the earth is permanently God's possession by right of creation, and nothing can ever alter that fact. "The earth is the Lord's, and the fulness thereof; the world, and they that dwell therein. For he hath founded it upon the seas, and established it upon the floods" (Psalm 24:1, 2). In the type, this was signified by God's permanent gift of a portion of His land to each family among His chosen people. "The land shall not be sold for ever: for the land is mine; for ye are strangers and sojourners with me. And in all the land of your possession ye shall grant a redemption for the land. If thy brother be waxen poor, and hath sold away some of his possession, and if any of his kin come to redeem it, then shall he redeem that which his brother sold" (Leviticus 25:23-25).

Just as an Israelite could sell or lose his land for a time, so apparently Adam lost his God-given dominion over the earth. Satan became the "god of this world" (2 Corinthians 4:4). But this situation could only be superficial and temporary, for "the earth hath he given to the children of men" (Psalm 115:16).

A lost estate in Israel could be redeemed by any kinsman with the purchase price. The only one able to redeem the earth, however, is the Creator Himself, and to be a kinsman of Adam, He must first become a man, the second Adam. The redemption price, furthermore, cannot be mere money. "Forasmuch as ye know that ye were not redeemed with corruptible things, as silver and gold, from your vain conversation received by tradition from your fathers; but with the precious blood of Christ, as of a lamb without blemish and without spot: Who verily was foreordained before the foundation of the world, but was manifest in these last times for you" (1 Peter 1:18-20).

The sinless Lamb of God must take away the sin of the world (John 1:29). But even after the price was paid, the great usurper must still be expelled from the redeemed estate before the redemption of the purchased possession would be complete. For a long time, however, the Lamb of God, the rightful owner, has been away in heaven, preparing a great city as a home for his redeemed ones, to bring back with Him when He returns to take possession of the earth.

This aspect is also pictured typologically in the Old Testament, this time in terms of the long absence of the whole nation of Judah from its land during the Babylonian captivity. In token of his faith that God would eventually restore the land to them, the prophet Jeremiah purchased a tract of land which he had the right as a kinsman-redeemer to buy, even though he knew the Babylonian invaders would usurp the land for seventy long years (Jeremiah 25:11).

The evidence of the transaction was to be buried until such time as the invaders were expelled and the rightful heirs could return to claim it. "And I subscribed the evidence, and sealed it, and took witnesses, and weighed him the money in the balances. So I took the evidence of the purchase, both that which was sealed according to the law and custom, and that which was open: And I gave the evidence of the purchase unto Baruch the son of Neriah, the son of Maaseiah, in the sight of Hanameel mine uncle's son, and in the presence of the witnesses that subscribed the book of the purchase, before all the Jews that sat in the court of the prison. And I charged Baruch before them, saying, Thus saith the Lord of hosts, the God of Israel; Take these evidences, this evidence of the purchase, both which is sealed, and this evidence which is open; and put them in an earthen vessel, that they may continue many days. For thus saith the Lord of hosts, the God of Israel; Houses and fields and vineyards shall be possessed again in this land" (Jeremiah 32:10-15).

The deed of sale was written and sealed. A duplicate was also made, the latter remaining open so as to bear testimony to what was in the sealed copy, and to be available for records and reference. The sealed copy, however, could only be opened by the rightful owner (as identified on the open copy), and the transaction was not fully consummated until he came forward to break the seals and exhibit the official title deed and right of ownership. In Jeremiah's case, both copies were buried together, since there was no safe place for records to be kept, and Jeremiah knew that God would somehow direct his heirs back to claim their inheritance.

Whose World Is This?

This is the background of the marvelous drama that now unfolds in Revelation. The Lamb has paid the price to reclaim the lost world and has delivered over the title deed, as it were, for safekeeping to its Creator God until He could return to cast out the invader and consummate the full redemption of His dearly purchased possession.

The heavenly title scroll is one rather than two, but the import is the same. Its contents are evidently brief, recording only the fact that the price for the whole world has been paid and the Lamb has right to the inheritance, but it is sealed tight with seven seals. However, the same brief information appears openly to all, written on the backside, or outside, so there is no need for two scrolls. The word has been published to the whole creation if men would only believe it, that the Lamb is the Redeemer and some day will return to claim his possession and to be acknowledged universally as King of kings.

Revelation 5:2.   And I saw a strong angel proclaiming with a loud voice, Who is worthy to open the book, and to loose the seals thereof?

First, however, it must be established in sight of all the heavenly host, as well as all the redeemed, that there was no one else qualified to claim the inheritance. An angel—no ordinary angel, but one of the highest in the heavenly host, perhaps Gabriel himself, a "strong" angel—proclaims with a thunderous voice, audible throughout the mighty company, that the time is at hand. The world has been plundered long enough by the great Adversary and he must be defeated and banished with all his followers, both human and demon, forever. But who and where is one who is both Kinsman and Redeemer, one who has both the right and the ability to take over "the uttermost parts of the earth [for His] possession" (Psalm 2:8)?

Revelation 5:3.   And no man in heaven, nor in earth, neither under the earth, was able to open the book, neither to look thereon.

The identity of the rightful heir must be determined, and the description is very specific, perhaps spelled out clearly on the open side of the seven-sealed scroll. For one thing it must be a man, rather than an angel, for it was man's lost estate that must be reclaimed. None of the angelic hosts in heaven, and certainly not the demonic hordes of Satan, can qualify.

But there are billions of men, including many of the saved, now in heaven around the throne. None of these, however, could qualify as the Redeemer because their very souls are included in the estate to be redeemed. Since man's sin was the cause for which the world was lost, no man who is or was a sinner can buy it back. The price is a life of perfect holiness, with that life being offered through the shedding of its blood in substitutionary suffering and death for the world of sinners, "In whom we have redemption through his blood, the forgiveness of sins, according to the riches of his grace" (Ephesians 1:7).

In all the world's history, there has been "none righteous, no, not one" (Romans 3:10). And if there are none in heaven who are qualified, still less qualified are the unredeemed still on the earth or under the earth in Hades. They are still *in* their sins. "For all have sinned, and come short of the glory of God" (Romans 3:23).

None of the saints around the throne could even bring himself to dare *look* at the book, just to see whether he would qualify. They had all experienced the purifying fire of Christ's presence and had been *made* like Him (Romans 8:29). But this was by His grace only—not any merit of their own. The one who could open the scroll must do so by right of His own demonstrated—not imputed— merit.

Revelation 5:4.   And I wept much, because no man was found worthy to open and to read the book, neither to look thereon.

John, as one of the raptured saints, views the scene in awe—but also in increasing concern. All had seemed in readiness to proceed with the expurgation of the great invader and his hosts of demonic and human followers on earth, but the rightful claimant to earth's title had not been found. The scroll remained sealed, and the judgments could not proceed until it was opened. John, in great emotion, and somehow still not of sufficient confident faith, despite all he had heard and seen, began to wonder whether the work of redemption might even yet fail of completion, and finally to weep and sob in near despair.

Revelation 5:5.   And one of the elders saith unto me, Weep not: behold, the Lion of the tribe of Juda, the Root of David, hath prevailed to open the book, and to loose the seven seals thereof.

It is significant that it was not the angel, but an elder, who came to meet John's need at this point. The elder was a redeemed and raptured saint, like John, and understood the intensity of his concern better than any angel could but he, unlike John, had long been in heaven with the Savior, having been among those rescued by Him from Hades at the time of Christ's resurrection. As an "elder," he had presumably lived his pilgrimage on earth before John was born, with the unique perspective such long experience had acquired for him.

It may be he is one of the ancient patriarchs—possibly even Judah himself! Who would know better the implication of Jacob's dying prophecy concerning the coming Savior? "Judah is a lion's whelp. . . . The sceptre shall not depart from Judah, nor a lawgiver from between his feet, until Shiloh come; and unto him shall the gathering of the people be" (Genesis 49:9, 10).

By John's time, the Romans had destroyed Jerusalem and the Jews were in dispersion: the scepter had indeed departed from Judah. Therefore, Shiloh had already come, the promised King, the Lion of Judah's tribe. But perhaps it had not been fully understood in those ancient times what "the gathering of the peoples" might mean.

Now all understood. All the redeemed peoples of all the nations of all the ages had been gathered together unto Him and were intensely awaiting His appearance as the great conquering Lion.

In the tribe of Judah, the chosen family was Jesse and the anointed king was David. He who had created David—"the root of David" was also the "offspring of David" (Revelation 22:16). He had "come whose right it is" (Ezekiel 21:27).

That it was His right had been proved because He had prevailed to open the book. This is the same word used for "overcome" in the letters to the churches, and also for "triumphed" in Colossians 2:14, 15: "Blotting out the handwriting of ordinances that was against us, which was contrary to us, and took it out of the way, nailing it to his cross; and having spoiled principalities and powers, he made a shew of them openly, triumphing over them in it." Not only was He the Son of man, He was the Lion of Judah and the Root of David; He had put away sin by the sacrifice of Himself on the cross and had prevailed over the powers of the wicked one who had usurped His Father's creation. John's tears ceased, as he turned to see the great prevailing Lion prepare to burst the seals.

Revelation 5:6.   And I beheld, and lo, in the midst of the throne and of the four beasts, and in the midst of the elders, stood a Lamb as it had been slain, having seven horns and seven eyes, which are the seven Spirits of God sent forth into all the earth.

Instead of the great Lion which he anticipated, however, John saw a Lamb standing in the midst—the meekest of all God's animal creation instead of the fiercest. The Lamb, like the Lion, is obviously symbolic, but the symbolism is clear.

When John had first seen the glorified Son of man (Revelation 1:13-16) the symbol of the Lion would have been fitting. But now in the rainbow light encircling the throne appeared the same divine person in different garb. The conquering King had first become the suffering Servant. It is in His capacity as the Lamb of God that the price of redemption had been satisfied. Therefore it is as the Lamb that He must receive the title scroll from the hand of Him who had held it in safekeeping throughout the age of grace.

Note also the Lamb stood "as it had been slain," and yet He *stood,* and was living. His death wounds were still visible, but He was "alive for evermore" (Revelation 1:18).

The Lamb's appearance was remarkable in another respect—"seven horns and seven eyes." The seven eyes represent the sevenfold Holy Spirit, as noted before. (Revelation 1:4 and 4:5). There is also a reference, however, to Zechariah 4:10: "For who hath despised the day of small things? for they shall rejoice, and shall see the plummet in the hand of Zerubbabel with those seven; they are the eyes of the Lord, which run to and fro through the whole earth."

Zerubbabel was in charge of building the temple after the Jews returned from the Babylonian captivity, thus serving also as a type of the Redeemer returning to His possession. The "small things" of the restored temple were a type of the whole earth, which would one day be restored, and the "seven eyes," seeing the whole earth as the Lord sees it reminded Zerubbabel, as they did John, of that great future day.

Zerubbabel's contemporary and colleague was Joshua, the high priest. God gave a similar message to him: "Hear now, O Joshua the high priest, . . . for, behold, I will bring forth my servant the BRANCH. For behold the stone that I have laid before Joshua; upon one stone shall be seven eyes: behold, I will engrave the graving thereof, saith the Lord of hosts, and I will remove the iniquity of that land in one day" (Zechariah 3:8, 9).

The "BRANCH" is the "root of David" again, a name for the coming Savior. In token of this promise, God gave Joshua an engraved stone with the "seven eyes." To Zerubbabel the seven eyes betokened restoration of the earth; to Joshua they symbolized its future purification. Both restoration and purification would be accomplished some day by the coming Redeemer.

The "seven horns" may be an antitypical reference to another Joshua (The name *Joshua,* of course, is the same as *Jesus*). When the children of Israel first entered the land of Canaan to claim it for their own as God had promised, they encountered a wicked city barring their way. When in accord with God's command, the priests took "seven trumpets of ram's horns," the walls of Jericho tumbled down and the city and its alien inhabitants were destroyed. Thus, these "seven horns" on the Lamb may well have recalled to John the seven ram's horns of Joshua, and their effectiveness in enabling the people of God to enter on their inheritance in God's land of promise. Further, their use as trumpets surely reminded John also of the trumpet that had called him up to God's throne.

Thus the seven horns and seven eyes on the heavenly Lamb would call to John's remembrance all the great promises of salvation, both to Israel and to the whole world. In fact Jesus Himself is called "an horn of salvation for us in the house of his servant David" (Luke 1:69).

Revelation 5:7.   And he came and took the book out of the right hand of him that sat upon the throne.

The dramatic moment for which John and the great assembly had waited was finally here. The Lamb came to take the title book, and the One on the throne gave it to Him, thus acknowledging before the universe that the slain, yet living, Lamb was the world's Redeemer.

Daniel saw the same great event in a vision. "I saw in the night visions, and, behold, one like the Son of man came with the clouds of heaven, and came to the Ancient of days, and they brought him near before him. And there was given him dominion, and glory, and a kingdom, that all people, nations, and languages, should serve him: his dominion is an everlasting dominion, which shall not pass away, and his kingdom that which shall not be destroyed" (Daniel 7:13, 14).

Daniel saw only a vision, and therefore not the complete sequence of events involved. John saw the actual events, because He was *there,* caught up with the saints into God's presence. John's "Lamb" is the same as the Son of man in Daniel, and the dominion given Him must actually be enforced by Him as the seals on the title scroll are opened.

When the Angels Sing

Revelation 5:8.   And when he had taken the book, the four beasts and four and twenty elders fell down before the Lamb, having every one of them harps, and golden vials full of odours, which are the prayers of saints.

This was the signal the rapt assembly had been waiting for. The Lamb who had purchased their redemption was back again, and soon would open the seals to complete the work.

"Thy kingdom come; thy will be done on earth, as it is in heaven." Thus had the Lord taught His disciples to pray, and thus had millions of His people prayed through century after century. Countless other prayers had ascended which had not yet been answered. Yet the Lord had promised: "If ye shall ask any thing in my name, I will do it" (John 14:14). The believing prayers of godly saints will all be answered, though many will not see all the answers before the Lord returns. It will be as though the prayers were stored up in bottles of precious incense, awaiting the proper time for the Lord's personal attention.

The daily prayers of the saints are indeed like sweet incense to the Lord. David said: "Let my prayer be set forth before thee as incense; and the lifting up of my hands as the evening sacrifice" (Psalm 141:2). In the tabernacle in the wilderness was an altar of incense, just outside the veil before the mercy seat, and the high priest was to "burn incense upon it, a perpetual incense before the Lord throughout your generations" (Exodus 30:8). This beautifully pictured the prayers of believers continually appearing before the presence of the Lord. "By him therefore let us offer the sacrifice of praise to God continually, that is, the fruit of our lips giving thanks to his name" (Hebrews 13:15).

The twenty-four elders, representing all the saints, have each apparently been given a golden bowl of incense, representing all the unanswered prayers of the ages to offer before the Lamb. They also have harps with which to praise Him in song. In song and prayer, falling down in worship, they (that is to say, *we!*) will begin an eternal ministry of joyful service to their Redeemer.

And, amazingly enough, the four "living ones" are with them in prostration before the Lamb. Even the mightiest of all the "angels desire to look into" the great mysteries of God (1 Peter 1:12), and rejoice with the "heirs of salvation" to whom they have ministered (Hebrews 1:14) when they are revealed and fulfilled.

Revelation 5:9.   And they sung a new song, saying, Thou art worthy to take the book, and to open the seals thereof: for thou wast slain, and hast redeemed us to God by thy blood out of every kindred, and tongue, and people, and nation.

The twenty-four elders, presumably accompanied by all the saints, will then proceed to sing, and it will be a song such as the cosmos has never yet heard. Even at the creation, when all the newly-created angelic host shouted for joy as they sang together (Job 38:7), there was nothing like this. For now, the renewed voices of billions of redeemed saints will join in a mighty anthem of praise to their strong Redeemer and King. Perhaps the song will even be heard on earth, as was the praise of the angels at the birth of Christ (Luke 2:13).

The song is new not only in magnitude but in words and music. A billion harps will accompany the golden voices of their singers, and the theme is that of gratitude to the worthy Lamb.

That more than just twenty-four are singing is evident from the song: "Thou hast redeemed us to God by thy blood out of *every* kindred, and tongue, and people, and nation." There are thousands of languages among men, and here is a gracious promise that God does have His elect hidden away in every tribe and people.

It has been pointed out that the pronoun "us" is not found in one of the oldest manuscripts, thus raising a question as to whether the elders are actually human beings. It does occur in practically all, however, so there is really no legitimate reason to question it.

It is noteworthy, too, that the heavenly host is not embarrassed (as are many modern congregations) to sing a hymn extolling the blood of Christ. The very price of the world's redemption was the shed blood of the Savior.

Revelation 5:10.   And hast made us unto our God kings and priests: and we shall reign on the earth.

Three times in the Book of Revelation it is said that believers are to be made kings and priests (Revelation 1:6; 5:10; 20:6). These functions apply particularly in the millennial kingdom, when there is still need for them. This, indeed is a part of the Christian's reward. "And he said unto him, Well, thou good servant: because thou hast been faithful in a very little, have thou authority over ten cities" (Luke 19:17). The people still in the flesh are on the earth, during the millennium, but the saints, in their glorified bodies, have their homes in the heavenly places, possibly in the New Jerusalem, hovering over the atmospheric heavens. Nevertheless, they have rapid access to the earth, as needed in the course of their kingly duties. As priests (1 Peter 2:5), they will offer up spiritual sacrifices, the sacrifice of praise continually (Hebrews 13:15). Perhaps there will also be ministries of intercession and of evangelism, in relation to those yet unsaved during the millennium. In any case, the promise of Christ is that we shall reign *over* (better than "on") the earth.

Revelation 5:11.   And I beheld, and I heard the voice of many angels round about the throne and the beasts and the elders: and the number of them was ten thousand times ten thousand, and thousands of thousands.

As John shared in the anthem of the redeemed multitudes, he next became aware of an even greater group joining in the heavenly chorus. The tremendous host of heaven was there too. The term "ten thousand" is actually "myriad," so that the number of angels is said to be "myriads of myriads, and thousands of thousands." This is not meant to be a precise count, of course, but simply to convey the thought of "innumerable." In fact, the same word ("myriad") is translated "innumerable" in Luke 12:1 and Hebrews 12:22. The latter reference, in fact, probably looks forward to this very gathering. "But ye are come unto Mount Sion, and unto the city of the living God, the heavenly Jerusalem, and to an innumerable company of angels, to the general assembly and church of the first-born, which are written in heaven, and to God the Judge of all, and to the spirits of just men made perfect, and to Jesus the mediator of the new covenant, and to the blood of sprinkling, that speaketh better things than that of Abel."

Whatever the number of saved men and women there may be—quite possibly several billion at least—the number of angels must be still greater, since every believer probably has several angels assigned to his care in addition to all the angels with other ministries. The number is no doubt a finite number, but is so great it cannot be even estimated. And all this numberless host of mighty angels, assembled from the far reaches of the cosmos there at the throne in the heavenly city, suspended high above the earth, will be united with the redeemed saints in singing beautiful praises to the worthy Lamb.

Revelation 5:12.   Saying with a loud voice, Worthy is the Lamb that was slain to receive power, and riches, and wisdom, and strength, and honour, and glory, and blessing.

The great congregation, with a "loud" voice (loud indeed, with unnumbered billions of voices joining the refrain), thus sings a mighty sevenfold ascription of praise to the Lamb. The first doxology (4:11), with a threefold ascription to the Lord, was for God's work of creation. This sevenfold anthem is for His work of redemption (5:9).

For His work of creation, "glory and honor and power" were invoked. These are all attributes of majesty. The Lamb merits not only these, however, but also "riches, wisdom, strength and blessing." For additional insight into the tremendous scope of this description of the attributes of the Lamb, consider some typical parallel passages using the same Greek words:

1. "power" (Gr. *dunamis*). Revelation 1:16. " . . . as the sun shineth in his *strength.*"

2. "riches" (*ploutos*) Philippians 4:19. "But my God shall supply all your need according to his *riches* in glory by Christ Jesus."

3. "wisdom" (*sophia*) 1 Corinthians 3:19. "For the *wisdom* of this world is foolishness with God."

4. "strength" (*iskus*) Mark 12:30. "And thou shalt love the Lord thy God . . . with all thy *strength.*"

5. "honor" (*timee*) Hebrews 2:9. " . . . crowned with glory and *honour.*"

6. "glory" (*doxa*) 1 Peter 4:11. " . . . to whom be *praise* and dominion for ever."

7. "blessing" (*eulogia*) Romans 15:29. "the fulness of the *blessing* of the gospel of Christ."

Revelation 5:13.   And every creature which is in heaven, and on the earth, and under the earth, and such as are in the sea, and all that are in them, heard I saying, Blessing, and honour, and glory, and power, be unto him that sitteth upon the throne, and unto the Lamb for ever and ever.

It is not sufficient that all the angels and all the redeemed saints should join in singing praise to the Lamb. The redemption price was adequate and the title deed established, which covered the whole earth and all its inhabitants, animal as well as man. God had originally placed all creatures under Adam's dominion (Genesis 1:28) and had confirmed the same to Noah, the covenant with whom was everlasting and with "every living creature of all flesh that is upon the earth" (Genesis 9:1, 2, 9, 10, 16). But, because of man's sin and Satan's investiture of the earth, "the whole creation groaneth and travaileth in pain together until now" (Romans 8:22).

Thus it is now, however, that the whole creation praises and rejoices in song together when the Lamb receives the scroll. Its millennia of travail are soon to end, and every creature sings in anticipation (with the implied exception, no doubt, of those evil ones *from* whom the world is to be redeemed).

Those creatures referred to as "on the earth, and under the earth, and such as are in the sea" must refer either to holy angels appointed to serve in these regions or else to the animal creation—more likely the latter. A similar scene is depicted in Psalm 148:7-10: "Praise the Lord from the earth. . . . Beasts, and all cattle; creeping things, and flying fowl." The reverberations from the heavenly anthem, finding an echo in the divinely-empowered instinctive response of the vast animal creation, make it seem to John that the entire universe is praising the Lamb —as indeed it is, in a figure.

Revelation 5:14.   And the four beasts said, Amen. And the four and twenty elders fell down and worshipped him that liveth for ever and ever.

When the great anthem was finished, the great assemblage of redeemed bowed down in worship (the phrase "him that liveth for ever and ever" is omitted in most manuscripts, and was possibly added inadvertently by transcribers from Revelation 4:10). In any case, it is obvious that the object of their adoration is the mighty redeeming Lamb in the midst of the throne.

This brief description by the Apostle John of what will be an almost indescribably magnificent gathering in the heavens in the imminent future only summarizes its high points. No doubt much will happen there which John did not record.

For example, there is considerable evidence that Psalms 146—150 (the last five chapters in the book of Psalms) refer to this scene. Each of the psalms begins and ends with the exhortation: "Praise ye the Lord!" This phrase is the Hebrew *hallelujah*. In the New Testament, the word is used only four times—all in Revelation 19 (verses 1, 3, 4, 6) and all in connection with the praises of this same heavenly assemblage.

The first of these last five psalms begins with the great exhortation "Praise ye the Lord," and the response of each believer is: "Praise the Lord, O my soul. While I live will I praise the Lord: I will sing praises unto my God while I have any being" (Psalm 146:1, 2). Then, the final psalm concludes with the glorious exhortation: "Let every thing that hath breath praise the Lord. Praise ye the Lord" (Psalm 150:6).

The detailed study of these last five psalms in the context of this great future meeting in the air and the events on earth which will accompany it will yield rich insights and spiritual blessings. A partial commentary in this vein is found in the writer's book *Sampling the Psalms* (San Diego: Creation-Life Publishers, 1978).

The assembly at the throne in heaven is seen again from time to time in Revelation (7:11; 11:16-19; 14:3; 19:1-6). Finally, this great congregation of the saints all will march out of the heavens with the risen Lamb, now become the conquering Lion, openly manifest as the eternal Word of God, acknowledged by all as King of kings and Lord of lords, reclaiming the earth and the whole creation for its Redeemer (Revelation 19:11-16).

6

The Great Day of God's Wrath

(Revelation 6)

The Opening of the Seals

The time of singing has finally ceased, for the hour of judgment has come. The Lamb, whose right it is, has received the earth's title deed and now must begin to take possession of His kingdom. The scroll whose writing is within had been rolled and sealed with seven seals. Before the great claim can be verified officially, the seals must be broken and the writing openly displayed. By the same token, the invaders of earth and their human lackeys must be expelled before the Lamb's divine ownership will ever be openly recognized. Thus, the opening of the seals coincides with the judgments on the earth. As each successive seal is broken, the wrath of God takes successive toll on the earth and its inhabitants.

Thus begins a seven-year period of the most severe troubles the world will ever know. This is "the day of the Lord," the time when God breaks His agelong silence and speaks from heaven in mighty power. The great judgments of this period are described in words of fire by the prophets of the Old Testament, especially Isaiah and Daniel. It requires the Book of Revelation, however, to provide a basic topical and chronological framework which enables us to sort them all out and put them in right perspective.

This seven-year period (see Chapter 1) is clearly also the same as Daniel's famous "seventieth week" (Daniel 9:24-27). With respect to the unbelieving nation of Israel, it is to be "the time of Jacob's trouble" (Jeremiah 30:7). For the unbelieving Gentiles, it is the time of "the indignation of the Lord upon all nations" (Isaiah 34:2).

The scene as described in Revelation 6 is from the perspective of heaven, where John is waiting with the assembled saints. The events taking place on earth are given in further detail from earth's perspective in the parenthetical chapters (7, 10, 11, 13). In heaven, the symbolism of four great horses and their fearsome riders is employed; on earth, the terrible judgments which they unleash are very literal and real.

Revelation 6:1.   And I saw when the Lamb opened one of the seals, and I heard, as it were the noise of thunder, one of the four beasts saying, Come and see.

The Lamb had received the title scroll from the right hand of Him on the throne, a ceremony which had precipitated the magnificent cosmic anthem of praise to the Redeemer. Now that the anthem is finished, the Lamb proceeds to open the seals. The noise of thunder, as though presaging the tremendous storms about to break on the earth, emanates from the throne, from one of the four cherubim, and then the mighty cherub speaks.

The voice thundered: "Come!" In the King James Version, the rendering is "Come and see" and, in view of the large number of manuscripts which support this reading, this may well be the correct one. It should also be acknowledged that "Come!" could just as well be translated "Go!" In any case, the one who is speaking, that is, the "living one," the cherub, is calling and sending the first mighty messenger of judgment.

The Invasion of Israel

On the earth, in the meantime, momentous events have been taking place which, to many of the men and women still on the earth, will be highly encouraging and optimistic. After decades of war and inflation, political tensions of unrelieved complexity, and a whole host of global ills, almost overnight it seems most of the world's major problems have been resolved.

The baleful threat of Russia and her program of global conquest have been removed by a complex of amazing natural catastrophes which have decimated her military machine. The story had been recorded prophetically long ago, in Ezekiel 38 and 39, and had finally come to pass. In order to understand the events that follow in Revelation 6, it is necessary to digress at this point to give a brief summary of these two remarkable chapters.

Ezekiel 38 foresees a sudden invasion of the land of Israel in "the latter days" (Ezekiel 38:8, 16), at a time when Israel has returned to her own land out of the nations and apparently dwelling safely there. The threats from her immediate Arab neighbors had been neutralized in some way (possibly through nonaggression pacts with Egypt, Arabia, and others, or possibly by the development of new weapons systems which made invasion by the usual methods impracticable).

The Russian bear far to the north, however, was still Israel's implacable enemy, and had been gradually extending its power through a ring of puppet nations surrounding Israel. These are enumerated in Ezekiel 38:2-6. The prophecy is as follows:

"Son of man, set thy face against Gog, the land of Magog, the chief prince of Meshech and Tubal, and prophesy against him, and say, Thus saith the Lord God: Behold, I am against thee, O Gog, the chief prince of Meshech and Tubal: And I will turn thee back, and put hooks into thy jaws, and I will bring thee forth, and all thine army, horses and horsemen, all of them clothed with all sorts of armour, even a great company with bucklers and shields, all of them handling swords. Persia, Ethiopia, and Libya with them; all of them with shield and helmet: Gomer, and all his bands; the house of Togarmah of the north quarters, and all his bands: and many people with thee."

Gog is evidently the name of the commander of these armies, and he hails from the region originally settled by Japheth's song, Magog. This name is probably equivalent to modern "Georgia" and Gog's name thus may refer to his homeland. Stalin, for example, was from the Soviet republic of Georgia (the prefix "ma" means "land of," and "Georgia" may be read "Gog-ia"), and his first successor was named "Georgi" (Malenkov). In fact, Gog could well be a general title, like Pharaoh, derived from the ancestral home of the vast northern nations. Meshech and Tubal were also sons of Japheth, and both ancient and modern ethnologists have recognized their names to have been preserved in the modern names Moscow (or Muscovy) and Tobolsk, the chief cities of western and eastern Russia, respectively. Finally, many scholars have stressed that "chief prince" is actually "prince of Rosh," and that Russia actually derives its modern name from this very verse. Thus, there is little doubt that the leader of this latterday anti-Israeli alliance will be Russia.

The other nations form a clockwise ring around Israel and the entire Middle East. Persia is, of course, modern Iran. Ethiopia includes the modern land known as Ethiopia, but may also include a part of the Arabian peninsula across the Red Sea, where the ancestral Ethiopians first settled. Libya, of course, still has the same name today. Gomer, another son of Japheth, gave his name to the Cimmerians, the Crimea, and Germani. Thus, the reference to "Gomer and all his bands" may refer to all the peoples that settled from the Black Sea to eastern Germany. Similarly, "Togarmah of the North quarters and all his bands" probably refers to Armenia and Turkestan in general. It is significant that many of these nations today are Moslem nations and all of them are under Russian domination, even though nominally independent. All of them are strongly anti-Israel.

The sudden invasion of Israel will be resisted verbally, though not militarily, by "Sheba and Dedan, and the merchants of Tarshish, and the young lions thereof" (Ezekiel 38:13). Sheba and Dedan were in Arabia, and this passage suggests that the wealthy Arab oil states, themselves the objects of Russian cupidity, may still at that time be outside Russian control. Tarshish is probably the same as Carthage, founded by the Phoenicians. "Tarshish" means "smeltry," and the ancient Phoenicians, the first great mariners, founded iron smeltries, mines, and settlements in many lands, including at least Spain and England, and quite possibly even in America. Thus "the merchants of Tarshish and their young lions," in modern equivalence, most likely are the western nations in general. The original Phoenicia is modern Lebanon, and this nation also will probably be aligned with Israel.

The attackers will be "like a cloud to cover the land" (38:9) coming from all directions, possibly great waves of paratroopers, as well as cavalry. Their weapons will be mostly of wood—probably one of the new forms of very light, but very strong wood (39:9), like lignostone. Perhaps Israel's advanced weapons technology will have developed laser or microwave beams which render metallic components inoperable. The overwhelming numerical strength of the invading hosts, a number sufficient to require seven months of work by the whole population just to bury (39:12, 13), would seem to be irresistible.

But then God will intervene in an unprecedented way! A tremendous complex of earthquakes, hailstorms, volcanic eruptions, and pestilence, supplemented by fighting among the invading armies themselves, will overwhelm the hosts of Gog, destroying five men out of every six (38:19-22; 39:2-4). Simultaneously, great fires devastate Russia itself, along with the coastlands of its confederates (39:6), so that it will be completely eliminated as a world power as will its various satellite nations.

The "coincidences" will be so remarkable (even though the catastrophes are all natural phenomena) that all the nations will know they were sent by God (38:23). Israel, in particular, will give up the atheism which has dominated the Zionist movement and the modern Israeli nation in general and will "know that I am the Lord their God from that day and forward" (39:22).

It is quite probable that this great event will give Israel both the desire and the opportunity finally to rebuild their ancient temple and reinstitute the ancient worship. The Moslem "Dome of the Rock" will be razed and a magnificent temple constructed (Revelation 11:1, 2). With all this, however, the Israeli people will still reject Christ (except for a remnant that will be especially prepared by God), even though they are seeking to restore the worship of the God of their fathers.

The other nations of the world will also quickly seek to take advantage of the vacuum left by Russia's fall. Quickly forgetting the obvious role of God in the affair, the nations of the western alliance—possibly the NATO nations and/or the nations of the European Common Market—will forge a vast politico/commercial/religious alliance designed to dominate world affairs. Ten of these nations—all with cultural and legal ties to ancient Rome (Daniel 2:40-43; 7:24; Revelation

17:12)—will unite together, first in a loose alliance, later in a united empire.

With Russia and the Moslem nations no longer a problem, and the oil resources of the Middle East under their jurisdiction, these western nations will anticipate a tremendous era of peace and prosperity. In one of these nations, a tremendously capable and charismatic leader will have come into power (Daniel 7:23-25), and he and his nation will quickly enter into a treaty with Israel, which had so recently been in mortal danger. The Scriptures do not indicate the terms of the covenant except that it is for a seven-year period and possibly guarantees the safe construction of the temple and establishment of its worship (Daniel 9:27).

At some point in this sequence of events, the Lord will descend from heaven to the earth's atmosphere, and the great resurrection of the Christian dead and rapture of the living believers will take place. It is impossible to say with certainty, however, whether it will take place before or after the Russian invasion, since the rapture is always imminent. Since the seven-year period of the treaty almost certainly corresponds to the seven years covered in Revelation 6-19, the rapture must take place no later than the date of its activation, but it may occur anytime before that. It is possibly also significant that the wooden weapons of Gog's devastated armies will serve as fuel for the Israeli people for a period of seven years (Ezekiel 39:9, 10).

In any case, when the rapture does occur, there will undoubtedly be a great flurry of excitement in the world, particularly in those nations where there are many Christians whose sudden disappearance will be newsworthy. Probably there will be enough people left with adequate knowledge of biblical eschatology to deduce what has happened, and many and heated will be the letters to the editor. Liberal pastors will preach sermons to their liberal congregations deploring the rapture theory and trying to explain all the disappearances as some sort of capitalist plot. Many others will claim that aliens from outer space have spirited them away in their spaceships. With all the other excitement in the world, the missing Christians will soon be forgotten, at least for a time, and the world will get caught up in the euphoria of anticipated prosperity and peace.

All of this will be the immediate background of the events in Revelation 6. On the earth will be the vivid memory of Russia's recent destruction. The focus of interest will be increasingly on Israel and the Middle East, and the vanished Christians will soon be forgotten.

The rapture will have had one other major effect on the world. No longer will there be any significant voice for morality and righteousness in the world, and the pursuit of pleasures and vices of every description will be unrestrained (2 Thessalonians 2:6-12).

But then the blow will fall. "For when they shall say, Peace and safety; then sudden destruction cometh upon them, as travail upon a woman with child; and they shall not escape" (1 Thessalonians 5:3).

Revelation 6:2.   And I saw, and behold a white horse: and he that sat on him had a bow; and a crown was given unto him: and he went forth conquering, and to conquer.

This is the first of the famous "Four Horsemen of the Apocalypse." These horses, of course, are clearly symbolic. There are no horses in heaven. Further, the first is quite different from the others as no specific plagues are associated with its rider, as are the others (war, famine, and pestilence, respectively).

For some reason, most futurist commentators take the rider on the white horse to be the coming Antichrist. This interpretation, however, fails to recognize that all four horsemen are sent forth directly from the Lamb, as judgments on the wicked men on the earth, of whom the *most* wicked is Antichrist himself. Furthermore, although this great "man of sin" does indeed attempt to conquer, he certainly is not to be allowed to conquer. He will quickly be conquered himself—by none other than this same rider on the white horse (see Revelation 19:11-20), who Himself is none other than King of kings and Lord of lords.

At this tremendous moment in history, "the Son of God goes forth to war," as the Lamb breaks the first seal. The seven seal judgments follow, then the seven trumpets, then the seven bowls. However, the seventh seal includes all the seven trumpets and the seventh trumpet leads into the seven bowls. The entire series thus represents the Lamb's successive forays into the invader's strongholds until finally the enemy is driven out completely. The climax comes at the battle of Armageddon, when the great Rider appears once again on His white horse to win the final victory (Revelation 19:11, 19).

This horseman is the only one with a crown, and it is the victor's crown (Greek *stephanos*) He is "to conquer"; He is the King. He is armed with a great bow, but the bow does not speak of warfare; for that is the province of the second horseman. The word "conquer" is the same as "overcome" used so frequently by the Lord in the letters to the churches. To the last church, the promise to the "conquering" Christian was that he would share His throne, since He also had "conquered" (Revelation 3:21).

There may be a suggestion in Habakkuk 3:9. "Thy bow was made quite naked, . . . even thy word. Selah." Like the sword "which proceeded out of his mouth" (Revelation 19:21), the bow perhaps speaks of His conquering the hearts of men through His Word, while at the same time He is defeating the rebellions of wicked men by the same Word. In any case, "when thy judgments are in the earth, the inhabitants of the world will learn righteousness" (Isaiah 26:9). As the seals are broken, the trumpets blown, and the bowls poured out, the wicked are indeed defeated but at the same time a great multitude will be won to Christ (Revelation 7:9). The bow, like the rainbow, speaks of mercy in the midst of judgment. The judgments are both preceded and followed, begun and ended, by the one who "is called The Word of God" (Revelation 19:13).

War and Famine

Revelation 6:3.   And when he had opened the second seal, I heard the second beast say, Come and see.

As the white horse receded from John's field of vision, riding forth to conquer the world with His great bow, John looked again at the Lamb in the midst of the heavenly throne. The rider on the white horse had been a vision, representing the Lamb's control of the judgments that were about to break forth on the earth. Indeed, this first horseman and the Lamb both represented none other than John's beloved Lord, the one who as Lamb of God took away the sin of the world (John 1:29) and who as the great Rider on the white horse was now riding forth to purge away the sinners of the world.

And then, when the Lamb broke the second seal on the title deed to the world, the second great cherub—the one appearing first to John like a calf, or an ox—spoke with a voice like thunder, and the second horseman prepared to ride.

Revelation 6:4.   And there went out another horse that was red: and power was given him that sat thereon to take peace from the earth, and that they should kill one another: and there was given unto him a great sword.

There had been a time of peace on the earth, but it was brief and illusory. The second rider, this one on a blood-red horse, was commissioned by the Lamb to take away their peace. "Wars and rumors of wars" (Matthew 24:6) again broke out, as nation rose against nation and men again undertook to "kill one another."

It is an amazing thing that men, created in the image of God, should become so blinded with hate or lust or ambition or envy that they should seek to destroy the precious lives of others. Yet the very first man born in the world slew his brother, and men have followed in the way of Cain ever since. Not only the barbarians of Genghis Khan, but the sophisticated butchers of Nazi Germany and Red China and Stalinist Russia in the enlightened twentieth century have murdered millions. The genocides in Cambodia and Viet Nam and in various African nations continued the same pattern.

Men have longed for peace. There have been peace treaties, disarmament conferences, leagues of nations, peace prizes, demonstrations for peace—all seeking somehow to bring in lasting world peace. But all had failed.

Then, with the sudden disintegration of Russia and its Moslem allies, there had been a tremendous surge of optimism and the world anticipated a long period of peace and prosperity. The troublesome Christians had also disappeared, and there was nothing to restrain full enjoyment of all the pleasures and indulgences of the sinful hearts of mankind.

But it could not last. In spite of themselves, men soon were fighting each other again. This was true not only in terms of actual wars between countries. Racial strife increased, as did labor troubles. Civil wars erupted within nations, and organized crime was rampant. Individual feuds generated waves of murders, and soon a state almost of anarchy prevailed. Police forces and armies were of little avail as they also were engaged in strife internal and external. Nothing seemed to help and men began to fight almost in spite of themselves. God had sent "strong delusion" (2 Thessalonians 2:11) and the Red Horseman had taken peace from the earth, his great sword, invisibly but lethally, plunging into its heart.

Revelation 6:5.   And when he had opened the third seal, I heard the third beast say, Come and see. And I beheld, and lo a black horse; and he that sat on him had a pair of balances in his hand.

The first horseman carried a great bow, the second a great sword. The third held merely a pair of balances, but this also symbolized a great weapon. The balances depict trade and commerce, the determination of price equivalents for goods. The power of commerce, to generate prosperity or calamity, inflation or depression, opulence or starvation, has been understood and manipulated by politicians and merchants and bankers for thousands of years, beginning back in ancient Babylon. The Sumerian tablets, probably the oldest of all known archaeological artifacts, reveal mercantile and commercial practices quite similar to those of today.

There is a remarkable prophecy in Zechariah apparently dealing with this same theme. In his vision, Zechariah saw an "ephah" going forth through all the earth, finally being carried to "the land of Shinar" (Zechariah 5:5-11). The ephah was the standard measure for wheat and other commodities, roughly equivalent to a bushel. An actual balance had been outfitted, with a container designed to hold an ephah attached to the balance. Zechariah saw a woman sitting in the ephah, however, with a talent of lead (that is, a circular lead weight) covering the mouth. One woman was in the ephah, with two winged women bearing it back to Sumer (same as "Shinar") where the whole system of worldly wealth and commerce was first developed and whence it had spread throughout the earth. "This is wickedness," said the angel (Zechariah 5:8), and it was being transported back to Babylon "to build it an house in the land of Shinar: and it shall be established, and set there upon her own base" (Zechariah 5:11). The great Babylonian harlot is seen again in Revelation 17 and 18, where apparently this system of wickedness has indeed been set again upon its original base, where she will once again control and manipulate world wealth and commerce.

Babylon is now largely in ruins, but it is quite near to Baghdad, the capital of Iraq. Iraq is today the center of tremendous oil reserves and has profited even more than Iran and Saudi Arabia from her great underground wealth. For years water control projects have been harnessing the waters of the great Tigris and Euphrates Rivers flowing through Iraq, and from time to time there has been talk of someday building a new Babylon.

Babylon would be ideally situated to serve as a world trade and communications center and indeed even as a world capital. An I.C.R. computer study some years ago demonstrated that this region is very close to the geographical center of all the world's land areas. In view of the clear indication that Babylon may indeed be the actual capital of the world empire of the Beast in the last days (see comments on Revelation 17 and 18), it may well be that the decision to rebuild Babylon (first as a trade center, later to become the capital) could be made at about the same time the decision is made to rebuild Jerusalem's temple. By that time, the economic influence of the American nations (already much in decline) may be much less significant than during the past century. With the defeat of Russia and the increasing importance of the Persian Gulf and the Indian Ocean, it may well be that the world's industrial leaders and international bankers will decide that an internationalized capital of commerce should be established in an ultra-modern new metropolis arising out of the ruins of earth's first metropolis. Possibly even the United Nations Organization will decide to move from the so-called "Babylon-on-the-Hudson" to the primal Babylon on the Euphrates.

Wherever they are centered, these international capitalists will begin to use the new period of peace as an opportunity to gain full control of the great oil resources of the world as well as its food resources and its money supply. The Black Horseman, however, will thwart their plans in considerable measure, as a worldwide famine suddenly strikes the world.

This is the period during which God's two Witnesses call for a worldwide three and a half-year drought (see comments on Revelation 11:3-6). Tremendous famines, then shortages and hunger, quickly follow.

Revelation 6:6.   And I heard a voice in the midst of the four beasts say, A measure of wheat for a penny, and three measures of barley for a penny; and see thou hurt not the oil and the wine.

This is an amazing revelation. The voice speaking out of the midst of the four living ones can hardly be other than God Himself, specifying commodity prices. Evidently the voice is directed to the Black Horseman, and perhaps also the various angels who control the winds and rains and other natural agents influencing agricultural growth, to instruct them as to precisely how severe the famine is to become.

The "measure" is the Greek *koinix,* about 1½ pints, and the "penny" is the *denarius,* a coin which was a day's wage of a laborer. This price represents severe conditions of shortage, conditions which will allow wage earners barely to survive. If they are unemployed, or if they have a family, some probably will not survive, without using their savings or being fed by government dole.

The instruction not to hurt the oil and wine is grimly sarcastic. Oil and wine represent luxuries rather than necessities such as wheat and barley. Normally these are expensive, mostly indulgences of the rich. They will at that time be available in ample supply despite the shortages of basic foodstuffs. The demand for luxuries normally drops in times of inflated prices for necessities.

It is barely possible that the "oil," instead of referring to olive oil, as it normally does, could refer to petroleum, which was unknown in New Testament days but is extremely important to the modern world. It could be still more important to the future world empire of the coming Antichrist. Wine has been the world's great intoxicating beverage for thousands of years, although it may in this context represent all intoxicating beverages. Thus, it may be that God's instruction here is to preserve the world's fuels and intoxicants. This would allow men to indulge their sinful appetites to the fullest, even while suffering from shortages of necessary food, to demonstrate the justice of their coming condemnation.

In either case, the overriding characteristic of the world after the third seal is broken is one of violence and near anarchy, along with severe famine and food shortage.

The Blood of the Martyrs

Revelation 6:7.   And when he had opened the fourth seal, I heard the voice of the fourth beast say, Come and see.

The last of the four living ones now issues his invitation, and the fourth horseman of the Apocalypse rides forth. Many previous writers have called attention to the analogy of the four beasts (respectively appearing like a lion, an ox, a man, and an eagle) to the four Gospels (Matthew, Mark, Luke, and John) which respectively portray the Lord Jesus Christ in His fourfold capacity as King of Israel, Suffering Servant, Son of man, and Son of God. Each of the Gospels, as it were, invites all men to "come and see" the Lord Jesus as He has left His glorious heavenly throne to come to earth as the atoning Lamb of God to take away the world's guilt. Now, each of the four mighty cherubim, as it were, invites all creation to come and see the Lamb of God returning again to earth to take away the world's sin by His mighty judgments.

Revelation 6:8.   And I looked, and behold a pale horse: and his name that sat on him was Death, and Hell followed with him. And Power was given unto them over

the fourth part of the earth, to kill with sword, and with hunger, and with death, and with the beasts of the earth.

The fourth horse was green (Greek *chloros*), the same word used to describe the color of grass in Mark 6:39, Revelation 8:7, and Revelation 9:4. Green is the color universally associated with *life,* yet the rider on the horse is called Death. The symbolism probably is intended as prophetic irony. The humanistic optimism generated by recent events will lead the ungodly world to rejoice in the imminent attainment of the utopian life of peace and luxury it had been seeking for ages.

But the good life they anticipate will quickly become ashes as the judgments of God begin to devastate the earth. "Life" is overcome by "Death" and "Hades" follows quickly to swallow the souls of those who die.

The judgments associated with this fourth horseman include those brought by the second and third ("sword" and "hunger"), and all are directed by the conquering rider on the first horse. That Christ Himself is directly responsible for the ravages of Death and Hades as they range over the earth is evident from His assertion that He has the keys of Death and Hades (Revelation 1:18).

In addition to the worldwide violence and famine, this last deadly rider also brings "death" and "the wild beasts of the earth." The word for "death" is the Greek *thanatos,* the same word as used for the name of the rider. It does not mean "pestilence" (Greek *loimos*), as often interpreted, though this may be implied. Violence and famine do lead frequently to pestilence but the term itself includes all causes of death. Everything from old age to traffic accidents or suicide may be a cause of death, and all are included. Although the world population will be the greatest in all history, so will the death rate. In fact, one fourth of all people in the world will die. This will evidently be at least a billion people since the world's present population is at least four billion. Furthermore this all will take place in only a year or two, during the first part of the three-and-a-half years covered in Revelation 6-11.

An intriguing additional specific cause of this great toll of death is said to be "the beasts of the earth." Since practically all the beasts really dangerous to man have either become extinct or are now rare and endangered species, it seems unlikely that wild animals could multiply enough in a couple of years in the last days to become a really serious threat. However, the term is also used in Acts 28:4, 5 to refer to a poisonous serpent, and it is possible that this passage portends a sudden proliferation of venomous snakes all over the earth.

The word "beast" here is the Greek *theerion,* and does indeed mean a wild, or dangerous, or venomous beast. It is different from the word *zoon,* translated "beast" in connection with the "living ones" around God's throne. It is remarkable, however, that *theerion* is used no less than thirty-eight times in Revelation, and in every other instance the word is used as a symbol for an ungodly, powerful, evil leader. Thus "the beasts of the earth" in this verse could well refer to latter-day political and military dictators whom the Lord allows for a time to subjugate and persecute their respective subjects.

Revelation 6:9.   And when he had opened the fifth seal, I saw under the altar the souls of them that were slain for the word of God, and for the testimony which they held.

With the four horsemen riding forth and the great judgments of God unleashed on the earth, the opening of the fifth seal by the Lamb introduces a strange and different scene. Like the Horsemen, the altar seen by John may be symbolic and the same may be true of the souls beneath it. Nevertheless, the martyrs are real and their cry is real.

The figure of the shed blood under the altar is taken from Leviticus 4:17, 18. "And the priest shall. . . . pour out all the blood at the bottom of the altar of the burnt offering, which is at the door of the tabernacle of the congregation." The blood under the Levitical altar was from the atoning sacrifices for sins, and "the life of the flesh is in the blood" (Leviticus 17:11). The Hebrew word for "life," *nephesh,* is often translated "soul." The blood was innocent blood, spilled in substitution for those who deserved to die, foreshadowing the sinless blood of the Lamb of God, crucified by those whom He came to save. The souls under the altar likewise had offered their lives in testimony for the sake of their Savior, their blood shed by those whom they sought to lead to salvation.

But who were these martyrs? All the "souls" of believers had been clothed with glorified bodies on the great resurrection day when Christ first descended from heaven to the earth's atmosphere (1 Thessalonians 4:16, 17). The reasons for this interpretation have already been discussed and they seem conclusive. Thus, the martyrs seen at this time can only be those who were put to death for Christ's sake during the first years of the seven-year period. This in turn means they had become believers during that same period, since all living believers had been raptured into Christ's presence at the time of the resurrection.

As noted above, there is some reason to believe that the "beasts of the earth" (verse 8) may refer to evil rulers who will put many to death as they take and consolidate their particular regimes during this period. Whether or not this is the particular meaning of that verse, the martyrs, slain "for *that* testimony which they held" (literal rendering) must have been victims of religious persecution either ordered or allowed by such leaders.

This, in turn, means that something has generated a great revival of belief in the true God and His Christ during this period in spite of the fact that there were *no* believers remaining on the earth at its beginning. For one thing, God will have sent his "two witnesses" (Revelation 11:3) into the world, prophesying and calling forth mighty miracles. Somehow also there will be 144,000 Israelites "sealed" for God's service during this period (Revelation 7:4). The result will be a "great multitude" saved (Revelation 7:9).

It is quite possible that there will be other *silent* witnesses as well whose testimony will finally be heeded. Millions upon millions of copies of the Bible and Bible portions have been published in all major languages, and distributed throughout the world through the dedicated ministries of the Gideons, the Wycliffe Bible Translators, and other such Christian organizations. Removal of believers from the world at the rapture will not remove the Scriptures, and multitudes will no doubt be constrained to read the Bible in those days. Furthermore, there has been in recent years a great revival of the doctrine of creation, and the long intellectual dominance of evolutionary humanism has been seriously undermined by the many books, lectures, debates, and other activities of creationist scientists. With the sudden disappearance of the Christians, followed by the miraculous preaching of the two witnesses and the great catastrophes coming on the earth, great numbers of people will acknowledge that there really is a God and Creator who has finally come to judge and cleanse the world He created. Thus, multitudes will turn to their Creator and Savior in those days, and will be willing to give their testimony for the Word of God and even to give their lives as they seek to persuade the world that the calamities it is suffering are judgments from the Lord.

Revelation 6:10.   And they cried with a loud voice, saying, How long, O Lord, holy and true, dost thou not judge and avenge our blood on them that dwell on the earth?

When Christ rose from the dead, He escorted the souls of believers back with Him to heaven (Ephesians 4:8-10). At His return, both dead and living believers had received their resurrection bodies (Philippians 3:20, 21; 1 Corinthians 15:51-53), and were thenceforth to be with Him forever (1 Thessalonians 4:16, 17). The unsaved dead remained in Hades, and the souls of all others who die outside of Christ in the future will also abide in Hades until the resurrection of all those under the dominion of Death and Hades just prior to the final judgment (Revelation 20:13).

But this leaves unsettled the question of the condition of those who die in Christ during the period after the resurrection of the saints. Apparently their souls will be translated to the vicinity of the Lord's throne, where they will rest at some location analogous to "the base of the altar" in the Levitical tabernacle, there to await the resurrection of *their* bodies. The latter in turn will evidently take place after the final completion of God's judgments on the earth.

Their prayer for vindication appeals to the Lord as "holy and true," whose holiness and truth can hardly endure much longer the wickedness of man and the lies of the evil one. God, however, is longsuffering, and there are still many more who will turn to the Lord as the judgments intensify on the earth.

Revelation 6:11.   And white robes were given unto every one of them; and it was said unto them, that they should rest yet for a little season, until their fellowservants also and their brethren, that should be killed as they were, should be fulfilled.

The "white robes" are symbolic of their righteous deeds (see Revelation 19:8), as well as the imputed righteousness received by them through their faith in Christ. It is most probably the same assemblage described as wearing white robes at the throne (Revelation 7:9), who are said to "have washed their robes, and made them white in the blood of the Lamb" (Revelation 7:14).

But how can "souls" actually wear white robes? This is a question that cannot be fully answered by mortals. It must be remembered, however, that the Lord Jesus Christ ascended to heaven in a physical body, and will descend from heaven in the same glorified physical body (Acts 1:9-11). In the interim, He is in heaven, preparing a glorious *"place"* for His disciples (John 14:2, 3). A place has spatial reality, and thus physical reality. That place is where the glorified Christ is spending the time between His first and second comings, and it is that place which He will bring with Him when He returns to the air and finally to the new earth (Revelation 21:1-3).

Somehow even today, when the souls of believers depart to be with Christ, they are "clothed upon" with a heavenly "tabernacle" and are somehow recognizable (2 Corinthians 5:1-8), even though their bodies are still in the grave. In like manner, the souls of these tribulation believers will be arrayed in white robes as they await their own resurrection.

There were still at least five years to go in the tribulation period, and many more who would yet turn to God. Most of these likewise would be slain for their faith and testimony and would then join those already beneath the altar, clothed with their own white robes in the heavenly tabernacle.

Shaking Terribly the Earth

Revelation 6:12.   And I beheld when he had opened the sixth seal, and, lo, there was a great earthquake; and the sun became black as sackcloth of hair, and the moon became as blood.

The opening of the next seal marked another great catastrophe on earth. This one, however, was not a continuing condition, as under the four horsemen of the first four seals, but a single great complex of physical convulsions on the earth. In its brevity and intensity, however, it spoke more clearly and eloquently to the inhabitants of the earth than had any of the others. They had already been experiencing war and famine and pestilence as well as general violence in the world. For that matter, even earthquakes had been occurring "in divers places" for many years. But most men had refused to see in these a divine warning.

The Lord Jesus Christ had even told his disciples that a worldwide state of war, accompanied and followed by famines, pestilences, earthquakes, fearful sights from heaven, and general troubles, would be a great sign of His coming and the end of the age (Matthew 24:7; Mark 13:8; Luke 21:11). All these, He said, would constitute "the beginning of travail" (that is, the first birth pains, presaging the imminent coming of the new age) This complex of events, in fact, seemed to occur for the first time in history in connection with the first World War, with a second and similar "birth pang" occurring in connection with World War II.

The same combination of troubles will be repeated in the world for at least the third time as the seals are opened by the Lamb, but the calamities will be far more severe than ever before. Especially is this true of the great earthquake described here, which—for the first time in history—is worldwide in scope.

Seismologists and geophysicists in recent years have learned a great deal about the structure of the earth and about the cause and nature of earthquakes. The earth's solid crust is traversed with a complex network of faults, with all resting upon a plastic mantle whose structure is still largely unknown. Whether the crust consists of great moving plates is a current matter of controversy among geophysicists, so the ultimate cause of earthquakes is still not known. In all likelihood, the entire complex of crustal instabilities is a remnant of the phenomena of the great Flood, especially the breakup of the fountains of the great deep.

In any case, the vast worldwide network of unstable earthquake belts around the world suddenly will begin to slip and fracture on a global basis and a gigantic earthquake will ensue. This is evidently, and naturally, accompanied by tremendous volcanic eruptions, spewing vast quantities of dust and steam and gases into the upper atmosphere. It is probably these that will cause the sun to be darkened and the moon to appear blood-red.

Joel apparently speaks of this same time: "And I will show wonders in the heavens and in the earth, blood, and fire, and pillars of smoke. The sun shall be turned into darkness, and the moon into blood, before the great and the terrible day of the Lord come" (Joel 2:30, 31). Many other prophets speak of the darkness of the day of the Lord: "That day is a day of wrath, a day of trouble and distress, a day of wasteness and desolation, a day of darkness and gloominess, a day of clouds and thick darkness" (Zephaniah 1:15). "Behold, the day of the Lord cometh, cruel both with wrath and fierce anger, to lay the land desolate: and he shall destroy the sinners thereof out of it. For the stars of heaven and the constellations thereof shall not give their light: the sun shall be darkened in his going forth, and the moon shall not cause her light to shine" (Isaiah 13:9, 10).

Revelation 6:13.   And the stars of heaven fell unto the earth, even as a fig tree casteth her untimely figs, when she is shaken of a mighty wind.

The "earthquake" of verse 12 actually includes more than the solid earth. The word (Greek *seismos*) literally means "shaking," and can apply to the air or sea, as well as the land. In Matthew 8:24, it is translated "tempest." To those on the earth it will seem that the sky is shaking as well as the earth, and it will appear as though the stars themselves are being shaken loose from their moorings in the heavens and then plummeting to earth. "For thus saith the Lord of hosts; Yet once, it is a little while, and I will shake the heavens, and the earth, and the sea, and the dry land; and I will shake all nations, and the desire of all nations shall come" (Haggai 2:6, 7).

The word "star" (Greek *aster*) refers to any luminous body in the sky other than sun and moon. Obviously the "stars" here are not the distant stellar objects we today call stars, but the language of the text seems to denote more than the meteorites commonly today called "falling stars," which were already, no doubt, as familiar to John as they are to us.

The most likely identification of these particular falling stars is that of a great swarm of asteroids that pummel the earth. Such an event has never occurred in historic times, but scientists have long speculated about the probability of either past or future earth catastrophes caused by encountering a swarm of asteroids.

Such an encounter is a real possibility, and would cause great devastation on the earth near the various points of impact. A shower of giant meteorites might have much the same effect. It might even be the trigger that will set off the global earthquake.

Revelation 6:14.   And the heaven departed as a scroll when it is rolled together; and every mountain and island were moved out of their places.

This enigmatic prophecy reflects Isaiah 34:4: "And all the host of heaven shall be dissolved, and the heavens shall be rolled together as a scroll; and all their host shall fall down, as the leaf falleth off from the vine, and as a falling fig from the fig tree." The "host of heaven" is a phrase commonly used in Scripture for the stars. The stars of heaven will never actually be "dissolved," because the Scriptures say they will shine forever (Psalm 148:3-6). However, they will appear to dissolve for the same reason that the sun and moon are darkened. The dust and gases from the "pillars of smoke" erupting from the earth's depths will screen and refract the light from all heavenly bodies.

The departing of the heavens like a scroll is more difficult to understand. There seem to be two possibilities. One is that the clouds of dust will gradually spread across the sky, making it appear that the sky is being "rolled up." However, the use of the graphic term *"departed,"* seems to indicate something more spectacular even than this. The other possibility is that the earth's crust, highly unstable ever since the great Flood, will be so disturbed by the impacting asteroids, the volcanic explosions, and the worldwide earthquakes, that great segments of it will actually begin to slip and slide over the earth's deep plastic mantle. Geophysicists for many years have been fascinated with the idea of "continental drift" (although strong evidence has been accumulating against any such phenomenon occurring in the present age). Several have published theories of a past naturalistic catastrophism involving what they call "the earth's shifting crust." Some such phenomenon may actually be triggered under this judgment of the sixth seal, dwarfing the damage occasioned by all the mighty earthquakes of the past. Those who reside in regions above such shifting crustal plates will observe the heavens appearing to move in the opposite direction, and it will seem as if they are being "rolled up."

And, in the process, "*every* mountain and island [islands are submerged mountains] were moved out of their places." It would seem that such an amazing phenomenon must be caused by some such area-wide slippages of the crust.

Revelation 6:15.   And the kings of the earth, and the great men, and the rich men, and the chief captains, and the mighty men, and every bondman, and every free man, hid themselves in the dens and in the rocks of the mountains.

Such a mighty display of cosmic power will finally gain the attention of the ungodly world, including all its political, industrial, intellectual, and military leaders—the very ones who had ignored the warnings of the previous judgments and were persecuting and slaying those who were trying to bear witness to the world that the judgments were due to the wrath of the Lamb.

And if the leaders were awed and frightened by the terrifying convulsions, even more so were ordinary people—both those who still enjoyed a measure of freedom and those who were in bondage (the word *doulos* could apply both to slaves and to those who, as subjugated peoples, were forced to work in occupations not of their own choosing, such as in Red China and other slave nations). Wherever possible, people—particularly the leaders—will flee to the great underground civil defense shelters that had been originally designed as protection against nuclear attack or to the great natural caverns such as Mammoth Cave, hoping to escape the falling stars and other devastations on the surface.

Revelation 6:16.   And said to the mountains and rocks, Fall on us, and hide us from the face of him that sitteth on the throne, and from the wrath of the Lamb.

The inhabitants of the world—including even their leaders—are finally convinced of the foolishness of atheism and evolutionary humanism, acknowledging that the God of Creation is indeed on His heavenly throne. They also will reluctantly recognize that He whom they had rejected (Psalm 2:1-3) is now speaking to them in His wrath and vexing them in His sore displeasure (Psalm 2:4, 5). The testimony of those who had borne witness to them of this fact had been silenced by execution, but now the Lamb Himself was angry and "his wrath is kindled but a little" and they were all about to "perish from the way" (Psalm 2:12). These kings and judges of the earth were no longer boasting and threatening, but were quivering in their holes in the earth.

They were not safe even there, as the sliding crust and quaking rocks caused many of their shelters to collapse on top of them. Even this, however, now seemed preferable to facing further judgments from the Lamb, and they even prayed for such quick destruction.

Revelation 6:17.   For the great day of his wrath is come; and who shall be able to stand?

At least it was salutary that men were finally willing to acknowledge God and His omnipotence. It is absurd for a creature to "imagine a vain thing" (Psalm 2:1), thinking he can dethrone his Creator, and this terrifying physical upheaval had forced them to recognize this fact. But like the devils, they merely believed in God and *trembled* (James 2:19), still refusing to turn to Him for forgiveness and salvation.

Isaiah also foresaw this day: "Enter into the rock, and hide thee in the dust, for fear of the Lord, and for the glory of his majesty. The lofty looks of man shall be humbled, and the haughtiness of men shall be bowed down, and the Lord alone shall be exalted in that day.... And they shall go into the holes of the rocks, and into the caves of the earth, for fear of the Lord, and for the glory of his majesty, when he ariseth to shake terribly the earth" (Isaiah 2:10-19).

But then, amazingly, even this would pass. After these few terrifying days, the stars stopped falling and the terrible shakings ceased. The survivors emerged from their shelters and began again to rationalize their resistance to God. After all, these awful calamities could be explained scientifically, so perhaps they had been too quick to attribute them to God's wrath. They quickly set about rebuilding their damaged structures and became more resolute than ever in their opposition to the gospel of Christ.

Nevertheless there were many who had really believed and were saved. They fearlessly gave a renewed testimony to the Word of God and the imminence of His judgments, and thus quickly they also joined the ranks of the martyrs at the heavenly tabernacle.

7

Saints in the Great Tribulation

(Revelation 7)

Angels and the Natural World

The seventh chapter of Revelation is interposed between the opening of the sixth and seventh seals on the great scroll, and thus does not necessarily participate in the chronology of the preceding and following chapters. On the other hand, it begins with "And after these things I saw . . . ," which seems to indicate that its events do not begin until after the great earthquake described in Revelation 6:12-17, when the sixth seal was opened. The termination of the chapter, however, seems to anticipate eternity, so that to some extent it represents an expository digression given for John's encouragement (and ours) just prior to the breaking of the last seal and the resulting judgments of the seven trumpets. As a whole, therefore, the chronology of Revelation 7 seems to pick up right after the earth convulsions of the preceding chapter. Though it also looks back to the beginning of the seven-year tribulation period, it looks forward to the end of the great tribulation and even to the eternal state in the new earth.

Revelation 7:1.   And after these things I saw four angels standing on the four corners of the earth, holding the four winds of the earth, that the wind should not blow on the earth, nor on the sea, nor on any tree.

After he had seen "these things" (the judgments under the first six seals), John saw another amazing situation. There, standing on the four "corners" of the earth, he saw four mighty angels holding back the four winds of the earth.

This verse has long been derided as reflecting a naive "prescientific" concept of earth structure, one that supposedly viewed the earth as flat with four corners. However, it is the same word (Greek *gonia*) which is translated "four quarters" of the earth in Revelation 20:8. In terms of modern technology, it is essentially equivalent to what a mariner or geologist would call the four quadrants of the compass, or the four directions. This is evident also from the mention of the "four winds" which, in common usage, would of course be the north, west, south, and east winds.

Parenthetically, accurate modern geodetic measurements in recent years have proved that the earth actually does have four "corners." These are protuberances standing out from the basic "geoid," that is, the basic spherical shape of the earth. The earth is not really a perfect sphere, but is slightly flattened at the poles. Its equatorial bulge is presumably caused by the earth's axial rotation, and its four "corners" protrude from that. The meaning of this verse, however, is undoubtedly that the angels located in four different key positions on the earth, perhaps one at each pole and two at opposite ends of a strategic equatorial diameter, are able to control the great atmospheric circulation which governs the winds of the earth.

This verse offers a remarkable insight into one of the abilities and functions of God's mighty angels. As created beings, they are not omnipotent, but they do "excel in strength" (Psalm 103:20). In obedience to God, with great wisdom and power they are able to comprehend and control to some degree the systems and forces of God's natural creation. When John first saw these four angels in particular, they were already engaged in the remarkable labor of restraining the great wind systems of the earth, keeping the winds from blowing on either land or sea. The circulation of the atmosphere is a mighty engine, driven by energy from the sun and from the earth's rotation. The tremendous powers involved in this operation become especially obvious when they are displayed in the form of great hurricanes and blizzards and tornadoes. These winds of the earth make life possible on earth through the hydrologic cycle, transporting waters inland from the ocean with which to water the earth. Yet the angels—only four of them—had turned off this gigantic engine.

This situation had apparently existed for some time before John noted and recorded it. It presumably ties in with the great famine which the world was experiencing under the judgment of the third seal (Revelation 6:5, 6), and was part of the means by which God was miraculously supporting the judgment called forth by His two Witnesses (Revelation 11:3-6) that there should be no rain on the earth for the first three-and-a-half years of the tribulation period. Without earth's wind systems on the earth, there could be no rain. Waters evaporating from the oceans would simply rise up into the higher atmosphere, eventually to spread out as a high vapor canopy around the earth.

The atmospheric disturbances caused by the bombardment of meteorites or asteroids under the sixth seal may have occasioned the precipitation of some of these vapors, or they may simply have driven them farther upward. Furthermore the volcanic activities accompanying the global earthquake must also have emitted vast quantities of water vapor, spewing them into the upper atmosphere. Both phenomena would contribute to the reestablishment of some of the "waters above the firmament" (Genesis 1:7) which had formed the earth's primeval thermal vapor blanket before the great Flood.

In the meantime, a great calm prevailed in the lower atmosphere of the earth. No breezes blew on the land, no leaves rustled in the forests, no waves broke on the shores.

Revelation 7:2.   And I saw another angel ascending from the east, having the seal of the living God: and he cried with a loud voice to the four angels, to whom it was given to hurt the earth and the sea.

John then saw another great wonder. A still mightier angel appeared on the eastern horizon. Some have even suggested this angel could be Christ Himself. Slowly, like the sun, the angel ascended from the east and, as he ascended, called out in a great voice, loud enough to reach the four angels stationed at the four quarters of the earth.

The four angels, restraining the winds as they were, had the power to "hurt" both the earth and the sea. The drought which they were generating would eventually dry up the rivers and lakes and scorch the trees and grass, leading finally to widespread suffering and starvation.

But the great angel from the east, though rising like the withering sun, had a message of grace for the servants of God. Furthermore he came bearing the seal of the living God.

The nature of this seal is not specified except that it was to identify certain special servants of God. These servants were to be protected thereby not only from the immediate judgments but from later judgments of God on the earth (Revelation 9:4). They evidently had a special ministry to fulfill and were to be protected, at least from physical judgments sent by God, until that ministry was accomplished. This was analogous to the protection of the ancient Israelites from the physical judgments sent by God upon the Egyptians (Exodus 9:6, 26; 10:23; 11:7).

The Holy Spirit is called the seal of God, at least during the Church Age (note 2 Corinthians 1:22, Ephesians 1:13; 4:30), assuring every genuine believer that his soul will indeed by preserved safe in Christ until the day of final redemption. He is omnipresent, of course, and will still be "sealing" new believers in this way even during the tribulation period. This may be, at least in part, the meaning of this work of the angel.

This particular sealing, however, while no doubt incorporating the salvational sealing of the Holy Spirit, clearly had as a further purpose the actual physical protection of those who were sealed, preventing God's judgments on the earth from destroying them with the wicked.

Revelation 7:3.   Saying, Hurt not the earth, neither the sea, nor the trees, till we have sealed the servants of our God in their foreheads.

After the judgments under the sixth seal (earthquakes, stars falling, etc.) there was thus to be a brief respite on the earth. This would give God's enemies an opportunity to recover from their fears and to rationalize their experiences naturalistically, fixing them more firmly than before in their wickedness. Its main purpose, however, was to give those who had come to believe in God an opportunity to understand their new faith, to study His Word, and to realize the cosmic significance of the events through which they were passing. A great multitude of new believers had emerged, even in the fiery furnace of affliction. The ancient prayer of Habakkuk was being answered: "O Lord, revive thy work in the midst of the years, in the midst of the years make known; in wrath remember mercy" (Habakkuk 3:2).

In particular was this to be vital for the preparation of a very special group of God's servants. They were to have a key role in witnessing to the world in the latter years of the tribulation period and then in the millennial age to come. They must both be prepared spiritually and then protected physically, if they were to accomplish their important ministry. They must therefore be "sealed in their foreheads."

This unusual procedure is perhaps partly in reference to the special instruction and understanding they must acquire in their minds (the forehead perhaps includes a cryptic reference to the brain's frontal lobe) before they can be effective witnesses and leaders in the years just ahead. They would need a concentrated time of study in the Scriptures and in their significance to an understanding of God's great purposes in creation, redemption, and the current cataclysmic judgments.

The seal, however, may also imply an actual physical mark on their foreheads, identifying them to all who would encounter them as God's special servants, under His special protection. This procedure would soon be blasphemously imitated by the coming world dictator, the beast, who would require all *his* followers "to receive a mark in their right hand, or in their foreheads" (Rev. 13:16). Ultimately, however, it would become a wonderful badge of identification and unity for all the saints, throughout eternity, when " . . . his servants shall serve him: And they shall see his face; and his name shall be in their foreheads" (Revelation 22:3, 4).

Exactly how the angel will affix the seal to their foreheads and what the insignia will be are not revealed. Nor is it indicated just how the recipients of the seal are to be selected. There was, however, a somewhat parallel instance in ancient Israel during the time of God's angry judgment on His people as they were being sent into captivity. All in Jerusalem were to be slain except those upon whose foreheads God had set His mark. The latter were "the men that sigh and that cry for all the abominations that be done in the midst thereof" (Ezekiel 9:4). Jerusalem was to be destroyed for its wickedness, except for those who had cried out against its wickedness.

Possibly this will be the criterion in the future judgment as well. Multitudes will turn back to God during these first years of the tribulation period. Especially will this be true in Israel, where the remarkable deliverance from Gog (Russia) will have had a traumatic effect on the whole nation even before the period of judgment begins. Many such believing Israelites will go further, believing in Christ as their Messiah and Savior. They will soon begin a forthright witness for Him, seeking to lead their countrymen, and indeed the world, to accept Him before it is too late, in the manner of Psalm 2:10-12 and Romans 1:16. It is probably such as these upon whom the Lord, through the angel, places His seal.

Revelation 7:4.   And I heard the number of them which were sealed: and there were sealed an hundred and forty and four thousand of all the tribes of the children of Israel.

Although there were great numbers of Gentiles who were being saved, God chose to seal Israelites only. "Thou shalt arise, and have mercy upon Zion: for the time to favour her, yea, the set time, is come" (Psalm 102:13). The new temple was under construction (Revelation 11:1). It was almost time for Isaiah's prophecy to be fulfilled. "And the Redeemer shall come to Zion, and unto them that turn from transgression in Jacob, saith the Lord" (Isaiah 59:20). An adequate cadre of faithful and prepared Israelites must be called for a strategic ministry of witness and leadership.

But why such emphasis on the number 144,000? This is the only mention of such a number in the Bible, and it obviously is based upon the twelve tribes of Israel, with 12,000 chosen from each tribe. The number twelve is also that of the apostles chosen by the Lord, and it is *their* names which are to be inscribed upon the foundations of the New Jerusalem (Revelation 21:14). The names of the twelve tribes of Israel are to be inscribed on its gates (Revelation 21:12), as well as on the gates of the millennial city of Jerusalem (Ezekiel 48:3-35).

The Lord had promised that in the millennial age His twelve apostles would "sit upon twelve thrones, judging the twelve tribes of Israel" (Matthew 19:28). Even though most of the people in the tribes had been long dispersed, and many today speak of ten of the tribes as the "lost tribes," God has kept the genealogical records and will be able, in His own good time, to identify *all* the tribes once again. Each will have his own geographical boundaries assigned in the millennium (see Ezekiel 48).

Thus, during the millennium, each tribe will have its own land, and one of the twelve apostles to serve as its judge. The latter, however, are resurrected and glorified men, whose true citizenship is in heaven (Philippians 3:20), and so can be only partially identified with the earthly tribes. There will also be need for an actual earthly member of each tribe to serve as its leader, perhaps for communication with its heavenly representative, the assigned apostle. If there are 12,000 prepared leaders for each tribe, then each could serve in this capacity for one month, twelve per year, throughout the thousand years of the kingdom age. Although this is only speculative, it could at least suggest a possible reason for God's preparation of the 144,000 in this way. There may be other good reasons known only to God at this time.

The Witnesses

Revelation 7:5.   Of the tribe of Juda were sealed twelve thousand. Of the tribe of Reuben were sealed twelve thousand. Of the tribe of Gad were sealed twelve thousand.

As the tribes are enumerated, twelve thousand sealed per tribe, John records the names of each tribe and the order in which they were sealed. Although Reuben was the oldest son of Israel, Judah is named first. The reason is discussed in 1 Chronicles 5:1, 2. " . . . Reuben the firstborn of Israel (for he was the firstborn; but, forasmuch as he defiled his father's bed, his birthright was given unto the sons of Joseph the son of Israel: and the genealogy is not to be reckoned after the birthright. For Judah prevailed above his brethren, and of him came the chief ruler; but the birthright was Joseph's:) . . ."

To Judah, the fourth son of Joseph, was given the "sceptre" (Genesis 49:10), and "it is evident that our Lord sprang out of Juda" (Hebrews 7:14). The twelve apostles, each of whom will judge one of the tribes of Israel, were all themselves from Judah's tribe, so far as known. It is appropriate, therefore, that the 12,000 Judahites would be the first sealed, with Reuben second. Why Gad (the seventh son of Jacob, and the firstborn of his concubine Zilpah) is mentioned third is not known. Jacob's prophecy concerning him was that "he shall overcome at the last" (Genesis 49:19).

Revelation 7:6. Of the tribe of Aser were sealed twelve thousand. Of the tribe of Nephthalim were sealed twelve thousand. Of the tribe of Manasses were sealed twelve thousand.

Asher and Naphtali were the eighth and sixth sons of Jacob. Manasseh was the first son of Joseph, Jacob's eleventh son. They were respectively the sons of Zilpah, Bilhah, and grandson of Rachel. Again there is no obvious reason for the order of enumeration. Perhaps it is this order in which the respective tribes will be gathered to the land of Israel in the last days to receive the sealing.

Neither does there seem a clear reason for the full repetition of the statement about the sealing of each tribe. It would seem one or two verses might have sufficed to give all the same information. Nevertheless, God does nothing without reason, nor would John have recorded this detailed enumeration unless he considered it significant. Evidently it is important that everyone know, beyond any question, that every single tribe of Israel has been preserved by God through the ages and that He also knows to which tribe each modern Israelite belongs (as reckoned, no doubt, by the male genealogy throughout the generations), even though the individuals themselves do not know.

It is noteworthy that the twelve tribes of Israel are formally listed many times in Scripture (almost thirty, in fact) and the order of enumeration is different in almost every case. If nothing else, this tells us that—except for Judah—the order is irrelevant. They are all equally important in the sight of God.

Revelation 7:7. Of the tribe of Simeon were sealed twelve thousand. Of the tribe of Levi were sealed twelve thousand. Of the tribe of Issachar were sealed twelve thousand.

Simeon and Levi, Jacob's second and third sons, are frequently listed together. However, Levi was the priestly tribe and had no geographical region originally assigned to his descendants in the promised land. As priests and Levites, they were given particular cities in all of the various tribal areas. As the spiritual leaders of Israel throughout the centuries, it would be expected and appropriate that they would be included among those sealed for this special service.

On the other hand, none from the tribe of Dan are listed at all, the inference perhaps being that none of the latter-day Danites were available or ready for this ministry. That the tribe of Dan has been preserved, however, is evident from the fact that it is listed as the very first in the division of the lands in the millennial kingdom (Ezekiel 48:1). Dan was the first tribe to lapse into idolatry in the promised land (Judges 18:30, 31), and this pagan inheritance is evidently still manifest even in the hundredth generation (note the warning in Deuteronomy 29:18-21).

There will come the time, however, when even Dan will be converted. "And so all Israel shall be saved: as it is written, There shall come out of Sion the Deliverer, and shall turn away ungodliness from Jacob" (Romans 11:26).

Revelation 7:8.   Of the tribe of Zabulon were sealed twelve thousand. Of the tribe of Joseph were sealed twelve thousand. Of the tribe of Benjamin were sealed twelve thousand.

Benjamin, the youngest of Jacob's sons, is listed last, as Judah was the first. Judah and Benjamin had been the two tribes left in the kingdom of Judah after the ten tribes separated to form the northern kingdom, Israel, in the days of Rehoboam and Jeroboam (1 Kings 12:16-24). The northern kingdom was often called Ephraim, the latter tribe having become dominant among the ten tribes in Israel. Ephraim, however, was the son of Joseph, as was Manasseh, Joseph having been granted the double inheritance forfeited by Reuben. Thus Ephraim and Manasseh had traditionally each been recognized as one of the twelve tribes, with Levi not considered as one of the twelve. In this enumeration, however, Ephraim is called Joseph, probably to stress the fact that all twelve tribes are united again. In the millennial geographical division (Ezekiel 48:1-29), all thirteen (including Levi, Dan, Ephraim, and Manasseh) will have a portion. At the last, however, the final recognition (that is, the names on the gates of Jerusalem) will be of the twelve original tribes, the actual twelve sons of Jacob (Ezekiel 48:31-35) and presumably this will be the case in the eternal new Jerusalem as well (Revelation 21:12).

The Tribulation Martyrs

Revelation 7:9.   After this I beheld, and lo, a great multitude, which no man could number, of all nations, and kindreds, and people, and tongues, stood before the throne, and before the Lamb, clothed with white robes, and palms in their hands.

John had observed the sealing of the 144,000 for a ministry on earth; now he saw another great drama in heaven, once again at the throne of the Lamb. On earth he had seen twelve thousand from each tribe of Israel; in heaven, standing before the throne, he saw such a great throng that it would be impossible for any one man to count.

These were not Israelites but Gentiles, coming from every nation, tribe, people, and language. Christ's great commission had been to "teach all nations" (Matthew 28:19), promising that when His gospel of the kingdom of God had been preached "for a witness unto all nations" (Matthew 24:14), then the end of the age would finally come. At this point, the gospel apparently *has* been preached "unto the uttermost parts of the earth" (Acts 1:8) and some have indeed been won to Christ from every tribe and language.

The fact that these are all arrayed in white robes suggests that they included the martyred saints of the early part of the tribulation period, since they had been given white robes. They were to be arrayed along with others who would be slain for their testimony and would join them (Revelation 6:11). The fact that they are no longer beneath the altar but standing before the throne waving palm branches (perhaps the antitype of the first "Palm Sunday"), indicates that John's vision in this case was of the still future time when all the martyred saints, to the very end of the tribulation period, had been gathered together at the throne.

Although the text does not say so explicitly, the fact that John sees the great redeemed multitude immediately after he sees the 144,000 Israelites sealed for special service strongly suggests a causal connection. Jews who are truly saved and become "completed Jews," born again through faith in the Lord Jesus, become strong witnesses for Christ. We are justified in inferring that the testimony of these 144,000, supplemented by the worldwide impact of the two witnesses of Revelation 11, along with the sobering effect of the great troubles in the world, is largely the explanation for the conversion of the great hosts of Gentiles now at the throne.

Revelation 7:10.   And cried with a loud voice, saying, Salvation to our God which sitteth upon the throne, and unto the Lamb.

Such a vast multitude could indeed cry with a *loud* voice. The doxology— "Salvation to our God," is essentially the same as the cry "Hosanna!" which another multitude had voiced on the Sunday of the so-called triumphal entry, when they also waved palm branches and acknowledged Christ as King (John 12:13).

Revelation 7:11.   And all the angels stood round about the throne, and about the elders and the four beasts, and fell before the throne on their faces, and worshipped God.

A similar shout and anthem of praise around the throne had been recorded earlier by John (Revelation 5:9-14). On that occasion, as shown earlier, all the resurrected and raptured believers, specifically represented by the twenty-four elders, joined with all the holy angels, the time being just prior to the first judgments of the seven-year tribulation period.

On this occasion, all these are joined by a new host gathered from every nation and tribe on earth. These are clearly different from the elders and, therefore, from the group of resurrected believers represented by the elders. This is a group which has reached the heavenly throne *after* the beginning of the tribulation. As noted before, they apparently consist of those martyred for Christ after becoming Christians during the tribulation.

133

Revelation 7:12. Saying, Amen: Blessing, and glory, and wisdom, and thanksgiving, and honour, and power, and might, be unto our God for ever and ever. Amen.

This time, the great assembly breaks into a sevenfold doxology, beginning and ending with "Amen." Each of the ascribed attributes is, in the original, preceded by the definite article—"*the* blessing, and *the* glory, ..."—thus emphasizing that God is deserving of *all* the blessing and glory that exists. He is the Creator of all, and Savior of all, therefore, deserving of all.

The testimony of praise in Revelation 5:12 contains the same seven attributes as the ascription of praise here in 7:12, with one exception. In 5:12, the Lamb is adjudged worthy to receive "riches." In 7:12, God receives "thanksgiving." The martyred, but redeemed, tribulation saints, knowing that God indeed owns all the riches of the universe, find it more appropriate and satisfying to offer Him "thanksgiving."

Revelation 7:13. And one of the elders answered, saying unto me, What are these which are arrayed in white robes? and whence came they?

Here there is an obvious distinction between the white-robed multitude and the crowned elder. The question asked John by the elder is obviously rhetorical, intended as an opportunity for an important item of instructional information. John has not yet seen the events on earth in the later years of the tribulation period, and so had seen neither the multitudes who came to believe in Christ nor the terrible persecutions which would result in their martyrdom. Rather, in this parenthetical vision, he is carried forward to the end to see the final result in the great redeemed multitude.

Revelation 7:14. And I said unto him, Sir, thou knowest. And he said to me, These are they which came out of great tribulation, and have washed their robes, and made them white in the blood of the Lamb.

John, recognizing the rhetorical nature of the elder's query, and acknowledging his preeminent position among the glorified saints (addressing him as "*kurios*," translated "sir," but often also rendered "lord"), expectantly awaits the answer. The amazing fact is, he is told, this tremendous throng has come out of "*the* great tribulation." It is not just that they (like many Christians before them) have endured great tribulation in their life and service for Christ. Nor have they gone *through* the tribulation. Rather they were translated to the throne in the heavens "out of" (Greek *ek*) "the tribulation—the great one" (literal rendering).

The great tribulation spoken of must refer to the same period mentioned by the Lord Jesus in His prophetic discourse on the Mount of Olives, shortly before His crucifixion (as recorded in Matthew 24, Mark 13 and Luke 21). "For then shall be great tribulation, such as was not since the beginning of the world to this time, no, nor ever shall be" (Matthew 24:21).

The word "then" in this reference, ties back to Matthew 24:15: "When ye therefore shall see the abomination of desolation, spoken of by Daniel the prophet, stand in the holy place, (whoso readeth, let him understand:)." That is, the great tribulation will follow immediately when the "abomination" is placed in the holy place—that is, in the place established for God to meet with the high priest, in the temple. The term "abomination" has particular reference to idolatry.

There is much further discussion of this theme in Revelation 13. Here the important point is that the great tribulation is a definite future chronological period, beginning with the setting up of the abomination in the holy place and ending with the return of Christ to the earth to set up His kingdom. "Immediately after the tribulation of those days . . . shall appear the sign of the Son of man in heaven: and then shall all the tribes of the earth mourn, and they shall see the Son of man coming in the clouds of heaven with power and great glory" (Matthew 24:29, 30).

It is *this* great tribulation from which the multitude in heaven will come. It is remarkable that the period of greatest suffering and persecution the world will ever see is to be also the time of the greatest wave of genuine conversions the world will ever see.

A strong word of caution and exhortation is in order, however. This redeemed multitude will come from among those who were still unsaved at the time of the rapture, when living believers were taken out of the world to be with the Lord. But they will almost certainly not include those who had heard and knowingly rejected the gospel before the rapture. This seems to be the teaching of 2 Thessalonians 2:10-12, which deals with this same period: " . . . because they received not the love of the truth, that they might be saved. And for this cause God shall send them strong delusion, that they should believe a lie: That they all might be damned who believed not the truth, but had pleasure in unrighteousness."

Just as death terminates the day of possible salvation for those who reject Christ, so in all probability will the rapture. Nevertheless there are perhaps at least two billion people in the world today who have never heard and understood enough of the gospel either to accept or reject it. It is among these that the great numbers of tribulation converts will be gleaned. The testimony of the 144,000 sealed Israelites, as well as the Bibles and volumes of true Christian literature left in the world by the raptured believers, along with the great calamities occurring in the world, and perhaps other influences, will be used to lead these people to saving faith in Christ. Many, perhaps most, will lose their lives before the end of the tribulation, and their souls will be arrayed in white robes with the others at the heavenly altar (Revelation 6:9-10). Those who survive will live on into the millennial period— but more on this subject in connection with Revelation 20.

These martyred tribulation saints have "washed their robes and made them white in the blood of the Lamb." The white robes of the victorious saints are later said to represent "the righteousnesses of saints" (Revelation 19:8). Even the righteous acts of believers, however, are meritorious only because of the shed blood of Christ, the Lamb of God. Those who are saved during the tribulation period will be saved on exactly the same basis as those before the tribulation period and, for that matter, in every age, which is by the atoning death and justifying resurrection of the Son of man.

Revelation 7:15.   Therefore are they before the throne of God, and serve him day and night in his temple; and he that sitteth on the throne shall dwell among them.

Martyrs have a special reward, called "the crown of life" (James 1:12; Revelation 2:10). In addition these tribulation martyrs will have the special privilege of dwelling in the very presence of God during the coming millennial age, serving Him "day and night in his temple." This promise looks beyond their immediate circumstances as souls under the altar, but does not look on to their eternal state. In the new earth there will be "no temple therein" and "no night there" (Revelation 21:22, 25). Consequently, this particular promise must be fulfilled during the millennium. At that time, there will indeed be a great temple in Jerusalem, where the Lord will dwell (Ezekiel 43:1-7). All the glorified saints will serve as kings and priests with Christ during His thousand-year reign (Revelation 20:4-6), but these tribulation saints ("beheaded for the witness of Jesus") will have this special place and service of blessing.

Revelation 7:16.   They shall hunger no more, neither thirst any more; neither shall the sun light on them, nor any heat.

During the most intense persecutions of the tribulation period, it will be illegal for believers to buy food or drink (Revelation 13:17), and they will be slain whenever they can be apprehended (Revelation 13:15; 20:4). No doubt many of these, like their Jewish Christian brethren, will have to flee into wilderness areas, living off the land as best they can, suffering from heat and hunger and thirst (compare Revelation 11:14; Matthew 24:16; Isaiah 26:20, 21), most of them eventually dying under these sufferings. It is conceivable that these are the ones specifically mentioned by the Lord in connection with His coming judgment of the nations at the end of the tribulation period. "Then shall the King say unto them on his right hand, Come, ye blessed of my Father, inherit the kingdom prepared for you from the foundation of the world: For I was an hungred, and ye gave me meat: I was thirsty, and ye gave me drink: I was a stranger, and ye took me in. Naked, and ye clothed me: I was sick, and ye visited me: I was in prison, and ye came unto me. . . . Inasmuch as ye have done it unto one of the least of these my brethren, ye have done it unto me" (Matthew 25:34-40).

The kingdom of which He speaks here is probably the millennial kingdom. Those who, at great danger to themselves, will help those being persecuted as above during the tribulation, may thus be privileged to enter (still in their natural physical bodies) this great kingdom on the earth.

Revelation 7:17.   For the Lamb which is in the midst of the throne shall feed them, and shall lead them into living fountains of waters: and God shall wipe away all tears from their eyes.

This is surely one of the most beautiful sentences and most gracious promises in the Word of God. "Living fountains of waters!" There will be an abundance of refreshing waters in the new Jerusalem, and its inhabitants will never thirst again. A river of pure water will flow in copious supply from the very throne of the Lamb, becoming a great river (Revelation 22:1, 2) which will water the entire earth. John himself had seen a fountain of both blood and water emerge from the side of the smitten Lamb when He was on the cross (John 19:34, 35), and with amazement had commented on it. Later, he wrote of the united witness of "The Spirit, and the water, and the blood" (1 John 5:6-8), all speaking of God's gracious gift of eternal life to all who believe—the Spirit imparting it, the water sustaining it, the blood securing it.

And that living fountain, opened on Calvary, will still flow eternally, from the Lamb Himself, in the midst of the throne. The water is physical water, but also spiritual water, such as the Lord had long ago promised the poor woman at the well (John 4:10-14). He Himself is the water of life and will satisfy the thirst of the soul for ever, even as the physical water He created will satisfy the glorified bodies of His loved ones throughout eternity.

Even from the millennial temple will emerge a great flowing river of fresh waters (Ezekiel 47:1-5), possibly tapping vast underground reservoirs in the Jerusalem aquifers, established by the tremendous earth upheavals during the tribulation period. This literal river will constitute a type of the great river of life flowing from the Lamb in the new Jerusalem.

Not only will He remove all thirst but also all hunger and all tears. The slain Lamb becomes the great Shepherd, who will "feed his flock" (Isaiah 40:11). He will wipe away all tears from their eyes (Revelation 21:4). Christians have shed many tears throughout the ages, especially in times of persecution, seeing their possessions stolen away, watching loved ones put to death, experiencing the scornful rejection of those they desired to lead to Christ and salvation. Finally, however, in the new earth, all tears will be wiped away by God Himself, and the former things will "not be remembered, nor come into mind" (Isaiah 65:17-19) in the joy of Christ's presence (Psalm 16:11) for ever.

These promises apply to all believers, as is evident from their repetition and amplification in the last chapter of Revelation. There is no doubt, however, that they will be peculiarly precious and encouraging to those new, but suffering, believers who will be reading them in their wilderness retreats and hidden cellars during the terrible days of the great tribulation that may soon be coming on the earth.

8

The Earth in Trauma

(Revelation 8)

The earth had enjoyed a brief respite from the plagues suffered when the first six seals of the great scroll were opened. There had been wars and violence, famine and drought, and then tremendous earthquakes. It had finally become so fearful that men had cried out hysterically for deliverance from God's wrath.

But then had come a reprieve, as it were, while the Lord had called and prepared His 144,000 witnesses from Israel. From his heavenly vantage point John had seen prophetically the great multitude of believers who would emerge, partially through the testimony of these witnesses, during the remaining years of the awful tribulation period which were still ahead of them.

The respite would be brief, however, and when the judgments began again to fall, they would be increasingly severe. There was only one seal yet unopened, but it would unleash more fury than all that had gone before.

Silence in Heaven

All eyes at the heavenly throne were now drawn irresistibly to the Lamb once more. An expectant hush settled on the multitude as He prepared to open the final seal. They perhaps did not all realize that its unveiling would set into action an entire series of further judgments, with mighty angels sounding trumpets of woe and pouring out great bowls of fiery wrath on the trembling earth.

Revelation 8:1. **And when he had opened the seventh seal, there was silence in heaven about the space of half an hour.**

As each of the other seals had been opened, the judgments corresponding to them had immediately begun to act on the earth and its inhabitants. The opening of the seventh seal, however, was followed by awful silence. The angelic hosts stood mute and the resurrected saints watched in intense concern.

Before this time and after, heaven and earth had been filled with sound. The joyful noises of praise and singing had poured forth from the hosts at the heavenly throne. On earth were the noises of battle and of nature in turmoil, with shouts of fear and blasphemy and challenge echoing through the world.

But suddenly an intense silence—the only one noted in the whole book of Revelation—seems to overwhelm the whole creation. It does not last long. John timed it as about half an hour. But it will seem like an eternity. In fact, it gives opportunity once again for all to consider eternity. Those in heaven meditate and pray. Those on earth, somehow sensing the hush in heaven, must consider anew whether to repent before God's judgments again bombard the earth or whether to harden their hearts yet further against the Lamb of God. Many will turn in repentance toward God and faith toward Christ, and will thus become part of the redeemed throng emerging from the great tribulation, as John already had seen prophetically. But most will continue to rebel and to increase in ungodliness.

The silence in heaven, and the brief respite on earth, will not last long. Quickly the cosmic drama gets under way once more.

Revelation 8:2.   And I saw the seven angels which stood before God; and to them were given seven trumpets.

That the number *seven* is truly a number of special divine significance is again indicated in the fact that God has designated exactly seven *archangels* whose privilege it is to stand in His immediate presence. The prefix "arch" means "first," and these are evidently so designated because they, of all the "principalities and powers" in the angelic hierarchy, have first access to God.

Angels are created beings, of course—not eternal, like God. They, like all other creatures, were made during the six days of God's creation week (Exodus 20:11). They are not mentioned in the Genesis creation narrative, except by implication, as part of the "host of heaven" alluded to in Genesis 2:1. But they are among the "sons of God" who are said to have "shouted for joy" when God "laid the foundations of the earth" (Job 38:4-7). The latter, no doubt, were "laid" on the third day of creation week, when God caused the "dry land" to "appear" out of the primordial waters which had originally maintained all elements in a solution or suspension which was "without form."

In all probability the angelic host was created on the very first day of creation week, immediately after God had created the space/time cosmos and had set His throne in its midst. This is the inference derived from Psalm 104:1-5 in particular. There we are told that after God had "[stretched] out the heavens," then He made "his angels spirits," and later "laid the foundations of the earth." Presumably, the seven "presence-angels" were assigned their positions at this time of their creation.

The name of one of the archangels is known to be Michael, since he is called "the archangel" in Jude 9. He is also mentioned in Daniel 12:1 as "the great prince," and as "one of the chief princes" in Daniel 10:13. He is said to command the vast heavenly army in Revelation 12:7.

Gabriel is certainly another of those "first angels." He identified himself to Zacharias as "I . . . Gabriel, that stand in the presence of God" (Luke 1:19). Gabriel also was sent direct from God's presence to Daniel (Daniel 8:16; 9:21-23) and to Mary (Luke 1:26).

The other five chief angels are not mentioned by name in Scripture. Jewish tradition (e.g., the apocryphal book of Enoch) does suggest names for four of them Raphael (mentioned also in the book of Tobit), Uriel, Sarakiel, and Raguel. One might also think of the possibility that four of these angels could be the four cherubim (or "living creatures"), since these latter are also always seen as in the immediate presence of God. They were directly involved in the opening of the first four seals (Revelation 6:1, 3, 5, 7), so it might be that they could also be involved in the sounding of the trumpets. This is unlikely, however, since they seem always to be carefully distinguished from other angels (e.g., Revelation 5:11, etc.; esp. Revelation 15:7).

In any case, these seven angels are granted the privilege of sounding seven mighty trumpets, which will signal the unleashing of a series of unprecedented physical judgments on the earth. These trumpets are not, however, the same as the "trump of God" (1 Thessalonians 4:16) which will *accompany* "the voice of the archangel," or the "last trump" of 1 Corinthians 15:52, which calls the dead forth from the grave. Both the terminology and the effects of these other trumps are quite different from those accompanying the trumpets of the seven angels, though a number of expositors have attempted to equate the "seventh trumpet" in particular, with the "last trump."

Revelation 8:3.   And another angel came and stood at the altar, having a golden censer; and there was given unto him much incense, that he should offer it with the prayers of all saints upon the golden altar which was before the throne.

Before the angels began to sound their trumpets, however, John saw another still higher angel make his appearance at the altar before the throne. This mighty angel was assuming nothing less than the role of the great high priest before the altar, preparing to present the intercessions of God's people to God Himself.

That this angel is higher than even the archangels is evident from his function. He transmits the prayers of the saints to God on the throne, and thus, like the ancient high priest of Israel, is a mediator between men and God. The priest's role was symbolic only, however, for there is really only "one mediator between God and Men, the man Christ Jesus" (1 Timothy 2:5). We are thus justified seeing in this angel none other than the Lord Jesus Christ appearing here in yet another of His many offices, this time in His gracious ministry of intercession, of conveying our own prayers to His Father, "now to appear in the presence of God for us" (Hebrews 9:24).

The prayers, however, must first be purified and made fragrant by the holy incense, mixed with them and offered in sacrifice upon the altar. But the incense itself is nothing else than the "odours" (Revelation 5:8—same word in the Greek) "which are the prayers of saints," contained in the golden vials held by the twenty-four elders at the throne. The prayers of these saints are thus mixed together with the prayers of *all* saints (Revelation 8:3) and all offered in the fire on the golden altar. Beneath the altar, in fact, John had already heard the cry of the martyred saints praying for God to avenge their blood, and these prayers also are about to be answered (Revelation 6:9-11).

It is, in fact, reasonable to see in this scene the gathering of all the unanswered prayers of God's suffering saints in all ages. Before God, these prayers, offered in faith and praise to God even though suffering, have been "an odour of a sweet smell, a sacrifice acceptable, well-pleasing to God" (Philippians 4:18). When Noah offered sacrifices on the first altar, after the awful judgment of the Flood, "the Lord smelled a sweet savour" (Genesis 8:21).

It was all this that the altar of incense in Israel (Exodus 30:1) was intended to portray, as Aaron the high priest was to "burn incense upon it, a perpetual incense before the Lord throughout your generations" (Exodus 30:8). David cried, "Let my prayer be set forth before thee as incense; and the lifting up of my hands as the evening sacrifice" (Psalm 141:2).

God is pleased when we pray in faith and praise, and these prayers will receive an answer—perhaps not on the same day on which they are offered, but at least in that day which John saw, if not before. "By him therefore let us offer the sacrifice of praise to God continually, that is, the fruit of our lips giving thanks to his name" (Hebrews 13:15).

Revelation 8:4. **And the smoke of the incense which came with the prayers of the saints, ascended up before God out of the angel's hand.**

In the hand of the angel was a golden censer, in which burned incense with fire from the altar. The Greek word for "censer" in this case is derived from the word for "frankincense," the main ingredient in the divinely-prescribed incense used in the holy tabernacle of Israel (Exodus 30:34), an incense so sacred that its profane duplication for sensual enjoyment was punishable by death. It was no accident that, in God's providence, the descent of His Son from heaven was acknowledged by a special offering of frankincense (Matthew 2:11), for He was Himself to become the sacrifice burned on the altar, thence to ascend up to heaven on our behalf. He is both altar and incense, both sacrifice and priest. "Seeing then that we have a great high priest, that is passed into the heavens, Jesus the Son of God, let us hold fast our profession. For we have not an high priest which cannot be touched with the feeling of our infirmities; but was in all points tempted like as we are, yet without sin. Let us therefore come boldly unto the throne of grace, that we may obtain mercy, and find grace to help in time of need" (Hebrews 4:14-16).

Because He was the one sacrifice for sins for ever, our daily sacrifices of praise and intercession are acceptable to a holy God. The smoke from the fiery altar of His awful suffering becomes the sweet incense which carries our prayers all the way to the heavenly throne. In the hand of our great High Priest, wounded with the nails of our transgressions, are held aloft our cries of confession and petition, and God hears and answers.

Revelation 8:5.   And the angel took the censer, and filled it with fire of the altar, and cast it into the earth: and there were voices, and thunderings, and lightnings, and an earthquake.

The same golden censer from which the prayers of the saints are wafted heavenward now becomes a fiery weapon discharging judgment earthward. The altar fires which consumed the divine sacrifice for sins now become the flames of God's wrath on a world of sinners. All who spurn God's loving forgiveness must receive His righteous vengeance. "For if we sin wilfully after that we have received the knowledge of the truth, there remaineth no more sacrifice for sins, but a certain fearful looking for of judgment and fiery indignation, which shall devour the adversaries" (Hebrews 10:26, 27).

Jesus Himself said, while still on earth in the days of His flesh: "I am come to send fire on the earth; and what will I, if it be already kindled? But I have a baptism to be baptized with; and how am I straitened till it be accomplished! Suppose ye that I am come to give peace on earth? I tell you, Nay; but rather division" (Luke 12:49-51).

His fiery baptism at the cross has divided men into two great companies. The one participates with Him in His sufferings, (though never in the same degree) and enters with Him forever into the kingdom of God; the other is offended by His righteousness, and even more by His grace, and thus must depart from Him forever in the fires of wickedness. "He that despised Moses' law died without mercy under two or three witnesses: Of how much sorer punishment, suppose ye, shall he be thought worthy, who hath trodden under foot the Son of God, and hath counted the blood of the covenant, wherewith he was sanctified, an unholy thing, and hath done despite unto the Spirit of grace?'' (Hebrews 10:28, 29).

Those who are offended at the cross become themselves an offending plague which must finally be purged with fire: "The Son of man shall send forth his angels, and they shall gather out of his kingdom all things that offend, and them which do iniquity; and shall cast them into a furnace of fire: there shall be wailing and gnashing of teeth" (Matthew 13:41, 42). Furthermore, those who themselves have suffered because of their faith in Christ and their service for Him will finally, like the martyrs under the altar, see their prayers answered, and righteous judgment on the enemies of Christ who became their enemies because of Him: "Seeing it is a righteous thing with God to recompense tribulation to them that trouble you: And to you who are troubled rest with us, when the Lord Jesus shall be revealed from heaven with his mighty angels, in flaming fire taking vengeance on them that know not God, and that obey not the gospel of our Lord Jesus Christ" (2 Thessalonians 1:6-8).

And so fire is cast to the earth! This comes after a quiet interlude, during which most men undoubtedly will have hardened their hearts still further toward God, thinking that somehow earth's brief respite from judgment had betokened victory over Him. But now the silence is broken. The first embers from the altar begin to reach the earth, in the form of a great world storm of thunder and lightning, but still no rain. A fearful sight this will be, with lightning bolts crashing from the sun-filled sky and leaden atmosphere. Atmospheric physicists will be called on to explain the strange phenomenon, and perhaps will venture some hypothesis that will calm the disturbed "voices" of the frightened populace for a time.

But then another great earthquake strikes around the world, and the voices of alarm become more clamorous. There had also been lightnings and thunderings and voices around the throne (Revelation 4:5), but these seem to be on the earth, to foretoken the great judgments about to fall when the seven mighty archangels sound their trumpets.

The Trumpet Judgments

The brief and foreboding silence in heaven was now broken. The prayers of the saints had all been presented to God, and they must now be answered. The inhabitants of earth had been warned anew that terrible judgments were about to break, both by the testimony of a multitude of new believers and by the sudden strange storm and earthquake, but they repented not.

Revelation 8:6.   And the seven angels which had the seven trumpets prepared themselves to sound.

The angels had apparently been waiting in readiness with their trumpets for half an hour, as John had watched. But suddenly there was activity. They "prepared themselves." The sound of *their* trumpets would not be an uncertain sound.

No doubt, these angels had been waiting for this particular ministry for a long time. As "ministering spirits, sent forth to minister for them who shall be heirs of salvation" (Hebrews 1:14), all of Christ's mighty angels (2 Thessalonians 1:7) are intensely occupied with the progress of His work of salvation on earth, "which things the angels desire to look into" (1 Peter 1:12). The seven "presence angels" were surely the most concerned of all, and they were fully prepared. The sounding of their trumpets would signal into action a vast host of heaven to set about the task of purging and purifying the earth. The angelic hosts have far greater understanding of nature's systems and processes than the most advanced scientists on earth and are able to exercise much control over their times and places and rates of operation, in response to God's commands (Psalm 103:19-21). The archangels, signaling, as it were, a great military advance by the armies of heaven when the trumpets blow, will thereby trigger the most tremendous physical upheavals experienced by the earth since the great Flood.

Revelation 8:7.   The first angel sounded, and there followed hail and fire mingled with blood, and they were cast upon the earth: and the third part of trees was burnt up, and all green grass was burnt up.

The inhabitants of earth had just experienced an amazing electrical storm plus a violent earthquake, and now followed a mighty storm of hail. Accompanying the pelting hailstones were balls of fire and drops of blood (possibly blood-colored water—blood itself is over 90 percent water). Such a phenomenon had never been seen by them before, and it will be terrifying.

Once before in history a somewhat similar calamity had overtaken one particular land. "And Moses stretched forth his rod toward heaven: and the Lord sent thunder and hail, and the fire ran along the ground; and the Lord rained hail upon the land of Egypt. So there was hail, and fire mingled with the hail, very grievous, such as there was none like it in all the land of Egypt since it became a nation" (Exodus 9:23, 24).

Men have attempted various naturalistic explanations for this unique event in ancient Egypt. Immanuel Velikovsky attributed it to discharges from an encroaching comet; others have suggested the fire running along the ground was the rare phenomenon known as "St. Elmo's fire." None of these suggestions has been fully satisfactory, and the record of Moses himself describes it as a miracle from the Lord sent in response to Moses' prayer when he stretched his rod upward. It did involve existing natural phenomena (thunder, hail, fire, rain) and so presumably was a *providential* miracle (special organizing of factors influencing natural phenomena, possibly through angelic agencies) rather than a *creative* miracle (direct creation of matter or energy or organization, requiring the personal power of the Creator Himself).

Whatever the exact nature of this Egyptian plague may have been, it could not have been the same as the coming judgment when the first trumpet blows. The latter will be worldwide rather than local and, further, will be "mingled with blood." It is even more unlikely that we can find a naturalistic parallel in this case than in the former case. It will certainly be so unusual—even unique—that men will have to recognize it as a divine judgment.

It may be possible that angelic hosts will divert the path of one of the many comets with which the solar system abounds so that the earth will pass through its tail. The most spectacular comet with which we are familar—Halley's Comet— would not need to stray too far from its normal orbit to envelop Earth in its fiery train. Whether such an experience would produce the phenomena described in this passage we do not know, since our scientists have no experimental data to go on yet.

Another possibility might be that of worldwide volcanic explosions, a normal consequence of a worldwide violent earthquake. The masses of water vapor blown skyward might well condense in the intense updrafts as hailstones, and showers of burning lava might well be "cast upon the earth with them." The blood of entrapped men and animals might be mingled with them, or possibly showers of liquid water drops might be so contaminated with dust and gases as to appear blood red.

This is all obviously highly speculative. There are little observational data with which to compare such a catastrophe, and it is likely that the avenging angels will so reorder natural processes as to produce an event entirely new in natural history, the better thereby to impress men that God Himself is speaking to them.

The fires so generated will ignite the trees and grasses of the world, already parched from the prolonged drought, and will leave the ground scorched, with fully a third of the world's forest burned to the ground. Whether or not any loss of human life is occasioned by this particular judgment is not revealed, but at least it must create great alarm among men everywhere and tremendous property damage.

Revelation 8:8. **And the second angel sounded, and as it were a great mountain burning with fire was cast into the sea: and the third part of the sea became blood.**

Scarcely had the hail ceased falling and the fires stopped burning when an even greater shock was felt on the earth. A fiery mass like a great mountain crashed into the sea—probably the Mediterranean Sea.

Again it is impossible to determine with certainty what this "mountain" is since the earth has not hitherto experienced any such catastrophe. It is probably not an actual terrestrial mountain—say, the crest of an exploding volcano—or John would have recognized it as such. He said, instead, that it was *like* a great mountain. A mighty mass of rock hurtling toward the earth, surrounded by combustible gases which ignite as they enter the atmosphere, steered earthward by the angelic host of heaven, seems the most likely physical explanation accessible to us at this time. Maybe a giant meteorite, or asteroid, or even a satellite orbiting one of the other planets, could conceivably be propelled earthward by cosmic forces of which we have little knowledge as yet.

Although its actual collision with the sea will be in only one impact location, it is evident that the entire world will know about it. People will observe it for some time approaching from space, then entering the earth's gravitational field and spiraling inexorably to the surface itself. Most likely television cameras will be focused on it and the actual splashdown will be seen on TV screens all over the world.

The mighty explosion on impact will dwarf that of an atomic bomb and will be terrifying beyond imagination. The destruction of life in the sea will be tremendous, and the poisoned waters, like a great "red tide," will spread out soon to the waters of all other oceans so that a third part of the sea "became blood."

Again there had been a somewhat similar phenomenon experienced long before in Egypt, when "all the waters that were in the river were turned to blood" (Exodus 7:20). The cause of that former limited plague, however, was not indicated, except as due to Moses' rod, and it had been imitated by the magicians of Egypt as well. By analogy, perhaps that local poisoning may have been produced similarly by meteorites or cometary ices being directed into the Nile and the other waters of Egypt, not only by God's angels in response to Moses' prayer, but also by demonic angels responding to the magicians' desperate pleas to *their* master.

The ability to turn water into blood, either by filling it with the actual blood of dead animals or, more likely, by transforming it chemically or biochemically into blood-red water, poisoned by multitudes of dead microorganisms (as in the well-known "red tides" which occur infrequently in modern oceans), made such an impression upon ancient Israel that it was recounted in their songs (Psalm 78:44; 105:29). The impression made upon the world's inhabitants in this great future day when, suddenly, fully a third of the world's oceans became as blood, can well be imagined.

Furthermore, the psychological effect will be all the greater in view of the fact that God's "two witnesses"—the same ones who had called for the worldwide drought which was already plaguing the world—were also known to have forecast and prayed for this very thing. "These have power to shut heaven, that it rain not in the days of their prophecy: and have power over waters to turn them to blood, and to smite the earth with all plagues, as often as they will" (Revelation 11:6).

There can be no doubt that the earth dwellers will be well aware of the claim that all these great plagues are being sent by God in judgment on their wickedness, but most will merely stiffen their self-righteous and rebellious necks and continue on their collision course with hell.

Revelation 8:9.   And the third part of the creatures which were in the sea, and had life, died; and the third part of the ships were destroyed.

If a third of the waters were poisoned, it is not surprising that a third of the fishes and other marine organisms died, thus adding to the poisoning and the stench and horror. Though no mention is made of land animal life, there is no doubt that this also will be grievously injured. The grass was scorched and a third of the trees burned up under the first trumpet, and a third of the marine organisms die under the second trumpet. These constitute the lowest and most basic components of many of the world's food chains, so their destruction must produce a domino effect on many higher forms of life.

But how could all this destroy "a third part of the ships?" The answer probably is that the same gigantic impact which poisoned the waters would also have generated mighty tsunami waves which would batter to pieces great numbers of ships anchored on shore, even though producing little effect (except in the immediate vicinity of the impact) on ships in the open ocean. The loss of human life still will be minimal in spite of the vast destruction in the biosphere and hydrosphere. Economic losses will be great, of course, and these events surely give a tremendous warning to mankind of great tragedy imminent for those who persist in rebellion against God and His Christ.

Revelation 8:10.   And the third angel sounded, and there fell a great star from heaven, burning as it were a lamp, and it fell upon the third part of the rivers, and upon the fountains of waters.

Then, before the people of the earth can recover from the shock of the last bombardment from the skies, astronomers identify still another of the "fearful sights and great signs from heaven" (Luke 21:11). Under the second trumpet, a great mountain fell to the sea; under the third trumpet, a great star falls from heaven. Both seem to be heavenly intruders, but one is mostly solid (a *mountain*), the other is mostly fluid, burning like a lamp. One was a solid mass, crashing into the sea; the other falls apart as it nears the earth, scattering its burning blobs over land and sea, everywhere over the earth.

As noted before, the term "star" in the Bible can refer to any heavenly body. There are other references to stars falling from heaven in the last days (Matthew 24:29; Mark 13:25; Revelation 6:13), but this is the most detailed and specific, even giving the name of the star.

In this case, the fragments of the star fall not only on the waters of the sea, but also on the rivers, poisoning a third of them as well. The deadly chemicals penetrate even to "the fountains of waters." The Greek word for "fountain" also means "well" and is so translated in John 4:6, 14. It thus refers to the subterranean sources of water, received through springs and wells. Even these are contaminated by the effusions of this deadly projectile from outer space.

Revelation 8:11.   And the name of the star is called Wormwood: and the third part of the waters became wormwood; and many men died of the waters, because they were made bitter.

The poisoning of the waters of the sea by the previous judgment had produced lethal results on the animals of the sea, but little direct effect on human beings. This new judgment will poison the drinking waters of men as well as many people will die.

The "wormwood" is, literally, the deadly liquor ingredient known as absinthe, from the Greek *absinthos*. The word is used in the New Testament only in this one verse, so that its derivation and precise meaning are uncertain. The term "wormwood" is also used several times in the Old Testament where it is the translation of the Hebrew *laanah* (once translated in the King James as "hemlock"). There it is suggested that it is a poison derived from a root of some kind (Deuteronomy 29:18), that it is very bitter (Proverbs 5:4), and that it produces drunkenness (Lamentations 3:15) and eventual death. It is associated with another poison known as "gall" (Deuteronomy 29:18; Lamentations 3:19). This substance was used to produce a stupefying drink for Christ on the cross (Psalm 69:21; Matthew 27:34) which, however, He refused to drink.

Whatever the exact nature of the substance of this deadly star may be, it is obviously lethal to drink, and many men will die as a result of drinking water from the rivers and wells contaminated by it. As a result, the star is actually given the official astronomic (or popular) name of "Wormwood," probably in retrospect and in commemoration of its death-dealing nature. It is barely possible that spectrographic analysis of its light while approaching the earth will give astronomers sufficient knowledge of its composition to enable them to christen it with this appropriate name and to warn people about it even before it strikes the earth. If this is the case, however, their warnings to not suffice, for many will die from the poisoned waters anyway.

Note also the "coincidence" that a third part of the rivers and their waters were poisoned. This recurring one-third proportion, experienced through several of the phenomena already, should also have given earth's inhabitants still further proof that the various calamities were not random events of nature, but controlled divine judgments.

Revelation 8:12.   And the fourth angel sounded, and the third part of the sun was smitten, and the third part of the moon, and the third part of the stars; so as the third part of them was darkened, and the day shone not for a third part of it, and the night likewise.

While the earth and its inhabitants were still reeling from the effects of the judgments under the first three trumpets, with scientists and politicians trying desperately to find naturalistic explanations for their causes and emergency remedies for their effects, yet another blast from the heavenly trumpets was sounded. This time the physical phenomena produced are so extraordinary as to defy all scientific understanding.

As the trumpet sounds, the vast heavenly host of angels responds by "smiting" (this word is used only this once in the New Testament, and its etymology and meaning are somewhat uncertain) the sun and the moon and the stars. The light of the sun in the daytime is reduced by one third, as are the light of the moon and stars at night. This phenomenon cannot be explained merely by clouds or haze in the sky, however, since it is specifically said to be caused by a smiting of the heavenly bodies in such a way as to reduce their light output by one-third.

The moon and the planets shine by reflected light, of course, so that their light would be reduced if the sun's light were reduced. But how could the burning reactions of the sun and stars possibly be affected in this strange way?

Furthermore, the effect is only temporary, since some time later the sun's burning is actually intensified (Revelation 16:8, 9), far beyond its normal energy output. Incidentally the repeated phrase "the third part" is only one word in the original and could better be rendered simply "a third."

The simplest explanation of all this ("simplest" in the sense of economy of explanation, not of scientific understanding, of which we have none at this time) is that, somehow, the visible luminaries in the heavens for a time, maybe a day, maybe several days, slow down their internal reactions in such a way as to reduce their power output by a factor of one-third. The day and night, as a result are only two-thirds as bright as normal, even though the skies are completely clear of haze or anything else to obscure the light.

A naturalistic scientist might object that such a thing is impossible. This, however, would be to say more than he knows. The nature of both the internal reactions in the sun and the external reactions on the sun's surface are still unknown. Solar physicists, until recently, were confident that the sun's output of radiant energy resulted mainly from thermonuclear fusion processes in the sun's interior. Now, however, the absence of the flux of solar neutrinos from the sun, which should be generated by such reactions, is causing a complete rethinking of the whole problem. Recent evidence that the sun is measurably shrinking in size apparently means that much of the sun's energy output results from gravitational collapse. Presumably this would be true of other stars as well.

Thus, if the gravitational shrinking of the sun could be slowed down for a time, possibly its light output would also be slowed down. Can angels somehow reduce the gravitational forces in the sun's mass? Since no one knows exactly what gravity is anyhow, who is to say they can't?

Since solar physicists even yet do not really comprehend either the full nature of gravitational processes or of solar radiation processes, and since it is at least plausible that God's mighty angels *do* understand such things (or at least *God* does, and He can instruct them), we are safe in assuming God's hosts are quite capable of accomplishing this tremendous hiatus in the normal operation of all the heavenly bodies.

By the same token, the amazing nature of the phenomenon can hardly be overlooked by the skeptical scientific naturalists on earth. Furthermore, the sudden loss of solar heat will surely cause a severe drop in world temperatures and a vast upset in all the earth's meteorology and climatology. Unpredictable and violent atmospheric storms may follow, as well as interruptions in botanical and biological cycles. More than ever will Jesus' prophecy be fulfilled: "And there shall be signs in the sun, and in the moon, and in the stars; and upon the earth distress of nations, with perplexity; the sea and the waves roaring; men's hearts failing them for fear, and for looking after those things which are coming on the earth: for the powers of heaven shall be shaken" (Luke 21:25, 26).

Revelation 8:13.   And I beheld, and heard an angel flying through the midst of heaven, saying with a loud voice, Woe, woe, woe, to the inhabiters of the earth by reason of the other voices of the trumpet of the three angels, which are yet to sound!

Four of the seven trumpets had blown, and great and amazing calamities had been imposed on the earth as a result. But now there is another brief interruption. John reminds us that he is an actual spectator of all these great future events, as well as an auditor ("I beheld, and heard").

And what he sees and hears is still another angel, with another special ministry. This angel is flying through the sky, crying out to the "inhabiters of the earth" (literally, "earth dwellers"), warning them of even greater woes to come. The scene itself is frightening. The inhabitants of earth, after all the fearful events of recent days, are suddenly confronted with the unbelievable sight of an angel of God flying to and fro across the midst of heaven, from one place to another, crying in such a tremendous voice that all below can hear. The news spreads rapidly and, no doubt, the scene quickly appears on television screens all over the world.

Any remaining humanistic skeptics in the world are bound to be convinced by this amazing sight that the unseen, supernatural world, which they have denied so long, is very real after all. There, before their eyes, flying through the heavens, they see and hear an actual angel!

And the message of the angel is one of threefold woe. He informs the inhabitants of the earth that the four fearsome physical upheavals through which they had passed recently had been sent directly from God, through the four archangels at the sounding of their trumpets.

Furthermore there were three more angels and three more trumpets, each ready to signal an even greater woe than any yet experienced, and this was the warning sounded by the flying angel. God is "longsuffering . . . not willing that any should perish, but that all should come to repentance" (2 Peter 3:9), and He is still graciously warning and calling them, but at this stage, there are few who will hear.

It is possible that this angel may actually be a flying eagle, as some of the older manuscripts have it and as most of the modern versions render it. However, eagles don't speak in human language, and the account becomes almost juvenile if this flying messenger is nothing but a bird. It is more probable that the King James text is correct, and the messenger is indeed an angel.

There is one other possibility. Maybe, *both* texts are correct—he is both angel and eagle. The four mighty cherubim, the "living creatures" of Revelation 4, are indeed high in the angelic hierarchy, even ranking above the archangels, in all probability (Satan himself had been the highest of all cherubim before his fall). The fourth of these is said to have an appearance "like a flying eagle" (Revelation 4:7). It may be that *this* mighty angelic cherub is the "eagle flying" through the midst of heaven with the warning message of the three woes. Whether angel or cherub or eagle, of course, it is the unique form and substance of the warning that arrests the attention of the earth, as its inhabitants fearfully await the sound of the next trumpet.

9

The Demonic Plagues

(Revelation 9)

Up until this point, the great devastations that had rocked the earth seemed directed against the physical world itself, affecting man only indirectly. Under the judgment of the first trumpet, the trees and grass were devoured by the hail and fire and blood. Next, the creatures in the sea and the ships moored along the coasts were destroyed by the impact of a burning mass from outer space.

When the third trumpet blew, another missile from space had poisoned the waters of the world. Then the energy-generating processes of the sun and stars had been reduced for a time. All of these judgments struck fear into human hearts and indirectly led to pain and death for many, but undoubtedly most survived with relatively little personal suffering.

After a few days the sun resumed its normal shining, the grass began to grow, the water supplies were quickly treated and made potable, and men went back to their own personal concerns, again ignoring the voice of God. When the next trumpet would sound, however—the first of the three great woes predicted by the angelic messenger they had seen flying through the heavens—every single person would indeed experience directly the mighty sting of judgment.

The Opening of Hell

For ages Satan and his host of fallen angels have hated mankind. Man, in fact, was the very occasion of their fall and the awful fate which they know is awaiting them.

Satan had once been the highest of all the angels, "the anointed cherub that covereth" (Ezekiel 28:14), the "son of the morning" (Isaiah 14:12). He was "full of wisdom, and perfect in beauty" (Ezekiel 28:12), and was in a place of unsurpassable privilege at the very throne of his Creator. He was not an eternal being like God, however, but had indeed been *created* (Ezekiel 28:15). In fact, he and all the angelic principalities and powers under his oversight had been created for the specific function of serving as ministering spirits, sent forth to "minister for them who shall be heirs of salvation" (Hebrews 1:14).

They had been created prior to man's creation, probably on the first day of creation, in order to be ready for this service when God was ready to create man on the sixth day. Man, unlike the angels, was to be made in the very image of God, with the created ability to reproduce his own kind. Although the angels were "innumerable" (Hebrews 12:22), their number was fixed and finite, whereas there was no limitation of this sort to be placed on man.

Whether for these or other reasons, Satan was not content with the exalted position for which he had been created. He wanted to exalt his throne above that of "the stars of God" (Isaiah 14:13) and to "be like the most High" (Isaiah 14:14). The term "stars" is frequently taken as synonymous with "angels" in the Bible (Job 38:7), possibly because angels have their domicile, as it were, in the stars of heaven, but Satan desired a still higher throne, and was able to incite a third of the angelic hosts to rebel with him against God (Revelation 12:3, 4, 7).

Satan and all his hosts, of course, could not prevail against their Creator, and they were cast to the earth (Ezekiel 28:17; Revelation 12:9). They should have learned obedience from this but unfortunately they did not, and they have continued in their rebellion through the ages. The only rationale for such irrational behavior on the part of one who was "full of wisdom" is that he has strangely concluded that God is not his Creator, after all, and that he therefore may yet be able to mount a successful revolt against Him. The tragic delusion of an eternal cosmic evolution must have had its first expression in the mind of Satan himself, attempting to rationalize his mad presumption that he could actually hope to defeat God.

But why was he banished to Earth, out of all the infinite array of created material bodies in the universe? Evidently because Earth was the abode of man, and because he had rebelled against his ministry of service to mankind, he was to be allowed to test man, thus determining whether man also would rebel against his Creator.

And rebel he did, believing the same satanic deception, doubting that God was really God! "*Ye* shall be as gods," said Satan. "God is not uniquely the Creator and Ruler of all things, as He claims. He is like us, and therefore we can be like Him. We were all made by natural processes out of the eternal cosmic matter. Therefore, join me in my campaign against His despotic rule. With your ability to procreate, we can soon generate a mighty host that, together with my own angelic followers, can rout His loyal angels and we shall all be gods!''

But again God intervened. ''Back to the dust!'' said God to Adam. ''The woman's Seed will crush you forever!'' said God to Satan. Once again, Satan's resistance to God's plan for man had led to awful judgment on him from God.

There was yet another time. When men multiplied on the earth, Satan tried to corrupt all mankind to such a degree that God's purpose for man would be thwarted. The sons of God possessed women, and they bare to them mighty men (Genesis 6:2-4). A race of ungodly men and women became easy prey to demonic possession, and the satanic spirits thereby also controlled the progeny of such unions, developing them into monsters in both size and wickedness. Satan evidently was again hoping to amass a mighty human army, possessed and controlled by his host of fallen angels (demons) to assault the loyal host of heaven. If this were unsuccessful, he would at least thwart God's purpose for man by thus corrupting all flesh on the earth.

But again He failed! ''Noah found grace in the eyes of the Lord,'' and though all others perished in the waters of the cleansing Flood, the line of the promised Seed was preserved. The bodies of the demon-possessed men and women perished in the waters of the great sea which received the Flood waters, and their lost souls were imprisoned in Sheol, or Hades. The angels who participated in this further act of rebellion received a special judgment, however. ''The angels which kept not their first estate [same word as ''principality''], but left their own habitation, he hath reserved in everlasting chains under darkness unto the judgment of the great day'' (Jude 6). ''God spared not the angels that sinned, but cast them down to hell [Greek *Tartarus*, the lowest hell], and delivered them into chains of darkness, to be reserved unto judgment'' (2 Peter 2:4).

Satan's host was thus significantly depleted, even though he still controls a great army of evil ''principalities [and] powers, . . . rulers of the darkness of this world, . . . spiritual wickedness in [the heavens]'' (Ephesians 6:12).

With all these defeats by God, all occasioned by his resistance to God's purpose for man, it is small wonder that Satan's hatred of mankind now is indescribably bitter. He would torment and destroy every last human being if God would allow it, but the great Restrainer, the Holy Spirit, will permit him only so much latitude. ''Messengers of Satan'' buffet men (2 Corinthians 12:7), demons possess and attempt to destroy men (Mark 9:17-27, etc.), Satan himself, ''as a roaring lion'' (1 Peter 5:8), devours whom he can. Yet God, in mercy, again and again gives grace and healing and protection against Satan's devices, and the hatred of Satan and his angels for men intensifies more and more.

Finally, the restraints will be relaxed, however, and the hosts of darkness will be unleashed to torment the age-long cause of their frustrations and resentments. But even this is no victory for Satan, God simply using it as one of His means of judgment on rebellious men.

Revelation 9:1.   And the fifth angel sounded, and I saw a star fall from heaven unto the earth: and to him was given the key of the bottomless pit.

The "bottomless pit" is the "pit of the abyss" (Greek *abussos*) deep in the interior of the earth. Since Hades is also revealed to be a great pit in the heart of the earth, it is probable that the pit of the abyss is either the same as Hades or at least connected directly with it. It seems clear that there are a number of different prisons in Hades. Tartarus, where the twice-fallen angels are confined, is one of these. Before the cross, the spirits of the lost and the spirits of the saved, were separated by "a great gulf" (Luke 16:26). The "pit of the abyss" is possibly still another compartment of Hades, in which have been stored a horde of fearsome creatures waiting to be unleashed. The legion of demons allowed by Christ to enter the herd of swine had urged Him not to send them to the abyss (Luke 8:31). Possibly these demonic beings could even be the fallen angels of Genesis 6 and Jude 6, bitterly resenting their confinement and chafing to take vengeance on men, whom they regard as proximate causes of their unhappy circumstances.

And so the judgment of the fifth angel, more fearsome than all before it, will involve giving these demons their freedom to torture those men who are still on the earth. When the trumpet sounds, it will be followed merely by Christ turning over the key to their prison to one who will release them.

But who is this mysterious star from heaven? That it is not a physical "star" falling from the sky, as under the two previous trumpets, is evident from the context—"to *him* was given the key." Satan, the daystar (or "Lucifer"), son of the morning (Isaiah 14:12) had long ago been cast out of heaven, as soon as iniquity was found in him (Ezekiel 28:15). The Lord Jesus Christ had described this scene to his disciples: "And he said unto them, I beheld Satan as lightning fall from heaven" (Luke 10:18).

The key is the perfect tense of the verb, which should be translated "fallen" (instead of "fall," as in the King James). It refers to action completed in the past. John beheld, not a falling star, but a *fallen* star. He had fallen from heaven long ago, though he evidently still was permitted some access to the one on the throne, in order to receive the key (Christ alone now possesses all the *keys* to death and Hades, as He asserted in Revelation 1:18, and so any such key must be obtained from Him).

Though one cannot be absolutely certain on this point, it does seem most probable that Satan is indeed this fallen star. That he does indeed have limited access to God's presence is evident from Job 1 and 2. It is only as man's accuser that he is granted such audience, however; in fact, his very name (Satan) means "Adversary." He is the "accuser of the brethren," accusing believers before God day and night (Revelation 12:10). He is our Adversary at the bar of God's justice, but Jesus Christ is our Advocate (1 John 2:2), and none of Satan's charges will ever stand against the efficacious shed blood of the Lamb.

Satan will have to watch all these proceedings in heaven and earth with deep chagrin and frustration. His angry bitterness will increase as he stands by helplessly when Christ calls the dead from their graves and the living believers with them up to His throne in the heavens. He will still be able to manipulate to considerable degree the nations on earth, but he will know his time is almost gone and will have great wrath (Revelation 12:12). He will also see with exasperation the conversion of a great multitude even during these first months of the tribulation period, and will be desperate indeed when Christ finally gives him the key to the great pit.

Revelation 9:2.   And he opened the bottomless pit; and there arose a smoke out of the pit, as the smoke of a great furnace; and the sun and the air were darkened by reason of the smoke of the pit.

This bottomless pit which he forthwith unlocks is literally "the pit of the abyss." The word "abyss" comes from roots meaning "without depth" and so is properly translated "bottomless." It is apparently at the very center of the earth and so, in truth, has no bottom. Its boundaries in all directions are all ceilings; one cannot go "down" in any direction. The *pit* of this abyss of Hades is apparently one of its imprisoning cells, and it is only this one to which Satan actually receives the key.

But when he opens the gate, an amazing phenomenon occurs. Great billows of subterranean smoke pour forth on the earth, spreading around until it darkens the air worldwide, even dimming the sun's light. This indicates that there must be somewhere on the earth an opening leading to a great shaft, leading down from the earth's surface, through the crust, the mantle and the core, all the way to Hades and the pit itself. Man has never discovered this shaft because it is apparently blocked at its exit, but this does not mean it doesn't exist. It has been "ordained of old" by God and its walls are impregnable, from within or without, designed by the Creator to withstand all rupturing pressures, natural or supernatural. But when the key is finally turned, great billows of smoke, presumably from the earth's internal heat and pressure, flow toward the surface and finally out to surround the earth itself.

Flying Scorpions from Hell

Revelation 9:3.   And there came out of the smoke locusts upon the earth: and unto them was given power, as the scorpions of the earth have power.

The first time in Scripture where smoke is seen is found in Genesis 19:28. There, when God sent fire from heaven to destroy Sodom and Gomorrah, Abraham observed the awful holocaust from afar and to him it seemed the whole country was afire, with smoke ascending like "the smoke of a furnace." Here, once again, this time near the very end of the age, smoke ascends like the smoke of a great furnace, and spreads across the whole world.

As if this were not sufficiently terrifying, out of the smoke the inhabitants of the earth see emerging wave after wave of hideous flying creatures like locusts. John is the one who describes the scene for us, from his vantage point in the heavenly places, and his description breathes amazement. Never were such creatures seen before on earth, though the prophet Joel had apparently seen them in a vision (Joel 1:6; 2:25). John must call them locusts—there were no other comparable creatures in his vocabulary—but they were not locusts in the entomological sense. They swarmed and darkened the sky like locusts, they had emerged from the earth like locusts, and they left misery in their wake like locusts.

But they had emerged from Hades itself. The center of the earth is hardly a breeding place for locust larvae, and the strange appearance and even stranger activities of these locust-like hordes prove their demonic character.

How long these creatures wreak their vengeance on men is not revealed, though it was presumably long enough for all to feel their vicious stings. For, unlike ordinary locusts, they had received the ability to inflict tormenting stings on men, stings so painful they could only be compared to scorpion bites. There are a number of varieties of scorpions, with some more poisonous than others, but the scorpion of the mideastern deserts is said to produce the most painful sting known to man.

Historical interpreters of Revelation have had great sport with these locusts, as with the other judgments recorded herein. They have imagined them to be everything from the armies of the Saracens to a plague of false teachers in the church. Such interpretations only serve to prove that Revelation was not written to tell us about church history. They can hardly be newly formed creatures. God does not *create* creatures that are not good (Genesis 1:31), not even as vehicles of judgment and, even if He had, He would not then place them under satanic jurisdiction. Satan would not have created them, because he is not the Creator, and therefore cannot *create* anything. They are obviously not real insects, because of their unique source and abilities.

There seems no escaping the conclusion that these locusts from hell are, indeed, demonic spirits, long confined in the pit of the abyss but now released for a little season perhaps so men would understand the fearful consequences of the choice they were making by continuing to reject God's great salvation. Men surely knew by now that Christ was in heaven, the raptured saints were in heaven, the holy angels had even been seen by them flying through heaven, and they knew the wrath of the Lamb was being visited on earth. Yet they persisted in their hatred of God, choosing Satan instead, and so God would allow them to experience a little direct fellowship with their future coinhabitants of the lake of fire.

Whether these "locusts" are the fallen sons of God of Genesis 6 or some other cache of demons confined because of venturing beyond God's permitted bounds is not revealed. If the former, they had already heard Christ's proclamation of victory when He descended into Hades after His death on the cross. There He had "preached [literally "heralded"] to the spirits in prison, which sometime were disobedient, when the longsuffering of God waited in the days of Noah" (1 Peter 3:19, 20). That Christ actually had descended into this same abyss is clearly implied in Romans 10:7, where Paul asks the rhetorical question: "Who shall descend into the [abyss]? (that is, to bring up Christ from the dead)." Christ alone can do this, of course, and that He did, freeing the captive saints, heralding His victory to the imprisoned rebellious angels and returning with all the keys to Hades and death.

The malignant swarm knew all this as they surged forth from their prison. Possibly they hoped, with Satan, that they could still somehow gain victory over their own divine tormentor, but in any case they eagerly seized the opportunity to vent their long-pent-up rage by tormenting men as long as He would allow them. Whether or not they could once again control the bodies of men by possessing them, as they had long ago, they could at least torment their bodies and perhaps even destroy them before Christ could save them.

Revelation 9:4.   And it was commanded them that they should not hurt the grass of the earth, neither any green thing, neither any tree; but only those men which have not the seal of God in their foreheads.

This command makes it still more clear that these are not any kind of locusts which men have ever seen before. It is precisely the trees and grass and green things that ordinary locusts ravage, but these locusts must scrupulously avoid such things. A third of the grass and the trees had already been burned under the first trumpet judgment, and the earth's vegetation was to be spared for a time as it tried to reestablish its growth.

The mission of the locusts was single. They were to hurt men only, and this assignment they were more than willing to undertake.

However, those men whom they most desired to destroy, the witnessing servants of God, they were forbidden to touch. This proscription doubtless infuriated them still more, but they knew from long and bitter experience the folly of transgressing the bounds set by God on their activities, and so they carefully discriminated between the saved and unsaved in their attacks.

God's 144,000 special servants had been specifically marked in some way for this very purpose (Revelation 7). But what about the great multitude that had been won to Christ through their witness? It would hardly seem that God would allow these to be so grievously injured either.

It is possible that these latter will be caught up to heaven in a new "rapture," or, more likely, that they may all have been martyred by this time. Still more probably, though the Scripture does not say, they also may have been so sealed in virtue of their faith.

Revelation 9:5.   And to them it was given that they should not kill them, but that they should be tormented five months: and their torment was as the torment of a scorpion, when he striketh a man.

It had been given to these demons that they could torment men and they had been given an ability to impose excruciating scorpionlike stings for this purpose. But it was also given to them (that is, a *commandment* was given to them) that no man must be killed by such stings. This was, no doubt, another grievous restriction, but they were powerless to act beyond their authority. Whether they were compelled by God only to inject so much poison as would torment without killing, or whether their venom was so compounded by God, we are not told.

Furthermore a five-month limitation was placed on their freedom. Presumably, when the five months had expired, they would be swept back down to their deep prison to be locked up again until the last great judgment. Five months (150 days) was, significantly, the duration of the rising Flood waters in the days of Noah (Genesis 8:1). Men had once suffered and all died during this former five-month judgment. Now, as in the days of Noah, men would again suffer five months, but none would die. In both cases, the agents of their suffering were these rebellious sons of God. Formerly, no doubt, they had appeared as "angels of light" (2 Corinthians 11:14). But this time they appeared in a manifestation more appropriate to their character, as agents of cruelty, locusts of darkness, scorpions of torment, striking men with their stings instead of deceiving men with their lies.

Revelation 9:6.   And in those days shall men seek death, and shall not find it; and shall desire to die, and death shall flee from them.

Five months will be ample for men to experience this awful judgment. They will flee to the mountains, to the seas, to the deserts; they will bar the windows, cringe in cellars. But there is no escape. These are spirit beings and not even solid walls deny them access. In their fury, they swarm over the earth, penetrate fortresses, swooping on men and women wherever they can flee, and none escape.

The plague is so dreadful and the pain so fearful that people will utterly despair. They will even seek death, futilely hoping that the grave might relieve their suffering, even though they surely know by now that hell is waiting for them, and these very creatures of torment will be there too. But they can't even commit suicide. Guns misfire, knives slip from their grasp, poisons lose their potency;

men cripple and injure themselves but somehow they can't kill themselves. And before they can try again, they must suddenly flee another of these ubiquitous pursuing locust-like demons.

One can hope that some of these tormented men and women will finally break down and repent and call on God for forgiveness and salvation. God's long-suffering desire for their repentance (2 Peter 3:9) is probably the very reason He will not allow them to die during this unspeakable five months.

More likely, however, Satan, that old serpent, that most subtle of all creatures, will use this judgment to gain converts of his own. When he cannot deceive men for his own ends, he will frighten them into submission. By this time, people will all have come to realize that Satan is a real being as well as Christ, and they will understand something of the real nature of the cosmic conflict between the Serpent and the Savior. Christ is still calling men to repentance through His judgments, but Satan is seeking active recruits, completely committed to him, to join his armies in the soon-coming battle of Armageddon.

There is no more time for deception, the old "angel of light" routine. People through the centuries, particularly in the animistic religions, have found it more expeditious to placate the spirits who infest their lives than to serve a far-off high God of whom they are only vaguely aware. This may well become Satan's strategy here. The diabolical locusts may promise to leave their victims alone if they will only sell their souls to Satan. Whether such a stratagem is employed, or how successful it proves, is obviously a matter of speculation.

That people are today being prepared for an irruption of demons, however, seems very probable. The plethora of movies, television programs, and books with demonic themes, along with the latter-day mushroom growth of occult religions and practices, are all surely conditioning men to a widespread belief in Satan and his demons. Furthermore, none of this is driving men to refuge in Christ, as one might at first suppose it would. Rather, it accentuates a morbid fear complex and drives them further away from Christ. It no longer seems at all far-fetched to suppose that fear of demons will eventually drive multitudes of men and women into satanic slavery.

Revelation 9:7.   And the shapes of the locusts were like unto horses prepared unto battle; and on their heads were as it were crowns like gold, and their faces were as the faces of men.

The historical school of interpretation and even many of the futurist school have produced many strange and wonderful ways of identifying these locusts and their remarkable appearance. What do these "horses" and "crowns" and "man-faces" represent? Interpreters grope here for possible meanings to these symbols.

But these are not written as symbols. The text does not say that the locusts were horses with human faces and golden crowns on their heads. Such a statement might indeed initiate a search for hidden meanings, since it could not possibly be taken literally. John, however, is merely describing what he saw, and seems almost to be searching for words capable of conveying the amazing sight to his readers. The demon locusts were shaped like battle horses; there were appendages on their heads that looked like crowns; their faces had humanlike features, thus expressing the intelligence and purpose in their malignant behavior. These were not merely a strange new variety of insects that had swarmed out from some hitherto unknown breeding ground but demon spirits from hell.

The prophet Joel had long ago had a vision of devouring locusts (Joel 1:4) which had apparently a partial fulfillment in his own time in an actual plague of locusts. However, many Old Testament prophetic visions merge such near fulfillments with distant fulfillments, and Joel's vision may well have also gradually shifted its focus, ultimately coming to rest on the distant invasion seen here by John. Note Joel's dire warning:

"A day of darkness and of gloominess, a day of clouds and of thick darkness, as the morning spread upon the mountains: a great people and a strong, there hath not been ever the like, neither shall be any more after it, even to the years of many generations. The appearance of them is as the appearance of horses; and as horsemen, so shall they run" (Joel 2:2, 4).

The demonic invaders can fly like locusts, can run like horses, and sting like scorpions. The terror which such creatures could generate is easily imagined. No wonder men seek death.

Revelation 9:8.   And they had hair as the hair of women, and their teeth were as the teeth of lions.

John continues the amazing and fearsome portrait. The creatures had manlike faces and womanlike hair (if this were all, one might be tempted to think of the male hair styles of the current generation, but the rest of the description goes far beyond this). Evidently they could rend with their teeth as well as sting with their tails. Joel also, in his doublevision had noted these lionlike teeth. "For a nation is come up upon my land, strong, and without number, whose teeth are the teeth of a lion, and he hath the cheek teeth of a great lion" (Joel 1:6).

Revelation 9:9.   And they had breastplates, as it were breastplates of iron; and the sound of their wings was as the sound of chariots of many horses running to battle.

Again compare John's graphic pictorialization to that of Joel. "Like the noise of chariots on the top of mountains shall they leap, like the noise of a flame of fire that devoureth the stubble, as a strong people set in battle array" (Joel 2:5). The army is invincible, immune to weapons. "When they fall upon the sword, they shall not be wounded" (Joel 2:8).

As stressed before, there is no way that these can be understood as mere insects, however fierce. Neither can they be allegorized away as some human army of the past or future. They can only be hordes of demonic spirits, released from a deep cavern in Hades, yet somehow embodied in these fearful locustlike, horse-like, lionlike, scorpionlike, womanlike, manlike forms.

Though this seems the only possible meaning (John is merely describing what he sees) such a meaning is not easily appropriated. Are these strange bodies real bodies or ghostly apparitions? If only spectres, induced in the minds of their victims by hypnosis or drugs or witchcraft, how do they inflict tormenting stings? But if they are real physical bodies equipped with true sacs of venom, whence was their creation? Only God can create—not even Satan can manufacture living bodies for his angels to indwell, and surely God would not oblige Satan with this convenience.

Or would he? After all, this invasion was initiated as a deliberate judgment of God on wicked and rebellious men, called forth by the sounding of a trumpet by His holy angel. Satan may hope to turn it to his own ends and may gain many victims, but God will overrule as always. There seems no alternative to concluding that God, satisfying the age-long desire of those wicked spirits to possess bodies of their own, has created bodies for them, bodies appropriate in demonic appearance to the character of their demonic inhabitants.

Revelation 9:10. **And they had tails like unto scorpions, and there were stings in their tails: and their power was to hurt men five months.**

Assuming that the strange bodies of these creatures had indeed been specially created by God for this particular judgment, it is easy enough to understand one other peculiar attribute. Their venom, inflicted through their tails in the same manner as used by real scorpions, was able to cause extreme pain but was never fatal. They were to hurt men, but not to slay men.

Furthermore the plague was to endure for five long months, but no longer. The grotesque stinging locusts were to vanish as suddenly as they had come, giving mankind still another brief respite in hope that some would repent. As in the ancient plagues on Egypt, however, this would merely result in most people "hardening their necks" more stiffly than ever when the demons departed, forced back presumably into their infernal pit.

Like the legion of demons permitted by Christ to enter the bodies of the two thousand swine (Mark 5:13), who then proceeded to destroy the very animals they possessed, these wicked spirits will no doubt destroy the hideous bodies of the giant insects they were using, as soon as the holy angel terminated their authority to use them. Perhaps the scientists of the world had been desperately attempting to develop an exterminating pesticide to cope with the invading creatures but, if so, nothing availed until their time was up. Then, as suddenly as they had appeared, their winged attacks ceased, and their carcasses littered the ground. Joel possibly refers to the results: "His stink shall come up, and his ill savour shall come up, because he hath done great things" (Joel 2:20).

Revelation 9:11.   And they had a king over them, which is the angel of the bottomless pit, whose name in the Hebrew tongue is Abaddon, but in the Greek tongue hath his name Apollyon.

The bodies of the invading army of demon locusts may have perished but the spirits themselves are destined for residence in the "everlasting fire, prepared for the devil and his angels" (Matthew 25:41). And so they must for the time be herded back into the abyss. This particular host of fallen angels is under the command of one mighty angel named Abaddon or Apollyon (both the Hebrew and Greek names meaning "the destroyer"). Many have thought he was Satan himself, but it must be remembered that Satan commands a hierarchy of "principalities" and "powers" (Ephesians 6:12; Colossians 2:15). Satan's present domain is not in Hades, but in the heavenly places. He is the "prince of the power of the air" (Ephesians 2:2).

Abaddon, on the other hand, with all the bevy of wicked spirits under his command, has apparently been incarcerated with them in their abyssal prison ever since their presumptuous attempt to destroy mankind in the days of Noah (the phrase used in this verse is not "pit of the abyss," as in verse 1, but merely "abyss," or "the place without bottom," which is thus evidently the abode of Abaddon.

That he and his angels were already locked in Hades at the time of Job, soon after the great Flood, is implied in Job 26:6: "Hell [i.e. "Hades"] is naked before him, and destruction [i.e. "abaddon"] hath no covering." Abaddon is evidently the chief of those fallen spirits already in prison (1 Peter 3:19, 2 Peter 2:4), but even he can only be "uncovered," when God so orders.

The Angels of the Euphrates

Revelation 9:12.   One woe is past; and, behold, there come two woes more hereafter.

After the fourth trumpet, the flying angel had warned of three great "woes" that were coming. The first one had now prevailed on the earth for five long months and woeful indeed had been the experience. And now, even though the terrifying swarms of devilish scorpions are dead and gone, a great voice from heaven—possibly from the same flying angel—warns of two more woes about to come, and these will be even worse. The first was painful; the second would be lethal!

Revelation 9:13.   And the sixth angel sounded, and I heard a voice from the four horns of the golden altar which is before God.

The second woe is the sixth trumpet. Each time the trumpet sounds, the judgment that follows is more severe than the previous one. Long ago Isaiah had prophesied that "when thy judgments are in the earth, the inhabitants of the world will learn righteousness" (Isaiah 26:9). No doubt, therefore, each succeeding judgment will uncover a few reluctant "learners," but those that remain unconverted are still more stubborn and thus each visitation must increase in severity.

When the sixth trumpet sounds, John again hears a voice from the divine altar before the throne, as he had earlier (Revelation 8:3-5). This time, however, it specifically originates from the four "horns" of the altar, at the four corners. On the brazen altar of Israel's earthly tabernacle, which was modeled after the heavenly tabernacle, the four horns were continually being touched with the blood on the finger of the priest who was burning the fat of the sacrifice on the altar (Leviticus 4:17, 18). On the altar itself inside the four horns, the priest maintained a perpetual fire (Leviticus 5:12, 13). The blood and the fire, of course, continually portrayed the divine requirement that sin be judged by fire and redeemed by blood. If innocent blood be not shed in atonement for sin, then the blood of the guilty must be shed in a fiery judgment on sin, and the earth is about to undergo the most widespread destruction of wicked men in all its sad history. Men in past ages have clung to the horns of the altar seeking mercy (1 Kings 1:50) but this time the voice of the avenging angel (or perhaps even of the Lamb Himself) is heard from within the horns pronouncing judgment.

Revelation 9:14.   Saying to the sixth angel which had the trumpet, Loose the four angels which are bound in the great river Euphrates.

Since the angels with the trumpets are those who stand immediately in God's presence (Revelation 8:2), presumably only God gives them orders. It seems likely, therefore, that the voice from the horns of the altar is indeed the voice of the Lamb of God, still in the process of taking away the sin of the world (John 1:29).

Here we are introduced to four more angels who have been *bound,* and thus heretofore restrained from carrying out their subversive desires. The command from the One on the altar to the mighty presence-angel is to unleash these other rebel angels so that they also can take their long-awaited vengeance on mankind.

But who are these, and how is it that their prison had been the great river Euphrates?

These four angels seem to have charge of still another great demon horde, distinct from those captained by Abaddon in the great abyss. The Scriptures give little specific information elsewhere concerning this intriguing question, but one speculative possibility exists.

The first rebellion of Satan and his angels against the will of God occurred soon after God's week of creation. Their fall initially resulted in their being cast out of heaven to the earth, as discussed earlier. Since the number of these fallen angels ("demons" or "evil spirits") is said to be "a third" of an "innumerable company" (Hebrews 12:22; Revelation 12:4-7), the number available for Satan's deployment was (and still is) extremely large.

However, his ill-fated attempt to corrupt all mankind in the days of Noah did take out of action one significant segment of his followers. Those rebellious "sons of God" (Genesis 6:2) were consigned to Tartarus, in chains of darkness, awaiting final judgment (Jude 6). As just discussed, however, these might well have been temporarily unchained for five months, used by God to implement His judgment under the fifth trumpet.

But here is another horde, 200 million strong, bound with their four captains in the river Euphrates, of all odd places. Their temporary release is later than that of Abaddon and his band, and so may have been their rebellion and incarceration.

The primeval Euphrates emerged from the garden of Eden (Genesis 2:10-14) evidently drawing its flow not from rainfall (Genesis 2:5, 6) but from vast underground reservoirs of pressurized waters, controlled and energized by the earth's internal heat deep below the surface.

At the time of the Flood, however, this "great deep" broke up (Genesis 7:11), and earth's pristine geography was utterly changed (2 Peter 3:6).

After the Flood there arose entirely new continents, and vast open oceanic reservoirs had replaced the subterranean reservoirs where the Euphrates originally flowed. But now a new river Euphrates was formed with its source high on the slopes of Mount Ararat, derived from water in the permanent ice cap that soon formed on its summit. This river wound its way down the slopes and emerged (with the Tigris, its sister) on the great Mesopotamian plain, thence to flow eventually to the new sea.

It was here that the descendants of Noah soon settled (Genesis 11:2), the region evidently being the most nearly like the ancestral home in Eden which they could find in the barren postdiluvian world. They named the two Mesopotamian rivers Euphrates and Tigris in memory of the Edenic rivers which they resembled and there proceeded to build the great city of Babylon, under the leadership of mighty Nimrod (Genesis 10:8-10).

But as the Cainitic civilization which developed near the primordial Euphrates soon became intolerably corrupt, so also did the Nimrodian civilization (the earliest Symerians, or Shinarians) which grew along the new Euphrates. As Satan had entered Eden, now he entered Babel, and once again a widespread corruption of mankind ensued. A great temple tower was erected "unto heaven" (Genesis 11:4), where men could assemble to worship the host of heaven. There no doubt was initiated the vast complex of pagan religiosity embracing astrology, pantheism, polytheism, idolatry, spiritism, and naturalistic philosophy which ever since has corrupted every nation. Satan, through his rebellious "host of heaven," communicated somehow with Nimrod and his deputies, instructing them in the occult secrets which would rationalize and energize still another great rebellion against God. Their temple shrine at the apex of Babel's tower was emblazoned with the great signs of the heavens, representing the stars and constellations, which in turn were identified with the pagan gods and goddesses who, in reality, were none other than the demonic hosts they soon began to worship and follow. This pagan evolutionistic complex of religious philosophies and corrupting behavior eventually was transported to every region of the world, and has dominated human thought ever since, so that Satan's host had acquired almost as much control over the thoughts and actions of men as they had in the days of Noah.

There had been another divine judgment as a result of Nimrod's rebellion. The languages had been confused and the families all dispersed, some eventually reaching the regions farthest removed from Babel and Ararat (Genesis 11:9). Although no mention is made of such a thing, it would at least be likely that God would also punish the legion of satanic angels that had instigated *this* rebellion as well, in manner analogous to His imprisonment of the antediluvian angels.

This may be the origin of those demonic hordes who are here implied to be bound in the river Euphrates, though, of course, we cannot be certain. This ancient river had been the locale of this most recent universal corruption of mankind by the devil and his angels, as had also been the case with that earlier rebellion before the Flood. It would be singularly appropriate to confine them at the very site of their rebellion, in the Euphrates itself.

Exactly *how* they are bound there is a mystery, of course. How anything—particularly disembodied spirits—could be chained for four thousand years in a flowing river is unknown, to say the least. Possibly their proximity might help explain the perpetual opposition of Babylon and its people to God and His people through the ages, but this supposition has no bearing on the question of how they are bound there. No doubt God is equal to the needs of the occasion, however, and can bind them in some quite appropriate and effective manner.

There is another intriguing possibility, of course. Maybe the Euphrates mentioned here is the antediluvian Euphrates rather than the Babylonian Euphrates. It is barely possible that, deep in the earth, remains the underground storage chamber which controlled the primeval flow into the garden of Eden. Though most of these caverns broke up when their fountains (controlled exit conduits) erupted to help produce the Flood, or at least in the earth's isostatic readjustments after the Flood, it just may be that the primeval source of Eden's rivers is still intact, designed so securely by God at the time of its creation that it never collapsed under the great stresses of the Flood period.

If this could be the case, it would provide an appropriate prison for these fallen angels. It would then be literally true to say they were bound in the great river Euphrates. In any case, wherever they are, they are now summoned forth by their four captains, as God's holy angel calls them out with his trumpet.

Revelation 9:15.   And the four angels were loosed, which were prepared for an hour, and a day, and a month, and a year, for to slay the third part of men.

The previous plague had lasted only five months, though it must have seemed interminable to those bombarded by it, but this will continue for just over thirteen months. The definite article in the original, *"the* hour," indicates that the time had been set long before, and the imprisoned spirits were chafing to be released, long awaiting their chance for partial vengeance on mankind.

Under the previous trumpet judgment, men had sought death but could not find it. Under this one, they can hardly escape it. A third of all men and women on earth—presumably over a billion people will be killed by this terrible army.

The fifth and sixth trumpet plagues will occupy a total of eighteen months. The first four trumpet judgments, plus those of the six seals, would surely encompass nearly an additional two years, so the sixth trumpet will presumably bring the world to the middle of the great tribulation period.

Revelation 9:16.   And the number of the army of the horsemen were two hundred thousand thousand: and I heard the number of them.

The tremendous horde released with the four bound angels was far too great for John himself to count. However, someone—perhaps the voice from the altar —said the number was 200 million, far greater than any army ever amassed before in human history, a number almost equal to the entire population of the United States.

However, this is not an army of human horseman, despite the preponderance of published interpretations to that effect. Although it might be possible for an earthly army of this size to be assembled, the description which follows cannot legitimately be equated to anything human.

Revelation 9:17.   And thus I saw the horses in the vision, and them that sat on them, having breastplates of fire, and of jacinth, and brimstone: and the heads of

the horses were as the heads of lions; and out of their mouths issued fire and smoke and brimstone.

The host seen by John appeared like a tremendous cavalry, with both horses and riders stretching almost endlessly across the earth. The King James translators called it a "vision" but the same word is also translated "sight." It is used only one other time in Revelation, " . . . in sight like unto an emerald" (Revelation 4:3). Its meaning is simply that of an unusual sight, not necessarily a vision. The sight seen by John was indeed remarkable, but it was real—not a dream or vision. Nevertheless it will be a sight never seen on earth before or after.

Like the scorpion-locusts under the preceding trumpet, this will be a demonic legion of nightmarish animals indwelt by evil spirits, hitherto bound up in the Euphrates with their four evil overlords. It must be that these frightful "horses" and "horsemen" are demon-possessed creatures whose bodies are specially created by God for the awful judgment which they are thereby enabled to inflict upon mankind. Their bodies are real physical bodies, capable of generating physical fire and brimstone and causing the physical death of those men and women whom they attack. This suggests that the bodies are specially created right at the time of the release of the unclean spirits from their prison, and are then immediately taken over by the ascending spirits.

Like a great storm, they spread forth from their pit, raging over the earth to take vengeance on mankind, whom they regard as responsible for their miserable circumstances. No longer constrained as they once were by the need of some kind of physical body wherewith to enslave men, they now are able to use their newly-secured bodies to destroy men.

And fearful bodies they are! Appropriately designed for the malignant spirits who will use them for thirteen months, they themselves will eventually be destroyed when their function has been served.

They are not horses, but their bodies are "like" horses, and their heads are said to be "as" the heads of lions. Perhaps they are like the fabled Centaurs— horses with humanlike heads and upper bodies, in appearance like men riding horses except that the horses ridden by them are also their own bodies. In this case, the heads are like lions rather than men and, since no other description of the "horsemen" is given, the implication is that the lionlike heads are atop the riders whose bodies merge into the bodies of the steeds.

It is a fearsome sight, whatever its aspect, and it must strike indescribable fear into the hearts of men as they watch them swarm forth. This fear is well justified, for the creatures are as deadly as they look. Armored with breastplates of jacinth (a hard gemstone, probably zircon), they have the appearance of burning fire and brimstone (usually interpreted as sulphur; however, its Hebrew root is related to the resin from the gopher wood used in Noah's ark, and its Greek form seems to come from roots meaning "divine appearance"). Evidently sulphur is considered the natural substance whose burning most nearly fits such apocryphal specifications, but its exact composition is unknown. The lion-faces actually breathe out fire and smoke and nauseous brimstone, as though clothed in the very aura of hell itself.

Skeptics who deny the existence of a literal hell often are heard to rationalize that men make their own hell right here on earth. They don't realize how literally true such sophistries will become. With two hundred million creatures, all arrayed in fire and brimstone, sweeping over the earth, it will indeed appear that the fires of hell have enveloped the earth.

No doubt all this sounds fantastic and impossible, so commentators have invented all sorts of figurative meanings to apply to these deadly horses. But these are not the first fire-breathing animals the earth has seen. Ancient nations everywhere describe fire-breathing dragons which formerly existed on earth, and the Bible describes at least one such creature, called Leviathan (Job 41:19-12). There are many indications that these dragons were actually dinosaurs, and the fossil evidence does show structures on at least some dinosaurs that could well have served as mixing chambers for flammable chemicals that could be expelled in the form of fire and smoke. John is merely describing what he actually saw.

Revelation 9:18.   By these three was the third part of men killed, by the fire, and by the smoke, and by the brimstone which issued out of their mouths.

All three of these deadly exhalations of the roaring mouths of the lionlike heads of these creatures are lethal. Men will be consumed in the flames, suffocated by the smoke, poisoned by the sulphurous gases. As the panic-stricken citizens of the world's nations, hardly recovered from the five-month terror of the locusts, hysterically flee and seek to hide, multitudes will be slain.

No doubt some of the animals will themselves be slain, as various weapons are turned against them. The scene will be like one of the monster movies dreamed up by science fiction writers and Hollywood moguls, but it will be real. Eventually, perhaps, government and military leaders will become organized to combat these invaders and finally, after thirteen terrible months, will manage to destroy them. The jacinth-stone breastplates are essentially bullet-proof however, and it will take many powerful weapons to defeat them. Once the animals are dead, their carcasses will deface and pollute the landscape, and their demonic occupants will again be without bodies. Whether they are then herded back to some pit in Hades or allowed to roam the earth as disembodied spirits through the remainder of the tribulation has not been revealed.

But the human carnage left in their train is almost incredible. One-third of the world's population at the time will be dead. Even with all the previous judgments, this undoubtedly means that about 1.2 *billion* people are slain, averaging about six victims per horseman.

Revelation 9:19.   For their power is in their mouth, and in their tails: for their tails were like unto servants, and had heads, and with them they do hurt.

But there had been one more amazing feature of these grotesque animals, which John now mentions almost as an afterthought. Not only was there death in their mouths but also in their tails. Like the demon scorpions which had preceded them, they can inflict tormenting pain with their slashing tails as well. John, however, does not liken them to scorpions in this case but to serpents, with fangs rather than stingers. No animal like this had ever been observed before (and it is good for mankind through the ages that they had not), but that hardly means the omnipotent Creator is incapable of producing them.

Furthermore, these animals had not come under the Noahic prescription that they would fear and dread man (Genesis 9:2), for they did not exist in the days of Noah. Newly created for the very purpose of judgment, and energized by wicked spirits, these animals will soon become the objects of man's fear and dread.

But finally the plague will end (evidently near the midpoint of the seven-year tribulation period) and the two-thirds of mankind who survive can now enjoy a brief respite once more. And surely, one would think, this monstrous experience, coming on top of all the other judgments, and with no more room for doubt as to the existence of God and Satan and the real meaning of the cosmic conflict, will drive all men to their knees in repentance and submission to God.

Not so! Human ingenuity and power had once more conquered, they will rationalize. The invasion had been stopped, and now they were secure.

Stone Hearts and Stone Idols

Revelation 9:20.   And the rest of the men which were not killed by these plagues yet repented not of the works of their hands, that they should not worship devils, and idols of gold, and silver, and brass, and stone, and of wood: which neither can see, nor hear, nor walk.

By this time, those men and women who had not already been converted through the testimony of God's two witnesses (Revelation 11:3), the 144,000 Israelites (Revelation 7:4-8), and the great divine judgments on the earth (Isaiah 26:9), all perhaps supplemented by the great wealth of Christian literature (not to mention Bibles) left behind when the pretribulation saints were called into heaven (Revelation 3:10; 4:1), had become so hardened against God that (with few exceptions) they were unreachable "vessels of wrath fitted to destruction" (Romans 9:22). They had continued relentlessly treasuring up to themselves "wrath against the day of wrath and revelation of the righteous judgment of God; who will render to every man according to his deeds" (Romans 2:5, 6).

Even though one-third of all such unrepentant rebels had perished in this most recent judgment, the survivors were more hardened against God than ever. As a matter of fact they had by now become open Satanists, worshiping devils. They knew by now that the judgments were from God (Revelation 6:16, 17), and that Christ was up there in the heavens preparing to return to earth with His resurrected saints (Revelation 12:12; 13:6), but had decided to cast their lot with Satan, believing that they could with him defeat even the hosts of heaven (Revelation 13:4).

No longer will there be atheists and humanists who deny the existence of God and His holy angels. They will have seen the latter flying across the sky and proclaiming judgment (Revelation 8:13; 14:6, 7), but will still reject God as true Creator, believing with Satan that even the angels and God Himself are more evolutionary products of an eternal self-existing universe of matter and energy. They will thus have become set in their adherence to Satan's monstrous self-deception that he can become God (Isaiah 14:12-14) and that they, through following him and his demonic hierarchy, will themselves become "as gods" (Genesis 3:5), no longer restrained from anything they wanted to do (Genesis 11:6; Romans 3:18).

Those sophisticates of western culture who had long deluded themselves in the unscientific sophistries of modern evolutionary humanism will quickly revert to the more satisfying practices of ancient evolutionary polytheistic pantheism, acknowledging the demonic powers which operate in the earth and its atmosphere under "the prince of the power of the air, the spirit that now worketh in the children of disobedience" (Ephesians 2:2). This acknowledgment will be even easier for those multitudes who had been devotees of Asian and African cultures, for these already were either pantheistic or animistic or both.

For many years prior to Christ's return for His saints, there will have been a revival of occultism, astrology, spiritism, and kindred "doctrines of devils" (1 Timothy 4:1; 2 Timothy 3:13), even in western cultures, preparing the minds of men everywhere for a worldwide return to pagan idolatry in the final days of the cosmic rebellion. Great worship centers will then be erected, with grotesque images of modern art depicting the various cosmic and terrestrial forces and processes presumably controlled by the principalities and powers of the wicked one (Ephesians 6:12; 1 John 5:19), and these will become objects of worship, with men and women in effect thus worshiping those evil spirits which they portray and represent. Worshiping of idols of gold and silver, brass and stone, and wood is of course the same as worshiping the demons who are associated with them (1 Corinthians 10:20).

The idols themselves are nothing but inanimate matter, with no life of their own, and it is absurd to believe that such as these can meet the personal needs of their adherents. Yet nations everywhere have practiced idol worship since the dawn of history. Modern philosophers and scientists, with all their arrogant intellectualism, believe the even more ridiculous fantasy that inanimate matter in an imaginary primeval formless state has somehow evolved into all the complex systems (even living systems) of the universe. "In the beginning, Hydrogen . . . ," they say, with all seriousness. Somehow, from eternal matter have evolved galaxies and planets, plants and animals, men and angels.

How absurd! How can it be that intelligent men, created in God's image, can put their faith in lifeless matter, "Saying to a stock, Thou art my father; and to a stone, Thou hast brought me forth" (Jeremiah 2:27)?

Once again will they find, in these terrible days that are coming on the earth, that neither evolutionary humanism nor evolutionary superhumanism—neither matter nor men nor angels—can save them. "But where are thy gods that thou hast made thee? let them arise, if they can save thee in the time of thy trouble" (Jeremiah 2:28). "And when they shall say unto you, Seek unto them that have familiar spirits, and unto wizards that peep, and that mutter: should not a people seek unto their God?" (Isaiah 8:19). But they will not!

Revelation 9:21.   Neither repented they of their murders, nor of their sorceries, nor of their fornication, nor of their thefts.

And here is the reason. Why do men insist on serving the powers of darkness rather than their Creator? "For every one that doeth evil hateth the light, neither cometh to the light, lest his deeds should be reproved" (John 3:20). Such pagans, Paul says, walk "in the vanity of their mind, having the understanding darkened, being alienated from the life of God through the ignorance that is in them, because of the blindness of their heart: Who being past feeling have given themselves over into lasciviousness, to work all uncleanness with greediness" (Ephesians 4:17-19).

These people who are idolatrous demon worshipers are also murderers and drug users and sexual profligates and thieves, and they do not want to change.

Ever since the beginning of the tribulation, when the red horse rode forth (Revelation 6:4), there had been violence and anarchy on earth. The rider had been sent to "take peace from the earth, and that they should kill one another." Forces for the maintenance of law and order had become ineffectual at best, and men were free to rob and steal and kill as they would, and they took full advantage of such license. The religious restraints on sexual freedom had likewise been removed, so that adultery, fornication, orgiastic revelries, sodomy, and lesbianism, and every other form of sexual perversion, had become commonplace.

Associated with all these forms of wickedness, and helping to dull any pangs of conscience which they might engender, there had been a tremendous upsurge in the use of drugs. The word translated "sorceries" is the Greek *pharmakeia,* which basically means "druggings." It is the source of our English words "pharmacy" (who would have thought a few years ago that the term "*drug* store" could have sinister connotations?) and "pharmaceutical." The Greek word is also translated "witchcraft" (Galatians 5:20, where it is inserted in a long list of fleshy sins right between "idolatry" and "hatred").

Stupefying and hallucinatory drugs have been associated with sorcery and witchcraft for ages, yielding to their users strange visions and hallucinations, which they could interpret as oracles for the guidance of their clients. Also, however, and more important, they divested their users of the control of their own minds, making them easily available for possession and control by evil spirits, who could through them convey whatever corrupting counsel served their purposes.

The Scriptures have repeatedly warned against all such forms of occultic worship and consultation for this reason. It is not surprising that the tremendous upsurge of drug use in recent years has been accompanied by a rise in occultism (astrology, witchcraft, spiritism, transcendental meditation yoga, and various Eastern and African religions).

During the awful days of the tribulation, the breakdown of law and order will mean that there will be no more restraints on drug use. Furthermore, the fearful judgments on the earth will drive many to drugs as a form of escapism. The merchants of the earth will gladly cooperate because of the great profits involved. The same word is used in connection with the sales activities of these international profiteers in Revelation 18:23: "For thy merchants were the great men of the earth; for by thy sorceries were all nations deceived."

Since Satan "deceiveth the whole world" (Revelation 12:9), it is obvious that he will use these "drugs" as a means of inserting his deceptions into the minds of many. The merchants do not care: their profits are enlarged and, as a matter of fact, they traffic in the "souls of men" (Revelation 18:13). It is probably that many of the murders and thefts of these people (especially during this time of unprecedented famine and want) are the result of the need to pay for the "druggings," and much of the fornication is likewise, at least as far as the women are concerned.

The scenario drawn for us by John is appalling. If there is any reader of these lines who is undecided about his eternal future, perhaps a time of meditation on the implications of his choice may help him decide. If the gracious love of Christ as expressed on the cross of Calvary, is not sufficient to draw him in repentance and faith to the Savior, then perhaps a realization of the coming wrath of Christ, as expressed in this unspeakable time of tribulation, may constrain him to come. "And of some have compassion, making a difference: And others save with fear, pulling them out of the fire" (Jude 22, 23). "It is a fearful thing to fall into the hands of the living God" (Hebrews 10:31).

10

A Bitter-Sweet Inheritance

(Revelation 10)

The earth is ravaged, multitudes are slain, and the world's inhabitants are benumbed with both wickedness and fear. Yet the cosmic and terrestrial rebellions continue. The tribulation period is only half consummated and there is one mighty trumpet yet to sound.

All the terrifying judgments throughout the first half of the tribulation had ensued when the Lamb received the title scroll from the hand of God on His heavenly throne (Revelation 5:7). The inheritance of the world was His, by right of both creation and blood redemption. He was the rightful heir of all things (Hebrews 1:2) though He must still wrest His dominion from the great usurper and pretender, Satan, with all his host of fallen angels and wicked men.

It is appropriate that at this midpoint of Christ's work of reclamation, as it were, John be given, and through him to us, a fresh vision of the mighty Redeemer and His sure victory. He (and we) would now be ready to comprehend the fuller meaning of the great conflict of the ages and its imminent consummation. This is the grandeur of the beautiful drama in Revelation 10.

The Rainbow Crown

John had already witnessed a glorious coronation. The four and twenty elders had received golden crowns (Revelation 4:4), which they had all laid down before the throne of the Creator (Revelation 4:10), acknowledging that He alone was worthy to be crowned with many crowns. Then, after the Lamb had received the Book (the title deed to the redeemed creation) John had watched Him receive a glorious crown as He rode forth on the great white horse of heaven, to conquer and regain His dominion (Revelation 6:2).

And now once again He sees the mighty Conqueror, with the most glorious crown one could ever imagine gracing His head. Once He had worn a crown of thorns, but now He was crowned with God's rainbow.

Revelation 10:1.   And I saw another mighty angel come down from heaven, clothed with a cloud: and a rainbow was upon his head, and his face was as it were the sun, and his feet as pillars of fire.

This mighty angel can be none other than the Lord Jesus Christ. Both in the Old Testament and in the Book of Revelation, in His preincarnate state and in His postresurrection state, respectively, Christ is presented a number of times as a glorious angel (or "messenger") of the Lord.

That this angel is not one of the created angels (not even one of the seven powerful angels that stand in God's presence) is evident from the context in general and from His appearance in particular. John saw Him coming *down* from heaven, thus to reach the earth itself. He is Creator, Redeemer, and Heir of earth and now is symbolically coming down to lay claim to His possession. Whether or not He is ready yet to *take* possession, He must at least let those in heaven and on earth know His claim.

That He is the same glorified Son of man seen by John at the beginning of the Apocalypse is clear from three striking marks of identification. As He descended from heaven, He was arrayed in a glory cloud, His face was like the sun (it was not the sun, but "as it were" the sun), and His feet were "as pillars of fire."

Those are precisely the characteristics noted by John in the first chapter of Revelation. "Behold, he cometh with clouds" (Revelation 1:7) was the initial testimony there. Furthermore, when He had first ascended into heaven (John had also been present then), it was recorded that "a cloud received him out of their sight" (Acts 1:9), and that He would someday return to earth "in like manner" (Acts 1:11). He had already descended from heaven to meet His redeemed ones "in the air" (1 Thessalonians 4:17) but now, for the first time, He will stand again on the earth, and He comes in a cloud.

Similarly, John had noted when He first saw the glorified Christ that "his countenance was as the sun shineth in his strength" (Revelation 1:16), and "his feet like unto fine brass, as if they burned in a furnace" (Revelation 1:15), with the appearance of glowing-hot boots, thus making his feet seem as pillars of fire.

But there is something new this time. The beautiful rainbow had been seen first by John above the throne of God, speaking (as it did in days of Noah) of grace and salvation even in the midst of judgment. But now it encircles the head of Christ, the mighty angel. It is as though the rainbow had been above His head when He was seated on His throne and then had traveled with Him as He descended to earth.

In any case, it is singularly appropriate that His crown should be God's beautiful rainbow. The definite article in the original—*"the* rainbow"—indicates that it is the bow specially associated with God. In the first biblical reference to the rainbow, right after the great Flood, God spoke to Noah of *"my* bow" (Genesis 9:13). As noted earlier, the bow had also been seen by Ezekiel about God's throne (Ezekiel 1:28).

In the Old Testament, the same word is used both for the rainbow and for the weapon ("bow" and arrow). Perhaps there is thus a suggestion in the rainbow that God is a God of both grace and judgment. That is, even in the midst of judgment, God's grace is still extended and multitudes will be saved out of the great tribulation (Revelation 7:14). By the same token, those who spurn God's grace must experience His wrath. "Of how much sorer punishment, suppose ye, shall he be thought worthy, who hath trodden under foot the Son of God, and hath counted the blood of the covenant, wherewith he was sanctified, an unholy thing, and hath done despite unto the Spirit of grace?" (Hebrews 10:29).

What a marvelous sight it will be! John saw Him (and so shall we) coming down from heaven, arrayed in a cloud of glory and crowned with the beautiful bow, to stand once again on the earth.

The Little Book and Seven Thunders

Revelation 10:2. **And he had in his hand a little book open; and he set his right foot upon the sea, and his left foot on the earth.**

When the mighty Lord reaches the earth, He will stand astride the earth and the sea, thus claiming ownership of both. He was, after all, their Creator. "The sea is his, and he made it: and his hands formed the dry land" (Psalm 95:5).

But He is also their Redeemer, and their Inheritor, having purchased it all back with the blood of His cross (Colossians 1:20). Furthermore, we who are His by right of redemption are joint heirs with Him (Romans 8:17; Hebrews 9:15). When He reclaims and rules the earth, therefore, we shall reign with Him (2 Timothy 2:12; Revelation 1:6; 2:27).

This, apparently, is the meaning of the "little book" open in His hand. This is not the same "book" which He had previously received from the One on the throne (Revelation 5:7). That book (or scroll), sealed with seven seals, had by now been completely opened, with all the seals broken, one by one. As discussed earlier, this great scroll represents the "title deed" to the earth, and it was only the Lamb who had the right to receive and open it. He is now laying full claim to its ownership as He stands on both land and water.

The little book in His hand is a different book, however. The "book" is the

Greek *biblion,* but the "little book" is the Greek *bibliaridion,* recognized as a diminutive of *biblion.* In English, we might use the terms "book" and "booklet."

When one inherits or purchases a large tract of land, it is permissible and common to subdivide that tract into many smaller lots, which can then either be sold to many subsequent buyers or transmitted to many subsequent heirs. Thus, many may eventually acquire an interest in the one grand original inheritance.

It is most likely, therefore, that this "little book" is a "little title deed," that portion of Christ's inheritance which is to be awarded to His joint-heir, the Apostle John, who appears here in the capacity of a representative Christian believer caught up to heaven at the time of the rapture. This diminutive title scroll was not sealed, as the grand title scroll had been, but was already opened. The purchase price had already been fully paid and Christ can thus award freely and graciously any such portion of His inheritance as He may choose, to His own joint-heirs.

Revelation 10:3.   And cried with a loud voice, as when a lion roareth: and when he had cried, seven thunders uttered their voices.

Here is another link to the description of Christ as given in Revelation 1, both passages noting the sonorous majesty of His voice. There His voice was likened to that of a great trumpet and to "the sound of many waters" (Revelation 1:10, 15). Here it is compared to the roaring of a lion. There is no record of what He cried with a loud voice, but the context would indicate that it was a mighty proclamation of ownership, calling on earth's inhabitants to reject the great usurper and to submit to their true Lord.

There is no recorded human response to His cry, and the dwellers on earth, despite all the terrible judgments they had experienced, continue blindly in their rebellion. The only response was a great sevenfold thundering from heaven. These thunders were not mere physical phenomena, however, such as the thunder following a lightning flash; for the sounds carried intelligible messages—voices.

John had earlier noted that there were thunderings proceeding from God's throne (Revelation 5:5) along with voices. It is probable that these seven thunderous voices which followed the great cry of the Lord as He stood on earth, therefore, were nothing less than seven pronouncements from the very throne of God.

The rainbow has already reminded us of the Flood, and now the seven thunders do the same, for thunder was first heard by man at the Flood, even as the rainbow was first seen then. Before the Flood, there had been no rain (Genesis 2:5), and thus no rainbow and no thunder.

The seven thunders, roaring forth from God's throne, clearly correspond to the sevenfold "voice of the Lord," as recorded in Psalm 29. This psalm is a magnificent vision of the terrestrial and celestial phenomena which occurred at the great Flood. See my book, *Sampling the Psalms* (San Diego, CA: Creation-Life

Publishers, 1973) pp. 38-43, for a full exposition. Its association with the Noahic Deluge is certified by its tenth verse: "The Lord sitteth upon the flood." The word here is the word *mabbul,* which elsewhere applies uniquely to that specific cataclysm.

In this psalm, the phrase "voice of the Lord" occurs seven times, each introducing a new phase of the Flood. The first is at verse 3, introducing the first great peal of thunder ever heard by man: "The voice of the Lord is upon the waters: the God of glory thundereth: the Lord is upon many waters." Since then, there have been other occasions when God's voice was heard through a thundering (John 12:28-30).

At this point the judgments of God will have been visited on the entire earth almost as severely as in the waters of the Deluge, and the worst trumpet is yet to blow. It would be appropriate for a similar sevenfold thundering to pour forth from God's wrath at such a time.

However, there was mercy in that judgment and so will there be in this. In fact, the very crown of Christ—the majestic rainbow—is itself the testimony and assurance that God still spares the earth.

As a matter of fact, the final thundering or "voice of the Lord" in Psalm 29, called forth new life out of the buried earth, dispersing the floodwaters and beginning a new world. "The voice of the Lord maketh the hinds to calve, and discovereth the forests: and in his temple doth every one speak of his glory" (Psalm 29:9). This "resurrection" thundering seems to be an echo of that in Psalm 104:6, 7, which also describes the retreat of the Flood. "Thou coveredst it with the deep as with a garment: the waters stood above the mountains. At thy rebuke they fled; at the voice of thy thunder they hasted away."

We are not told what the seven thunders from the throne uttered, though John apparently understood the messages. It was God's design for us to know they had spoken, however, and John was thus allowed to record that fact. The very context demands that the message be one of great physical judgment, as it had been long ago when they spoke at the Flood, but the rainbow also demands that the judgment be tempered with mercy, as it had been at the Flood. Indeed there is a hint that the judgment of universal destruction is even to be postponed for a little season.

Revelation 10:4.   And when the seven thunders had uttered their voices, I was about to write: and I heard a voice from heaven saying unto me, Seal up those things which the seven thunders uttered, and write them not.

This seems at first to be a strange command. Had God merely wanted to restrain John from recording the commands of the seven thunders, there would seem no need to have him mention them at all.

Evidently, God wanted us to know not only that the seven thunders had spoken, but also that the fulfillment of their utterances had been delayed. It is as though the time for final destruction of the ungodly had come and the thunders were ready to call it forth, just as they had at the great Flood. Christ had descended from heaven and proclaimed His ownership of land and sea. But then God intervened once more. Despite man's continued, and now seemingly implacable, rebellion, God is still long-suffering, still extending His open arms and waiting for repentant sinners. Even after the thunders have spoken, He delays their validation. "Yet seven days," He had told Noah (Genesis 7:4), giving the antediluvians one last opportunity. Now He seems to say again, "Yet a little longer." As in the days of Sodom, He will spare the world even for even a few righteous.

There is a very similar scene at the end of Daniel's prophecy—possibly the same scene. Daniel had heard the angel speak of the terrible tribulation that would come just before his people would be delivered and resurrected (Daniel 12:1, 2). But then, like John, he had been told to "shut up the words, and seal the book, even to the time of the end" (Daniel 12:4). In response to the question, "How long?" (Daniel 12:6), another angel "held up his right hand and his left hand unto heaven, and sware by him that liveth for ever that it shall be for a time, times, and an half" (Daniel 12:7).

From other Scriptures (Daniel 4:16; 7:25; Revelation 12:14; 13:5), it seems clear that the "time" referred to is a "year," so that one time plus two times plus half a time means three-and-a-half years. Daniel then was told again "the words are closed up and sealed till the time of the end" (Daniel 12:9).

Both Daniel and John seem to have heard terrible words of final judgment on the world of wicked men in the very last days, but both were told to withhold them for a while. It would be yet three-and-a-half years before their final imposition. Meanwhile, the judgments would intensify, and men could still choose to flee from the even greater wrath yet to come.

Revelation 10:5.   And the angel which I saw stand upon the sea and upon the earth lifted up his hand to heaven.

God manifests Himself in varied ways, though always through His Son (John 1:18). To John, He has already been seen or heard as the glorified Son of man (Revelation 1:13), as the Creator on His throne (Revelation 4:2, 11), as the Lamb in the midst of the elders (Revelation 5:6), as the angel with the prayers of all the saints (Revelation 8:3), as a great voice from heaven (Revelation 4:1; etc.), and now as the seven thunders and the mighty angel of the rainbow crown. He is both infinite and finite, omnipresent and localized, many yet One, Son of God and Son of man.

John has just heard Him as the thunders, then as the heavenly voice instructing Him to seal up the words of the thunders, and now again his attention is directed to Him as the angel astride the land and sea. This time he watches the angel lifting His hand heavenward, preparing to speak to and for the One on the throne.

This act of lifting His hand identifies him yet more clearly with the man, or angel, seen by Daniel, as noted above (Daniel 12:7). In the next verse here in Revelation, we are told that He "sware by him that liveth for ever and ever," exactly as the man seen by Daniel had done.

This fact constrains us to inquire more exactly into the description given of Him by Daniel and, when we do, we find indeed that He is, once again, none other than our glorified Lord and Savior Jesus Christ. Daniel identified Him as "the man clothed in linen" (Daniel 12:7), the one he first saw after three weeks of fasting and prayer, when he himself was an aged man in the court of King Cyrus. Note the description: "Then I lifted up mine eyes, and looked, and behold, a certain man clothed in linen, whose loins were girded with fine gold of Uphaz: His body also was like the beryl, and his face as the appearance of lightning, and his eyes as lamps of fire, and his arms and his feet like in colour to polished brass, and the voice of his words like the voice of a multitude" (Daniel 10:5, 6).

The identification is beyond doubt. This man is the same one seen by John at the very beginning of Revelation. Note the marks of correspondence:

DANIEL 10:5, 6	REVELATION 1:13-16
clothed in linen	clothed with a garment
girded with fine gold	golden girdle
body like beryl	head and hair white as snow
face as lightning	countenance as the sun
eyes as lamps of fire	eyes as a flame of fire
arms and feet like polished brass	feet like fine brass
voice like a multitude	voice as many waters

There is almost perfect correspondence. The only significant difference seems to be that Daniel described His body as like a beryl, a brilliant crystallike stone. However, He was clothed with a garment to the foot, so that the only visible parts of His body were His head and hands and feet. John described His head as white like snow, and both described His limbs as like glowing brass, so that even these descriptions agree. Daniel saw Him as a "man," but obviously far greater than mortal man, and John said He was like unto the "Son of man." John "fell at his feet as dead" (Revelation 1:17) and Daniel "retained no strength" (Daniel 10:8). Clearly the two are the same.

But there is one great difference. In Daniel's case, he "saw this great vision" (Daniel 10:8), a theophany. It was Christ in preincarnate state, arraying Himself for a time in the form He would, after Calvary, enter to inhabit forever. John saw

Him, however, not in a vision but in reality. It was John who was translated forward in time, to participate directly in the great events of the end times, events which had been given to Daniel only in prophetic vision. John saw Christ not in a preincarnate theophany, but "alive for evermore" (Revelation 1:18).

Time No Longer

And now this same Christ, seen by both John and Daniel, is also identified plainly as the mighty angel, claiming ownership of earth and ocean (having already, as the slain Lamb, purchased it with His blood), lifting up His hand to heaven, swearing by the eternal one on the emerald throne.

Revelation 10:6.   And sware by him that liveth for ever and ever, who created heaven, and the things that herein are, and the earth, and the things that therein are, and the sea, and the things which are therein, that there should be time no longer.

The one who "liveth for ever and ever" is, of course, the Creator on His throne (Revelation 4:10, 11), and also the Lamb (Revelation 5:13). There can be none greater. "Because He could swear by no greater, he sware by himself" (Hebrews 6:13).

Although the final judgment has been deferred, as it were, for yet a time and times and half a time, there will be no delay beyond that. This is the meaning of the statement that "there should be time no longer." The space/time universe has been established forever, and there could be no ending of time as such without the annihilation of space as well. As a matter of fact, time will still be measured by months in the new earth (Revelation 22:2). It is just that the time when "the mystery of God shall be finished" is near at hand.

The identification of the Creator is very explicit, and carries us back to Genesis 2:1. "Thus the heavens and the earth were finished, and all the host of them." Even more explicitly is there a reference to the wording of the fourth commandment. "For in six days the Lord made heaven and earth, the sea, and all that in them is" (Exodus 20:11).

It is significant that the sworn assurance that there will soon be a consummation of all things appeals to the fact that there was a creation of all things. A universe without a creation would necessarily be one with no purpose. Since it did begin in creation, however (and creation means special creation, of course. Natural creation is a vacuous concept, since the laws of nature are conservative or destructive, never creative), and since the Creator, by definition, cannot be capricious, therefore the universe does have a divine purpose, and that purpose will surely be consummated.

God indeed is long-suffering. He has accomplished a wonderful and winsome plan of redemption, and desires all men to come to repentance and salvation (2 Peter 3:9). He has waited year after year, and century after century, for lost men to accept their Savior, but He will not compel them against their will. Finally, He has, against His own will, it almost seems, reluctantly initiated the terrible judgments of the day of the Lord. But even in these, many are saved, and He will joyfully receive those who come to Him out of the great tribulation.

But those who have persisted in hardening their hearts throughout the successive waves of chastisement for three and a half years are surely beyond hope, it would seem. Nevertheless, our "God of all grace" (1 Peter 5:10) will endure such vessels of wrath yet another three and a half years, exhausting every last drop of His cup of patience. But *that* will be the last delay; *then* cometh the end.

Revelation 10:7.   But in the days of the voice of the seventh angel, when he shall begin to sound, the mystery of God should be finished, as he hath declared to his servants the prophets.

John receives the promise that there will be no more delay. The seventh trumpet will echo for three and a half years, as the same Christ had told Daniel in his preincarnate state, but that would be the end. That this final trumpeting is to be prolonged is suggested by the reference to "the *days*" of the voice [Greek *phone*, meaning "sound"] of the seventh angel."

The word for "begin" actually means "about." In the same way that John was "about to write" (Revelation 10:4) the seventh angel is "about to sound." He is not yet quite ready, however. The second "woe" has not yet quite run its course (Revelation 11:14) and only then will the seventh angel sound his trumpet (Revelation 11:15). The mighty angel has assured John that, even though the final devastations proclaimed by the seven thunders have been delayed, it will only be for a brief time. The seventh trumpet is almost ready to blast forth, and while its sound is still echoing throughout heaven, specifically for three and a half years, the mystery of God "shall also be completed."

But what is this "mystery of God?" This word (Greek *musterion*) was used commonly to refer to the secrets imparted to the initiates in the Greek mystery religions. Even though a precisely equivalent term does not appear in the Old Testament, the prophets are said to have been assured of the ultimate completion of the mystery of God.

Although there are a number of mysteries referred to in the New Testament, the context here seems strongly to indicate that this mystery of God refers to the whole purpose and plan of God. Why has a holy God allowed evil to thrive for so long? Why do the righteous suffer? What is God's ultimate purpose for Israel, for the Gentiles, for the Church? These and many other such questions pertaining to the ultimate reconciliation and accomplishment of God's many purposes in creation will someday all be answered, and it is perhaps the combination of all these that is called here "the mystery of God." In any case, all such mysteries of God's dealing with men will finally be resolved and understood during these days of the sounding of the final trumpet.

The prophets had, indeed, received such promises long ago. To Daniel had been promised that "all these things shall be finished" (Daniel 12:7). To Zechariah had been promised: "In that day shall there be one Lord, and his name one" (Zechariah 14:9). The Psalms had prophesied: "His name shall endure for ever: his name shall be continued as long as the sun: and men shall be blessed in him: all nations shall call him blessed" (Psalm 72:17).

The End Not Yet

Although the consummation is sure, and the end glorious, John must still wait longer. The martyred saints in heaven must wait also (Revelation 6:9-11), as must the persecuted saints on earth. Furthermore, those who are redeemed, both those already in heaven and those still on earth, must still wait to receive their own inheritance, even as the Lord Jesus Christ still defers to take full possession of His. They can share to a degree in its privileges and responsibilities even while waiting, however, and this seems to be the theme of the next scene.

Revelation 10:8.   And the voice which I heard from heaven spake unto me again, and said, Go and take the little book which is open in the hand of the angel which standeth upon the sea and upon the earth.

This great voice from heaven speaks again to John, now for the third time (Revelation 4:1; 10:4), instructing him now to take what seems to be a most presumptuous action. The mighty angel, still standing astride land and sea, still thereby claiming right of ownership of all things, the one who had just proclaimed the imminent consummation of all God's purposes in creation—*that* is the one whom John is commanded to approach and from whom he must take the book.

The book is still open and still in his outstretched hand, evidently the same hand which had just been lifted up to heaven with the oath of certain consummation. The "booklet," as noted above, seems most likely to represent the particular lot of Christ's inheritance which is to be awarded to John and, in principle, representing also the appropriate share for each believer.

In the parallel section in Daniel to which we have been referring, that prophet also awaits an inheritance. The Book of Daniel closes with exactly such a promise. "And he said, Go thy way, Daniel. . . . till the end be: for thou shalt rest, and stand in thy lot at the end of the days" (Daniel 12:9, 13). In analogous fashion, long ago did Joshua (whose name is the name as "Jesus") divide up God's promised inheritance in the land of Canaan, apportioning by lot the sections for each tribe and family (Joshua 19:51).

Revelation 10:9. And I went unto the angel, and said unto him, Give me the little book. And he said unto me, Take it, and eat it up; and it shall make thy belly bitter, but it shall be in thy mouth sweet as honey.

John, quick to obey the voice from heaven, no matter how presumptuous it might seem, immediately approached the angel to request the book. After the rapture, believers will all have glorified bodies like that of Christ (Philippians 3:20, 21), and thus will be able to move rapidly across space in whatever direction desired, as well as to see and hear events at great distances. Our present bodies are so constructed as to be governed by present physical force systems—gravitational forces, electromagnetic forces and nuclear forces. The resurrection body of Christ, however, although real and physical, was not so constrained. He could move quickly from earth to heaven and pass through walls. Presumably, since we shall be like Him (1 John 3:2), we shall also have such capabilities. John, translated forward in time in such a state, could thus move from heaven to earth as commanded. He "went unto" the angel in this way.

The angel (that is, Christ), receiving his request for the little book, will immediately give it to him. It is, after all, his inheritance. However, there are serious consequences; it involves sober and bitter responsibilities, as well as great blessings.

He is instructed by the angel to *eat* the book, seemingly a most strange command. Yet he would recognize this as something familiar to the experience of other prophets before him. David had said that God's Law was "sweeter also than honey" (Psalm 19:10), and another psalmist had likewise compared God's words to honey (Psalm 119:103). Jeremiah 15:16 gives similar testimony.

Ezekiel was given a "roll of a book" to eat, a book containing "lamentations, and mourning, and woe." When he ate it, as commanded, it was sweet as honey to the taste, though its message was bitter, and would embitter all Israel against him, as God's prophet (Ezekiel 2:8-34).

Not only the prophets, but every faithful witness of God through the ages can testify to similar experiences. The Word of God and the teaching thereof are a great joy, sweeter than honey, a rejoicing of the heart to the one who truly knows and serves the Lord. But others reject it bitterly and seek to oppose and destroy its testimony, sometimes even slaying those who bear its witness.

And if this situation has been true in former ages, it will be more so than ever during the tribulation period, for all those servants of Christ who are still living on the earth at that time. John, however, represents the raptured saints in heaven, who no longer can be harmed by human persecutors. The roll he eats thus represents his own inheritance, in particular, not the words of the Lord in general.

Even so, as a glorified joint-heir with Christ (Romans 8:17), he must also "suffer with him," even in the responsibilities of the inheritance. This is why the title scroll is wonderfully sweet to the taste but bitter to the belly. Joint-heirship with Christ involves not only reigning with him but also *judging* with Him. We must participate—at least in observation, if not in implementation—in the remaining judgments, climaxed when we come to earth with Him at Armageddon (Zechariah 14:5; 1 Thessalonians 3:13; Jude 14; Revelation 19:14).

The Lord will have no pleasure in the death of the wicked (Ezekiel 18:23; 33:11), and neither shall we. He is long-suffering, and so we should be, but the time will come when the wicked must be judged. Whether those remaining unconverted are friends or loved ones or merely the great multitudes for whom Christ died and whom we should have sought to win, they must finally be judged.

And evidently, beginning at this midway point in the tribulation, when John (representing us) receives and appropriates to his own life the title-deed of his inheritance, all the resurrected saints must participate with Christ in these final judgments. "Do ye not know that the saints shall judge the world?" (1 Corinthians 6:2). This will be a necessary, but bitter, bitter experience.

"Let the high praises of God be in their mouth, and a two-edged sword in their hand; to execute vengeance upon the heathen, and punishments upon the people; to bind their kings with chains, and their nobles with fetters of iron: to execute upon them the judgment written: this honour have all his saints. Praise ye the Lord" (Psalm 149:6-9).

That is not all. The martyred tribulation saints will finally be resurrected; "and judgment was given unto them" (Revelation 20:4) as well. Then all the saints, from before and during the tribulation "reigned with Christ a thousand years" (Revelation 20:6). Each overcoming believer "shall rule them with a rod of iron; as the vessels of a potter shall they be broken to shivers: even as I received of my Father" (Revelation 2:27). Yet another duty of judgment follows this. "Know ye not that we shall judge angels?" (1 Corinthians 6:3).

Revelation 10:10.   And I took the little book out of the angel's hand, and ate it up: and it was in my mouth sweet as honey: and as soon as I had eaten it, my belly was bitter.

Sharing in Christ's inheritance will not be all sweetness and joy, at least not until after the final judgment. This symbolic act of eating the little book was given to stress vividly to John, and to all other believers as well, the true bittersweet nature of the great honor of sharing in His inheritance. We will know, in that day, after the resurrection and our own purging at His judgment seat (1 Corinthians

3:11-15) both the full demands of His righteousness and the great depths of His mercy and love. As we participate in the necessary judgments of fallen angels and unrepentant human beings, we will fully acquiesce in their justice but also weep with Christ when they die.

Note that the roll turned bitter as soon as it was eaten. This indicates further that both the sweet and the bitter aspects of the joint-inheritance were to begin immediately. The first half of the tribulation period apparently, as far as the raptured saints are concerned, will be a time of observation and preparation for their service. The second half will require full participation.

Revelation 10:11.   And he said unto me, Thou must prophesy again before many peoples, and nations, and tongues, and kings.

The Lord Jesus Christ finally, in the person of the rainbow-crowned angel, issues a final word to His servant John. After viewing the awful judgments of the seals and trumpets, then seeing the Lord descend from heaven to assert His heirship over the earth, and finally hearing the roaring proclamations of the seven thunders, John might well have assumed his more immediate ministry of writing in a book what he had seen (Revelation 1:11) was about ended.

But the task was only half finished. He must not only participate in the bitter judgments yet to come, but write about them as well. He, of course, was writing "what he had seen"—that is, history. But to those who would read what he had written, it would be prophecy.

Therefore, he must take up his pen once again. The word "before" (Greek *epi*) is better rendered simply "of." There were still many peoples, nations, languages, and rulers about whom he must write, those who would be the climactic objects of the cumulated wrath of God through the ages. In spite of all the devastating plagues, there were still multitudes of people in the world, and these were all uniting for one final, desperate assault against God. Further, there were still many witnessing Christians alive, and many unsaved who might still somehow be reclaimed, with hearts not yet irretrievably hardened. He must write of these also —possibly even *for* these, as they might yet read the Scriptures in these closing days.

11

God's Two Witnesses

(Revelation 11)

In the eleventh chapter of Revelation we encounter one of the most extraordinary events and one of the most fascinating chapters in the book. The chapter division is arbitrary, since the scene is a continuation of that in Chapter 10. The second woe (the plague of demonic horselike creatures) is just finishing its thirteen-month course, and the Lord Jesus Christ, appearing as the angel with the rainbow over his head, is still speaking to John.

The New Temple

At the time of John's experience on Patmos, the magnificent temple that had once been the beauty of Jerusalem was merely a twenty-five-year old memory. John, in fact, had been present on the Mount of Olives when Christ had prophesied its destruction, saying: "There shall not be left here one stone upon another, that shall not be thrown down" (Matthew 24:2). The prophecy had been fulfilled by the Roman armies in A.D. 70.

And yet the old prophets had often written of the holy temple as it would be in the last days (Ezekiel 40-48; Amos 9:11; Micah 4:1; Haggai 2:9; and Zechariah 6:12, 13). Somehow the temple must therefore some day be built again.

Though John could not know this when he wrote, over nineteen centuries would come and go after his death, before the temple would reappear. The holy city would be "trodden down of the Gentiles," even seeing a Moslem mosque erected where the temple should be, for year after long year.

But one day it would be built again, and this is the temple in the Book of Revelation that John was allowed to see.

Revelation 11:1.   And there was given me a reed like unto a rod: and the angel stood, saying, Rise, and measure the temple of God, and the altar, and them that worship therein.

The angel, as shown before, is Christ, and he is ultimately the one who has allowed the new temple to be constructed. However, on earth, it will apparently be authorized by a treaty made by the Israeli government with the head of a confederation of European nations. As noted in Chapter 6 (see pages 110, 111), this coming king will make a seven-year covenant with the Jewish leaders (Daniel 9:27), allowing them to rebuild the temple and reinstitute their ancient worship, including the sacrificial offerings.

Orthodox Jews have long dreamed of this day and have been making plans for decades to rebuild the temple when opportunity allows. The miraculous defeat of Russia and her Moslem allies (Ezekiel 38) will provide the opportunity and they will make the most of it. Construction crews will quickly raze the Islamic "Dome of the Rock" which now stands on the temple site and then erect a magnificent new temple edifice as rapidly as possible. When it is completed and dedicated, the Levitical rituals and offerings will be restored, and many of the faithful orthodox Jews will begin to take part.

But this will all seem like a strange anachronism to many, not only to the Gentile world at large but no doubt even to many of their Jewish brethren. That sophisticated modern men and women would actually start offering the blood of bulls and goats on a sacrificial altar once again will be too much for many to take. Even though the period will have begun with Israel held in worldwide awe because of her miraculous deliverance from the Russian hosts, the old prejudices and resentments will soon surface again.

It is questionable whether all, or even most, of the Jews will actually practice the ancient worship. Although even the most atheistic of the Zionist Jews had been profoundly impressed by God's intervention on their behalf, many will be unwilling to participate in the animal sacrifices that will be instituted by the ultra-orthodox.

There are many who will, however, and it is these to whom the angel directs John's attention. By the time the temple is built, and the sacrificial offerings activated, much of the first three-and-a-half-year period of the tribulation will have been completed, and it is at this point that John is sent to the scene.

He had just been told that he would have to prophesy again of peoples and kings—this time of those who would be prominent in the last half of the tribulation, during the time of the sounding of the last trumpet. And the first of the nations of whom he must prophesy is Israel.

The instruction is somewhat cryptic: "Measure the temple, and the altar, and the worshipers." The measuring "reed" with which he was to do this (Greek *kalamos*) was commonly grown in the Jordan valley, and had many uses, one of which was as a measuring rod. In smaller lengths it was used as a "pen," and the word is so translated in 3 John 13. In the Septuagint, it was used to translate the Hebrew *kaneh,* meaning "rule."

There is obviously more to this measuring process than merely determining the size of the temple. The latter is not given at all. Furthermore, the worshipers were to be measured as well as the temple.

But how does one measure a worshiper? Evidently this type of measurement has to do with spiritual standards rather than physical. The temple and its altar and its worshipers are to be evaluated in terms of their conformity to God's spiritual criteria, and John is to be the one who measures (or *judges*) them.

This responsibility is evidently given because, as a joint-heir with Christ, John is (along with all the redeemed) to participate in the work of judgment (see the discussion in the preceding chapter). Just as Israel is the first nation of whom John is to "prophesy again," so Israel is the first to be judged. "For the time is come that judgment must begin at the house of God" (1 Peter 4:17).

This is always the order. God judges His own people first to cleanse and purify them. Then He judges His enemies to punish and banish them. The judgment seat of Christ, where Christians are purged and prepared for eternal service in the kingdom of God, takes place a thousand years before the judgment of the great white throne, where unbelievers are separated from God forever in the lake of fire.

The reconstructed temple in Jerusalem is based on a covenant made by Israel with a godless dictator. The new altar is an insult to the Lamb of God, who had offered one sacrifice for sins forever; and the worshipers in the temple, though professing to honor God, have rejected Christ. Therefore, all come short, when the measuring rod of God's standard is applied.

Israel is, therefore, about to enter the time of her greatest suffering. God will use the heavy hand of wicked Gentile nations to chastise His people, but the process will purify them. It will be the "time of Jacob's trouble" (Jeremiah 30:7), the "time of trouble, such as never was since there was a nation" (Daniel 12:1), the "great tribulation, such as was not since the beginning of the world" (Matthew 24:21). This final great judgment on Israel is initiated in Revelation 11:13, but most of the rest of the book is devoted to God's judgments on the Gentiles. The details of Israel's judgment had already been outlined in the prophets (Zechariah 14:1) and by Christ Himself (Mark 13:14-20).

Revelation 11:2.   But the court which is without the temple leave out, and measure it not; for it is given unto the Gentiles: and the holy city shall they tread under foot forty and two months.

Traditionally, Gentiles were allowed to enter the outer courtyard surrounding the temple but never into the temple itself. This area, therefore, was not to be included in John's measurement. That is, it was the judgment of Israel, not that of the Gentiles, with which he was to be concerned at this point. Jerusalem first, Babylon later, would feel God's wrath. Purification of His people first, then punishment of His enemies.

Gentiles, furthermore, would retake Jerusalem and would still "tread it under foot" for three and a half years. All the time the sounding of the seventh trumpet continued to echo across the world. The Jews had finally possessed the temple site and much of the city itself but now the Gentiles would wrest it all back once more.

This temple, in fact, is the fourth temple built in Jerusalem—the first by Solomon, the second under Zerubbabel, the third by Herod. Each in turn had been destroyed by invading Gentiles, with the third temple (the one in which John himself had worshiped) having been leveled to the ground by the Roman armies commanded by Titus in A.D. 70. Ever since that time, the temple and Jerusalem itself had been under Gentile domination.

Christ had prophesied of the Jews' long exile in the following words: "And Jerusalem shall be trodden down of the Gentiles, until the times of the Gentiles be fulfilled" (Luke 21:24). Israel had finally been reestablished as a nation in 1948 and had regained most of the city of Jerusalem itself in the Six Day War in 1967. However, the temple site, the most vital part of Jerusalem, remained under Moslem control.

Then, finally, it had seemed that the great prophecy was fulfilled when the Western Prince made a seven-year covenant with the Israeli government allowing them to build their temple and reinstitute their ancient worship. By the time of Revelation 11, the pact had been in operation for three and a half years, and the Jews no doubt were feeling happy and secure.

Nevertheless, the city and the temple were theirs only by sufferance of the great Prince who was rapidly gaining control of the world's nations. Furthermore, he was becoming increasingly irritated with them; their worship of their Creator (even though they still had not identified Him as Christ) was inimical to the humanistic worship promoted by the dictator, and their bloody sacrifices were an offense. Furthermore 144,000 of these Israelites had actually accepted Christ and were preaching the gospel everywhere, seemingly immune to all the plagues and persecutions that were afflicting the world.

The Days of Their Prophecy

This will be the situation when the tribulation period nears its midpoint. The Israelis' enjoyment of their freedom will be brief, and the Gentiles are soon to drive them out of their temple and city once more. For another forty-two months, Jerusalem must be trodden down of the Gentiles before their judgment would come and the times of the Gentiles be finished.

Revelation 11:3.   And I will give power unto my two witnesses, and they shall prophesy a thousand two hundred and threescore days, clothed in sackcloth.

The mighty angel appears suddenly to change the subject, speaking of *"my two witnesses."* The assertion that these two witnesses are peculiarly His witnesses is further proof that the angel is Christ. Furthermore their witness was to be in the form of prophecy. They were true prophets, speaking by divine revelation under the authority of Christ and the duration of their prophetic testimony was set at 1260 days, corresponding to forty-two months of thirty days, or three-and-a-half years.

They are obviously prophets of judgment. The mohair sackcloth which serves them as clothing has for ages symbolized suffering and grief. Furthermore their prophecy is clearly worldwide in scope, with people everywhere aware of their message of warning and doom. They preach to both Jew and Gentile. In fact, this two-fold division of mankind is probably why there are two witnesses, and why they are suddenly introduced at this point in the narrative. John is himself to prophesy concerning both Jews and Gentiles, and the witnesses are prophesying against both Jews and Gentiles. The burden of both sets of prophecies concerns the imminent judgments, first on the Jews, finally on the Gentiles. The duration of their prophecy is given in terms of days, probably to emphasize that they are not once-a-week preachers. Every single day, for three-and-a-half years, their testimony of judgment to come is conveyed to a rebellious and resentful world.

The identity of the two witnesses has been a matter of much speculation. Many have suggested that they represent the Law and the Prophets, but both the narrative and the context show clearly that they are real men who speak and perform miracles and then die and rise again. Many commentators conclude that they are two great future prophets whom God calls in the last days but whose names are unimportant and therefore unrevealed. This is a possibility, but seems unlikely in view of Christ's special identification of them as "my" witnesses, as though they were somehow known to Him and serving Him long before. The reference to Zechariah's prophecy of the olive trees and candlesticks (verse 4) suggests the same.

That they are men, however, and not angels is obvious from the fact that they die. The most likely conclusion is that they are two of God's faithful witnesses from former ages, sent back to witness again in the final age.

This is strongly supported by the remarkable prophecy concerning Elijah: "Behold, I will send you Elijah the prophet before the coming of the great and dreadful day of the Lord: And he shall turn the heart of the fathers to the children, and the heart of the children to their fathers, lest I come and smite the earth with a curse" (Malachi 4:5, 6). This prophecy is all the more remarkable in that it contains the very last words of the Old Testament.

Some assume that this prophecy was fulfilled in John the Baptist but John the

Baptist himself denied it. "And they asked him, What then? Art thou Elias? And he saith, I am not" (John 1:21). John did indeed come "in the spirit and power of Elias" (Luke 1:17), but he was not Elias, and his coming did not fulfill Malachi's prophecy. Jesus Himself confirmed this. "Elias truly shall first come, and restore all things" (Matthew 17:11).

Elijah was taken into heaven without dying (2 Kings 2:11). God must have had a reason for such a remarkable action; Elijah was no more deserving of such a privilege than many other saints before and since. Evidently, God had a ministry for Elijah which required that he still remain living in his natural body. There he has remained ever since, awaiting the time at the end of the age when he would return to earth to complete his prophetic mission to the people of Israel just "before the coming of the great and dreadful day of the Lord."

But if Elijah is one of the witnesses, who is the other? The majority of commentators believe it is Moses, primarily because Moses appeared with Elijah on the mount of transfiguration (Matthew 17:3), and also because both Moses and Elijah had called forth miracles from heaven in the form of plagues on God's enemies and could effectively represent both the Law and the Prophets.

However, there do seem to be serious problems with this solution. Moses was not taken into heaven as Elijah was, but died and was buried (Deuteronomy 34:5, 6). The appearance of Moses with Elijah on the mountain was not an actual physical descent from heaven but was merely a "vision" (Matthew 17:9). Despite the mysterious reference to Michael's dispute with Satan over Moses' body (Jude 9), it is likely that Moses' spirit, like all others who died before Calvary, was in Sheol, at least until the time of Christ's resurrection.

The greatest problem, however, with the assumption that Moses is one of the witnesses is that this would mean Moses would die twice, which would contradict Hebrews 9:27: "It is appointed unto men once to die." Furthermore, both Moses and Elijah were prophets to Israel, whereas the two witnesses of Revelation 11 are prophets of judgment to the whole world, both Jew and Gentile.

All of these considerations point clearly to the great antediluvian patriarch Enoch as the second of the two witnesses. Enoch is the only other man in all human history, besides Elijah, who was taken directly into heaven in his natural body without dying. "By faith Enoch was translated that he should not see death" (Hebrews 11:5). Neither he nor Elijah were given immortal bodies when they were translated, however, because it was necessary for Christ first to die for their sins and rise again. "For as in Adam all die, even so in Christ shall all be made alive. But every man in his own order: Christ the firstfruits; afterward they that are Christ's at his coming" (1 Corinthians 15:22, 23).

Thus Enoch and Elijah have been waiting in heaven in their natural bodies through all the intervening ages since their respective translations. Therefore, although we cannot be absolutely certain, it does seem most probable that these are Christ's two witnesses, sent to earth again in the last days to complete their prophetic testimonies to an ungodly world just before Christ returns. Enoch's testimony, given to the antediluvians, could well be the essence of his message to the world in the tribulation period: "Behold, the Lord cometh with ten thousands of his saints, to execute judgment upon all, and to convince all that are ungodly among them of all their ungodly deeds which they have ungodly committed, and of all their hard speeches which ungodly sinners have spoken against him" (Jude 14, 15).

Enoch and Elijah are uniquely appropriate selections for this peculiar ministry in the last days. For approximately the first 2,000 years of human history (Adam to Abraham), God was dealing with the world of mankind as a whole. For approximately the second 2,000 years of history (Abraham to Christ), He was dealing primarily with the chosen nation Israel. It is significant that Enoch's prophetic ministry was to the first group and that he preached and was translated during about the middle of the "Gentile" (or "nations") epoch of history. Elijah's ministry was to Israel, and he preached and was translated at about the middle of the period from Abraham to Calvary.

The third major period of history is the Church Age, also about 2,000 years in duration, during which the members of Christ's Church, through the prophetic written Word, preach to both Jews and Gentiles. This age is terminated by the rapture of the Church. During the tribulation, with the Church no longer on earth, God will send back His two greatest prophets of the two former ages to renew and to complete their respective testimonies to Gentiles and Jews, proclaiming to the whole ungodly world the mighty judgments of God. After living in their natural flesh in heaven for an average of over three-and-a-half thousand years, they will preach again on earth for a final three-and-a-half years, and then finally be put to death for three-and-a-half days.

Revelation 11:4.   These are the two olive trees, and the two candlesticks standing before the God of the earth.

Here is another intriguing evidence that these two witnesses have been living in former ages. They are said also to have been "standing before God" back in the days of Zechariah.

Zechariah had been granted a series of remarkable visions, which evidently had a twofold application, first to the current project of temple rebuilding and second to the end times. In Zechariah's time (between the times of Ezra and Nehemiah), the rebuilding of the temple, though authorized in the days of Ezra, was languishing and Zechariah's mission was to encourage Zerubbabel the governor and Joshua the high priest to proceed with the task.

One of these visions was of a golden candlestick (or lampstand) with seven lamps, flanked by two olive trees yielding golden oil for the lamps. The olive trees were interpreted as "the two anointed ones [or "the ones with the oil"], that stand by the Lord of the whole earth" (Zechariah 4:14). The phraseology is obviously the same. Thus the two witnesses were "standing before" or "standing by" the Lord long before John's time.

These two great men were peculiarly men accustomed to being in God's presence. When they were on earth before, it was said that Enoch "walked with God" (Genesis 5:24) and Elijah first introduced himself thus: "As the Lord of Israel liveth, before whom I stand" (1 Kings 17:1). They have continued close in his presence throughout the ages. They had been specially anointed as God's prophets to the nations and the chosen nation, respectively, and their concern for their responsibilities has been no less immediate and passionate in heaven than it had been on earth.

Zechariah had seen them in vision as two mighty olive trees, each bearing an especially strong and fruitful "branch" which perpetually emptied its golden oil into a golden bowl on the apex of a golden lampstand, from which coursed the oil through seven pipes to the seven lamps on the lampstand. The whole apparatus thus symbolized the divine Light to and through the chosen nation Israel, all energized by the Spirit of God. The message to Joshua (same name as "Jesus") was that the blessing and power for the nation must be received through "my servant the BRANCH" (Zechariah 3:8) which, in turn, was the name of the man who would ultimately build the eternal temple and would be both its priest and king (Zechariah 6:12, 13). The message to Zerubbabel was that all this would come "Not by might, nor by power, but by my spirit" (Zechariah 4:6), as symbolized by the flowing oil. The branch is Christ, the oil is the Spirit, but both were conveyed, as it were, to Israel by the two anointed ones, said specifically by the Lord to be represented by Zechariah's two olive trees, and also by the two witnesses here in Revelation 11.

But the witnesses also were called "the two candlesticks" as well as "the two olive trees," whereas in Zechariah there was only one candlestick. The reason probably is that one candlestick represents Enoch's witness to the nations, the other Elijah's witness to Israel.

The Lord Jesus Christ called them "my two witnesses," indicating that these bore a special relationship to Him which was not shared by other witnesses. These were the two that had stood by Him for long ages, sharing His great concern and love for those who loved Him, but also sharing His wrath against those who despised and rejected Him.

They had stood by Him in the days of their flesh, in the midst of their own ungodly generations. After their translation to heaven, they stood by the Lord in His dealings with their brethren through the centuries, with just this intriguing glimpse provided for us here in Zechariah's vision: "These are the two anointed ones that stand by the Lord of the whole earth" (Zechariah 4:14). Note that, even though the immediate situation was concerned only with Israel (thus there was only one candlestick in the vision), it was still important for Zechariah's hearers to remember that God was Lord of the whole earth.

Although it is obviously speculation, it seems possible that they may even have stood by Him when He came to earth, or at least at the climax of that visit when He died and rose again. On the morning of the empty tomb, it is remarkable that there were two men standing by. "And they entered in, and found not the body of the Lord Jesus. And it came to pass, as they were much perplexed thereabout, behold, two men stood by them in shining garments" (Luke 24:3, 4).

Similarly there were two men standing by at His ascension back to heaven. "And while they looked stedfastly toward heaven as he went up, behold, two men stood by them in white apparel" (Acts 1:10).

The time had finally come, however, when Christ's two faithful witnesses must return to earth to "finish their testimony" (verse 7). They had stood by Him: now, surely, He would stand by them.

Revelation 11:5.   And if any man will hurt them, fire proceedeth out of their mouth, and devoureth their enemies: and if any man will hurt them, he must in this manner be killed.

Like the 144,000 Israelite witnesses (Revelation 7:3; 8:4) these two chief witnesses will be protected from all harm during the three-and-a-half years of their testimony. Their daily pronouncements of condemnation and warning, in addition to the miracles of judgment which they called forth on the earth, will make them feared and hated above all men before them, and many attempts will be made on their lives. But they will be invulnerable and, furthermore, they will have the power to slay their enemies merely by a spoken word as though a consuming fire were leaping from their tongues. Such power is manifest otherwise only by Christ Himself (2 Thessalonians 2:8; Revelation 2:16; 19:15). Furthermore, in whatever manner anyone seeks to hurt them, he himself will be slain by an analogous judgment.

Elijah, in fact, had been able long before to call down fire from heaven with his spoken word (1 Kings 18:37, 38; 2 Kings 1:10, 12), and had been invulnerable then as well. He was recognized, in his day, as the one who summoned "the chariot of Israel, and the horsemen thereof" (2 Kings 2:12).

Revelation 11:6.   These have power to shut heaven, that it rain not in the days of their prophecy; and have power over waters to turn them to blood, and to smite the earth with all plagues, as often as they will.

Not only do the two prophets have miraculous power to defend themselves against all enemies, but also to call forth great plagues on the earth. First of all, they call for the greatest drought ever experienced on earth. The "days of their prophecy" are "a thousand, two hundred and threescore days" (verse 3), so it will "rain not" for three-and-a-half years. As Elijah had called for a three-and-a-half-year drought in the land of Israel (James 5:17), so now he and his fellow prophet inflict the same on the whole world.

Such a drought obviously will generate worldwide famine. This seems clearly to correspond to the judgment already described under the third seal, right at the beginning of the tribulation (Revelation 6:5, 6).

This fact is one indication that the three-and-a-half-year period of the prophecy of the two witnesses corresponds to the first half of the tribulation. More significantly, the forty-two-month period of Gentile tyranny over the holy city (Revelation 11:2) and of absolute rule by the beast (Revelation 13:5) apparently becomes possible only by the execution of the two witnesses by the beast (Revelation 11:7). As long as the witnesses exercise such power over both men and nature, it is impossible for the beast to acquire absolute world power. Thus it seems necessary to conclude that John is here being given a retrospective view of the ministry of the witnesses, from the chronological standpoint of the middlle of the tribulation. As a matter of fact, each of the sub-histories of these parenthetical chapters (11, 12, and 13) will be seen to begin with a retrospective review of the background events leading up to the midtribulation turning-point, then to continue with a preview of events yet future.

Almost simultaneous with the beginning of the drought, was the restraint of the world's atmospheric circulation (Revelation 7:1). Such a combination of meteorologic phenomena will result in a gradual reestablishment of the prediluvian waters above the firmaments, and thus help to prepare the world for the idyllic environment of the millennium.

Note also that the ability of the prophets to turn waters into blood corresponds to the judgments of the first and second trumpets (Revelation 8:7-9). In fact, they were also responsible for "smiting the earth with all plagues."

All the seal judgments and the trumpet judgments were also called "plagues" in the summary statement of Revelation 9:20. Since the two witnesses were empowered to smite the earth with all plagues, it is evident that, as far as the earth-dwellers were concerned, the judgments through which the earth had been passing had been directly caused by the imprecations of the witnesses.

Thus the various plagues had both a heavenly cause and an earthly cause. John had seen the horsemen and angels and other emissaries of judgment sent forth from heaven. Now he learns that they had also been announced on earth by the two witnesses. These two prophets were *Christ's* witnesses, still in perfect harmony on earth with His will in heaven. Whatever they asked on earth was done for them in heaven (Matthew 18:19).

No wonder the ungodly men and women on earth had come to fear and hate these witnesses with such intensity. Right from the first, they had been told that the plagues had been sent as punishment from God for their wickedness and continuing rebellion against Christ.

It is, of course, difficult for us to understand how these two prophets could live for 3,000 and 4,000 years, respectively, in heaven in their natural bodies without dying. Furthermore, how could they get there and return from there in bodies controlled by the normal gravitational forces that control all matter in our existing space-time cosmos? We can perhaps understand in part how angelic bodies, or resurrection bodies, could do this, since they are not controlled by such forces, but how can natural material bodies be transported from earth to heaven (wherever that is) in any reasonable time? As a matter of fact, science does not yet understand gravity itself.

The Victory of the Beast

To such a question we can have no answer at this time except that a miracle may be involved. There may, of course, be some type of anti-gravitational energy implicit in nature (as Peter's walking on the water and Philip's being "caught away" from the Ethiopian eunuch by the Lord) which is simply undiscovered as yet by modern science. Whether this is the case or whether such events are purely miraculous, it is obvious that they are well within the capabilities of God. The one who created all natural laws is able to utilize them or modify them according to His own will.

Revelation 11:7.   And when they shall have finished their testimony, the beast that ascendeth out of the bottomless pit shall make war against them, and shall overcome them, and kill them.

Their testimony and the judgments which they inflict have been ordained by God to last for three-and-a-half years. During that time, despite all manner of opposition by the ungodly hosts of the nations, especially of the great leader who has organized the nations of the west in a great confederation, they have proved invulnerable. In fact, all the police and military forces sent to arrest them have themselves been destroyed. Assassins dispatched to execute them have fallen by the same means they were preparing to use. They seem indestructible, and the terrible plagues unleashed by them have raged through the world without restraint. Furthermore, multitudes have been converted to Christ by believing their testimony, along with that of the 144,000 sealed Israelites who also receive miraculous protection.

But now, for the first time in Revelation, we meet an amazing character known as "the beast." Much additional information is provided concerning him, notably the fact that he is a man, not a demon, even though he has ascended out of the great abyss and is Satan-controlled (Revelation 13:2, 18).

He is introduced at this point in the narrative without any word of explanation, as though John already knew of him. Indeed, even though this is the first mention of this beast in Revelation, John did know of him through the prophet Daniel. Daniel's vision (Daniel 7) involved four great empires symbolized by wild beasts, the fourth of which was the same as this one. In particular, the final king that would acquire control over this fourth kingdom of Daniel's prophecy is the one whom John now recognizes as the beast here in the Apocalypse.

Furthermore, this is the same as Daniel's "prince that shall come" (Daniel 9:26), the one who had made the seven-year covenant with Israel permitting the reconstruction of their temple. During this first half of the tribulation period, he has been involved in consolidating his own worldwide political power, well aware that it is the great dragon, Satan himself, who is enabling him to gain such power (Revelation 13:2). However, he has been hindered and thwarted again and again by the two witnesses and their followers, both by their condemnatory preaching and by the devastating plagues which they bring on the world.

Finally, he will decide to mount an all-out war against them. He must be rid of them at all costs, regardless how many of his own followers perish in the process. This is also the time of the plague of the sixth trumpet, when the hordes of demonic "horsemen" are slaying the third of the world's population. They are desperate days calling for desperate measures and the beast dispatches great armies both to fight the horsemen and, more importantly, to kill the two prophets.

And, finally, he is successful. Somehow, his forces manage to penetrate the hitherto invincible wall of fire about the witnesses and to slay them. At the same time, the last of the demonic horsemen are destroyed, and suddenly the people of the world think that all their troubles are over. Satan's man has conquered God's men, and now the people of the world are finally free to live as they please, without fear of retribution from a suddenly-impotent Christ. They "repented not," (Revelation 9:20), but rather rejoiced in the great victory of the beast. Little will they understand the fact that the two witnesses have merely "finished their testimony." The 1260 days are completed; otherwise, not even the armies of the beast would have been able to touch them.

But who is this beast? John merely says at this point that he had ascended out of the abyss. Daniel 9:26 says that his "people" were the ones who would destroy Jerusalem, which suggests that his nationality will be Roman, or at least from one of the nations that came out of the old Roman empire.

Because of these factors, many ancient and modern commentators have suggested that the beast would be the emperor Nero returned from the dead. Some in modern times have proposed Mussolini as a candidate for such a resuscitation. Others have suggested Nimrod or Judas. All such suggestions overlook the fact, however, that Satan is not the Creator and would therefore be unable to create "resurrected" bodies in which the departed spirit of some great Antichrist leader of the past could return.

On the other hand, Satan is extremely powerful and capable of manipulating natural processes in many marvelous ways, short of actual creation. Many cases have been reported from eastern and other occult religions, for example, of mystics who have apparently "died," and have remained in a state of suspended animation for a time before reviving. In various such cases, as well as in certain remarkable tales of those who testify of UFO encounters, the "dead" person has returned to tell of amazing journeys on which he had been taken while in such a condition.

In the case of the beast, it may be that John recognized him as one who had recently been "slain," but had returned to his body after a brief interval and had been telling the remarkable story of a trip to the great abyss, where he had received great power from Satan, including a commission to rule all nations.

Such an experience would be an impressive counterfeit of the resurrection of Christ, and will persuade multitudes (already impressed with his political abilities) to follow him. He is not a false Christ, however, but *Anti*Christ! He will not pretend to be Christ, but will openly blaspheme and oppose Christ, boasting that he has received his authority from Satan and that he and his master will soon depose God and His Christ.

By studying the relevant Scriptures (note especially Revelation 13:1-6), it seems that his pseudoresurrection may have occurred near the end of the first half of the tribulation. When he returns boasting of his encounter with Satan, and then demonstrates his great power by suddenly putting an end to the career of the two witnesses, the whole world will marvel and gladly submit to his authority.

Revelation 11:8.   And their dead bodies shall lie in the street of the great city, which spiritually is called Sodom and Egypt, where also our Lord was crucified.

The Lord Jesus said one time, in sad irony: "I must walk to day, and to morrow, and the day following: for it cannot be that a prophet perish out of Jerusalem" (Luke 13:33). "O Jerusalem, Jerusalem, thou that killest the prophets, and stonest them which are sent unto thee . . . Behold, your house is left unto you desolate" (Matthew 23:37, 38).

Jerusalem, the holy city, the city of peace and the temple of God, is also the city where God's prophets die and their Lord is crucified! These two greatest prophets must also die in Jerusalem, their testimony refused even by God's chosen people. It is there the armies of the beast finally will apprehend and slay them and leave their bodies unburied in the street for all their enemies to see.

An indication of the moral degeneracy of Jerusalem at this time is indicated by its "spiritual" name, Sodom and Egypt. The same word (*pneumatikos*) is used elsewhere only in 1 Corinthians 2:14, where the things of God's Spirit are said to be "spiritually" discerned. The holy city of Jerusalem, even with its rebuilt temple and renewed worship, has become so wicked that it is called by the Holy Spirit and

all spiritually-minded believers by the name associated with its terrible behavior—
"Sodom and Egypt," Sodom, whose very name has been identified for 4,000
years with sexual perversion, and Egypt, associated ever since Moses with the
persecution of God's people, indicate pungently the wicked character which the
city of Jerusalem had taken on, even in the brief period since its great deliverance
from the armies of Gog.

The city had also probably become an international center by this time, filled
with commercial speculators and political adventurers of every stripe, together
with a deluge of tourists and tourist-oriented entertainment complexes, with all
their associated evils. All of this may well have vexed the souls of the religious
Jews in the city, even as with Lot in the days of the original Sodom (2 Peter 2:7, 8),
but they no doubt enjoyed the resulting prosperity and managed to rationalize it.
With all their rejoicing over God's deliverance and the renewal of the ancient
religious system, they still had not repented of their rejection of Christ. And now,
in the same streets through which Christ had long ago walked to His crucifixion,
the bodies of His two faithful witnesses lay dead.

**Revelation 11:9.   And they of the people and kindreds and tongues and nations
shall see their dead bodies three days and an half, and shall not suffer their dead
bodies to be put in graves.**

Although the two prophets, like Christ, had returned to Jerusalem to die, their
preaching and the plagues they invoked had affected all nations everywhere. They
had been regarded for three-and-a-half years as the greatest enemies of the entire
human race and had been feared and hated like none else before them. The news of
their conquest and execution spread immediately throughout the world, carried by
satellite to television screens in homes and public places everywhere. Believers
who tried to give the bodies a proper burial were driven away.

The gloating of the happy spectators knew no bounds. "Free at last!" they
thought, and the beast who had rid them of their tormentors quickly became an
international hero. Day after day they kept the bodies in the street, blaspheming
their God and defying His vengeance. His most powerful prophets were dead, and
their plagues at an end.

**Revelation 11:10.   And they that dwell upon the earth shall rejoice over them, and
make merry, and shall send gifts one to another; because these two prophets
tormented them that dwelt on the earth.**

It is like Christmas. Worldwide merrymaking is in order and a great holiday
celebration gets under way. Sales boom again and gifts are exchanged freely. Joy
to the world, the Lord is dead! Men once celebrated the birth of Christ in such a

manner; now they will rejoice in His death. No more will they have to hide in caves of the earth from the wrath of the Lamb. Nevermore will angels fly across the sky, warning those who dwell on the earth of great woes about to fall. The stinging scorpion-locusts and the frightful horse-demons are a bad memory that will never torment them again.

The great prince has conquered Christ, and no one can make war with him anymore (Revelation 13:4). Henceforth his power is invincible, and he will rule, in Satan's name, forever. He has even been to hell and back, and death itself has been vanquished by him. His greatest human enemies, the two tormenting prophets, lie still in the streets of Jerusalem, and all the peoples of the world are rejoicing in his victory. His triumph is complete.

Revelation 11:11.   And after three days and an half the Spirit of life from God entered into them, and they stood upon their feet; and great fear fell upon them which saw them.

The television cameras continue their daily vigil at the scene of triumph, beaming the spectacle onto every picture tube in the world, at the daily news hour. Men and women continue in an orgy of revelry, their frenzy increasing every time they view the dead prophets in Jerusalem.

But as Christ was three days and three nights in the heart of the earth so will his prophets rest three days and three nights on a street in Jerusalem. As the testimony of their grim prophecies was heard for three-and-a-half years, so will the testimony of their silent bodies be seen for three-and-a-half days.

Then, as the drunken revelers watch in horror, the bodies will begin to stir. Slowly the old prophets rise to their feet and the Jerusalem mob shrinks back in astonishment. The cameras zoom in on their glowing faces, and four piercing eyes glare out of 100 million television screens.

Rejoicing quickly is transformed into shock. "Great fear" the Scripture calls it, and it could just as well be translated "exceeding terror." Revelry becomes hysteria and once again will "men's hearts [fail] them for fear, and for looking after those things which are coming on the earth" (Luke 21:26). Probably many will die of heart failure and stroke, and perhaps many others in the ensuing panic and mob hysteria that no doubt will follow.

Revelation 11:12.   And they heard a great voice from heaven saying unto them, Come up hither. And they ascended up to heaven in a cloud; and their enemies beheld them.

But not only did the viewers see the spirits of the prophets return from God into their bodies. They also heard a thunderous voice roar from heaven, speaking to the risen saints. Having finally died, Christ's two witnesses are now alive forevermore, like He is. Their service on earth is done, and they now can return to His presence.

"Come up hither," the voice cried. This is the same message John himself had heard (Revelation 4:1), adding still further to the evidence that the latter is nothing less than the great resurrection call (John 5:28, 29), and that John's experience was indeed that of actual participation in the rapture of the Church when Christ returns, as he was miraculously translated forward in time to that great day.

Now the rapture is repeated, at least for the two witnesses. Like Christ at the ascension (Acts 1:9), and like believers at the rapture, they will ascend in a cloud (1 Thessalonians 4:9) to meet their Lord in the air. This time, however, it will not be done in the twinkling of an eye (1 Corinthians 15:52); instead, every eye will watch them as they rise—first to their feet, then to the skies.

And all their enemies, all those who had rejected their word and rejoiced when they died, especially the beast who had hunted them to death, all these will gaze transfixed as they watch them ascend far up into the heavens and into the presence of their Lord. The word for "beheld" (Greek *theoreo*) is a strong word, implying a transfixed stare. The sight will be enough to strike terror into the hearts of the most arrogantly rebellious of their enemies. A moment before, such men were rejoicing in supreme confidence that Christ was finally defeated and Satan's man was on the victor's throne. But now Christ had triumphed again. The ascent of the prophets into heaven was a dire prediction that even greater judgments were about to descend from heaven. The three-and-a-half-day festivities were about to be followed by another three-and-a-half years of judgments more severe than ever.

Revelation 11:13.   And the same hour was there a great earthquake, and the tenth part of the city fell, and in the earthquake were slain of men seven thousand: and the remnant were affrighted, and gave glory to the God of heaven.

So there could be no question as to cause-and-effect; while the people were still staring into the heavens in awe, the earth began to quake terribly, just as it had at the resurrection of Christ (Matthew 28:2). No one could doubt that the One whose voice had come from heaven a few moments before had also sent the earthquake. This could be none other than the very God of heaven—the one whose defeat they had been proclaiming with great revelry the past three days, but who now was demonstrating again His power.

The two witnesses had stood by "the God of the earth" (Revelation 11:4). Now "the God of heaven" had stood by them. The unbelieving multitudes had been forced to give glory to the God of heaven, though they had put to death His servants. Unfortunately, their sudden "conversion" would be short-lived. In a little while they would again start to "blaspheme the God of heaven" (Revelation 16:11) as they again experience His fearful judgments.

As a token of what is to come, the earthquake will cause 7,000 fatalities in Jerusalem alone, with a tenth of the city falling. If the 7,000 are men only, as the text implies, this suggests a population in the city of about 300,000 at that time. Actually the word "fell" could as well be translated (and often is) "fell down," indicating a direct physical plunge to the ground, thus suggesting that the earthquake caused 10 percent of the city's buildings to collapse. It was in any case sufficient to cause great fear among those who were left as they realized that they were about to see even greater judgments coming on the earth.

Revelation 11:14.   The second woe is past; and, behold, the third woe cometh quickly.

This announcement probably marks the midpoint of the seven-year tribulation period. The ministry of the two witnesses, which had endured for three-and-a-half years (verse 11:3), is now at an end, and the full reign of the beast will occupy the last three-and-a-half years (Revelation 12:6, 14; 13:5).

It is doubtful that this announcement was made for John's benefit only. More likely, it was made from heaven by the same angel who had first pronounced the coming of the "three woes" to "the inhabiters of the earth," calling it out with a loud voice, "flying through the midst of heaven" (Revelation 8:13). The first woe had been the plague of demonic scorpion locusts (Revelation 9:12). The second had occupied over thirteen months, including the scourge of the 200 million devilhorsemen as well as the continuing judgments of the two witnesses and, finally, the great earthquake that had fallen on Jerusalem.

And now the last woe is about to come. It will be worse than any previous judgment, since it is the same as the judgment of the seventh trumpet, which will include all seven of the "vial judgments" (Revelation 16), spanning the entire last half of the tribulation, climaxing in the destruction of all wicked men, and the complete purging and renewal of the earth itself.

The Seventh Trumpet

Revelation 11:15.   And the seventh angel sounded; and there were great voices in heaven, saying, The kingdoms of this world are become the kingdoms of our Lord, and of his Christ; and he shall reign for ever and ever.

Here, finally, is the sounding of the last of the seven trumpets. The first six had ushered in various events on the earth during the first half of the tribulation

(Revelation 8 and 9). The last will echo throughout the entire second half, the period of great tribulation.

There is an important reference to "the last trump" in 1 Corinthians 15:52. There it is said that, at this last sounding of the trumpet, the resurrection of the dead and the immortalizing of the living saints will take place. In Revelation 11:15, and following, there is no specific reference to resurrection. On the other hand, there *is* (verse 18) a reference to the judgment of the dead and the giving of rewards to His servants, both of which presuppose a resurrection.

However, the "last trump" of this passage in 1 Corinthians is obviously the same as the "trump of *God*" of 1 Thessalonians 4:16, 17, whereas the seventh trumpet of Revelation is the "trump of the angel." These are obviously two different trumpets. In addition, of course, it has already been demonstrated that the resurrection and rapture of those who are in Christ, as described in 1 Corinthians 15 and 1 Thessalonians 4, must take place *before* the tribulation period, whereas the seventh angel will sound his trumpet at the middle of the tribulation period.

But if that is the case, why is the trumpet of 1 Corinthians 15:52 called the last trump, when at least the seven trumpets of Revelation will all be sounded later? Furthermore there is even a trumpet which is to be blown near the end of the tribulation by God Himself. "And the Lord shall be seen over them, and his arrow shall go forth as the lightning: and the Lord God shall blow the trumpet, and shall go with whirlwinds of the south" (Zechariah 9:14). In context, this is a reference to God's supernatural deliverance of Israel right at the end of the tribulation. This event is probably the same one mentioned by Christ in Matthew 24:29-31. "Immediately after the tribulation of those days . . . he shall send his angels with a great sound of a trumpet, and they shall gather together his elect from the four winds, from one end of heaven to the other."

Thus, trumpets will be blown both by angels and by God Himself after the "trump of God" which is the "last trump" in 1 Corinthians 15:52. The terminology in this passage is clearly intended not to imply an absolute chronology of trumpets, but one which is relative to its context. Similarly the "last day" of such verses as John 6:40 ("I will raise him up at the last day"), John 11:24 (" . . . in the resurrection at the last day"), and others is not the final day of the cosmos, for time will never end.

The "last day," in which the resurrection occurs, is the last day of the Church Age, and the last trumpet, which signals the resurrection, is the last trumpet blown by God at the end of the Church Age, but this does not preclude another last trumpet to terminate the tribulation, or even another last trumpet to end the millennium and gather all the unsaved for judgment at God's throne. Or, perhaps, one could infer that the "last day" will encompass over a thousand years (2 Peter 3:8), thus including all the resurrection events both before the tribulation, during the tribulation, after the tribulation, and after the millennium (Revelation 20:4-6) within its scope. By the same token, the last trump may not merely be one brief burst of sound, but a trumpet whose sound continues long, as did the divine trumpet on Sinai (Exodus 19:19), enduring throughout the entire duration of the thousand-year long "last day."

In any case, this passage certainly provides no justification for so-called "posttribulationists" and others to contend, as they do, that the "last trump" of 1 Corinthians is identical with the seventh trumpet of Revelation. The latter is sounded by an angel releasing great judgments, but the former is the mighty trump of God which raises the dead.

The sounding of the seventh trumpet is accompanied by a great chorus of voices at the heavenly throne rejoicing in the approaching climax of the Lamb's great work of reclamation. The earth which He created, and which He redeemed with His blood, will soon be His own once more, never to be lost again.

The testimony given by the voices in heaven anticipates and summarizes the results of the events set in motion by the seventh trumpet. Like the assurance that there would be no more delay (Revelation 10:6), so the ascription of eternal dominion in this verse looks forward to the ultimate fulfillment, in certainty that it will be accomplished and that the events which will assure it have now been inexorably set in motion.

Note the implied reference to Psalm 2, as quoted in Acts 4:26: "The kings of the earth stood up, and the rulers were gathered together against the Lord, and against his Christ" (Acts 4:26). The age-long rebellion of the kingdoms of this world against the Lord and His Christ has been allowed because God is long-suffering, desiring men to come to repentance rather than to judgment, but He is not eternally suffering! The time is coming soon when all these kingdoms will become His kingdoms, and He shall rule forevermore.

Revelation 11:16. **And the four and twenty elders, which sat before God on their seats, fell upon their faces, and worshipped God.**

The four and twenty elders had last been noted at the beginning of the tribulation (Revelation 5:14), and now again at its midpoint (the reference to them in Revelation 7:11 is looking forward to the end of the tribulation, with all the tribulation saints gathered in heaven).

As discussed earlier, these elders represent men and women who had been redeemed and raptured, believers of the ages prior to the return of Christ. During all the judgments of the first three-and-a-half years, the elders had remained seated on the thrones, intently observing events on earth. Just before the opening of the first seal on the great scroll, they had fallen on their faces to worship God (Revelation 5:14). Now once again they dismount their thrones, falling down on their faces to praise the Lord. This will happen once again at the end of the tribulation (Revelation 19:4).

207

Revelation 11:17.   Saying, We give thee thanks, O Lord God Almighty, which art, and wast, and art to come; because thou hast taken to thee thy great power, and hast reigned.

Even though the Lord is not yet literally reigning, the resurrection of His two witnesses has demonstrated beyond question, at least to those in heaven, that He has power to do so. The last great judgments, irrevocably inaugurated by the blowing of the seventh trumpet, will certainly accomplish His purposes. The elders and all the saints in heaven acknowledge Him again as the Almighty One, the only self-existing God, the one who alone has been God from eternity, before the world was.

And this God, of course, is none other than the Lord Jesus Christ. The same identity, in the same terminology, was claimed by the glorified Christ at the beginning of John's encounter with Him (Revelation 1:4, 8). The one on the heavenly throne had also been described in the same terms by the four cherubim (Revelation 4:8).

The term "reigned" is better rendered "shown thyself as king." Christ at this point has not yet actually taken the earthly kingdoms and inaugurated His millennial reign, but He has demonstrated Himself to be the eternal and omnipotent Creator, and therefore absolute sovereign of all.

Revelation 11:18.   And the nations were angry, and thy wrath is come, and the time of the dead, that they should be judged, and that thou shouldest give reward unto thy servants the prophets, and to the saints, and them that fear thy name, small and great; and shouldest destroy them which destroy the earth.

Seven great events are thus anticipated by the elders as they worship on their faces before Christ, the Almighty Lord:
1. He has displayed His mighty power over all creation;
2. He has demonstrated Himself to be king of all kings;
3. He has observed the implacable anger of all nations against Himself;
4. He has manifested His righteous wrath against all those living in rebellion;
5. He has prepared the final judgment for all the unsaved dead;
6. He has provided a gracious reward for all who believe and obey Him;
7. He has ordained eternal destruction for all who have corrupted the earth.

This is the same Lord Jesus who was meek and lowly (Matthew 11:29) and from whose lips proceeded words of grace (Luke 4:22). But He is also the one to whom all judgment is committed (John 5:22) and who will tread the great winepress of the wrath of God (Revelation 14:19, 20; 19:15).

The nations have all sealed their rejection of Christ by willfully yielding their own sovereignty to His greatest enemy, the beast, the one who executed His two witnesses (see Revelation 13:7; 17:13). Though there may be still some hope of snatching individuals from the fire, as it were, the nations as such have all passed far beyond the point of no return and can only experience now "a certain fearful looking for of judgment and fiery indignation, which shall devour the adversaries" (Hebrews 10:27).

The time (or "season") of the dead, when they will be raised for judgment, is not to be consummated for a thousand years (Revelation 20:11-15), but the time is set and the judgment sure. The rewards for His prophets, and the saints, and for all who fear His name, have in some measure already been given at the judgment seat of Christ (Romans 14:10-12; 1 Corinthians 3:11-15; 2 Corinthians 5:10) which followed the rapture, but there are still tribulation saints and millennial saints who are to be rewarded, possibly at or near the end of the tribulation and the end of the millennium, respectively.

It is significant that special attention is called to the judgment of those who "destroy the earth." God's first great commandment to mankind had included an injunction to "subdue the earth" (Genesis 1:28). Man was to exercise dominion over all the earth, but this was to be a dominion of stewardship and service—not one of despotism and exploitation. Adam and his descendants were to organize and utilize the creation for man's benefit and God's glory.

Furthermore, this great commission had been renewed to Noah after the Flood, and it has never been withdrawn. Mankind is still responsible under God and this primeval mandate to exercise proper stewardship over the earth and all God's creation.

But instead, men have all but destroyed the earth. Instead of caring for the animals and plants committed to his dominion, man has become their enemy, and many kinds have been exterminated. Wars have devastated the forests and scorched the lands. Human greed has yielded polluted waters and noxious air. Nutrients have been leached from the soils and lands have been overcultivated and overgrazed. Landscapes have been blighted with open mines and urban slums.

All of these deteriorative processes have even been hastened by God's judgments on man's sin. The great Flood, for example, had not only demolished the ideal antediluvian environment which God had created for man's use, but had left behind tremendous numbers of dead plants and animals in the thick sediments deposited by the deluge. Many of these had, as a result of intense heat and pressure, been converted through various physical and chemical processes, into materials which, in the latter centuries of man's occupation of earth, would be burned as his fuels. These so-called "fossil fuels" are notoriously inefficient and pollution-generating, for God had certainly not created at least His animals for such purposes.

Worst of all had been man's wickedness, both to his fellowman and against God. The word "destroy" is the same, actually, as "corrupt." Man had destroyed the earth by corrupting the earth, using it not for God's glory, but instead to satisfy his own greed and lust. Therefore God must finally destroy the destroyers and corrupt the corrupters. "He that is unjust, let him be unjust still," he will say; "and he which is filthy, let him be filthy still" (Revelation 22:11). For it is He who "is able to destroy both soul and body in hell" (Matthew 10:28).

Revelation 11:19.   And the temple of God was opened in heaven, and there was seen in his temple the ark of his testament: and there were lightnings, and voices, and thunderings, and an earthquake, and great hail.

John's attention is still directed heavenward, where he has just heard the praises of the twenty-four elders bowing before the throne. Shortly before, however, the Lord had called his attention to the earthly temple in Jerusalem (Revelation 11:1-2) which now had been completely taken over by the beast for his own uses.

It is in this context that John first sees (or at least writes about) the temple in heaven. He had noted the throne and the sea of glass (Revelation 4:6) as well as the altar (Revelation 6:9; 8:3-5). He had also made reference to the future service which would be rendered by the tribulation saints in the heavenly temple (Revelation 7:15). Here, however, he first calls attention to the temple itself and to its chief component, the holy place.

That there is indeed a temple in heaven is confirmed in both Old and New Testaments. Isaiah the prophet saw it in his vision (Isaiah 6:1), and the writer of Hebrews makes it clear that the earthly tabernacle (and, later, Solomon's temple) had been patterned after "the true tabernacle, which the Lord pitched, and not man" (Hebrews 8:2). The service of the priests in the temple on earth were "unto the example and shadow of heavenly things" (Hebrews 8:5). The sacrifices on the earthly altar were mere types of the one sacrifice for sins forever on the heavenly altar, for it was "necessary that the patterns of things in the heavens should be purified with these; but the heavenly things themselves with better sacrifices than these. For Christ is not entered into the holy places made with hands, which are the figures of the true; but into heaven itself, now to appear in the presence of God for us" (Hebrews 9:23, 24).

This is a real physical temple, in a real physical city, where Christ now appears in His real physical, glorified resurrection body. The city, with its temple, had been brought with Him by Christ when He "descended from heaven" (1 Thessalonians 4:16) to resurrect and rapture His saints into His presence there.

And, like the earthly temple when the price for sin had finally been paid (Matthew 27:51; Hebrews 10:19-20), the very holiest place in the inner heart of the temple is now opened, in the heavenly temple as well.

There, in the holy of holies, where God Himself dwells (and where He met with the high priest in the earthly tabernacle), John saw an amazing thing. There was the ark of the covenant! The ark was the most sacred aspect of the temple, for it was there that God could commune with His people, above the mercy seat which covered the ark, between the overshadowing cherubim. Within the ark was a pot of manna, and Aaron's rod, and (most importantly) the two tables of God's law (Hebrew 9:3-5).

The ark of the covenant disappeared when Nebuchadnezzar destroyed the temple and carried Judah captive into Babylon 600 years before Christ. At that time "all the vessels of the house of God, great and small, and the treasures of the house of the Lord" were also taken to Babylon (2 Chronicles 36:18), as were the brass and other metals that adorned the temple (2 Kings 25:13-20). No mention, however, was made of the ark, the most important and perhaps most costly (the ark was overlaid with pure gold, and the mercy seat and cherubim were of pure gold) item in the temple, as well as certainly the most significant item to the writers of the accounts in 2 Kings, 2 Chronicles, and Jeremiah (chapter 52, as well as the book of Lamentations). Neither was there any mention of the ark when Cyrus commissioned the rebuilding of the temple and sent back all its vessels as well (Ezra 1:1-11).

It seems impossible that God would have allowed the ark to be destroyed. When it was captured earlier by the Philistines, in the days of Samuel, Saul, and David, God saw that it was providentially kept for almost a hundred years until David finally returned it to the tabernacle in Jerusalem (1 Samuel 4:4, 11, 22; 1 Chronicles 15:28; 16:1).

Men through the centuries have been almost as intrigued with the search for the ark of the covenant as they have with the search for Noah's ark. The ark was not in the restoration temple, nor the temple of Herod, nor in the tribulation temple. Neither is there any mention of it even in the millennial temple described in Ezekiel 40—48. People have rumored it is preserved somewhere in a cave in Ethiopia, or in the Arabian desert, or somewhere else.

But there is no mystery as to where it is. God showed John, when He revealed to him the Apocalypse, that it was safely stored in the heavenly temple. No doubt the two tables of the Ten Commandments are there as well. If God could translate Enoch and Elijah to heaven, and if the resurrected Christ could ascend to heaven, He would be quite able to have an angel remove the ark from Jerusalem before Nebuchadnezzar's armies sacked the temple, and then have him carry it safely to the true tabernacle in the New Jerusalem under construction in heaven.

And there it will remain, until after the millennium, when the New Jerusalem (which itself is the true tabernacle—Revelation 21:3) will descend from God out of heaven to the earth. Since the city is itself a tabernacle, and especially "the Lord God Almighty and the Lamb are the temple of it" (Revelation 21:22), there will be no temple within the city. But the ark of God's covenant will be there, with its mercy seat possibly constituting His very throne, or at least representing the throne whereon He will meet with His people forevermore.

Accompanying this grand revelation once again are manifested lightnings and voices and thunderings in heaven, accompanied by a great earthquake and hailstorm on earth. These heavenly phenomena occur at the beginning of the tribulation (Revelation 4:5), here at the middle of the tribulation, and finally at the end of the tribulation (Revelation 16:18).

The great storm and earthquake that occur at this time presumably affect the whole earth, supplementing the earthquake in Jerusalem at the resurrection of the two witnesses. The latter had pronounced a three-and-a-half-year drought on the earth, and the inhabitants had cried for rain. But the drought is broken instead with a great hail. The angels who had restrained the winds and rains suddenly release them as the witnesses return to heaven, resulting in a terrible storm on earth which still further testifies of God's power and His wrath against all ungodliness of men.

12

The Conflict of the Ages

(Revelation 12)

This chapter begins the second half of the Book of Revelation, just as it marks also the beginning of the second half of the tribulation period, the final three-and-a-half years before the coming of Christ to the earth to reign in power and great glory. The trumpet of the seventh presence-angel has sounded, and its echo will continue to resound throughout this last awful period, the great tribulation.

The Seed of the Woman

However, the remarkable vision seen by John in this chapter looks back first of all to the very beginning of earth history, then races forward to the time of Christ and finally to the events still to be consummated in this final period. This review was necessary for John (and for us) to comprehend the full significance of the great sign about to be unveiled.

Revelation 12:1.   And there appeared a great wonder in heaven; a woman clothed with the sun, and the moon under her feet, and upon her head a crown of twelve stars.

The word "wonder" is the same as "sign" in the Greek, John thus informing us that the immediate vision is symbolic rather than literal. No woman in the strict physical sense could be arrayed with the sun and standing on the moon.

It is significant, however, that John feels it necessary to call this fact to our attention even when its very description makes this fact amply obvious. Evidently he would imply that *most* of Revelation is to be taken literally. This chapter is figurative and plainly so, but John nevertheless is at special pains to mention it.

Furthermore, even when a passage in the Bible is intended to be understood figuratively, as in this case, there is always ample information, either in the immediate context or in the broader context of background Scripture, to enable us to discern its full meaning. The complete message of this great chapter is of such grand scope that it can only be fully appropriated and appreciated through this use of symbol.

In his vision, as John gazed toward the heavens, it seemed that the sun was the brilliant apparel of a beautiful woman. On her head, above the shining sun, was a circle of twelve stars, forming as it were a diadem for the woman. Low along the horizon appeared the moon, seeming to form a footstool for her feet.

Since the meaning of this sign is not explained in the context, we must look elsewhere in Scripture for its interpretation. There is, in fact, another "heavenly" woman mentioned in the New Testament—"Jerusalem which is above is free, which is the mother of us all" (Galatians 4:26). The specific connection of the sun and moon and twelve stars, however, is found elsewhere only in Joseph's dream (Genesis 37:9), where Joseph understood them as representing his father, mother, and eleven brothers, who would someday bow down to him.

Also, the nation Israel is occasionally represented in the Old Testament as a woman, sometimes as the symbolic "wife" of Jehovah (Isaiah 54:5, 6; Jeremiah 31:32; Hosea 2:19-23), and even as a woman in travail (Isaiah 66:7-9; Micah 4:10—5:3). Though none of these usages conform precisely to the symbology here in Revelation 12, they seem to suggest, when taken all together, that the woman seen by John may represent Israel, the true Israel, that is, the remnant in the nation that had believed God's promises and sought to obey His Word throughout their generations.

However, the subsequent emphasis on the seed of this woman would carry us back not just to the beginning of the nation of Israel (in Joseph's dream, the woman seems to have represented his mother Rachel, although Rachel was already dead at the time; actually, Rachel's sister Leah was the mother of Judah, from which tribe eventually came the Messiah), but back to the protevangelic promise in the garden of Eden itself. There God had predicted an agelong conflict between the Serpent and the Woman, and between the seed of the serpent and the seed of the woman (Genesis 3:15), and it is that conflict which is in view in this chapter.

The woman, therefore, includes Israel (the faithful remnant in Israel, that is) but must go beyond Israel, back to the beginning. Eve (not Rachel, or Jerusalem) is the true "mother of us all" in the physical sense, and it was concerning her that the protevangelic promise ("the seed of the woman will someday crush the head of the serpent") was given. The woman thus represents the whole body of believers. As the true Israel was symbolized as the wife of Jehovah and the true Church as the bride of Christ, so the great woman must represent all true believers, beginning with Eve herself.

Her clothing is the sun, with the moon under her feet. The glory of the sun is a picture of the glory of Christ, who is "the light of the world" (John 8:12). Believers are all to "cast off the works of darkness" and to "put on the armour of light"—that is to say, "put ye on the Lord Jesus Christ" (Romans 13:12, 14). Christ Himself is our glorious apparel, and this fact seems to be the primary meaning of the great symbol of the woman clothed with the sun.

By the same token, the moon under feet must represent the works of darkness which are cast off. The moon is not a true light, as is the sun, since it only counterfeits that light, not shining of itself but merely reflecting the sun's light. Whenever objects are depicted as "under the feet" in Scripture, they are represented as subjugated, trodden down, held in bondage (Psalm 91:13; 1 Corinthians 15:25).

Thus, the heaven-pictured woman in this verse seems most likely to picture the great body of the redeemed people of God through all ages. They have conquered the false "angel of light" (2 Corinthians 11:14), bruising him under their feet (Romans 16:20), and have hidden themselves in Christ's righteousness so that they "shine forth as the sun in the kingdom of their Father" (Matthew 13:43).

The twelve-starred crown on the woman's head seems to represent either the twelve tribes of Israel (Revelation 21:12) or perhaps their respective angels (angels often are called "stars" in Scripture) or else the twelve apostles of the Lamb (Revelation 21:14), or possibly both. Just as Christ had said the righteous would shine forth as the sun, so the angel had told Daniel that "they that turn many to righteousness [shall shine] as the stars for ever and ever" (Daniel 12:3).

The common interpretation that the woman of Revelation 12:1 is Israel is, thus, clearly too constricted an interpretation for the magnificent context in which this scene is placed. Israel is certainly included, but so are all the people of God throughout the ages, beginning with Eve herself.

Revelation 12:2.   And she being with child cried, travailing in birth, and pained to be delivered.

The original evangelical promise was made by God in the garden of Eden: "And I will put enmity between thee and the woman, and between thy seed and her seed; it shall bruise thy head, and thou shalt bruise his heel" (Genesis 3:15). These words were directed to Satan, that old serpent, the very one who is central in this chapter of Revelation. There was to be perpetual enmity between Satan and "the woman" (that is, *all* believing women), and between the serpent's seed (that is, all those who, like Cain, would reject God and His Word) and the woman's seed (that is, all those who, like Abel, would believe and therefore obey God and His Word, no matter the cost).

But someday there would come the prototype "seed of the serpent," one who would be the very incarnation of Satan, completely embodying the character of his father, the father of lies (John 8:44). He will be "that man of sin, the son of perdition" (2 Thessalonians 2:3), whose evil career is a major theme of the Book of Revelation.

The one who will conquer this final and greatest seed of the serpent will be the prototype and only perfect "seed of the woman," the Son of God, born not of the seed of man but born of the virgin. Before He can crush the head of the serpent, however, the serpent must wound His heel, and this conflict requires that He enter the human family through the divinely ordained process of conception and birth (in His unique case, of course, it would be by miraculous conception and virgin birth). It is this birth that is particularly in view in this great sign of the woman in the sky.

But the woman is not only the virgin Mary. This woman in the vision is womankind in general. Mary was merely representative of all godly women through the ages, any one of whom could as well have been chosen by God to serve as the vehicle for the entrance of His Son into human life. All such women have shared the curse of Eve, the sorrow and pain experienced in conception and childbirth (Genesis 3:16). Nevertheless, in submitting, through faith in God's promise, to this responsibility, believing women have been blessed abundantly "Notwithstanding [they] shall be saved in chidbearing, if they continue in faith and charity and holiness with sobriety" (1 Timothy 2:15).

In fact, in still another sense, this travailing woman pictures the whole creation, groaning under God's curse because of sin, but still certain of the fulfillment of God's promise of deliverance when the heaven-promised Deliverer would come: "Because the creature itself also shall be delivered from the bondage of corruption into the glorious liberty of the children of God. For we know that the whole creation groaneth and travaileth in pain together until now" (Romans 8:20-22). When she is delivered of the child, then she herself can ultimately be delivered.

God's gracious promise of the coming Savior, the seed of the woman, given to all mankind, had eventually to be fulfilled in a particular chosen nation, a chosen tribe, a chosen family, and finally a chosen woman. Thus the promise to the world became the promise to Israel, then to the tribe of Judah, then to the family of David, and ultimately to the virgin Mary. The same heavenly woman prefigures all of these.

All of these, therefore, must travail in pain before the seed is born, and the promised deliverance eventually accomplished. The nation Israel in particular will suffer: "Be in pain, and labour to bring forth, O daughter of Zion, like a woman in travail: for now shalt thou go forth out of the city, and thou shalt dwell in the field, and thou shalt go even to Babylon; there shalt thou be delivered; there the Lord shall redeem thee from the hand of thine enemies" (Micah 4:10). "But thou, Bethlehem Ephratah, though thou be little among the thousands of Judah, yet out of thee shall he come forth [note again the figure of birth in this promise to Judah and the city of David] unto me that is to be ruler in Israel; whose goings forth have been from of old, from everlasting. Therefore will he give them up, until the time that she which travaileth hath brought forth: then the remnant of his brethren shall return unto the children of Israel. And he shall stand and feed in the strength of the Lord, in the majesty of the name of the Lord his God; and they shall abide: for now shall he be great unto the ends of the earth" (Micah 5:2-4).

There is much depending on the birth of this glorious Son. Not only will He redeem and rule Israel, but He shall deliver the whole creation into glorious liberty. "For unto us a child is born, unto us a son is given: and the government shall be upon his shoulder: and his name shall be called Wonderful, Counsellor, The mighty God, The everlasting Father, The Prince of Peace" (Isaiah 9:6).

That Old Serpent

Revelation 12:3.   And there appeared another wonder in heaven; and behold a great red dragon, having seven heads and ten horns, and seven crowns upon his heads.

Here is yet another sign in heaven. This is another symbolic enactment which John must understand if he would comprehend fully the great cosmic drama which had been taking place in heaven and earth since the very foundation of the world. In the protevangelic promise of Genesis 3:15 were two principal characters—the woman and the serpent. Likewise the two great miraculous signs (the words "miracle" and "sign" are both *semeieon* in Greek, as is "wonder" in these verses) which John now observed in the heavens centered on, first the woman, then the serpent.

The serpent is identical with the great red dragon, of course (see verse 9), and there is no question that he represents Satan. The fabled dragon of antiquity appears in the New Testament only in the Book of Revelation, but is mentioned often in the Old Testament (Psalm 91:13; Isaiah 34:13) and was evidently considered a real animal. There is an increasing amount of scientific evidence today that the great reptiles known as dinosaurs survived into fairly modern times (some marine dinosaurs may even survive today in the inaccessible depths of the oceans and deep lakes of the world), and it is likely that these provided the prototype animal to which to relate the great symbol of Satan seen by John in the sky.

This dragon was fiery red in color, perhaps anticipating the flames of his ultimate destination. However, this dragon, or dinosaur, was no ordinary dragon. Like the Gorgon of Greek mythology, it was a hydra-headed serpent, and thus all the more fearsome. Its seven heads all wore crowns, indicating kingly power. These are later interpreted (Revelation 17:10) as seven kingdoms of the past. The ten horns are interpreted (Revelation 17:12) as ten kings of the end times. A somewhat similar vision was seen by Daniel, except that the beast of his vision had only one head with ten horns (Daniel 7:7, 20, 24).

For the identification of these kings and kingdoms, see the exposition of chapter 17. For the present, it is enough to say that they do represent the kingdoms of this world and that such kingdoms by and large are indeed under the domain of Satan. Since the number seven throughout Revelation is used to symbolize completeness, it would seem that this vision confirms that all Gentile kingdoms of past and present have been largely under the control of Satan. He is the one "which deceiveth the whole world" (verse 9).

This, of course, was the very claim of Satan when he tempted Christ. "And the devil taking him up onto an high mountain, shewed unto him all the kingdoms of the world in a moment of time. And the devil, said unto him, All this power will I give thee, and the glory of them: for that is delivered unto me; and to whomsoever I will I give it" (Luke 4:5, 6).

It is sobering to realize that all governments of men are ultimately controlled by the devil, even though God Himself ordained the powers that be (Romans 13:1) and commands Christians to submit to their ordinances (1 Peter 2:13). There have been many godly men in positions of political power and these have had a restraining influence. Furthermore, to the extent that a government is founded upon law rather than men, and to the extent that these laws are based on the laws of God as revealed in Scripture, to such an extent will the government be in conformity with God's purposes rather than Satan's. There have been periods in the history of Israel, as well as in the history of England, the United States, and other nominally Christian nations, when this seems to have been largely the case. Sad to say, however, Satan's claim was so nearly the full truth that Christ Himself did not bother to refute it. John also had said in his epistle: "We know that . . . the whole world lieth in wickedness" (1 John 5:19). Practically all the past kingdoms of the world, symbolized by the seven heads, and the ten main final kingdoms of the world, represented by the ten horns, are organically united with the guiding spirit of the great fiery dragon.

Revelation 12:4.   And his tail drew the third part of the stars of heaven, and did cast them to the earth: and the dragon stood before the woman which was ready to be delivered; for to devour her child as soon as it was born.

The dragon has not only controlled the nations of the earth. He has even dragged the stars of heaven down to the earth.

As John observed this amazing phenomenon, he no doubt recalled his Lord's words. "I beheld Satan as lightning fall from heaven" (Luke 10:18). With all his power, Satan was inevitably to be defeated, for God had already cast him out of heaven, and his fall was so rapid as to be compared to lightning.

This is also the scene behind Isaiah 14:12-15 ("How art thou fallen from heaven, O Lucifer, son of the morning!") and Ezekiel 28:16, 17 ("I will destroy thee, O covering cherub . . . I will cast thee to the ground."). It had long been known that Satan had a host of angels under his control. Christ Himself had spoken of "the devil and his angels" (Matthew 25:41). Here, for the first time, we learn that these satanic angels constituted a third of all the angels. That the stars in the sign correspond to the devil's angels is evident from verses 7-9. When Satan was cast to the earth out of his position at God's throne, the great host of angels who followed him in his rebellion were also forced to follow him out of heaven, thereby all becoming "the rulers of the darkness of this world" (Ephesians 6:12). They are now "the principalities and powers" who were "spoiled" at the cross by the Lord Jesus Christ (Colossians 1:14, 15).

When Satan was cast to the earth, he quickly gained victory over Eve but then God had pronounced his own coming destruction by the seed of the woman. This initiated an agelong effort by Satan to thwart the fulfillment of the prophecy, either by destroying any who could possibly be the promised seed as soon after birth as possible or else by preventing the birth altogether.

He implanted his own seed in Cain's heart, and then led Cain to kill Abel. "Cain . . . was of that wicked one, and slew his brother" (1 John 3:12). When Lamech made what seemed to be a Messianic prophecy concerning his son Noah (Genesis 5:29), Satan made a bold attempt to poison the whole human race with his own deadly seed. "The sons of God came in unto the daughters of men, and they bare children to them" (Genesis 6:4). The context of this remarkable passage indicates that this was a tremendous outbreak of demonic possession. Satan's angels were able to indwell and control the minds and bodies of great numbers of the antediluvian men and women and then also their progeny.

In Abraham's time, Satan was apparently able to prevent even the conception of the son promised to Abraham until God intervened miraculously. The events that almost destroyed Jacob and that caused the rejection of Jacob's first three sons and the slaying of Judah's first two sons are further examples. At the time of Moses' birth, Satan became bold enough to seek, through Pharaoh, to destroy all the male children in Israel. The many attempts of Saul and others on the life of David, the repeated efforts either to corrupt or destroy the successive kings of Judah and their families, and finally the almost-successful campaign of Haman to destroy the entire Jewish nation when they were in captivity in the days of Queen Esther were the continuation of Satan's efforts to destroy the line of the promised seed before He could come into the world.

In the days of Isaiah, the primeval promise concerning the woman's seed had been made crystal clear: "Behold, a virgin shall conceive, and bear a son, and shall call his name Immanuel" (Isaiah 7:14). Finally, at the promised time in the promised place through the promised family, the chosen virgin gave birth to the promised seed. As he had in the days of Moses, Satan once again undertook, this time through Herod, to find and slay the child by slaying all male children in the region of Bethlehem, hoping thereby "to devour her child as soon as it was born." As always he failed, since God cannot fail.

Many times, Satan attempted to destroy Christ before He could go to the cross. When he was unable to destroy His holiness at the temptation, he attempted again and again to slay Him, but always without success. But when the proper hour had come, Jesus went to the cross, "that through death he might destroy him that had the power of death, that is, the devil" (Hebrews 2:14).

Through all the ages, Satan had attempted to prevent this promised mission of the seed from its fulfillment, continually standing before every woman in the line of promise from Eve to Mary, seeking to slay her man-child before he could accomplish God's mission. His failure has made him more bitterly angry than ever, and he continues in every way he can to persecute the symbolic woman and all her seed.

Revelation 12:5.   And she brought forth a man child, who was to rule all nations with a rod of iron: and her child was caught up unto God, and to his throne.

That the primary fulfillment of this promise relates to Jesus Christ is clear from the reference here to Psalm 2:7-9: "The Lord hath said unto me, Thou art my Son; this day have I begotten thee. Ask of me, and I shall give thee the heathen for thine inheritance, and the uttermost parts of the earth for thy possession. Thou shalt break them with a rod of iron; thou shalt dash them in pieces like a potter's vessel." Since the nations will not willingly submit themselves to God and His Anointed One (Psalm 2:2), He will have to subdue them forcibly, and then to reign over them with a scepter of iron. He is again identified thus when He finally conquers them as the victorious King of kings. "And out of his mouth goeth a sharp sword, that with it he should smite the nations: and he shall rule them with a rod of iron" (Revelation 19:15).

As noted before, however, this promise applies also in a secondary sense to all who genuinely believe on Him and are therefore included among those who conquer with Him. "And he that overcometh, and keepeth my works unto the end, to him will I give power over the nations: And he shall rule them with a rod of iron; as the vessels of a potter shall they be broken to shivers: even as I received of my Father" (Revelation 2:26, 27). Even as the woman in the great sign-vision applies ultimately to all the people of God before the birth of Christ, especially the nation Israel, so the symbolic man-child is fulfilled not only in Christ Himself, but in all who would believe on His saving name and who, therefore, are "in Christ."

The child of the woman, instead of being devoured by the dragon, was caught up to the throne of God in heaven. This, no doubt, refers mainly to the resurrection and ascension of Christ, who "is set down at the right hand of the throne of God" (Hebrews 12:2).

However, the words "caught up" are the same precisely as those used in connection with the rapture of believers at the return of Christ, when we "shall be caught up together with them in the clouds to meet the Lord in the air" (1 Thessalonians 4:17). It is thus very likely that, as the man-child includes both Christ and those who are redeemed by Him, so the catching away of the man-child refers not only to Christ's ascension but also to the rapture and glorification of His saints. It presumably also includes the rapture of His two witnesses (Revelation 11:12) and possibly other tribulation saints.

Revelation 12:6.   And the woman fled into the wilderness, where she hath a place prepared of God, that they should feed her there a thousand two hundred and three-score days.

Following the ascension of Christ and the later destruction of Jerusalem by the Romans, the Jewish remnant fled toward the Dead Sea wilderness and the storied mass suicide at Masada. This could hardly represent the event described in this verse, however. Furthermore this prophecy still awaited future fulfillment in John's day. Since it follows the catching up of the man-child, the latter must include the rapture of the Church and probably also that of the two witnesses, as noted above. Thus the 1,260 days when the woman is in the wilderness must refer to the second half of the tribulation period. This interpretation is also supported by the fact that the intense persecution of the woman by the dragon must correspond to the forty-two months of totalitarian depotism by the beast (Revelation 13:5, 7).

The woman, representing as she does the people of God out of whom came Christ and His Church, must at this point in time symbolize Israel, since believers of earlier times, including the Church, are no longer in the world. The 144,000 sealed Israelites are possibly in view. There is also a great multitude from all nations who will be saved during the tribulation (Revelation 7:9, 14); most of these, however, will no doubt be martyred (Revelation 6:9-11; 13:15), and those who escape would hardly have been in Jerusalem.

It will be recalled that Israel had been granted authority to rebuild their ancient temple and to reestablish their ancient worship, through a seven-year covenant made with the leader of the western and Mediterranean nations, after the miraculous defeat of Gog and Magog (Russia and her followers) in their attempted invasion of Israel (see discussion in Chapter 6). However, this treaty was broken by that ruler after only half of the treaty period had expired. The worship in the temple was stopped, and the holy city was to revert to absolute Gentile rule for forty-two months, the unfinished term of the treaty (Revelation 11:2).

Even though the majority of Israelites had not yet accepted Christ as their Messiah, they *had* renounced their atheism and liberalism, returning to orthodox Judaism, believing in the Old Testament Scriptures and in the God of their fathers. Many, no doubt, will be seriously examining the New Testament and the claims of Christ at this time, as a result of the testimony of the 144,000 witnesses, who had already become Christians.

The sudden breaking of the covenant would surely generate intense anger against the beast, who had seemed like their friend and deliverer at first but had now become their opponent and persecutor. Resenting the worship of any god but himself, he had demanded that both Christians and orthodox Jews renounce their faith and yield worship and obedience to him only. This they will refuse to do, unleashing a bitter war of extermination against them.

As Jesus had warned long ago: "When ye therefore shall see the abomination of desolation, spoken of by Daniel the prophet, stand in the holy place. . . . Then let them which be in Judaea flee into the mountains: . . . For then shall be great tribulation, such as was not since the beginning of the world to this time, no, nor ever shall be" (Matthew 24:15-21). The "mountains" spoken of by Christ must obviously be the "wilderness" spoken of in Revelation. "The woman" is now the godly Jewish remnant in Jerusalem, probably including many new Jewish believers in Christ, and she must quickly flee to the wilderness to survive.

The wilderness and the mountains may be either in the Sinai or in the mountains of Transjordan, or both. The Transjordan area, south and east of the Dead Sea, embraces the area occupied in biblical times by the Moabites and Ammonites (descendants of Abraham's nephew Lot) and the Edomites (descendants of Jacob's brother Esau).

Some have suggested that the "wilderness" would be all the nations of the world in which the persecuted Jews could scatter and hide. No doubt there will be many Jews in other nations who will also be subjected to persecution; but the immediate context clearly refers to the people in Jerusalem and Israel itself, who had been participating in the restored temple worship. The urgency of Christ's command to flee as soon as the abomination of desolation stands in the holy place (that is, the idolatrous image set up in the temple for humanistic worship of the beast—see Chapter 13) indicates that they must flee immediately—no opportunity for plane reservations, packing belongings, or anything else. The nearest desert area they can reach will be their only opportunity for survival.

The most quickly attainable desert area would be across the Jordan and Dead Sea into the regions of ancient Moab, Ammon, and Edom; and there are some intimations in Scripture that this is where they will go. Daniel, for example, in describing the end-time campaigns of the marauding prince, notes that only these three countries will escape his devastating armies (Daniel 11:36-45). Isaiah indicates that the Israelite remnant will flee into Moab and Edom, mentioning Sela (same as modern Petra) as their headquarters (Isaiah 16:1-5). Petra is the famous rock city, visited by countless Holy Land tours, which was at one time the almost impregnable Edomite capital.

Wherever they will be, whether concentrated in one location such as Petra or scattered over these vast wilderness areas south and southeast of Jerusalem, these godly Israelites will be under God's special protection and will receive his special provision. Isaiah foresaw this time in these words: "Come, my people, enter thou into thy chambers, and shut thy doors about thee: hide thyself as it were for a little moment, until the indignation be overpast. For, behold, the Lord cometh out of his place to punish the inhabitants of the earth for their iniquity" (Isaiah 26:20, 21).

In the "waste howling wilderness," there is surely no food for a multitude of desolate Israelites to eat for three-and-a-half years. Nevertheless the Lord had fed several million of His people for forty long years in the desert once before, and He can do it again. The manna was called "angels' food" (Psalm 78:25) and, no doubt, angels will again be the instruments God uses in meeting this need.

War in Heaven

That angels are indeed intensely concerned with all these events on earth has been evident throughout the Book of Revelation. It is the devil and his angels who are bent on persecuting the woman; therefore, it is Michael and God's angels who will protect and feed her. It may well be that this conflict will precipitate the great battle described in the next passage.

Revelation 12:7.   And there was war in heaven: Michael and his angels fought against the dragon; and the dragon fought and his angels.

Even though Satan had long ago fallen from his exalted position at God's throne in heaven, he and his angels are still allowed to function as "the prince of the power of the air" (Ephesians 2:2) and as "the rulers of the darkness of this world," "spiritual wickedness in high places" (Ephesians 6:12). They roam and rule the earth's atmospheric heavens, with free access to all the kings and kingdoms of the world. They may still have access in some degree to the sidereal heavens, as suggested by their occasional designation in Scripture as "the host of heaven," a term also applied to the stars.

In particular, Satan himself has regular access to the very heaven of God's presence, appearing there as accuser against God's people on earth. The familiar scenes in Job 1:6-12 and 2:1-7 give graphic descriptions of Satan's direct activity in the function of our "adversary" (the meaning of "Satan") and "slanderer" (the meaning of "devil"). He is "the accuser of our brethren . . . which accused them before our God day and night" (verse 10). He also is shown appearing before God against Joshua the high priest (Zechariah 3:1, 2). Furthermore Satan is not the only fallen angel who, at least occasionally, appears in God's presence. There was a "lying spirit" there in the days of King Ahab, for example (2 Chronicles 18:18-22).

But this situation is now about to be ended. No longer will Satan and his host befoul the heavens. "The heavens are the Lord's" (Psalm 115:16). Satan and his angels have been allowed to continue there for thousands of years, by God's grace and for man's testing, but the time has come to expel them. This battle probably began when the Lord and His holy angels descended from heaven to set up His judgment seat in the atmospheric heavens where the demonic powers had held sway for ages (1 Thessalonians 4:16, 17; Revelation 4:2). Long before, when the archangel Michael had attempted to come to Daniel, he had encountered serious resistance from a satanic principality whom he called "the prince of Persia," also mentioning "the prince of Grecia" (Daniel 10:12, 13, 20). Almost certainly the devil and his angels would offer strong resistance (but unsuccessful) to the great rapture of believers and the translation of God's throne to Earth's atmosphere, and this great "war in heaven" would become more intense than ever when Satan makes a last-ditch effort to destroy Israel and any remaining earthly believers. God had allowed him to send forth his demonic hordes from the great abyss on to the earth for a time, but these also were gone now, and Satan must engage in direct warfare with the heavenly hosts of Michael.

Revelation 12:8.   And prevailed not; neither was their place found any more in heaven.

God could, of course, have destroyed Satan and his angels merely with a word, but He instead will allow His faithful angels to battle the wicked angels. Long restrained from this vengeance, Michael is finally permitted to enter into direct conflict with his ancient rival.

They had met before, not only in heaven but on earth. "Yet Michael the archangel, when contending with the devil he disputed about the body of Moses, durst not bring against him a railing accusation, but said, The Lord rebuke thee" (Jude 9). Now Satan's privileges in the three heavens are to be withdrawn, however, and he is to be limited exclusively to the earth. Michael and his angels are commissioned to carry out this great expulsion and purification of the heavens, and they will gladly and vigorously enter into the battle, anticipating the time when even earth itself will finally be purged.

With what weapons and by what tactics this heavenly warfare will be waged is beyond our understanding. Angels cannot be injured or slain with earthly weapons, and such physical forces as we know about are not able to move spiritual beings. But these beings do operate in a physical universe, so there must exist powerful physico-spiritual energies of which we yet can have only vague intimations, energies which can propel angelic bodies at superluminary velocities through space and which can move mountains and change planetary orbits. It is with such energies and powers that this heavenly battle will be waged and the spectators in heaven (including John) will watch in awe. When Michael finally prevails, and Satan is forced forever out of the heavens, a tremendous cry of thanksgiving will resound through the heavens.

Revelation 12:9.   And the great dragon was cast out, that old serpent, called the Devil, and Satan, which deceiveth the whole world: he was cast out into the earth, and his angels were cast out with him.

Appropriately enough, this is the very middle verse of the Book of Revelation, and the event it describes marks again the middle of the tribulation period. The rapture of the two witnesses, the breaking of the Jewish temple treaty by the beast, the flight of Israel, the casting out of Satan and the appropriation of world power by the beast must all occur within a few days of each other at this midpoint of the tribulation.

The repetition of the names and titles of the wicked one in this verse is striking —the great dragon, that old serpent, the Devil, Satan. There can surely be no doubt as to his identity. The old serpent in Genesis is the great dragon in Revelation, as well as the Satan who tested Job and the Devil who tempted Christ. He is the great enemy of God and of God's people through the ages. He often appears deceptively as an angel of light and a minister of righteousness (2 Corinthians 11:14, 15), but he is really a hissing snake, and a fiery dragon, and a devouring lion (1 Peter 5:8).

Note especially the amazing assertion that he has been the deceiver of the whole world. Educated and ignorant, king and pauper, male and female, Jew and Gentile, strong and weak, young and old, black and white—all are deceived by him. All the world's high-sounding philosophies, conceived ever so brilliantly by profound thinkers—whether pragmatism, idealism, gnosticism, determinism, hedonism, materialism, transcendentalism, existentialism, deism, or any of countless others, and regardless of the eminence of the geniuses with whose names they are associated—Aristotelianism, Platonism, Hegelianism, Marxism, Maoism, Confucianism, Buddhism, Kantianism, Freudianism—*all* are man-originated, man-centered, and man-honoring, rather than God-originated, God-centered, and God-honoring. They are all merely varieties of humanism, rather than theism, exalting man rather than God and thus helping to carry out Satan's attempt to dethrone God.

Furthermore, they are all based on a denial of God's Word as supreme—true and final. They assert man's reason in judgment upon God's Word. "Yea, hath God said . . . ?" was Satan's first deception, as he tempted Eve, and he has followed the same procedure ever since. If he can persuade men to question, to doubt, to modify, to allegorize, to compromise God's Word, and then finally to disobey, reject, and destroy God's Word, he will thereby defeat God's purposes in creation, and God Himself will then no more be God.

But how can he thus deceive the whole world into rejecting God's Word and believing the lie of humanism? The answer, clearly, is by persuading men that God is not the ultimate reality, and that the universe itself is the only eternal entity. Space, time, matter, energy, motion—these are the only eternal absolutes, and

225

all other systems (organic or inorganic, cosmic or atomic, physical or spiritual) are in a perpetual state of evolutionary flux, ever changing and always relative.

Thus all the beliefs and philosophies of men are humanistic philosophies, denying the absolutes of God and His Word, and all humanism is based on the grand deception of evolutionism. Small wonder that all religions and philosophies of men, ancient or modern, naive or sophisticated, are fundamentally evolutionary systems, the only exceptions being those based on God's Word, the Bible.

The Devil has effectively deceived the whole world, therefore, utilizing the same monstrous deception with which he has deceived himself. He apparently believes that, since matter is the only ultimate reality, rather than the God who claimed to have created him, he can somehow succeed in dethroning God and placing himself on God's throne. This is the conflict of the ages.

Revelation 12:10.   And I heard a loud voice saying in heaven, Now is come salvation, and strength, and the kingdom of our God, and the power of his Christ: for the accuser of our brethren is cast down, which accused them before our God day and night.

When the heavens are finally cleansed of all the demonic powers and Satan himself is gone, this will be the signal for a glad cry of victory from all the multitudes assembled at the throne in the heavens. Probably this very throne will have been the objective of the attack by hell's angels, since it was this throne that Satan coveted, but now it is fully secure and the attacking hosts are gone.

The coming of God's kingdom and the reign of Christ, already celebrated a number of times by the redeemed throng in heaven, is again the object of their thankful praise. This time probably the celebration is more exciting than ever, since it has been demonstrated in direct conflict that not only the omnipotent God but even the holy angels are able to defeat Satan and his legions. Truly Satan is a defeated foe.

A special object of thanksgiving is the fact that Satan no longer will have personal access to God, which privilege he has abused for ages by continual accusations against the redeemed. Of course, when such accusations are made (no doubt often justified in part, though probably also distorted and magnified), the Lord Jesus Christ is our intercessor and advocate (Hebrews 7:25; 1 John 2:1), and His blood is a perpetual offering and cleansing agent for our sins (1 John 1:7; 2:2). Nevertheless, Satan's repeated presence and disturbing charges against fellow believers still on earth constitute an intensive irritant in heaven, and great will be the exultation when he is finally deposed completely.

Revelation 12:11.   And they overcame him by the blood of the Lamb, and by the word of their testimony; and they loved not their lives unto the death.

The saints at the throne in heaven, perhaps recalling all of Christ's gracious promises to "him that overcometh" (see Chapters 2 and 3), gladly give their witness to the faithfulness of the suffering saints who had just lately been experiencing demonic persecution on earth and satanic accusation in heaven. "But they overcame the Accuser!" is their testimony.

As always, victory over sin and Satan had been achieved by the two-edged sword of faith and confession. The blood of the Lamb had been the necessary and sufficient price of their forgiveness and redemption, and they had believed and received this in their hearts. But that same Redeemer had also said they must confess this faith openly on earth, thus proving it to be genuine faith, before He would confess them as His own to His Father at the throne in heaven (Matthew 10:32, 33).

This is the testimony of many Scriptures. "If thou shalt confess with thy mouth . . . and believe in thine heart . . . thou shalt be saved" (Romans 10:9). "Let the words of my mouth, and the meditation of my heart, be acceptable in thy sight, O Lord, my strength, and my redeemer" (Psalm 19:14). "But sanctify the Lord God in your hearts: and be ready always to give an answer to every man that asketh you a reason of the hope that is in you with meekness and fear" (1 Peter 3:15).

Furthermore these tribulation saints (like many others through the ages) had maintained their inward faith and outward testimony even in the face of martyrdom. Satan's slanders against the saints become hollow (as did his accusations against Job) and empty when they prove the genuineness of their faith even in the presence of opposition and ridicule, of suffering and death.

Revelation 12:12.   Therefore rejoice, ye heavens, and ye that dwell in them. Woe to the inhabiters of the earth and of the sea! for the devil is come down unto you, having great wrath, because he knoweth that he hath but a short time.

While all those who have been translated to heaven can experience great joy at Satan's final exile from heaven, it will be a great woe for those on earth. Those who are already believers there, both Jews and Gentiles (as well as those Bible-believing Israelites who have yet to acknowledge Christ) will undergo the most severe persecutions to which Satan and his angels can subject them, seeking either to slay them in his bitter resentment and wrath or at least to eliminate their usefulness to God on earth. All the other inhabitants of earth he knows must be organized quickly into a massive army against God. His angelic hosts have proven insufficient, but there may be the one last chance that these can be supplemented with the two billion or more ungodly men and women still left on earth. It is a foolish and desperate hope, but it is all he has. Furthermore, he well knows that God's calendar has only allowed him another forty-two months, so his time is running out. The inhabitants of the earth and sea must be quickly sealed in their own rejection of God, both to assure his control over them and to cheat God of any further souls for His kingdom.

But who are the "inhabiters of the sea?" Actually the words "the inhabiters of" do not appear in the oldest manuscripts, though they are in the received text. However, the pronouncement of woe on the land and sea merely in their physical structures would seem pointless, so that their inhabitants are at least included by implication. In any case, it is likely that the term applies to the not inconsiderable number of people who spend most of their time on the sea (fishermen, merchant seamen, navy personnel, houseboat dwellers). Both boat people and land dwellers are the objects of Satan's wrathful purposes. This is the pronouncement of the third "woe" (compare Revelation 8:13; 9:14). Satan's wrath and the sounding of the seventh trumpet both persist throughout the entire second half of the tribulation. This verse is the middle verse, not of the entire Book of Revelation (verse 9), but of chapters 4 through 19, which are the chapters comprising the tribulation period.

Return to the Wilderness

Revelation 12:13.   And when the dragon saw that he was cast unto the earth, he persecuted the woman which brought forth the man child.

No longer able to combat his enemies in heaven, either human or angelic, Satan will seek to vent his wrath on Israel. It is he, no doubt, who constrains the beast to break the covenant with Israel and to insist that men worship the beast's own image, and it will be Satan who will instruct his man of sin to seek to destroy the Jews when they refuse.

The Jewish people have been persecuted longer than any other nation in history, and this last persecution will have the purpose of their complete and final destruction. God, however, will once again intervene on their behalf, and they will be protected there in their place in the wilderness. Furthermore, God will use this time for intensive instruction and reconciliation with His ancient people, preparing them to receive the Lord Jesus as their Messiah and Savior when He comes to the earth again at the end of their three-and-a-half-year exile: "Therefore, behold, I will allure her, and bring her into the wilderness, and speak comfortably unto her. . . . . And I will betroth thee unto me for ever; yea, I will betroth thee unto me in righteousness, and in judgment, and in lovingkindness and in mercies. . . . and I will say to them which were not my people, Thou art my people; and they shall say, Thou art my God" (Hosea 2:14-23).

Revelation 12:14.   And to the woman were given two wings of a great eagle, that she might fly into the wilderness, into her place, where she is nourished for a time, and times, and half a time, from the face of the serpent.

The urgency of the woman's flight is reiterated here. In order to escape the wrath of the beast, she required special help, "two wings of a great eagle." The meaning of this figure is not clear except that it implies miraculous help. There is probably an allusion to Exodus 19:4. "Ye have seen what I did unto the Egyptians, and how I bare you on eagles' wings, and brought you unto myself." In this case, the figure certainly refers to the many miracles by which the Lord brought Israel out of Egypt. Thus the "eagle" symbol is appropriate for the angelic ministers who undoubtedly were involved in these miracles. Likewise here, the fleeing woman will be aided by miraculous protection afforded by an angelic eagle.

Once she reaches her place prepared by God, she will be "nourished" (same word as "feed" in verse 6), and this no doubt will also require miraculous provision. The duration ("time and times and half a time") is clearly the same period as the 1,260 days of verse 6. Thus a "time" in prophecy means a year. The use of this unusual terminology here is probably for the purpose of tying it in to Daniel 7:25 and 12:7, where the same terminology appears, also referring to the second half of the tribulation.

The Jewish remnant symbolized by the woman is kept secure in a definite place prepared for them by God. Whether this place is Petra, as some think, is not all certain, since it is not specifically named. However, it is known to the serpent (and, therefore, to the beast), as the woman is nourished in the very "face of the serpent." Try as he will Satan is unable to reach and destroy the woman in the wilderness.

Revelation 12:15.   And the serpent cast out of his mouth water as a flood after the woman, that he might cause her to be carried away of the flood.

Not able to reach the woman directly, the serpent resorts to long-range artillery, as it were, shooting forth a "river" from his mouth with which to flood her out of her haven. Again, the symbol is somewhat ambiguous. It can hardly be a literal river, since it comes from the symbolic "mouth" of the symbolic "serpent."

The most probably meaning of the sign is that of an overwhelming army dispatched by the beast, as instigated by the serpent. This would be the obvious reaction of the irate dictator when the Jews suddenly flee Jerusalem, and such a meaning is also consistent with the use of the same figure of speech in the Old Testament. For example, when the Egyptian armies came against Babylon, Jeremiah said: "Egypt riseth up like a flood, and his waters are moved like the rivers; and he saith, I will go up, and will cover the earth; I will destroy the city and the inhabitants thereof" (Jeremiah 46:8). Note also Jeremiah 47:2 and Daniel 11:26.

Whatever the meaning of the figure, Satan will mount what would seem to be an invincible attack against the godly remnant of Israel in their desert stronghold.

But God is equal to the need. "When the enemy shall come in like a flood, the Spirit of the Lord shall lift up a standard against him" (Isaiah 59:19). "If it had not been the Lord who was on our side, now may Israel say . . . Then the waters had overwhelmed us, the stream had gone over our soul; Then the proud waters had gone over our soul. Blessed be the Lord, who hath not given us as a prey to their teeth" (Psalm 124:1-6).

Revelation 12:16. And the earth helped the woman, and the earth opened her mouth, and swallowed up the flood which the dragon cast out of his mouth.

With all his wrath and all his cleverness and all his power, the old dragon cannot reach one who is under God's protection, for "greater is he that is in you, than he that is in the world" (1 John 4:4). The overflowing horde of men and weapons sent after the Jews in the wilderness by the beast (if that, indeed, is what the river from the serpent's mouth depicts), though infinitely superior to the unarmed refugees in might, is utterly unable to conquer them or even to reach them. A great chasm will open in the earth, already trembling and unstable from the worldwide earth movements of the tribulation period, and swallow them up.

Such a terrestrial miracle is quite appropriate in the context. The whole situation is analogous to the pursuit of the children of Israel by Pharaoh at the time of Exodus. When the Egyptian armies were drowned in the Red Sea, Miriam sang of the deliverance in these words: "Thou stretchest out thy right hand, the earth swallowed them" (Exodus 15:12). Not long afterward, a dangerous rebellion was thwarted thus, "And the earth opened her mouth, and swallowed them up . . . and the earth closed upon them" (Numbers 16:32, 33).

Whatever the exact fulfillment of this prophecy may entail, it is calamitous and devastating to the purposes of the beast and the dragon. By the same token, their miraculous deliverance and sustenance will be traumatically persuasive to the Jewish men and women, trembling in their place of refuge.

"As I live, saith the Lord God, surely with a mighty hand, and with a stretched out arm, and with fury poured out, will I rule over you: . . . And I will bring you into the wilderness of the people, and there will I plead with you face to face. Like as I pleaded with your fathers in the wilderness of the land of Egypt, so will I plead with you, saith the Lord God. And I will cause you to pass under the rod, and I will bring you into the bond of the covenant" (Ezekiel 20:33-37).

As the forty years in the wilderness prepared the people of Israel in olden times to enter the land of Canaan, so these three-and-a-half years in the wilderness will make them ready to receive Christ and enter the glorious kingdom age of the millennium.

But, although this Jewish remnant is to be the nucleus of the millennial kingdom of Israel, there are many other believers (or potential believers) still scattered around in all the nations of the world. These are also of concern both to the dragon and to the Lord.

Revelation 12:17.   And the dragon was wroth with the woman, and went to make war with the remnant of her seed, which keep the commandments of God, and have the testimony of Jesus Christ.

When the dragon cannot reach the woman herself (and certainly he can no longer touch the true seed, Jesus Christ), he will direct his full wrath against "the remnant of her seed." Thus, his age-long vendetta against "the seed of the woman" (Genesis 3:15) will continue right to the very end of the age and his final incarceration in the lake of fire.

When the Jews flee Jerusalem into the wilderness at the midpoint of the tribulation, there will undoubtedly be many who remain behind. Some will prefer compromise, some will be unaware of the danger or ignorant of the Scriptures, and some will simply be unable to flee for one reason or another. In any case, there will be considerable numbers of Israelis who will continue to live in Jerusalem and other parts of Israel; and these also are referred to in a number of biblical prophecies. Furthermore, there will still be many Israelites in other nations, and these too are included in the prophecies. All of these will undergo severe persecution at the end-times, by virtue of being Jews, and for refusing the mark of the beast.

It is remarkable that such a small and apparently insignificant nation as Israel could be the focus of so much attention and concern from all the great nations of the world. It is equally remarkable that the Israelites who have been scattered around the nations of the world for thousands of years still retain their national identity and still feel tht the land of Israel is their home land.

Even today world attention is focused on Israel, as well as on world Jewry. In the imminent prophetic future, as already discussed (Chapter 6) is the invasion of Israel by Russia, followed by the catastrophic defeat of Russia and the resulting rise of the western alliance (NATO and the Common Market) into a state of world preeminence. Even then, attention will still center on Israel, and a prominent leader of this alliance (soon identified also as the beast, the man of sin, the Antichrist, the final world dictator before the triumph of Christ) will make his seven-year treaty with Israel, then break it at its midpoint. Many Jews will have returned to Israel in the first three-and-a-half years, but many will still be scattered. And wherever they are, the beast will seek to persecute them, and God will thereby chastise them, in hopes they can be delivered from their unbelief and finally brought to acknowledge the Lord Jesus as their Messiah and Savior.

Many Scriptures deal with their great tribulation and final restoration. For example, Jeremiah says: "For, lo, the days come, saith the Lord, that I will bring again the captivity of my people Israel and Judah, saith the Lord: and I will cause them to return to the land that I gave to their fathers, and they shall possess it. ... Alas! for that day is great, so that none is like it: it is even the time of Jacob's trouble, but he shall be saved out of it. ... For I am with thee, saith the Lord, to save thee: though I make a full end of all nations whither I have scattered thee, yet will I not make a full end of thee: but I will correct thee in measure, and will not leave thee altogether unpunished" (Jeremiah 30:3-11).

Note also many other Scriptures to this effect (Leviticus 26:40-45; Deuteronomy 30:1-5; Isaiah 11:10-16; 27:6-13; Jeremiah 23:3-8; 31:7-11; 32:37-41; Ezekiel 34:11-16; 36:22-28; and Daniel 12:1). In fact, great portions of the books of the Old Testament prophets, especially Isaiah, deal with the sufferings and promised blessings of the scattered remnants of Israel during the tribulation period.

Apparently there will also be many Gentiles in the nations of the world who will become believers during this period. Revelation 7:9-14 speaks of a great multitude from all nations who come out of the great tribulation and will then be martyred during its second half. Some will survive, however, and will constitute the remnant who will populate the millennial world when Christ returns.

All of these, also, are included among the seed of the woman, with whom the dragon will engage in mortal combat during the last three-and-a-half years—the great tribulation. It is these who "keep the commandments of God, and have the testimony of Jesus Christ." The old serpent—as well as the beast, the serpent's seed, and all his other multitudes of demonic followers and human spiritual progeny—hate these people with diabolic passion, making war on them in unremitting intensity and ferocity.

But despite all such persecutions, they love not their lives unto death, maintaining "the testimony of Jesus Christ" and seeking to "keep the commandments of God." Some modern Christians, who carry dispensational distinctions to an extreme, would suggest that keeping God's commandments somehow mitigates against a testimony for Christ and salvation by grace, but these tribulation saints certainly find the two compatible, even in the most difficult circumstances that godly men and women will ever have to endure.

13

The Unholy Trinity

(Revelation 13)

This is another key chapter of the Revelation, describing the rise of two ungodly men who will play two extremely important roles in the climactic events of the end-times, epitomizing all the cleverness and wickedness of the long succession of tyrannical leaders before them, from Nimrod to Nero to Mao Tsc-tung. They are both called "beasts" in this chapter, though later the second is also called "the false prophet." Both receive their brilliance and power from Satan, the old dragon. Many writers have noted the parallel between this unholy trio and the divine Trinity. The dragon, the beast, and the false prophet seem almost intentionally to be counterfeiting the Father, Son, and Holy Spirit, respectively. In any case, these three willfully and maliciously pull out all stops in their last-ditch efforts to dethrone God and destroy His saints.

The Man of Sin

The first of these wicked men has, of course, already been mentioned in Revelation. God's two witnesses had been slain by the beast (Revelation 11:7), leading to his assumption of full power for the last forty-two months of the tribulation (Revelation 11:2; 13:5). He is mentioned often in earlier prophetic passages also. Daniel calls him "the prince that shall come" (Daniel 9:26), Isaiah calls him "the wicked" (Isaiah 11:4), and Christ called him "the abomination of desolation" (Matthew 24:16). The Apostle Paul designated him as "the man of sin, the son of perdition" (2 Thessalonians 2:3), perhaps the most definitive of all his titles.

Revelation 13:1.   And I stood upon the sand of the sea, and saw a beast rise up out of the sea, having seven heads and ten horns, and upon his horns ten crowns, and upon his heads the name of blasphemy.

John's gaze had been fixed, as it were, on the two great signs in the heavens, the sign of the woman and the sign of the dragon, watching the agelong conflict between them. Now, however, it seems as though he were standing on the sands of the seashore, observing a third great sign, this time on the sea. Even though the word "sign" is not used on this occasion, the whole context makes it evident that the scene is symbolic. The continuity with the sign of the dragon is evident by comparison of the description of the dragon "having seven heads and ten crowns and seven horns" (Revelation 12:3), with the description of the beast here in Revelation 13:1.

The beast rising out of the sea is not the same as the dragon, however, even though their appearances are similar. The dragon is Satan (Revelation 12:9), whereas the beast is a man (Revelation 13:8). Nevertheless the similarity is very significant, evidently stressing the similar character and purposes and activities of the beast and the dragon. In fact, the former is specifically said to have received his power and throne and authority from the latter (verse 2).

If the beast from the sea is symbolic, then the sea also must be symbolic. Usually the sea in Scripture, if not more specifically identified, is the great sea west of Israel, that is, the Mediterranean Sea. John sees what appears to be a great monster of the sea, like a hyra-headed plesiosaur, arising out of the depths of this great sea near the shore on which he stands.

Perhaps at first the similarity of the beast to the dragon would make John think of Isaiah's prophecy, where the Scripture speaks of "leviathan, the piercing serpent, even leviathan that crooked serpent . . . the dragon that is in the sea" (Isaiah 27:1). But then, as he looks more closely, he sees that the beast is not a reptile at all, but rather what appears to be a strange hybrid land mammal of some kind. A land mammal ascending from the Mediterranean Sea could only speak of some powerful personage emerging from the peoples of the Mediterranean lands, with the hybrid characteristics of the beast suggesting that he is somehow a product of all of them.

The obvious similarity of this frightful beast to the beasts in Daniel's vision is sufficient confirmation that the "sea" here represents the peoples of the lands around the sea (compare Daniel 7:3 and 7:17). Although the seven heads and ten horns clearly relate the beast to the dragon, the hybrid animal body just as surely identifies him with the four beasts of Daniel 7.

Daniel's vision consisted of four beasts representing four great nations striving for supremacy. The first was like a lion, the second a bear, the third a leopard, the fourth an unnamed animal, but very strong. It is the last animal (Daniel 7:7) that seems to be the same as the beast of Revelation 13:1, the key point of identification being its ten horns.

Both the four nations of Daniel 7 and the seven heads and ten horns of Revelation 13 seem obviously to entail a complex of nations and leaders under the domination of the great blasphemer Satan. On each head, therefore, is emblazoned an unnamed name, designed solely to exalt man as a god, thereby blaspheming the true God.

Revelation 13:2.   And the beast which I saw was like unto a leopard, and his feet were as the feet of a bear, and his mouth as the mouth of a lion: and the dragon gave him his power, and his seat, and great authority.

John would remind us again that he was actually witnessing this important sign as it developed. Though he does not mention it, it does become more obvious that the beast he sees is, at least in part, a composite of the beasts Daniel saw. With a leopard's body, a bear's feet, and a lion's mouth, this beast clearly partakes of the natures of Daniel's beasts. Thus, to understand the one, we must first understand the others.

It is usual to interpret the four beasts of Daniel 7 as the historical empires of Babylonia, Medo-Persia, Greece, and Rome, in order. This corresponds precisely to the meaning of the four parts of the image of Nebuchadnezzar's dream, in Daniel 2. Practically all Bible scholars agree on this, and the contextual chapters in Daniel confirm it at least as far as the first three empires are concerned, and as far as Nebuchadnezzar's image is concerned.

However, there are difficulties in applying the same interpretation to the beasts of Daniel 7. Although they do appear in order, the four beasts seem to be contemporaneous rather than sequential. The four appear first in correspondence to the parallel statement: "Behold, the four winds of the heaven strove upon the great sea" (Daniel 7:2). Furthermore, all four beasts continue to strive with each other to the end; in fact, the lives of the first three beasts "were prolonged for a season and a time" after the fourth beast had "his body destroyed, and given to the burning flame" (Daniel 7:11, 12). Finally all four beasts were still future at the time of Daniel's writing (Daniel 7:17), even though at that time Babylonia had already fallen and Medo-Persia had come into dominance.

Thus it seems probable that the four beasts of Daniel 7 represent four great kingdoms (or, possibly, confederations), one each from the north, south, east, and west, like the four winds striving over the sea. The beast of the west (the lion with eagles' wings) might, for example, represent the British lion and the American eagle, or the western alliance in general. The second is a great devouring bear, which could well be the Russian colossus and her communist satellites. The third is a four-headed, four-winged leopard, possibly symbolizing a future eastern alliance (Revelation 16:12 prophesies the coming of "the kings of the east" and Daniel 11:44 speaks of troublesome "tidings out of the east"). The leopard is the most wide ranging of the great carnivores and is yellow with black spots. The fourth beast, evidently unidentifiable in terms of animals known to Daniel, was "dreadful and terrible, and strong exceedingly," eventually dominating the other three beasts. It would then, presumably, as the "south wind," represent the Mediterranean nations themselves, occupying roughly the territory of the old Roman empire, both north and south of the Mediterranean Sea. It was "diverse from all the beasts that were before it [literally, 'confronting it']" and soon would conquer and assimilate the others, at least to a degree.

It is apparently this last beast that John sees emerging from the sea. By this time (the middle of the tribulation) this beast—*the* beast—had sufficiently subjugated the others that his body appears as a hybrid of all of them. He is part lion, part bear, part leopard, but also part dragon.

It was not by his own strength or his own strategy that the beast has come into such a position of world eminence. It is none other than Satan himself who has given him his great might and his throne and preeminent rulership over the other nations. How he will acquire such authority, humanly speaking, is only intimated in Scripture. Probably, he will seize the advantage of the leadership void left by the catastrophic defeat of Russia in Israel and the insipid response of the western nations to the Russian invasion (see discussion in Chapter 6). In any case, it is his dark league with Satan that really opens the way for him, the Devil making him appear so attractive as a world leader that other kings and presidents willingly submit to his authority in the stressful times just before and during the first half of the tribulation period.

The beast, as did the dragon who empowered him, was seen by John to have seven heads and ten horns. However the dragon had seven crowns upon his seven heads (Revelation 12:3) whereas the beast had ten crowns upon his seven heads (Revelation 13:1). During the long centuries corresponding to the sign of the dragon, there had been seven great kings, but the kings represented by the ten horns were still future and still uncrowned. In the time of the beast, the ten kings were now ruling, whereas the seven ancient kings survived only in their evil heritage.

That these seven heads represent seven historical kingdoms is indicated also in Revelation 17:9-11, where the beast again appears. The identity of these kingdoms is not specified, but it seems reasonable that they should be seven great world powers of past history. It is also probable that they represent the seven great powers that came into particular opposition to the plan of God as it was unfolding throughout history, as recorded in Scripture. Since the symbol assures their connection with the dragon, and since that old serpent has been perpetually attempting to thwart the divine program, we would expect to find these histories at least referenced in the Bible.

With these considerations in mind, the most likely identification of these seven historical kingdoms is as follows:

1. **Sumeria.** Under Nimrod, Babel in the land of Shinar became the first postdiluvian center of human rebellion.

2. **Egypt.** This ancient nation was Israel's first oppressor, leading to God's supernatural deliverance under the hand of Moses.

3. **Assyria.** The invading armies of Pul, Tiglath-Pileser, Shalmanezer, and Sennacherib devastated the land of Israel and carried the people of the northern kingdom into captivity.

4. **Babylonia.** Under Nebuchadnezzar, the later Babylonians revived Nimrod's empire and destroyed Jerusalem and its temple, carrying the people of Judah into captivity. Throughout Scripture, therefore, "Babylon" is synonymous with enmity to God, and Satan himself is adumbrated under the title "king of Babylon" (Isaiah 14:4-17).

5. **Medo-Persia.** As prophesied by Daniel (Daniel 2:39; 5:28), the Medo-Persian empire succeeded Babylonia in world dominance, and was the nation under which the Jews would have been exterminated by Haman, except for providential intervention through Queen Esther. It was also the nation which allowed them to return from their captivity.

6. **Greece.** Daniel also prophesied (Daniel 2:39; 8:21; 11:2, 3) that Greece would supersede the Persians, and this occurred under Alexander the Great. The Greek language became the language of the New Testament and Greek philosophy has dominated the Judaeo-Christian world ever since.

7. **Rome.** The greatest of the seven empires politically was Rome, which ruled at the time of Christ, and which destroyed the temple in A.D. 70, sending the Jews into their age-long dispersion. The Roman emperors, especially Nero, also severely persecuted the early Christians.

The above suggested identifications are not intended dogmatically, as there have been other great nations or groups of nations in history that have opposed either Israel or Christianity or both (Syria and Tyre before Christ, the Islamic Nations, Nazi Germany, Russia, and other Communist nations after Christ). In terms of their biblical emphasis, however, the seven mentioned above seem most probably the ones symbolized by the seven heads of the dragon and the seven heads of the beast, "crowned" in the first instance, "uncrowned" in the second. Further discussion on this subject is provided in Chapter 17, in connection with the parallel description of the "seven heads" in Revelation 17:3, 9-11.

Revelation 13:3. **And I saw one of his heads as it were wounded to death; and his deadly wound was healed: and all the world wondered after the beast.**

If the interpretation of the seven heads and seven kingdoms suggested above is correct, then one of them is apparently going to be revived in the last days. It is this revived head, no doubt, on which is based the ten horns and ten crowns, since they also refer to the last days. It is probably this head which speaks with the mouth of a lion (verse 2), though perhaps the others do also.

Which of the heads is revived is not stated, although many expositors consider this to be a reference to the revival of the old Roman empire.

It is interesting, as a matter of fact, that most of these ancient nations are today experiencing something of a revival. Egypt has attempted to become spokesman for the Islamic world and has been the first Arab nation to attempt rapprochement with Israel. Persia, which is modern Iran, has likewise captured world attention because of its oil resources and militant Moslem fundamentalism. Modern Iraq corresponds to ancient Babylonia and Assyria (the ruins of Babylon are near its capital city Baghdad) and it has become probably the strongest Arab nation militarily. Greece is still an important Mediterranean nation, as is Italy, and their religious cultures permeate the nations of the north and west through the various Orthodox churches and the Roman Catholic Church, respectively.

None of these "revivals," however, are sufficiently striking to make all the world "wonder after the beast." It will take something more than that, something almost miraculous. The NATO Alliance and the European Common Market have also been suggested as potential revivals of the Roman empire, but again neither of these is a really spectacular development. They may possibly be precursors of the "ten horns" which will give their power to the beast (Revelation 17:12, 13), but they are not the "revived head" and they are certainly not the beast.

The beast, of course, is a man, though he will become so identified with the empire he heads that the two are almost synonymous. It has been noted already (Revelation 11:7) that he "ascends out of the abyss," and that his ascent is marked by such satanically-imparted powers that he is able finally to put an end to the three-and-a-half-year influence of God's two witnesses. All of this will so enthrall the nations that he will quickly gain worldwide preeminence over them all. His experience with Satan "in the abyss," as he will claim, will be some kind of occult supernatural phenomenon whereby his body seemed to be dead (actually in suspended animation) while his spirit is taken by the devil for the impartation of the knowledge and powers he would need to fulfill his dark mission in the world.

Although he himself is not the wounded head of the beast (since he *is* the beast), his own recovery from the deadly wound (a wound not unto death but "as it were" unto death) will bear such striking analogy to the revival of the ancient nation represented by the head as to make a profound and stirring impression on every nation. He is also called "the beast that was, and is not, and yet is" (Revelation 17:8) and then also said to be one of the "seven kings" (Revelation 17:10, 11).

The head that will be revived will certainly be also the kingdom that will best epitomize the nature and purposes of the dragon who empowers the beast. It will serve as the center of his rule over all the nations—his capital, as it were.

It would seem that this could not be Rome, since Rome does not need "resurrecting." Rome had been one of the world's greatest cities ever since the Caesars. After the fall of the old Roman empire, the "Holy Roman Empire" succeeded it, and it has been the central capital of the quasi-political religious institution of the Roman Catholic Church ever since.

It will be noted that the middle head on the beast is Babylon which, from the point of view of symmetry at least, would most appropriately be the chief head on the beast. Babylon was defeated by the Persians over two-and-a-half millennia ago, but continued at least as an inhabited city for many centuries. Eventually it seemed to die completely, although various poor communities continued to exist in or near its environs. The ruins of its ancient glory are a top tourist attraction today.

The possibility of reconstructing Babylon has been seriously considered in recent years, both by the Iraqi government and by various internationalist organizations. It is ideally situated, being very near the geographical center of the earth's land masses, to serve as a world capital. Although we cannot be sure that this will happen, there are good reasons for believing that the beast may select this site as his world capital. Rapid construction, using the most advanced technologies, could almost overnight raise ancient Babylon back to life again. Not only could Babylon serve as the political center of the world, but also as its commercial, cultural, and religious center. Since the religious philosophy of Nimrod and the first Babylonians (that is, evolutionary humanistic pantheism) permeated every great empire from Sumer to Rome, such a renaissance would in effect be a restoration of all the heads of the beast. And since the beast himself would have also experienced a remarkable personal (pseudo) death and resurrection, all the world would indeed marvel at the great power of the beast and the magnificence of his capital city, together with the establishment of his great cultural and trade center. This would not merely be a revived Roman empire, which so many Bible teachers have postulated, but a revived Babylonian, Egyptian, Assyrian, Persian, and Greek empire, all comprising a mighty revival of ancient evolutionary paganism, humanism, and (ultimately) Satanism.

Revelation 13:4. **And they worshipped the dragon which gave power unto the beast: and they worshipped the beast, saying, Who is like unto the beast? who is able to make war with him?**

For many years prior to the rapture, a revival of various forms of ancient occultism (spiritism, astrology, witchcraft, eastern mysticism, and even Satan-worship) will have been developing. This movement will be tremendously accelerated with the departure of the multitudes of true Christians when Christ returns to meet them in the air just prior to the tribulation period. During the first three-and-a-half years of the tribulation, the preaching of Christ's two witnesses (along with that of 144,000 sealed Israelites and many others), combined with the great judgments of the seals and trumpets, will finally eliminate every vestige of the scientific skepticism that has dominated the intellectual world for two centuries or more.

Men and women will have seen and heard mighty angels flying through the skies. They will have seen and heard the miracles and the preaching of Christ's witnesses. Quite possibly such preaching, along with the testimony of the rapture itself, will have stimulated many to read the Bible and other Christian literature left behind. They will have had many other evidences which will finally convince even the most skeptical of the reality of both God and Satan. They will come to understand something of the true nature of the cosmic conflict of the ages, between the dragon and the woman.

But then they will choose Satan. They will elect to cast their lot with him, believing that his agelong rebellion against God will ultimately triumph. If Satan can resurrect the great prince, wounded to death as he had been, and impart to him such remarkable powers as to enable him to destroy God's two hitherto invincible witnesses, then he can also be trusted to give them eternal life and mighty power. Amazing and incredible as it seems, men will in great multitudes decide to worship the dragon. They will acknowledge him as the rightful king of the cosmos, and will consciously encourage and help him in his battle against God.

Furthermore, they will acknowledge that the dragon had indeed granted universal earthly authority to his human counterpart, the beast, and so will worship the latter as well. After all, if he can destroy the two mighty witnesses from heaven, then who else on the earth could possibly mount a successful battle against him?

For three-and-a-half years he had been striving for supremacy with other nations (west and north and east of his own domain) as well as with the two witnesses and their converts. Probably he had also been attempting to develop his great center and capital at Babylon. He had been hindered not only by these struggles but also by the devastating plagues from heaven. But now, finally, he is triumphant, and the whole world comes to look to him for its guidance and deliverance, trusting in his own master, Satan, for all needed power and wisdom. The three-and-a-half-year drought has been relieved, the plagues have stopped, the witnesses are gone; the beast is in charge, and the dragon and his angels have come to the earth.

Revelation 13:5. **And there was given unto him a mouth speaking great things and blasphemies: And power was given unto him to continue forty and two months.**

The mouth of the beast, like the roaring of a lion (verse 2), began to roar out great things. The dragon, who gave him his authority, also now gives him great pronouncements to make to the world. Counterfeiting God's divinely impaired prophets of old, he makes satanically-inspired proclamations and predictions, filled with blasphemies against the true God and His Christ, foretelling their imminent destruction and the freedom of mankind from all restraints of righteousness and fear of judgment.

Men will believe him, sad to say. With minds deceived and blinded by Satan (2 Corinthians 4:4; Revelation 12:9), further confused by drug addiction (Revelation 9:21) and benumbed by sins of every description, they will believe his blasphemies. They will believe "Even him, whose coming is after the working of Satan with all power and signs and lying wonders, and with all deceivableness of unrighteousness in them that perish; because they received not the love of the truth, that they might be saved. And for this cause God shall send them strong delusion, that they should believe a lie: That they all might be damned who believed not the truth, but had pleasure in unrighteousness" (2 Thessalonians 2:9-12). Actually, the definite article is present in the Greek—"they will believe *the* lie."

His authority was to endure for only forty-two months. Satan knew this was all the time he had left before the climactic battle (Revelation 12:12). This is obviously the same forty-two months during which the Gentiles would defile Jerusalem and the temple (Revelation 11:2).

It is also the same period in which God will specially protect His people in the wilderness (Revelation 12:6, 14) from the fangs of the serpent, in particular by destroying the army sent after them by the beast.

Revelation 13:6.   And he opened his mouth in blasphemy against God, to blaspheme his name, and his tabernacle, and them that dwell in heaven.

Not content merely to rail against God, the dragon-inspired beast must utter diatribes and obscenities against all He stands for (His name), defaming His holiness, His love, His law, His grace. He curses the heavens (the dragon has recently been expelled from heaven) where God dwells. Those who dwell with God in heaven, including not only the holy angels but also all the raptured saints, share in his vilifications. This continual barrage of slander must now take place on earth, since the Devil no longer has access to heaven where he used to accuse the brethren.

Daniel also prophesied of his vile mouth: "In this horn were eyes like the eyes of man, and a mouth speaking great things. . . . a mouth that spake very great things. . . . And he shall speak great words against the most High, and shall wear out the saints of the most High" (Daniel 7:8, 20, 25). And again Daniel says:

"And the king shall do according to his will; and he shall exalt himself, and magnify himself above every god, and shall speak marvellous things against the God of gods" (Daniel 11:36).

No doubt, one of the purposes of this campaign of vituperation will be to intimidate any on earth who might be followers or potential followers of the true God. The dragon can ill afford any other defections from his ranks.

The Kingdom of Man

Ever since Nimrod, there have arisen many powerful and ambitious men who have aspired to rule the world. Ruthless and evil almost to a man, such dictators have managed to enlist many followers and conquer many nations. In addition to those mentioned in the Bible, one thinks of Genghis Khan, Napoleon, Hitler, Stalin, and others. But one after another, they have failed. God would not allow Nimrod to establish a world government, nor has he allowed any other. Even the mighty Roman empire could not accomplish it. The Romans could not even subjugate the Parthian empire (Persians), let alone the great nations of Africa, the Orient and Northern Europe.

The idealists of the western world have also dreamed of world government. Tennyson, with his poetic "parliament of man," Woodrow Wilson and his League of Nations, the modern-day United Nations organization, all have tried and failed. Various conspiratorial societies (Communists, Illuminati, etc.) have hoped to bring it about, and the international banking/business establishment today seems to cherish such a goal. But God will never allow it.

Not until the very end of the age, that is. Finally, however, there will be a world government of sorts, but once again it will be merely a grand exercise in humanistic futility.

Revelation 13:7.   And it was given unto him to make war with the saints, and to overcome them: and power was given him over all kindreds, and tongues, and nations.

Before the beast can establish the world empire which he covets, he must subjugate both those who still resist him in his own kingdom and also those other nations which have not yet surrendered. His greatest resistance will be offered by "the saints," a great number of believers in the true God and His Christ who will have been converted during the first half of the tribulation. There is no indication that these offer armed resistance, but their moral resistance, coupled with the apparent immunity which they seem to have against the plagues that have been sweeping the earth, will make them the special object of his hatred and wrath. Many believers will be martyred during the first half of the tribulation and many more during the second half as a result of the beast's vicious campaigns against them.

Daniel speaks of this warfare against the saints: "I beheld, and the same horn made war with the saints, and prevailed against them" (Daniel 7:21). Particularly after the death and subsequent translation of the two witnesses (Revelation 11:7-12), the beast will systematically seek to destroy every one who worships the true God (or any god except himself and the dragon, for that matter), and the only ones who escape death must do so by fleeing and hiding. We have noted already that the "woman," mainly symbolizing at this time Israel's believing remnant, is supernaturally protected in a special wilderness retreat prepared by God (Revelation 12:6, 13-16). No doubt many others will survive by hiding in other places around the world, but multitudes will die as martyrs for their faith (see Revelation 6:9-11; 7:9-17; 12:10-11).

The beast must also conquer the other nations of the world and their armies and this conquest will occupy much of his attention during the first half of the tribulation. To some degree he must acquire a position of leadership at least among the Mediterranean nations even before the seven years of the tribulation itself actually begin. This period corresponds to the seven-year covenant which he will make with Israel (Daniel 9:27) as discussed previously (see Chapters 6 and 11). It is possible, of course, that he will rise to this position of prominence before the rapture of believers (1 Thessalonians 4:16, 17) takes place, but it is also possible that some period of time will elapse between the rapture and the signing of the seven-year treaty. The rapture is undated in Scripture and always imminent ("Watch!" commanded Jesus).

Some of the beast's struggles to attain supremacy over the nations are outlined in Daniel 7:3-8, 19-25, and Daniel 11:45. The account in Daniel 7 culminates its account of this struggle by stating: "And they shall be given into his hand until a time and times and the dividing of time" (Daniel 7:25). The account in Daniel 11 is concluded with the statement: "At that time shall Michael stand up . . . and there shall be a time of trouble, such as never was since there was a nation even to that same time" (Daniel 12:1). Then, in answer to the question, "How long shall it be to the end of these wonders?," the angel replies: "it shall be for a time, times, and an half" (Daniel 12:6, 7). Both accounts obviously take us up to the last half of the tribulation, indicating again that this "prince that shall come," the beast, will have attained his coveted position of world supremacy by the middle of the tribulation or very shortly thereafter.

Thus was "power" (the word actually means "authority") given to him over every nation, every language group within that nation, and every clan within the language group. This, no doubt, will be an uneasy reign. Many other ambitious leaders will submit grudgingly, and there will not be adequate time nor enough military police to completely consolidate these triumphs. Nevertheless, he will be the first man since Nimrod's abortive attempt at Babel long ago who is able to exercise even nominal rule over all people.

Revelation 13:8. And all that dwell upon the earth shall worship him, whose names are not written in the book of life of the Lamb slain from the foundation of the world.

We have already been told (verse 4) that "they" will worship both the dragon and the beast. Here we are told who are included in the term "they." *All* men and women everywhere, in every nation, will worship this very brilliant but very evil man. They will reject the true God as God, even though they no longer doubt His existence. But they will believe that this *man* (and his master, Satan) are greater and more powerful than God, and therefore they should be worshiped (that is, their will should be obeyed) rather than God. As did the ancient pagans, and as do modern evolutionists, they "changed the truth of God into a lie, and worshipped and served the creature more than the Creator" (Romans 1:25).

Here is humanism gone mad. Man desires human autonomy and so concludes that man himself is the pinnacle attained by the cosmic process of evolution and thus that man himself is God. But then he must have a visible representative of mankind to whom his representative worship can be given. In thus worshiping the world's greatest man, he is subliminally worshiping himself. Thus he gladly yields fealty to the monster of evil, finding vicarious satisfaction in the ability of a man like himself to attain such cosmic eminence. Also, of course, he can find practical release from any pangs of conscience due to the evil in his own heart and the wickedness of his own hands.

All will worship the beast, that is, except those whom the Lord has reserved for Himself. The terminology here is significant. Not all those whose names are written in the Lamb's book of life will have, to this point, made an open profession of faith in Christ. But they will in good time, (or at least may do so) since they are not among those who have submitted to the beast. (See the discussion on the significance of the "book of life" in Chapter 3, under Revelation 3:5.) Many of these are godly Israelites, preserved by God in the wilderness until such time as they come to understand and acknowledge the Lord Jesus Christ as their Messiah and Savior. In any case, there will even in these very last days be a substantial number of people who recoil at worshiping the beast, even though it may cost their lives.

Since the Lamb had, at least in principle and in God's foreknowledge, been slain from the foundation of the world, He had been able in perfect justice to write in His book of life the names of everyone who would someday be born. The redemption price which He would pay (His innocent blood, shed on the cross in substitution for the sins of the whole world) was of more than sufficient merit to cover every person, and so their names were written in His book before the world began. However, one name after another had been "blotted out of the book of life" as people had lived and died without validating their entry, as it were, through personal appropriation of Christ by faith. By far the majority of men and women through the ages have either rejected or neglected Him and thus died in their sins. This will be even more the case in the awful tribulation period, when men will have to worship the beast or die.

Revelation 13:9.   If any man have an ear, let him hear.

This is the same pleading message which John had earlier conveyed from the Lord to the angels of the seven churches. And if it was important for people in the churches of the Christian dispensation to heed such a message, how much more urgent it will be for people in this future age. In this case, the message was not addressed "to the churches," since there will be no organized churches as such in the fearful times of the tribulation. Nevertheless, the admonition is needed more than ever. If men will worship the beast, they have no part in the book of life, and thus face the certainty of an eternal hell. If they do not worship the beast, they will be persecuted and slain. It is a solemn choice they must make, and they need to hear and understand its implications. If any have been putting off this decision for some reason, the beast is about to force it. Refuse his mark, renounce his worship and die, or else accept his mark and worship him, hoping that he and the dragon can vanquish Christ and empty hell.

Other martyrs have fearlessly made a similar choice in the past, and the witness of their blood will bear its testimony to many last-day martyrs as they confront the beast and his minions.

Revelation 13:10.   He that leadeth into captivity shall go into captivity: he that killeth with the sword must be killed with the sword. Here is the patience and the faith of the saints.

The Lord graciously interjects here a word of encouragement to those saints who are being persecuted. Those who are the instruments of their suffering will soon be repaid in like measure. God long ago had enumerated such a principle (an eye for an eye and a life for a life), and He will diligently enforce it in these days of judgment. The day of grace is completely past, as far as these are concerned who become enforcers for the beast. Those police agents who pursue and imprison the suffering believers of the tribulation period will soon be thrown into a dungeon infinitely worse. Those who capture and execute men who refuse to worship the beast will themselves be slain—perhaps by the awful sword proceeding from the mouth of the coming conqueror (Revelation 19:15).

It is this promise and confidence which will help to sustain the saints through such a bitter time of persecution. *Here* (in this promise) rests the faith of the saints, making them patient in tribulation. The patience of which this verse speaks means "patient endurance." Like their Lord, "who for the joy that was set before him endured the cross" (Hebrews 12:2), they know that they "have in heaven a better and an enduring substance" and that their confidence in His promise "hath great recompence of reward" (Hebrews 10:34, 35).

In yet another sense, the emphatic *"Here!"* would urge us to realize that the awful stress of these final days will dwarf anything endured by believers in former days and will provide the greatest test of patience and faith ever experienced. Here patience and faith are defined.

The False Prophet

The sign of the dragon and the beast now veers to another aspect and wicked personage, the third member of the infernal trinity. In an evil parody of the Holy Spirit, who glorifies Christ (John 16:14), this third personage seeks to cause men to worship the beast, who has received his authority from the dragon. Although he is not identified by this name here (at this point he is merely called the "beast coming up out of the earth") he is three times later in Revelation called "the false prophet," and is directly associated with the beast and the dragon (Revelation 16:13; 19:20; 20:10).

Revelation 13:11.   And I beheld another beast coming up out of the earth; and he had two horns like a lamb, and he spake as a dragon.

John sees another (that is, "another of the same type") beast (Greek *therion*, "dangerous beast") arising from the earth, instead of from the sea like the first beast. Since the first beast is a man, so is the second, but their backgrounds are different. As noted previously, "the sea" probably refers to the Mediterranean, the implication being that the first beast comes from one of the Mediterranean kingdoms. In fact, Daniel 9:27 suggests that he comes from the people of the ancient Roman empire, possibly a direct descendant of the Romans. By the same token, the second beast must come from somewhere in the great land masses outside the Mediterranean nations, but we apparently have no other clue to his origin.

There has been much speculation as to the identity of this second beast. Since he is later called the false prophet, he apparently first comes to world attention as a miracle-working religious leader, professing to convey supernaturally inspired messages to mankind. His "prophecies," of course, are not from God but from Satan, though it may well be that he will first become known (possibly before the tribulation) as a man supposedly receiving messages from God. He professes to be a true prophet but is in reality a false prophet. Jesus warned of false Christs and false prophets (Matthew 24:24) in the great tribulation, and these two (the Antichrist and the false prophet) are the very prototypes of these two classes of deceivers.

Actually the term "antichrist" occurs only in the epistles of John (1 John 2:18; 4:3; 2 John 7) and is applied to anyone who deceives men by professing to serve God while at the same time denying the supernatural incarnation and the divine/human nature of Christ. However, the concept of "the Antichrist" does occur often in both ancient and modern Christian literature, usually referring to the great antichristian world dictator of these last days. The second beast is interpreted by some writers (as Scofield, in his reference Bible) as the Antichrist, but this seems arbitrary. In any case, John calls them the beast and the false prophet here in Revelation and it does seem significant that he, as the author of the only New Testament verses in which the term "antichrist" is used, does not apply it in Revelation to either of these men. He had already, in fact, said that anyone who denied the coming of Jesus Christ in the flesh is "the antichrist" (the definite article is used this way in the 2 John reference).

This second beast is clearly a religious spokesman of some kind and possibly he is the leader of the world religious system as it will culminate in the last days, coming into its ultimate character as the great harlot of Revelation 17.

The modern ecumenical movement, active first among apostate Protestant churches in the first half of the twentieth century, then essentially combining (or at least fellowshiping) with the Catholic and Orthodox churches in the second half of the twentieth century, will eventually amalgamate with all other world religions, especially after the departure of all true churches to be with Christ.

This second beast, or false prophet, will most likely emerge as the patriarch (or pope, or ayatollah, or guru or, more likely, simply "prophet") of this universal religion. He will originally counterfeit the gentle character of Christ ("two horns like a lamb"), but his "inspired" words will be those of Satan, the old dragon. First they will be sweetly deceptive words, soon they will become deadly, tyrannical, dragon words.

Revelation 13:12.   And he exerciseth all the power of the first beast before him, and causeth the earth and them which dwell therein to worship the first beast, whose deadly wound was healed.

The two Satan-empowered men had somehow become allies, probably at some time before the actual onset of the tribulation period. The alliance of religion and state has a long and sad record of despotism and suppression, but the ecclesiopolitical union of these to human beasts will culminate in the worst period of persecution in the history of the world.

By the time the political power of the first beast is reaching its zenith, the syncretistic religious union of world religions is also being concentrated under control of the second beast. Each leader assists and supports the other, the king enforcing the religious authority of the prophet and the prophet persuading the world's superstitious masses that the king should be worshiped and obeyed as a god.

With his worldwide reputation as a miracle-working prophet already established, he will see that the remarkable pseudo-resurrection of the beast is widely publicized and idolized in every church and temple around the world as the chief argument to persuade people to acknowledge him as divine and deserving of worship. The two will soon become an unprecedented team, working in partnership to establish universal control over all people everywhere.

Revelation 13:13.   And he doeth great wonders, so that he maketh fire come down from heaven on the earth in the sight of men.

The false prophet will be able to perform certain types of miracles by the power of Satan, and this will further enhance his reputation and authority. Among these wonders will be the ability to call down fire from the sky. Special understanding and control of atmospheric phenomena by satanic angels will probably be imparted to the false prophet to enable him to accomplish this and other miracles.

No doubt he will exploit his ability to produce fire from heaven because this had been one phenomenon which had been used by Christ's two witnesses to intimidate the unbelieving world for three-and-a-half years (Revelation 11:5). Even though the beast had prevailed against them and killed them, their resurrection and rapture was known around the world, and people still feared their power. It was important that men everywhere should see (perhaps on television) that the beast and false prophet had powers similar to those of the witnesses.

Revelation 13:14.   And deceiveth them that dwell on the earth by the means of those miracles which he had power to do in the sight of the beast; saying to them that dwell on the earth, that they should make an image to the beast, which had the wound by a sword, and did live.

Thirteen times in Revelation we read about those who "dwell on the earth," twice in this verse. These earth-dwellers easily are subject now to satanic deception and are especially impressed by the prophet's ability to perform miracles.

Men through the ages have always been profoundly awed by the supernatural. Often it is true that the more skeptical a person has been about the miracles of God the more gullible he will become when he sees a demonic miracle. Although neither Satan nor his angels can perform miracles of creation (since only God can create), they can and do sometimes manipulate natural processes so as to produce unusual and apparently inexplicable phenomena. Thus miracles (except for genuine miracles of creation) are not necessarily evidence of divine origin and must always be tested in relation to their purpose and fidelity to Scripture (Isaiah 8:20).

Especially in the last days will such demon-produced miracles be abundant. The Lord Jesus Christ warned: "For there shall arise false Christs, and false prophets, and shall shew great signs and wonders; insomuch that, if it were possible, they shall deceive the very elect" (Matthew 24:24). Paul, speaking probably of this same false prophet, says his "coming is after the working of Satan with all power and signs and lying wonders" (2 Thessalonians 2:9). His miracles are lying miracles, in that their purpose is to cause men to "believe the lie" (2 Thessalonians 2:11) that the "man of sin," with his image "sitting in the temple of God" is, as he is claiming, truly God (2 Thessalonians 2:3, 4).

Men have always been prone to idolatry, even in an age of science, desiring to see something or someone in whom they can place their trust. When intellectuals decide that no real God exists, they replace Him by evolution. Then, regarding man as the apex of evolution, they decide that man is God and idolize great men, worshiping at the feet of Darwin or Marx, Hitler or Stalin, Hirohito or Mao, Einstein or Schweitzer. They erect great statues to their honor, making long pilgrimages to see their tombs or their birthplaces, paying them homage.

This idolatrous system of evolutionary humanism will come to its climax and its ultimate culmination in the worldwide worship of the beast as the greatest of all men, the man who had conquered death and conquered the great witnesses of God and conquered the world. He is man in perfection, the great leader for whom all mankind had been searching for thousands of years, the king who would bring universal peace, prosperity and freedom from fear of God.

Now that the dream seems reality, and all the world is worshiping the beast and the dragon (verse 4), it seems fitting to formalize and systematize this worship. The prophet instructs people to make or purchase small statues of the emperor and to use them in their homes as reminders of his power and beneficence.

But all these household gods will be mere replicas of the great prototype image of the beast, an image which, like the great image of Nebuchadnezzar (Daniel 2:31; 3:1) will be set up in the most strategic place possible, symbolizing man in all his perfection, the most fitting object conceivable for humanistic worship of all men everywhere.

The establishment of this worldwide system of humanistic idolatry has at least two purposes: (1) satisfaction of the immense ego of the man of sin (the sin of pride is the sin of the devil, the root sin of all sin, and the man of sin will certainly be a man of pride); (2) consolidation of his rule by causing people to accept him as a god as well as king.

The great act of blasphemy was prophesied long ago by Daniel. "And he [that is, the prince that shall come] shall confirm the covenant with many for one week [that is, shall make a seven-year treaty with the Jews allowing them to reestablish their temple and ancient system of worship]: and in the midst of the week [that is, at the midpoint of the seven-year treaty period] he shall cause the sacrifice and the oblation to cease [break the treaty, terminating the sacrifices and worship ceremonies], and for the overspreading of abominations he shall make it desolate, even until the consummation, and that determined shall be poured upon the desolate" (Daniel 9:27).

The word "overspreading" here is the usual Hebrew word for "wings," commonly used for the overspreading wings of the cherubims, as they hovered over the ark of the covenant in the holy of holies in the temple. But now, instead of cherub wings, there will, in this holy place, be established the overspread arms of the great image of the man of sin. The term "abominations" means the worst types of crimes and pollutions men can commit, and is often in Scripture applied to the making and worship of idols. The prophecy thus anticipates the unspeakable blasphemy of making the temple and its holy place a "desolation" (the same word is used for "astonishment"), emptying it of its sacred furniture and true worshipers, and installing in their place a hulking statue of the beast to which all must bow.

The Lord Jesus Christ also referred to this coming event: "When ye therefore shall see the abomination of desolation, spoken of by Daniel the prophet, stand in the holy place, (whoso readeth, let him understand:) Then let them which be in Judaea flee into the mountains: . . . For then shall be great tribulation, such as was not since the beginning of the world to this time, no nor ever shall be" (Matthew 24:15-21).

This is undoubtedly also the event about which Paul wrote to the Thessalonians: "Let no man deceive you by any means: for that day shall not come, except there come a falling away first, and that man of sin be revealed, the son of perdition; Who opposeth and exalteth himself above all that is called God, or that is worshipped; so that he as God sitteth in the temple of God, shewing himself that he is God" (2 Thessalonians 2:3, 4).

The military and political might of the first beast is thus exploited by the religious cunning and wonder-working capabilities of the second beast. When the image is set up in the holy place, the temple is soon emptied of its worshipers and the Israelite remnant will flee into the wilderness (Revelation 11:2; 12:6), but most of the earth-dwellers will quickly be obediently worshiping the great man of sin and the devil himself.

Revelation 13:15.   And he had power to give life unto the image of the beast, that the image of the beast should both speak, and cause that as many as would not worship the image of the beast should be killed.

The false prophet next performs perhaps the greatest of all his feats of magic. Soon after the image is carved and installed in the temple, the image begins to speak.

This image is more then a mere robot with a computer voice. That would be no great marvel today, with all the accomplishments of automation and kine-metronics (or audio-animatronics). Millions of people have observed an image of Abraham Lincoln move and "speak" at Disneyland, but they were hardly moved to bow down in worship of his image.

The image of the man of sin will speak intelligibly and his words will not be preprogrammed. He will issue commands, among them the command to slay all who do not worship him. Those who observe this remarkable phenomenon, whether in person at Jerusalem or on another side of the world by television, will be convinced the image is really speaking of its own volition.

It does not actually possess life, of course (only God can create life). The word in the Greek is *pneuma*, meaning "spirit" or "wind." The false prophet is enabled (by his own master, Satan) to impart a spirit to the image, but that spirit is one of Satan's unclean spirits, probably a highly placed demon in the satanic hierarchy. This is a striking case of demon possession, with the demon possessing the body of the image rather than that of a man or woman. And, just as the evil spirit possessing a human being can use the vocal chords of that person to convey his own messages, so the spirit indwelling the image of the beast will utilize the complex "audio-animatronics" apparatus with which it will be equipped to convey Satan's messages. Possibly these will be relayed worldwide to receivers in the individual household replicas of the image so that everyone can hear the beast speaking.

Whether this is the exact means Satan will use remains to be seen, but the prophecy is entirely plausible in any case. In some way, the edict will be conveyed around the world that it will be considered a capital offense not to worship the beast via his image, and the dragon via the beast. It would also be feasible to have monitors installed in every home to feed information back to a centralized network of computers recording whether or not such worship is actually being rendered as well as any other information desired by the vast intelligence network of the beast.

Revelation 13:16. And he causeth all, both small and great, rich and poor, free and bond, to receive a mark in their right hand, or in their foreheads.

In order better to control the activities of the people of his vast dominion, each person is required to register and to receive a brand which will identify him as a loyal citizen of the world kingdom. This registration is intended to be absolutely universal, although one can imagine it will be carried out only with some difficulty in the far-flung lands of Asia and Africa. No one is excepted, no matter how wealthy or how eminent. No doubt registration centers will be set up in every community, and people will be instructed to report for registration and marking on or before a certain date.

The nature of the mark is not described, but the basic principle has been well established for years in various nations. The social security card, the draft registration card, the practice of stenciling an inked design on the back of the hand, and various other devices are all forerunners of this universal branding. The word itself ("mark") is the Greek *charagma*. Is it used only in Revelation, to refer to the mark of the beast (eight times), plus one time to refer to idols "*graven* by art and man's device" (Acts 17:29). The mark is something like an etching or a tattoo which, once inscribed, cannot be removed, providing a permanent (possibly eternal) identification as a follower of the beast and the dragon. One may contrast this mark with the protective "seal" (Greek *sphragis*) provided for the servants of God on their foreheads (Revelation 7:3). That seal is apparently the name of the Father (Revelation 14:1), and it seems the beast intends to imitate this by branding his name either on their foreheads or in their right hand.

Revelation 13:17.   And that no man might buy or sell, save he that had the mark, or the name of the beast, or the number of his name.

As far as convenience of enforcement is concerned, an openly visible mark is obviously much superior to a wallet card or other device. One would think that being branded would be so demeaning that widespread resentment and rebellion would hinder its implementation. No doubt there will be much grumbling and many will refuse to report to the registration centers. This will certainly be true of those who are still trusting in God, as they will understand the spiritual significance of this act and firmly reject such permanent identification with the beast.

But it will be extremely difficult to survive at all without the mark. Once the enforcement machinery is set up, no one will be able to get or hold any kind of employment, nor will he be able to conduct even a one-man sales business of any kind. Even if he has money or other valuable stored away somewhere, he will be unable either to spend his money or sell his property. No transaction of any kind will be legal unless all parties to the transaction can display either on their foreheads or in their right hands the mark of the beast. If one party does not have the mark, the other will surely report him to the ubiquitous police and that will be his death sentence, for the image of the beast has decreed that all who would live must worship the beast, and worship certainly includes obedience. Others, as enemies of the people, must die.

There will undoubtedly be many who survive by living off the land or by setting up secret communes in the wilderness or by other means, but it will involve extreme hardship and danger. The rural areas, with their produce and livestock, will offer the only potential havens, but the whole world will have just endured a three-and-a-half-year drought (Revelation 11:3, 6) and the famines associated with the judgment of the third seal (Revelation 6:5, 6). It is perhaps these traumatic times to which the Lord refers in Matthew 25:31-46, the so-called "judgment of the nations" (or "Gentiles"), when He will commend those who have provided help to His brethren, but will consign to everlasting punishment those who do not.

Evidently the brand may take any one of three forms, perhaps based on certain further categories into which the emperor wishes to divide his followers—say, perhaps, military, governmental, and civilian, with different types of privileges and duties applied to each. One group receives the mark, some peculiar design (or logo) which is appropriate for the beast, and this is probably applied to the bulk of the population. Another group is imprinted with the beast's own name, probably the group associated most closely with his purposes and actions. The third group is marked with a number, that number which is peculiarly fitting both for his character and for his own name. Unless a person can display one of these three brands, thus marking him permanently as committed to Satan, he is marked for privation and death.

Six Hundred Sixty-Six

Revelation 13:18.   Here is wisdom. Let him that hath understanding count the number of the beast: for it is the number of a man; and his number is six hundred threescore and six.

This concluding verse of this amazing chapter of Revelation is most intriguing. It is as though John were posing a puzzle, a challenge that would help people determine the identity of the beast. Once the tribulation begins, however, there will be no question as to his identity, since it is he who will make the seven-year covenant with Israel. Therefore, John evidently intended this clue for his initial readers in the seven churches of Asia, and therefore for all other believers before the Church is raptured prior to the beginning of the tribulation.

But why would he do this? If the Church is to be removed before the beast comes to power, then what difference would it make to them, except as an item for curiosity and gossip? And, if he felt people should know who the beast would be, why didn't he just give his name (after all, both Josiah and Cyrus were named prophetically long before they were born—note 1 Kings 13:2; 2 Kings 23:16; Isaiah 44:28—45:4; Ezra 1:1-4).

The answer to the first question is that the beast will evidently come into power gradually, and will become well known in the world long before the tribulation actually begins. He will, no doubt, be an extremely impressive personage, a leader of great ability and personal magnetism. His convincing new form of the philosophy of evolutionary humanism will be made immensely attractive, especially to the oncoming younger generation steeped in an older form of evolutionism in their schools, and he will become an international hero long before he acquires political leadership. Like Antiochus Epiphanes, the evil Syrian monarch of old whom Daniel made to be a type of this final man of sin, he will be a "vile person" who will "come in peaceably, and obtain the kingdom by flatteries" (Daniel 11:21).

Like the false prophets who would "deceive, if it were possible, even the very elect," he and people of similar kind will have a great influence even over true Christians. Long before the actual kingdom of Antichrist is set up, antichristian doctrines will have taken deadly toll even among true believers. Forewarned is forearmed, however, so that if his true character could be recognized and exposed before he actually comes to power, much harm to Christ's churches can be prevented. Hence, "here is wisdom," for Christians to recognize the beast before the world does.

As to why John doesn't give us the man's name plainly, the reason probably is that God reveals His mysteries only to those who really love His Word and search them out. In Proverbs this principle is enunciated: "My son, if thou wilt receive my words, and hide my commandments with thee; so that thou incline thine ear unto wisdom, and apply thine heart to understanding; yea, if thou criest after knowledge, and liftest up thy voice for understanding; if thou seekest her as silver, and searchest for her as for hid treasures: *then* shalt thou understand the fear of the Lord, and find the knowledge of God. For the Lord giveth wisdom: out of his mouth cometh knowledge and understanding" (Proverbs 2:1-6).

The concluding words of Daniel are to the same effect: " . . . and none of the wicked shall understand; but the wise shall understand" (Daniel 12:10). The Lord Jesus voiced a similar principle: In answer to the disciples' question: "Why speakest thou unto them in parables?" the Lord replied: "Because it is given unto you to know the mysteries of the kingdom of heaven, but to them it is not given" (Matthew 13:10, 11).

Evidently, the Lord wants his children to know the identity of the coming man of sin, but only in response to implicit faith in His Word and the willingness to act and study in obedience to it. Thus only those will learn his identity, discovering the secret knowledge which God's clue will provide, who will have the "understanding" to use such knowledge properly. "*Here* is wisdom!"

And here is the clue: "Count the number of the beast." But what is that? The previous verse tells us that it is "the number of a man."

That is, the beast is not a kingdom, but a man, and that man has a name, and his name has a number. We are to count the number of that man's name.

But how does one count the number of a man's name? In the English language, such an instruction would seem absurd, but not in the Hebrew or Greek language. In English, there are certain written characters (the Arabic numerals) for the different numbers. In Hebrew, and Greek, however (the original languages of the Old and New Testaments, respectively), each symbol used for a letter of the alphabet was also used for a number. The same is partially true in Latin (thus, V means "five," X means "ten," L means "50," etc.).

Since the Book of Revelation was written in Greek, it is probably the Greek language in which the instruction applies specifically. Every letter in Greek has a corresponding numerical value, so that each word likewise has a numerical value equal to the sum of the values of each letter in the word. Thus the Greek letter *alpha* (α) was also used for the number "one," *beta* (β) was used for "two," *iota* (ι) means "ten," *rho* (ρ) means "hundred," and so on.

To "count" the number of a name means, obviously simply to add up the numbers attached to all the letters in the name. If the man's name is Greek, this would be a straightforward operation. If his name is in some other language, then his name can be easily transliterated into Greek. We have noted that this coming prince may well be a descendant of the ancient Romans, though the prophecy of Daniel 9:27 might also be understood to apply to a person in any nation with a legal and cultural system traceable to Rome (that is almost any country in the western world), but Latin (the language of ancient Rome) is a "dead" language today, and only a few of the letters in Latin were used for numbers anyway.

Since there is essentially a one-to-one equivalence between letters of the Greek alphabet and letters of the English alphabet (as well as between Greek and French, Greek and Italian, etc.), it is possible to transliterate any name in one of the western languages into a corresponding number. For example, the name "Robert" becomes in the Greek:

rho omicron beta epsilon rho tau.

ρ o β ϵ ρ τ

The numerical values associated with this groups of letters are

$$100 + 70 + 2 + 5 + 100 + 300 = 577.$$

Similarly, every name has a certain numerical value associated with its Greek transliteration. The Greek word for "number," incidentally, is *arithmos* (from which we get our English word "arithmetic").

All of this suggests that whenever a particularly popular leader begins to figure prominently in world affairs (especially if he is antichristian in his thinking and counsel), Christians would be well advised to "count the number of his name." Then, if that number turns out to be "666," they should be extremely careful not to be influenced by him and try to warn others of his possible satanic associations.

It is obvious that there can be many names with the numerical value 666, of course, but only one man can be the Antichrist. For example, "Lyndon B. Johnson," when transliterated into Greek, adds up to 666, but President Johnson was not the Antichrist. In fact, probably the names of about one in every 10,000 people will total 666. This identification is not in itself a sure test, but it is at least a caution and an incentive to be more incisive in examining the teachings and private character of any new and charismatic international hero who shows up on the world scene.

The number 666 is significant in its own right. Since "six" is one short of the perfect "seven" and since man was made on the sixth day, the number six has long been associated with man in his imperfection. The three sixes together may be suggestive of the unholy trinity—the dragon, the beast, and the false prophet.

Further, 666 has the interesting characteristic of being the sum of the first 36 numbers $(1+2+3+ \ldots +36)$, and 36 is 6 x 6. This "number of man" seems to permeate the number 666, and so is uniquely appropriate for the beast to use as his number. It is also remarkable that John refers to him by the name "beast" exactly thirty-six times in Revelation.

It is bound to be significant that, in contrast to the number of the name of the beast, the number of the name of Jesus in Greek (that is Ιησους) is equal to 888. Just as the number "six" is associated with man, especially sinful man and the man of sin, so the number "eight" is associated with the second man, the perfect man, the God-man, Jesus. Each of His eight names, as used in the New Testament (that is, "Lord," "Jesus," "Christ," "Lord Jesus," "Jesus Christ," "Christ Jesus," "Lord Christ," and "Lord Jesus Christ") have numerical values which are multiples of "eight." As the first man, Adam, was made on the sixth day, so the second man, Jesus, was resurrected on the eighth day (the second first day of the week).

One other point of significance may be noted in connection with the number of the beast. Some men will be marked with his name, some with his mark, some with the number of his name. Although the Scriptures do not tell us what his mark will be (one may speculate that it might be a mark representing either his human likeness or the likeness of the symbolic beast depicted here in Revelation 13, but there is no way of knowing at this time), there is a strong possibility that the number of his name will be written as the Greek number *Chi Xi Stigma* (Χξς). The number value of X is 600, of ξ is 60, and of ς is 6. This would be the normal way of writing the number "666" in New Testament Greek.

Sinners of the world have been led into perdition time without number by antichrists who have appeared through the centuries. Mistaking them for great deliverers, people have followed their pernicious ways into destruction. The greatest of all of these false Christs, *the* Antichrist, will appear at the very end of the age, and will deceive and carry vast multitudes with him into hell. Outwardly he will appear as the most attractive, brilliant, strongest man of history—*the* Man. He seems to be the very highest pinnacle of the agelong evolutionary process which culminated in man.

But inwardly he is a venomous snake, a ferocious beast, the pseudoincarnation of the Devil himself! God wants His people to be forewarned against him, and so has graciously granted us this clue by which to recognize him as he slinks onto the world stage.

14

The Everlasting Gospel

(Revelation 14)

In stark contrast to the fearsome power of the beast and his evil purposes for the world, as described in the thirteenth chapter of Revelation, the fourteenth chapter assures us of the greater power of the Lamb and His holy purposes. It is as though John were echoing the psalmist: "I have seen the wicked in great power, and spreading himself like a green bay tree.... But the salvation of the righteous is of the Lord: he is their strength in the time of trouble. And the Lord shall help them, and deliver them: he shall deliver them from the wicked, and save them, because they trust in him" (Psalm 37:35-40).

Redemption of the Hundred and Forty-four Thousand

Before the great judgment trumpets began to blow, a remarkable event had been recorded by John. A protective seal had been placed on the foreheads of 144,000 chosen ones out of the tribes of Israel, assuring them of immunity to the plagues about to be unleashed on the earth-dwellers (Revelation 7:2-4; 9:4). But now the wicked one had commanded that all must die who would not receive his mark in their foreheads (Revelation 13:16, 17). The battle had been joined, but "he that is begotten of God keepeth himself, and that wicked one toucheth him not" (1 John 5:18).

Revelation 14:1. **And I looked, and lo, a Lamb stood on the mount Sion, and with him an hundred forty and four thousand, having his Father's name written in their foreheads.**

Ten times John uses the formula: "And I looked" (or "saw" or "beheld") and "lo" (or "behold") (Revelation 4:1; 5:6; 6:2; 6:5, 8; 7:9; 14:1, 14; 15:5; 19:11). Each time it serves as the introduction to a marvelous event, one which John himself could hardly have believed had he not seen it with his own eyes.

And surely no more amazing sight could have burst upon his vision than this. The most vicious persecutions of the beast and all his forces will be unable to destroy a single member of the 144,000 sealed ones, and John sees all of them congregating in a glorious assembly at the end of the great tribulation right on Mount Zion itself. The protecting seal, now revealed to be nothing less than the very name of the Father, has performed its good work. No longer will the Gentiles defile the holy city, for the chosen ones of the Father will lead a new nation into His glorious kingdom here on earth.

The Lamb is there with them, in their midst, on the holy mountain of Zion, having come finally not only to claim, but also to possess, His own dominion. John sees all this as certain to come to pass, despite the despotic rule and deadly purges just ordered by the beast and his prophet.

Many commentators spiritualize this passage, taking it to be a vision of heaven and glorified saints. Even futurist interpreters, for some reason, often consider the 144,000 servants of Revelation 7 to represent a different group than the 144,000 here in Revelation 14. "Mount Sion" is taken as the church triumphant or the heavenly home, or something similar. The fact is, however, that Zion (or Sion) always refers in Scripture either to the actual mountain on which Jerusalem was built, or to Jerusalem herself personified.

This generalization probably even applies to Hebrews 12:22-24, a passage often interpreted to refer to heaven: "But ye are come unto Mount Sion, and unto the city of the living God, the heavenly Jerusalem, and to an innumerable company of angels, to the general assembly and church of the firstborn, which are written in heaven, and to God the Judge of all, and to the spirits of just men made perfect, and to Jesus the mediator of the new covenant, and to the blood of sprinkling, that speaketh better things than that of Abel."

The word "come" in the above passage means basically to "draw near" (and is so translated in Hebrews 10:22) or "consent" (see 1 Timothy 6:3). The thrust of the above Hebrew passage is that the Jewish Christians to whom the epistle was addressed had not been content with only the doctrine emanating from Mount Sinai, speaking of judgment on sin, but had gone on to the doctrine of salvation through the blood of Jesus, and its ultimate promise of the restoration of all things. The city of the living God, the heavenly Jerusalem, will one day indeed come down out of heaven when the Lord returns to the air. Probably an earthly "model" of this new Jerusalem will then be established on Mount Zion, the literal mountain in Jerusalem, a promise often repeated in the Old Testament prophecies (Isaiah 2:3). The spirits of righteous men will not be "made perfect" at death, but at the resurrection and the judgment seat of Christ. Furthermore the great assembly of the church of the firstborn will be called together only when He returns.

Thus, both Hebrews 12:22-24 and Revelation 14:1-5 refer to the great future gathering of all the saints on Mount Zion in Jerusalem when Christ returns to earth at the end of the tribulation period. Most of the saints will have returned with Christ, after their resurrection and glorification (1 Thessalonians 3:13; Revelation 19:14), but the still-living saints who have survived the tribulation will also be there. And chief among these will be the 144,000.

Revelation 14:2. And I heard a voice from heaven, as the voice of many waters, and as the voice of a great thunder: and I heard the voice of harpers harping with their harps.

The last time the Lamb had actually been seen by John, He was in the midst of the heavenly throne (Revelation 7:17), surrounded by the multitude redeemed from the great tribulation, the implication being that they had been won to faith in Christ through the testimony of these same 144,000 witnesses. John had seen them in a prophetic vision immediately after the sealing of the 144,000, being translated forward to the end of the tribulation, apparently to a point in time immediately prior to the descent of the Lamb and all His saints from the throne in heaven to their work on earth.

In like manner here, he is again translated momentarily even further ahead in time to see the Lamb with His chosen witnesses who have survived the great tribulation still in the flesh, standing triumphantly on Zion's mountain in Jerusalem.

But then, having glimpsed the future glory, he is brought back to the present, that is, the middle of the tribulation, by the cry of a mighty voice from the midst of the throne in the skies. At this point in time, the Lamb is still there, with the elders and the living creatures. The 144,000 are still witnessing on earth, and the great multitude still are to come out of the great tribulation.

Once again the mighty voice from heaven seemed as the sound of thunder (Revelation 6:1) and the sound of roaring waters (Revelation 1:15). The voice this time, however, was not that of the cherub or even of the one on the throne, but of the entire assembly, chanting a beautiful song of majesty and holiness. The melodious sound of the harp also poured through the heavenly throng, accompanying the song of the host.

Revelation 14:3. And they sung as it were a new song before the throne, and before the four beasts, and the elders: and no man could learn that song but the hundred and forty and four thousand, which were redeemed from the earth.

The song was a new song, never heard before in earth or heaven. The theme of the song is not revealed but whatever it is, it is uniquely appropriate to the unique experiences of this unique body of 144,000 dedicated Christian witnesses. They had been redeemed by the blood of the Lamb, protected by the name of the Father sealed on their foreheads, and completely dedicated to His service and testimony. Many have been Christ's faithful witnesses and martyrs through the centuries, but never a group like this. The song which they would sing no one else could ever really "learn" (the Greek word means "experimentally understand"). The heavenly assembly could sing the words and the tune, but only the 144,000 could truly understand its meaning, for it was their new song.

The Scriptures tell of nine "new songs," and each one speaks of a glorious theme specifically designed for the singer of the song. The first six are in the book of Psalms (Psalm 33:3; 40:3; 96:1; 98:1; 144:9; 149:1) and one is in Isaiah 42:10. One of the new songs was that sung by the redeemed host at the throne of the Lamb when He received earth's title deed (Revelation 5:9). The last new song is here on this occasion. One other song is mentioned in Revelation, but it is not a "new song," being identified rather as "the song of Moses, and of the Lamb" (see on Revelation 15:3).

Although the words of the song of the 144,000 are not recorded, it surely dwells in part at least on the great truth that they had been "redeemed from the earth." Although in one sense all saved people have been redeemed from the earth, these could know the meaning of such a theme in a more profound way than others. They had been saved after the rapture, at that time in history when man's greatest persecutions and God's greatest judgments were on the earth. It was at such a time that they, like Noah (Genesis 6:8), had "found grace in the eyes of the Lord" and had been separated from "all that dwell upon the earth" (Revelation 13:8). Not only had they been redeemed spiritually but, precursively as it were, they had been redeemed from the very curse on the earth (Genesis 3:17), being protected from pain and death by the guarding seal. Further, they had apparently even been set free from the very presence of sin in their lives in order to accomplish the unique and demanding ministry ordained for them by the Lamb.

Revelation 14:4. **These are they which were not defiled with women; for they are virgins. These are they which follow the Lamb whithersoever he goeth. These were redeemed from among men, being the firstfruits unto God and to the Lamb.**

These identifying marks of the 144,000 are quite specific but commentators have been inclined to spiritualize them and make them apply to whatever group appeals to their own conceit. A number of cults (for example the Jehovah's Witnesses) maintain that they are the 144,000. Another popular opinion is that these are the outstanding servants of God selected from all generations (no doubt including among them those who advance this idea).

But the Scriptures are explicit. In the first place they are all male Israelites, 12,000 from each tribe. They are "servants of God" redeemed from among men, and they follow the commands of their Lord in all things, being disobedient in nothing. Further they are all virgins, not one having ever experienced sexual intercourse.

These constitute a rather rigid group of specifications, and one can search both history and the present world in vain to identify such a remarkable body of men. The conclusion is that they have not yet been called and sealed. The unique exigencies of the tribulation period will require a unique ministry of witness, and these must be specially prepared by God.

Some writers recoil at the phrase "defiled by women," noting the teaching of Scripture that "marriage is honourable in all, and the bed undefiled" (Hebrews 13:4). Therefore, they assume that the virginity spoken of is a spiritual virginity, as when Paul told the Corinthians he desired to present them "as a chaste virgin to Christ" (2 Corinthians 11:2), not defiled by idolatry and other forms of spiritual unfaithfulness to their heavenly bridegroom.

It must be remembered, however, that Paul himself remained unmarried and recommended such a state to these same Corinthians (1 Corinthians 7:1, 7) if they were so called and gifted. The Lord Jesus said that some men would "be eunuchs, which have made themselves eunuchs for the kingdom of heaven's sake. He that is able to receive it, let him receive it" (Matthew 19:12).

The fact is that the burden of this special ministry of witness during the tribulation period will be so demanding and so urgent that those who exercise it cannot be concerned with either personal comfort or family needs. They have no time for wives or children; they must follow the Lamb wherever He leads. "He that is unmarried careth for the things that belong to the Lord, how he may please the Lord" (1 Corinthians 7:32). Not only must they remain unmarried, but also they must have remained free from sexual sin in their youth as well. Even though the marriage bed is undefiled, being outside the will of God in any area of life is defilement and, in the case of these chosen ones, their virginity and complete single-mindedness have been God's will for them from their youth up.

They are called the "firstfruits to God and to the Lamb." This identification must obviously refer to the firstfruits of the tribulation period, and presumably the firstfruits of revived Israel. As far as those saved before the tribulation are concerned, Christ Himself is "the firstfruits; afterward they that are Christ's at his coming" (1 Corinthians 15:23). Long before the complete harvest of Israelite believers at the end of the tribulation however, when "all Israel shall be saved: as it is written, There shall come out of Sion the Deliverer, and shall turn away ungodliness from Jacob" (Romans 11:26), these 144,000 Israelites will be redeemed and prepared, as firstfruits, for their special service to their brethren and to others during the climactic years of the great tribulation.

Revelation 14:5.   And in their mouth was found no guile: for they are without fault before the throne of God.

Here is further testimony to the single-mindedness of those dedicated servants of God. Like their Master (1 Peter 2:22) "who did no sin, neither was guile found in His mouth," these witnesses are so devoted to Him and to the need of souls for whom He died that their tongues belong completely to His message.

And because there is no guile on their lips, there is no fault in their hands. "If any man offend not in word, the same is a perfect man, and able also to bridle the whole body" (James 3:2). No wonder no one else can learn their song!

How is it possible that 144,000 men—even redeemed men—could be so wholeheartedly perfect before the Lord? The answer can only be in terms of God's grace. Noah, for example, "was a just man and perfect in his generations" (Genesis 6:9) but, before such a testimony could be given of him, "Noah found grace in the eyes of the Lord" (Genesis 6:8). Like John the Baptist, who was "filled with the Holy Ghost, even from his mother's womb" (Luke 1:15), and like the Apostle Paul, who could testify that God had "separated me from my mother's womb, and called me by his grace" (Galatians 1:15), these had been called and prepared from birth. They had not been sinless, for all have sinned—even Noah and Paul and John the Baptist. But God had so prepared and protected them that they had never yielded to the sin of sexual defilement, being zealous toward God from infancy. Their redemption from among men had been foreordained from the foundation of the world but not effectuated until after the rapture of the believers of the Church Age.

Then their zealous Jewish eyes had finally been opened and they had recognized and received the Lord Jesus as the Messiah for whom they had been longing. Their sins had been forgiven so that they were now indeed "without fault before the throne of God," and were then enabled, still by God's grace, to continue in the things which they had learned. As the Apostle Jude had promised, God indeed is "able to keep you from falling, and to present you faultless before the presence of his glory with exceeding joy" (Jude 24).

Thus the days of great men wholly dedicated to God are not past. It will be a tremendous experience, at the coming great assembly of all the saints of all the ages on Mount Zion not only to meet the ancient godly patriarchs of former generations like Noah and Job and Daniel (Ezekiel 14:14), but also these equally strong and godly younger witnesses of the last generation. Their holy examples, both past and future, can convict and challenge and encourage us in our own witness in this present generation. Perhaps, in the grace of God, it might even be that what we do now will contribute in some way to the calling and saving of the 144,000 chosen men in the days to come.

The Gospel of Creation

Once again John's attention is directed back to the earth. The heavenly testimony concerning the 144,000 witnesses has been given, and the witnesses themselves are diligently laboring to bear God's testimony to a world in bondage under the beast and in turmoil under God's judgments. However, the two chief witnesses (probably, as discussed in Chapter 11, Enoch and Elijah) are gone, and the threat of death hangs heavy over any who would refuse the beast and follow Christ. Even though the 144,000 witnesses are under God's protection, they will no doubt be vigorously opposed wherever they go, and most people will be mortally afraid to heed their message or even to befriend them.

Revelation 14:6.   And I saw another angel fly in the midst of heaven, having the everlasting gospel to preach unto them that dwell on the earth, and to every nation, and kindred, and tongue, and people.

Six additional angels now appear on the scene, all with urgent messages or ministries to and concerning all earth-dwellers. One after another proclaims a vital testimony which should be of great interest to any who still have the slightest fear of God and concern about salvation.

The first performs an amazing mission. Christ had given the Great Commission to all His followers, commanding them to "preach the gospel" (Mark 16:15). The Apostle Paul had exclaimed: "Woe is unto me, if I preach not the gospel!" (1 Corinthians 9:16), and his own final admonitions had stressed the urgent command to "preach the word" (2 Timothy 4:2). The preaching of the wonderful gospel (a word meaning "good news") of Jesus Christ has always been the unique privilege and responsibility of Christian believers. Yet, at this point in history, conditions apparently have become so extreme as to require an entirely new method of preaching the gospel. Even though the 144,000 may still be on earth with their testimony, they no longer will have access to television or radio, and people will be mortally fearful of going to any kind of preaching service where they might hear them in person. There will be only one such witness for each 10,000 or more of earth's inhabitants, so it would humanly be impossible to reach them all with a personal ministry in the short time remaining. Furthermore, most of the efforts of the 144,000 Israelites will necessarily be directed toward evangelizing and discipling their own brethren, preparing them to receive their Messiah when He comes at the end of the tribulation.

On the other hand, as pointed out previously, the people on earth will no longer be ignorant of God. Not only have they had access to the Bibles and Christian literature left behind when believers were raptured but also they have heard the testimony of Enoch and Elijah for three-and-a-half years, have experienced many great divine judgments on earth, have seen and heard angels of God flying through the skies, and have realized at least in measure what is really happening in heaven and earth. Yet they still reject God and His Christ and are in imminent danger of receiving the mark of the beast and thus forfeiting all hope of repentance and salvation.

God, in His infinite grace, will thus send forth a mighty angel, flying back and forth across the skies, loudly proclaiming the gospel from one place to another, covering every nation and tribe and speaking in every language so that no one at the coming judgment would be able to say he hadn't heard.

Note also that the gospel he preaches is the "everlasting gospel." There is nothing new or different about it. Paul, in fact, had warned that if an angel from heaven came preaching some other gospel than the same gospel which he (Paul) had preached, that angel should be rejected as one accursed of God (Galatians 1:8). This, plus the fact that John himself, who certainly knew what the true gospel was, called the angel's message the everlasting gospel, is conclusive proof that this gospel is the true and only gospel.

Yet, strangely enough, many Bible teachers have insisted that there are several different gospels ("gospel of grace," "gospel of the kingdom," "everlasting gospel," etc.), a different gospel for each dispensation, perhaps. This type of hermeneutics, however well intentioned, makes Scripture contradict itself for the sake of maintaining a particular theological system. In effect, it denies to God the ability to say what He means, thus requiring a hermeneutist with the proper theological training to translate what God says into what He means, for the benefit of the "layman."

It is the gospel which we are to preach, which believers in all ages were commanded to preach, and which the angel will preach. The gospel is everlasting. It is good news from God, and is exceedingly broad in scope. Many descriptions cannot exhaust its meaning, even though they can give us many insights to its nature. It is the glorious gospel (2 Corinthians 4:4); the gospel of peace (Ephesians 6:15), the gospel of the kingdom (Mark 1:14), the gospel of God (1 Peter 4:17), the gospel of Christ (Romans 15:19), the gospel of the grace of God (Acts 20:24), the gospel of salvation (Ephesians 1:13), and a gospel of many other facets. But there is only one true gospel and that gospel is everlasting.

In fact, this is the very last use of the word in the Bible, which makes it especially significant that the Holy Spirit, through John, here calls it everlasting. It has never been, and will never be, any other gospel.

Revelation 14:7.   Saying with a loud voice, Fear God, and give glory to him; for the hour of his judgment is come: and worship him that made heaven, and earth, and the sea, and the fountains of waters.

The gospel is often defined as the substitutionary death, burial, and bodily resurrection of the Lord Jesus Christ, based on 1 Corinthians 15:1-4, where the word is used in its central occurrence (out of 101 total occurrences). Although this is surely the central focus of the gospel, it by no means exhausts the sweeping scope of its meaning, which encompasses the complete work of Christ from eternity to eternity.

It is significant that the first time the word is used (Matthew 4:23), it is in reference to "the gospel of the kingdom," looking forward to the great day when Christ will be universally acclaimed as King of kings. The final occurrence is here in Revelation 14:7, where it looks back to the creation. The gospel of Christ ("the good news about Christ") is that He is the Creator of all things (and therefore able to control and judge all things), the Redeemer of all things (and therefore able to save to the uttermost them that come unto God by Him), and the Heir of all things (therefore able and certain to bring the kingdom of God to earth as it is in heaven). The creation is the foundation of the gospel, the second coming is the blessed hope of the gospel, the cross and the empty tomb constitute the power of the gospel. A gospel without the creation and the consummation is as much an emasculated gospel as one without the cross and empty tomb. One does not really preach the gospel unless he places and teaches all these together in their true majesty and fullness.

The angel calls out with a tremendous shout, able to be heard over a large region on the earth below each time he speaks. His message is the everlasting gospel but the urgency of the situation demands that he emphasize the coming judgment "on them that know not God, and that obey not the gospel of our Lord Jesus Christ" (2 Thessalonians 1:8). Most earth-dwellers have repeatedly spurned the love of God, but there are still some who might respond to fear of judgment. "And others save with fear, pulling them out of the fire" (Jude 23). Therefore the flying angel prefaces his cry with words of warning. "Fear God!" "The time of judgment is at hand!"

God's right to judge men, of course, is founded on the fact of creation. "Give Him the glory," the angel shouts, "and bow down to the one who made all things."

Lest any think it strange or inappropriate that the gospel proclamation of the angel stresses creation, they should realize that the world's inhabitants had been indoctrinated for several generations with the godless philosophy of evolution which Satan and his followers had adopted as their intellectual rationale for refusing to worship God. Both lost men and fallen angels had rejected God as Creator, deceiving themselves into believing that the universe itself was the only eternal reality, worshiping and serving "the creature more than the Creator" (Romans 1:25). Having deceived themselves with this monstrous lie, they have ever since taught this falsehood to all who would hear until, as the Scripture says, Satan has deceived "the whole world" (Revelation 12:9). And if Christ is not the

Creator, He can hardly be the Savior or the coming King. These men of the last days must first be called back to believe in a true creation and therefore a real Creator God before they can ever be constrained to come to Him as Savior. Even after they realize that Christ is real and His hosts are waiting in the heavens, they still are wondering whether the beast and Satan can defeat Him. Thus the angel cries out repeatedly: "*God* is Creator! *He* will judge. Fear Him!"

The comprehensive formula so familiar from Scripture is rehearsed by the angel. "He made heaven, the earth, the sea" (note Exodus 20:11). The complex universe could not possibly have evolved itself from primeval chaos, but this is the absurd belief that has captivated and enslaved men for centuries. This time the angel adds "the fountains of waters" to the customary catalog of created entities, most probably because of their association with the earlier judgment of the great deluge, when "all the fountains of the great deep [were] broken up" (Genesis 7:11). These marvelous fountains leading from the pressurized reservoirs of water located deep beneath the earth's crust had been created by God to serve as the basis for the earth's primeval hydrologic cycle, but all this system, together with the earth's original land/water/atmosphere complex, had all been cataclysmically changed by the Flood. The angel's cry reminded men that as God had created all these things and then had destroyed them once before because of man's sin, so He was still able to control all things and that another great divine judgment was imminent.

Another reason for emphasizing the creation component of the gospel will be to reach those people whose isolated cultures have hitherto precluded them from contact with the Scriptures or knowledge about Christ. Such people can best be reached in terms of their own experience, limited so far to contact with the evidence of God in nature and in their own consciences. Paul, for example, always began with the Scriptures when he witnessed to his fellow Jews, who already knew and believed the Scriptures, needing only to convince them that Jesus was the Messiah promised in the Scriptures. When he witnessed to pagans, however, he first preached the gospel of creation (Acts 14:14-17; 17:22-30). This approach, whether for this or other reasons, was also the approach of the mighty flying angel, who gave forth a final urgent call to the lost multitudes on earth, urging them to turn back in simple faith to the one who had created them, trusting Him to save them.

Revelation 14:8.   And there followed another angel, saying, Babylon is fallen, is fallen, that great city, because she made all nations drink of the wine of the wrath of her fornication.

The second of the six angels apparently follows the first wherever he flies, proclaiming an important message of support for the everlasting gospel proclaimed by the first. The tremendous power and pageantry of the empire of the beast, centered in his magnificent capital at rebuilt Babylon, are impressive credentials and will serve greatly to intimidate all earth-dwellers, dissuading them from turning to Christ.

Therefore the second angel cries out to inform men that mighty Babylon and all she represents are doomed. Modern Babylon is merely a reincarnation of ancient Babylon, and her kingdom continues that established long ago by Nimrod, perpetuating the humanistic and "superhumanistic" (i.e., satanic) world system, set up at the first Babel, uniting mankind in a great religious, commercial, cultural, and political rebellion against God. This unspeakable spiritual adultery, worshiping and serving God's creatures instead of the true Creator, has been the deadly heritage received from Mother Babylon by all her spiritual children—all the nations of the world.

The figure of speech used in this verse is graphic and is taken from Jeremiah 51:7. "Babylon hath been a golden cup in the Lord's hand, that made all the earth drunken: the nations have drunken of her wine; therefore the nations are mad." It is picked up again in Revelation 17:2, where the theme of Babylon is developed in all its sad ramifications. The influence of Babylon, both ancient and future, is agelong and worldwide; its system of evolutionary pantheistic humanism has damned unnumbered souls through the centuries.

But Nimrod is dead and so are Nebuchadnezzar and Belshazzar, and the beast himself will very soon become an occupant of the lake of fire (Revelation 19:20). " . . . take up this proverb against the king of Babylon, and say, How hath the oppressor ceased! the golden city ceased! . . . Hell from beneath is moved for thee to meet thee at thy coming" (Isaiah 14:4-9).

Thus the angel both warns and encourages the inhabitants of earth. The fall of mighty Babylon is sure to come and it will come so soon that they could consider it as accomplished already. Twice the message is repeated for emphasis: "Babylon is fallen, is fallen!" The actual fall of Babylon will occur at the end of the tribulation, as described in Revelation 18, but the anticipatory pronouncement is made by the second angel, again and again assuring men on earth that Babylon will soon be destroyed.

Revelation 14:9.   And the third angel followed them, saying with a loud voice, If any man worship the beast and his image, and receive his mark in his forehead, or in his hand.

Then, immediately after the first two angels, a third follows in their train, warning the dwellers on earth still more urgently concerning the dangers of following the beast. His voice is loud enough for all to hear as he traverses the skies day after day, so that none can say they were not warned. Each message reinforces and emphasizes the one before. The first proclaims the everlasting gospel and warns of impending judgment; the second assures men that the mighty Babylonish empire of the beast, who seeks to bar men from the gospel, is about to fall; the third still more pointedly warns men against yielding individually to the commands of the beast.

The beast and his prophet, with all the force of the world's secular and religious systems behind them respectively, have threatened capital punishment to every person who refuses to obey the beast and to bow down to his image in the temple at Jerusalem. They have also demanded, on pain of death, that everyone receive the mark of the beast, branded on the hand or forehead. Without this mark, they can neither buy nor sell, and life will be so difficult that the pressure to submit will be overwhelming.

But the penalty for submission is infinitely worse! "And fear not them which kill the body, but are not able to kill the soul," said Jesus, "but rather fear him which is able to destroy both soul and body in hell" (Matthew 10:28).

Revelation 14:10. The same shall drink of the wine of the wrath of God, which is poured out without mixture into the cup of his indignation; and he shall be tormented with fire and brimstone in the presence of the holy angels, and in the presence of the Lamb.

The sentence to be pronounced upon those who receive the mark of the beast is fearsome indeed. As the nations have drunk of the wine of the wrath of Babylon's fornication, so now shall they drink of the wine of God's wrath. But God's wrath, for long ages tempered with grace and mercy, is now unadulterated and unmitigated, requiring a full draught by all who have chosen the beast and his dragon lord. The Lord Jesus Himself, as the Lamb of God, had once drained the cup of God's indignation, enduring all the fury of an offended Creator, substituting His own sufferings for those who deserved them. But now they had all willfully rejected His great sacrifice and so they must themselves drink the cup of God's wrath. "For in the hand of the Lord there is a cup, and the wine is red; it is full of mixture; and he poureth out of the same: but the dregs thereof, all the wicked of the earth shall wring them out, and drink them" (Psalm 75:8).

And because they had rejected the substitutionary suffering of the Lamb on God's heavenly altar they must themselves suffer in the very presence of the Lamb as well as that of the holy angels whose mediating messages and ministries they had likewise spurned. Further, their destined suffering is to be very real and severe, one of "torment" (a word sometimes also translated as "pain" and "toil"), and the torment is one of physical suffering in "fire and brimstone." This is clearly a reference to the lake of fire into which ultimately will be cast the Devil, his angels, the beast, the false prophet, and all people who die without Christ (Matthew 25:41; Revelation 20:10, 14, 15).

On the nature of "brimstone," see the discussion on Revelation 9:17, 18. Whatever this substance may be, there can be no question as to the reality of an environment of burning flames as the ultimate destiny of the wicked. This is such a frequent theme in Scripture (Daniel 7:11; Ezekiel 20:47, 48; Isaiah 66:24; Matthew 3:12; 13:50; Mark 9:43-49; and Jude 7) that it is folly to ignore it or to "spiritualize" it. The bodies of the unsaved dead are to be resurrected (Revelation 20:5, 12-15; John 5:29, etc.) and thus must be physical bodies, capable of being "tormented" in physical flames. Whether they will be burned up (as our present bodies would be) or will be so changed as to be nonflammable is not clear from Scripture. In any case, the spirits of unsaved men and women as well as the evil spirits who comprise the fallen angels will be confined to a place of eternal fire and torment.

Although this confinement will in one sense be so located as to be in the "presence" of the Lamb and the holy angels and can even be viewed by the redeemed (Isaiah 66:23, 24), these lost spirits will apparently be removed to some far-off region of the cosmos, "punished with everlasting destruction [that is, not "annihilation," but "ruin"] from the presence of the Lord, and from the glory of his power" (2 Thessalonians 1:9), cast into outer darkness, like "wandering stars, to whom is reserved the blackness of darkness for ever" (Jude 13). See the discussion on Revelation 19:20.

Revelation 14:11.   And the smoke of their torment ascendeth up for ever and ever: and they have no rest day nor night, who worship the beast and his image, and whosoever receiveth the mark of his name.

The doctrine of eternal punishment may be objectionable to modern intellectuals and cultists, but this resistance cannot offset the fact that the Bible clearly teaches it. Even if the fires of hell were not literal fires, their *torment* continues *forever,* whatever they are. Such is the unequivocal statement proclaimed by the angel as he flies through the atmosphere.

If perhaps the fires were not physical, or the resurrected bodies were not physical, at least the torment is real and eternal. It may be that the figure of physical burning is used because no other could so picturesquely convey the meaning of real and everlasting punishment. If so, the reality must be at least as terrible as its symbol.

The torment involves not only the fire and the smoke of burning but also eternal fatigue, with no prospect of sleep or respite. One of the delightful promises in heaven is that of *rest!* "There remaineth therefore a rest to the people of God" (Hebrews 4:9). "Rest from their labors," in fact, is promised in the very next verse to those who die in the Lord, and this is surely a precious promise to the weary pilgrim. But since true rest (especially from the guilt and consequences of sin) is found only in Christ (Matthew 11:28), there can be no rest to those outside of Him.

Since the context in this passage has to do with the beast-worshipers of the last half of the tribulation, the angel pointedly reminds them again that everlasting punishment awaits all who receive the mark. This explicit denotation in no way suggests, of course, that only those who actually receive this mark of the beast are destined for eternal torment in hell. It is the plain teaching of Scripture, in fact, that all unbelievers share the same lake of fire (Revelation 21:8) and that this punishment is everlasting. The beast and the false prophet, for example, are seen as still suffering in the fiery lake a thousand years after their first entry into it (Revelation 19:20; 20:2, 7, 10). If the unbelievers of any age had been subjected to the same conditions as those in this tribulation age, they also would have been every bit as willing as these to receive the mark of the beast and to give him their worship. God is both just and omniscient, and the punishment is prepared for all.

One other point is worth noting. Modern science has demonstrated the principle of conservation of matter and energy to be the most certain and universal principle of science. Matter and energy can change forms but can be neither created nor annihilated. And if mere physical matter cannot be annihilated, the far more important entity of the human soul/spirit complex (in particular the created "image of God" in man—note Genesis 1:27) can surely not be destroyed, as claimed by the so-called "annihilationists," or believers in "conditional immortality." Every human being ever conceived, possessing a divinely-created human soul and spirit, will exist forever somewhere.

Revelation 14:12.   Here is the patience of the saints: here are they that keep the commandments of God, and the faith of Jesus.

Apparently this is an interjection by John, designed to mitigate the awful pronouncements of judgment on earth with the reminder that the saints in heaven are still very concerned. It is this for which they have waited and suffered and with which their patience is finally rewarded.

The early Christians had been exhorted to patience and long-suffering, in confidence that God would eventually reward their faithfulness and judge their persecutors (Matthew 5:10-12; Romans 12:19; 2 Thessalonians 1:6-8; Hebrews 10:30-37; 1 Peter 1:6, 7). A very explicit promise to this effect had also been made to the martyred saints here in the tribulation period (Revelation 6:9-11).

"Here," says John, is the object of the agelong patience of all the saints. The gospel promises are accomplished, the judgment is come, the humanistic world system is fallen, and all the ungodly are in hell—this is the immediate prospect, and their patience is justified at last.

"Here," he says further, are all the godly. After the ultimate demise of all wickedness, the righteous shall shine forth in the kingdom of the Father (Matthew 13:43). Note the twofold ascription: "they that keep God's commandments *and*

the faith of Jesus." There have, sadly, been many antinomian teachers, in both ancient and modern times, who set these two in opposition, when they should be in apposition. Those who truly have the saving faith of the Lord Jesus love His commandments (1 John 5:3-5). Those who reject God's commandments (not as a means of salvation, of course, but as the expression of His unchanging holiness, which He seeks to produce in us) have only a superficial notion of the true faith of the Lord Jesus (1 Peter 1:14-16). If one truly believes on Jesus, he will keep His commandments (John 14:21). If one truly loves God's commandments, he will believe on Jesus (John 6:28, 29). These are two sides of the coin, as it were. Both works without faith, and faith without works, are dead. A living faith is an obedient faith and a long-suffering faith, destined finally for satisfaction and reward.

Revelation 14:13.   And I heard a voice from heaven saying unto me, Write, Blessed are the dead which die in the Lord from henceforth: Yea, saith the Spirit, that they may rest from their labours; and their works do follow them.

There is an important interval between the first three angels and the last three angels here in Chapter 14. The Holy Spirit speaks and the Son of man acts.

John had called attention to the imminent fulfillment of all God's promises to the faithful saints through the ages, but there is a particular promise to the martyrs of this last half of the tribulation, for there will never be a period of such intense and universal persecution as this. This is the second of the seven "beatitudes" of Revelation (the others in Revelation 1:3; 16:15; 19:9; 20:6; 22:7; 22:14), promising a blessing to those who die in the Lord "henceforth" (that is, after the tribulation midpoint, when the beast mounts his global program of humanistic world rule and suppression).

The promise is so important that it is conveyed to John by "a voice from heaven," commanding him to write it down. Twelve times in Revelation, in fact, is John specifically commanded, "Write!" (Revelation 1:11, 19; 14:13; 19:9; 21:5; in addition to the seven commands in the letters to the seven churches). There is no question of faulty memory or long tradition here. Everything was recorded immediately in this final book of the Holy Scriptures.

The voice from heaven which first pronounced the blessing is unidentified, but now comes an echoing response from none other than the Spirit of God. Except for the messages to the seven churches, this is the first of only two instances in the Book of Revelation where the Spirit speaks directly, the second being the very last gospel invitation in the Scriptures (Revelation 22:17).

The Spirit's message in this case is a very wonderful promise. Although applying specifically, as it comes from the heavens, to the tribulation martyrs, the principle surely can be taken to themselves by all who die in the Lord.

Once this life is done, whether at death or at the rapture, our labors are over, though our eternal service is just beginning (Revelation 22:3). We can know that our "labour is not in vain in the Lord" (1 Corinthians 15:58), for our labor here is the basis of our service there (Matthew 25:21). By the same token, those who seek ease and favor here will be barren there (1 Corinthians 3:14, 15).

One of the most blessed promises of Scripture is that the good works we do "in the Lord" while we are still in the flesh can still bear fruit and be credited to our "work record" even after we die. "Now he that planteth and he that watereth are one: and every man shall receive his own reward according to his own labour" (1 Corinthians 3:8).

One's reward is according to his labor, not the fruit from the labor, which may well come to fruition long after he himself has gone to be with the Lord. "Their works do follow them." Each tribulation martyr undoubtedly will leave an unforgettable testimony to all who observe their martyrdom. For our own part, still in the prerapture chronology of human history, one of the most challenging incentives to faithfulness in labor and seed-sowing is the possibility that some of our own ministries in these last days may bear fruit even after the rapture. Testimonies given, tracts and books distributed, letters and articles written, by God's grace, may be used to help win some of these tribulation saints. May He enable us to be faithful!

The Grapes of Wrath

The Spirit of God has spoken concerning the blessedness of believers, even those who give their lives because of their faith. It is time for the second group of three angels described in this chapter to bring their messages of judgment. The perspective is still that of the middle of the tribulation, looking forward to the coming climax at the end. The first three angels had warned the earth of imminent judgment; the last three speak of the implementation of that judgment, ordering and arranging the coming battle of the great day of God at Armageddon.

Revelation 14:14.   And I looked, and behold a white cloud, and upon the cloud one sat like unto the Son of man, having on his head a golden crown, and in his hand a sharp sickle.

Still in the interval between the two sets of three angels, but immediately after the comforting message of the Holy Spirit, John views an amazing scene. The same Son of man whom he had seen at the beginning (Revelation 1:13) appears again. In the interim between these two appearances, the Lord Jesus had appeared as the Lamb, as the rider, as the mighty angel, and in various other aspects, but now John sees Him again as He is and will be forever, as the glorified Son of man. It is as the Son of man that the nations will see Him come in glory

(Matthew 24:30) and reign in power (Matthew 26:64). They will see Him "coming in the clouds of heaven" and here John also sees Him on a glory cloud.

The sickle in His hand, of course, indicates He is coming in judgment and the crown on His head indicates He is coming to reign. As John had heard Him say long before, the Father "hath given him authority to execute judgment also, because he is the Son of man" (John 5:27). As Son of man, as perfect man, as resurrected man, He is also the Heir of all God's promises to man and is to have dominion over all the earth (Psalm 2:7, 8; 8:4-6).

The scene is obviously one of preparation for judgment and the figure of the reaping sickle is taken from Joel 3:13, "Put ye in the sickle, for the harvest is ripe: come, get you down; for the press is full, the fats overflow; for their wickedness is great." In context Joel also is prophesying of the coming great battle of Armageddon (Joel 3:9-16), reaching its climax when "the Lord also shall roar out of Zion, and utter His voice from Jerusalem."

Revelation 14:15.   And another angel came out of the temple, crying with a loud voice to him that sat on the cloud, Thrust in thy sickle, and reap: for the time is come for thee to reap; for the harvest of the earth is ripe.

The last three angels of the preview of judgment in this chapter now make their appearances in rapid succession. The first one emerges from a waiting period in the temple to cry out to the Son of man on the cloud. Whether this is the heavenly temple or the earthly temple is not stated, but it is probably the latter. The angel had perhaps been observing the abominable defilement of the temple by the beast and his image, and so cries up to the heavens, entreating the Lord not to delay any longer. The harvest of the wicked is ready for the threshing; the grapes of wrath on earth are full and ready for the reaping.

A created angel cannot, of course, command the Son of man to proceed with judgment, so that his cry should be regarded as a plea rather than as a demand. The holy angels, no less than the martyred saints, are appalled at the wickedness of men and devils and yearn for the time to come when the great rebellion will be forever put down and God's will shall be done in all His creation.

Revelation 14:16.   And he that sat on the cloud thrust in his sickle on the earth; and the earth was reaped.

In response to the plea of the angel guarding the holy temple (made unholy by the abomination of desolation standing in the holy place) the Son of man does begin His mighty reaping. The "reaping of the earth" is apparently something different than "gathering the vine of the earth" (verse 19), though the great sickle of judgment is used in both. The one precedes the other, and the latter is clearly a reference to the gathering of the armies of the beast and his followers to Armageddon. The first reaping is apparently a "harvest" of grain, the second a "vintage" of grapes. The first is cut and threshed, the second is gathered for the winepress. Probably the first refers to all the worldwide judgments of the second half of the tribulation, unleashed when the seven bowls of wrath pour out over the earth (Revelation 16), climaxing in the utter destruction of Babylon, the capital, and the entire Babylonish world-system. The second refers more specifically to the final judgment of the beast and all his followers at Armageddon.

The climax of this reaping of the earth at Babylon is described in Revelation 17 and 18, but was long ago prophesied also by Jeremiah and foreshadowed by the defeat of ancient Babylon. "For thus saith the Lord of hosts, the God of Israel; The daughter of Babylon is like a threshingfloor, it is time to thresh her: yet a little while, and the time of her harvest shall come" (Jeremiah 51:33).

The harvesting of Babylon will separate wheat and chaff. There are still some of God's people in the Babylonian system even at this late date and the final judgments will sift them out. "As therefore the tares are gathered and burned in the fire; so shall it be in the end of this world. The Son of man shall send forth his angels, and they shall gather out of his kingdom all things that offend, and them which do iniquity; and shall cast them into a furnace of fire: there shall be wailing and gnashing of teeth" (Matthew 13:40-42). Both the Old and New Testament prophecies of Babylon's fall contain exhortations to those of God's people who yet are clinging to their Babylonian comforts to escape her before the destruction falls (Jeremiah 51:45; Revelation 18:4).

Revelation 14:17.   And another angel came out of the temple which is in heaven, he also having a sharp sickle.

The harvest of the earth has been undertaken by the Son of man Himself, quite possibly because He is still seeking to save that which is lost. Though only a few corns of wheat can be found in a field choked with tares, He still cries in the midst of judgment, "Come out of her, my people!" And some still respond, coming out of the great tribulation, washing their robes white in the blood of the Lamb, refusing the brand of the beast, and willing even to become martyrs if the Lord so ordains.

To another angel, however, He assigns the task of reaping "the vine of the earth," casting these all into the trampling of the vintage of the great winepress of the wrath of God. This angel is called out of the temple in heaven, thus contrasting with the preceding angel in the earthly temple. Possibly this is one of the "presence angels" (see Revelation 8:2) since he was in the temple of God's presence in the heavenlies. Furthermore, he is assigned a ministry quite close to that of the Son of man Himself, wielding the great sickle of judgment. That it is a judgment sickle, speaking not of harvest blessing but of cutting destruction, is indicated by its description as sharp. No cluster of grapes ripe for the winepress will escape its keen edge.

Revelation 14:18.   And another angel came out from the altar, which had power over fire; and cried with a loud cry to him that had the sharp sickle, saying, Thrust in thy sharp sickle, and gather the clusters of the vine of the earth; for her grapes are fully ripe.

Finally the sixth angel of Revelation 14 appears and this angel, like the fourth, is on the earth, assigned evidently to attend the altar in the temple at Jerusalem. The Scriptures give us intriguing glimpses here and there of the particular duties and powers of the different angels of God, though all in one way or another minister somehow to the heirs of salvation (Hebrews 1:14). Here in Revelation, for example, we have encountered angels who can even restrain the winds (Revelation 7:1). This one has "power over fire," perhaps calling or restraining fires from heaven in relation to the altar as in the days of Elijah (1 Kings 18:17-41).

As the fourth angel had entreated the Son of man to thrust in His sickle and reap the harvest of the earth, so now the sixth angel will beseech the fifth angel, sent by the Son of man, to thrust in his sickle and gather the vintage of the earth. The grapes of wickedness and rebellion have ripened fully on the vine, and are fit now directly for the great winepress of the wrath of God.

The "vine of the earth" contrasts diametrically with the vine of heaven. Jesus said "I am the true vine" (John 15:1). The fruit borne by the branches of this true vine ("ye are the branches," said Jesus) is good fruit, fruit that "remains" (John 15:16). The fruit of the "vine of the earth," however, yields sour grapes and bitter wine and is about to be trampled in the divine presses. The false vine, with all its branches visibly joined to it by the tell-tale "mark," can only refer to the great counterfeit system of Antichrist, established by the beast and the false prophet in the power of the dragon. This is the final form of the cosmic rebellion against the Creator and this must finally be crushed forever.

As the blood of the Lamb once was shed by His enemies, so their blood now must be shed, wrung out to the last drop. When His blood was shed, however, it became the life-giving new wine of the kingdom, symbolized by the cup of remembrance at the Lord's supper. When their blood is shed, crushed out in the great vintage-trampling at Armageddon, it will merely provide "the supper of the great God" (Revelation 19:17) to the fowls of the air.

Revelation 14:19.   And the angel thrust in his sickle into the earth, and gathered the vine of the earth, and cast it into the great winepress of the wrath of God.

The thrusting of the sickle to cut the vine of the earth obviously speaks of a rapid displacement of all the followers of the beast from their home countries. They are to be gathered to one place. This is the great gathering spoken of in many other passages as well. "I will also gather all nations, and will bring them down into the valley of Jehoshaphat" (Joel 3:2). "For I will gather all nations against Jerusalem to battle" (Zechariah 14:2). "And he gathered them together into a place called in the Hebrew tongue Armageddon" (Revelation 16:16). "And I saw the beast, and the kings of the earth, and their armies, gathered together to make war against him that sat on the horse, and against his army" (Revelation 19:19).

The "winepress" into which they are to be cast is the place ordained for ages to be the locale of the last great conflict between Christ and Antichrist. Tremendous numbers of soldiers will be massed in the land of Israel for this final confrontation. Joel describes it thus: "Multitudes, multitudes in the valley of decision: for the day of the Lord is near in the valley of decision" (Joel 3:14).

Once gathered and cast into the winepress, these condemned multitudes can face only "a certain fearful looking for of judgment and fiery indignation, which shall devour the adversaries" (Hebrews 10:27). It is the "winepress of the wrath of God," and it is Christ Himself who executes the wrath, for "he treadeth the winepress of the fierceness and wrath of Almighty God" (Revelation 19:15).

Revelation 14:20.   And the winepress was trodden without the city, and blood came out of the winepress, even unto the horse bridles, by the space of a thousand and six hundred furlongs.

As John looks forward in his vision toward the end of the tribulation period and sees all the nations being drawn like a magnet to the land of the chosen people, he must sense the enormity of the calamity that is soon to overwhelm them. But he could hardly have anticipated the awful scene that eventually unfolds in his prophetic vision.

Nothing less than the sudden spilling of the blood of all the unnumbered multitudes massed together in a great phalanx extending through the whole land of Israel is the terrible sight entrusted to him. The bloodshed is so massive and so quick that the only apt comparison is the spurting of the juice from tremendous clusters of ripe fruit beneath the feet of the grape-tramplers in a winepress. The hordes of soldiers and civilians, many riding horses, no doubt many on foot, perhaps others on vehicles of one sort and another, thronging together as in a great trough, unable to flee, their gaze transfixed on an amazing scene in the heavens, suddenly explode like bursting grapes, and the blood pours from a billion fountains.

The bodies quickly are awash in their own blood, and will soon become carrion for the waiting flocks of vultures that darken the sky (Revelation 19:17,

18). Thus shall be the unspeakable end of those who worship the beast and receive his mark.

This vat of blood will extend for sixteen hundred furlongs (Greek *stadion,* with each stadion the equivalent of about 607 feet), or a distance of approximately 180 miles. Imagine, if you can, a massive army of 200 million men, stretched out for 180 miles in length and, say, a mile in width. This would allow each man an average area of only twenty-five square feet in which to maneuver. That is, every man would be separated by only five feet from the next man in front of him, behind him, and on each side. If they were on horseback, they would be packed like sardines.

That 200 million is not an impossible number is evident from the fact that this is the number of demon horsemen released from the River Euphrates under the sixth trumpet (see on Revelation 9:16) and the fact that, at this time, there will probably be still well over 2 billion people on earth. Most of the able-bodied men (possibly also women) will be drafted into the armies of the nations under the beast. If 10 percent of the world's population is gathered to fight under the beast in the Holy Land (and such seems appropriate in light of the superlatives employed in Scripture to describe this vast army), that would come to 200 million, and such a number would become a veritable sea of humanity, a mile wide and 180 miles long.

And when the blood suddenly bursts forth from the bodies of these multitudes, in addition to the blood of the horses on which they are mounted, the sea of humanity will become a sea of blood. The blood will drain toward the valley center, where it will literally reach to the horses' bridles.

All of this will take place "without the city," so that the Holy City itself will not be polluted with this bath of blood. The armies will have besieged Jerusalem, and to some extent have plundered it (Zechariah 12:2, 3; 14:1-3), but will be unable to occupy it and will withdraw toward their line down in the wilderness of Judaea and along the Jordan River and the Dead Sea, extending down into ancient Idumea, or Edom.

The great phalanx will project deep into Edom, in fact, at least as far as the ancient Edomite stronghold of Bozrah, which is about twenty miles southeast of the southern tip of the Dead Sea. On the north it will extend to and beyond the great plains of Esdraelon, or the valley of Jezreel, near the town of Megiddo, a region known since ancient times by the foreboding name of Armageddon, "the mount of Megiddo." The center of the phalanx will be concentrated in the Judaean wilderness opposite Jerusalem, in a region where King Jehoshaphat once won a great victory over the enemies of God's people (2 Chronicles 20:20-24) and thus later called in Scripture "the valley of Jehoshaphat."

The line from Bozrah through the valley of Jehoshaphat to Armageddon is roughly 140 miles in length, with Jerusalem closely opposite the middle of it. The 180 miles mentioned in this verse would allow the military forces of the beast to protrude about twenty miles beyond Bozrah and Armageddon. If the width of the encampment is 1⅓ miles instead of one mile, then the termini would be at Bozrah and Armageddon (assuming one person every five feet, as noted above). Whatever the precise numbers and areas may be, at least the biblical descriptions are eminently plausible, and may be taken quite literally.

It is this great valley in which the blood will, at its center, reach the bridles of the horses. "The sword of the Lord is filled with blood, . . . for the Lord hath a sacrifice in Bozrah, and a great slaughter in the land of Idumea" (Isaiah 34:6). "Who is this that cometh from Edom, with dyed garments from Bozrah? this that is glorious in his apparel, traveling in the greatness of his strength? I that speak in righteousness, mighty to save. Wherefore art thou red in thine apparel, and thy garments like him that treadeth in the winefat? I have trodden the winepress alone; and of the people there was none with me: for I will tread them in mine anger, and trample them in my fury; and their blood shall be sprinkled upon my garments, and I will stain all my raiment. For the day of vengeance is in mine heart, and the year of my redeemed is come" (Isaiah 63:1-4).

The winepress thus extends from Bozrah in Edom on the south. In the north it reaches to Armageddon (Revelation 16:14-16). "And he was clothed with a vesture dipped in blood: . . . and he treadeth the winepress of the fierceness and wrath of Almighty God" (Revelation 19:13-15). Its center converges on the valley of Jehoshaphat. "Let the heathen be wakened, and come up to the valley of Jehoshaphat: for there will I sit to judge the heathen round about. Put ye in the sickle, for the harvest is ripe: come, get you down; for the press is full, the fats overflow; for their wickedness is great" (Joel 3:12, 13).

But what is the occasion for such an unprecedented assemblage of the armies of the earth in the Holy Land? Why would such hordes be gathered against the pitiable remnants of the forces of Israel? Many Israelites had flown to the wilderness when the beast had taken over Jerusalem and the temple (Revelation 11:2; 12:6) and the remainder had been the objects of his decimating persecutions. Yet here we see the gigantic armies of the beast besieging Jerusalem (Zechariah 12:1-3) once again.

It is evident that something of great moment has happened in Jerusalem since the installation of the beast's image in the holy place at the middle of the tribulation. In some mysterious way the beast's deputies have been frustrated, the Israelis are again in control in Jerusalem, and the beast (presumably ensconced in his new Babylonian capital) is furious.

The precise fulfillment of this remarkable development is right at the end of the tribulation, of course, but John is permitted to look forward to it in his prophetic vision even though his immediate perspective is focused on the tribulation's midpoint. Although the Scriptures are not explicit as to how this will all be accomplished, the vision of the 144,000 Israelites on Mount Zion with which this chapter began implies that their return to Jerusalem has something to do with it.

Perhaps (and this is only a suggestion) the 144,000, after teaching their people in the wilderness for almost three-and-a-half years, preparing them for the coming of their Messiah, return to Jerusalem to meet Him there when He comes. Since they are under God's invincible physical protection (Revelation 7:3; 9:4; 14:1), the beast's forces would be unable to prevent their occupying the city and setting up an encampment on Mount Zion, where the Lamb will quickly come to meet them (Revelation 14:1).

Knowing that the final confrontation with the returning Redeemer is imminent, the beast (no doubt energized and guided by his master, Satan) will then desperately assemble all the armies he can muster, from all the kings of the earth, hoping against hope that he can thereby recapture Jerusalem and perhaps even defeat the armies of heaven as they return with Christ.

This last-ditch spasm of a defeated foe is utterly futile, of course. Although it will constitute the mightiest army ever assembled on earth, it is really only the gathering of the ripe fruit of the vine of the earth for a mighty blood-letting in the winepress of God.

The heaven-bathed sword (Isaiah 34:7) will "strike through kings in the day of his wrath. He shall judge among the heathen, he shall fill the places with the dead bodies; he shall wound [that is, "crush"] the heads over many countries" (Psalm 110:5, 6). It will not be a sword of steel which sheds the blood of the wicked, for "out of his mouth goeth a sharp sword, that with it he should smite the nations" (Revelation 19:15). "The Lord will roar from Zion" (Amos 1:2). "He shall smite the earth with the rod of his mouth, and with the breath of his lips shall he slay the wicked" (Isaiah 11:4). "And then shall that Wicked be revealed, whom the Lord shall consume with the spirit of his mouth, and shall destroy with the brightness of his coming" (2 Thessalonians 2:8). His powerful Word is "sharper than a two-edged sword" (Hebrews 4:12) when He finally speaks in judgment.

15

Prelude to Doomsday

(Revelation 15)

The fifteenth chapter of Revelation is, by far, the shortest chapter in the book, serving primarily as a prologue to the sixteenth chapter and the somber recital of the seven great bowls of wrath and the seven last plagues on the earth. Nevertheless it is of vital importance in its own right, providing another beautiful glimpse of the joy and glory at the heavenly throne.

The chronological framework of the seven-year history inscribed in Revelation is contained especially in Chapter 6 (the seal judgment, Chapters 8 and 9 (the trumpet judgments), and Chapter 16 (the bowl judgments). The seal and trumpet judgments occupy essentially the first three-and-a-half years, the bowl judgments the last three-and-a-half years. However, the seventh seal releases the seven trumpets (Revelation 8:1, 2) and the seventh trumpet calls forth the seven bowls (Revelation 11:15; 15:1, 7), continuing to reverberate across the skies as the bowls are emptied on the earth. The seventh trumpet is also equivalent to the third "woe" (Revelation 11:14; 12:12). Chapter 7 constitutes a parenthetical revelation, interjected chronologically between the seal and trumpet judgments but also looking forward to the trumpet at the end of the tribulation period. Chapter 10 similarly appears at the end of the trumpet judgments and also previews the remaining years of the tribulation. Chapters 11, 12, 13, and 14 are parenthetical chapters which expound agelong themes. Their perspective is that of the midpoint of the tribulation period but they also look back to the very beginning of the conflict between God and Satan and forward to its termination. In particular they outline key events and personages from the beginning of the tribulation period to its climactic end, even looking forward to the eternal ages to come.

Chapter 15, likewise, is partly parenthetical even though it provides the prelude to the resumption of the chronological plagues of Chapter 16. It contains backward glances to God's former judgments and also anticipates the glory to come, as it introduces the seven last judgments of God's bowls of wrath.

Song at the Glassy Sea

The chapter opens with a marvelous vision of the future, made all the more beautiful and glorious by its stark contrast with the unprecedented vision of slaughter and judgment in the last verses of the fourteenth chapter. Both of these are scenes brought by God before John's amazed eyes: "And I looked, and behold . . ." (Revelation 14:14). "And I saw . . . great and marvelous, . . ." (Revelation 15:1). The apostle would assure us again that he was not fabricating these visions. "I saw them!" he insists.

Revelation 15:1. **And I saw another sign in heaven, great and marvellous, seven angels having the seven last plagues; for in them is filled up the wrath of God.**

This is the third "sign" (Greek *semeion*) identified as such by John in Revelation. The same word is rendered "wonder" in its two parallel occurrences in Revelation and is frequently elsewhere translated "miracle." Even in the latter usage, however, its primary thrust is that of a sign. Certain miracles were signs of the unique power of God, and their purpose was both to attest to that power and also to teach a spiritual lesson suggested by the sign. Even the miracles performed by the false prophet (Revelation 13:13, 14) were intended by him as signs of his own mighty power.

The first divinely-given sign in Revelation was that of the great woman and the second that of the great dragon (Revelation 12:1, 3). Both of these were also "miracles" or "wonders" because they were specially-created pictorializations in the heavens, depicting the principal characters in the agelong conflict between the seed of the woman and the old serpent, Satan.

In the same way, this third sign is a miraculous scene in the skies, a preview of the great drama about to be played on earth and the majestic choir that will be prepared to sing the chorus at its triumphant conclusion. When the woman's conquering seed finally consigns that old serpent to the great pit (Revelation 20:2, 3), all those whom the beast had sought to destroy will reign with Christ instead (Revelation 20:4).

It is noteworthy how often in Scripture God has sealed His revelation to His prophets and ministers by such a threefold sign. This was done for Joseph (Genesis 37:5-11; 40:8-22; 41:15-40), for Moses (Exodus 3:2; 4:2-5; 4:6, 7), for Joshua (Joshua 4:22-24; 6:20; 10:10-14), for Gideon (Judges 6:36-40; 7:13-15), for Saul

(1 Samuel 10:1-7), for Elijah (1 Kings 19:9-13), for Elisha (2 Kings 2:14, 22, 24), for Hezekiah (2 Kings 19:20, 29-35; 36:8-11), for Ezekiel (Ezekiel 1:1; 3:22, 23; 8:4) and others. Thus also did John receive this special threefold sign (amidst all the others he had seen—note John 20:30, 31), and he has attested it to us.

This third sign was "great and marvelous," a phrase used elsewhere in Scripture only once again, and that just two verses hence. The sign was great and marvelous because the works of God which it depicted will be great and marvelous (Revelation 15:3). These seven last plagues are the greatest plagues. The seals visited great plagues upon the earth, the trumpets still greater plagues (Revelation 9:20), but these are the greatest and most awesome of all.

God had been speaking to men in His wrath, but they would not heed. Now He would vex them in His sore displeasure (Psalm 2:5). That these are the last plagues proves again that they are not mere reiterations of former plagues. The seals and trumpets and bowls are sequential, not parallel. In these plagues God's wrath is finally filled up (Greek *teleo,* translated "fulfilled" in verse 8, and "finished" in Revelation 10:7).

The word "plagues" conveys the idea of judicially inflicted pains, rather than sicknesses. It is frequently translated "stripes" (as in Luke 12:47). In Revelation 13:3, 12, 14, it is translated "wound." The great sign in the heavens pictures the overflowing wrath of a long-suffering judge finally breaking forth in fury, inflicting the severest punishments and deadliest blows which He can administer.

The seven angels administering His judgments are themselves also symbolic, being part of the sign. They probably represent all God's holy angels, since all are vitally concerned with this final fulfillment of God's great purposes (1 Peter 1:12). Seven specific "presence angels" (Revelation 8:2) had been given the seven judgment trumpets, but these angels of the last plagues evidently signify all angels.

However, there is an intriguing way in which these might be seven specific angels who could, at the same time, represent all angels. There were seven specific angels assigned to guard seven specific churches in Asia, the very ones to whom John was addressing the Apocalypse itself (Revelation 1:11). These angels were the "seven stars" in the right hand of the Son of man (Revelation 1:13, 16, 20), a position of unique significance and importance. Yet there is no question that these seven churches represent all churches, and thus their seven angels represent all angels (Ephesians 3:9-11). It may be that these seven angels could continue to represent all angels in their watch-care over the people of God on earth by thus administering the seven final judgments which will finally restore the earth to its rightful purposes under its good and faithful stewards. This possibility is further suggested by the fact that one of them shows John the judgment of the false bride, the harlot church (Revelation 17:1) and another shows John the eternal home of the Lamb's bride, the true Church (Revelation 21:9).

Whether or not these seven church angels are also the angels of the seven last plagues does not, of course, affect the significance of this third great sign in the sky. Furthermore, this is only a part of the sign. A very special part of God's people also are pictured there.

Revelation 15:2.   And I saw as it were a sea of glass mingled with fire: and them that had gotten the victory over the beast, and over his image, and over his mark, and over the number of his name, stand on the sea of glass, having the harps of God.

As John continues to gaze at the great and marvelous heavenly sign, he sees also a remarkable assemblage of redeemed men and women. As noted above, the seven angels represent all those holy angels whose ministry is to the "heirs of salvation" (Hebrews 1:14) and this particular body, coming out of the last half of the great tribulation, is the final installment, as it were, of the saints to be translated to heaven. Their lives in the flesh have been terminated by martyrdom during the very period when the seven last plagues are being visited on earth. It had been decreed that all must receive the mark of the beast and worship his image, on pain of death (Revelation 13:15-17). On the other hand, God had decreed that any who did worship the beast and receive his mark would be cast into eternal torment (Revelation 14:9-11). Physical death with eternal salvation or physical life with eternal damnation—that had been their bitter choice, and multitudes had opted for the brief continuation of their wretched lives on the earth, enduring all the judgments of God rather than the executioners appointed by the beast.

These, however, had gained the victory over the beast. They overcame him because they "loved not their lives unto the death" (Revelation 12:11). Their actual gathering must await their resurrection at the end of the tribulation (Revelation 20:4-6), but John could already see them, "as it were," in the heavenly sign along with the symbolic angels.

The sign also included, as it were, a remarkable sea of glass mingled with fire, with the martyred saints standing on it (the Greek *epi* could also be translated "by"). Although there was an actual crystal sea (Revelation 4:6) at the throne set in the temple in the heavens when Christ returned to the air, it must be remembered that the particular sea in the sign only symbolized the real sea, where the saints will sing together at the end of the tribulation.

There had been a sea in Solomon's temple (1 Kings 7:23), and the temple was also equipped with ten lavers (2 Chronicles 4:6), but both sea and lavers were used for washings in connection with the sacrificial offerings. The sea in the heavenly temple obviously pictures something more than this, however, since there is no need for cleansing the heavenly priests. The beautiful "sea of glass like unto crystal" of Revelation 4:6 is not really explained, but its purpose is at least partially clarified in its symbolic representation here. It has a memorial signification of great import to all the people of God through the ages, as seen in the next verse. It also speaks, through the mingled fire, of coming judgment.

This particular assemblage has also been given harps, or lyres. The trumpets of the angels and the harps of the saints (Revelation 5:8; 14:2) are the only heavenly musical instruments, at least as described in Revelation ("musicians and pipers," as well as "harpers and trumpeters" will be common in wicked Babylon, however, as noted in Revelation 18:22). In any case, there will surely be an abundance of music and singing in the holy city and the new earth.

Revelation 15:3.   And they sing the song of Moses the servant of God, and the song of the Lamb, saying, Great and marvellous are thy works, Lord God Almighty; just and true are thy ways, thou King of saints.

Gathered by the glassy sea, the redeemed saints in the sign are seen and heard by John to be singing two great anthems of victory and praise, the song of Moses and the song of the Lamb. It is this fact that gives us the necessary clue to the symbolic import of the sea itself, for the song of Moses had first been sung long before by the shores of a sea of deliverance and judgment.

In the new earth there will be "no more sea" (Revelation 21:1), but there will be the beautiful crystal sea surrounding the throne of God as a fitting memorial of what the mighty sea had once accomplished for God's purposes and God's people in the first earth. Water, for example, was used for cleansing—hence, the laver in the tabernacle and the sea in the temple. There will be no more need for cleansing in the new earth, however.

More to the point in this instance is the fact that the sea had been used by God as a vehicle for the deliverance of God's people and for judgment on their enemies. This was the theme of the original "song of Moses" (Exodus 15:1-21). "I will sing unto the Lord, for he hath triumphed gloriously: the horse and his rider hath he thrown into the sea. . . . . Thou in thy mercy hast led forth the people which thou hast redeemed: thou hast guided them in thy strength unto thy holy habitation. . . . The Lord shall reign for ever and ever."

Portions of this song, first composed over 3,500 years earlier, are thus peculiarly appropriate for these tribulation saints, and they might well recall the ancient song of Moses and the great deliverance of those first Israelites, when the same Red Sea which saved them also destroyed the armies of mighty Pharaoh. The horse and rider which were inundated in the sea of water might even be paralleled by the sea of blood extending to the horses' bridles (Revelation 14:20) which they had seen.

There was also another song of Moses (Deuteronomy 31:30), now preserved as Deuteronomy 32:1-43, which might well also be sung appropriately by these tribulation martyrs. Another possibility is the ninetieth Psalm, the psalm attributed to "Moses, the man of God." However, the most appropriate seems to be the actual song at the Red Sea, praising God for His great salvation.

Long before even that deliverance, there had occurred an even greater judgment and redemption by the waters of the sea, "when once the long-suffering of God waited in the days of Noah, . . . wherein few, that is, eight souls were saved by water" (1 Peter 3:20). The same waters which had destroyed an ungodly world had saved the believing remnant from destruction by that world. It is interesting also that the waters of baptism, symbolizing death to sinfulness and resurrection unto holiness, are compared both to the waters of the Red Sea (1 Corinthians 10:1, 2) and to the waters of the great Flood (1 Peter 3:20, 21).

Thus will the sea at the heavenly throne perpetually call to remembrance the waters of the Flood, the waters of the Red Sea, and the waters of baptism, all speaking both of God's judgment on the wickedness of rebellious men and His great salvation for those who trust Him and obey His Word. This last company of persecuted believers had experienced these also, in high degree, and so could join heartily in singing the ancient song of Moses.

But also they could gladly join all the other redeemed hosts (Revelation 5:8-14) in the great anthem of the Lamb. It was only because of His gracious work on their behalf that God was able to save them. They had been able to overcome the beast and the dragon not only because of their willingness to witness and to die for their faith, but first of all "by the blood of the Lamb" (Revelation 12:11).

There is surely no conflict, as some have taught, between the dispensations of Moses and the Lamb. The written law was given by Moses, and grace and truth came through Jesus Christ (John 1:17); both are integral components of God's will for man. The contrasting "but" of John 1:17 is not in the original. The redeemed saints could with equal faith and enthusiasm sing the song of Moses and the song of the Lamb.

Though neither of these songs, as recorded in Exodus 15 and Revelation 5, contains the precise ascriptions cited in this passage, the exalted words are perfectly consistent with both. His works (whether the mighty miracle at the Red Sea or the even greater miracle at Calvary and the empty tomb) are indeed "great and marvelous." His ways (whether the destruction of rebellious Pharaoh or the sacrifice of His sinless Son on a cross of substitution) are surely just and true. Whatsoever God doeth is right, and whatsoever He saith is true.

He is the "Lord God Almighty" (a term used five times in Revelation, and nowhere else). "Almighty" (Greek *pantokrator*) is a synonym for "omnipotent." He is also long-suffering, desiring men to come to repentance, but one day soon He will assume His great power and reign (Revelation 11:17). He is Creator of all—therefore Sovereign of all!

But also He is "King of saints." This title is used in no other passage, and a few of the manuscripts render it "King of nations," others "King of ages." However, neither of these two titles appears anywhere else either, and the King James rendition, based on the Received Text, best fits the context.

As king of all the saints (a term applied in the New Testament uniquely to true believers in Christ), the Lord Jesus will soon lead them forth to battle (Revelation 19:7-16). At this juncture He has not yet become king over all nations (note the next verse), but the saints all gladly acknowledge His rule, knowing from full experience that He is both just and true.

The crystal sea, speaking of a past watery judgment and deliverance, is also "mingled with fire," speaking of the impending fiery judgment and deliverance. The Apostle Peter likewise, first reminded men of a former watery cataclysm, purging the heavens and the earth, which were of old, and then warning them that "the heavens and earth, which are now," have been "reserved unto fire" (2 Peter 3:5-7). Water and fire do not commingle on the earth, but the great heavenly sign shows them mingled in heaven, both testifying of God's power and righteousness as well as His grace and truth.

Revelation 15:4.   Who shall not fear thee, O Lord, and glorify thy name? for thou only art holy: for all nations shall come and worship before thee; for thy judgments are made manifest.

This stanza continues the song of the martyred saints, reflecting the themes of both the song of Moses and that of the Lamb. "Who is like unto thee, O Lord, among the gods? who is like thee, glorious in holiness, fearful in praises, doing wonders?" (Exodus 15:11). "Worthy is the Lamb that was slain to receive power, and riches, and wisdom, and strength, and honour, and glory, and blessing" (Revelation 5:12).

The earth-dwellers had proclaimed: "Who is like unto the beast? who is able to make war with him?" (Revelation 13:4). These had made war with him and so could now answer, "Who shall not fear thee, O Lord?" Power over all nations had been given to the beast (Revelation 13:7), but soon all nations must bow to the Lord. God the Lord is the only true Holy One (Greek *hosios;* not the usual word for "holy," stressing absolute *rightness*). God alone is completely right—by very definition—and therefore, sooner or later, all must some day fear Him, glorify Him, worship Him.

His judgments (that is, His "righteous deeds and righteous words") shall soon be universally acclaimed as such. Someday everyone will understand and acknowledge that even God's punishments are deserved and righteous in the fullest degree. The terrible plagues that are about to burst on the earth are incalculably destructive but are wholly merited and perfectly designed for God's righteous purpose. "I have sworn by myself, the word is gone out of my mouth in righteousness, and shall not return, That unto me every knee shall bow, every tongue shall swear" (Isaiah 45:23).

Smoke in the Open Temple

This midpoint in Chapter 15 actually marks a change of scenes and themes. John has been describing the great sign in the heavens, with its vision of the seven angels and the host of tribulation saints singing their songs of victory and praise at the glassy sea. But now the narrative must return to the actual prosecution of the judgments which will warrant this future paean of glory. John's attention, therefore, is directed back to the actual temple and throne in the heavens where these actions are about to be implemented.

Revelation 15:5.   And after that I looked, and, behold, the temple of the tabernacle of the testimony in heaven was opened.

The phrase "And after that" clearly indicates this change in perspective, as John was constrained to fix his attention once again on the actual temple scene in the atmosphere rather than the great sign in the skies.

The unique terminology, "temple of the tabernacle of the testimony," deserves close attention. John had already been shown this "true tabernacle" (Hebrews 8:2), even recording the amazing fact that the long-lost ark of the covenant had apparently been translated there (Revelation 11:19), presumably at the time of the plundering of the earthly temple by Nebuchadnezzar (Jeremiah 52:12-23).

Within the ark, of course, had been placed the tables of the Decalogue, and the whole was established within the most holy place of the tabernacle. These were called the "two tables of testimony, tables of stone, written with the finger of God" (Exodus 31:18). Consequently the ark was commonly called "the ark of the testimony" (as in Exodus 25:22) and even the entire tabernacle was often called "the tabernacle of the testimony" (Numbers 10:11), stressing that the most important aspect of the tabernacle was as a dwelling place for God's Ten Commandments, the great "Testimony" which He "established in Jacob" (Psalm 78:5). These Ten Commandments constitute the great "witness" of God to man, revealing both God's own nature of perfect holiness *to* man, and also His standard of perfect holiness *for* man, created in the image of God. All the Scriptures are divinely inspired, but the Decalogue is divinely inscribed, written by the very finger of God on tables of stone, placed temporarily in an earthly tabernacle as the peculiar treasure of His chosen people, but then enshrined eternally in the heavenly tabernacle, as a continuing "testimony" of God through the ages to come.

The basic meaning of "tabernacle," whether in the Hebrew or Greek words so translated, is that of "dwelling place." In Israel, it was also the tent of meeting, where God would meet with His people (actually only with the high priest, properly prepared and cleansed to represent the people), but it was primarily a dwelling place for the ark of the testimony.

This is apparently the emphasis here in Revelation. The "tabernacle of the testimony" is the beautiful heavenly home of the ark of God's covenant. But, then, what is "the temple of the tabernacle of the testimony"? Actually there are two different Greek words commonly translated "temple" in the New Testament. One is *hieron,* referring to the entire precincts of the temple. The other is *naos,* referring particularly to the sanctuary itself, the shrine as it were. It is this latter word which is used here. Thus the thought of the entire phrase is: "the inner sanctuary of the dwelling place of God's ten commandments, His eternal testimony to man."

And now, at this climactic juncture in the history of God's dealings with man, John sees all this opened. In the earthly tabernacle, as later in Solomon's temple, the ark was always hidden from man, behind the thick veil of the temple in the Holy of Holies. "And after the second vail, the tabernacle which is called the Holiest of all; which had the golden censer, and the ark of the covenant overlaid round about with gold, wherein was he golden pot that had manna, and Aaron's rod that budded, and the tables of the covenant; and over it the cherubims of glory shadowing the mercy seat; of which we cannot now speak particularly" (Hebrews 9:3-5).

This holiest place of the tabernacle was not accessible to the people, or even to the priests. Only the high priest, once each year, could enter it (Hebrews 9:7). When the temple of Solomon was built later to replace the tabernacle, again Solomon placed the ark in the most holy place (2 Chronicles 5:7). By this time, for some reason, "There was nothing in the ark save the two tables which Moses put therein at Horeb, when the Lord made a covenant with the children of Israel, when they came out of Egypt" (2 Chronicles 5:10). Later towards the very end of Judah's kingdom period, Josiah caused the ark, which had by then been removed and almost forgotten, to be restored to its place in the temple (2 Chronicles 35:3). Not long afterwards, however, came the destruction and plundering of the temple, and nothing further is known of the ark and its precious contents after that. The next appearance is here in Revelation, in the heavenly tabernacle.

Thus, the temple of Herod, used by the Jews at the time of Christ, boasted beautiful outward form, but the most important contents of the first temple, the ark and the testimony, were missing. Whether God actually met there annually with the high priest as in former days is doubtful, especially in view of the corrupt character of the high priestly family at the time of Christ.

Nevertheless, the Herodian temple was still regarded by Christ as at least God's house of prayer (Matthew 21:13; John 2:16). At the time of His crucifixion, "the vail of the temple was rent in twain from the top to the bottom" (Matthew 27:51), clearly symbolizing the opening of the holy place in view of Christ's great sacrifice on the cross. "Having therefore, brethren, boldness to enter into the holiest by the blood of Jesus, by a new and living way, which he hath consecrated for us, through the vail, that is to say, his flesh; and having an high priest over the house of God; let us draw near with a true heart in full assurance of faith" (Hebrews 10:19-22).

Thus, since Christ, there is no more need for an earthly tabernacle, or sacrifices, or high priest, by which to come to God. In a figure, the holy place of His presence is always open to the believer, since Christ Himself is the tabernacle of God as well as the one sacrifice for sins forever and our eternal High Priest.

It is significant that these rare glimpses into the heavenly temple which God has given us in Revelation also show it as an open temple. There is nothing to keep man from God's presence if He comes through Christ. The human flesh of the Lord Jesus Christ is the veil that both contains the glory of God and conceals its unapproachable brilliance from sinful men.

But the law of God is eternal, and it applies to the Gentile nations as well as to the chosen nation. Here it appears again at the very end of the age as God prepares His final judgments on the earth. The temple is open, not only to confirm God's accessibility but also to reveal His awful holiness to a rebellious world. Both Jew and Gentile have gone out of the way, and the law of offended holiness is their condemnation. "There is no fear of God before their eyes. Now we know that what things soever the law saith, it saith to them who are under the law: that every mouth may be stopped, and all the world may become guilty before God" (Romans 3:18, 19).

All the world is guilty because all are under the law and have refused God's remedy. "For all have sinned, and come short of the glory of God; being justified freely by his grace through the redemption that is in Christ Jesus" (Romans 3:23, 24). Even if they have not read the law in the Scriptures, the same law is written in their consciences (Romans 2:14, 15), and the day has finally come "when God shall judge the secrets of men by Jesus Christ according to my gospel" (Romans 2:16). The opened temple of the tabernacle, displaying the testimony of God's ineffable holiness and righteousness in all its stark majesty, inscribed forever on tables of stone, must inspire awe in all the redeemed saints at the throne as they await the judgments.

Revelation 15:6.   And the seven angels came out of the temple, having the seven plagues, clothed in pure and white linen, and having their breasts girded with golden girdles.

Emerging from the temple (not the tabernacle, or "dwelling place" itself, but from the immediate vicinity, inside the inner room of the divine residence), are seen the seven angels selected to administer the seven last plagues to the earth. Each of these plagues will have to do with one or more of the "natural" physical processes of God's creation. As already observed, not only in Revelation but also in other Scriptures, the angels are spiritual beings of mighty power and extensive knowledge, understanding the many factors which affect the rates and intensities of such processes and able to control them and change them when circumstances warrant and God permits.

Their apparel is significant—white linen robes with belts of gold. There are four different words in the New Testament translated "linen," but this one, used only this one time, is *linon,* from which the English word itself is derived. A few of the ancient manuscripts have the word *lithos* ("stone") instead of *linon,* and thus many modern translations have the angels clothed in pure white stone instead of linen.

It seems easier to understand how careless copyists could substitute *lithos* for *linon,* however, than to understand why these angels would be dressed in stone, so it is probable that "linen" is the correct rendering. If, however, it should ever be proved that "stone" is the true original, then a possible interpretation could be that the plagues inflicted by the angels are based on the stone tables of God's testimony against a perverse world.

On the other hand it would be singularly appropriate for these angels to be arrayed in pure white linen, for this is the apparel of the redeemed and purified saints whom they represent and guard (Revelation 3:5, 18; 19:8, 14). Further, it is the clothing of the Son of man Himself, as seen by Daniel in a vision (Daniel 10:5-7) and by John in person (Revelation 1:13, 14), including in particular the golden girdles. The white linen speaks of righteousness; the belts of gold speak of riches and beauty. As God is perfect in holiness and will purge all wickedness, so He is also altogether lovely and possesses all earth's fulness, and so must eliminate eventually all ugliness and want.

Revelation 15:7.   And one of the four beasts gave unto the seven angels seven golden vials full of the wrath of God, who liveth for ever and ever.

The seven angels already have the seven plagues. Now they each receive also a golden bowl filled with God's wrath.

The word in the Greek is *phiale,* translated in the King James Version as "vial" and in most others as "bowl." Many think it refers to the shallow dishes used as censers for burning incense in the tabernacle or the temple. Its precise meaning is still doubtful.

Whatever may be the exact nature of the containers, they have been filled full of God's wrath. The overwhelming and terminal nature of the judgments might suggest that these bowls are massive urns, dipped deep into the fiery sea until overflowing with the wrath of an angry God. Or perhaps they are censers, burning not with sweet incense but with fire and brimstone.

The bowls of wrath are received from one of the four "living ones," who are (as shown in Chapter 5) the same as the "cherubim." These exalted beings had been active in signaling the judgments of the seals (Revelation 6:1-8) and now again appear on the scene to initiate the bowl judgments. The trumpet judgments had begun when the seven trumpets were given to the seven angels standing before God (Revelation 8:2) and it is likely that these also had been given to them by the living ones. The four mighty cherubim, associated from the very time of creation with the immediate presence of God, are perpetually concerned to do His will and administer His holy purposes in the creation.

But it is only God who has lived from eternity, "for ever and ever." This remarkable phrase (literally "for aeon after aeon") occurs twenty-one times in the New Testament, three times referring to the continuing punishment of the unsaved, once to the unending bliss of the saved, and seventeen times to the unique nature of God, who alone has existed from past eternity to future eternity. The one occasion when the phrase is applied to the saints is the very last: " . . . for the Lord God giveth them light: and they shall reign for ever and ever" (Revelation 22:5).

Revelation 15:8.   And the temple was filled with smoke from the glory of God, and from his power; and no man was able to enter into the temple, till the seven plagues of the seven angels were fulfilled.

As the bowls had been filled with wrath, so the temple was now filled with smoke. The term "smoke" (Greek *kapnos)* is used alike for the smoke ascending from a fire (as in Revelation 18:9), the smoke from sweet incense (Revelation 8:4), and the glory cloud from God's holy presence, as here.

Apparently, the temple had not been suffused with smoke heretofore, though God Himself dwells in light which no man can approach (1 Timothy 6:16). But with the spilling over of God's wrath, as it were, the brilliance of His holiness and the invincibility of His power—both about to be poured out without measure on a rebellious earth—generate billows of brilliant fiery clouds, impenetrable by any man or woman, even by the redeemed hosts near the throne.

There had been similar occasions on earth. When the tabernacle was established and dedicated to God's service, "a cloud covered the tent of the congregation, and the glory of the Lord filled the tabernacle. And Moses was not able to enter into the tent of the congregation, because the clouds abode thereon, and the glory of the Lord filled the tabernacle" (Exodus 40:34, 35). Similarly it was at the time Solomon's temple was dedicated, "when the priests were come out of the holy place, that the cloud filled the house of the Lord, so that the priests could not stand to minister because of the cloud: for the glory of the Lord had filled the house of the Lord" (1 Kings 8:10, 11).

Isaiah's vision of the heavenly temple encountered a similar scene. There he saw the seraphim (possibly identical with, or at least closely allied with, the cherubim), crying out: "Holy, holy, holy, is the Lord of hosts: the whole earth is full of his glory. And the posts of the door [that is, "the foundations of the threshold"] moved at the voice of him that cried, and the house was filled with smoke" (Isaiah 6:3, 4). Similarly "a great cloud, and a fire infolding itself" surrounded the four living creatures (or, the cherubim again) as the glory of the Lord approached Ezekiel by the river of Chebar (Ezekiel 1:4).

This glory cloud of celestial smoke, known by the ancient Hebrews as the "Shekinah" glory, is thus associated in Scripture with the intimate presence of God at times of great crises in God's dealings with men. No man can ever approach God in His ineffable omnipotent holiness, but the glory smoke assures man of the divine presence and the certainty of the divine accomplishment.

When the seven angels emerged from God's presence with His commission to administer the seven last plagues on earth, and when they had received from the chosen cherub the overflowing bowls of the divine wrath in which these judgments were to be imposed, then the glory cloud once again filled God's holy heavenly temple. This time it would not henceforth be removed at all until the earth was thoroughly purged and the eternal service of the new priesthood of redeemed men could begin its service in the heavenly sanctuary.

16

The Seven Last Judgments

(Revelation 16)

The seven chosen angels have been selected, appointed, and equipped as God's final messengers of judgment. The last half of the seven-year tribulation period is getting under way and rebellious men and women still can avail themselves of God's saving grace, even though few will do so. The Jewish remnant has fled to the wilderness, and the fierce purges of the beast are under way. Those who are refusing to be branded with the mark of the beast are fleeing for their lives, but multitudes are being caught and executed. The long drought and famine are still plaguing the earth, and food supplies are critically short. This is the world scene as the plagues recorded in Revelation 16 get under way.

Overflowing Bowls of Wrath

The seven angels not only have the ability and authority to impose seven unprecedented plagues on the earth, but also their great bowls have been filled to overflowing with the wrath of God. That is, the plagues are no longer primarily for the purpose of conviction and conversion but are a pure expression of the vengeance of a holy God.

Revelation 16:1. And I heard a great voice out of the temple saying to the seven angels, Go your ways, and pour out the vials of the wrath of God upon the earth.

The angels are given their final marching orders, as it were, signaling, by a great voice rolling out of the heavenly temple itself, the final attack of God on the earth. This voice can be nothing less than that of Deity, the same as the "great voice" which John heard at the beginning (Revelation 1:10). It is the voice of the glorified Christ, and it is He who is full of wrath. Again and again He has spoken to men in mercy and love, offering forgiveness and salvation, but finally His cup of wrath is full, and it must overflow.

No longer will God's wrath be restrained. With no further delay, the bowls of wrath must be poured out and the awful plagues must infest the earth. Yet each of the plagues, though deadly and painful to men in its own right, still has its own specific purpose. Each must be poured out in proper order and the cumulative effect of all seven will finally be the complete purging of human rebellion from the earth.

Revelation 16:2.   And the first went, and poured out his vial upon the earth; and there fell a noisome and grievous sore upon the men which had the mark of the beast, and upon them which worshipped his image.

As the first angel goes forth from the temple in heaven, his great bowl overflowing, he flies swiftly around the earth, tilting the bowl here and there until every portion of the earth has received some of its bitter contents. Finally the bowl is drained and the awful mixture proceeds to accomplish its ordained mission.

That work is to spread a hideous and painful infection on the bodies of men and women everywhere. This infection manifests itself as a loathsome ulcer of some kind, eating into the skin, seemingly malignant and unresponsive to medical treatment.

The record does not specify the exact nature of these sores, probably because they are unprecedented and therefore unnamed. The most amazing aspect of them, however, is that they (like the trumpet judgments, which did not affect those who had received God's seal) will not affect those who have refused the mark of the beast.

Although it is impossible to be certain, it may well be that the very process by which man had received this mark had rendered them susceptible to these unique sores. The mark had been permanently affixed to the skin, like a tattoo, and something in the chemicals or in the marking process (possibly a process of irradiation, because of the government's mandate to mark billions of people rapidly and permanently) may have entered the bloodstream. The angel with the plague, knowing the nature of this poison, could then release some other agent into the atmosphere which would specifically and quickly react with all human bodies so affected, causing them to break out in these "loathsome and penetratingly painful" sores.

This plague did not affect merely "a third part of men," as had some of the earlier plagues, but absolutely every person who had received the beast's deadly mark. Because they had refused to worship the true God and Creator, Jesus Christ (Revelation 14:6, 7), choosing rather to worship the great image of the beast, and its replicas throughout the world, the "hour of His judgment" had come on them. Would they be identified with the beast by his mark? Then God would add His own mark to their bodies, noisome sores which by their revolting appearance would truly reflect the character of the humanistic god they preferred. Were they fearful of the persecutions they would endure by refusing to worship the beast? Then God would send them far more intense suffering, of which the grievous sores were merely a painful surety of that which is to come. From this point on, no one who had received the beast's mark would be able ever to forget the consequences of the awful choice he had made.

And all of this will only infuriate them still more against the Lord Jesus Christ who has inflicted these judgments upon them. Since they cannot harm Him directly, their anger will be vented with great bitterness against those men and women who are not yet suffering as they are. Great pressures will be exerted—social pressures, business pressures, intellectual pressures—on all these to persuade them to join the crowd and receive the deadly mark. When these measures do not avail, they are summarily hunted down, arrested, tried, and executed if they will not yield.

Marvelous it is, therefore, that even out of this worst period of persecution in world history, this greatest tribulation of all, will come a "great multitude" of believers who refuse the mark of the beast and are redeemed by the blood of the Lamb (Revelation 7:9-14).

Revelation 16:3.   And the second angel poured out his vial upon the sea; and it became as the blood of a dead man: and every living soul died in the sea.

Under the judgment of the second trumpet, a "third part of the sea became blood," and one third of all living creatures in the sea died. This had resulted from the fall of a great burning mountain into the sea (review the discussion under Revelation 8:8, 9). Now, however, all of the sea will become blood, and every living creature in the sea will perish.

On that previous occasion the blood-poisoning of the sea had been accomplished by the propelling of a giant cometary or meteoritic body of some kind into it. Perhaps the same type of phenomenon is again induced, though this time on a grander scale. Instead of only one "burning mountain," possibly an entire swarm of these bodies attacks the earth, blasting into all the oceans of the world and thus rendering all waters bloody and noxious. If so, the metaphor of an angelic "pouring-out" of God's wrath into the sea would be singularly fitting.

Since such a heavenly bombardment is not specifically mentioned, however, it may be that some more subtle transmutation of the waters is implied. It should be remembered that, chemically speaking, the composition of sea water is almost identical to that of blood, so that only a relatively small modification would be necessary. Of course, the red color of blood flowing in human veins is imparted to it by the hemoglobin in the red corpuscles, due largely to its component of iron. In living flesh, these corpuscles transmit oxygen and other materials to all the cells of the body so that, truly, "the life of the flesh is in the blood" (Leviticus 17:11). In no way could sea water substitute for the blood of living flesh, but in this case the waters of the sea became as the blood of a dead man. It is merely a chemical solution, water containing iron and other chemicals which give it a blood-red appearance, but there is no longer life therein. In fact, it brings death to every living creature in the sea.

Exactly what chemical reactions take place to produce this lethal transformation of the waters of earth's vast oceans we do not know, though chemists could offer speculative suggestions. We can be sure, however, that the "angel of the waters" knows far more about water chemistry than any modern organic chemist and is well able to initiate and maintain such reactions until, indeed, all the earth's great and wide seas are filled with a deadly solution having the appearance and chemical components of the noxious blood of a human corpse.

In this toxic ocean nothing can survive, and soon all the billions of fishes and marine mammals and marine reptiles and the innumerable varieties of marine invertebrates will perish, thus still further poisoning the oceans and contaminating the sea shores of the world. The oceans will have effectively completed their age-long function in earth's physical economy, and will die. As God had created every living soul in the waters (Genesis 1:21), so now every living soul died in the sea.

In the new earth, there will be "no more sea" (Revelation 21:1), and thus no more sea animals. In the present world, sea organisms provide the basis for the world's great "food chains," and the ocean itself (at least in the postdiluvian world) is the anchor of the earth's essential hydrologic cycle. But this will be unnecessary in the new earth, and apparently the millennial earth is to be, in considerable measure, a prototype of the new earth, combining in some degree features of both the old and the new.

The transition, however, will be exceedingly traumatic for the earth and its inhabitants. When men who know of the true existence of God refuse to glorify Him as God and are not thankful for the great gifts of His creation (Romans 1:20), God will finally give them up (Romans 1:24), so that even the creation itself turns against them. The sea and its creatures had once been a spring of life; now it becomes a turgid pool of death.

Revelation 16:4.   And the third angel poured out his vial upon the rivers and fountains of waters; and they became blood.

298

The poisoning of the ocean would not in itself destroy human water supplies, for the hydrologic cycle could still function to maintain a fresh water supply for the rivers and springs of the world. However, the hydrologic cycle itself had malfunctioned throughout the first half of the tribulation period, as God's two witnesses had caused the rains to be restrained (Revelation 11:6) and the angel of the winds had caused the movements of the atmosphere to cease (Revelation 7:1). To some degree, at least, the cycle had resumed its activity when the ministry of the witnesses ceased as there had at least been a fall of hail at that time (Revelation 11:19).

It is thus possible, at least, that there had been a brief ending of the drought, though in the form of violent thunderstorms and hail, and this would have helped to replenish depleted stream and groundwater levels so that water storage reservoirs had been partly refilled. Evaporation from the oceans would remove its harmful solutes, so that any precipitation would have been pure water. The rivers and springs may thus at this time again be flowing with fresh water.

But now comes a third angel, an "angel of the waters," and his bowl of wrath is emptied on all the rivers and springs so that they also become blood. Again, whether this transmutation is effected by introducing a shower of particles from space or simply by new chemical reactions between the waters and the organisms and boundary materials in contact with them is not known, but we can be confident this mighty angel of the waters will be able to accomplish it.

Apparently, the water of the rivers and springs, even though transformed effectively to the composition of blood, will not be as toxic as the waters of the ocean, since people will still be able to drink it (verse 6). It will be bitter and repulsive, but perhaps by expensive treatment can be made potable. Possibly some fresh water can still be salvaged by use of cisterns to catch such rain as falls. At best, human survival will be made far more difficult than it has ever been before, when all the waters become blood.

Revelation 16:5. And I heard the angel of the waters say, Thou art righteous, O Lord, which art, and wast, and shalt be, because thou hast judged thus.

Men may fret and whine when they receive the just reward of their deeds, but all who truly know God are intensely aware that the great Judge of all the earth invariably acts in perfect righteousness (Genesis 18:25). In fact, what God does is the very definition of righteousness. No doubt there will be a great outcry of bitter complaint and resentment against their Creator, when men are forced to drink blood to survive, and these recriminations will be laced with blasphemies (verse 9). But complaining is not repenting, and so will avail them nothing.

The powerful angel equipped by God with the understanding necessary to induce this strange reaction in the waters will clearly see the justice of such a remarkable plague. He will give a great testimony, a doxology ascribing to his God all praise for the unique appropriateness of the judgment rendered. Not blinded by sin and self-interest, as are fallen men and fallen angels, he can comprehend and eulogize the mighty Creator and Judge.

And John hears his testimony, and would have us know that he hears it. It is a testimony that every man needs to hear and to burn into his heart. God is a righteous God, and He will judge unrighteousness in a wholly righteous way.

Since He is also a merciful God, He is willing to forgive man's wickedness, but only because the terrible penalty of wickedness has been exacted already, when the Son of God died in substitutionary propitiation as God's sacrificial Lamb. But when men proceed to despise this sacrificial blood of God's sanctifying covenant (Hebrews 10:29), there remains no more sacrifice for sins (Hebrews 10:26) and God's holy wrath must be poured out.

There are no dispensational distinctions in either righteousness or mercy. The God who was is the God who is and the God who will be. "Jesus Christ the same yesterday, and to day, and for ever" (Hebrews 13:8). Saved men have always been judged in righteousness and saved by grace. To refuse grace is to choose unrighteousness, and God will allow this for a time, but men should remember the final consequences of such a foolish choice. God is not mocked.

Revelation 16:6.   For they have shed the blood of saints and prophets, and thou hast given them blood to drink; for they are worthy.

The peculiar righteousness of God's vengeance is attested in the peculiar nature of His punishment. Not only had men despised the atoning blood of the Lamb; they had also shed the blood of His saints and prophets. As the Lamb had been acclaimed worthy to receive the eternal inheritance because He had offered His blood for its redemption (Revelation 5:9), so now those who refuse Him are held worthy to drink a pseudoblood for their own wretched survival a few days more. They did not hesitate to shed righteous blood; now they must drink the blood of judgment.

Even though most men had not participated directly in the act of bloodshed, they had done so vicariously. The people of the earth had rejoiced when God's two witnesses were finally slain by the beast (Revelation 11:10), and had uttered no protest when the beast instituted his campaign of destroying all who would not worship his image.

So it has always been. The effete religious leaders of the Jews were too dainty to drive the nails themselves when they urged the crucifixion of Jesus, but they cried, "His blood be on us, and on our children" (Matthew 27:25). So said all the people. The Lord Jesus said that the people of His own day were guilty of the blood of the righteous men even of previous generations. "That upon you may come all the righteous blood shed upon the earth, from the blood of righteous Abel unto the blood of Zacharias'' (Matthew 23:35).

Men and women who recoil in righteous indignation against capital punishment, and who deplore the crime of murder and the horror of war, are nevertheless guilty in God's sight of bloodshed if they reject Jesus Christ and the Word of His grace. "They crucify to themselves the Son of God afresh, and put him to an open shame" (Hebrews 6:6). Even professing Christians, who mock the Lord's supper by retaining known sin in their lives while they partake of the communion elements "shall be guilty of the body and blood of the Lord" (1 Corinthians 11:27).

Similarly those who acquiesce—even by their silence—whenever His witnesses are scorned and repudiated and silenced, are in effect exhibiting the attitude of persecutors. To the most imposingly educated and religious people of His earthly generation, Jesus said: "Ye shut up the kingdom of heaven against men: for ye neither go in yourselves, neither suffer ye them that are entering to go in. . . . [Ye] say, If we had been in the days of our fathers, we would not have been partakers with them in the blood of the prophets. Wherefore ye be witnesses unto yourselves, that ye are the children of them which killed the prophets. Fill ye up then the measure of your fathers. Ye serpents, ye generation of vipers, how can ye escape the damnation of hell?" (Matthew 23:13, 30-33).

Many and fierce have been the persecutions of believers and witnesses in both past and present, but none have ever been so universal and unremitting as will be those conducted by the beast in this final period. Therefore it is peculiarly fitting that this final generation should be compelled to drink the blood which they so exulted in shedding. They will especially deserve it.

Revelation 16:7.   And I heard another out of the altar say, Even so, Lord God Almighty, true and righteous are thy judgments.

Not only does the angel who executed this judgment bear witness to its righteousness. John immediately hears still another voice proclaiming the same testimony. This voice is not identified, though it does not seem to be that of another angel. No doubt every other angel in heaven could and would say "Amen" to the testimony of the angel of the waters, so there would be no point in thus recording the affirmation of some unknown angel at the altar.

Some of the manuscripts, in fact, omit the words "another out of," so the text in these reads: "I heard the altar say." Obviously a physical altar cannot speak, but this could well be an appropriate metaphor for a great voice arising from the multitude under the altar, sounding to John indeed as though he were hearing "another voice" emanating from the altar itself.

In Revelation 6:9-11, John had described as "under the altar" the souls of the martyrs of the early part of the tribulation. They had "cried with a loud voice," imploring God to avenge their blood, but had been told to rest a while longer.

Since that time their numbers had been greatly augmented, with multitudes more yielding up their blood in the persecutions of the last part of the tribulation. One can easily imagine their mounting excitement as this final series of divine judgments is poured out over the earth. Then, as they observe the sudden turning of the oceans and rivers and springs into blood, everywhere, always, reminding men on earth of the blood they had shed, the waiting souls under the altar cannot restrain themselves. In unison a great cry ascends from their resting place under the heavenly altar: "The judgments of God, though long delayed, are true judgments and righteous judgments when they finally come!"

The appropriate name they ascribe to the great Judge is "Lord God Almighty," the same as in the great song at the glassy sea (Revelation 15:3) and in the song of the cherubim (Revelation 4:8). Seven times in Revelation is Jesus called both "Lord" and "Almighty." In the first (Revelation 1:8), He introduces Himself as "the Lord, which is, and which was, and which is to come, the Almighty." In all the others (Revelation 4:8; 11:17; 15:3; 16:7; 19:6; 21:22), He is simply addressed in praise as "Lord God Almighty," or "Lord God Omnipotent" (same Greek word). Because of who He is, His judgments and ways are what they are—true and righteous altogether (Psalm 19:9).

Revelation 16:8.   **And the fourth angel poured out his vial upon the sun; and power was given unto him to scorch men with fire.**

Hitherto all the plagues have affected only the earth and its atmosphere. God, however, owns the sun as well as the earth; He made it, and can do with it what He wills. As a matter of fact, He is Creator of heaven and earth and all things that therein are (Revelation 10:6).

Though the sun is not part of the earth, it serves the earth. It was created specifically to "give light upon the earth" and to "be for signs, and for seasons, and for days, and years" (Genesis 1:14, 15). The sun has indeed been a good servant to man, and all of earth's physical and biological processes derive their energy ultimately from the sun. "His [out-radiations] are from the end of the heaven, and his circuit unto the ends of it: and there is nothing hid from the heat thereof" (Psalm 19:6).

But the sun, like the Lord Jesus Christ, whom it symbolizes as "the light of the world" (John 8:12) can be an enemy as well as a servant. It can both quicken and slay with its enormous power. And now is the time for judgment, when those plants without root or fruit will be revealed for what they are: "And when the sun was up, they were scorched; and because they had no root, they withered away" (Matthew 13:6).

There was an angel of the winds, an angel of the waters, and now an angel of the sun. To this angel has God entrusted the great energy conversion processes of the solar engine. Whatever the ultimate fuel is (scientists today, convinced at one time that it was atomic fuel, functioning through the process of thermonuclear fusion are now for various reasons uncertain; except that it would indicate the sun's age as much too short for evolution, the current weight of evidence strongly favors actual gravitational shrinking and chemical burning processes), this angel understands the components of the process and how to accelerate or decelerate it, thus either warming or cooling the earth.

When he pours out the contents of his great bowl on the sun, it will heat up to great intensity and the solar radiation will pour forth in great waves of scorching heat on the earth. The prophet Malachi, in the last chapter of the Old Testament, wrote of this: "For, behold, the day cometh, that shall burn as an oven; and all the proud, yea, and all that do wickedly, shall be stubble: and the day that cometh shall burn them up, saith the Lord of hosts, that it shall leave them neither root nor branch" (Malachi 4:1). Isaiah adds this comment: "Therefore hath the curse devoured the earth, and they that dwell therein are desolate: therefore the inhabitants of the earth are burned, and few men left" (Isaiah 24:6).

This is probably also the time of which Isaiah writes when he says: "Moreover the light of the moon shall be as the light of the sun, and the light of the sun shall be sevenfold, as the light of seven days, in the day that the Lord bindeth up the breach of his people, and healeth the stroke of their wound" (Isaiah 30:26). The night will be as bright as day, with the moon reflecting the seven-times greater light from the sun.

The inhabitants of the earth are thus tormented still more. The burning heat is bad enough in itself, but it becomes like coals of fire on the ulcerous sores in their skin. Furthermore, there is little relief at night and it is difficult to rest or sleep. Some can retreat to air-conditioned buildings, perhaps, but these offer only partial and shortlasting benefits. Water supplies are critical and must be allocated only to the most essential uses, and then only after expensive purification treatments. The whole situation will be traumatic and maddening, and it will be difficult for men even to think rationally anymore.

Furthermore the intense solar radiation will again evaporate great quantities of water from the oceans and other water surfaces, lowering sea level and water tables everywhere. Even if the angels of the winds (Revelation 7:1) are no longer restraining the winds, the temperatures everywhere will soon become constantly hot and this in itself will inhibit the normal functioning of the water cycle. Thus, more and more water vapor will remain aloft, strengthening the greenhouse effect and still further slowing any atmospheric movements. Such rain and hail as do reach the surface will probably be in the form of violent thunderstorm and tornado cells, adding yet more to earth's misery.

The general lowering of water levels will also render the lands more unstable, especially along the great continental shelves and continental slopes, which have been somewhat unstable ever since the postdiluvian uplift of the continents. Extensive submarine coastal earthslides will ensue from time to time, each not only creating havoc in coastal cities but also generating devastating tsunami waves that also attack the coasts.

However, the intense heat of the sun will also produce another effect which will, at least for a time, somewhat compensate for oceanic evaporation. That is, the great ice sheets on Greenland and the continent of Antarctica will melt. There is enough ice stored in these great reservoirs, it is estimated, to raise the world's sea levels about 200 feet if it were all melted.

Such melting is imminent even under present environmental conditions, as the global greenhouse is being augmented by the burning of fossil fuels. It is probable that the ice sheets would melt before the sea level could be lowered much by evaporation. Thus the most immediate hydrologic effect of this fourth bowl of wrath would likely be a rapid rise of sea level, to be followed later by the great drop in level already suggested.

This phenomenon may be intimated in certain Scriptures. "He casteth forth his ice like morsels. . . . He sendeth out his word, and melteth them . . ." (Psalm 147:17, 18). "Hast thou entered into the treasures of the snow? or hast thou seen the treasures of the hail, which I have reserved against the time of trouble, against the day of battle and war?" (Job 38:22, 23). The word "treasures" in the latter passage could as well be translated "storehouses," so the verse refers to great storage reservoirs of snow and hail which have been reserved for "the time of trouble" (the period of tribulation?).

Also consider Amos 9:5, 6: "And the Lord God of hosts is he that toucheth the land, and it shall melt, and all that dwell therein shall mourn: and it shall rise up wholly like a flood; and shall be drowned, as by the flood of Egypt. It is he that buildeth his stories in the heaven, and hath founded his troop in the earth; he that calleth for the waters of the sea, and poureth them out upon the face of the earth: The Lord is his name."

Although the writers of the Bible presumably had never seen an ice sheet and thus could not write of them in the language of their own experience, as is the case in other parts of Scripture, such references could well refer cryptically to far-off storehouses of snow which will someday be melted and sent forth by the Lord to cause the waters of the sea to pour out in judgment along the sea coasts of the world.

If, indeed, the great ice caps should suddenly melt one day, many of the world's greatest cities (such as New York, Tokyo, London, Los Angeles, Rio de Janeiro, Buenos Aires, Amsterdam, Leningrad, Rome, Athens, Beirut, Calcutta, Shanghai, Singapore, Hong Kong, and numerous others) would be largely inundated and destroyed. Most of these large coastal shipping metropolises have been notorious centers of corruption and immorality, and would be appropriate candidates for divine judgment, especially after their complement of believers has been removed by the rapture.

Revelation 16:9.   And men were scorched with great heat, and blasphemed the name of God, which hath power over these plagues: and they repented not to give him glory.

Again a tragic commentary on human nature. No longer could there be a possible doubt by any one on earth that these shattering judgments afflicting the earth are from its offended Creator God. But they have elected to believe that the old dragon, together with his two evil allies, the beast and the false prophet, can somehow defeat and dethrone God.

Because they refused to love the truth that they might be saved, they are under the spell of a deadly delusion, believing an incredible lie (2 Thessalonians 2:10, 11). Not even the awful plagues on the earth or the pain in their bodies will bring them to repentance. Knowing that only God could remove the plagues, they nevertheless continue to defy and blaspheme His holy name. Maddened by a terrible conglomerate of sin-darkened minds, oppressive evil spirits, addiction to drugs, devastated environment and now intense pain and heat, all they can think of is hatred of God, pressing forward to a final confrontation which they yet believe will deliver them from His power and judgment, freeing them to live in the wickedness which they love.

Revelation 16:10.   And the fifth angel poured out his vial upon the seat of the beast; and his kingdom was full of darkness; and they gnawed their tongues for pain.

Secure in his Babylonish capital (the two great cities of Jerusalem and Babylon are at sufficient elevation to be safe from the sea level rise occasioned by melting ice caps), the beast himself, and his immediate coterie, have hitherto been spared at least the worst of the suffering experienced by most men. With the best medical attention both human and demonic, with the best food and water still available, with air-conditioned palaces, and safe behind powerful armies and impregnable walls, the beast and his prophet continue to direct their global campaign of enslavement and consolidation. Not even the unprecedented sunlight and moonlight impress them, confident that their satanic master is himself a mighty angel of light and could duplicate such miracles if it served his purpose.

But now a fifth bowl of wrath is emptied, this time spilling its contents on the very throne of the beast himself. The result is a thick darkness beginning in the throne room and then permeating the palace and other administration buildings, finally covering the whole of the capital city until a heavy darkness fills the royal city everywhere, night and day.

How such a region of thick darkness can be produced, especially in the midst of a world which everywhere else is brilliant with sevenfold sunlight, is a mystery as impenetrable as the darkness itself. In Pharaoh's Egypt, the demon-possessed magicians could imitate certain of Moses' miracles, but their enchantments could not generate the supernatural darkness which distinguished between the Egyptians and the Israelites (Exodus 10:21-23). Perhaps some kind of energy barrier will be erected invisibly surrounding and covering the city, able to reflect all incoming radiation.

Regardless of how this remarkable phenomenon is produced, it constitutes a striking testimony, even to the beast, of the power of the God he hates. Neither he nor his master, Lucifer, can bring light to his dwelling. While all the outside world is almost blindingly illuminated with God's searing sunlight, the kingdom of the beast is in gross darkness. Such an obvious spiritual parable can hardly be escaped by the earth-dwellers. They know beyond question that God is light and Satan is darkness. Nevertheless, men love darkness rather than light, because their deeds are evil (John 3:19).

Some writers prefer to interpret the darkness as worldwide rather than as limited to the capital of the beast. The Scripture says only that the bowl was poured out on the throne of the beast and the darkness filled his kingdom. The first bowl had been poured on the earth, the second on the sea, the third on the rivers, the fourth on the sun. If the darkness of the fifth bowl were intended to cover the whole earth, parallel usage would seem to require the bowl to be emptied on the earth rather than on merely the beast's throne.

Actually "the kingdom of the beast" does not refer to the whole world but only to his own particular kingdom, the base from which he later will acquire control over all other kingdoms. The national background of the beast and the identity of his original kingdom have long been a matter of controversy among Bible commentators. Rome, Greece, Syria, Assyria, Russia, the United States, and others have all had their advocates. The fact is that it is impossible to make such an identification at this time. The Bible specifically says that *"then* shall that wicked [One] be revealed" (2 Thessalonians 2:8). A number of events must occur before this takes place, most important of which is the resurrection of the dead and the translation of living saints when Christ returns to the earth's atmosphere (1 Thessalonians 4:16, 17). The Scriptures have intentionally left this matter unrevealed (a fact abundantly proved by the very number of speculative identifications that have been published), probably to avoid the opprobrium that would otherwise attach itself to that kingdom and its people *before* the Wicked One arises among them.

Wherever he comes from, it does seem that, after he gains world dominion, he will build a great world capital at Babylon (see the discussion in Chapters 17 and

18). There his throne will be centered, and thus it is there that the supernatural darkness will fall. Whatever may be the extent of his kingdom at this time (as distinct from all the kingdoms of the nations over which he acquires control), the darkness surely will center particularly upon the capital city. It may extend somewhat further, but the context makes it unlikely that it will extend throughout the world.

In any case, it will constitute one more, very powerful, evidence that God is still God; the reign of the beast is outwardly impressive and global in extent but will be soon forgotten, when Christ finally establishes His kingdom on the earth.

The tongues that now speak blasphemies against God's name will soon be silenced. Even at this time, their tongues can hardly frame rational words of blasphemy while they are gnawing these same tongues for pain. The torment of the loathsome sores and the bitter water, the burning heat and then the heavy darkness, are becoming almost unbearable to many, and there is gnashing of teeth and gnawing of tongues.

Revelation 16:11.   And blasphemed the God of heaven because of their pains and their sores, and repented not of their deeds.

Despite all the pain and trauma, almost incredibly, the blasphemous vituperations continue. There are some today who believe that ungodly men will have a second chance after death to repent and believe, and that the sufferings of hell (or purgatory) may lead them to such repentance. This passage, however, should certainly disabuse anyone of such a notion.

Note also that the men who were afflicted with sores when the first bowl was poured out are still suffering with the same sores after the fifth bowl. This is an obvious refutation of the historical theory of interpretation, which would refer all these bowls to various historical events occurring over the centuries since Christ.

Call to Armageddon

Every new judgment on the earth has merely hardened still further man's unrepentant heart. It is as though men have become so possessed with hatred for God that they are eager for a final confrontation, a great battle that will determine forever who will be king of the universe, its gracious Creator or the great rebel, the old serpent. They have irrevocably chosen the dragon and received the mark of the beast, still believing that he will ultimately deliver them from the fearful plagues and judgments of the God of heaven. But they cannot endure the pains of the plagues much longer, and eagerly press toward the great contest.

And if the distressed nations on earth are eager for the final confrontation, the same is even more true of the beast. Satan, most of all, has been preparing for this battle for ages and now his time is short and the day of decision is near.

Revelation 16:12.   And the sixth angel poured out his vial upon the great river Euphrates; and the water thereof was dried up, that the way of the kings of the east might be prepared.

The seven bowl judgments were also called the seven last plagues (Revelation 15:1), and at first it is not apparent how the drying up of a single river could be called a plague. This calamity has overtaken many rivers throughout history. Sometimes people have migrated elsewhere as a result, but the world as a whole was not much affected. All the other plagues produce profound effects worldwide, but how could any comparable impact be produced merely by drying the Euphrates?

The Euphrates, however, is no ordinary river. Its flood plain was the site of the first human city (Babel) after the great Flood and it was the site of Nebuchadnezzar's magnificent capital city Babylon in the days of Daniel the prophet. On its shores will apparently be erected the even more magnificent New Babylon to serve as the capital of the beast in his brief but unprecedented worldwide reign in the great tribulation. It is called "the great River Euphrates" five times in the Bible and is, indeed, one of the great rivers of the world. In Bible times the Nile was its only known rival in terms of length and magnitude.

At this point in the chronicle, the tribulation will be rapidly approaching its climactic end. The throne of the beast, and probably all of great Babylon, has just been plunged into gross darkness. However the power plants presumably still function, so artificial lighting can maintain essential operations in the city.

The water supply of the new Babylon (as was true of ancient Babylon) no doubt will depend on the Euphrates. In ancient times, an extensive network of dams and canals utilized the waters of the Euphrates to sustain the advanced agricultural and urban economy of the Babylonians. The modern nation of Iraq has, with British and American assistance, developed in the past several decades extensive water supply, flood control, and hydropower works on the Euphrates, as well as considerable work toward rebuilding Babylon itself. Thus there is little doubt that the great new capital of the beast likewise will depend almost entirely on the Euphrates for its water supply. Not only water for drinking and other personal uses, but cooling water for generating plants, water for air-conditioning systems and industrial processes, and for a multitude of other essential operations, will depend on the river Euphrates.

Thus the sudden drying up of its water would indeed constitute an almost lethal blow to the city. The power generating plants would soon have to shut down and the only lights in the dark city will be lamps and candles (note Revelation 18:23). Any stored water still available would have to be conserved for such vital necessities as drinking.

As a matter of fact, the flow of water in the river will already have been significantly depleted before this sixth plague is put into effect. The three-and-a-half-year drought of the first half of the tribulation will surely have decreased river flows everywhere. Then, the reactions which transmuted the fresh waters of the world into blood (verse 4), will have made costly treatment necessary for the waters remaining. Finally, the scorching heat of the fourth bowl judgment will surely have evaporated much of the water still in the rivers and reservoirs. Thus, the flow of the river will already have been seriously depleted.

All of the above conditions will prevail all over the world, of course, with water supplies as well as food supplies drying up everywhere. But now another judgment attacks the great river Euphrates in particular and it dries up completely. No doubt the sudden desiccation of the river includes its tributaries as well and also the ground water table feeding into it. Although the Scripture does not say so explicitly, it is likely that any physical phenomenon which would so attack the Euphrates would attack its sister river, the Tigris, in the same way.

Thus the water supply of the magnificent new capital city of the beast, along with that of the region around which supports it, already affected seriously by the general shortage, is quickly dissipated. The mighty headquarters of the world, the magnificent capital of the proud man of sin, quivers in dense darkness and thirsts for water.

How the sixth angel operates to dry the Euphrates is not stated, but it is possible that tectonic forces are involved. The tribulation period, since its very beginning, is characterized also by earthquakes and volcanism. The next succeeding judgment, in fact, is destined to be the greatest earthquake of all time. The whole region has been tectonically unstable throughout history, and it is conceivable that earth movements could cause deep underground caverns and channels to open and drain off the surface waters. Another possibility would be intensive local winds and accelerated evaporation. Whether these or other known phenomena are involved, the angel of the sixth plague is certainly able to direct any or all such processes to cause the sudden draining and drying of the proud Euphrates.

There is one other intriguing possibility. Both the Euphrates and the Tigris Rivers have their sources on or near the high slopes of Mount Ararat, ultimately in the snow and perennial ice cap near its 17,000-foot summit. The region of Ararat (biblically, the same as Armenia) is high and rugged terrain, unstable and volcanic in nature, and is covered with snow throughout the winter. The highest mountain, Mount Ararat, is capped with a permanent ice cap which melts only partially during the summer. The melting snows of the highlands provide most of the water for the Euphrates-Tigris system. The world's most venerable rivers, that is, have their source in the same region which is mankind's birthplace after the great Flood, the mighty Mount Ararat region, where Noah and the animals disembarked from the ark. But these snows and glaciers will melt along with the great ice sheets of Greenland and Antarctica during the great drought and especially from the intense solar heat of the fourth bowl judgment. This in itself will substantially dry up the river, since the waters that fed its source will be gone.

It is here on Mount Ararat that Noah's ark landed, and it is here, in a stationary glacier at about 15,000-foot elevation, that many explorers, ancient and modern, claim to have glimpsed the prow of the ark protruding from the melting ice cap at the end of a long hot summer. Scientific expeditions however, attempting to verify these reports by documented evidence and systematic measurement, have failed, usually because the particular summers in which they searched were to mild to melt back the ice enough.

It may be that the Lord is withholding this discovery for an optimally strategic time. If not before, at least at this time of the sixth plague, the ice cap will be permanently melted and the ark revealed, serving as a great witness to God's truth and His sovereign judgment in the very last days.

But what is this mysterious reference to kings of the east? There are no less than nine references in Revelation to "the kings of the earth," but this is the only one to "the kings of the east." In the prophecy of Daniel there is a cryptic reference to "tidings out of the east and out of the north" which trouble the king, who is evidently the same as the beast in Revelation (Daniel 11:44). However, the context in Daniel places this event earlier in the tribulation, when the king was still in the process of conquest and consolidation of his world empire.

As discussed earlier (see Chapter 6), a major factor contributing to the rise of the despotic king who is called the beast was the catastrophic defeat of the northern confederacy headed up by Gog near the beginning of the tribulation. The great coalition of Russian and Arab forces was decimated there, giving the European and western nations the opportunity to consolidate their own power. Somewhere out of these emerged the beast as leader. Thus, most of the political and military developments to this point, as outlined especially in Daniel, Ezekiel, and Revelation, seem to focus on the nations of north or south or west.

But there are great nations in the east as well—China, Japan, India, and many others. These are every bit as antichristian as the nations in other parts of the world. For ages they have been dominated by religions (Buddhism, Confucianism, Hinduism, and others) which are fundamentally evolutionary religions. That is, they all envision an eternal universe, with no concept of a transcendent, omnipotent, personal God who created all things. Their emphasis is solely on present behavior. To them history consists mostly of interminable cycles, without beginning or ending.

Associated with these pantheistic systems was (and is) always the worship of spirits. Whether these are understood as spirits of ancestors or as the spirits of trees and other natural objects, such worship is in reality worship of demons, or fallen angels. Such religions thus are also commonly associated with idolatry. This eastern religion—whatever specific form it may assume in a particular time or place—is essentially the same old worship of idols which God's prophets continually condemned. Comprising a monstrous complex of evolutionary, pantheistic, polytheistic, idolatrous, astrological, animistic humanism, it is merely a variant of the primeval religion introduced by Nimrod at Babel and promulgated throughout the world by the confusion of tongues and subsequent worldwide dispersion from Babel.

By its very nature, it lends itself to control of its devotees by demonic influence. Nevertheless, through the centuries, many have been won to Christ out of these pagan religions, much gospel seed has been sown, and it is probable that a great harvest of souls will be gathered from them to Christ during the tribulation times.

Those who are not so converted, however, will become more subject to demon influence and manipulation than ever, and will quickly follow the evil spirits to Armageddon when the time comes. The kings of the east in particular, and all the kings of the earth in general, will lead their multitudes of followers to converge on tiny Israel, there finally to meet the heavenly armies of Christ in mortal conflict.

And it is the kings of the east whose armies are the greatest in numerical strength, with all the billions of Asia to draw from. Soon great multitudes will be coming from China and Japan, from India and Indonesia, from Malaysia and Viet Nam, streaming past Babylon and across the Euphrates, drawn like moths to the flames of hell at Armageddon.

The drying up of the Euphrates is not, of course, necessary before these eastern hordes can cross it, except perhaps as a symbol that Kipling's ancient barrier between east and west has finally been breached. The Euphrates was the ancient boundary between Assyria and Babylonia and, at the time of John the Apostle, was the eastern boundary of the Roman empire. It is also the eastern boundary of the land promised to Abraham (Genesis 15:18).

Other than as a symbol, its crossing surely does not require its emptying. Ancient armies crossed it many times, and modern motorized armies could easily cross on the many bridges which now span the river.

How does its drying, then, "prepare the way" of the eastern kings? This is a mysterious statement and a dogmatic explanation is impossible at this time. It is probable, however, that there is a connection between this reference to the Euphrates and the only other New Testament mention of the Euphrates, the equally mysterious statement in Revelation 9:14. There the judgment of the sixth trumpet unleased from the Euphrates four evil angels and their horde or 200 million demon horsemen, to slay the third part of men. Here, four years later, the judgment of the sixth bowl dries up the Euphrates, preparing the way for a horde of human horsemen to hasten to their final doom in the great plain of Armageddon.

The Euphrates has for ages been viewed as the boundary between east and west, a tradition probably dating from the primeval dispersion there at Babel. This idea will surely be greatly reinforced by the construction of new Babylon and the great world capital there. The most awesome aspect of the Euphrates, however, especially to the spirit-appeasing multitudes of the nations of the far east in these tribulation years, will be the memory of the terrible horde of deadly demon horsemen that had swarmed out of the Euphrates four years earlier. The lethal toll of these lion-headed, serpent-tailed horses, particularly in the densely populated cities of the east, had been indescribably great, and must have shrouded the great river with a superstitious aura which would be more effective than an iron curtain in turning back any from the east who would cross to the west.

But suddenly the mighty river is dry and the exposed sand and rocks of its bed are barren of demons or any form of life at all. It seems as though the river itself is inviting men to cross and speed on their way to Armageddon. No more are long-imprisoned evil spirits stalking human prey. All the legions of hell are ready to converge on the long-prophesied spot where Christ will soon appear, and they need all the reinforcements they can gather from among mankind. The brand of the beast has been implanted on the hands and foreheads of men and women and, when the dragon hisses, they must follow.

Revelation 16:13.   And I saw three unclean spirits like frogs come out of the mouth of the dragon, and out of the mouth of the beast, and out of the mouth of the false prophet.

As John watches the rapid change in the Euphrates, his attention is somehow directed back to darkened Babylon. There an amazing council is being held in an inner chamber of the candlelit capital. As in a midnight seance, the two beasts—the ruler and his prophet—are listening to a strange visitor. This is the *real* king of Babylon (Isaiah 14:4), the one who has given the beast his throne (Revelation 13:2). This malevolent spirit is old Lucifer (Isaiah 14:12), often through the centuries appearing to men as an angel of light (2 Corinthians 11:14) but clearly apparent now to John as the great dragon.

The council reaches its decision. The situation has become desperate, and the course of events now in motion is irrevocable. The unholy trinity has an appointment with a Man called Faithful and True (Revelation 19:11), and He will not wait. The agelong conflict is soon to be decided, and they must quickly assemble every possible recruit for the battle if they are to have any hope of victory.

With one voice they speak, and all the principalities and powers of darkness spread out from the darkness at Babylon into the nations of the world. As when darkness settles on a quagmire, and suddenly the clamorous croaking of frogs pierces the night air in every direction, so these three evil spirits—unclean, ugly, and clamorous like frogs—go forth to lead an innumerable multitude of lesser spirits out into all the world, rasping out their guttural messages in the world's dark night. These "seducing spirits," with their "doctrines of devils" (1 Timothy 4:1), spread lies and deceptions, as they have for millennia, one more time. And the kings of the earth, already irrational with their drug-distorted perceptions and with the pain of God's plagues, listen to their deceptions one more time.

Revelation 16:14. **For they are the spirits of devils, working miracles, which go forth unto the kings of the earth and of the whole world, to gather them to the battle of that great day of God Almighty.**

These demonic spirits have no physical bodies of their own, of course, but it is a simple matter for them to use the voices of the host of demon-possessed men and women whose bodies they have taken control of during (or even before) these tribulation years. The multitude of "false prophets" (Matthew 24:24) and "false teachers" (2 Peter 2:1) who contaminate the last days will gladly "give heed to seducing spirits and doctrines of devils" (1 Timothy 4:1) and lend their voices and intellects and physical strength to the demons who possess them.

Furthermore, if they should encounter questionings or resistance from those kings and judges of the earth whom they seek to persuade, they will perform miracles both to establish their own credibility and to assure men of the invincible power of the dragon and the beast and the false prophet whom they represent. As the Lord Jesus Himself prophesied, they "shall shew signs and wonders, to seduce, if it were possible, even the elect" (Mark 13:22). Once the kings and presidents and generals of the nations of the whole world are convinced, they in turn undertake whatever means are appropriate among their own constituencies to persuade the people as well. In this they are aided by the marvel-displaying sorcerers and spellbinding "prophets" who have proliferated everywhere. And the people, suffering under the plagues and already bitter against the true God, are not hard to convince. In droves they enlist and prepare to go to war.

What is the message conveyed by these evil spirits through their host of willing oracles? It is this: "Prepare war, wake up the mighty men, let all the men of war draw near; let them come up: Beat your plowshares into swords, and your pruninghooks into spears: let the weak say, I am strong. Assemble yourselves, and come, all ye heathen, and gather yourselves together round about: thither cause thy mighty ones to come down, O Lord. Let the heathen be wakened, and come up to the valley of Jehoshaphat" (Joel 3:9-12).

And so they begin to come, heading toward Jerusalem, streaming from Africa, Asia, Europe, and America. The armies of the nations fly and march and ride and sail, using all the means of military transport at their disposal. But fuel and ships and planes are in short supply, so the multitudes of untrained recruits come however they can. Autos, trucks, and busses creep along the highways until the gas tanks run dry (most drilling and refining operations probably have been suspended because of the critical water supplies and intense heat). Commandeering horses and asses and camels, many will ride on such animals as are available. Those who must walk may (fortunately for them) be left behind, but soon there are great multitudes, both of professional warriors and untrained (but angry) civilians assembling in the great chain of plains and valleys on the east of Jerusalem. In desperation they are eager to do battle with Almighty God, knowing

Christ and his heavenly army will shortly come to earth near Jerusalem, and He is the one responsible for their awful sufferings. Having rejected Him as their Savior, their only hope is to destroy Him before He becomes their Judge. Surely they realize that their human arms are insufficient, but they have confidence in the superhuman powers of the beast and dragon whom they worship (Revelation 13:4), and the great host of evil spirits who accompany them.

Revelation 16:15.   Behold, I come as a thief. Blessed is he that watcheth and keepeth his garments, lest he walk naked, and they see his shame.

Since verse 16 obviously continues the theme of verse 14, the insertion of this divine promise in verse 15 seems at first to be out of place, having nothing directly to do with the context either before or after. It is obviously not addresed to the multitudes of demon-led men and women enroute to Armageddon, and certainly not to their leaders, either human or demonic. It is addressed clearly to Christian believers.

Similar promises in the Gospels and in the epistles (Matthew 24:42-44; Luke 12:35-40; 1 Thessalonians 5:2-4; 2 Peter 3:10; Revelation 3:3) refer to the always-imminent return of Christ and the resultant need for readiness and watchfulness. At this point, however, the rapture is already past. Furthermore, Christ's return to the earth to judge the nations will not be "as a thief," for they are all now awaiting it and "every eye shall see him" (Revelation 1:7) when He comes.

Thus there is something special and unique about this particular promise in this particular context. Evidently there are still many at this time, both Jew and Gentile, who have refused the mark of the beast, and have somehow managed to survive, probably by fleeing to various wilderness retreats, in a manner analogous to the fleeing of the Jewish remnant to the wilderness near Jerusalem, as described in Revelation 12 and other Scriptures. Many of these have trusted in Christ as Savior; others (especially Jews) may not yet be born-again Christians but do believe in the true God and so refuse to worship the beast and bow to his image.

It is probably such as these to whom the Lord speaks this time. Although they themselves have been spared the suffering of the angelic bowls of wrath, they can hardly fail to be distressed and fearful, not only because the agents of the beast have been seeking to find and slay them but because of the strange demonic fury of the multitudes as they hasten to do battle with God in the land of Israel. They themselves need a special word of instruction and comfort from the Lord, encouraging them to continue in their stand.

The Lord has not forgotten them. He has protected them from the fiery plagues and supplied their needs. But, they may wonder, what will happen to them when the Lord returns in power and great glory to judge the nations? And so God graciously sends to them a special message from heaven just at this time. He will come for them too, even as He did for His saints before the tribulation. As for those earlier saints, He will come as a thief at some time unannounced.

Therefore they must remain watchful and ready, as clothed for a journey, not as undressed and indifferent. As it would be frightfully embarrassing to be suddenly compelled to take a trip without even the time to put on any clothing, so would it be to be transported into the holy presence of Christ when one is arrayed, as it were, only in the filthy rags of careless indulgence instead of in the fine linen of righteousness which He provides for His saints. "And now, little children, abide in him; that, when he shall appear, we may have confidence, and not be ashamed before him at his coming" (1 John 2:28).

Whether this particular coming will be, in effect, another rapture, with resurrection of dead believers and glorification of living saints, is uncertain. More likely it will be translaltion of the living to join with their brethren in the holy city just before the Lord returns to earth. "Gather my saints together unto me; those that have made a covenant with me by sacrifice. And the heavens shall declare his righteousness" (Psalm 50:5, 6).

Revelation 16:16.   And he gathered them together into a place called in the Hebrew tongue Armageddon.

Having interjected this special word of comfort and exhortation from the Lord to the tribulation saints still surviving in the troubled world, John returns to the immediate narrative of events. The previous verse tells that the nations are being gathered together to a climactic battle. This verse tells us where they are being assembled.

"Armageddon" is from "Har-megiddo," or "Mountain of Megiddo." Megiddo is an ancient town about sixty miles north of Jerusalem, overlooking the plain of Megiddo on the west and the plain of Esdraelon (or valley of Jezreel) on the northeast. This area was the scene of many ancient battles (Judges 5:19; 2 Chronicles 35:22), and would be the obvious location for a bivouac area from which to mount an assault on Jerusalem.

It is to this area that the multitudes come. However, even such a great plain as the plain of Esdraelon cannot contain them all, and soon great numbers are being deployed on down into the Jordan valley and the valley of Jehoshaphat, toward Jerusalem. Soon the vast column protrudes along the shores of the Dead Sea and down into Idumea, even beyond Bozrah (see the discussion on Revelation 14:20). Possibly their ranks are augmented by others marching up toward Jerusalem after disembarking from seagoing vessels on the Red Sea or Gulf of Akaba. On the north, the multitudes assembling at Armageddon are perhaps reinforced by contingents arriving at the nearby port of Haifa.

Some might wonder why, if the object of this unprecedented army is Jerusalem, it is necessary to plan such a massive attack by land. It would seem far easier to launch a missile or air attack. Jerusalem could quickly be obliterated by nuclear bombs, or leveled even with conventional bombs.

One can only surmise that the beast has rejected such a strategy for what he believes are good reasons. Even though he hates bitterly those Jews who have refused to worship his image, especially the 144,000 sealed Israelites who have encamped on Mount Zion (Revelation 14:1), he realizes that his primary enemy is the Lamb, with His armies in heaven, and these enemies cannot be reached by bombs and missiles. Also, he knows by sad experience that the 144,000 at least, are invulnerable with God's protecting seal on their foreheads.

It is quite possible also that his vanity persuades him not to try to level Jerusalem. What infinite satisfaction it would be, after he has destroyed the Lamb and established universal control for himself, to take over the holy city which God had chosen and then to establish his own throne there. As it is, he has already placed his great image in the holy place in the temple. He would not want to see his image destroyed with the city. Consequently, he desires to capture the city rather than to raze it.

The great deceiver thinks it is he who has gathered the nations together against Jerusalem but it is actually God who has used him to do so. The beast does actually invade Judah and lay siege to Jerusalem (Zechariah 12:2). For a brief while, he even gains a pseudovictory over the city. "For I will gather all nations against Jerusalem, to battle; and the city shall be taken, and the houses rifled, and the women ravished; and half of the city shall go forth into captivity" (Zechariah 14:2). "And they have cast lots for my people; and have given a boy for an harlot, and sold a girl for wine" (Joel 3:3). As they pass through the land of Judah, his armies rout many of the inhabitants of the land (Isaiah 10:28-31). The pitiable forces in Judah and Jerusalem obviously are incapable of significant resistance.

But *then!* "Then shall the Lord go forth, and fight against those nations, as when he fought in the day of battle" (Zechariah 14:3). "The Lord also shall roar out of Zion" (Joel 3:16). "Therefore wait ye upon me, saith the Lord, until the day that I rise up to the prey: for my determination is to gather the nations, that I may assemble the kingdoms, to pour upon them mine indignation, even all my fierce anger: for all the earth shall be devoured with the fire of my jealousy" (Zephaniah 3:8).

So Mighty an Earthquake

While the demonic spirits were spreading their lies around the nations, and the multitudes were beginning their hasty trek to Armageddon, there was still one more bowl of wrath waiting to be spilled on the earth. The angel of the seventh plague was waiting for the arrival of these multitudes in the valley of decision, and then would come pouring down on the earth the terrible potion in the final bowl.

Revelation 16:17.   **And the seventh angel poured out his vial into the air, and there came a great voice out of the temple of heaven, from the throne, saying, It is done.**

Here is the last and greatest plague of the seven last plagues. The bowls had been poured, respectively, on the land, on the sea, on the waterways, on the sun, on the throne of the beast and on the river Euphrates. This bowl is poured upon the atmosphere, and thus its contents are spread to every portion of the globe.

The climactic and terminal significance of this final strike of God against a rebellious world is certified by a great testimony from heaven, a voice proceeding from the temple and thence from the very throne of God. John has heard many great voices in heaven, from many sources, but this is the first that is said to emanate directly from the throne in the temple in heaven. It is none other than the voice of God, and the pronouncement issuing from His voice is of supreme significance.

"It is done!" He says. This is the final judgment that will have to be visited upon the earth before the coming of the Lord. The earth will be fully prepared for His coming and His great millennial kingdom. The word is the same as in Hebrews 4:3: "The works were *finished* from the foundation of the world." Just as God had absolutely completed His mighty work of creating and making all things in His first six days (Genesis 2:1-3), so now He has absolutely completed His work of purging and changing the earth and its physical systems, enabling it to fulfill its great purposes in the kingdom age which is about to begin.

Yet once more will He make such an announcement. Even the millennial world, as beautiful and perfectly designed as it will be, is still imperfect, because men who live therein are still sinners, and there must therefore be one more purgation at the end of the millennium. Christ will make a new earth and a new heavens out of the purified elements of the old, and then He will make one more announcement, saying again, for the final time: "It is done!" (Revelation 21:6).

But now we must learn how this final plague accomplishes such a mighty work of God. Already there have been vast changes in the earth. Lands and seas, marine life and plant life, atmosphere and even the sun and moon, have all been greatly affected, but one more grand transformation remains to be accomplished.

Revelation 16:18.   **And there were voices, and thunders, and lightnings; and there was a great earthquake, such as was not since men were upon the earth, so mighty an earthquake, and so great.**

Thrice before had John heard "voices and thunderings and lightnings" (Revelation 4:5; 8:5; 11:19) in heaven, just before the seal judgments, the trumpet judgments and the bowl judgments, respectively. On the last two occasions there had also been an earthquake on the earth. Thus are the three sets of seven judgments, each bounded, as it were, by a threefold turmoil at the heavenly throne —great voices, lightning, and thunder. The three sets of judgments are then terminated, as it were, by a great earthquake on the earth.

But this final earthquake is without precedent or parallel! Through the ages there have been earthquakes "in divers places," ever since the mighty tectonic movements that ended the great Flood (Psalm 104:5-9). The earth has been in a state of stress and instability and, now and again, here and there, this unstable equilibrium yields to great earth movements, sometimes with devastation to man and his works. The first Flood was a worldwide flood, followed through the centuries by a multiplicity of local floods. Conversely a multiplicity of local earthquakes through the centuries is climaxed and terminated by a worldwide earthquake. All of them, floods and earthquakes alike, are ultimately attributable to the first great Flood, with the topographical and atmospheric changes which it caused.

The effect of all these deteriorative changes in the earth's physical regimen must somehow be rectified in the tribulation, so that the beautiful antediluvian world can be revived in the millennium. The mighty global earthquake of the seventh bowl is the final event which brings this about.

The movements of the earth have already been great and convulsive during the seven years of the tribulation. The sixth seal had unleashed a great earthquake which evidently caused a slipping of the very crust of the earth (Revelation 6:12-14). After the earthquake at the beginning of the trumpet soundings (Revelation 8:5), the earth was bombarded with huge objects from space (Revelation 8:7-10). At the tribulation's midpoint was another great earthquake (Revelation 11:13, 19; 12:16).

But none was like this earthquake. The old prophets also had foreseen such a day. "For thus saith the Lord of hosts: Yet once, it is a little while, and I will shake the heavens, and the earth, and the sea, and the dry land; And I will shake all nations, and the desire of all nations shall come: and I will fill this house with glory, saith the Lord of hosts" (Haggai 2:6, 7). "Fear, and the pit, and the snare, are upon thee, O inhabitant of the earth. . . . for the windows from on high are open, and the foundations of the earth do shake. The earth is utterly broken down, the earth is clean dissolved, the earth is moved exceedingly. The earth shall reel to and fro like a drunkard, and shall be removed like a cottage; and the transgression thereof shall be heavy upon it; and it shall fall, and not rise again. And it shall come to pass in that day, that the Lord shall punish the host of the high ones that are on high, and the kings of the earth upon the earth" (Isaiah 24:17-21). "The Lord also shall roar out of Zion, and utter his voice from Jerusalem; and the heavens and the earth shall shake" (Joel 3:16).

This mighty earthquake will not only change the topography of every nation, of course, but will largely destroy all earth's proud cities. Especially will this be true of mighty Babylon, the most magnificent of all.

Revelation 16:19.   And the great city was divided into three parts, and the cities of the nations fell: and great Babylon came in remembrance before God, to give unto her the cup of the wine of the fierceness of his wrath.

Under the shattering blows of the unprecedented global earthquake, all the chief cities plummet to the ground. As previously discussed, many of the world's great cities along the coasts of the continents may already have been inundated by the sea level rise accompanying the rapid melting of the ice caps under the scorching sun of the fourth bowl. Now the cities at higher elevations also perish. On every continent—Chicago and Mexico City, Caracas and São Paulo, Johannesburg and Cairo, Peking and New Delhi, Moscow, Berlin, and Paris—all go tumbling down.

The earthquake even affects "the great city," dividing it into three parts. However, this city is not destroyed, as are all the cities of the nations (or "Gentiles"). Since it also is distinguished from Babylon (and since Babylon, like the other cities of the Gentiles, is to be completely destroyed—note Revelation 18:21), the necessary conclusion is that the "great city" is none other than Jerusalem, the "holy city." Jerusalem is, in fact, called "the great city" in Revelation 11:8, and the new Jerusalem is called "the great city" in Revelation 21:10.

Jerusalem alone, of all the great cities of the earth, is thus to be spared destruction by the earthquake at the end of the tribulation. It is the one eternal city, and will survive as long as the earth endures in its present form, finally being replaced as the new Jerusalem, in the new earth. "For David said, The Lord God of Israel hath given rest unto his people, that they may dwell in Jerusalem for ever" (1 Chronicles 23:25). "They that trust in the Lord shall be as mount Zion which cannot be removed, but abideth for ever" (Psalm 125:1). "And the Lord shall reign over them in mount Zion from henceforth, even for ever" (Micah 4:7).

But even Jerusalem is to be significantly changed when the great earthquake strikes. Immediately after the promise that the Lord will go forth and fight the nations which are gathered together against Jerusalem, Zechariah says: "And his feet shall stand in that day upon the mount of Olives, which is before Jerusalem on the east, and the mount of Olives shall cleave in the midst thereof toward the east and toward the west, and there shall be a very great valley, and half of the mountain shall remove toward the north, and half of it toward the south" (Zechariah 14:4).

Thus, two of the three parts into which the great city will be divided by the earthquake will evidently be Mount of Olives (north) and Mount of Olives (south). Perhaps the third is Mount Zion itself, which is now separated from the Mount of Olives by the Kidron Valley, with the Brook Kidron meandering its way down to the Dead Sea. It seems likely that the cleavage of the Mount of Olives will stop at Kidron, since Zechariah does not imply that the new valley cleaves Mount Zion as well. In fact, the Scriptures (note above) seem strongly to assert that Mount Zion (the complex of hills on which most of the old city of Jerusalem was constructed) will stand forever (that is, as long as the earth stands).

But Zechariah goes on to record another intriguing prophecy: "And it shall be in that day, that living waters shall go out from Jerusalem; half of them toward the former sea, and half of them toward the hinder sea: in summer and in winter shall it be" (Zechariah 14:8). Even though Mount Zion is left unscathed by the great earthquake, somehow a great artesian spring will open up in the mountain, generating a large river. This will evidently be the source of the water that flows from the millennial temple (Ezekiel 47) down to the Dead Sea, healing the waters of that saline lake.

The water from Jerusalem will flow both to "the former sea" and "the hinder sea." One of these is certainly the Dead Sea; the other must be either the Sea of Galilee or the Mediterranean Sea. The latter is more probable since, with respect to the temple, the Mediterranean is due west and the Dead Sea due east. "Former" seems clearly to imply the polar opposite of "hinder." Since Jerusalem is essentially on the divide between the Mediterranean and the Dead Sea, it would be quite reasonable for the mysterious new spring on Zion to drain off into both the eastern and western seas.

The location of the marvelous artesian aquifer which the earthquake rift will pierce and whose pressurized waters will then be released in such copious supply to Jerusalem is unknown. God knows where it is, however, and precisely what subterranean channel needs to be opened by the earthquake to convey the waters upward to Zion.

Thus, while other cities are destroyed by the mighty earthquake, God's holy city is rendered more beautiful and perfectly situated than ever. "Beautiful for situation, the joy of the whole earth, is mount Zion, on the sides of the north, the city of the great King" (Psalm 48:2).

The fate of great Babylon, however, is diametrically different. All the other cities of the nations fell, evidently lying in ruins but potentially renewable and rebuildable during the millennium. Babylon is not so. She is the very special object of God's wrath and must be made to serve as an object lesson to all mankind forever. She must be made to drink the wine from the trampled grapes of the wrath of God (see the discussion on Revelation 14:18-20), and will be thrown down with violence and so dismembered as to leave no remains at all (Revelation 18:21).

The theme of great Babylon is so important, however, that John was led to devote two entire chapters of his Book of Revelation to its full story. We shall return to this theme in Chapter 17.

Revelation 16:20.   And every island fled away, and the mountains were not found.

Under the judgment of the sixth seal (Revelation 6:12-14), the earthquakes were so great that "every mountain and island were moved out of their places." The earth's crust became so unstable that, for a time at least, it was slipping across the deep mantle. The relative motion involved was such that, to people at certain points on the earth, "the heaven departed as a scroll when it is rolled together." The worldwide devastation was terrible.

Nevertheless, the mountains and island (which are undersea mountains) were still in existence when the earth movements ceased. The topography was vastly changed, and many of the highest mountains had been broken up. The accelerated desiccation of lakes and rivers, and even ocean bodies, with the prolonged drought of the tribulation years, had contributed further to subsurface landsliding, so that submarine sediment deposition was occurring at the highest rate for thousands of years. The topography was rapidly being smoothed out, with the high elevations cut down and the deep basins filled up.

But what had been only a rapid change, now, under this last great plague, will become cataclysmic. Before, the mountains and islands had only moved out of their places. Now, "every island fled away, and the mountains were not found!" The great mountains and islands of the world will vanish, with all their great masses of granite and limestone and sandstone broken up and transported to the bottom of the sea. The deep ocean basins, conversely, will be built up, thus restoring sea levels to their former higher elevations, but with much of their previous waters now elevated above the troposphere, spread out in a great canopy of water vapor as it had been back at the time of creation (Genesis 1:7).

These, indeed, were traumatic changes for those on the earth, both for the tremendous armies arrayed against Jerusalem in the great phalanx from Armageddon to Idumea, and also for the multitudes still scattered around all the continents. Nevertheless, the new effect of all these changes on the earth's surface was ameliorative, preparing it for the beautiful environment of the millennial age soon to come.

The great prophecy of Isaiah was being fulfilled. "Every valley shall be exalted, and every mountain and hill shall be made low: and the crooked shall be made straight, and the rough places plain: And the glory of the Lord shall be revealed, and all flesh shall see it together: for the mouth of the Lord hath spoken it" (Isaiah 40:4, 5).

The gentle rolling topography of the world as originally created will be restored. No more will there be great inaccessible, uninhabitable mountain ranges or deserts or ice caps. The physical environment of the millennium will be, in large measure, a restoration of the antediluvian environment. This is discussed more fully in Chapter 20. Though it will be of great benefit to the world's future inhabitants, these terrestrial convulsions will be incredibly fearful to its present inhabitants.

Revelation 16:21.   And there fell upon men a great hail out of heaven, every stone about the weight of a talent: and men blasphemed God because of the plague of the hail; for the plague thereof was exceeding great.

The most grievous aspect of the unprecedented earthquake, evoking again a torrent of blasphemy from the men experiencing it, will be a great hail of stones falling from the sky. This hail will not be the usual form of hail—that is, ice produced by violent updrafts in atmospheric storm cells. The Greek word *(chalaza)* means simply something which falls. It is used in the New Testament only in Revelation (8:7; 11:19), and can apply to any objects falling from the sky. The nature of this particular hail is specified by use of the term "stone" (Gr. *lithinos*), always used elsewhere only for true rock materials.

The awful scene, therefore, is one of incredible horror and carnage. The violent earth movements necessarily will be accompanied by tremendous volcanic explosions scattering not just ash but large rock fragments over great areas. The only apt description will be that of a hail of great rocks falling on men from the sky.

These rocks are not mere pebbles, but boulders. Each one on the average weighs a "talent," which is an ancient, and somewhat variable, unit of weight, always on the order of a 100 pounds or more. We are to visualize, therefore, a rain of 100-pound boulders pelting down from the sky, along with the greatest earthquake of all time—mountains falling, great fissures opening, structures crumbling, tsunamis attacking the coasts, devastations everywhere. This plague, indeed, is "exceeding great!"

The probability is, of course, that the hail of stones rains with particular intensity on the massed millions ready for the battle with Christ and His returning saints. For these, there is no escape—only bitter cries of invective and blasphemy. Aligned in the complex of valleys and plains from Armageddon to Edom, encamped together in great density, they are utterly helpless against the heavenly bombardment.

It may be that this is the meaning of the graphic figure in Revelation 14:19, 20, where these masses are said to be cast into God's great winepress of wrath, there to be trodden without the city until blood flows even to the horse bridles. Perhaps the men and their mounts are the grapes, and the boulders the treading feet. Possibly intense cyclic waves of atmospheric high and low pressures resulting from the earth shocks also contribute to the bursting of blood vessels and spilling of blood. Whatever the details may be, the utter horror of the scene is beyond imagination. God is long-suffering, but the day of the Lord will come. "Thou shalt break them with a rod of iron; thou shalt dash them in pieces like a potter's vessel" (Psalm 2:9).

17

Mystery Babylon the Great

(Revelation 17)

There have been two earlier and somewhat cryptic references in Revelation to the city of Babylon, as well as two similarly mysterious references to the Euphrates River. There is, as we have seen, good reason to take these references literally even though the large majority of previous commentaries on Revelation take the position that this great city, Babylon, is not a real city at all. If they do accept it as a real city, they take it to be Rome, or New York, or some other city, but not Babylon.

What is the explanation for this reluctance to believe that John meant Babylon when he wrote "Babylon"? Even at the time John was writing, Babylon was still a viable city, with a substantial colony of Jews (the famous Babylonian *Talmud* originated in or near there, about 500 years after the time of Christ) and there was a significant Christian church there as well (1 Peter 5:13). At the very least, it would be confusing to John's first century readers, as well as to later generations, for him to write so much about Babylon when he really meant Rome (Paul was not afraid to speak directly about Rome in his writings, so why should John be?) or "the false church" (all the apostles, including John, wrote plainly and scathingly about false teachers and false doctrines in the church and would not need to hide their teachings by symbols).

It must be stressed again that *Revelation* means "unveiling," not "veiling." In the absence of any statement in the context to the contrary, therefore, we must assume that the term Babylon applies to the real city of Babylon, although it also may extend far beyond that to the whole system centered at Babylon as well.

The fact that the major structures of Babylon would eventually (though temporarily) fall into almost complete disuse would hardly take God by surprise, and it is certainly possible that divine omniscience could also foresee a time when Babylon would eventually again exhibit its former eminence and grandeur. Even at this present writing the Iraqi government is busily attempting to rebuild the great city, primarily as a tourist attraction. Once the resources of the United Nations (or, even more likely, a future true world government) are thrown behind the project, mighty Babylon can easily be established once again. As we progress in the study of Revelation 17 and 18, it will become increasingly more obvious that the great world capital of the beast will indeed be centered either directly on, or in the immediate vicinity of, the strategic site of ancient Babylon.

Mother of Harlots

Babylon is mentioned by name six times in Revelation. In Revelation 14:8 it is called "that great city"; in Revelation 16:19, it is "great Babylon"; it is called "Babylon the great" in 18:2; "that great city Babylon, that mighty city" in 18:10; and "that great city Babylon" in 18:21. Only in Revelation 17:5 is she called "Mystery, Babylon the great." The later term clearly conveys something different from the others, yet there is no doubt (as we shall see) that all six terms refer to the same basic subject and that this subject at least includes the real city of Babylon. In addition to the passages specifically naming Babylon, it is called a "city" four times (Revelation 17:18; 18:16, 18, 19). Yet this city is also associated with a great "Mystery," a mystery which relates to the baleful influence of that city over all the nations of the earth.

Revelation 17:1.   And there came one of the seven angels which had the seven vials, and talked with me, saying unto me, Come hither; I will show unto thee the judgment of the great whore that sitteth upon many waters.

As the unprecedented global earthquake which comprised the last plague was leveling the cities of the world, it had been called to John's attention that one of those cities—great Babylon—was about to undergo some exquisite special judgment appropriate to her unparalleled wickedness (Revelation 16:19, following Revelation 14:8). Because Babylon had made all nations drink her wine of fornication, God would give Babylon His wine of fierce wrath. One of the angels of the plagues—probably the seventh—now gives John a special bidding to come to observe this judgment.

Only he calls it "the judgment of the great whore that sitteth upon many waters." This picturesque pejorative is used here for the first time, and yet in such a way as to imply that John was already aware somehow of her character and influence. Babylon indeed had been the enemy of God's people for centuries, and her

324

idolatries had infected many nations. Perhaps John was reminded by this statement of such a passage as Jeremiah 51:7. "Babylon hath been a golden cup in the Lord's hand, that made all the earth drunken: the nations have drunken of her wine; therefore the nations are mad." Or perhaps he would think of Isaiah 47:5. "Sit thou silent, and get thee into darkness, O daughter of the Chaldeans: for thou shalt no more be called, The lady of kingdoms."

In context, the prophecies in Isaiah and Jeremiah concerning Babylon had been directed primarily against the Babylon of their own day. To considerable degree these prophecies had been fulfilled as the Persians and later the Greeks had invaded and sacked Babylon. Now, however, John learns that these prophecies (like numerous other Old Testament prophecies) have both a near and a distant fulfillment, with the first a type and precursor of the last. Babylon may have seemed weak and impotent in John's day, but she was not dead. Her unclean and idolatrous ways had survived through the other nations she had contaminated, and she herself, through them, would one day revive in greater wickedness than ever.

The word "whore" (Greek *porne*) is the same as "harlot" (verse 5) and is related to *porneia* ("fornication") and *pornos* ("fornicator" or "whoremonger"). It does not refer only to women who sell their bodies but simply to any who commit fornication. In the Old Testament, especially, physical fornication and adultery were often considered as symbolic of spiritual fornication—that is, of serving and loving other gods than the true Creator. This is undoubtedly also the primary thrust here. Babylon as a nation could not have literally committed fornication with other nations (though this particular sin was very common among her people) but she did indeed lead many nations away from God.

Revelation 17:2. With whom the kings of the earth have committed fornication, and the inhabitants of the earth have been made drunk with the wine of her fornication.

The allusion both here and in Revelation 14:8 to Jeremiah 51:7 is obvious. Since the latter clearly refers to literal Babylon, so must this passage. But how could it really be that Babylon had made *all* nations and their inhabitants drunk with the wrath of her fornication? Nebuchadnezzar, with whom Jeremiah's prophecy had been immediately concerned, was a great king and his later Babylonian empire was the greatest of his day, but his kingdom was long gone even in John's day, and so were the empires of Persia and Greece that followed him. Furthermore, there were great nations even in Nebuchadnezzar's day—the nations of the Far East and of the Americas, for example—who had never even heard of Nebuchadnezzar and the Babylonian empire. How could he have infected *them?*

To understand this situation, it should be remembered that Nebuchadnezzar's Babylon was not the original Babylon. As a matter of fact, Nebuchadnezzar himself had been eminently concerned with the restoration of Babylon's earlier culture and religion. He rebuilt temples and reinstituted the ancient worship of the older Babylonians of the time of Hammurabi and earlier.

Thus it is not the Babylon of Nebuchadnezzar that made all nations drunk with the wine of her spiritual fornications. Nebuchadnezzar's Babylon did transmit much of its culture to the Medo-Persian, Greek, and Roman empires which succeeded it (as implied by the great image of Nebuchadnezzar's dream in Daniel 2), and it was of profound importance in the history of Israel, since it was Nebuchadnezzar who carried them into their seventy-year Babylonian captivity. But what it transmitted, it must have first received from its own progenitors. Furthermore, the great number of similarities between the idolatrous worship of the ancient Chinese, the Hindus, the Incas, and other peoples far removed from Babylon, with the Babylonian worship could not have come from Nebuchadnezzar's kingdom.

Nebuchadnezzar reestablished the worship of Marduk as the chief god of the Babylonian pantheon. This name is also commonly written as Merodach, and the strong probability is that this name was ultimately derived from *Nimrod*.

The data of archaeology and secular history became increasingly speculative as their antiquity increases. Unfortunately the earliest of these periods have been especially confused because of the false concept of evolution and erroneous dating techniques (for example, radiocarbon) that have clothed them with a spurious antiquity. It is generally agreed, however, even by secular archaeologists and antiquarians, that the earliest known civilizations are those of Sumer and Akkad, both of which were located in Mesopotamia and both of which contributed culturally and religiously to the old Babylonian empire which succeeded them. Almost as old is the Assyrian nation which was contiguous to them and often intertwined with them.

In view of the many uncertainties of the monuments and secular records, it is sad that the authorities pay so little attention to the true record of the origin of these ancient nations and cities. The inspired account in the Bible beautifully fits all known facts concerning these events.

"And the beginning of his [i.e., Nimrod's] kingdom was Babel, and Erech, and Accad, and Calneh, in the land of Shinar. Out of that land went forth Asshur [or, probably better, "he went forth into Assyria"], and builded Nineveh, and the city Rehoboth, and Calah" (Genesis 10:10, 11).

Nimrod, therefore, was the founder of Babel, as well as Accad (Akkad, Agade), Erech (Uruk, a prominent city of ancient Sumeria), Assyria (and its capital, Nineveh), and the kingdom of Sumer (Shinar, a synonym of Babylonia, as confirmed in Daniel 1:2). In Micah 5:6, Assyria is called "the land of Nimrod," and the Assyrian and Babylonian empires are treated occasionally in Scripture as almost one entity. The city of Calah, which has been excavated about twenty miles from Nineveh on the Tigris River, is still called "Nimrud" by the inhabitants of the region. The remains of a great step-tower, or ziggurat, in Borsippa, a suburb of Babylon, are still called "Birs-nimrud" ("the tower of Nimrod") by the Arabs.

We are well justified biblically, therefore (and the Bible is our authority), in inferring that the religious system established at the original Babylon (or "Babel") by its founder and first king, Nimrod, is the root source of the later Assyrio/Babylonian complex of religion and philosophy. This inference is also supported by many parallel indications in archaeology, ethnology, and cultural anthropology, when these are divested of their evolutionary distortions.

Furthermore, with the confusion of tongues and resultant dispersion (Genesis 11:9), this religious system was carried by the scattering tribes into every region of the world. Each had its own cultural distinctives, and the names of the pantheon of gods and goddesses were different in each nation, because the languages were now different. But the basic system was still the same everywhere.

This is the reason why every nation and tribe of the past or present (except those whose cosmogony is based on Genesis 1 and 2, such as Christianity, Judaism, and Islam) has a religious system which is fundamentally pantheistic (believing that the physical universe, rather than the transcendent Creator of that universe, is the ultimate reality), polytheistic (believing that this deified cosmos manifests itself locally as various forces and systems of nature, which are personified as "gods" and "goddesses"), evolutionary (believing that these personified forces of nature somehow generate higher and higher orders of beings, including man and—in many cases—even spirits), animistic/spiritistic (believing that the spirits so generated, including the spirits of dead men and women, continue to survive and perhaps evolve into still higher beings), astrological (believing that the highest beings so developed either inhabit or are identical with the starry host of heaven, so that these stars control events on earth), and idolatrous (believing that these gods and goddesses, or personified forces and systems of nature, should be worshiped through images constructed to represent them and which they then possess and energize). This monstrous system of evolutionary, polytheistic, pantheistic, spiritistic, astrological idolatry has permeated practically every culture in the world in one form or another. Even modern evolutionary scientism is nothing but this same ancient paganism in more sophisticated garb. All religions and philosophies except those founded on special creation as revealed in Genesis worship and serve the creation more than the Creator (Romans 1:25) and thus are under God's condemnation. They are either humanistic (worshiping man as the highest attainment of the cosmic process) or "superhuman-istic" (worshiping spiritual beings as still higher attainments of evolution than man). Since they are inexcusable in such an arbitrary rejection of their Creator, God has given them up (Romans 1:24, 26, 28) to uncleanness, to vile affections, and a reprobate mind. Thus have all the inhabitants of earth been made drunk with the wine of Babel's primeval fornication, as Nimrod chose Satan rather than God.

Revelation 17:3.   So he carried me away in the spirit into the wilderness: and I saw a woman sit upon a scarlet coloured beast, full of names of blasphemy, having seven heads and ten horns.

The angel had invited John to see the judgment on great Babylon, but first he must be instructed concerning the nature and the deeds of Babylon and the events preceding her judgment. Therefore, once again John is translated "in the Spirit" (note Revelation 1:10; 4:2) to another time and place.

His observations had been focused on the earth right at the end of the tribulation, as it was rocked with the terrible global earthquake. Now, however, John is translated far back in time, evidently to observe the whole history of the Babylonian corruption. The aspect of the land and sea becomes vastly different—it is nothing but "wilderness" (the definite article is absent in the original).

The most likely time for such a scene is immediately after the great Flood. The world emerging from the watery cataclysm was indeed a vast wilderness, barren and inhospitable, tremendously changed from the idyllic world of the antediluvians. However, it was a purified world, with all the ungodly rebels purged out of it and only Noah and his immediate family as survivors. The wicked "sons of God" who had led the ungodly world into such a morass of corruption that only a global bath could cleanse it (Genesis 6:4-6) had all been bound in chains of darkness (Jude 6). Mankind had opportunity for a new beginning, with every incentive to obey God, knowing so traumatically the terrible price of sin. With the hosts of ungodly men and demonic spirits both purged, the new race of humans could surely stay true to God.

But Satan had not been bound, and he still had a host of demonic principalities and powers available to command. Immediately he resumed his opposition to the work of God, but his strategy this time would be more subtle. John had previously seen the sign of the great red dragon in heaven, leading a third of the angels to follow him in his rebellion against their Maker (Revelation 12:3, 4). He had also seen the beast rising out of the sea, with the same seven-headed, ten-horned aspect as the dragon (Revelation 13:1), exercising the power and occupying the throne given him by the dragon (Revelation 13:2).

Now John sees the same symbol once again, emerging from the great wilderness. This time, however, the symbolic beast seems to combine the characters of both the dragon and the beast of Revelation 13. Like the latter, he has names of blasphemy on his heads (compare 13:1) and, like the dragon, he is red in color (compare 12:3). Presumably the sign represents both the dragon and the earthly governments and kings which he possesses and uses for his evil goals. It will be recalled that the beast of Revelation 13:1 is the same as the beast of Daniel 7:7, and there had been three similar beasts which preceded him (Daniel 7:4-6). Similarly, this beast of Revelation 17 is said to be the eighth, with seven similar kings preceding him (Revelation 17:11). Putting these data all together, it seems most likely that this beast, on which the woman rides, is symbolic of the historical succession of world governments, which are raised up and empowered by Satan.

This, in fact, was Satan's strategy after the Deluge. God had instituted the principle of human government (Genesis 9:6) but had decidedly not instituted the principle of a one-world government. In fact, His specific command to mankind had been to scatter worldwide (Genesis 9:1, 7), which meant that governmental systems would be simple and localized, serving the purpose of maintaining peace and freedom for each community. Instead, Satan had raised up Nimrod to conquer all others and to establish a one-world autocratic government centered at the first Babylon (Genesis 10:8-12; 11:2-4).

It seems, therefore, that this beast of Revelation 17 depicts the principle of dictatorial world government, as continually instigated and energized by the old dragon, Satan. Since the first such government was that of Babylon, under Nimrod, since the same spirit of Babylon has motivated and animated other conquering rulers following him, and since the last such government will again be centered at Babylon, it is most probable that the primary meaning of the beast in the passage is that of political Babylon. It would be controlled and empowered by the dragon for the main purpose of maintaining a humanistic and governmental center of opposition to God and His plan for human government and His ultimate purpose in history.

Who, then, is the unclean woman riding this beast? The angel called her "the great whore sitting upon many waters," but when John saw her, she was sitting on the beast. Presumably the beast was himself on the waters, which are said to symbolize the various nations of the world (verse 15). As the beast is symbolic, so must be the woman, and she herself is identified as Babylon the great, except that she is Babylon in mystery form (verse 5).

As the dragon empowers the beast, so the beast supports the harlot. The woman in turn makes the beast appear outwardly beautiful, thus making it easier for him to attain the control he seeks over mankind. Instead of following the true spiritual bride, the Jerusalem which is above, the mother of us all (Galatians 4:26) most men prefer to pursue the spiritual harlot, the false bride, Babylon, the deceiver of us all. The harlot Babylon is a contrasting type of the chaste Jerusalem and, in one sense, the whole course of history is essentially a tale of these two spiritual cities. Thus, as the beast represents political Babylon, the great whore is religious Babylon. The one is governmental rebellion and confusion, the other is spiritual rebellion and confusion. As Jerusalem is the City of Peace, Babel is the City of Confusion.

Revelation 17:4.   And the woman was arrayed in purple and scarlet colour, and decked with gold and precious stones and pearls, having a golden cup in her hand full of abominations and filthiness of her fornication.

Arrayed like a beautiful queen, the harlot is decked in rich jewelry and magnificently colored garments. Almost irresistibly attractive to ungodly men, she perpetually seduces and tempts them to depart from the true God and to partake of her pleasures. With a beautiful golden cup full of sparkling wine in her extended hand, her invitation is tendered, age after age, nation after nation, and multitudes are deceived and lost thereby. "For the lips of a strange woman drop as an honeycomb, and her mouth is smoother than oil: But her end is bitter as wormwood, sharp as a two-edged sword. Her feet go down to death; her steps take hold on hell" (Proverbs 5:3-5).

This is the way of false religion. Masking the dearth of real spiritual life by outward ostentation and sensual satisfactions, the state religion, supported by the political power (religious Babylon riding upon political Babylon), impresses its devotees with ornate temples and golden images, jeweled garments, marble statues, hypnotic music, and delightsome incense. In many religious systems of past and present, these luxuries are further augmented by temple prostitutes and sexual debauchery, in the name of the god or goddess of the particular cult.

Such religious worship, usually approved and supported by the state, both panders to man's religious nature and appeals to his sensual feelings. It is a powerful opiate, to use the famous Marxist metaphor, and indeed has itself in many cultures even been further stimulated by use of various drugs. In all its essentials, it is the religious system established by Nimrod, and probably revealed to him by Satan back at Babel long ago, as modified and adapted to suit the tastes of varied cultures at different times and places.

Multitudes through the ages have partaken of the harlot's golden cup and been made drunken with the wine of her fornication. Instead of lifegiving wine from heaven, the cup has contained a stupefying concoction of foolishness and filthiness, abominable idolatry and unspeakable wickedness, even the blood of persecuted saints of God; and all have been blasphemously offered to men in the name of religion.

Revelation 17:5.   And upon her forehead was a name written, MYSTERY, BABYLON THE GREAT, THE MOTHER OF HARLOTS AND ABOMINATIONS OF THE EARTH.

Did ever a woman have such a name as this? It was the custom in some places in ancient times that prostitutes should covertly display their names on their foreheads or on their clothing, but this matriarch of all harlots and all idolatries in John's vision is seen with a proud name and lengthy title boldly emblazoned for all to see. She is the great city BABYLON, and is the fountainhead of all spiritual fornication and all false worship, with all the appurtenant evil practices.

The word "abominations" (Greek *bdelugma*) is specifically associated with idol worship. It is the same word used by Christ when he prophesied of the blasphemous image which would be set up in the temple by the beast, calling it "the abomination of desolation" (Matthew 24:15). The worship of idols has been so endemic in false religions through the ages that the prophets of God were forced continually to utter denunciations and warnings against its corrupting influence—even on the true worship of the true God. The first two of God's Ten Commandments were directed against it (Exodus 20:1-6) and the very last word of John's own epistle had warned Christian believers against it (1 John 5:21: "Little children, keep yourselves from idols").

Many intellectuals of the past and present (whether ancient Greek philosophers or modern American academics) have rightly ridiculed the worship of sticks and stones but they have, to all intents and purposes, worshiped mental constructs of their own imaginings, and this is an even worse form of idolatry, with each man becoming his own god. And what is modern evolutionary humanism but flagrant idolatry, deifying man and his corporate self-worship?

It is very significant also that the Bible identifies covetousness with idolatry (as in Ephesians 5:5; Colossians 3:5). As the first two Commandments forbid idolatry, so the last forbids covetousness. The underlying motive of the covetous person is that of rejection of God and His will, discontent with what God has supplied, and a desire for things instead of God. Giving anything priority over the true God and His perfect will is idolatry in God's sight. Jesus said: "Ye cannot serve God and mammon" (Luke 16:13). The Pharisees to whom this particular exhortation was directed derided Him because they "were covetous." To them Jesus said: "Ye are they which justify yourselves before men; but God knoweth your hearts: for that which is highly esteemed among men is abomination in the sight of God" (Luke 16:14, 15). Here is the same word again, and Jesus thus identified these hypocritical religionists as spiritual descendants of the mother of abominations. Even though they piously decried idolatry in the form of image-worship, they used their religion as a cloak for covetousness and thus were more culpable in their idolatry than the Gentiles they despised.

Many Bible teachers have identified this harlot not only as spiritual Babylon but also, more explicitly, as the Roman Catholic Church, noting that many of the doctrines and sacraments of the Babylonian religion were transmitted to pagan Rome and thence ultimately to papal Rome. The most detailed exposition of this teaching can be found in the venerable work by Alexander Hislop entitled *The Two Babylons*.

There is no doubt that many of the doctrines and practices of the Roman Catholic Church, as well as the various Orthodox churches and similar ancient churches, are based on tradition rather than Scripture. There are many striking parallels between many of these and the corresponding doctrines and practices of ancient paganism, which can in turn be generally traced back to their origins in Babylon. The old harlot has indeed caused all nations to imbibe her abominable wine, including even Christian nations.

But to say that spiritual Babylon is either Rome or the Roman Catholic Church is to grossly underestimate the agelong global impact of this great mystery, Babylon the Great. Babylon is the mother of all the harlots and abominations of the earth. From her have come ancient paganism, Chinese Confucianism, Asian Buddhism, Indian Hinduism, Shamanism, Taoism, Shintoism, animism, astrology, witchcraft, spiritism, Sikhism, and all the world's vast complex of "gods many, and lords many" (1 Corinthians 8:5).

Of more direct concern in twentieth-century America is the direct descent of modern scientism and evolutionary humanism from this ancient mother of harlots. As noted before, modern evolutionism is in no way scientific, being contradicted by all true facts of science, but is merely a revival of ancient Greek (and ultimately Babylonian) evolutionary pantheism. This current manifestation of Babylon's philosophy has to considerable degree subverted Christian doctrine, not only in the Catholic Church but in most other Christian sects and denominations. Furthermore the ornate covetousness, the ritualistic sensualism, the hypnotic appeals to the physical senses, the revival of occultism, and other aspects of ancient paganism—in addition to the baleful influences of evolutionism and uniformitarianism—have significantly undermined sound biblical doctrine in many churches of all kinds today.

This development has also been taking place in other great religions which had originally developed in reaction against the practice of idolatry and which sought to acknowledge a true Creator. That is, not only Christianity, but also Judaism, Islam, Zoroastrianism, and other such monotheistic faiths have today been largely contaminated by modern evolutionism and modern covetousness (consider the Arab oil cartels, for example). The various pseudo-Christian cults (such as Mormonism and Christian Science) are all composed of various mixtures of paganism and Christianity and can all be traced to the same Babylonian source. Furthermore, even those who do acknowledge God as true Creator have largely rejected Him as Savior, relying on their own works for salvation, and so also are humanistic in the last analysis. This "mystery" aspect of Babylon has indeed infected every nation with its substitute religion and repudiation of the true Creator and Redeemer.

Revelation 17:6.   And I saw the woman drunken with the blood of the saints, and with the blood of the martyrs of Jesus: and when I saw her, I wondered with great admiration.

Not only is spiritual Bablyon a false and corruptive religion, it is fiercely intolerant. When it cannot subvert by infiltration and false teaching, it will seek to destroy by persecution.

One of the most amazing aspects of religious history is the hatred of other religions against Christ and His followers. Wherever Christianity has gone, preaching the gospel of the love of Christ and salvation by God's grace, it has been resisted. Perhaps more often than not, it has been resisted by bitter persecution, at least for a time. Why this unreasoning animosity against a loving Creator, a holy standard, and a gracious salvation? The only answer is the old dragon and his enmity against the seed of the woman, the true God and Creator and Savior, Jesus Christ. He has energized the political power (the beast) which controls the religious power (the whore), and they everlastingly do all they can to resist and destroy the work of God.

Therefore, through the ages, multitudes of true believers have shed their blood in the cause of Christ, not in wars of aggression, as have many Muslims and Communists and others, but in maintaining a faithful witness against the threats and recriminations of those who would silence their testimony. The blood of the saints (the martyrs before Christ) and the blood of the martyrs of Jesus have been mixed in the golden cup in the woman's hand with all her own concoction of idolatry and wickedness, and the resultant mixture is a deadly potion which renders both her and the inhabitants of the earth drunken and irrational.

The sight of this drunken harlot and her blood-strewn history filled John with great "admiration"—not in the twentieth-century meaning of the term, but in the older sense of "awe" or "amazement." Such a history is indeed enough to cause anyone to shudder in awe. Perhaps John had never realized before the amazing scope of Babylon's baleful influence, but now he sees this unspeakable woman drunk with her fornication and idolatry and the blood of all the martyred saints, and he (as we) can only marvel at the amazing revelation.

The Seven Heads

Revelation 17:7.   And the angel said unto me, Wherefore didst thou marvel? I will tell thee the mystery of the woman, and of the beast that carrieth her, which hath the seven heads and ten horns.

John's amazement had been directed toward the woman and her influence, but the angel mildly rebukes him. The "mystery" of great Babylon involves not only the woman (that is, the religious system established at Babylon) but also the beast that carries her (that is, the totalitarian system of unified government established at Babylon). Perhaps the gentle rebuke also suggests that John (and Christians in general) should have been more aware of these great world movements and influences than they had been heretofore. It is, indeed, sadly true that most Christians tend to be so involved with their own personal needs and activities that they are little aware of the great plan of God and their own place in that plan.

333

In any case, the mystery is about to be unveiled. Not only the characters of the woman and the beast, but their relation to the seven heads and ten horns needs also to be understood. This is not incidental, but vital, information for our guidance in the last days.

Revelation 17:8.   The beast that thou sawest was, and is not; and shall ascend out of the bottomless pit, and go into perdition; and they that dwell on the earth shall wonder, whose names were not written in the book of life from the foundation of the world, when they behold the beast that was, and is not, and yet is.

At first this angelic revelation still seems very enigmatic, and it has led to a number of quizzical interpretations. Various candidates for the Antichrist, in the minds of various expositors of the past, including Nimrod, Judas Iscariot, Nero, and others, are expected by them to return from their incarceration in Hades, rise from the dead, and assume leadership of the last world empire. Such interpretations ignore the fact that after men die in their sins, they will not rise until the last judgment (Hebrews 9:27; Revelation 20:4-6, 12). Satan does not control the keys of Hades and death (Revelation 1:18). Only Christ can bring men back from the grave, and there is no suggestion in Scripture that He would allow such a thing in the case of such ungodly men as these.

As we have seen, however, the beast is not an individual but a despotic world kingdom, raised up and energized by Satan. This kingdom existed in the past, does not exist in the present, and will be revived in the future. It could hardly be the revived Roman empire, as some expositors teach, however, since the Roman empire never has actually ceased, but continues in the various kingdoms and political systems which developed out of it.

The Babylonian empire, on the other hand, perfectly meets all the biblical specifications for this beast. It was the world's first great empire and continued as an important power for almost two millennia. Although the city survived to a small degree after its fall to the Persians, it was of little world significance in John's day, and now, in our day, Babylonia is almost forgotten. Yet, as we have seen, the Bible indicates that its great capital city will one day again be the capital of a world empire. It is a kingdom that was, and is not, and yet is (or, better, "will be" in the coming days of John's vision).

Of course, kingdoms as such neither enter the abyss nor ascend from it. This whole scene, however, is symbolic, and these "beast kingdoms" have all, in a figure, come from the wicked one. Isaiah prophesied the fall of Nebuchadnezzar's Babylon in the following striking words. "That thou shalt take up this proverb against the king of Babylon, and say, How hath the oppressor ceased! the golden city ceased! . . . Hell from beneath is moved for thee to meet thee at thy coming: it stirreth up the dead for thee, even all the chief ones of the earth, it hath raised up from their thrones all the kings of the nations. All they shall speak and say unto thee, Art thou also become weak as we? art thou become like unto us?" (Isaiah 14:4-10).

The wicked king of Babylon (Belshazzar perhaps), descending into Hades, is treated as symbolic of the fallen kingdom of Babylon. But the human king of Babylon is really directed by Satan himself, who raised him up, possessed, and energized him. Thus the "proverb against the king of Babylon" (Isaiah 14:4) proceeds (in verses 12-15) to look beyond the human king to the real king of Babylon, the great rebel Lucifer. He (Satan or Lucifer) accompanied the fallen king down to the abyss of Sheol, and will eventually be cast permanently into the lake of fire.

However, that beast, specifically Satan, but symbolically the kingdom of Babylon that fell at the time its king was cast into Sheol, will someday ascend out of the abyss, and become a great world kingdom again (Daniel 5:22-30).

This will be a most remarkable development in history, that a long-dead world kingdom and its great capital should suddenly be raised from the dead, as it were. It will excite "wonder" (essentially the same word as "admiration" in verse 6) among those worldly-minded men and women who will shortly accept the mark of the beast. The opulent beauty of rebuilt Babylon will probably contribute to the attraction that the beast has over the earth-dwellers.

Almost incidentally in this context appears a remarkable clause: "whose names were not written in the book of life from the foundation of the world." These latter people apparently do not wonder at the beast, presumably because they have been instructed already, probably through reading this very section of the Apocalypse, to expect such a revival. Those who receive the mark of the beast will thereby irrevocably reject Christ and be consigned to perdition (Revelation 14:9-11), thus having their names erased from the book of life in which they had been entered at the time of their conception (see discussion on Revelation 3:5; 13:8). In the eternal counsels of God, however, who created both space and time and sees all things everywhere in all time at once, the blotting out of the names is concurrent with the writing of the names. Thus, in God's perspective, it is as though their names had never been entered at all. Those whose names are not destined to be blotted out of the book, therefore, are those whom God has chosen and who have chosen Him.

Revelation 17:9.   And here is the mind which hath wisdom. The seven heads are seven mountains, on which the woman sitteth.

Those whose names are in the book of life also have minds of wisdom, and so can discern the nature, not only of the beast, but also of the harlot woman riding the beast. This is similar terminology to that in Revelation 13:18: "Here is wisdom. Let him that hath understanding count the number of the beast." In this latter passage, the spiritually-minded person is given the clue which will enable him to determine the identity of the beast as a man, before he is openly identified by the world.

Now also, the mind that possesses biblical wisdom is given the needed clue concerning recognition of the beast's kingdom and of the corrupt religious system which it fosters and uses, before the rest of the world can realize what is happening.

The seven heads of the beast are said to represent seven mountains on which the woman sits. This has been widely interpreted as the "seven-hilled city of Rome," with the woman correspondingly identified as the Roman Catholic Church.

Such an identification is wrong, however, for several reasons. The Roman Catholic Church does not sit on the seven hills of Rome. Its churches are all over the world and its headquarters only in Vatican City. Furthermore, many cities have seven hills, and Rome itself has more than seven. Besides that, a "hill" (Greek *bounos*) such as in Rome is not a "mountain" (Greek *oros*), and it is the latter word that is used here.

The clearest interpretation is shown in the very next verse, which identifies the seven mountains as seven kings, with one being the beast mentioned in this chapter. The latter we have already seen to represent a Satan-controlled kingdom, the first (and last) in a series of similar kingdoms, all comprising political Babylon. Thus the scarlet-arrayed harlot is seen as supported through the ages by seven kingdoms.

Revelation 17:10. **And there are seven kings: five are fallen, and one is, and the other is not yet come; and when he cometh, he must continue a short space.**

The seven heads of the beast on which the harlot rides are thus interpreted as seven mountains, but these in turn are interpreted as seven kings. The equating of mountains with kings requires yet another link in the chain to conform to scriptural example elsewhere. That is, mountains often represent kingdoms, and each kingdom is usually equated with some prominent king at its head.

For example, prophesying of the messianic kingdom coming in the millennium, Isaiah says "And it shall come to pass in the last days, that the mountain of the Lord's house shall be established in the top of the mountains, and shall be exalted above the hills; and all nations shall flow unto it" (Isaiah 2:2). Speaking of the same kingdom, the prophet Daniel said: " . . . and the stone that smote the image became a great mountain, and filled the whole earth" (Daniel 2:35). The interpretation of this mountain, which (in the emperor Nebuchadnezzar's vision) had destroyed the great image representing the age-long succession of great world kingdoms, was as follows: " . . . the God of heaven [shall] set up a kingdom, which shall never be destroyed: . . . and the kingdom . . . shall break in pieces and consume all these kingdoms, and it shall stand for ever" (Daniel 2:44).

The symbolic nature of the beast and the whore requires the associated items in the vision also to be symbolic. Whenever the meaning of a symbol is not explained in the immediate context, it should be found in related passages of Scripture. The prophecies of Isaiah and Daniel, of course, provide background for much of the Apocalypse, and it is certainly reasonable to conclude from such passages as the above that the mountains in the vision represent kingdoms.

The question is which kingdoms? Again the image of Daniel 2 provides the key. The golden head of the image was Nebuchadnezzar's great empire centered at Babylon (Daniel 2.37, 38); the silver breast and arms were the Medo-Persian empire which displaced Babylon (Daniel 2:39; 5:28; 8:20); the brass belly and thighs represented the Grecian empire which superseded Persia (Daniel 2:39; 8:21). Following the same progression, the legs of iron clearly represented the great Roman empire which would conquer Greece and most of the known western world (Daniel 2:40). The Roman empire was still in power in John's day so it must be the kingdom that "is."

Though none of these empires ever actually ruled the whole world, each was the greatest kingdom of its own time, particularly in reference to the land and people of Israel and these kingdoms' opposition to the proclamation of God's Word and the accomplishment of His purposes in the world. And before these four (Babylon, Persia, Greece, and Rome), there had been two other great kingdoms, Egypt and Assyria, both of which also had been perpetual enemies of God, His Word, and His people.

These, of course, have not been the *only* kingdoms that have been at enmity with God and His purposes. In this category could also be placed such kingdoms as Syria, Edom, Moab, Midian, and many others, but none of these were empires of great size and influence. On the other hand, there were other great and powerful empires in the ancient world—China, India, and the Incas, for example—but these had only peripheral contact with the Word of God and the chosen people. There were only six kingdoms that met both criteria up to the time of Christ and the apostles. Furthermore, all six of these were not only legitimate heirs of political Babel but also of religious Babel as well. Babylonia, Egypt, Assyria, Persia, Greece, and Rome were all strongholds of the world religion of evolutionary pantheism and idolatrous polytheism. Thus, they appropriately are represented as six heads on the great beast that supports the harlot.

But what kingdom, arising after John's day, is represented by the seventh head? There have been a goodly number of strong kingdoms that have opposed both Jews and Christians since the days of the Romans (the Mongol, Moslem, Fascist, and Communist nations, for example). However, the particular kingdom prophesied here will exist for only "a short space," in contrast to the first six, each of which continued over many centuries. Further, like the other six, it must continue to support the great false religious system symbolized by the woman riding the beast.

The reason why it is difficult to identify this seventh kingdom is probably because it is still future. The various relevant prophecies in Daniel, especially the image prophecy of Daniel 2, indicate that the Roman empire continues for a long time. The two "legs" of the image, the eastern and western divisions of the empire, were eventually perpetuated mainly in the two politico/religious cultures coming out of the originally monolithic empire. Thus in a sublimated sense, the old Roman empire still exists, though in a different form, surviving in what today we call "east," the Communist nations dominated by Russia, and "west," the capitalist nations led by the United States and, to a lesser degree, by England, France, and Germany. The two feet of Daniel's image, partly iron and partly clay (Daniel 2:33, 41-43) quite possibly correspond to this particular stage of history.

In this sense, therefore, the mighty empire of Rome existed as the key world kingdom both in the days of John's lifetime and in the days to which John was translated in his vision. It is the kingdom that "is."

The one which "is not yet come" must, therefore, correspond to the *toes* of Daniel's image, the ten kingdoms which, in the last days, arise out of the "foot" stage of the image. These are also the "ten horns" mentioned in this passage. Since these have not yet arisen, it is probably premature to speculate as to their identity, although many current teachers are assuming the nations of Europe's Common Market will be involved. As discussed in Chapter 6, the political chaos that will follow the miraculous defeat of Gog and Magog in Israel, probably shortly before the beginning of the seven-year tribulation period, will probably lead to the emergence of a strong new western alliance of ten kingdoms, possibly including some of the Communist nations who refuse to participate in Gog's invasion of Israel. This seventh kingdom of John's particular vision is probably this alliance, or possibly whichever nation dominates the alliance. Some may choose to call this the "revived Roman empire" or, perhaps better, the "revised Roman empire."

These nations and cultures of Europe and America, while nominally Christian, especially in the "foot" stage of Daniel's image, "partly strong and partly broken," have been also the chief repository for the esoteric perpetuation of the religion of the great harlot. As noted earlier, the modern religion of evolutionary humanism and occultism has permeated and dominated the schools and other institutions of all these nations for many decades, and has in fact been exported to all other nations as well. But this is merely a modernized version of the same age-old pagan system introduced at Babel by Nimrod. It may seem like a glamorous and sophisticated lady, clothed in the pseudo-scientific garments of intellectualism, religious ritualism, and opulent materialism to meet the tastes of the twentieth century, but underneath she is the same ancient whore.

This seventh kingdom, composed of the ten-kingdom alliance, will not last very long. Probably its duration is essentially the three-and-a-half years of the first half of the tribulation. John has already learned (Revelation 13:7) that, at the midpoint of the tribulation, the Satan-empowered beast will then be given power over all kindreds, tongues, and nations. This is further confirmed in the following verses.

Revelation 17:11.   And the beast that was, and is not, even he is the eighth, and is of the seven, and goeth into perdition.

At first there seems here to be an anomaly. There are only seven heads on the beast, representing seven kings and their kingdoms. But now there appears an eighth king, or kingdom, which is "of the seven." Furthermore, this latter king turns out to be the beast himself. So we have the entire beast somehow arising from the seven heads of the beast. This strange cycle answers to the equally strange description of the beast as one who "was" and "is not" and yet "shall be" (verse 8). It seems almost an attempt to counterfeit the resurrection of Christ, or at least to imitate the description of Him as the one who "liveth, and was dead; and, behold, [is] alive forevermore" (Revelation 1:18).

We have already been warned that this beast, this man of sin, will indeed present himself in just such a fashion. He will receive a deadly wound, apparently die and descend into Hades, then suddenly seem to be resurrected and tell marvelous tales of his ascent from the great abyss (note Revelation 11:7; 13:3-6, 12; 17:8).

The anomaly is resolved when we see that this beast is both a king and a kingdom, and that both are apparently resurrected, even though neither actually died. The man of sin will indeed receive a wound which appears to be lethal—a "deadly" wound—but the Scripture does not say he actually dies. Had he actually descended into Hades, he could not have returned, for Christ holds the key to Hades, not Satan. Nevertheless, Satan is not yet bound there (Revelation 20:2, 3) and he can and does descend into the abyss to the extent Christ permits, likewise ascending from the abyss to continue his warfare in the heavenly places. Satan also, as noted before, is symbolized by this beast, since he indwells and energizes him. Probably the statement that he ascends from the abyss (or "bottomless pit") applies specifically only to Satan. While the beast lies apparently dead, he is really only in a deep trance or state of suspended animation, receiving from Satan revelations about Hades and his future role in the world as the dragon's incarnation.

In parallel and strikingly analogous fashion, the beast's kingdom will also suddenly be revived. Since it is "of the seven," it partakes of the character of all of them, in a sense marking the resurrection of all these ancient nations, from Babel to Rome. This is not surprising, since all manifest the same characteristics, political and religious, and all together are identified as Babylon the Great in mystery form.

In various Old Testament prophecies, this final Antichrist is identified in one way or another with all six of these ancient empires. He is identified with the Romans in Daniel 9:26, which notes that "the people of the prince that shall come" are the people who will destroy Jerusalem and the temple after Messiah's rejection by the Jews. The head of one of the four divisions of the Greek empire which preceded Rome was Antiochus Epiphanes, the "vile person" of Daniel 11:21, whose wickedness and violence against Jerusalem are taken as a type of the beast of the last days (note Daniel 8:23-25; 11:31-33).

Among the Persians, the traditional "enemy of all the Jews" was Haman the Agagite (Esther 9:24), whose plot to annihilate them makes him also an appropriate type of the beast (compare Esther 3:8-10, 13 and Revelation 12:17; 17:14). The Egyptians, likewise, were enemies of God's people from the time of Abraham to the time of Jeremiah and especially in the time of Moses. The Pharaoh of the Exodus, who also attempted to destroy all the children of Israel, becomes thereby also a type of the Antichrist. Pharaoh is called "the great dragon that lieth in the midst of his rivers" in Ezekiel 29:3, and is said to be "like in glory and greatness among the trees of Eden" (Ezekiel 31:18), but he and his people (like the beast) will be brought down to "the nether parts of the earth." More directly to the point, the Antichrist is specifically called "the Assyrian" in a number of passages (e.g., Micah 5:5, 6; Isaiah 30:31; 31:8), possibly because of the close association of Assyria with Babylon in their origin and history (note Isaiah 23:13; Micah 5:6). As far as Babylon is concerned, not only is Nimrod a type of the beast and Nebuchadnezzar's image (Daniel 3:1-7) a type of the beast's image, but the beast himself is here directly identified with Babylon the Great.

It is also noteworthy that all those ancient nations will experience a measure of physical and political renewal in the last days, and presumably will continue as nations in the millennium. Egypt and Assyria, for example, are specifically mentioned in such a context (Isaiah 19:23-25). Persia is mentioned as one of the nations confederate with Gog and Magog in the latter days and Elam (essentially the same as Persia in the Bible) is going to be brought again from captivity in the latter days, according to Jeremiah 49:39.

Greece and Rome have continued active through the centuries, no longer as great political empires but nevertheless as viable nations, and all western nations still manifest their philosophical and cultural influence. Of course, Egypt and Persia also still exist as nations today, and apparently all of these will be active nations during the coming millennium, except Babylon.

Babylon will indeed be resurrected as a great city, capital of a worldwide empire. She will be the eighth of these great kingdoms of the earth, arising out of them even as they all are also reviving. Yet in mystery form, Babylon the Great has existed ever since Nimrod. She has never actually died, even in a physical sense, and the great prophecies of her utter desolation in Isaiah and Jeremiah have never yet been really fulfilled. But they will be! Egypt and Assyria will be thriving nations in the millennium, but not Babylon. "And Babylon, the glory of kingdoms, the beauty of the Chaldees' excellency, shall be as when God overthrew Sodom and Gomorrah" (Isaiah 13:19). Just as her last and greatest king will be despatched into perdition, so will mighty Babylon finally become and remain a desolation as long as the earth endures.

The Ten Horns

Revelation 17:12.   And the ten horns which thou sawest are ten kings, which have received no kingdom as yet; but receive power as kings one hour with the beast.

As discussed above, the ten horns on the seventh head of the beast probably constitute an end-time confederation of kingdoms arising out of the remnants of the sixth kingdom, the Roman empire. This confederation is the seventh in the historical succession of empires extending from Babylon to Rome, and will endure for a brief time, probably three-and-a-half years. Though the individual nations in some cases have existed for centuries (for example, nations such as the United States, England, France, Italy, and Germany in the west and Poland, Hungary, Greece, Yugoslavia, and Rumania in the east could satisfy the prophetic specifications here, particularly after the destruction of Russia and her allies in Israel as described in Ezekiel 38), they would not come to power as a united kingdom until this future federation is implemented. The ten nations listed above are, of course, speculative and illustrative only; there is no way of identifying them precisely until world events lead to its formation, and this may well be after the rapture of the Church.

At some time, however, this seventh great kingdom will be formed almost overnight. The ten will receive power as "co-kings" in the kingdom "at one hour." It seems likely that some great event, possibly the sudden destruction of Gog and Magog, will bring to a climax previous political movements, appearing to facilitate the imminent solution to all world problems through the formation of such a confederation, and it will all be accomplished in short order.

Prominent in these plans and negotiations will be the head of one of these ten nations, the man destined just a few years hence to be recognized as world dictator, the beast, the heir of the seven kingdoms of history and the ten kingdoms of the present. He will attract much attention and praise for his efforts and, among other things, he will consummate a seven-year treaty with Israel, allowing the reestablishment of their temple and their ancient religious system in Jerusalem. Initially, however, he and his kingdom will only be one of the ten, all of whom at the same hour will yield their individual sovereignties to the "United Nations," a kingdom which presumably will be ruled by a ten-man security council (one vote for each nation) at the helm.

Revelation 17:13.   These have one mind, and shall give their power and strength unto the beast.

Although these ten start out as equals, they will gradually come to acknowledge the superiority of the beast and will soon set about to cede all sovereignty to him. The meaning of "mind" in this passage is "will" or "purpose." Whatever resistance they may encounter from their own or from other people, it becomes their set purpose to surrender all to him.

This surrender will include both their armaments and their authority ("power and strength"). This is an amazing phenomenon, that ten important and strong nations should all voluntarily yield their sovereignty and their military forces to one man! He must indeed be a tremendously brilliant and intimidating individual, a man of extraordinary charisma and political insight, inspiring both awe and confidence in the ungodly men and women of the world.

This will not take place overnight, of course, as the ten-nation kingdom will endure for three-and-a-half years. In fact, parallel prophecies in the Old Testament indicate that considerable resistance is encountered at first. The "ten horns" of Daniel 7:7 are clearly the same ten kings as here in Revelation. Apparently three of these need to be "persuaded" before they also have "one mind." "And the ten horns out of this kingdom are ten kings that shall arise: and another shall rise after them; and he shall be diverse from the first, and he shall subdue three kings" (Daniel 7:24).

While this internal dissension is being quelled, the federated kingdom also must battle against outside nations. Daniel 11:40-44 apparently describes this period and indicates that there will be struggles with both "the king of the south" and "the king of the north." The first of these seems to be a federation of nations in northern Africa and the Near East (Egypt, Libya, Ethiopia, Edom, Moab, and Ammon are mentioned). The king of the north may include the remnants of the Russian confederation. Also troublous "tidings out of the east" are mentioned, suggesting that the vast hordes of China and other far eastern nations are displeased at the formation of these western "United Nations."

While all of this is going on, however, it must not be forgotten that the great judgments of the seals and the trumpets are plaguing all nations, causing much distraction from their political goals and military pursuits. The plagues are seen, humanly speaking, as emanating from God's two great witnesses (Revelation 11:6), and there is tremendous persecution mounting everywhere against new Christian believers as a result.

Then, suddenly, two events will take place which will galvanize all nations into rapid submission to the beast. The first will be his amazing "resurrection" from Hades. One of his enemies will stab him to death, and probably his funeral will be viewed via television all over the world. Thus multitudes will be watching

342

when he suddenly returns to life, recounting amazing stories of his supposed victory over death and Hades. Then, he will be successful in overcoming and killing God's two witnesses, who had previously been invincible and unapproachable.

Such amazing events, occurring in a world already half irrational through pain, environmental cataclysms, drugs, and general turmoil, will be more than enough to silence all opposition to his assuming absolute power. Not only the ten kingdoms of the western federation, but also all that dwell upon the earth, will worship him, except those whose names are in the book of life (Revelation 13:8).

Revelation 17:14.   These shall make war with the Lamb, and the Lamb shall overcome them: for he is Lord of lords, and King of kings: and they that are with him are called, and chosen, and faithful.

This is surely one of the great mountain-peak verses of the Bible. The beast may, in his unprecedented triumphs here at the midpoint of the tribulation, deceive himself into thinking that he has now exhibited himself to be the greatest man in history. He is the first world dictator, and all the world now worships him. He has even conquered death, and has slain the two greatest servants of the God of heaven, men who themselves had lived in heaven for thousands of years. With the help of his dragon master, he can now even plot to conquer the Lamb Himself, who he realizes is preparing to return to earth to claim His inheritance.

But the old dragon has deceived the whole world, even his own man of sin! He is *not* the greatest king after all. The Lamb is King of *all* kings! The Lamb is the Son of God. As the Lord, He created all men (Revelation 4:11); as the Lamb, He died to redeem all men (Revelation 5:9). The dragon is not a match for God's Lamb.

He may mobilize all these kings of the earth, and their armies, as indeed he will very shortly, but it will be only to their doom. The Lamb will overcome them with only a spoken word. The Lord Jesus is not only King of kings and Lord of lords, but also Conqueror of conquerors. He is the great Overcomer and in Him we also overcome. "And this is the victory that overcometh the world, even our faith" (1 John 5:4).

The beast has vast armies at his control, but the Lamb also has armies, with armor of fine linen, white and clean (Revelation 19:14), the righteousness of saints. These are not the clamorous rabble of the earth, but the very elite of creation, carefully selected and proven, "called and chosen and faithful." The three Greek words are, respectively, *kletos, eklectos, pistos.* God calls many according to His purpose (Romans 8:28), and from these, He selects some for special ministry. "Many are called, but few are chosen" (Matthew 22:14). Then, sadly, only some of these are faithful. Only some will hear His "Well done, good and faithful servant" (Matthew 25:23). There are some who are saved, but who receive no reward (1 Corinthians 3:15). "My reward is with me, to give every man according as his work shall be" (Revelation 22:12).

Such judgments and discernments must be left to the Lord. In any case, these who are with Him as He overcomes the armies of the beast are men and women who have been called and chosen and faithful. Perhaps other believers remain regretfully at the heavenly throne while these, like Gideon's 300, go to war. As believers who have been entrusted with His service, we have been called and chosen. May we also, as good stewards, be found faithful (1 Corinthians 4:2).

Revelation 17:15.   And he saith unto me, The waters which thou sawest, where the whore sitteth, are peoples, and multitudes, and nations, and tongues.

The angel who had carried John back, and then forward, through time in order to show him the great sign of Mystery Babylon (verse 1) and had then undertaken to explain its meaning (verse 7) now speaks again, this time to tell him the fate of spiritual Babylon, the scarlet-dressed woman in the sign. The harlot had been seen as sitting upon a scarlet-colored beast, symbolizing political Babylon as energized by Satan, but this beast had previously been seen (Revelation 13:1) as emerging from the sea. Thus the woman was also seen by John upon the waters.

These waters are now explained as symbolic of the many peoples of the world. The woman is also sitting, of course, on the seven heads of the beast, representing seven mountains and thus seven kingdoms. The meaning apparently is that these great world empires are her immediate support, but also that, secondarily, she is further and ultimately supported by *all* the peoples of the world. All nations have been deceived by Satan (Revelation 12:9), worship the beast (Revelation 13:8), and are preparing to fight the true God (Revelation 16:14).

The waters of the troubled sea symbolize the ungodly nations of the world in other Scriptures as well (Daniel 7:3; Isaiah 57:20). The Lord Jesus, in fact, described the last days as a time when there would be "upon the earth distress of nations, with perplexity; the sea and the waves roaring" (Luke 21:25).

There are several other scenes in Revelation where large numbers of people are mentioned (Revelation 5:9; 7:9; 10:11; 13:7; 14:6) but this is the only one in which "multitudes" are listed as a separate category from "peoples and nations and tongues." The latter three all represent coherent groups of people—clans, nations, linguistic groups. Perhaps this passage suggests that there are also large groups among the world's ungodly people who will organize around other than tribal, ethnic, and linguistic criteria in these last days. Unions, commercial and mercantile associations, cultic societies, secret political internationals, and other such groups might be examples of the "multitudes" which are included in the global milieu out of which the great harlot emerges. She sits on these waters. They support her and partake of her fornications and share in her guilt.

Revelation 17:16.   **And the ten horns which thou sawest upon the beast, these shall hate the whore, and shall make her desolate and naked, and shall eat her flesh, and burn her with fire.**

Then, suddenly, the ancient whore, right at the moment of her greatest triumph, reigning proudly over the peoples of the whole world, meets her end. In every land have been erected great churches and temples and mosques and shrines and images in her honor. In the schools and homes her philosophy is taught and her rituals are practiced. Priests and monks and counselors in wide variety teach the people and receive their gifts. Tax monies also accrue to the monstrous system, political Babylon amply supporting the opulence of religious Babylon, and the syncretistic union of all the world's complex of humanistic religions is soon accomplished.

With the departure of all believers in the true churches before the beginning of the tribulation period, organized religion will quickly be forged into a powerful tool for the support of the political power. Religious Babylon has always been attached in some degree in an unequal yoke with political Babylon. "Church and state" have only rarely in history been clearly and properly separated. Each has always sought to use the other to attain its own ends, with considerable success on both sides.

During the first half of the tribulation, while the beast is attempting to establish his supremacy over his colleagues in the ten-kingdom federated empire, he quickly realizes he can use man's religious nature to help implement his own ambitions. Through the special genius of his colleague, the false prophet (the second beast, announced in Revelation 13:11), he is able soon to gain a considerable following in many nations through promoting a cultic worship of himself throughout the world. With the earth-dwellers already naturally inclined to humanistic man-worship, it is easy for the prophet, even using miracles as a means of persuasion, to seduce great multitudes into idolizing the brilliant and charismatic king who has so rapidly risen to world prominence.

Then, when he finally attains his goal of global dictatorship at the midpoint of the tribulation, the members of the world's religious hierarchy no doubt hope they will share richly in the fruits of conquest, continuing to exercise much power over the people and even over their leaders. However, these religionists will no longer be needed once the beast becomes world emperor. All men will then soon worship the beast, and his image will be seen and revered all over the world. It will no longer even be necessary to use religious intermediaries of any kind, since men will openly acknowledge and worship Satan as well as the great super man (Revelation 13:4).

The beast and the false prophet will quickly let it be known that they neither want nor need this vast humanistic religious complex any more, possibly serving as a rival to their own power. The ten kingdoms in the federation, with their respective heads of state, will no doubt also have long resented the power and influence of the religious system. The alliance of church and state, while always useful to both parties, has also always been resented by both parties, each side wanting all the power. Possibly the ten kings also will develop a special antipathy toward this particular religious hierarchy as they have so recently seen it used to help bring the beast to power over themselves.

Consequently, they will eagerly jump at the chance to destroy this despised harlot once the beast gives permission. Already a persecution has been mounted against Christians and Jews—why not get rid of all religion at the same time? No more vestiges of Buddha worship or veneration of Confucius, no more praying to Allah or appeasement of assorted angels and demons—certainly no more vestiges of pseudo-Christian or Jewish worship—are to be tolerated.

Even though the masses have been persuaded to abandon their various religions and worship the beast only, the religious leaders will probably wish to hang on to their positions of eminence and influence, and so will try to resist these orders. With that, the campaign of annihilation will be mounted in full. All the riches of the temples will be confiscated, the buildings and accoutrements burned with fire, the leaders executed. Soon the old whore will be left desolate and naked, and even her naked "flesh," meaning, presumably, whatever of real substance might have remained in her religious system after all its ornate trappings had been removed, will have been utterly consumed by the political powers who hate her. The kings will mourn the later destruction of political Babylon (Revelation 18:9) but will exult over this destruction of her religious parasite.

Revelation 17:17.   For God hath put it in their hearts to fulfil his will, and to agree, and give their kingdom unto the beast, until the words of God shall be fulfilled.

Herein is an amazing thing, that men should fulfill God's will even while they oppose His will! "Surely the wrath of man shall praise thee: the remainder of wrath shalt thou restrain" (Psalm 76:10). When these ungodly kings consented to cede their kingdoms to the beast, their very motivation was that they could thereby more effectively aid Satan in his opposition to God. Instead, however, they are really doing exactly what God led them to do!

It was like the men who crucified Jesus. "The kings of the earth stood up, and the rulers were gathered together against the Lord, and against his Christ. For of a truth against thy holy child Jesus, whom thou hast anointed, both Herod, and Pontius Pilate, with the Gentiles, and the people of Israel, were gathered together, for to do whatsoever thy hand and thy counsel determined before to be done" (Acts 4:26-28).

God used these ten kings, first of all, to destroy the age-old pseudoscientific system of religious Babylon, which had deceived and damned multitudes throughout the centuries. They did this for their own utterly selfish and wicked motives, of course, but nevertheless they accomplished the will of God in the process. One should note in passing that God's decisions are not contingent on man's will, nor is His will contingent on man's decisions. Rather, men make their decisions in accord with God's will, even when they intend otherwise.

At this point, though the kings certainly do not have such a thing in mind, God is constraining them to unite in this way under the beast in order that His own words might be fulfilled. In order for "all nations" to be "gathered together" for judgment and destruction at the day of the Lord (note Joel 3:2; Zechariah 14:2), as God had promised long ago, there must first be established a human agency to implement such a convocation. Nothing could ever accomplish this except an all-powerful world government. Hence, the kings of the earth must first yield their sovereignty to such a commander. God's Word must be fulfilled, whether men intend it so or not.

Revelation 17:18.   And the woman which thou sawest is that great city, which reigneth over the kings of the earth.

The final word of the angel to John is that the woman whom he had shown to John in the sign was to be understood as "that great city." And what city is that? The woman herself had blatantly displayed the answer to this question on her forehead; she is "Babylon the great."

As a system, religious Babylon began at Babel, whence it permeated every nation on earth, maintaining its special character and influence not only in both ancient Babylon and later Babylon, but also in Egypt, Assyria, Persia, Greece, and Rome, the others in the succession of great nations which transmitted the Babylonian heritage of heresy down through the ages. It finally will reach its zenith of power in rebuilt Babylon, the capital city of the final world empire, the kingdom of the beast. There the old harlot will again, though very briefly, become that great city which reigns over all the kings of earth. But it is also there that these same kings will turn on her and destroy her.

Political Babylon must then, also quickly fall. The two have been so entwined together through the ages that the fall of one can only presage the fall of the other. And when the capital falls, the kingdom must also quickly fall. The end of all things is at hand.

But first it must be emphasized again that Babylon is a city. Further, the city is Babylon. It says so, plainly, in Revelation 18:10 and 18:21. Commentators, even futurist and literalist commentators, seem strangely reluctant to accept this fact. They argue that since Isaiah and Jeremiah prophesy of Babylon's permanent destruction, it is impossible for Babylon to be rebuilt in the tribulation.

Babylon, indeed, will be permanently destroyed, as recorded in the very next chapter (18:21), but this has not happened yet. The prophecies of Isaiah and Jeremiah also refer to this future destruction, not merely to Babylon's present-day condition, as is evident from the following considerations, among others: (1) The destruction will take place in the time that the stars and sun are darkened (Isaiah 13:1, 9, 10). (2) The city will become as desolate as Sodom and Gomorrah, burned completely, with no remains whatever (Isaiah 13:19; Jeremiah 50:40). (3) It shall become desolate forever, with neither man nor beast entering it any more (Isaiah 13:20; Jeremiah 51:62). (4) It will be a time of judgment not only for Babylon but for all nations (Isaiah 13:11-13; Jeremiah 51:49). (5) Its destruction will be followed by universal rest and peace (Isaiah 14:7, 8). (6) Its destruction is directly associated also with the casting of Lucifer into Sheol (Isaiah 14:12-15). (7) Babylon's stones will never be used in future construction elsewhere, whereas the present-day ruins of Babylon have been frequently plundered and reused in later constructions (Jeremiah 51:26).

It is true that these famous Old Testament prophecies of Babylon's destruction (Isaiah 13:1—14:27; Jeremiah 50:1—51:64) contain many sections that deal specifically with the Medo-Persian conquest of Babylon and her eventual decline and desolation in the centuries following. Like a great many other Old Testament prophecies, however, these have both a near fulfillment and a far fulfillment, with the first a type and precursor of the second. From the prophet's perspective, both were in the future and thus tended to merge together as he recorded his vision. This is a very common phenomenon in the Old Testament, and the seven considerations above make it abundantly evident that this is the case here as well. One can, by careful study, discern the two clearly as he reads the words of these visions with the advantage of a perspective between the two stages of their fulfillment. He will find there are no contradictions, and since so many predictions have already been fulfilled in the past, he can be confident the rest will be fulfilled in the future.

This, however, will require that Babylon somehow be restored to its former magnificence and prominence. As noted previously, Babylon continued as a viable city for many years, even through several centuries of the Christian era. Even today the town of Hillah is a substantial community occupying at least a portion of the area of ancient Babylon. However, much of the ancient city is in ruins, and has been in a semidesolate condition for centuries. It seems at first like a very improbable candidate for any kind of urban renewal program.

Nevertheless, Babylon is indeed a prime prospect for rebuilding, entirely apart from any prophetic intimations. Its location is the most ideal in the world for any kind of international center. Not only is it in the beautiful and fertile Tigris-Euphrates plain, but it is near some of the world's richest oil reserves.

The nation of Iraq, which includes Babylon in today's geography, is the wealthiest and strongest of the Moslem nations. Its engineers, associated with top consultants from other nations, have developed the water supplies of the two great rivers through a series of dams and canals so that its agricultural and hydroelectric resources are rapidly expanding, as are its manufacturing industries. Realizing the tremendous tourist potential in a restored Babylon, the Iraqis have already made considerable progress on its reconstruction.

However, the instabilities of the Middle East situation, the radical nature of the Iraqi government and its Russian connections, plus the hostility of Iraq and other Moslem nations to Israel, all make this current venture uncertain. The real potential of Babylon is in the more distant future and involves far more than tourism.

Computer studies of the Institute for Creation Research have shown, for example, that Babylon is very near the geographical center of all the earth's land masses. It is within navigable distances of the Persian Gulf and is at the crossroads of the three great continents of Europe, Asia, and Africa.

Thus there is no more ideal location anywhere for a world trade center, a world communications center, a world banking center, a world educational center, or especially, a world capital! The greatest historian of modern times, Arnold Toynbee, used to stress to all his readers and hearers that Babylon would be the best place in the world to build a future world cultural metropolis.

With all these advantages, and with the head start already made by the Iraqis, it is not far-fetched at all to suggest that the future capital of the "United Nations Kingdom," the ten-nation federation established at the beginning of the tribulation, should be established there. The idea of locating the capital in any one of the ten kingdoms would undoubtedly be resisted by the other nine, so that a "neutral" location would be needed. With the defeat of Gog (Russia), along with its Moslem allies, including particularly Iran, Turkey, and Libya, plus Ethiopia and, probably, East Germany, as described in Ezekiel 38, as well as many other peoples not named, Iraq may well be sufficiently "neutralized" to make such a project politically desirable and feasible.

Whatever may prove to be the exact sequence of events, Babylon will surely be rebuilt. As the beast becomes more and more powerful, he will push the project vigorously. He will have spiritual motives as well as political, in view of his alliance with Satan, whose center of earthly activities began at Babel and has apparently continued near there through the ages.

With modern construction equipment and unlimited wealth at his disposal, the beast can rebuild mighty Babylon almost overnight once he gets approval to push the project in earnest. By the end of the first half of the tribulation, there is every possibility that Babylon once again will be a city of great size and splendor. Then, when the beast takes over as world dictator, Babylon will immediately become, if it isn't already, the center of all kinds of government offices, schools, and communications networks, and will be the hub of world trade and finance. It will also be a city of all kinds of vice and wickedness, proudly flaunting its godlessness for all in heaven and earth to see.

But "great Babylon" will soon come "in remembrance before God, to give unto her the cup of the wine of the fierceness of his wrath" (Revelation 16:19).

18

Requiem over Babylon

(Revelation 18)

Never has a great world city had such a meteoric rise as New Babylon, and never will one experience such a cataclysmic and total fall. As discussed in the preceding chapter, Babylon-on-the-Euphrates had lain dormant and foreboding for centuries. There were still reminders of the demonic spirits that once roamed there in the promulgation of its idolatrous pantheism. As Isaiah had prophesied, "Wild beasts of the desert shall lie there; and their houses shall be full of doleful creatures; and owls shall dwell there, and satyrs shall dance there. And the wild beasts of the islands shall cry in their desolate houses, and dragons in their pleasant palaces" (Isaiah 13:21, 22).

But mighty Babylon is not really dead. It appeared to John as the beast "that was, and is not, and yet is" (Revelation 17:8). Suddenly it will arise, as it were, from the grave, and become a "great city" once again. Under the impact of overwhelming geopolitical needs, it will be authorized and implemented by the unprecedented building program undertaken by the federated ten-kingdom empire of the west, then pushed to dynamic completion by the beast. Finally it will be inaugurated as the great world capital of the beast, who will have become king of all the kingdoms of the globe.

Exit from Babylon

The fall of great Babylon is to be even more sudden than its rise. In common with all the rest of the world, the citizens of New Babylon soon will begin to experience the plagues of the bowls of wrath (Revelation 16), the sores, the bloody waters, the intense heat, and the battering hail. John had already witnessed these dreadful scenes on earth before one of the angels of the plagues had taken him back in time to learn the meaning of the age-long Babylonian conspiracy. He had finally observed the fall of the religious component of Babylon, at a time approximately the midpoint of the tribulation, just prior to the initiation of the seven last plagues.

Now, however, John is returned to the scene from which the angel had taken him. The seven plagues have been completed, climaxed by the gigantic earthquake that destroyed all the other cities of the earth and leveled all the mountains and islands of the earth (Revelation 16:18, 20). And now comes Babylon's remembrance.

Revelation 18:1.   And after these things I saw another angel come down from heaven, having great power; and the earth was lightened with his glory.

Here is a new angel, not one of the angels with the seven last plagues, and apparently one not yet participating directly in earth's judgment, an angel reserved explicitly for the final judgment on Babylon. Perhaps he is the same angel whom John had heard earlier (Revelation 14:8) forecasting the coming fall of Babylon. In any case, he is one of the highest angels, a being of great power and of such luminous energy as to illumine the whole land (same word as "earth").

It will be recalled that Babylon had been shrouded in perpetual darkness under the judgment of the fifth bowl (Revelation 16:10). Now, suddenly, the land is illumined with great brightness, but any fleeting relief felt by the inhabitants will quickly turn to terror as they see the source of the illumination, an angel of mighty power coming down from heaven.

Somehow, Babylon had been the only one of earth's great cities (except Jerusalem) that had not fallen in rubble under the mighty earthquake. Her unique position on the Babylonian plain between the dried-up Tigris and Euphrates Rivers may have contributed to this, but the real cause was the control by the seventh angel of the directions and intensities of the global tremors.

Babylon had only been spared for a still greater judgment, however. Not only must she fall, like the other cities, but she must disappear forever, like the mountains. And first she must burn, and then must she lie desolate for a while, and then eventually be found no more at all.

Revelation 18:2.   And he cried mightily with a strong voice, saying, Babylon the great is fallen, is fallen, and is become the habitation of devils, and the hold of every foul spirit, and a cage of every unclean and hateful bird.

The angel not only manifests tremendous light energy but also sound energy, crying mightily with a loud voice. As all can see him, so can all hear him, and the words they hear are terrible and searing words.

The announcement of great Babylon's fall is made and repeated, exactly as the angel had done at the midpoint of the tribulation (Revelation 14:8). At that time it had been a warning and promise for the future, and perhaps also a reference to the fall of religious Babylon. Now it is an announcement of the final fall of political Babylon—Babylon the Great.

The result of her destruction will be complete annihilation of the inhabitants, followed by utter desolation, a desolation comparable to that prophesied by Isaiah, as cited earlier in this chapter (Isaiah 13:21, ??). The "satyrs" mentioned by Isaiah are from the same Hebrew word as the "devils" of Leviticus 17:7 and 2 Chronicles 11:15. The "dragons" may be dinosaurs, but also may refer to evil spirits, as may the "doleful creatures." In any case, the desolation experienced by Babylon in recent historical times is to be briefly repeated near the end of the tribulation, the first being a type of the second.

One can imagine the triumphant blasphemies as great Babylon is rebuilt. Its long desolation had been superseded by an even more splendid metropolis than Nebuchadnezzar had built, and God's judgment on Babylon had seemingly been set aside by the greater power of the beast. So they will boast, with malicious glee.

But their triumph will be very short-lived. In only a few days, perhaps, the desolation will be even greater and will last forever. None will be left there except a horde of demons and evil spirits. These, no doubt, had exercised great influence over the men and women of wicked Babylon, but now they are merely disembodied spirits. The bodies they had possessed had burned to embers and their souls departed to Hades.

There will also be a swarm of unclean birds fouling the ruins, feasting on the charred flesh of the inhabitants. These may well be from the great flocks following the armies of the east trooping across the dried-up Euphrates (Revelation 16:12). God has bidden them to the great supper at Armageddon (Revelation 19:17, 18), just as they had feasted on the armies of Gog in Israel seven years earlier (Ezekiel 39:17-20), but these unclean and hateful birds will gladly postpone their westward flight in order to perch in the ruins of Babylon for a time.

Revelation 18:3.   For all nations have drunk of the wine of the wrath of her fornication, and the kings of the earth have committed fornication with her, and the merchants of the earth are waxed rich through the abundance of her delicacies.

Here is the same indictment as in Revelation 17:2: "With whom the kings of the earth have committed fornication, and the inhabitants of the earth have been made drunk with the wine of her fornication." It is the same as in Revelation 14:8: "She made all nations drink of the wine of the wrath of her fornication." It is evident that the "Babylons" of Revelation 14, 17 and 18 must all be the same Babylon.

Yet, as we have seen, there must also be a difference. There must be a religious Babylon, the great whore, and a political Babylon, the scarlet beast. They are like two sides of the same coin; each is part and parcel of the other and each supports the other. Each is the great city Babylon, long dead and now risen from the dead, yet never really dead. When the woman finally dies, burned in the fiery wrath of the "horns of the beast," as the ten kings who hate her put the torch to her, she still survives as the great city imbued with the adulterous and covetous spirit of the old harlot. The false church, the prostitute religion with all her golden trappings, is burned, but the commercial and political harlotry continues more than ever. The religious worship of the ungodly world is no longer focused on mystic rituals and demonic doctrines, but is frankly fixed on the great god Mammon, and Babylon lives! The international bankers and the corporation directors and the mercantile barons and the shipping magnates and all their host of money-worshiping, power-seeking underlings, who once traversed their orbits around New York and Geneva, London and Paris, Moscow and Berlin, Johannesburg and Tokyo, now find it gloriously profitable to center it all in great Babylon. Babylon is the great capital of the world, and all the capital of the world flows in and out of Babylon. Even in the midst of all the terrible plagues of the tribulation, it is business as usual for the merchants of the world. Shortages abound, and inflation is rampant, but the money kings know how to turn it all to their advantage, and their riches increase still more. It will not be for long, however.

"Go to now, ye rich men, weep and howl for your miseries that shall come upon you. Your riches are corrupted, and your garments are motheaten. Your gold and silver is cankered; and the rust of them shall be a witness against you, and shall eat your flesh as it were fire. Ye have heaped treasures together for the last days" (James 5:1-3).

This movement of the commercial capital of the world back to Babylon, together with its religious and political capitals, was foreseen long ago by the prophet Zechariah, in his *ephah* vision (Zechariah 5:5-11). The ephah was the primary volumetric measure (roughly equivalent to a bushel) and was often used as a symbol of commerce in the ancient world. In his vision, Zechariah saw a woman in the ephah, sealing its mouth with the lead weight.

Covetousness is idolatry, and the ancient center of both had been at the great city of Babylon. Zechariah's prophecy, however, was written after the Jews' return from captivity, with the heyday of Babylon's glory long past. The Jews had given up their affinity to Babylonian idolatry, but had returned instead with a strong infusion of Babylonian mercantilism and covetousness. It was this sin, symbolized by the woman in the ephah, that the angel called "the Wickedness" (the definite article is in the original). The fall of Babylon had caused the world trade and banking center to be shifted to other nations, and Judah herself had been imbued with this spirit.

But then Zechariah saw a remarkable drama unfold in his vision. "Then lifted I up mine eyes, and looked, and, behold, there came out two women, and the wind was in their wings; for they had wings like the wings of a stork: and they lifted up the ephah between the earth and the heaven. Then said I to the angel that talked with me, Whither do these bear the ephah? And he said unto me, To build it an house in the land of Shinar: and it shall be established, and set there upon her own base" (Zechariah 5:9-11).

The two winged women were not angels, since angels are always in Scripture denoted as masculine. Thus the transportation of the ephah to Shinar was not a divine mission but an evil one. The two women possessed the great wings of an unclean bird, the stork, with the wind (or, better, "the spirit") aiding their wings. The women must somehow also bear the character of the woman who is wickedness, since they are translating her by means of some unclean spirit back to the land of Shinar whence she had come. It may be that they represent the twofold character of the great harlot, political and religious Babylon.

The woman in the ephah, however, along with the entire symbol, obviously depicts the theme of commerce and the spirit of covetousness. Something similar to this scene—that is, winged women carrying the standard of weights and measures—has often been used around the world as a symbolic emblem of international commerce. The reason why a woman is used to symbolize covetousness, the same as why a woman was used to symbolize Babylon, is undoubtedly because of the need to depict birth. As the woman in the Apocalypse is "the mother of harlots and abominations," so the woman in the ephah represents the idolatry of Mammon, the love of which is "the root of all evil" (1 Timothy 6:10).

Zechariah's vision thus clearly foretells a time when the center of world finance and commerce will be removed from its bases in New York and Geneva and other great cities and transported quickly across the world to a new foundation and headquarters in the land of Shinar. The land of Shinar, of course, is simply a biblical term for Babylon, and has been ever since Babel was first erected there (Genesis 11:2. Note also Isaiah 11:11; Daniel 1:2).

Though there is nothing intrinsically wrong with money and commerce, it often and easily becomes the object of inordinate affection, even leading to theft and murder and all kinds of wickedness. It is easy to understand the scriptural identification of covetousness with idolatry. Even after religious Babylon is destroyed by the kings of the earth, it lives on as commercial Babylon, whose later destruction is mourned by these same kings.

As the kings of the earth have engaged themselves illicitly with the harlot through the ages, so the great merchants and financiers of the earth, often more powerful even than kings, have enriched themselves through the "abundance" (or "power"; Greek *dunamis*) of her "delicacies" (or "luxuries," literally "strainings"; Greek *strenos)*. There is great power in wealth, and such men have abounded in it.

Revelation 18:4.   And I heard another voice from heaven, saying, Come out of her, my people, that ye be not partakers of her sins, and that ye receive not of her plagues.

This voice was not that of an angel, but of the Lord Jesus Himself, calling urgently to "*My* people." It is surprising, at this late stage, that there are believers living in Babylon itself, the very source and center of the worldwide persecutions that will have been unleashed on believers. The time context is evidently shortly after the midpoint of the tribulation, however, before the intensive program of beast-worship, with the mark of the beast imprinted on the foreheads or right hands of all who buy or sell, had been effectively implemented.

But the awful plagues of the seven bowls of wrath are about to begin, and some of these will fall most severely on Babylon itself, especially the plague of darkness and then the final utter devastation and eventual complete eradication of the city. The Lord Jesus, in His grace, provides a special warning to any in Babylon who may yet believe on Him.

It is evidently about this same time, in fact, that three angels are seen and heard throughout the whole world, warning men to turn back to God (Revelation 14:6-12). One of these preaches the "everlasting gospel" of God as Creator, the second warns of the coming fall of Babylon, the third warns men not to receive the beast's mark, on penalty of hell. In such a context, the special warning to believers in Babylon is pungently appropriate. It is in the capital city that the deadly decree of the false prophet (Revelation 13:15-17) will undoubtedly be imposed first of all and most severely of all. Even if believers residing in Babylon should somehow escape the purges of the beast, they would still be affected by the awful plagues that are coming on Babylon. Thus the Lord's urgent warning to believers to flee Babylon immediately.

But, as a matter of fact, why should there be any believers living in Babylon in the first place? Surely they should have known they were out of place in such an environment, right at the very hub of anti-Christianity. God had even given believers the key to identifying the Antichrist before he would ascend the throne of the world (Revelation 13:18).

As a matter of fact, "Mystery" Babylon has also always had a strange attraction for believers. One of the saddest commentaries on the Christian witness through the ages has been its perennial dilution through compromise with the world system of evolutionary humanism. The wistful desire of Christian intellectuals, of Christian entertainers, of Christian business and professional people, even of Christian ministers, for recognition and approval by their colleagues in "Babylon" has been the downfall of innumerable Christian individuals and institutions over the years. God has repeatedly had to deal with this problem of compromise. "Be ye not unequally yoked together with unbelievers: for what fellowship hath righteousness with unrighteousness? and what communion hath light with darkness? And what concord hath Christ with Belial? or what part hath he that believeth with an infidel? . . . Wherefore come out from among them, and be ye separate, saith the Lord, and touch not the unclean thing" (2 Corinthians 6:14-17).

Apparently the same worldly allure will attract many believers to this final stage of the Babylonian apostasy. The appeal of salary and prestige will entice many capable Christian business and professional men—architects, engineers, merchants, doctors, accountants, and others—to participate in the planning and activation of this exciting and dynamic new metropolis. Christian workers in many construction and other trades will follow the enticement of high wages. No doubt many of these Christians will rationalize their move to Babylon by the opportunity thus afforded to "have a witness" in the world's most important city, to its most important people.

What such Christians have always failed to recognize is that an effective witness is never mediated through compromise. God's message in circumstances like these is not "Be like her, my people, thereby to appease and attract her," but rather "Come out of her, my people, that ye not partake of her sins!" The parallel passage in Jeremiah records the warning from the Lord in these words: "My people, go ye out of the midst of her, and deliver ye every man his soul from the fierce anger of the Lord" (Jeremiah 51:45).

Revelation 18:5.   For her sins have reached unto heaven, and God hath remembered her iniquities.

Nimrod led the first Babel rebels in a great temple building project "unto heaven," but the only thing that reached heaven was the stench of their rebellion. God had to "go down" to see this project and punish their sin (Genesis 11:4, 7). Similarly, the great king of later Babylon dreamed himself to be a great and strong tree "whose height reached unto the heaven" (Daniel 4:20), but the tree was cut down, and proud Nebuchadnezzar had to live like an animal for seven long years (Daniel 4:30-33). Neither the tower of ancient Babylon nor the tree of later Babylon could really reach heaven. Therefore, "her judgment reacheth unto heaven, and is lifted up even to the skies" (Jeremiah 51:9).

Although God is long-suffering, He does not forget and He knows her measure of wickedness is full. Babylon's rebellion has been long and deep and wide, and the time has come to drink the cup of wrath.

The Divine Imprecation

Revelation 18:6.   Reward her even as she rewarded you, and double unto her double according to her works: in the cup which she hath filled fill to her double.

In response to the voice from heaven, which had exhorted the Lord's people to flee Babylon, there comes a responding prayer of imprecation, exhorting the Lord to punish Babylon. Whether this prayer comes from the believers in Babylon, now experiencing the persecution which they should have anticipated (but did not) when they elected to reside in Babylon, or directly from John himself, is not stated.

In any case, the imprecation urges the Lord to repay Babylon in kind, and with double vengeance. "Render to her what she rendered to you!" Babylon's double fall (verse 2) answers to her doubled repayment and the doubled filling of her cup. Further, it is a double reminder of the dual character of Babylon. Harlot Babylon has been burned with fire, and merchant Babylon is about to be utterly destroyed by fire and then to disappear in the sea (Revelation 17:16; 18:8, 21).

This is the sixth reference in Revelation to the cup of wickedness with which both Babylon and all the nations of the world have been made drunken (Revelation 14:8; 17:2, 4, 6; 18:3, 6). It is also the third reference (Revelation 14:10; 16:19; 18:6) to God's cup of wrath, and it is amazing that God turns the one into the other. "Babylon hath been a golden cup in the Lord's hand, that made all the earth drunken: the nations have drunken of her wine; therefore the nations are mad" (Jeremiah 51:7). "And I will make drunk her princes, and her wise men, her captains, and her rulers, and her mighty men: and they shall sleep a perpetual sleep, and not wake, saith the King, whose name is the Lord of hosts" (Jeremiah 51:57).

Revelation 18:7.   How much she hath glorified herself, and lived deliciously, so much torment and sorrow give her: for she saith in her heart, I sit a queen, and am no widow, and shall see no sorrow.

The imprecatory prayer concludes with the petition that torment and sorrow be visited upon Babylon in the same proportion as the self-glorifying pride and luxurious life-style which she had flaunted in the past. The word "deliciously" is essentially the same word as "delicacies" in verse 3, both referring to an ostentatious and offensively luxurious standard of living, supported evidently by the lucrative common market of the world banking and mercantile system centered at Babylon.

In contrast to pride and luxury, the divinely-inspired prayer invokes pain and mourning. The word "torment" is one implying physical pain, and could even be translated "torture." Similarly the word for "sorrow" is also commonly translated "mourning." Thus pride and luxury are to be suddenly changed to pain and mourning.

The beautiful new buildings and avenues of rebuilt Babylon, perhaps with the famous hanging gardens of Nebuchadnezzar restored, and with finely manicured parks irrigated from the Euphrates, the ornate capital indeed sits like a proud queen in the broad plains of Shinar. With all the world's military and economic might as well as its cultural and religious systems centered at Babylon, it does appear to be built for the ages.

The figure of speech is taken from Isaiah 47. "Come down, and sit in the dust, O virgin daughter of Babylon, sit on the ground: there is no throne, O daughter of the Chaldeans: for thou shalt no more be called tender and delicate.... Sit thou silent, and get thee into darkness, O daughter of the Chaldeans: for thou shalt no more be called, The lady of kingdoms.... And thou saidst, I shall be a lady for ever.... Therefore hear now this, thou that art given to pleasures, that dwellest carelessly, that sayest in thine heart, I am, and none else beside me; I shall not sit as a widow, neither shall I know the loss of children: But these two things shall come to thee in a moment in one day, the loss of children, and widowhood" (Isaiah 47:1, 5, 7-9). As noted before, the prophecies of Isaiah and Jeremiah against Babylon have both a precursive partial fulfillment in the Babylon of Belshazzar and a final complete fulfillment in the restored Babylon of the Antichrist.

The principle applies, of course, not only to Babylon as a city, but also to Babylon as a system as well as to anyone imbued with the spirit of Babylon. "Pride goeth before destruction, and an haughty spirit before a fall" (Proverbs 16:18). "Wherefore let him that thinketh he standeth take heed lest he fall" (1 Corinthians 10:12).

Revelation 18:8.   Therefore shall her plagues come in one day, death, and mourning, and famine; and she shall be utterly burned with fire: for strong is the Lord God who judgeth her.

Here is the divine response to the imprecations of verses 6 and 7. Like the imprecatory psalms of the Old Testament (such as Psalm 35), this prayer had been divinely inspired, reflecting the judgment and desires of God himself. Consequently, the prayer is certain to be answered, and so the response begins with the divine *"Therefore."*

Proud Babylon had boasted that she would "be a lady for ever," that she would "see no sorrow," and that she had "lived deliciously." But then the plagues of the bowls of wrath come, and the very first day they strike (that is, the plague of the terrible sores first, followed by all the others, as recorded in Revelation 16), the wicked residents of Babylon begin to experience death and sorrow and hunger.

"She shall be utterly burned with fire!" As the seven last plagues run their course, Babylon suffers under them like all the rest of the world. Two of them, in fact, seem to affect Babylon especially, the plague of the darkness and the plague on the Euphrates (Revelation 16:10, 12). The final plague had been the global earthquake, which had overthrown all the cities of the world, except Jerusalem and Babylon. The latter's sturdy and costly new construction, situated on the Mesopotamian plain, had somehow enabled her to withstand the awful shaking. But then, "great Babylon came in remembrance before God" (Revelation 16:19).

Burned utterly (one word in Greek, *hatakaio*). The Scriptures do not describe the source of such a devastating fire, but it surely can be no ordinary fire. The buildings of Babylon will certainly be of fireproof construction, yet they will be completely incinerated. Possibly the earthquake belches fire and brimstone from the earth's mantle. Possibly nuclear missiles stored in Babylon are somehow detonated. Perhaps it is all strictly supernatural fire from heaven.

The kings of the earth had burned Mystery Babylon, the harlot religious system, with fire, but these same kings mourn the burning of commercial Babylon (Revelation 17:16; 18:9), so obviously these are not the same burnings. One is the foreshadowing of the other, but the last is utter destruction by fire.

The probability that the fire is supernatural—or at least supernaturally triggered and released—is strengthened by the final clause of this verse. "Strong is the Lord God who judgeth her."

Revelation 18:9.   And the kings of the earth, who have committed fornication and lived deliciously with her, shall bewail her, and lament for her, when they shall see the smoke of her burning.

The holocaust that consumes Babylon is quickly known throughout the world. In the rubble of the quake-devastated cities, there was still confidence that somehow the great world leaders at the capital, with their supernatural abilities, would be able to restore order and prosperity in the earth. But then all hopes are dashed to pieces with the news of Babylon's burning.

It seems probable that there will be a brief period between the global earthquake and the subsequent destruction of Babylon, sufficient time to reestablish a semblance of normalcy. Communications will be critical, so all efforts will be concentrated on their reactivation. Soon radio and television will begin transmitting news and orders. The armies that were on their way to Armageddon, temporarily thrown into disarray by the earthquake, soon will be on their way again.

Then, suddenly, the awful fire strikes great Babylon. The terrible moment will evidently occur as people all over the world, especially the kings and other leaders of the nations, are watching on television. Perhaps all have been instructed to watch, as important announcements and instructions are being given concerning the world crisis. The beast himself, however, along with the false prophet, will already have left Babylon to take charge of the armies as they assemble near Jerusalem.

As the kings and great men of the earth watch in horror, they see on the video screens a tremendous burst of flame, engulfing the whole city of Babylon in a gigantic fireball. These kings of the earth all had, only a few short years before, turned over their kingdoms to the beast (Revelation 17:17). They had enjoyed the luxuries and great prosperity which the Babylonian system had brought, for a brief period, to the world. They had become increasingly concerned as their kingdoms had felt the impact of the great plagues, but still maintained their confidence in the beast and his master, the old dragon.

Now, however, they must watch in utter dismay as Babylon burns and as a giant mushroom cloud of smoke ascends high into the sky. When they begin to realize the enormity of the calamity that has befallen the world, not only destroying its political capital but also its financial and commercial center, a great and bitter lament is heard all over the world.

The terms "bewail" and "lament" are graphic. The first describes uncontrollable sobbing and the second beating the breast in anguish. What an activity for mighty kings of the world!

Revelation 18:10.   Standing afar off for the fear of her torment, saying, Alas, alas, that great city Babylon, that mighty city! for in one hour is thy judgment come.

These great kings of the earth, wailing and shaking, are visibly terrified by what they see. Knowing that they have placed all their hopes for time and eternity on the beast and the dragon (understanding well the divine condemnation on all who received the beast's mark), they are fearfully aware that Babylon's torment may soon be theirs. It is possible that some of these kings may be with their armies in their trek toward Armageddon and thus may actually see the great pillars of smoke (note Joel 2:30) through their telescopes from a great distance. Most of them, however, will probably view it via television satellite transmission, standing, indeed, *afar* off! However they observe it, anguish and fear in their hearts is the result.

The English word "alas" only partly conveys the feeling in the Greek *ouai*, the very sound of which bespeaks grief and terror. It is the same word translated "woe" elsewhere (as in Revelation 8:13). Aghast at the sudden fate of the newest and richest and most important city in the world, coming so soon after the fall of other cities in the cataclysmic earthquake, they can only sob and cringe, dreading the awful confrontation they know awaits them in the valley of Jehoshaphat.

Judgment is coming, and they must face the Judge. God is long-suffering, but the day of repentance is past, and the hour of His judgment is approaching quickly. The hour of Babylon's judgment has already come. The beast has headed for Armageddon with his false prophet, and the dragon himself will be there with his demonic hordes. The only remaining hope of these forlorn kings, futile though it be, is to amass their own armies there too, trusting that the infernal trinity of their leaders can somehow save them.

Revelation 18:11.   And the merchants of the earth shall weep and mourn over her; for no man buyeth their merchandise any more.

Not only do the kings of the earth "bewail and lament" Babylon's fall, but also the merchants of the earth "weep and mourn" for her. "Bewail" (v. 9) is the same Greek word as "weep." "Mourn" is the verb form of "sorrow" (v. 7) or "mourning" (v. 8). The reaction of the merchants of the earth is very similar to that of the kings of the earth.

As a matter of fact, these merchants are also "kings" in a sense. They are not ordinary shopkeepers, but are kings of banking, shipping, construction, and communications, captains of industry, giants of commerce. These merchants are "the great men of the earth" (v. 23). Previously, during the early judgments of the tribulation period, these "kings of the earth, and the great men" had sought to hide from "the face of him that sitteth on the throne" (Revelation 6:15, 16). Now they know there is no place to hide, and they must meet Him soon.

The word for "merchants" (Greek *emporos*) is used only here in Revelation 18 (four times) and refers particularly to wholesalers, those who deal in large quantities of trade items involved especially in international commerce. It is highly appropriate to list these two categories of world leaders (kings and merchants of the earth) in such close juxtaposition. Such international magnates and financiers constitute, more often than not, the power behind the throne. Kings and presidents often attain and keep their authority by sufferance of those who finance their undertakings. In turn, these great men of the earth receive land grants and trade monopolies and tax loopholes and innumerable other favors from those whom they establish in political power, all to enrich themselves still further.

This Babylonish system of covetousness (which is idolatry, the worship of Mammon instead of God) has been the source of unspeakable evil through the ages (note vv. 23 and 24). The Apostle Paul said: "For the love of money is the root of all evil" (1 Timothy 6:10). Not only unbelievers, but countless Christian believers have also been deceived thereby. To them Paul says: "Having food and raiment let us be therewith content. But they that will be rich [that is "desire riches"] fall into temptation and a snare, and into many foolish and hurtful lusts, which drown men in destruction and perdition" (1 Timothy 6:8, 9).

These great merchants of the earth do not weep over their sins, nor do they mourn the violent death of their colleagues in the city of Babylon. Their crying and sorrowing is for only their own financial losses. No one will buy their merchandise any more. The well of their profits is dry. Their great industrial empire is collapsing before their eyes, and their one interest in life is being taken away, so they mourn and weep.

Revelation 18:12.   The merchandise of gold, and silver, and precious stones, and of pearls, and fine linen, and purple, and silk, and scarlet, and all thyine wood, and all manner vessels of ivory, and all manner vessels of most precious wood, and of brass, and iron, and marble.

Here follows a remarkable catalog of the items of merchandise which had enriched the great men of the earth. A total of twenty-eight categories are listed, fourteen in this verse and fourteen in the next. The vocabulary is one appropriate to the first century, even though John was actually seeing events of the last century of the age. The items listed, in fact, are items that have been valuable and costly in every age.

The fact that twenty-eight commodities are itemized (that is, four sevens) suggests that the list is representative, rather than specific and exhaustive. Seven as the number of completeness and four as the number of the whole expanse of the earth (north, south, east, and west), thus combine to symbolize all the world's items of treasure on earth. All the endless variety of materialistic possessions which men and women have sought through the ages—for which they have labored and schemed and even stolen and killed—are symbolized here as the merchandise of Babylon, the system that has suddenly vanished in a great ball of fire and pillar of smoke.

First are listed the chief items of timeless value, the precious metals and jewels that have always served as the very measure of value and the basis of monetary systems. Especially in times of inflation, such as in the years of the tribulation, men seek to protect their savings by investing in items of intrinsic value—gold, silver, gemstones, and pearls—and trade in such commodities as these has always been and will continue to be uppermost in the plans of international merchants.

Next are listed four kinds of valuable cloth for the apparel of the world. The two most valuable materials, fine linen and silk, and the two most esteemed colors, purple and scarlet, are listed evidently as representative of the tremendous commerce in clothing around the world.

There is always a great demand for materials of all kinds, for all kinds of domestic and industrial uses. Six of the most valuable kinds of materials are enumerated here as of poignant concern to the merchants who can no longer trade in them. For fine furnishings and ornaments no materials have been more prized than ivory and fine woods. Thyine wood is a very hard and aromatic coniferous wood that was especially valued for such uses by the Romans. All other valuable woods are mentioned, as well as the most costly construction material, marble. "All manner vessels" is a term broad enough to include all types of furniture, housing, construction, ornamentation and other uses.

The two most important metals for practical uses are also included. "All manner vessels of brass and iron" is a term sufficiently comprehensive to cover not only metal structures and furnishing, but also musical instruments, appliances, machinery, tools, weapons, and endless other metallic implements.

All of the items have been prized by men of both ancient times and modern times. Trade in such commodities has been the focus of human greed and the basis of the wealth of great merchants all through the ages and into the future.

Revelation 18:13.   And cinnamon, and odours, and ointments, and frankincense, and wine, and oil, and fine flour, and wheat, and beasts, and sheep, and horses, and chariots, and slaves, and souls of men.

Next are listed representative luxury items, such as spices, perfumes, ointments and incense, all costly and prized items of the export-import trade.

Of special interest, at least to latter-day readers of the Apocalypse, is the inclusion of wine and oil in the catalog of valuable commodities. These were noted as specially important during the time of the seal judgments (Revelation 6:6). As with previous items, it would seem that wine is representative of another broad class of items, namely intoxicating beverages. Every nation in every age has been contaminated with drunkenness ever since the primeval sin of Noah (Genesis 9:20, 21). We can be certain that, in the wicked and terrifying days of the tribulation, ungodly men will turn to intoxicants and drugs far more than ever in history. That drugs are also a major item is evident from the reference to "sorceries" in verse 23. As noted before (Revelation 9:21), this term is a translation of the Greek word from which we transliterate the English word "pharmaceutics." The great demand for intoxicants and drugs in these coming days will surely be further stimulated by the ungodly and covetous merchants who profit so greatly from them.

And oil is there in the listing too. In the apostolic period, a reference to oil would have been understood as olive oil, or some similar natural oil used primarily for anointing and medicinal purposes. However, "ointments" have already been listed, so it seems possible that some other type of oil is intended here. Although petroleum was essentially unknown in the ancient world (bitumen was known, but not the substance we now call "oil"), it does seem probable, in the context of the tribulation, that this is a prophetic reference to that kind of oil which would come to dominate the economies of the world in the latter times. Oil has today become a vital necessity for all the world's transportation and industrial systems, and the oil-producing nations have become strategically able to wield great influence over other nations by exploiting their need for oil. The great oil cartels must therefore surely be included among these weeping merchants. Babylon itself had been strategically located to control the oil production and exports of the most important oil-bearing lands of the globe, but now that control has been destroyed.

Perhaps the only commodity more important than oil today in terms of international trade is that of wheat, so it is not surprising that "fine flour and wheat" are next listed. The "fine flour" (Greek *semidalis*) is mentioned only this one time in the New Testament, and is believed to refer to the finest grade of wheaten flour. The term "wheat" (Greek *sitos*) is translated "corn" as well as "wheat." In the context here, it can best be understood as representing all kinds of agricultural products that are important in world trade.

Not only agricultural commodities but also livestock trading is of great commercial importance, and this too has been precipitously stopped by the fall of Babylon. The "beasts" mentioned in the list (Greek *ktenos)* include any kind of domestic animals, whether beasts of burden or meat animals for slaughter. "Sheep" are listed separately, as are "horses." The first is vital for its wool as well as its meat. The second is the most prized animal, traditionally as a beast of burden, giving its name to the standard industrial measurement of power—i.e. "horsepower," but in modern times more valuable as an animal for riding, both for recreational and military uses.

The inclusion of "chariots" in the list is also intriguing. This term connoted a certain type of vehicle to the ancient world. The Greek word *(rheda)* means a four-wheeled wagon for traveling, not a two-wheeled war chariot, and could very appropriately be interpreted to include modern-day four-wheeled transport vehicles. Thus this term probably refers here specifically to the great auto industry of the last days.

Finally there is a sadly climactic reference to "slaves and souls of men" as one of the items of commerce which has been wrested from control of the earth's "merchants" by Babylon's destruction. The slave trade of antiquity was vital to the Romans, as it continued to be even in "Christian" nations into the nineteenth century. Furthermore slavery has not even yet been really abolished (especially in African and Asian countries) and it may well be that it will be revived in other nations during the tribulation.

However, the reference more probably refers to the so-called "white-slave trade." The Greek word translated "slaves" is *soma,* meaning "body" and usually so translated. The international traffic in forced prostitution, both of men and women, is a tragic but financially lucrative business of modern times and will undoubtedly become even bigger in the evil days ahead. These vice barons are particularly venomous "great men" of the earth, not only amassing great wealth for themselves, but destroying both the "bodies and souls" of the hapless girls and boys who come under their control. Babylon is the "mother of harlots," both spiritual and physical, and fornication of all varieties will be rampant in these last days (Revelation 9:21). But God's judgment on such abominations will finally and totally and suddenly fall.

Revelation 18:14.   And the fruits that thy soul lusteth after are departed from thee, and all things which were dainty and goodly are departed from thee, and thou shalt find them no more at all.

The dirge continues. Men and women through the ages have lusted after "dainty and goodly things," never content, as Paul has exhorted, with "food and raiment." Achan so coveted a "goodly Babylonish garment," when the Israelites conquered Jericho, that it cost his life and the lives of all his family (Joshua 7:21, 25). Especially the kings and great men of the earth, instead of using their wealth for purposes that would honor God, have squandered fortunes on costly foods and wines, on lavish homes and furnishings, on personal adornment, expensive statuary and paintings, on stables of horses or chariots, cars or yachts or airplanes, and innumerable other prerequisites of wealth and luxury. That which they could not spend on themselves, or their families, or their mistresses, they have reinvested to attain even more wealth. The "soul" of Babylon, age after age, "lusteth after" *things,* and is never satisfied. It "saith not, 'It is enough.' "

But now Babylon and all her effete luxuries are gone forever. The great city Babylon, both in ancient times and in future times harboring the world's greatest accumulation of wealth and power ever assembled in one place, has been weighed in God's balance and found wanting. And with her, the entire Babylonian complex of world commerce and idolatrous humanism, wherever it is found all over the world, must soon perish too.

The conflagration has consumed everything. In former times, great merchants and kings, great corporations and conglomerates, when suffering financial losses, could always hope to gain them back again. At least their successors or usurpers could take over their wealth, and the basic system could be perpetuated. But this time the loss is total and the damage irreparable. Everything, everything, is "departed from thee" and Babylon "shall find them no more at all." Not only the adulterous religious system of Babylon, not only the great capital city of the beast's kingdom, not only the world's great empire of trade and finance, but everything connoted to God and men by Babylon is gone, never to be seen again as long as time exists.

Furthermore, the destruction has come suddenly, before they had tasted the anticipated results of man's great project. The "fruits" are actually the "ripe-fruits," to be plucked at summer's end, but the judgment fell with the fruit yet on the vine. The "dainty things" are, literally, the "plump and lusty things," and the "goodly things" are more precisely the "gorgeous, sumptuous things," but destruction has come with these sought-for products of the Babylonian system still found only in their covetous souls, never realized in actual experience.

Revelation 18:15. **The merchants of these things, which were made rich by her, shall stand afar off for the fear of her torment, weeping and wailing.**

The enormity of their losses presses more and more upon the merchants of the earth. The kings of the earth had been quicker to realize the hopelessness of the situation and its ominous implications for their own future. They are standing afar off for the fear of her torment (v. 10). Now the merchants are also seen standing afar off. All over the world the news travels and in every troubled, fallen city of the nations, financiers tremble and cry.

"For what is a man profited, if he shall gain the whole world, and lose his own soul?" the Lord had said (Matthew 16:26). Men accustomed to dealing in profit-and-loss calculations should have spent more care with that calculation. They had carelessly added wrong, mistakenly thinking they had been made rich, placing far too small a valuation on God and on their own souls. Now that these are lost forever, the enormous deficit in their accounts confronts them and they know they have entered eternal bankruptcy, never to rise again.

Wall Street (if it still exists at this time) will panic, and so will Fleet Street, and the Sorbonne, and the bankers of Zurich. The Rockefellers and the Rothschilds will see their supranational corporate empire collapse before their eyes, and they will weep and wail.

"Go to now, ye rich men, weep and howl. . . . Ye have lived in pleasure on the earth, and been wanton; ye have nourished your hearts, as in a day of slaughter. Ye have condemned and killed the just; and he doth not resist you" (James 5:1, 5, 6). This prophecy of the Apostle James is set in the context of the last days and, most likely, is anticipating this very event. His admonition to believers, in contrast, is: "Be patient therefore, brethren, unto the coming of the Lord. Behold, the husbandman waiteth for the precious fruit of the earth, and hath long patience for it, until he receive the early and latter rain. Be ye also patient; stablish your hearts: for the coming of the Lord draweth nigh. Grudge not one against another, brethren, lest ye be condemned: behold, the judge standeth before the door" (James 5:7-9). The impatient Babylonians will perish before the fruit can be plucked. The believers, in "the patience of the saints" (Revelation 14:12), will one day enjoy all the precious fruit of the earth which was lost by Babylon. The great Judge is soon to enter the door.

Revelation 18:16. **And saying, Alas, alas that great city, that was clothed in fine linen, and purple, and scarlet, and decked with gold, and precious stones, and pearls!**

Like the kings, the merchants also cry, *"Ouai, ouai!"* (Greek for "woe"). Yet, with all their agony and mourning, there is not a single note of repentance or of sorrow for sin, or even of acknowledgment that Babylon's destruction is a divine judgment. There is no regret for the bodies and souls of the multitudes of men whom they had abused in their insatiable worship of wealth and power.

All they can think about in their great mourning is the loss of their wealth and luxury. The beautiful apparel and bejeweled ornamentation, both of Babylon as a whole and her proud residents in particular, are all suddenly lost and this is their only concern. The genius of sin is such that it becomes its own judgment.

With consciences seared as by a hot iron (1 Timothy 4:2), men who repeatedly repudiate the convicting ministry of the Holy Spirit will one day find He no longer strives with them (Genesis 6:3) and they have no more desire or ability to do righteousness. "He which is filthy, let him be filthy still!" is the awful declaration of God as men depart into hell (Revelation 22:11). Ruled solely and entirely by self-interest, and by the things which they can amass to satisfy their own covetous lusts, they are utterly confused and desolate when the things are gone.

"Thou fool!" said the Lord; "this night thy soul shall be required of thee: then whose shall those things be?" (Luke 12:20). Multitudes of rich men and great men and mighty men will hear such a voice from heaven in that day of gloom and darkness, and loud and bitter will be their cry. All their cherished gold and jewels are going to another city. "Neither their silver nor their gold shall be able to deliver them in the day of the Lord's wrath; but the whole land shall be devoured by the fire of his jealousy: for he shall make even a speedy riddance of all them that dwell in the land" (Zephaniah 1:18).

The brilliant apparel and bejeweled adornment of the burning city had also been the trappings of the old harlot of Babylon (Revelation 17:4) and the trade in these same commodities had enriched the merchants of the earth (v. 12), but now it is all in ashes. One day, however, there will be established another City, with pearly gates, and golden streets and jeweled foundations, whose inhabitants dress in fine linen, and it shall never pass away. Instead of "Woe, woe!" the echoing cry will be "Alleluia; amen!"

Revelation 18:17.   For in one hour so great riches is come to nought. And every shipmaster, and all the company in ships, and sailors, and as many as trade by sea, stood afar off.

Men had, not many years before, marveled at the rapid rebuilding of great Babylon, resurrecting it from a thousand-year sleep, as it were, and paralleling the seeming resurrection of its proud ruler, the beast, after his professed descent into Hades. Little did they know how brief would be their glory! In one hour the one is utterly burned with fire, and shortly the other will be translated into an unending burning in the lake of fire.

The mourning cries heard thus far have been chiefly from the kings and great merchants of the earth, whose political and international commercial empires had suddenly collapsed with Babylon. But now multitudes of others join in the great lament, as they also begin to realize the enormous loss they have suffered. Most obviously affected are those who have their employment in shipping-related industries, since Babylon is the central focus of all trade and the repository of global wealth.

The captains of ships cry, and the officers of shipping and warehousing firms cry, and then the officers of all the mercantile and longshoremens' unions begin to cry, and all those who travel by ship cry (probably "ships" here also includes "airships," since much international travel and trade is now centered in the world's vast airline industries). Soon all the sailors and shipping clerks, as well as importers and brokerage houses—all whose profits and wages stem from international commerce—as they watch the awful scene on television screens set up amidst the rubble of their own quake-devastated cities, sob and weep with a great and bitter cry.

Revelation 18:18.   And cried when they saw the smoke of her burning, saying, What city is like unto this great city!

These also, like the kings and great men, were filled with amazement and fear as they watched, from all over the world, the awful mushroom of smoke ascending high over burning Babylon into the stratosphere. A few days earlier, their own cities had reeled and crumpled under the mighty global earthquake, but their proud capital had survived, giving its assurance that the beast would yet be victor in the coming cosmic confrontation.

But now Babylon has not merely fallen in ruins, it is burned to ashes, and all hope is gone. If Babylon cannot endure, then no city can, because there never was a city like this great city.

God has spoken clearly. It has never been His plan that men would congregate in great cities. They were to spread out and "replenish [fill] the earth" (Genesis 1:28), tilling the ground, enjoying and using God's great creation for man's greatest good and for God's glory. After the Flood, God again had given commandment to fill the earth (Genesis 9:10). In both cases, rebellious men had chosen rather to settle in great cities and to make a "name for themselves, rather than calling on the name of the Lord." Cain had built the first city (Genesis 4:17) and Nimrod had built Babel (Genesis 10:10), and the great urban centers of the Cainitic and Nimrodian civilizations, before and after the Flood, respectively, had led men away from God. Finally Babel, the greatest city of all, had fallen completely, along with all the other cities of the nations, and the world is ready at least to receive another city, that "city which hath foundations, whose builder and maker is God" (Hebrews 11:10).

Revelation 18:19. **And they cast dust on their heads, and cried, weeping and wailing, saying, Alas, alas, that great city, wherein were made rich all that had ships in the sea by reason of her costliness! for in one hour is she made desolate.**

The extremity of their despair is indicated by this bizarre expression of agony, gathering up handfuls of dirt from the ground and pouring it on their heads. This was a practice in ancient times (as in Lamentations 2:10, Job 2:12), but would seem strange today. Nevertheless it is appropriate, proclaiming symbolically their fear that the earth shall soon cover their own dead bodies, and they will go back to the dust.

This is the final verse of this final and unique lamentation of Scripture (vv. 9-19). Containing four references to bewailing their awful fate (vv. 9, 11, 15, 19) and three references to the unprecedented destruction in "one hour" (vv. 10, 17, 19), this mournful elegy expresses perhaps better than anything in all literature the hopeless lament of souls who know they are lost and doomed but are unable even to acknowledge or care about the sin of unrepenting unbelief which put them there. Their only thought is one of lost wealth and power.

And their last sad comment about the great city Babylon still deals with her opulence and the riches that her centralized world commerce and finance had made possible for the materialistic multitudes. "Lo, this is the man that made not God his strength; but trusted in the abundance of his riches, and strengthened himself in his wickedness" (Psalm 52:7).

The great system Babylon, seducing multitudes through the ages through her humanistic religion and her promise of wealth and luxury and delicious licentiousness, has finally been brought to utter desolation, suddenly and totally.

Joy in Heaven

The Lord Jesus had said long before: "There is joy in the presence of the angels of God over one sinner that repenteth" (Luke 15:10). When a lost man or woman turns in repentance and faith to the Savior, heaven indeed rejoices with great joy, because a sinner has thereby been delivered from hell and assigned eternally to heaven.

But if such sinners become instead irrevocably hardened and unbelieving, leading many others to perdition with them, then there is also another kind of joy in heaven when such as these are finally brought to judgment. Neither saints nor heavenly angels of course, delight when men are consigned to hell, but they must rejoice when such people are thereby constrained from causing still others to turn away from God. "As I live, saith the Lord God, I have no pleasure in the death of the wicked" (Ezekiel 33:11). Yet the Scripture also says: "When it goeth well with the righteous, the city rejoiceth: and when the wicked perish, there is shouting" (Proverbs 11:10).

There is thus a remarkable change in tone at this point. From the mournful dirge of the earth-dwellers over Babylon's sudden demise, the mood shifts instantly to one of joy and thanksgiving in heaven because of that demise. The last five verses of Revelation 18, in contrast to the elegy of verses 9-19, constitute a paean of triumph and answered prayer.

Revelation 18:20. Rejoice over her, thou heaven, and ye holy apostles and prophets; for God hath avenged you on her.

This exhortation presumably comes from the same heavenly voice heard earlier by John (vv. 4, 8). Or, possibly, it is John himself who utters it, caught up in the excitement of mighty Babylon's demise.

In any case, the cry is one of exultation, addressed to all the saints assembled at the throne in heaven. The specific salutation is simply to "heaven," used here in a generic sense including all who are in heaven, both angels and resurrected men and women from all the ages. Men on earth lament the fall of Babylon, but those in heaven rejoice.

Though all in heaven are included in the exhortation, there are two classes who will experience special joy, the "holy apostles and prophets." These have borne a special ministry for God on earth, and have suffered special privations and persecutions. Their heavy burdens are lifted now, and their testimony vindicated, for Babylon is fallen.

The word "holy" (Greek *hagios*) is the same as "saint," with the basic meaning that of being "set apart," or "consecrated." Many manuscripts include an extra conjunction here, so the phrase is frequently translated "ye saints and ye apostles and ye prophets." However, this might seem redundant, since the "apostles" and "prophets" are also "saints." Roman Catholic ecclesiology may distinguish "saints" as a particular category of unusual Christians, but the Scriptures make no such distinction. In the Bible all true believers are "saints." Also, as noted above, the term "heaven" itself surely includes the saints.

Thus it is probable that the King James Version has the best rendition, "ye holy apostles and prophets," just as it stands. In fact, this same phrase, "his holy apostles and prophets," had been used by the Apostle Paul in Ephesians 3:5, in reference to the new revelations given by the Lord in the Church Age to His holy apostles and prophets, in that they had both been "set apart" for this special ministry of receiving God's new revelation in the establishment of Christ's Church in the New Testament dispensation.

All of the apostles had suffered great persecutions and finally (except in John's case) martyrdom; the same was undoubtedly true of the New Testament prophets (Stephen, for example, was a "prophet," receiving a marvelous revelation from God as well as a divinely inspired message, in the great sermon of Acts 7, before he was stoned to death). They had all preached faithfully and forcefully against "Babylon," that is, the humanistic idolatry and covetous materialism of the world system, when they were on earth, and yet had seen it apparently triumph over them as it hounded them all to a martyr's death. Thus their joy was great as they could now observe from the vantage point of heaven the final and complete and permanent destruction of Babylon, both the capital city and the system it stood for through the ages. The great prophets of the Old Testament must likewise have shared their triumphant rejoicing, and for the same reason.

"Vengeance is mine," the Lord had said (Romans 12:19). As the Lord had promised concerning the false religionists even among His own people back at the beginning of their history: "To me belongeth vengeance, and recompence; their foot shall slide in due time: for the day of their calamity is at hand, and the things that shall come upon them make haste" (Deuteronomy 32:35).

Revelation 18:21.   And a mighty angel took up a stone like a great millstone, and cast it into the sea, saying, Thus with violence shall that great city Babylon be thrown down, and shall be found no more at all.

Here yet another angel comes upon the scene, with another testimony concerning Babylon. The second of the six angels in Revelation 14 had conveyed a prophetic warning to the earth concerning the imminent fall of Babylon (Revelation 14:8), so perhaps this is the same angel.

The action described here is evidently some days, or even weeks, after the burning of Babylon. Enough time has elapsed for Babylon's ruins to become the habitation of wild animals and demons, as described in the prophecies of Isaiah 13:20-22 and Jeremiah 50:39, as well as in Revelation 18:2. But then even the very remembrance of Babylon is finally to be cut off so that not even her ruins can be found. As a heavy stone thrust into the sea will sink to the bottom never to be seen again, so Babylon also will be thrown down to everlasting oblivion. This is pictured by the casting of a great stone by the angel into the sea, possibly the Persian Gulf, into which Babylon's Euphrates empties.

John particularly noted that the appearance of the stone was like that of a millstone. The casting of a millstone into the sea is such an unlikely figure of speech that it suggests a special reason why John would use it. Possibly he was reminded of the day many years before when the Lord Jesus had used a similar figure of speech in instructing His assembled disciples: "But whoso shall offend one of these little ones which believe in me, it were better for him that a millstone were hanged about his neck, and that he were drowned in the depth of the sea" (Matthew 18:6). Babylon, the greatest offender of all, though once arrayed in scarlet and decked with gold, now has nothing but a great millstone for her apparel, hanging around her neck and carrying her headlong deep beneath the sea.

A similar fate is described at the end of Jeremiah's prophecy concerning Babylon: "And it shall be, when thou hast made an end of reading this book, that thou shalt bind a stone to it, and cast it into the midst of Euphrates: And thou shalt say, Thus shall Babylon sink, and shall not rise from the evil that I will bring upon her: and they shall be weary. Thus far are the words of Jeremiah" (Jeremiah 51:63, 64).

Probably this will be brought about by an aftershock of the global earthquake that had occurred just a few days or possibly weeks before. Suddenly the whole Mesopotamian plain will drop down, as a great chasm opens in the deep crust. The entire Euphrates valley will be inundated as the waters of the Persian Gulf roar up into the gaping hole. Babylon will thus sink into both the Euphrates and the encroaching sea, and all her proud buildings will lie unseen far below the waves as long as the world endures.

"How is Babylon become an astonishment among the nations! The sea is come up upon Babylon: she is covered with the multitude of the waves thereof" (Jeremiah 51:41, 42). Darkness and demons, fire and flood, then everlasting death. Not only has Babylon been slain in the sea; very soon now "he shall slay the dragon that is in the sea" (Isaiah 27:1).

Revelation 18:22.   And the voice of harpers, and musicians, and of pipers, and trumpeters, shall be heard no more at all in thee; and no craftsman, of whatsoever craft he be, shall be found any more in thee; and the sound of a millstone shall be heard no more at all in thee.

The angel's message of judgment continues. As verses 12 and 13 had given a remarkable insight into the former commerce of Babylon, so verses 22 and 23 give a picture of the former daily life of Babylon. It had been a place of much music, probably loud and sensual music, of the type that had become so influential in the latter days. The specific categories listed—harpers, pipers, trumpeters—are undoubtedly meant to be typical rather than exhaustive. The harp represents stringed instruments, of which there are many. Pipers, probably synonymous with "flutists," and trumpeters represent the even more numerous wind instruments. The "musicians" probably refer especially to singers.

Babylon was also a city of skilled artisans, as indicated by the terms "craft" and "craftsman." This reflects the desire of its inhabitants for luxurious living. The reference to millstones suggests the manufacture of "fine flour" (v. 13) and perhaps other costly products.

There is another striking passage in Isaiah which seems to refer to this unique and climactic event. "The new wine mourneth, the vine languisheth, all the merry-hearted do sigh. The mirth of tabrets ceaseth, the noise of them that rejoice endeth, the joy of the harp ceaseth. They shall not drink wine with a song; strong drink shall be bitter to them that drink it. The city of confusion is broken down: every house is shut up, that no man may come in" (Isaiah 24:7-10; see entire chapter, in fact).

Although Babylon is not mentioned by name in this chapter, the entire context seems to fit perfectly, and the reference to "the city of confusion" seems to confirm it. There also are parallel references to the mirth and music. In addition to the stringed and wind instruments noted in the chapter of Revelation, here in Isaiah percussion instruments ("tabrets") are also mentioned. The abundance of wine and drunkenness is emphasized as well.

But all of Babylon's activities—whether lucrative commerce or opulent living or raucous pleasure—are still and silent. None will ever be heard or seen any more.

Revelation 18:23. **And the light of a candle shall shine no more at all in thee; and the voice of the bridegroom and of the bride shall be heard no more at all in thee: for thy merchants were the great men of the earth; for by thy sorceries were all nations deceived.**

The terminal refrain continues: *"No more!"* No more sales of profitable merchandise (v. 11), no more dainty and goodly things (v. 14), no more Babylon (v. 21), no more music or fine crafts or sound of industry (v. 22) and now (v. 23) no more light and no more social affairs. The phrase "no more" or its equivalent occurs eight times in this sonorous passage.

For some time prior to this final judgment, Babylon had been in darkness. Under the judgment of the fifth bowl of wrath (Revelation 16:10), the throne of the beast and his kingdom had been plunged into unrelieved darkness. No doubt the city will have been designed with ultramodern illumination facilities, but the probability is that the power stations serving the city will malfunction under the impact of the plagues. Any hydroelectric plants will be helpless as the water supplies are exhausted, climaxed by the complete drying up of the river Euphrates. Solar-energy plants will be useless with the city in perpetual darkness. Nuclear and oil-driven plants will be unable to function without a copious supply of cooling water. Transmission lines from other regions will probably be rendered inoperative by the intense heat of the fourth plague and then will completely collapse under the shocks of the global earthquake. Thus the city of Babylon, for some period of time at least, will finally have to rely strictly on candlelight or kerosene lamps for its illumination. It will be a miserable and desperate place during its final days.

But now, not even the light of a candle shines in Babylon. To Babylon and its doomed inhabitants "is reserved the blackness of darkness for ever" (Jude 13).

When Babylon had been first restored in all its gaudy glory, it had been the pride of the nations. Its citizenry soon boasted the elite from every nation, men and women of wealth and intellect and power. Marriages uniting prominent world families would be common, and Babylon would naturally become a real melting-pot of nations. Wedding customs of a wide variety of cultures and religions would be freely integrated under the aegis of the world humanistic religious system (Mystery Babylon) which now had its headquarters in the great capital of the beast and the false prophet. At last the world had achieved a truly "United Nations" and a truly humanistic culture, with all nations, tribes, races, and creeds fully integrated, Babylon itself being the prototype showplace of this greatest achievement of mankind. Probably the wedding ceremonies of its citizens would provide the finest opportunities for ostentatious display of its wealth and revelry. Marriage vows would mean little in terms of fidelity, since sexual license was common everywhere (Revelation 9:21; 14:8), but they would mean much in political and economic and cultural terms.

But now all weddings and other social and cultural events have ceased forever in Babylon. The "beautiful people" are dead, the powerful families are broken, the palatial homes are burned, and the city itself has disappeared under the onrushing sea. Her citizens had been earth's elite, the greatest merchants and financiers and intellectuals and rulers that an ungodly culture could produce, but now their greatness is past.

Long ago God had used Babylon to execute a similar judgment against His own people, who had gone after other gods, calling Nebuchadnezzar, the king of Babylon, "my servant" (Jeremiah 25:9), and saying: "Moreover I will take from them the voice of mirth, and the voice of gladness, the voice of the bridegroom, and the voice of the bride, the sound of the millstones, and the light of the candle" (Jeremiah 25:10). Eventually, however, after the full judgment on His own people, God would give the same cup of fury to Babylon and all the nations (Jeremiah 25:15). "Thus saith the Lord of hosts, Behold, evil shall go forth from nation to nation, and a great whirlwind shall be raised up from the coasts of the earth. And the slain of the Lord shall be at that day from one end of the earth even unto the other end of the earth" (Jeremiah 25:32, 33).

Finally the twofold reason for Babylon's awful judgment is repeated. First, it was by her sorceries that all nations had been deceived. The harlot of Babylon, with her false religion of satanic evolutionary humanism, had corrupted literally every nation in the history of the world since Nimrod. It was through her that Satan had deceived the whole world (Revelation 12:9). All earth's inhabitants had, to one degree or another, been intoxicated with her corrupting wine (Revelation 17:2).

Furthermore, as noted before (see Revelation 9:21) the "sorceries" actually involve inducement of religious visions and states of altered consciousness by use of drugs. The Greek word translated "sorcery" and "witchcraft" is *pharmakeia,* meaning "drug" or "potion" or "medication." Thus this verse states in effect that all nations have been drugged by Babylon, deceived into believing a lie. Whether using actual hallucinatory drugs in the modern revival of occultic super-humanism, or the intellectual soporific of evolutionary humanistic scientism, the Babylonian harlot had deceived all nations into worshiping another God.

Revelation 18:24.   And in her was found the blood of prophets, and of saints, and of all that were slain upon the earth.

The harlot's golden cup was outwardly beautiful, but the contents were a filthy mixture of blood and abominations, and Babylon herself was drunk with blood (Revelation 17:4, 6). This is the second reason for Babylon's fearful destruction. Not only was she the mother of harlots, spawning every false religion and philosophy in mankind's history of apostasy from the Creator, but she was also the mother of persecutions. Whom she could not deceive and corrupt, she would pursue and slay.

In every generation, the people of God have been persecuted by the enemies of God. Sometimes this has been done in the name of a pagan pantheistic poly-theism, such as in the kingdoms of ancient Egypt, Assyria, Persia, and Rome. Modern pagan nations have done the same (as Japan, China, Tibet, and Mongolia). Even more severe have been the persecutions of the pseudomonotheism of the Islamic nations. Not infrequently some form of corrupt Christianity, compromising with paganism, has been the instrument of persecution (such as the Romanism of the medieval period and the Anglicanism of later British history). Most vicious of all have been the mass executions instigated in the name of humanistic socialism, whether the system of a totalitarian fascism (as Hitler's Germany) or of revolutionary communism. It is estimated that, since Marx, more than one hundred million people have died in communist purges. This monstrous fruit of the bitter root of evolutionary atheism has, of course, destroyed multitudes of people who were not Christians at all, but it is God's true witnesses who have been the objects of its special hatred.

All of these systems and many others have their roots in Babylon. The terrible indictment has been written: the source of human murder and warfare and all other "slayings" in the long, sad saga of earth history, and particularly the killing of God's own saints and prophets, is Babylon. The Babylonish system, and now its mighty capital, have been judged, condemned, and finally consigned to everlasting destruction and oblivion. "All these things shall come upon this generation" (Matthew 23:36).

19

The King Triumphant

(Revelation 19)

The great conflict of the ages is almost over. Babylon is gone forever, and the nations of the ungodly are retreating to their final stand at Armageddon. The dragon and the beast and the false prophet are themselves en route to lead their followers into the last great battle of the long warfare between heaven and hell. They have dispatched their legions of wicked spirits (Revelation 16:13, 14) to gather all the kings of the earth and their armies to the climactic confrontation at the great day of God Almighty. The hordes are assembling in the tremendous column extending across Israel, from Armageddon to Edom, and there have already been sieges and skirmishes throughout the land, especially at Jerusalem (see discussion on Revelation 14:18-20).

Preparations for the battle are also underway in the heavens. The holy angels are there, and the raptured saints are there, and all have been watching the terrible judgments on the earth, knowing that they very soon will also march forth to follow their King as He returns to earth.

The Fellowship of Praise

John, in the spirit, is also there. After observing and recording all the awful plagues on earth, and then the final fiery holocaust at Babylon, it is with great relief that he turns now to see the heavenly throng, exulting and rejoicing at the throne of God in the temple in the city in the heavens.

Revelation 19:1.   And after these things I heard a great voice of much people in heaven, saying, Alleluia; Salvation, and glory, and honour, and power, unto the Lord our God.

Often before had John heard the heavenly multitude sound forth in a great chorus, but never quite like this. This is the mighty "Hallelujah Chorus," when the innumerable host in the heavens spontaneously break forth in a great response of praise.

"Hallelujah," like "Amen," seems to be one of those words which is the same in many languages. In Hebrew it comes from *hallal* ("praise") and *Yah* (short for *Jehovah)*, thus meaning "Praise ye the Lord." It is used twenty-two times in the Book of Psalms and, in particular, is both the opening and closing exhortation in each of the last five psalms.

In the New Testament it occurs only in this one chapter, being used four times in verses 1 through 6. It may well be, in fact, that this unique occurrence in the New Testament, when there is so much else in the New Testament that could warrant the same doxology, is intended specifically to tie these "hallelujah psalms" to the same great scene in the heavens which John is describing here.

The context would certainly fit. The Book of Psalms is divided into five "books," each of which ends with an epilogue in the form of a doxology (see Psalm 41:13; 72:19; 89:52; 106:48; 145:21). Then, the last five psalms correspondingly provide a beautiful epilogue to the entire Book of Psalms, exhorting men and angels and all creation to praise the great Lord and Savior.

In any case, there is much for which to praise the Lord in this great assembly in the heavens. They have already praised Him for His creation (Revelation 4:11) and for His redemption (Revelation 5:12, 13). Now they can praise Him for complete deliverance and salvation as well.

When praising Him for His creation, they ascribed to Him glory and honor and blessing. When praising Him for His redemption, they ascribed to Him power and riches, wisdom and strength, honor and glory and blessing.

Now, finally, they are able also to praise Him for *salvation*. Not only is the redemption price paid but they know beyond any further uncertainty that Babylon is fallen and the whole satanic empire is collapsing before their eyes. Therefore they cry out that salvation, as well as glory and honor and power, belong to the Lord. This great cry had already been heard by John much earlier in the tribulation period when he had been given the vision of the tribulation's end, with the multitude of tribulation saints praising the Lord for His salvation (Revelation 7:10, 12). Now the vision is rapidly being fulfilled, with the souls of these martyred saints joining with all the resurrection saints and the angelic hosts, in the great song of praise.

Revelation 19:2.   For true and righteous are his judgments: for he hath judged the great whore, which did corrupt the earth with her fornication, and hath avenged the blood of his servants at her hand.

The ascription of praise continues with the testimony that God has acted in perfect righteousness and truthful judgment in His awful vengeance on Babylon. There are no doubt many of squeamish temper and equivocal discernment who would recoil today at the ferocity of the divine anger against Babylon, not understanding or caring about the atrocities inflicted on God's people by Babylon nor her blasphemies against His holy name. Of similar character are those in this present dispensation who moralize against capital punishment for cold-blooded murderers.

But these who have experienced both Babylon's wickedness and God's holiness have no such supercilious reservations. *They* know that God has already been almost infinite in His longsuffering and that His plenteous mercy has been both unwanted and unrequited. Babylon and all her inhabitants are eminently deserving of every last dreg of the bitter cup of judgment they have been compelled to drink, nor would any further mercy or call to repentance have availed an iota.

Again there is a last reminder of Babylon's spiritual harlotry, corrupting and destroying nation after nation, age after age, with her deadly apostasy and rebellion against the Creator. Unnumbered multitudes of lost souls, inhabiting the eternal lake of fire, will be there because of the seductions of Babylon's man-exalting, nature-worshiping, evolutionary pantheism.

And the long plea for God to avenge his own elect (Luke 18:7, 8) has finally been heard and answered. "Vengeance is mine; I will repay," the Lord had promised (Romans 12:19). The impatient saints had cried, "How long?" (Revelation 6:10), but God alone has known when His patient long-suffering would no longer avail against the stubborn hearts of men. The time has finally come, and nothing is left for beast-marked earth-dwellers except "a certain fearful looking for of judgment and fiery indignation, which shall devour the adversaries" (Hebrews 10:27).

Revelation 19:3.   And again they said, Alleluia. And her smoke rose up for ever and ever.

The second "Hallelujah" resounds throughout heaven. The brief but deeply felt doxology thus begins and ends with the hallelujah cry, just as do the five hallelujah psalms (Psalms 146-150).

While the heavenly multitudes are still rejoicing over the fall of Babylon, John interjects the sad observation that the smoke of the burning city will continue ascending eternally. The literal city was indeed burned with fire (Revelation 18:8), but its own literal fires will not burn forever. In fact, as noted in the preceding chapter, the ruins of Babylon will eventually disappear beneath the encroaching sea.

While it was burning, however, the plume of smoke rose to great heights in the atmosphere. Like the water vapors ascending from the falling water levels, ascending high above the troposphere to reestablish earth's primeval vapor canopy, the column of smoke, heated more and more by the intensified radiation of the sun, will be propelled finally above the stratosphere and into outer space, its particles never falling again to earth. Babylon is to be so completely wiped from earthly memory that even the particles of soot produced in her burning are to be translated ever farther away from earth.

In a secondary sense, the statement also applies to Babylon's inhabitants. When these, along with other unsaved souls, are resurrected for the last judgment, they will be cast into the lake of fire, there to burn forever. The Lord Jesus Himself said, and repeated it twice, that in that fearful destination, "their worm dieth not, and the fire is not quenched" (Mark 9:44, 46, 48). Of those who would worship the beast and receive his mark, and this company certainly included the Babylonians, the angel had already warned that "the smoke of their torment ascendeth up for ever and ever" (Revelation 14:11).

They also, like the ever-ascending smoke of Babylon's burning, are to be translated to the farthest reaches of the universe, "punished with everlasting destruction from the presence of the Lord, and from the glory of his power" (2 Thessalonians 1:9). Before this dreadful day comes—and it will come, exactly as John has written—let everyone still residing in Babylon, that is, in "Mystery Babylon," the false religion of the apostate world, no less than in the future literal restored Babylon, capital of the beast's world empire, heed the urgent warning of the mighty voice from heaven: "Come out of her, my people, that ye be not partakers of her sins, and that ye receive not of her plagues" (Revelation 18:4).

Revelation 19:4.   And the four and twenty elders and the four beasts fell down and worshipped God that sat on the throne, saying, Amen; Alleluia.

As the hosts in heaven finish their great testimony of praise, all their leaders prostrate themselves before the glorious presence on the throne. The twenty-four elders represent all the redeemed saints, and the four cherubim represent all the holy angels, so all in heaven worship God through them.

To *worship,* in the Bible, means to bow down to the will of God, acknowledging that what He says is true and what He does is right. Many and long had been the years when it seemed that God didn't care about the sufferings of His people nor about the blasphemies of Babylon, and many had even claimed that God was dead.

How often has a discouraged believer, pressed hard by bitter circumstances and unable to see the way out, cried out to God in tears, seeking to understand the mysteries of His will and the reasons for His seeming silence. Such a time is designed for true worship, bowing down in obedient faith, even when the way is dark and the reason fails. The will of God may be difficult, but the will of God is best, and one day God's will is to be fully manifest in all its perfect wisdom. Finally, when God's gracious long-suffering has run its full course, Babylon will vanish, all prayers will be answered and His kingdom will come. And in that glad day, with tears of joy and songs of praise, will every last saint in heaven worship God.

Nor could any words be more fitting or more heartfelt as an expression of universal worship than the two universal exclamations, *Amen, Hallelujah*—"So be it—praise the Lord!" No longer can there ever be any question that God's will is perfect. He is long-suffering, not willing that any should perish, but the day of the Lord will come! (2 Peter 3:9, 10). The Hallelujah Chorus in the heavens continues, and is rising now to a grand climax, as the realization of what is about to happen surges through the multitudes.

Revelation 19:5.   And a voice came out of the throne, saying, Praise our God, all ye his servants, and ye that fear him, both small and great.

The voice out of the throne is most likely that of the Lord Jesus Christ Himself. The "voice from heaven" of Revelation 18:4, calling to "my people," was certainly that of God, though it may not be certain which of the three divine Persons of the Trinity, as was the "voice from the temple" (Revelation 16:1) and the "voice from heaven" of Revelation 11:12. Here, however, the voice comes from the royal throne itself, where God is seated (see the previous verse). The Lamb is said to be seated on the throne, with the Father (Revelation 3:21; 5:13; 7:15, 17; 22:3).

The identification of the voice as that of the Savior is further confirmed by the command to praise God. In the Book of Psalms, the great "praise book" of the Bible, the first occurrence of the verb "praise" (Hebrew *hallal*) is at Psalm 22:22, right at the very climax of the suffering of Christ on the cross, as described prophetically in that great messianic psalm. At this point, the suffering Lord cries out, "I will declare thy name unto my brethren: in the midst of the congregation will I praise thee. Ye that fear the Lord, praise him" (Psalm 22:22, 23).

In the midst of "the great congregation" will the slain Lamb thus become our great "praise leader," exhorting all the servants of God, those who fear Him, those who are His spiritual seed (compare Psalms 22, 25, 30) to praise Him. All the redeemed will be "His servants" there, no matter how great or small had been their position in their previous earthly lives; and His servants shall "serve Him" in that new earth which He will create, forever (Revelation 22:3). But first there will be a great time of praise in His presence, and then the wedding, where they will be established to "ever be with the Lord"(1 Thessalonians 4:17).

Revelation 19:6.   And I heard as it were the voice of a great multitude, and as the voice of many waters, and as the voice of mighty thunderings, saying, Alleluia: for the Lord God omnipotent reigneth.

John then hears, in response to Christ's exhortation to the great congregation, a mighty chorus of praise resounding through the heavens. The words "great multitude" here are the same Greek words as for "much people" in verse 1 (also the same as in Revelation 7:9).

Their praise now is not merely for their own personal salvation and deliverance from Babylon. No longer focusing on themselves, they rejoice in the very fact of God's glorious person and His rightful place on the throne of the cosmos.

The voice of the Lord had been like the sound of many waters (Revelation 1:15; 14:2) and like mighty thunderings (Revelation 14:2), and now the sound of the praises of His redeemed hosts displays the same majestic quality. The saints have been made like Him (1 John 3:2, 3; Philippians 3:20, 21) and even the very tones of their united voices echo the same beautiful doxologies.

This is the fourth and final "Hallelujah" of this chapter (and of the New Testament). The great testimony that follows the "Hallelujah" speaks of the kingdom of God and the marriage of the Lamb. Similarly, the five great hallelujah psalms which climax the Book of Psalms, each beginning with "Praise ye the Lord" (that is, in Hebrew, *hallelujah*), also have as their primary themes the coming eternal reign of God over the universe and His unending union and fellowship with all His creation, especially the redeemed saints.

The Marriage of the Lamb

This nineteenth chapter of Revelation is surely one of the mountain-peak chapters of Scripture, as well as one of the most magnificent in all literature. From the great Hallelujah Chorus in heaven to the long-awaited union of Christ and His Bride, then on to His glorious return to earth and finally to the cataclysmic battle of the ages, this amazing chapter proceeds from one majestic theme to another, climaxing in the termination of the long, sad day of man and bringing in the glorious kingdom of God on earth.

The second of these grand themes is introduced by the heavenly chorus, as the time nears for the heavenly Bridegroom to be united in endless bliss to His Bride, a Bride whom He had purchased long ago, with His own blood on Calvary, as the spotless Lamb of God. Finally His Bride is ready and the marriage song begins.

Revelation 19:7.   Let us be glad and rejoice, and give honour to him: for the marriage of the Lamb is come, and his wife hath made herself ready.

After praise, joy comes. The "great multitude" in heaven had echoed forth its great doxology, praising the Lord for His mighty power and His imminent reign. But then the awareness that His kingdom is about to come suddenly brings the realization, as it were, that His holy marriage is also about to come, and this causes gladness and joy unspeakable. Yet in all their joy, they are careful also to ascribe honor to the heavenly Father of the Bridegroom. The Son whom He loves has been given to the Bride whom the Bridegroom loves. Age after age, He has waited, but at long last the Bride is ready, the marriage date is set, and the marriage feast is being prepared.

The grand union of time and eternity, of man and God, has always been portrayed by the very institution of marriage itself. When man and woman were first created, God made man's body from the physical elements of His created cosmos, then woman's body from the living flesh and bone of man (or, perhaps, from the *blood,* which sustains both flesh and bone) and then the solemn pronouncement was made: "Therefore shall a man leave his father and his mother, and shall cleave unto his wife: and they shall be one flesh" (Genesis 2:24).

This passage was taken literally by the Lord Jesus Christ and then used by Him as the basis of His teaching that marriage (therefore also the institution of home and family) was intended by man's Creator to be permanent and monogamous (see Matthew 19:3-8; Mark 10:2-12). Even more significantly, the Apostle Paul showed that marriage was not only permanent but was a picture of the indissoluble and perfect union of Christ and His Church. This is the theme of the beautiful passage in Ephesians 5:22-33. For example: "Husbands, love your wives, even as Christ also loved the church, and gave himself for it; that he might sanctify and cleanse it with the washing of water by the word, that he might present it to himself a glorious church, not having spot, or wrinkle, or any such thing; but that it should be holy and without blemish" (Ephesians 5:25-27). And then, quoting from the Genesis record: "For we are members of his body, of his flesh, and of his bones. For this cause shall a man leave his father and mother, and shall be joined unto his wife, and they two shall be one flesh. This is a great mystery: but I speak concerning Christ and the church" (Ephesians 5:30-32).

Although this beautiful simile finds its fullest and ultimate expression here in the New Testament union of Christ and His Bride, the Church, it is familiar throughout the Bible.

For example, the Lord referred to the people of Israel as His own wife, whom He loved dearly but who often was an unfaithful and adulterous wife. The prophecy of Hosea is largely built around this concept. After rebuking Israel for her unfaithfulness, the prophet says: "And she shall follow after her lovers, but she shall not overtake them; and she shall seek them, but shall not find them: then shall she say, I will go and return to my first husband; for then was it better with me than now" (Hosea 2:7).

Then, when Israel finally returns to the Lord (as we have already seen will happen during the tribulation), the Lord will gladly receive His erring "wife" back into His loving fellowship. "And I will betroth thee unto me for ever; yea, I will betroth thee unto me in righteousness, and in judgment, and in lovingkindness, and in mercies" (Hosea 2:19, 20).

Similarly Jeremiah says: "Behold, the days come, saith the Lord, that I will make a new covenant with the house of Israel, and with the house of Judah: Not according to the covenant that I made with their fathers in the day that I took them by the hand to bring them out of the land of Egypt; which my covenant they brake, although I was an husband unto them, saith the Lord" (Jeremiah 31:31, 32).

Isaiah also uses the same figure: "For thy Maker is thine husband; the Lord of hosts is his name; and thy Redeemer the Holy One of Israel: The God of the whole earth shall he be called" (Isaiah 54:5).

In the New Testament, the Church is symbolized as the pure and faithful Bride of Christ: "For I am jealous over you with godly jealousy: for I have espoused you to one husband, that I may present you as a chaste virgin to Christ" (2 Corinthians 11:2).

Whether a clear-cut distinction should be made, in interpreting this great future wedding, between Israel as the restored wife of the Lord and the Church as the virgin Bride of the Lord has long been a matter of disagreement between expositors. Although there is surely a difference between an adulterous wife and a chaste bride, so far as the figure of speech goes, there is not such a clear distinction between actual individual believers before Christ and after Christ. There were many godly and faithful Jewish believers in ancient times just as there are multitudes of compromising carnal Christians today.

Whatever fine distinctions may be warranted at this great future gathering, surely the primary truth is the final, perfect eternal union between Christ and His people. All sin will have been purged and cleansed, and full fellowship reestablished, as far as the resurrected saints are concerned, whether Jew or Gentile. Probably the restoration of the earthly people of Israel (that is, those who survive the tribulation and enter the millennium in their natural physical bodies) is a sort of earthly reflection of the heavenly union between Christ and all glorified believers. The restored wife or earth may thus be a type of the newly married Bride in heaven.

The testimony is also given that "his wife hath made herself ready." On the earth the unfaithful wife, Israel, will have prepared herself through the purifying furnace of affliction in the great time of introspection in the wilderness, to which she had fled from the face of the dragon (Revelation 12:6). When Christ returns in power and great glory to His people, and they look on Him whom they pierced (Zechariah 12:10), they will completely submit to Him in full repentance and faith.

At the same time, in heaven, at the judgment seat of Christ, all the raptured saints of the ages will have been purified and made like Christ (1 John 3:2, 3; Romans 8:29). In the figure, the Bride will have put on her appropriate bridal garments, prepared to meet her Bridegroom and to be joined forever to Him.

Revelation 19:8.   And to her was granted that she should be arrayed in fine linen, clean and white: for the fine linen is the righteousness of saints.

The fine linen garments, white and clean, of course speak of the full preparation of the Bride to accompany her Bridegroom. The old clothing has been abandoned and all is new and pure as she enters His holy presence forever. "I will greatly rejoice in the Lord, my soul shall be joyful in my God; for he hath clothed me with the garments of salvation, he hath covered me with the robe of righteousness, as a bridegroom decketh himself with ornaments, and as a bride adorneth herself with her jewels" (Isaiah 61:10).

The Bride's old garments of self-righteousness, which once had seemed so fine and attractive, had become in her sight like filthy rags (Isaiah 64:6), and she had gladly put them aside for the pure white linen provided by her Savior. "Wherefore, my brethren, ye also are become dead to the law by the body of Christ; that ye should be married to another, even to him who is raised from the dead, that we should bring forth fruit unto God" (Romans 7:4).

Whenever a man or woman receives the matchless gift of salvation offered by the Lord Jesus Christ, this is the way it is. He saves us, not by our works, for we are his workmanship created unto good works (Ephesians 2:9, 10). Then, in turn, the good works in which He has before ordained that we should walk become the "righteousness of saints."

The word here is plural and could better be translated "the righteous deeds of saints." Here is a paradox, yet a paradox which is utter reality. No believer is saved, or made fit to enter his Savior's presence, by virtue of his righteous acts. Yet, once having been saved by grace through faith, he then is both enabled and constrained to walk in righteousness, and these righteous deeds in some marvelous transmutation become the clean white linen robe of righteousness provided by the Savior for His people.

Mystery or no, it will be blessedly real in that day. In unfathomable grace, the Lord Jesus will reward us for all righteous acts done in His name, and these will equip us to stand in His presence. Yet these very acts are only by His enabling, identifying in some wonderful way with the garments of salvation and robe of righteousness which He himself has purchased and provided for His Bride.

Furthermore, all sin and remnant self-righteousness will have been exposed, judged, and cleansed at His judgment seat in the heavens (2 Corinthians 5:10). Thus will His wife make herself ready, and accompany her Lord in clean raiment.

Revelation 19:9.   And he saith unto me, Write, Blessed are they which are called unto the marriage supper of the Lamb. And he saith unto me, These are the true sayings of God.

Since the closest possible antecedent of "he" is apparently the "voice from the throne" (v. 5), it may be that the Lord Himself is renewing His command to John at this point to write what he was seeing and hearing. More likely, however, the instruction came from the angel (see v. 10). This was to be the true record of future history, to be written for the guidance and encouragement of all the generations of Christians who would come after John.

That which he was specially admonished to write at this point was the fourth of the seven great "beatitudes" of Revelation. It would become a great blessing and strength to all the suffering saints through the ages, exhorting everyone who would be a member in Christ's growing Church (His Bride) to anticipate their glorious future union with the heavenly Bridegroom.

And again the figure of the "marriage" or "marriage supper" is used to depict that union. The "marriage" of the Lamb is mentioned in verse 7, and the "marriage supper" of the Lamb here in verse 9, but both the usage of these words and also the wedding customs of John's time regarded the marriage and marriage feast as essentially the same.

The betrothal was normally arranged by the parents long before the actual wedding. The marriage contract was effected by the payment of a dowry by the bride's parents. Months, or perhaps years, later when the bride and groom were ready for marriage, the date for the wedding feast would be set. At the appointed time, the bridegroom and his friends would set forth from his home to her home to claim his bride.

There she, his chaste virgin bride, would await his coming with her own friends, all virgins, who would accompany her to the wedding supper, sumptuously provided at great expense by the father of the bridegroom. Upon the arrival of the bridegroom, the bride would be surrendered to him by her parents, and he would carry her back to his own home with great joy and anticipation. They would be followed by their friends, who would then join them in the happy wedding celebration at the home of the groom's father.

From that time on, the bride and groom were united, never to be parted until death if God's ideal plan for marriage were accepted and followed by them. Thus did the marriage supper consummate the marriage.

It is this beautiful custom which apparently is in view here in this striking picture of the marriage of the Lamb. The marriage had been engaged long ago when the heavenly Father essayed to claim a Bride for His Son from the world of lost mankind. In this case, however, the Bride had no dowry to offer for a husband and was quite unworthy of such a wedding. Therefore the Son offered to pay the price Himself. He became the Lamb of God, taking away the sin of the world (John 1:29), and His shed blood became the purchase price that made the Bride fit to enter the home of His father. The garments of salvation, her robes of righteousness provided by Him, replaced her own filthy rags, and she became His espoused Bride.

It was a long time, however, before He could actually go forth to claim His Bride. Finally the day had come and He had received her to Himself from the home of her parents, taking her with Him to the place of the wedding. The time en route (corresponding to the time between the "rapture" and the actual wedding supper) would be a time of fellowship and also a time of further cleansing and purification in His presence (corresponding to her appearance at His judgment seat). But now, at last, it was almost time for the wedding.

The figure of the wedding feast is familiar in the parables of Christ. For example, in the parable of Matthew 22:1-14 (also Luke 14:16-24) Jesus said: "The kingdom of heaven is like unto a certain king, which made a marriage for his son. And sent forth his servants to call them that were bidden to the wedding: and they would not come." The major thrust of this parable, of course, is directed against those who refuse Christ's invitation. All have been invited to His wedding, but most people decline His gracious call. Whatever the excuse, it does not satisfy the king, and He sends into the highways and hedges to find those who will come to the wedding. When the wedding feast is finally ready, "the wedding was furnished with guests" (Matthew 22:10). Further, the host provided all with the proper garments for the wedding, no matter how torn or filthy may have been their own clothing. When one man appeared at the feast without a garment, however, he was cast out. He, like all the others, had been invited and had rejected the formal terms of the invitation, preferring instead to participate on his own terms, rather than those of the host. This is impossible, of course, and he will therefore be cast out with all those who had refused even to come at all.

A different, though related, emphasis is found in Christ's parable of the ten virgins (Matthew 25:1-13). "Then shall the kingdom of heaven be likened unto ten virgins, which took their lamps, and went forth to meet the bridegroom. And five of them were wise, and five were foolish."

The foolish virgins were shortsighted, too much concerned with their immediate interests and comforts to prepare for the great privilege of participating in the wedding of the king. They had not declined the invitation and, in fact, were planning to be in the entourage of the bride herself, but were simply careless and self-centered, not being sufficiently concerned to make adequate preparations for the great opportunity they had been offered. The generous host would send the needed garments for their clothing, but not the oil for their lamps. They had ample time to prepare but slept instead, and the bridegroom came upon them unawares. "And while they went to buy, the bridegroom came; and they that were ready went in with him to the marriage: and the door was shut." To the foolish virgins, when they finally came, He said, "I know you not" (Matthew 25:10, 12).

In the one parable, many are excluded from the wedding by their own choice. In the second parable, half of those who want to come are excluded by their own negligence. Those who do get there are there by their own choice, by their submission to the terms of the invitation and by virtue of their diligence in making the needed preparations. All three are apparently essential qualifications for those who come to the great wedding supper.

Many interpreters believe the oil for the lamps symbolizes the Holy Spirit, with the excluded virgins representing those professing Christians who are not truly born again by the Spirit. This is doubtful, however, for two reasons. First, there is no specific reference anywhere in Scripture which states that oil is symbolic of the Holy Spirit. Specifically, in this parable of the ten virgins, there is no suggestion that the oil, as such, is a symbol of anything at all. Second, the presence or absence of the Holy Spirit in an individual does not depend upon his own effort, but the parable speaks of the need for going to the market and buying the oil. Every true believer receives the Holy Spirit at the same moment he receives Christ's "garment" of righteousness, through his faith in Christ as Savior, and nothing else.

At the same time, "faith without works is dead" (James 2:20). Genuine faith is evidenced, first of all, by a spiritual "wisdom" which is careful, rather than careless, toward the Lord. The word "wise" in the parable of the virgins is the Greek *phronimos,* which means, literally, "thoughtful." The word "foolish" (Gr. *moros*) has the sense of "heedless." The foolish virgins demonstrated that they did not really know the Lord (and, therefore, He knew them not) by their attitude of indifference toward Him.

In summary, the consistent teaching of the parables and of all relevant Scripture is that those who will participate in the great wedding feast of the Lamb are all those who have responded in true saving faith to the gospel invitation, manifesting outwardly that inward faith by an attitude of thoughtful concern for the things of God. They are all clothed in clean, white linen, which speaks of the "righteousness" of the saints (Revelation 19:8).

But what distinction, if any, is to be made between the guests at the wedding and the attendants of the Bride, or between these and the Bride herself? Many and ingenious have been the interpretations proffered, but it is significant that none of these are offered in the biblical texts themselves.

It is certain that all who were saved, both before and after Christ, will be with Him, eating and drinking with Him in the kingdom of God. "And I say unto you, That many shall come from the east and west, and shall sit down with Abraham, and Isaac, and Jacob, in the kingdom of heaven" (Matthew 8:11; see also Luke 3:29). "But I say unto you, I will not drink henceforth of this fruit of the vine, until that day when I drink it new with you in my Father's kingdom" (Matthew 26:29).

Furthermore, the New Jerusalem is identified as the Bride of Christ (Revelation 21:9, 10), no doubt because it is the eternal home of all who are saved (Revelation 21:24), those who collectively constitute His Bride. But this city has twelve gates, inscribed with the names of the twelve tribes of Israel, and twelve foundations, in which are the names of the twelve apostles of the Lamb (Revelation

21:12, 14). This surely means that within the city are both the redeemed of ancient Israel and the redeemed of the later Church of Christ. And this in turn must mean that all of these are somehow a part of "the bride, the Lamb's wife."

The Bride, therefore, represents and includes all her attendants and all the wedding guests as well. The symbolism in the parables cannot be pressed beyond its purpose. The real message is that all believers in the true God, both Creator and Redeemer, of all the ages, will one day be restored to perfect fellowship with Him and united with Him forever. Glorious will be the great wedding feast, and blessed indeed are all who are called unto it.

Whatever distinctions may exist between the saints of the pre-Abrahamic period, the saints in Israel before Christ, the saints among the Gentiles from Abraham to Christ, the saints of the tribulation, and the saints in the churches from Christ to the rapture (and no doubt these will continue to be identifiable groups even in the ages to come) such distinctions are secondary to the great primary truth that all will be there by virtue of the saving work of Christ and their personal trust in the true Creator God and His provision of salvation. There is only one God (not one God identified with Israel and one God associated with the Church) and that one triune God will be in personal fellowship forever with all the redeemed saints of all the ages. He will dwell with them in the Holy City forever (Revelation 21:2, 3).

The blessedness of the great union and the feast accompanying it is so great and so important that it is emphasized again to John that these sayings are *true,* for God is their author. On two later occasions is a similar testimonial assertion made (Revelation 21:5; 22:6), and all three speak of the blessedness of the redeemed in glory. Such promises are deemed by God to be of such paramount importance as to warrant a special surety that they are from God Himself.

Revelation 19:10.   And I fell at his feet to worship him. And he said unto me, See thou do it not: I am thy fellowservant, and of thy brethren that have the testimony of Jesus: worship God: for the testimony of Jesus is the spirit of prophecy.

So magnificent was the mighty angel who had conducted John through the great scenes, and so overwhelming his revelation, that the apostle felt a sudden compulsion to bow down in worship before him. John later made the same mistake again (Revelation 22:8, 9). On both occasions, the angel reminded him that only God should be worshiped. No created thing or being—not even the greatest man or most exalted angel—is ever to be worshiped, for worship (that is, literally, "bowing down" to do the will of another simply on the basis of his intrinsic power and authority) belongs only to God.

This was, indeed, a mighty angel, but he would only claim to be a fellow servant, with John, of the One to be worshiped. Angels are merely "ministering" (that is, *serving*) spirits (Hebrews 1:14). In fact, the angel here claimed actually, literally, to be a fellow slave of John's, so wholly dedicated was he to doing God's will. Like John and his Christian brethren, the angel himself maintained and proclaimed the same "testimony of Jesus" which they proclaimed, nothing more.

This phrase is very significant, with a different connotation than the somewhat more common phrase "testimony of Christ," or "testimony of Jesus Christ." The emphasis here is on His human name and thus the testimony has specifically to do with His humanity. The angel knew full well the fact of Christ's deity. In fact, he knew and believed that He was nothing less than the Creator, so that "all the angels of God worship him" (Hebrews 1:6). Of His deity there was no question, but that God would become man was hard to believe and would need the faithful and consistent testimony of both holy angels and godly men. It is this testimony that is opposed by the rebel angels, the demonic spirits, and it was for this "witness of Jesus" *(witness* is the same Greek word as *testimony)* that the tribulation saints had been beheaded (Revelation 20:4).

It was the spirit of opposition to this inestimable significant truth of the incarnation (the Word made flesh, as per John 1:14) that John in his epistle had already recognized as the spirit of Antichrist (1 John 4:3), and now he had seen Antichrist himself seeking to destroy all who maintained the testimony of Jesus Christ (Revelation 12:17). The "testimony of Jesus" is the spirit of true prophecy. It contradicts the testimony of false prophets. "Beloved," John had warned, "believe not every spirit, but try the spirits, whether they are of God. . . . Every spirit that confesseth that Jesus Christ is come in the flesh is of God: And every spirit that confesseth not that Jesus Christ is come in the flesh is not of God" (1 John 4:1-3). "Who is a liar but he that denieth that Jesus is the Christ? He is antichrist, that denieth the Father and the Son" (1 John 2:22).

It was for his faithful proclamation of this testimony that the mighty angel desired John to recognize him, not the marvelous revelations concerning the future judgments which he had been privileged to show John. To him, the most amazing of all revelations was that the Almighty Creator had become the man Jesus, to save His people from their sins.

The King of Kings

The saints have now all been called to the wedding feast and provided with the proper garments, fine linen, white and clean. But the supper itself must be held on earth, and the earth is still in bondage to the kings of the earth, and they in turn to the dragon and the beast and the false prophet. Babylon has been destroyed, but the armies of the kings have been assembled at Armageddon. They know that Christ is about to return and are determined to wage a final, all-out battle to prevent His regaining sovereignty over the earth.

Not only are the multitudes of human armies assembled there. All the principalities and powers of darkness are also there, following their master, Satan, the god of this world. They know their time has come, and the climactic battle of the ages is about to be joined.

Revelation 19:11.   And I saw heaven opened, and behold a white horse; and he that sat upon him was called Faithful and True, and in righteousness he doth judge and make war.

John several times before had seen "heaven opened," but never a scene like this. Emerging from the temple in the city in the heavens appeared a great white horse and a majestic Rider, with all the armies of the gloriously arrayed saints following him (v. 14).

This is evidently the same symbolic horse and Rider that John had seen going forth "to conquer" at the very beginning of the tribulation (Revelation 6:2) and now he sees Him setting forth in the great event of final conquest. The earlier vision had not specifically revealed His identity, but here He is openly proclaimed as the Faithful and True One, with His war of victory based on perfect righteousness and His punitive judgments founded on divine holiness.

He is called Faithful and True because He is "the faithful and true witness, the beginning of the creation of God" (Revelation 3:14). He will keep His Word, for His Word is true; He is very faithfulness and very truth. And because He is true and faithful and must act in righteousness, He must finally, after long ages of grace and mercy, become the Judge and the Warrior. As the Judge, He has pronounced the sentence; as the Warrior, He will carry it out. The rebels have been condemned (in fact, have condemned themselves, by deliberate choice); now they must be executed.

This is the first of three magnificent names accorded the Lord Jesus as He returns to earth in power and great glory, as ascribed in this section. His name is Faithful and True; then His name is the Word of God (v. 13), and finally His name is recognized as King of kings and Lord of lords (v. 16).

Revelation 19:12.   His eyes were as a flame of fire, and on his head were many crowns; and he had a name written, that no man knew, but he himself.

There is no room for doubt as to the identity of this conquering Commander on the great white steed. His eyes are the same eyes of flame John had seen in the beginning (Revelation 1:14) when he recognized Him as the Son of man. But now adorning His snowy white head were many diadems. These crowns were not the same crowns which the elders had cast at His feet (Revelation 4:10), nor did they include the crown given Him when He first rode forth to conquer (Revelation 6:2). These latter are translations of the Greek *stephanos,* whereas the crowns He is wearing as He parades in triumph are the crowns (Greek *diadema)* which had once been usurped by the kings of the earth (Revelation 12:3; 13:1; 17:9-12).

No longer will alien rulers despoil His creation. It is He whose right it is (Ezekiel 21:26, 27), not only as Creator but also as Redeemer. As the Lamb, He was the only one worthy to break the seals on the scroll conveying ownership of the earth (Revelation 5:9), unleashing the great series of purging judgments that had finally wrested control from the rebel kings. Now He wears their crowns as He rides forth in triumph. "Gird thy sword upon thy thigh, O most mighty, with thy glory and thy majesty. And in thy majesty ride prosperously because of truth and meekness and righteousness; and thy right hand shall teach thee terrible things" (Psalm 45:3, 4).

It is apparently across these diadems that a name was written. John could see the writing, but he could not decipher it. Nor could anyone read this name, written evidently in characters of some angelic script, beyond the learning of mortal men. It was not one of the other names ascribed to Him in this passage (verses 11, 13, 16) for all these names are all well known to believing men. It is probably the name which is above every name (Philippians 2:9), not the name "Jesus" but the name "given to Jesus" (Philippians 2:10, literal meaning), when He was raised from the dead and exalted "far above all principality, and power, and might, and dominion, and every name that is named" (Ephesians 1:21).

The names assigned to the Lord Jesus Christ in Scripture are many and beautiful (such as the Light, Master, Messiah, King of Israel, Son of man, Son of God, Lamb of God, Prince of Peace). But all of them together cannot exhaust the infinite meaning of His ineffable name. We know Him in many wonderful attributes, but we can never know Him in His incomprehensible fullness. He is all and in all and we, even in the glorious resurrection, can never learn everything concerning Him, though no doubt our knowledge of Him will continue to grow throughout eternity. The fullness of His mighty name, only He can know!

Revelation 19:13.   And he was clothed with a vesture dipped in blood: and his name is called the Word of God.

The blood-dipped vesture, of course, speaks of the shed blood of His enemies. As noted before, the great valley filled with the armies of the kings will flow with blood to the bridles of the horses (Revelation 14:20), and He is seen as riding triumphantly through this vale of slaughter. Beginning from its southern end in Edom (Isaiah 63:1), He rides north to Jerusalem and on to Armageddon, "red in thine apparel, and thy garments like him that treadeth in the winefat" (Isaiah 63:2).

There is a fine mixture here of graphic symbolism and stark reality. The heavenly horses may be symbolic visions, of course, and so may be the blood-dipped vesture. But the slain multitudes are real, and the conquering Redeemer is real. This is the "glorious appearing of the great God and our Saviour Jesus

Christ" (Titus 2:13). This is the great "sign of the Son of man in heaven" when all men "shall see the Son of man coming in the clouds of heaven with power and great glory," and "all the tribes of the earth shall mourn" (Matthew 24:30).

As the majestic Rider reaches Jerusalem, "his feet shall stand in that day upon the Mount of Olives" (Zechariah 14:4), and the mountain will split in two. "And I will shake all nations, and the desire of all nations shall come: and I will fill this house with glory, saith the Lord of hosts" (Haggai 2:7). "But who may abide the day of his coming? and who shall stand when he appeareth? for he is like a refiner's fire, and like fullers' soap" (Malachi 3:2). "The Lord Jesus shall be revealed from heaven with his mighty angels, in flaming fire taking vengeance on them that know not God, and that obey not the gospel of our Lord Jesus Christ" (2 Thessalonians 1:7, 8).

In His glorious appearing, it is appropriate to remember that the mighty Conqueror is none other than the incarnate Word of God. It was by the Word of the Lord that the heavens were made (Psalm 33:6) and the *aeons* were framed (Hebrews 11:3). It is by the same Word that the heavens and earth are kept in store (2 Peter 3:7). That Word which was in the beginning (John 1:1) is also the Omega, and will dwell forever with His people (John 1:14, Revelation 21:3-6).

Revelation 19:14.   And the armies which were in heaven followed him upon white horses, clothed in fine linen, white and clean.

Like a mighty general conducting his triumphant armies through the streets of an earthly capital, the victorious Rider is followed by a tremendous stream of warriors, all in gleaming white uniforms and all on beautiful white horses. The fine linen apparel symbolizes the righteous deeds of all these followers of the Lamb (v. 8) and the whole procession is a glorious vision vouchsafed to John to indicate to him and to us the unprecedented majesty and glory of the Lord when He finally returns to earth.

Although the horses and white linen armor may be symbolic (and perhaps even these are literal; God could surely create divinely-energized creatures of whatever type He chooses), they do speak of a great victory and glorious homecoming which will literally take place on the earth. Both the Lord Jesus Christ and all the multitudes of the redeemed will descend from the region of the throne in the sky, from where the Lord Jesus has been directing the events of the tribulation period, and will engage the armies of the beast in a brief climactic battle to consummate the judgments and to establish His kingdom here on earth.

This glorious coming of the Lord with His saints has been prophesied since the dawn of history. "And Enoch also, the seventh from Adam, prophesied of these, saying, Behold, the Lord cometh with ten thousands of his saints [or "myriads of saints"], to execute judgment upon all, and to convince all that are ungodly among them of all their ungodly deeds which they have ungodly committed, and of all their hard speeches which ungodly sinners have spoken against him" (Jude 14, 15).

The great event was likewise foretold by the prophets of Israel. "Then shall the Lord go forth, and fight against those nations. . . . And the Lord shall be king over all the earth" (Zechariah 14:3-9). "Let the saints be joyful in glory. . . . Let the high praises of God be in their mouth, and a two-edged sword in their hand; to execute vengeance upon the heathen, and punishments upon the people. . . . To execute upon them the judgment written: this honour have all the saints" (Psalm 149:5-9).

Likewise had it been prophesied by the Apostles: "To the end he may stablish your hearts unblameable in holiness before God, even our Father, at the coming of our Lord Jesus Christ with all his saints" (1 Thessalonians 3:13). What a magnificent procession that will be, when all the angelic host of heaven and all the multitudes of redeemed and purified saints of God accompany their victorious Redeemer back to earth again! After long ages of rule by the old serpent, the god of this world, with his powers of darkness and his legions of Christ-rejecting human dupes, the diseased and fevered earth will finally be scoured and purified, and Christ will reign supreme.

Revelation 19:15.   And out of his mouth goeth a sharp sword, that with it he should smite the nations: and he shall rule them with a rod of iron: and he treadeth the winepress of the fierceness and wrath of Almighty God.

John had seen this sharp sword before (Revelation 1:16), the piercing sharpness of the lethal words of judgment leaping from the mouth of the wrathful Son of man. Isaiah also had prophesied of this: "He shall smite the earth with the rod of his mouth, and with the breath of his lips shall he slay the wicked" (Isaiah 11:4). "[That wicked one] the Lord shall consume with the spirit of his mouth, and shall destroy with the brightness of his coming" (2 Thessalonians 2:8).

The "sword" is, specifically, a sabre or a long, broad cutlass. Symbolically it can be used for any weapons of intense battle, and here of course it refers to the fiery words of judgment from the Lord. The "nations" to be smitten thus are the Gentile nations ("Gentiles" and "nations" are translations of the same Greek word, *ethnos*). The Jewish nation will already have undergone its own judgment during the "day of Jacob's trouble," the tribulation period, and will have accepted Christ as their long-rejected Messiah when He returns.

During the imminent millennial age, these Gentile nations will be ruled with a rod of iron (see also Revelation 12:5). The word for "rule" is actually "shepherdize" or "pastor." Christ will be their pastor, but He will demand absolute obedience. It will be a dictatorship of love, but a dictatorship nonetheless. The terminology comes originally from Psalm 2:8, 9: "I shall give thee the heathen for thine inheritance, and the uttermost parts of the earth for thy possession. Thou shalt break them with a rod of iron."

This promise was given by the heavenly Father to His Son (Psalm 2:7) but the Lord Jesus also extended it to each person that "overcometh, and keepeth my works unto the end" (Revelation 2:26, 27). As the psalmist noted: "This honour have all his saints" (Psalm 149:9).

Once again there is a return to the figure of the overflowing winepress and the blood-dipped vesture. This was the graphic picture of Revelation 14:14-20, but here we are told specifically that the one who treads the winepress is Christ Himself. Further, He treads it alone (Isaiah 63:3), so that only His vesture is dipped in blood.

The winepress depicts the fierceness and wrath of Almighty God. The word for "fierceness" (Greek *thumos*) is also translated "indignation" and "wrath." The word here for "wrath" (Greek *orge*) is also rendered "anger," "indignation" and "vengeance." Thus the two terms are essentially synonymous and express with doubled intensity the unleashed ferocity of a long-suffering God, whose unrequited patience has endured for ages the wickedness and rebellion and blasphemy of the men and women He had loved and sought to redeem. "Because I have called, and ye refused; I have stretched out my hand, and no man regarded; but ye have set at nought all my counsel, and would none of my reproof: I also will laugh at your calamity; I will mock when your fear cometh; when your fear cometh as desolation, and your destruction cometh as a whirlwind; when distress and anguish cometh upon you" (Proverbs 1:24-27).

A mighty wind will sweep through the long valley where the armies of the millions are gathered, the sharp sword striking forth from the mouth of the offended King. Bursting arteries will spew their blood until the great trough flows in blood and the press is full. "Put ye in the sickle, for the harvest is ripe: come, get you down; for the press is full, the fats overflow; for their wickedness is great" (Joel 3:13).

Revelation 19:16.   And he hath on his vesture and on his thigh a name written, KING OF KINGS, AND LORD OF LORDS.

Here is yet another wonderful name of Christ, written both on His blood-dipped vesture and also, in lieu of a two-edged sword, upon His thigh (compare Psalm 45:3). In the days of His flesh, the minions of earth's greatest king had cast lots for His vesture (John 19:24); now His vesture dripped with the blood of all such blasphemers and was inscribed with the testimony that He was King over all such earthly kings and Lord over all terrestrial lords. He needed no sword at His thigh, like earthly conquerors, because His sword proceeded out of His mouth, so here also was placed the glorious ascription.

This title was used earlier by the Apostle Paul speaking of the future "appearing of our Lord Jesus Christ." Paul seemed to glimpse this very scene: "Which in his times he shall shew, who is the blessed and only Potentate, the King of kings, and Lord of lords" (1 Timothy 6:15). Speaking earlier of these earthly kings, while writing about the harlot Babylon, John had recorded the testimony of the angel. "These shall make war with the Lamb, and the Lamb shall overcome them: for he is Lord of lords, and King of kings" (Revelation 17:14). He is King of time and King of space, King of all creation. How can mere creatures, whether men or angels, or even Satan himself, presume to oppose Him!

The Great Battle of Armageddon

The spirits of demons, working miracles, have now persuaded all the kings of the earth to send their armies to Armageddon (Revelation 16:13-16), there to be ready to fight their great Enemy, in one final desperate attempt to confirm the beast as king of the earth, and to enthrone Satan as king of the cosmos. They know Christ is about to descend to earth, and they have experienced His awful judgments, one after the other. But there is no longer either desire or opportunity for salvation, so they must either fight or perish. And so they march and skirmish with the people of the lands and fight with the remnant Jews in Jerusalem, and wait fearfully for the heavens to open and Christ to come.

Revelation 19:17.   And I saw an angel standing in the sun; and he cried with a loud voice, saying to all the fowls that fly in the midst of heaven, Come and gather yourselves together unto the supper of the great God.

An invitation had gone out long ago to come to the marriage supper of the Lamb, and many had responded. Now an invitation is issued to another feast, the supper of the great God, but what a difference in the two suppers! The guests at the one are the redeemed saints of the ages, joyfully feasting in the presence of the Redeemer. Those invited to the other are the birds of prey and the carrion-eating fowl from all over the world, and their dinner is to be the flesh and blood of the slain multitudes at Armageddon.

The angel who called out this amazing invitation was "standing in the sun." Perhaps this means, merely, that the angel was in the sunlight, or else standing on the earth with the sun behind him but it would seem unnecessary to mention it at all if that were the meaning.

More likely, the angel was actually *in* the sun. Angels are commonly identified with stars in the Scripture, and it is not far-fetched to suppose this angel has his own assignment, in God's great dominion, on the sun itself. As such, he would have special concern for the earth, since it is energy from the sun that maintains the physical and biological processes taking place on the earth. It may well have been this same angel who was responsible (see Revelation 16:8, 9) for causing the sun to heat up so severely during the latter days of the tribulation period.

But the task of cleansing the earth of the awful carnage at Armageddon will be more than unaided solar energy can accomplish, no matter how much intensified. Accordingly, he calls out in a mighty cry, reaching all the way from the sun, capable of being heard and understood by the hawks and ravens, the crows and vultures, from all over the world.

The call is to a great gathering-together of the fowls of the heavens. The armies of the heathen had first been gathered together (Joel 3:2, 11; Zephaniah 3:8; Zechariah 12:3; 14:2; Revelation 16:16) on the ground, in a great column from Bozrah in Edom up through the valley of Jehoshaphat and over the plains of Jezreel at Armageddon. Now the birds of prey also begin to gather together, but in the air, circling over the masses of humanity stretched out below them, darkening the sky and undoubtedly filling the hearts of the armies on the ground with great gloom and dread. "For wheresoever the carcase is, there will the eagles be gathered together" (Matthew 24:28). "Hold thy peace at the presence of the Lord God: for the day of the Lord is at hand: for the Lord hath prepared a sacrifice, he hath bid his guests" (Zephaniah 1:7).

Revelation 19:18.   That ye may eat the flesh of kings, and the flesh of captains, and the flesh of mighty men, and the flesh of horses, and of them that sit on them, and the flesh of all men, both free and bond, both small and great.

Mighty kings and mighty warriors, great men and small men, all men, will become carrion for the vultures. Thus will the haughtiness of men be brought low. "For the day of the Lord of hosts shall be upon every one that is proud and lofty, and upon every one that is lifted up; and he shall be brought low" (Isaiah 2:12).

This scene is very similar to that described in Ezekiel 39:17-20. "And, thou son of man, thus saith the Lord God; Speak unto every feathered foul, and to every beast of the field, Assemble yourselves, and come; gather yourselves on every side to my sacrifice that I do sacrifice for you, even a great sacrifice upon the mountains of Israel, that ye may eat flesh, and drink blood. Ye shall eat the flesh of the mighty, and drink the blood of the princes of the earth, of rams, of lambs, and of goats, of bullocks, all of them fatlings of Bashan. And ye shall eat fat till ye be full, and drink blood till ye be drunken, of my sacrifice which I have sacrificed for you. Thus ye shall be filled at my table with horses and chariots, with mighty men, and with all men of war, saith the Lord God."

Because of the similarities, many commentators have taken the battle of Gog and Magog, of which this Ezekiel passage is an aftermath, to be the same as the battle of Armageddon. This is very unlikely, however, though the one may well be intended as a type of the other. One is on the mountains of Israel, the other on the plains of Armageddon and in the valley of Jehoshaphat. One includes all the animals of the land, the other only the men and their horses. The destruction in the first is caused by divinely controlled nature, the second directly by Christ Himself. Further, as discussed in Chapter 6, the battle of Gog and Magog almost certainly will take place at the beginning of the tribulation, Armageddon at its end.

Reports have been widely published stating that there has been a great increase in the population of such birds of prey in recent years in the lands of the Middle East. Whether or not this is really so, there are indeed two great banquets due one day soon to be spread for the birds of the air, one of the armies of Gog, the other those of the beast.

Revelation 19:19.   And I saw the beast, and the kings of the earth, and their armies, gathered together to make war against him that sat on the horse, and against his army.

The last time the beast and the kings of the earth were seen together was as recorded at Revelation 17:13, where the kings had deeded their power and strength over to the beast. This was at the middle of the tribulation so that, for the last three-and-a-half years, the beast had been essentially king of the world. Under the impact of the ensuing bowl judgments, the beast and the false prophet, as instructed by the old dragon, had finally sent forth their call to all the kings to gather their armies together to Armageddon (Revelation 16:13-16). Shortly thereafter, the great capital city at Babylon had been destroyed, and all these kings of the earth had mourned greatly over her loss (Revelation 18:9, 10).

But now they are all gathered together at Armageddon, with their hosts extending in great multitudes down past the Dead Sea deep into the ancient territory of the Edomites, awaiting the coming of Christ and His army of saints from heaven. The dragon also is there, with all his demonic hordes, poised for one last mighty assault on the King of creation, still hoping against hope that God can be defeated. The day of final confrontation is almost here. "Multitudes, multitudes in the valley of decision: for the day of the Lord is near in the valley of decision" (Joel 3:14). "Come near, ye nations, to hear; and hearken, ye people: let the earth hear, and all that is therein; the world, and all things that come forth of it. For the indignation of the Lord is upon all nations, and his fury upon all their armies: he hath utterly destroyed them, he hath delivered them to the slaughter" (Isaiah 34:1, 2).

Revelation 19:20.   And the beast was taken, and with him the false prophet that wrought miracles before him, with which he deceived them that had received the mark of the beast, and them that worshipped his image. These both were cast alive into a lake of fire burning with brimstone.

398

The multitudes in the armies of the kings of the earth had placed great faith in their leader, the beast, believing that he would indeed prove out to be greater than Christ. They had been willing even to receive the mark of the beast, knowing that this choice would irrevocably cut them off from any subsequent desire to change their minds and turn to Christ (Revelation 14:9-11). To considerable degree, they had been influenced to make this fateful decision by virtue of the charismatic personality of the beast and the amazing miracles wrought by his lieutenant, the world's preeminent religious leader and prophet. This false prophet had persuaded men that he could even give life to the great image of the beast set up in the temple at Jerusalem, so that all men should bow down to this image, either the prototype image in Jerusalem or the replicas of the image installed in household shrines all over the world.

With the beast and the false prophet there to exercise their brilliant leadership and miraculous powers, respectively, the earthly armies still hoped desperately that the Lamb and those following Him could be defeated when they descended from their great space platform in the skies. Furthermore they knew that the dragon whom they worshiped (Revelation 13:4) was also there with all his hosts. Despite the circling vultures and the fresh memory of the global earthquake and the fall of mighty Babylon, somehow they still hoped that they would be delivered. The Devil that deceived them, through the demonic miracles of the prophet, still held sway.

How unspeakably terrifying, then, to see their great leaders suddenly and unceremoniously snatched from their midst! Whether Christ dispatched a band of angels to take them or whether they were simply caught up in response to His omnipotent Word is not recorded. Whatever the means, these two mighty men, the most powerful and most feared men in all the world, were gone. The assembled multitudes were suddenly left exposed and helpless, with no one to lead them. Their confusion and fright were unbounded, as they watched in an absolute trauma the grand approach of the armies of heaven.

But their fright was nothing compared to that of the beast and the prophet, as they were suddenly siezed and translated at unimaginable speed to a vast fiery lake boiling with brimstone. There, while still alive in their human bodies of flesh and blood, they were hurled into the flaming cauldron, where they would remain throughout eternity.

This is the first specific mention in Scripture of the lake of fire, at least by this name. Needless to say, the location and character of this terrible place has been the subject of much controversy throughout the centuries. Are the fires in the lake literal or symbolic? If they are literal fires, how can human bodies continue to exist in them forever? If they are symbolic, what do they symbolize? Would God leave such an important figure of speech unexplained, if indeed they are figurative?

The lake of fire is clearly not the same place as *Hades,* or *Sheol,* which terms are often translated as "hell" in the New and Old Testaments, respectively. This is obvious by the fact that the unsaved dead in Hades are first resurrected from Hades and only then cast into the lake of fire (Revelation 20:13-15).

As we have already seen (note discussion on Revelation 1:18; 9:1), Hades is a great abyss in the center of the earth, where the spirits of unsaved men are confined until the "second" resurrection takes place (Revelation 20:5, 6, 13). Furthermore, there are apparently hordes of demonic spirits confined there as well, in compartments of Hades called Abaddon and Tartarus (see discussion on Revelation 9:1-3, 11, 16-18).

Wherever the lake of fire may be, the beast and the false prophet will become its first occupants. Later the Devil and all unbelieving men and women will join them there (Revelation 20:10, 15).

The concept of a place of fire into which ungodly men and women will ultimately be consigned does appear occasionally in the Old Testament. Isaiah says that the Lord will make new heavens and a new earth and, in the same passage, says that as far as "the men that have transgressed against me" are concerned, "their worm shall not die, neither shall their fire be quenched" (Isaiah 66:22, 24). Daniel said, concerning the beast: "I beheld even till the beast was slain, and his body destroyed, and given to the burning flame" (Daniel 7:11).

In the New Testament, the Lord Jesus Christ Himself spoke of this place of "everlasting fire, prepared for the devil and his angels" (Matthew 25:41), into which shall also be cast the unsaved. He spoke of this place as "hell," a place of "fire that never shall be quenched: Where their worm dieth not, and the fire is not quenched" (Mark 9:43-48). The word for "hell" in these passages is not *Hades*, but *gehenna*. This place of unquenchable fire is clearly identical with the "everlasting fire" and the "lake of fire."

Christ also spoke of *gehenna* in a number of other passages as well. "Whosoever shall say, Thou fool, shall be in danger of [*gehenna*] fire" (Matthew 5:22). "Fear him which is able to destroy both soul and body in [*gehenna*]" (Matthew 10:28). See also Matthew 5:30; 18:9; 23:15; Luke 12:5.

There are also a number of other references in the New Testament, to these everlasting fires. For example: "As therefore the tares are gathered and burned in the fire; so shall it be in the end of this world. The Son of man shall send forth his angels, and they shall gather out of his kingdom all things that offend, and them which do iniquity; and shall cast them into a furnace of fire: there shall be wailing and gnashing of teeth" (Matthew 13:40-42). "The chaff he will burn with fire unquenchable" (Luke 3:17).

There is no question, therefore, that the Bible teaches that the ultimate destiny of all the unsaved is to be cast into the "everlasting fire, prepared for the devil and his angels" (Matthew 25:41). Furthermore this fiery environment is to be their eternal prison. Those who are incarcerated there will be "tormented with fire and brimstone in the presence of the holy angels, and in the presence of the Lamb: And the smoke of their torment ascendeth up for ever and ever" (Revelation 14:10, 11).

The beast and the false prophet are thus evidently the very first to be cast into gehenna, the lake of fire. As the greatest and most blasphemous of all human rebels against their Creator, they will be given the distinction of being the first to be separated forever from His presence. Initially they will be taken to gehenna by the holy angels, and in their presence and in the presence of the Lamb whom they have despised, they will be "tormented," a word which comes from a root meaning "placed under foot." Their knees must bow and their tongues confess that Jesus Christ is Lord (Philippians 2:10, 11), and then they "shall be punished with everlasting destruction from the presence of the Lord, and from the glory of his power" (2 Thessalonians 1:9). Following this, in other words, the Lord and His angels will withdraw forever from their presence, leaving them in this unending torment of bitterness and defeat, like "wandering stars, to whom is reserved the blackness of darkness for ever" (Jude 13).

Initially they will be cast alive into the lake of fire. Assuming that the fire is literal fire (and in view of the abundance of Scriptures referring to this fire, as listed above, it would be presumptuous to think otherwise at this point), their bodies will be quickly burned up and they will die, in the physical sense. This is confirmed in Daniel 7:11. "The beast was slain, and his body destroyed, and given to the burning flame."

However, their spirits, like those of all men, are eternal spirits, initially created in the image of God. As unsaved spirits, these wicked men, like the evil spirits of the fallen angels, will then continue to occupy the lake of fire forever. For a thousand years, they will be its sole occupants, and one can well imagine their unspeakable loneliness, the bitter recriminations, the implacable hatred which will consume their thoughts during this period. We will reserve discussion of the nature and location of the fiery lake, however, until the section on Revelation 20:10-15, when all other lost spirits will join them there.

Revelation 19:21.   And the remnant were slain with the sword of him that sat upon the horse, which sword proceeded out of his mouth: and all the fowls were filled with their flesh.

When their great leaders, the supposedly invincible king and his miracle-working seer (the Scriptures call them the beast and the false prophet), were suddenly siezed and carried away from their command post, the armies which had followed them were left in utter dismay and confusion. This is the scene particularly foretold in Luke 21:26, 27. "Men's hearts failing them for fear, and for looking after those things which are coming on the earth: for the powers of heaven shall be shaken. And then shall they see the Son of man coming in a cloud with power and great glory."

Knowing now that all hope was completely gone, the frightened multitudes will await their own fate. They will not have to wait long. A mighty cutting wind sweeps across their ranks, up the 180-mile column of massed men and horses, proceeding like a slicing sword directly from the powerful Word of the majestic Rider as He rides up from Edom. Like grapes trampled in a winepress, the blood bursts from their veins and death is instantaneous. Soon the great trough is flowing with blood and His vesture dips therein while He treads the winepress alone. The spirits of the slain multitudes depart into Hades, there to await the judgment of the great white throne.

This is the great climactic battle of the ages, long foreseen by the prophets. "The Lord at thy right hand shall strike through kings in the day of his wrath. He shall judge among the heathen, he shall fill the places with the dead bodies; he shall wound the heads over many countries" (Psalm 110:5, 6). "The wicked shall be turned into hell [i.e., *sheol*], and all the nations that forget God" (Psalm 9:17).

The language of Isaiah's prophecy is awesome: "Their slain also shall be cast out, and their stink shall come up out of their carcases, and the mountains shall be melted with their blood. . . . The sword of the Lord is filled with blood . . . for the Lord hath a sacrifice in Bozrah, and a great slaughter in the land of Idumea" (Isaiah 34:3-6).

The prophet Jeremiah gives a similar message: "I will call for a sword upon all the inhabitants of the earth, saith the Lord of hosts. . . . The Lord shall roar from on high, and utter his voice from his holy habitation; he shall mightily roar upon his habitation; he shall give a shout, as they that tread the grapes, against all the inhabitants of the earth. . . . Thus saith the Lord of hosts, Behold, evil shall go forth from nation to nation, and a great whirlwind shall be raised up from the coasts of the earth. And the slain of the Lord shall be at that day from one end of the earth even unto the other end of the earth ["earth" in this passage could legitimately, and probably better, be translated "land," as, for example, in Jeremiah 25:20— "the *land* of the Philistines"]: they shall not be lamented, neither gathered, nor buried; they shall be dung upon the ground" (Jeremiah 25:29-33).

Through Zephaniah the Lord had pronounced: "I will bring distress upon men, that they shall walk like blind men, because they have sinned against the Lord: and their blood shall be poured out as dust, and their flesh as the dung. Neither their silver nor their gold shall be able to deliver them in the day of the Lord's wrath; but the whole land shall be devoured by the fire of his jealousy: for he shall make even a speedy riddance of all them that dwell in the land" (Zephaniah 1:17, 18). See also Zephaniah 3:8.

It is apparently at this time, as the conquering Christ comes up from Edom to Jerusalem, smiting all the assembled armies as He comes, that the Jews who have returned to Jerusalem finally will receive Him as their Messiah and Savior. The prophet Zechariah tells us about it: "And in that day will I make Jerusalem a burdensome stone for all people: all that burden themselves with it shall be cut in pieces, though all the people of the earth be gathered together against it. In that day, saith the Lord, I will smite every horse with astonishment, and his rider with madness. . . . And it shall come to pass in that day, that I will seek to destroy all the nations that come against Jerusalem. And I will pour upon the house of David, and upon the inhabitants of Jerusalem, the spirit of grace and of supplications: and they shall look upon me whom they have pierced, and they shall mourn for him, as one mourneth for his only son, and shall be in bitterness for him, as one that is in bitterness for his firstborn. . . . In that day there shall be a fountain opened to the house of David and to the inhabitants of Jerusalem for sin and for uncleanness. . . . They shall call on my name, and I will hear them: I will say, It is my people: and they shall say, The Lord is my God" (Zechariah 12:3, 4, 9, 10; 13:1, 9).

It is probably at this time that He will stand triumphantly on Mount Zion, with the 144,000 chosen Israelites, who will have returned to Jerusalem with their Jewish converts from their sojourn in the wilderness (Revelation 12:6; 14:1). He will also "stand in that day upon the mount of Olives" (Zechariah 14:4), from which He had ascended long ago (Acts 1:9-12), thereby triggering the great earthquake which will open the healing springs and rivers (Zechariah 14:4, 8).

Whether or not He then will continue on up to Armageddon, to complete the trampling of the winepress, as it were, we are not informed, but the awful slaughter is indeed quickly accomplished. Millions upon millions of dead bodies lie fallen upon the ground, awash in their own blood. "For by fire and by his sword will the Lord plead with all flesh: and the slain of the Lord shall be many" (Isaiah 66:16).

Then will the great cloud of ravenous birds swoop down from the heavens, gorging themselves on the flesh and blood of the once high-and-mighty rebels against a long-suffering God. Gradually the earth will be cleansed of its pollution, leaving the bones soon to disintegrate and scatter with the winds.

The terrible scene of carnage and death depicted in these verses may at first offend the sensibilities of those who think of God only as a loving and patronizing grandfather. He is indeed a God of great mercy and forgiveness, not willing that any should perish, but that all should come to repentance. His love for a lost world is so great that as the sacrificial Lamb of God He suffered and died on the cross to save men from their sins.

But when they adamantly refuse His salvation, denying His Word and blaspheming His name, there must one day come a time of reckoning. "To every thing there is a season, and a time to every purpose under the heaven" (Ecclesiastes 3:1). The time is surely coming when God's great purpose for His creation must be brought to its consummation and this requires that it be purged from sin.

20

The Millennial Age

(Revelation 20)

The twentieth chapter of Revelation has been the major battleground of the various basic competing systems of biblical eschatology. In general, the way in which this chapter is interpreted seems to determine how the entire Book of Revelation and, to a large extent, how biblical prophecy as a whole is interpreted. It is in this chapter that the record appears of a thousand-year period when Satan is bound and the world is ruled in righteousness by Christ and the people of God.

But the question is whether, and to what extent, this record should be taken literally. Is this thousand-year period exactly 1,000 years, or is the number merely a symbolic number? Is Satan literally imprisoned and powerless during this time, or is he bound only in a relative sense by the liberating power of the gospel? Is Christ to reign in a direct sense over the earth, on a literal throne, or is this only a figure of speech referring to the eventual conversion of the world to righteousness through the work of the Church and the preaching of the gospel?

Although there are variants within each system, the three major approaches to eschatology are as follows: (1) *Premillennialism,* which takes a fully literal approach to the interpretation of this passage. Premillennialism teaches that Christ's personal return to the earth in glory, as described in Revelation 19, is followed by the literal binding of Satan in Hades and a literal thousand-year reign of Christ and the resurrected saints on the earth. (2) *Postmillennialism,* which takes a partially literal approach, teaching that there will be a literal period of Christian righteousness on the earth. Christ's reign, according to this teaching, will be spiritual, through His Church, which will have won the world to Him through its worldwide ministry of evangelism and teaching under His Great Commission. His personal return to earth will be at the end of the millennium, when the new earth is established. (3) *Amillennialism,* which takes a fully spiritual approach, equating the Millennial Age with the Church Age. Christ's kingdom was established in a symbolic sense on the earth when Satan was defeated and bound by the Lord's substitutionary death, resurrection, and ascension, and with His personal return to earth scheduled at the end of this Church Age for a general judgment.

As pointed out in the Introduction to this commentary, and as consistently followed throughout its expositions, the only proper interpretation is, in our judgment, the fully literal approach. This necessarily entails the premillennial position, as defined above. Further reasons for taking this approach, especially with reference to the pivotal question of the millennium itself, will be developed in this chapter.

The Reign of Christ on Earth

The narration of Chapter 20 follows directly from that of Chapter 19, beginning with the conjunction "and." It is a continuing record of actual events, and the chapter division here is almost misleading. In fact, the emphasis on a literal succession of future historical events in this *Revelation Record* is pointed up by the use of this conjunction (Greek *kai)* to begin almost every verse in Chapters 19 and 20. The chapter structure and content surely have the appearance, at least, of a straightforward record of real events.

Revelation 20:1.   And I saw an angel come down from heaven, having the key of the bottomless pit and a great chain in his hand.

Apparently this event will follow immediately after the destruction of the assembled armies. With all the human rebels and their leaders vanquished, only the demonic hosts remain opposed to the will of the conquering Lamb of God. Now they also must be dealt with and the decision is to bind them in Hades for the time being, along with all the other spirits of rebellious men and angels already there.

As previously noted (see on Revelation 9), various groups of fallen angels had long ago been locked in various compartments in the great cavity at the center of the earth. There were still legions of evil spirits free to do their master's bidding, however, and they had been especially active during the years of the tribulation. They had long feared being cast into the abyss (translated "deep" in Luke 8:31), but finally the dreaded time had come for them also to join their fellows in Hades (note Matthew 8:29). Although these malevolent spirits are not mentioned specifically in this passage, the binding of Satan necessarily assures that all those under his command will be put away as well.

The angel who accomplishes this mission is not identified by John except that he has the key of the bottomless pit. There is a possibility that the angel is Christ Himself, once again assuming the form of an angel (note on Revelation 8:3; 10:1). Christ had uniquely claimed to have the keys of Hades (Revelation 1:18) and it would be fitting for Him to dispatch Satan there directly and personally. On the other hand, He had on at least one occasion (Revelation 9:1) given the key to another angel, and there does seem a contextual intimation that "him that sat upon the horse" (Revelation 19:21) and the "angel come down from heaven" (Revelation 20:1), being mentioned in two successive verses, are probably two different persons. If the angel is not Christ, it may possibly be the great angel Michael, who had long been a particular enemy of Satan's (Jude 9; Revelation 12:7). He and his angels had cast the Devil and his angels to the earth at the middle of the tribulation; it would be appropriate for them now to thrust them all the way to Hades.

In addition to the keys to the abyssal pit, the angel held a great chain in his hand; with which to "bind the strong man" (note Mark 3:27). This chain is obviously not a physical chain, since a spirit could hardly be restrained merely by a chain of iron. Whatever its nature, it will suffice to keep the Devil restrained in Hades throughout the millennium.

Revelation 20:2.   And he laid hold on the dragon, that old serpent, which is the Devil, and Satan, and bound him a thousand years.

There is no doubt as to who is being bound. It is the dragon, the persecutor of Christ and of God's people (Revelation 12:17). It is the same old serpent who had tempted Eve (2 Corinthians 11:3). It is the Devil ("accuser," "slanderer"), the originator of sin (1 John 3:8). It is Satan ("adversary"), the wicked prince of darkness who has tried by every means to destroy the work of Christ (Mark 1:13). He had been identified before by all four of these names (Revelation 12:9), where he also had been acknowledged as leader of a third of the created angels, who had followed him in his rebellion (Revelation 12:4). But now he is finally to be bound.

Here is the first explicit reference to the "thousand years." The most obvious reason for taking this term literally is that there is nothing in the context to indicate otherwise. The word "thousand" or "thousands" is used frequently in the New Testament, but never before in any kind of symbolic sense. Occasionally it is used in an indefinite way, for the purpose of conveying the idea merely of a large number rather than that of a precise count, but never in such a figurative sense as would be required by the amillennial view. If the latter interpretation is followed (that is, if the millennium corresponds to the Church Age), the "thousand years" has already become almost two thousand actual years.

Furthermore, this period is said to be "a thousand years" no less than six times in this passage (Revelation 20:2-7). It is as though John (and the Holy Spirit) wanted us to know as emphatically and plainly as possible that Satan was to be bound, and Christ and the saints to reign on earth, for a real chronological period of a thousand years!

Furthermore, the "binding" of Satan hardly squares with the nonmillennial viewpoint. For the two thousand years of Christianity, it would seem that Satan has been more active than in all previous history, attempting, often very successfully, to hinder and thwart the preaching of the Word and the strengthening and spiritual growth of God's people. "Be sober, be vigilant; because your adversary the devil, as a roaring lion, walketh about, seeking whom he may devour" (1 Peter 5:8). This warning surely gives no suggestion that Satan is presently bound and powerless. Neither are his wicked hosts, with whom we must "wrestle" constantly (Ephesians 6:11-13) in order to "stand against the wiles of the devil."

Revelation 20:3.   And cast him into the bottomless pit, and shut him up, and set a seal upon him, that he should deceive the nations no more, till the thousand years should be fulfilled: and after that he must be loosed a little season.

Somewhere deep in the center of the earth a prison cell has been reserved for a special prisoner, a cell in the remotest recesses of the bottomless pit. The Greek word for this central cavity is *abussos,* meaning literally "without depth" or "bottomless." Modern translations call it the "abyss," but "bottomless" is a more precise derivation. Located at the very middle of the earth, one could not fall any deeper down, and every boundary is a ceiling. It seems that such a place will be Satan's confine during the millennium, as far removed from human beings as is possible to be on this planet. He who is the father of lies (John 8:44) and the deceiver of the whole world (Revelation 12:9) will be absolutely shut off from exercising his wiles (Ephesians 6:11) for a thousand years.

Not only will he be hurled to the center of the earth, but he will be shut up in his cell, with its entrance invincibly sealed so that he cannot even direct his own demonic hosts while so restrained. These latter will presumably likewise be bound in appropriate compartments of Hades or the abyss, as will the spirits of lost men and women, there to await the judgment of the great day. A central cavity no more than ten miles in diameter could easily confine the spirits of all the fallen angels and of all lost humanity through the ages, even if each spirit still required as much space as a human body. It is doubtful whether such a cavity could ever be detected by scientific measurements made by geophysicists on the earth's surface, but the Bible says it is there.

Eventually, toward the close of the millennium, Satan "must" be released for a brief period, apparently because the people born during the millennium must be tested. Incidentally, this is further proof that the binding of Satan is more than a relative semi-restraint on his power by virtue of Christ's victory over him at Calvary. It is true that on the cross the Lord Jesus despoiled principalities and powers (Colossians 2:14, 15) but if this is all that is meant by the millennial binding of the Devil, then what is the meaning of his subsequent unleashing? Is the victory at Calvary to become defeat again? Such an idea is preposterous.

In the meantime, with Satan bound for a thousand years, the world will be freed from its most virulent source of evil. The awful physical trauma through which the earth had just passed during the seven years of its tribulation will not only have purged it of its human demonic corruption but also, in considerable measure, of its natural deformities. Thus it will be prepared to serve appropriately as the physical setting of the great millennial messianic kingdom.

The violent earthquakes and upheavals will have leveled all the polluted cities of a sinful world, the better to facilitate the erection of new, clean, peaceful communities at the beginning of the millennium. These great land movements will also have eliminated the great mountain ranges and islands of the world, filling up the ocean depths and restoring gentle, globally habitable topography and geography all over the world, as it had been in the antediluvian age, before the cataclysmic upheavals of the great Deluge. As Isaiah the prophet had foretold, "Every valley shall be exalted, and every mountain and hill shall be made low: and the crooked shall be made straight, and the rough places plain" (Isaiah 40:4).

This reversal of the topographic upheavals of the Flood, however, will not send waters over the continents again, since much of the waters of the oceans will already have been reelevated above the atmosphere, restoring in some measure the antediluvian "waters above the firmament." The worldwide drought of the first half of the tribulation, the cataclysmic splashdowns of bodies from the heavens during the trumpet judgments and the intensified solar radiations of the bowl judgments will all have contributed to the translation of vast quantities of water vapor far into the skies.

Quite probably, the immense tectonic movements, eruptions, and landslides may also have trapped vast quantities of water beneath fresh sedimentary and volcanic deposits, reinstating in partial degree the primeval pressurized reservoirs of "the great deep," facilitating the birth of copious artesian springs, including one which will feed the vast river emerging from the millennial temple in Jerusalem (Ezekiel 47:1-12; Zechariah 14:8).

Thus the seas of the millennial world will be relatively narrow and shallow once again, as in primeval days. Furthermore, the restoration of the vapor canopy should, in large measure, restore the globally pleasant warm climate of the antediluvian period to the earth again. No longer will great atmospheric movements generate violent rainstorms, blizzards, hurricanes, and tornadoes, because the uniform temperatures of the global greenhouse will inhibit air mass movements of more than local extent.

In the original world, the only rains were gentle mists, from localized daily evaporation and precipitation (Genesis 2:5), keeping the world everywhere at comfortable temperatures and humidities, and supporting an abundance of plant and animal life in all regions of the globe. There were no deserts or ice caps or uninhabitable mountain heights. It was all "very good" (Genesis 1:31). The cataclysm of the great Flood destroyed that beautiful world, but the global upheavals of the great tribulation will restore it, at least in measure.

For example, note Joel's prophecy: "Fear not, O land; be glad and rejoice: for the Lord will do great things. Be not afraid, ye beasts of the field: for the pastures of the wilderness do spring, for the tree beareth her fruit, the fig tree and the vine do yield their strength. Be glad then, ye children of Zion, and rejoice in the Lord your God: for he hath given you the former rain moderately, and he will cause to come down for you the rain, the former rain, and the latter rain in the first month" (Joel 2:21-23; see also Hosea 6:3, and Zechariah 10:1).

The redistribution of earth's topography and restoration of its vapor canopy will soon result in an elimination of many, if not all, of its wastelands and deserts: "The wilderness and the solitary place shall be glad for them; and the desert shall rejoice, and blossom as the rose. . . . for in the wilderness shall waters break out, and streams in the desert. And the parched ground shall become a pool, and the thirsty land springs of water" (Isaiah 35:1-7; note also Isaiah 30:23; 32:15; 51:3; Ezekiel 34:26; 36:33-35; etc.).

Somehow there will also come a great healing of the lands and waters of the earth. Before the great Flood, the soils were rich in all needed nutrients, and the drinking waters all came pure and fresh from artesian springs fed from deep underground reservoirs. The destruction of these deep fountains and the devastating land erosion of the great Flood largely destroyed God's primeval terrestrial ecology, leaving the lands depleted and waters polluted. Originally all animals, as well as man, were to derive nourishment only from plant foods (Genesis 1:29, 30), but under the far more rigorous conditions of the postdiluvian environment, God authorized man to eat animal flesh as well (Genesis 9:2-4). Evidently for the same reason many animals also had to become carnivorous.

These conditions were further aggravated during the long centuries after the Flood, with the lands becoming further impoverished and the waters further contaminated, requiring increasingly great expenditures on fertilization and purification. The traumatic upheavals of the tribulation period had brought these conditions to a climax, with devastating famine conditions and with terrestrial waters so depleted and poisoned that all the animals of the sea had perished. Had such conditions been allowed to persist much longer, all life on earth would soon have become impossible.

In some marvelous way, however, God will use the physical convulsions of that awful period of purging to cleanse the lands and waters of the earth as well as its moral and spiritual climate. Possibly the tectonic and volcanic upheavals, and perhaps even the atmospheric bombardments, will implant new supplies of needed nutrients and trace elements in the soils. Even the multitudes of dead animals and plants in the lands and oceans, as well as the skeletons of the millions of dead men and horses at Armageddon and elsewhere, may well become fertilizing agents for the lands as their remains are scattered far and wide.

The unprecedented global earthquakes and eruptions will trigger vast and violent landslides and showers of dirt and rocks, entrapping tremendous volumes of ocean waters beneath great overburdens of solid materials which will rapidly become pressurized, lithified, and partially sealed.

This will likely produce at last two important effects. In the first place, the sea bottoms will be raised to higher elevations than at present, compensating for the great losses of water caused by the restoration of the atmospheric canopy and by the entrapment of vast volumes beneath the huge landslides and rock showers. The entire crust itself will, to some unknown extent, have shifted and slipped over the earth's mantle, rearranging the various continental plates to a more nearly uniform distribution of land and sea surface areas, but with relatively greater land areas than at present.

Second, this extensive rearrangement of topography and formation of large pressurized subterranean water pockets will facilitate the development of a new terrestrial system of springs and spring-fed rivers, the waters of which will be purified by the processes of heating and percolation. "I will open rivers in high places, and fountains in the midst of the valleys: I will make the wilderness a pool of water, and the dry land springs of water" (Isaiah 41:18).

Whether or not the ocean population of fishes and other marine organisms will somehow be replenished is uncertain. The second bowl judgment (Revelation 16:3) had caused the death of "every living soul . . . in the sea," so that at least those fishes requiring a marine environment had apparently been eliminated from the so-called food chain. The third bowl judgment had similarly affected the fresh waters, except that no reference was made to death of fresh-water organisms (Revelation 16:4) so that probably many of these had survived, and they would be more important for the future millennial economy.

In the description of the great millennial river in Jerusalem, for example, the following intriguing statement appears: "And it shall come to pass, that every thing that liveth, which moveth, whithersoever the rivers shall come, shall live: and there shall be a very great multitude of fish, because these waters shall come thither: for they shall be healed; and every thing shall live whither the river cometh" (Ezekiel 47:9). This river will emerge from the new temple (Ezekiel 47:1) and may well contain health-giving minerals acquired from source beds deep under the city. Perhaps also it may be artificially purified and fortified as it issues from its spring in the temple, using the knowledge and ingredients obtained from the accumulated research of the greatest minds of the ages, now redeemed and perhaps instructed by Christ Himself.

The scenario inferred in the foregoing is bound to be incomplete and may well be incorrect in many respects. Further study and research on these fascinating possibilities are in order, but the most important point is to realize that God is somehow going to revitalize this tired old planet and make it ready for the glorious kingdom of Christ on earth.

And, in order to do all this, the god of this present age, the old dragon, Satan, must be completely restrained from continuing his nefarious and baleful influence over the earth. He must be bound, and then the dominion usurped by him can be unbound. "No man can enter into a strong man's house, and spoil his goods, except he will first bind the strong man; and then he will spoil his house" (Mark 3:27). "Because the creature [better translated as "creation"] itself also shall be delivered from the bondage of corruption into the glorious liberty of the children of God" (Romans 8:21).

Revelation 20:4.   And I saw thrones, and they sat upon them, and judgment was given unto them: and I saw the souls of them that were beheaded for the witness of Jesus, and for the word of God, and which had not worshipped the beast, neither his image, neither had received his mark upon their foreheads, or in their hands; and they lived and reigned with Christ a thousand years.

Four times in this chapter, John says: "And I saw" (verses 1, 4, 11, 12), thus stressing that he was an eyewitness of these amazing events which are to come. Immediately after he saw the beast and the false prophet cast into the lake of fire and Satan cast into the bottomless pit, he saw a vast array of thrones waiting to receive their kingly occupants. Then, as he watched, "they" sat upon them and the authority to act as rulers and judges was assigned to them.

But who are these kingly judges, and who are they to judge? In terms of the narrative just preceding, there can be only one answer as to the identity of the judges. They are the same saints, dressed in fine white linen, appropriate not only for the wedding feast but also for judicial robes, who comprised the armies accompanying Christ as He returned to earth (Revelation 19:8, 14, 19). All those who had been redeemed by His blood, resurrected from the grave, raptured into His presence, and evaluated for their rewards at His judgment seat will apparently be assigned individual thrones of authority and judgment, unless they are deemed undeserving of any reward at all (1 Corinthians 3:11-15).

This remarkable situation is promised in many Scriptures, both directly and in parables. "Do ye not know that the saints shall judge the world?" (1 Corinthians 6:2). "Judgment was given to the saints of the most High; and the time came that the saints possessed the kingdom" (Daniel 7:22).

The twelve apostles have already been assigned their own specific jurisdiction. "When the Son of man shall sit in the throne of his glory, ye also shall sit upon twelve thrones, judging the twelve tribes of Israel" (Matthew 19:28). Other realms of authority will be assigned in proportion to faithfulness, according to the parable of the pounds (Luke 19:11-27) and the parable of the talents (Matthew 25:14-30).

Even in the introduction to the Book of Revelation, this future role of the saints is implied: "[He] loved us, and washed us from our sins in his own blood, and hath made us kings and priests unto God and his Father" (Revelation 1:5, 6; 5:9, 10). Furthermore, such authority is to be executed rigidly, conforming to the "iron scepter" principle already noted (see Revelation 2:26, 27) under the direct command of Christ Himself (Revelation 19:15). In fact, as the verse under discussion plainly says: this reign of the saints will be with Christ.

Nor will the tribulation saints be forgotten in this assignment of jurisdiction, even though they were not among those resurrected and raptured at the beginning of the tribulation. They are, in fact, accorded very special recognition, in view of the unique circumstances which they have suffered. They had maintained a faithful witness for the Lord Jesus and the truth of His Word under some of the most severe difficulties ever experienced. All official or semiofficial toleration of Christianity by the governments of the nations had been withdrawn soon after the rapture, and those who dared to accept Christ had very soon faced fierce persecution everywhere. Many had been slain even in the early years of the tribulation (Revelation 6:9). Then a systematic extermination of believers had become the official policy of the world government when the beast acquired total power at the middle of the tribulation. Those who refused to worship the beast and receive his mark had been relentlessly hunted and executed.

John now saw the "souls" of all these who had died for their faith, just as he had seen the souls of some of them under the heavenly altar near the beginning of the tribulation. As each had been martyred during the tribulation, the soul of each had been translated to the heavenly temple, there to await *this* moment!

Finally now, they also participate in the glorious resurrection of the dead. They "lived"! This simple declaration is the climax of all their sufferings, and far more than compensates for all they had endured as they witnessed for Christ and His Word. They had cried "How long?" and now their blood had been avenged (Revelation 6:10).

The statement that they "lived" can only refer to the resurrection of their bodies. Amillennialists like to interpret this as referring to a resurrection of the soul at the time of conversion, but this is obviously a case of forced exegesis. Souls do not die and, hence, cannot be resurrected. The souls of these martyrs all along had been very much alive and aware and able even to speak, but now their bodies also "lived again" (v. 5), so that they also could reign with Christ. The resurrection thus includes the resurrection of Christ as the firstfruits, then the resurrection of those who had died before His second coming in the air, and finally the resurrection of those who die between the time He comes to the air and the time He finally returns to earth.

Thus will these tribulation saints also be installed on millennial thrones with appropriate spheres of authority, there to reign over the earth with Christ for a thousand years. In Revelation 5:10 the throng assembled at the heavenly throne had anticipated this coming privilege and responsibility, singing: "Thou hast made us unto our God kings and priests: and we shall reign over the earth."

The declarative statement in this verse of the millennial reign of Christ and His saints is sparse in details concerning the nature of that reign and conditions in the world at that future time. Such information has already been provided, however, in previous passages of both Old and New Testaments, so is not repeated here by John. One very vital item of information *is* given here for the first time, however, namely, the duration of this period. *That* bit of information is given here no less than six times, in fact, so there should be no doubt that this wonderful future "dispensation," also known by some as the "mediatorial kingdom," will endure for a thousand years.

The period will apparently be initiated by an event known as the judgment of the nations, described in Matthew 25:31-46. Its chronology is clearly just following the tribulation. "Immediately after the tribulation of those days . . . they shall see the Son of man coming in the clouds of heaven with power and great glory" (Matthew 24:29, 30). Then, in the next chapter, the narrative part of this great Olivet discourse continues: "When the Son of man shall come in his glory, and all the holy angels with him, then shall he sit upon the throne of his glory: And before him shall be gathered all nations [or, "Gentiles," which is the same Greek word, *ethnos*]: and he shall separate them one from another, as a shepherd divideth his sheep from the goats" (Matthew 25:31, 32).

The account in Revelation has given us the further information that, before this assumption of His glorious earthly throne, Christ has already slain the armies massed at Armageddon and resurrected His tribulation martyrs. Thus the only ones left on earth are those followers of the beast who were not in the armies at Armageddon and who had not already perished in the plagues, as well as those who had managed somehow to escape the beast's executioners while still refusing to receive his mark. These are evidently the goats and the sheep, respectively.

These will all be gathered to His throne from the ends of the earth by the holy angels (Matthew 24:31). There will not be too many, though the exact number is unknown. "Behold, the Lord maketh the earth empty, and maketh it waste, and turneth it upside down, and scattereth abroad the inhabitants thereof. . . . Therefore hath the curse devoured the earth, and they that dwell therein are desolate: therefore the inhabitants of the earth are burned, and few men left" (Isaiah 24:1-6).

Superficially the basis of the judgment of these survivors of the tribulation period may seem legalistic, but actually it is very realistic in the context of the tribulation. Those who were adjudged as "goats" had refused succor "to the least of these my brethren," when they had suffered for lack of food or drink or clothing, or were even languishing in prison, no doubt awaiting execution, either because they were afraid to help or because they agreed with their persecutors, or both. Both attitudes characterized people who either had, or would have, if the beast's minions had reached them, received the dread "mark" of the beast. Consequently, in view of the dire warning of Revelation 14:9-11, they must be condemned. No doubt, they, like their compatriots at Armageddon, will then be slain, with their souls despatched for a time to Hades. Ultimately, these must depart into "everlasting fire, prepared for the devil and his angels" (Matthew 25:41).

The "sheep," on the other hand, had been both compassionate and courageous, rendering such help as they could to these persecuted "brethren" of the Son of man, at the risk of their own lives. Such people would undoubtedly have refused the mark of the beast if his emissaries had reached them, and thus had exhibited that attitude of faith toward their Creator and His Word which either had resulted in their acceptance of Him as their Lord and Savior or would have as soon as the true gospel of Christ was made known to them.

The immediate destiny of these, however, was not departure to heaven, but to "inherit the kingdom prepared for you from the foundation of the world" (Matthew 25:34). Eventually, of course, their great faith, which had manifested itself in such gracious and courageous works, like the great men and women of faith catalogued in Hebrews 11, would assure also their entrance into "life eternal" (Matthew 25:46).

The "brethren" of whom the Lord had spoken could only be the persecuted tribulation martyrs, both Jew and Gentile. Jesus said: " . . . my brethren are these which hear the word of God, and do it" (Luke 8:21). Jesus called His disciples "my brethren" (Matthew 12:49; John 20:17), but never the Jews, as a nation. Prophetically He said: "I will declare thy name unto my brethren, in the midst of the church will I sing praise unto thee" (Hebrews 2:12).

The "goats," no doubt, at this time are composed almost exclusively of Gentiles (hence the "judgment of the Gentiles"), since the nation Israel has been undergoing its "day of Jacob's trouble," with the final result of its complete national conversion at the glorious return of Christ (Zechariah 12:10; 13:1; Romans 11:26). These redeemed of Israel will also, of course, at this time "inherit the kingdom," and thus enter the millennium, ready to enjoy the fulfillment of all God's ancient promises to their fathers.

From each nation, with Israel at the head, will thus come a remnant to rebuild their devastated countries. Even though the initial population of each nation will be small, the conditions and incentives will be present to encourage large families, and the populations will grow rapidly. Furthermore, antediluvian longevity will be restored. "There shall be no more thence an infant of days, nor an old man that hath not filled his days: for the child shall die an hundred years old; but the sinner being an hundred years old shall be accursed" (Isaiah 65:20). This may be accomplished partially by the restoration of antediluvian climatological and agricultural conditions and partially by new technologies developed by millennial scientists. In fact, scientific and technological research will thrive as never before, as mankind seeks as never before to fulfill its primeval commission to "subdue the earth" (Genesis 1:28).

415

Israel, of course, will be the chief nation of the world during the millennium. "And many nations shall come, and say, Come, and let us go up to the mountain of the Lord, and to the house of the God of Jacob; and he will teach us of his ways, and we will walk in his paths; for the law shall go forth of Zion, and the word of the Lord from Jerusalem" (Micah 4:2).

Other nations will be expected to honor Israel and to center their worship there: "And it shall come to pass, that every one that is left of all the nations which came against Jerusalem shall even go up from year to year to worship the King, the Lord of hosts, and to keep the feast of tabernacles. And it shall be, that whoso will not come up of all the families of the earth unto Jerusalem to worship the King, the Lord of hosts, even upon them shall be no rain" (Zechariah 14:16, 17). A great temple will be established in Jerusalem, as described in Ezekiel 40-46, and a form of the ancient worship instituted again, complete with priestly orders and sacrificial animal offerings. The worship will not be mere ritual, however, as it often was in pre-Christian Israel. "Yea, every pot in Jerusalem and in Judah shall be holiness unto the Lord of hosts: and all they that sacrifice shall come and take of them and seethe therein" (Zechariah 14:21).

Such animal sacrifices had been, of course, set aside after the death and resurrection of Christ, for "he had offered one sacrifice for sins for ever" (Hebrews 10:12). During the Christian dispensation, the gospel of salvation by grace through faith in Christ needed no animal sacrifices either as evidence of faith or as aid to faith. In the millennium, however, it will be different. It will be easy to believe in Christ—in fact almost impossible *not* to believe. No longer will one suffer ridicule or persecution if he takes a stand for Christ, nor will he ever be led astray by evolutionary teachings in the schools or by overt temptations to sin by his peers.

In every dispensation, salvation is offered only by the grace of God on the basis of the substitutionary death of Christ for sin. Before His first coming people had given evidence of their faith in God's promised redemption by offering sacrificial animals in atonement for their sins. In that case, the sacrifices had served both as a significant aid to faith and as a testimony to their faith. Even in the Christian age "faith without works is dead" (James 2:20), but that faith is exercised in the person and finished work of Christ, as confirmed and recorded in the Holy Scriptures of the New Testament.

In the Millennial Age, with the glorified Christ and His resurrected and reigning saints personally present and with Satan and his hosts out of the way, there will be no room whatsoever for intellectual doubt as to the deity of Christ and the truth of His Word. Nevertheless, salvation will still require a *personal* faith and commitment to Christ and, more than ever, the genuineness of such faith must be evidenced by works. It may well be that this is at least part of the reason for the reinstitution of animal sacrifices. In the days of His humiliation, it requires strong faith to believe in His coming glorification. In the days of His glory, it will be difficult to remember and believe in His humiliation and death, and yet it is still as important as ever that men and women understand and believe that they are sinners and can only be saved through the substitutionary death of Christ for their sins. Thus, the animal sacrifices will be a memorial and reminder of the great saving work of Christ, and thus will also serve both as an aid and evidence of faith.

Revelation 20:5.   But the rest of the dead lived not again until the thousand years were finished. This is the first resurrection.

The "rest of the dead," of course, refers to the unsaved men and women whose souls are imprisoned in Hades. This statement (that they "lived not again") makes it crystal clear that the "resurrection" of which these verses speak is a bodily resurrection. At the end of the millennium, Hades delivers up these spirits so that they also live again in the body (v. 13). Their souls had never ceased to have conscious existence (see for example, Luke 16:23, as well as Revelation 6:9, 10). So the phrase "live again" would be quite meaningless except in terms of the body.

The resurrection of the unsaved will be the "resurrection unto damnation," which was distinguished as a separate resurrection from the "resurrection of life" by the Lord Jesus Christ in John 5:29. He also implied that "the resurrection of the just" was a distinct event (Luke 14:14). Here, finally, it is revealed that the "first resurrection" precedes the second by a thousand years.

This resurrection of the souls of the tribulation martyrs thus completes the first resurrection. In the final sentence of this verse, the word "is" appears in italics (KJV) indicating its absence in the original. The sense of the sentence is simply, "This *completes* the first resurrection."

The word "resurrection" in Greek is *anastasis,* meaning literally "standing again." It is used forty times in the New Testament, and always refers most naturally to a bodily rising from the dead (John 11:24; Acts 4:33). There is certainly no warrant for taking it to mean something else in this passage.

The "first resurrection" does occur in more than one stage, according to 1 Corinthians 15:20-23. The resurrection of the dead began with Christ Himself, as the "firstfruits of them that slept," followed immediately by "many bodies of the saints" which "came out of the graves after his resurrection" (Matthew 27:52, 53). Next comes the rapture, when "the dead in Christ shall rise" along with the living saints (1 Thessalonians 4:16, 17). At the middle of the tribulation the two witnesses rise (Revelation 11:11) and now finally all the rest of the tribulation martyrs.

Revelation 20:6.   Blessed and holy is he that hath part in the first resurrection: on such the second death hath no power, but they shall be priests of God and of Christ, and shall reign with him a thousand years.

No matter which stage of the first resurrection one may participate in, he is thereby assured that his future life will be one of blessedness and holiness. He may have experienced the pains of death, but these will all be forgotten in the glorious resurrection, and he will never die again. The awful second death which awaits the unsaved at the "second" resurrection cannot touch him any more than it could the body of the risen Christ (Revelation 1:18).

On the other hand, the obverse side of this fifth of Revelation's beatitudes suggests that the second death *does* have the "authority" in the case of all those who do not participate in the first resurrection. Their future is one of misery and corruption, forever, in the lake of fire, rather than one of eternal blessedness and holiness in the fellowship of Christ.

Not only will the saints reign with Christ a thousand years, but also they will be His priests (Revelation 1:6), thus directing both the civil government and spiritual instruction for the millennial populations. Christ is High Priest, as well as King of kings, and all the resurrected saints will exercise varied religious and political functions under His supreme command throughout the millennium, in accord with the faithfulness of their service in this present life.

The detailed manner and variety of these administrations is yet to be revealed. The resurrected saints have their citizenship in heaven, not on earth (Philippians 3:20), and it is likely that once they have been awarded the heavenly "mansion" prepared for them by Christ (John 14:2, 3), they will never again reside on earth— at least not until their heavenly city descends from heaven to the renovated earth at the end of the millennium (Revelation 21:2). Presumably at proper times, however, they will appear on earth to exercise prescribed duties with respect to their earthly charges. For example, the resurrected apostles of the Lord have been promised that they will be assigned earthly thrones from which they will judge the twelve tribes of Israel (Luke 22:28-30). It seems also that the resurrected King David may be placed over the entire nation of Israel (Ezekiel 37:24, 25; Jeremiah 30:9; Hosea 3:5). Some will be assigned jurisdiction over ten cities, some over five (Luke 19:17, 19). Apparently there will be a hierarchy of authority assigned to the saints in either civil or religious duties or both.

It may appear at first that the hosts of resurrected saints, including all the redeemed of all the ages, will so far outnumber the depleted population of the earth at the beginning of the millennium, that there will be more "kings and priests" than "subjects." Although the Scriptures give very little specific information about this intriguing topic, there are a number of factors at least to be considered. In the first place, not all the saints will receive a reward. Many will "scarcely be saved" and "shall suffer loss" (1 Corinthians 3:15), so that the opportunity they might have had for fruitful service in the millennial age will be given to others (Luke 19:24-26). Thus there may even be many of the raptured and glorified saints who will still themselves need some measure of supervision and guidance during at least the first years of the millennium. Those who had attained a higher state of spiritual knowledge and effectiveness in the days of their flesh may well serve as teachers and leaders for those who died as "babes in Christ," at least for the early years when the human population on earth is still low.

Furthermore their ministries will be needed for all those who had died while still too young (many men still in the fetal state) to have even reached the so-called "age of accountability." They must surely be allowed to grow to maturity somehow, both physically and spiritually, and many of the more mature saints may well have assignments to train and tutor these. Possibly the Lord may assign many of these specific duties to godly redeemed women in the heavenly city.

There is no way to know precisely how many resurrected saints will be there in heaven in these glorious days to come during the millennium, but a reasonable guess might be about 4 billion. This is roughly equal to the present population of the world and is 10 percent of what seems to be a plausible figure for the total number of men and women who have lived since Adam (probably about 40 billion). Since the large majority of people die in an unsaved condition (Matthew 7:13, 14), the 10 percent figure seems at least reasonable.

Whatever the number may be, it will undoubtedly be much larger than terrestrial populations at the beginning of the millennium. However, the conditions favorable to human fertility and longevity will have been restored, as discussed earlier, and it will not take many years before God's primeval command to "fill the earth" (Genesis 1:28; 9:1) will be essentially accomplished, with numbers of people like "the sand of the sea" (verse 8). There will by *that* time be such an abundance of people on earth as indeed to provide adequate challenge for *all* the saints, both those who were prepared for such responsibilities at the beginning of the thousand years and those who had required further training during its early years.

There is one other intriguing possibility. There exists "an innumerable company of angels" (Hebrews 12:22) and these were created to be "ministering spirits, sent forth to minister for them who shall be heirs of salvation" (Hebrews 1:14). This relationship presumably will continue forever, since there is no intimation in Scripture that it will be changed in the new earth.

Many of these angels have rebelled against God, following Satan, and these will all be consigned to everlasting fire (Matthew 25:41). Those who had remained faithful to their calling, however, and who thus will still be subservient to the will of Christ, will probably also be under the direction of those who will "reign with Him." This is likely the meaning of the rather cryptic reference in 1 Corinthians 6:3. "Know ye not that we shall judge angels? how much more things that pertain to this life?"

Gog and Magog

One of the most amazing commentaries on the fallen human nature to be found in all the Word of God is right here in this passage. After one thousand years of a perfect human environment, with an abundance of material provisions and spiritual instruction for everyone, no crime, no war, no external temptation to sin, with the personal presence of all the resurrected saints and even of Christ Himself, and with Satan and all his demons bound in the abyss, there are still a multitude of unsaved men and women on earth who are ready to rebel against the Lord the first time they get a chance.

Revelation 20:7.   And when the thousand years are expired, Satan shall be loosed out of his prison.

Note that Satan does not escape from his prison. The Lord Jesus Christ is on the throne of the cosmos, with all power in heaven and earth belonging to Him. Even though the saints are reigning with Him, it is His authority which they exercise, and Satan is firmly bound in his prison, utterly helpless to interfere.

Even though King David, in his resurrection body, may have been assigned immediate jurisdiction over Israel (Ezekiel 34:23, 24), the Son of David, Jesus Christ, actually rules over the whole world from the throne of David in Zion, and will do so for ever (Isaiah 9:7; Luke 1:31-33; Revelation 11:15; Isaiah 2:2-4). He will be in absolute control, ruling all nations with a rod of iron (Psalm 2:6-9).

And yet, according to verse 3 of this chapter, Satan must be loosed a little season. During the wonderful Millennial Age, any crime and overt wickedness will have been rigidly prevented. Although ample time will be provided for such flagrant sinners to repent, they likely will be exposed to capital punishment if they have not done so by age 100 (Isaiah 65:20).

Furthermore, everyone will be well exposed to the truth concerning the Lord Jesus Christ as their Creator, Redeemer, and King. They will probably be able to see Him personally if they wish, as well as the glorified saints who are more directly accessible to them as their own kings and priests. They will be well instructed in the necessity of substitutionary sacrifice for salvation from sin, as each nation must regularly send delegates to Jerusalem to offer memorial animal sacrifices, keeping ever before them the remembrance that, long ago, their great King in Jerusalem had Himself borne their sins in His own body as He died on the tree of Calvary to save their souls (1 Peter 2:24).

And yet, with all these privileges, with every possible incentive to believe on His name and to love and serve Him, there will still be multitudes who will reject Him in their hearts. These will not be those who first enter the millennium, of course, but will come from the generations of those who follow them. These, for the most part, will refrain from overt acts of sin and rebellion, but this restraint for many will be one of fear, not love.

To men and women who have been born and raised in such an ideal environment, so that all they have ever known is peace, prosperity, and righteousness, the stories told them about the former ages by their parents and by their heavenly rulers and teachers will sound increasingly fanciful as the centuries go by. Soon those ancient times will begin to seem glamorous, with their supposed freedom and excitement, and many in the younger generations will begin inwardly to resent the constraints under which they must live. Even though Satan is bound, and there are no external temptations to doubt God or to disobey His will, they are not innocent, like Adam and Eve in the garden. Their hearts are naturally "deceitful and desperately wicked" (Jeremiah 17:9), simply by virtue of genetic inheritance, and they must consciously accept Christ as personal Savior if they are to be saved just as their ancestors did. With so little contact with overt sin and with provision of every material need so easily available, this may be even more difficult for them than it had been for their forebears.

It is apparently for such reasons that the Devil, and presumably all his hosts, must be released for a little season. All these millennial generations, all of which are living, must also be confronted with a clearcut choice. Will they trust their great Savior and King in Jerusalem, or will they, when finally they have the opportunity, choose sin as their life-style and Satan as their god?

This will be mankind's last and greatest test. In former ages, men had used their environmental problems, such as poverty, pornography, war, intellectual pressures, and sickness as excuses for rejecting Christ. But with all these suppressed for almost a thousand years, there is no more excuse but their own sinful hearts, and these must be exposed.

Revelation 20:8.   And shall go out to deceive the nations which are in the four quarters of the earth, Gog and Magog, to gather them together to battle: the number of whom is as the sand of the sea.

Satan has always been the great deceiver and even a thousand years in the bottomless pit will not change either his character or goals one iota. Once again, even after all his defeats, he will set out to destroy God, using the same old strategy of deception to enlist his human allies. This time, his prospects are actually greater than they have ever been, because the human population will have reached its highest number in history. Mankind will finally, as a result of a thousand years of longevity and perfect environment, "fill the earth," and the population will be practically innumerable, like the sand of the sea.

But even the old Devil may be surprised at his success. He will find the various nations much as he had known them for thousands of years, but more ripe for his deceptions than they had ever been before. Certain of the nations had begun to neglect their duty to go to Jerusalem for the feast of tabernacles, for example, and had been punished by a serious drought in their lands. Egypt had even experienced a plague (Zechariah 14:16-19).

As Satan dispatches his demonic emissaries once again to the human kings of the earth, he will be delighted at his quick and wide success (compare Revelation 16:13-16). No doubt, the demonic surge will be resisted by the resurrected saints serving as kings and priests to the nations, but not even they will be able to stem the wholesale defections of the world's multitudes, eager for a chance to escape the bondage of righteousness. The age-old deceptions will again accomplish their deadly mission and gullible masses will soon return to the evolutionary faith of their fathers, rejecting all the incontrovertible proofs that God is Creator and Savior, preferring to hope that the universe itself is the only eternal entity, out of which had emerged both God and Satan.

Needing human leadership for his demon-possessed armies, Satan will find the most receptive minds and hands among those ancient enemies of the Lord, Gog and Magog. Babylon, of course, had been completely destroyed just before the millennium, but the great northern kingdom of Magog had again become strong and prosperous, like the other nations, and was ready to take the lead once again in opposing God.

Magog, grandson of Noah and second son of Japheth, had founded the great kingdom north of the Black and Caspian Seas which became known as Scythia and eventually as Russia. His name seems to have been faintly preserved in the name of the ancient nation of Georgia. Similarly, Magog's brothers, Meshech and Tubal, who also migrated into these northern regions, are probably still slightly recognizable in the names Moskva (Moscow) and Tobalsk.

There is little in the Scriptures about the histories of these people, except Ezekiel 38 and 39, and not much light yet from archaeology. But everything that is known does point to the complex of peoples who would become the progenitors of the great Russian empire of the latter days. The two key chapters describing Israel's invasion by Gog and Magog and their cataclysmic destruction have already been discussed in Chapter 6.

Because of the reappearance at this point in Scripture of the striking names Gog and Magog, it is not surprising that many commentators interpret this section of Revelation 20 as the same event narrated in Ezekiel 38 and 39. However, the two have practically nothing in common except the names. In Ezekiel the armies attacking Israel are from several specifically named countries surrounding Israel; in Revelation, they come from all over the earth. In Ezekiel they are destroyed by a great earthquake and volcanic eruption, in Revelation by fire from God out of heaven. In Ezekiel, the destruction is followed by a seven-month burial and a seven-year bonfire of weapons. In Revelation, it is followed by the renovation of the earth and the last judgment.

We have already noted the reasons for believing that the events in Ezekiel 38 and 39 occur near the beginning of the tribulation period and thus must have taken place over a thousand years earlier than the battle of Gog and Magog described in Revelation 20. Even though most of the Magogites (or Russians) had been destroyed during the tribulation, with their great commander Gog buried with his armies in Israel even before the tribulation, there had been a godly remnant who had been spared, the same as in the other nations.

The descendants of these, however, had multiplied rapidly, so that Russia had soon again become a great millennial nation, possibly even readopting its ancestral name of Magog. One can suppose that after several generations the younger Magogites had begun to rankle over the history of the destruction of their fore-bears, and especially to resent the Israelites, both because it was in Israel that Gog's empire had been destroyed and because the Israelites now occupied the premier place among the nations. The armies of the other nations had been de-stroyed in Israel later, at Armageddon, and now their descendants also began to share the same resentment.

But the new Magogites and their new Gog were the readiest of all to rebel. Therefore Satan and his demons will use them to organize and lead one last army against the Lord.

Revelation 20:9. **And they went up on the breadth of the earth, and compassed the camp of the saints about, and the beloved city: and fire came down from God out of heaven, and devoured them.**

The narrative does not say how long a period of time will be occupied with this final rebellion, only that it begins *after* the thousand years. The pace of the record at least suggests that it all transpires quickly. Once Satan is released, his deceptions will find quick and ready acceptance in disobedient minds and hearts throughout the world. Gog and Magog will send their agents everywhere, as will Satan, probably through the mechanism of demon-possessed men and women. During the millennium no weapons of warfare will have been allowed (Micah 4:3), but it will no doubt be a time of unprecedented scientific and technological ad-vance, so it may not take long, once circumstances allow, for the rebels to devise means by which they think they can quickly conquer the great capital, Jerusalem the beloved, where Christ is reigning with David and the apostles.

In great multitudes they will swarm from every direction to surround the "camp of the saints" as well as the city of Jerusalem. The word for "camp" is also translated "castle" or "army," and refers to an organized structure or system for military defense. These "saints" are the same who had come from heaven with Christ to reign with him on earth. Evidently, when the dimensions of the human rebellion reach global proportions, all of the redeemed and reigning saints will join their Lord at the beloved city of the great King. Presumably the people of Israel will remain faithful to their Messiah this time, perhaps also godly remnants from the other nations as well. All who are faithful to the Lord, whether people in their natural bodies, resurrected saints, or holy angels, will be gathered together in or near Jerusalem. Surrounding them for miles in all directions, perhaps even above them in hovering aircraft, the innumerable multitudes of Gog and Magog, instigated and energized by the great Adversary of the ages, will prepare one final great assault on Christ and His saints.

And now, finally, after ages of grace and patience and mercy, God's long-suffering comes to an end. When mankind is so quick to rebel against Him even after a thousand years of an all-but-perfect world, providing every material blessing and even the personal presence of Christ Himself, there is nothing else that the Lord can do to encourage and draw men to receive Himself as Savior. With all the greatest gifts of His love repudiated, and with multitudes choosing to follow Satan instead, God will finally ring down the curtain.

Suddenly it will seem that the very heavens are on fire. "For, behold, the day cometh, that shall burn as an oven; and all the proud, yea, and all that do wickedly, shall be stubble: and the day that cometh shall burn them up, saith the Lord of hosts, that it shall leave them neither root nor branch" (Malachi 4:1). A falling ring of fire will surround the holy city and the legions of the saints, radiating outward in all directions until every last unregenerate human being is engulfed and burned to death in the descending and surging sea of flames.

This is but a foretaste of what will shortly become the rebels' eternal fate after their bodies are resurrected and cast into the lake of fire. In the meantime, their disembodied souls will commingle for a brief interlude with the raging demons of Satan, whose last and greatest effort to dethrone God has terminated in abject failure. Even after their release from the pit and their easy seduction of the multitudes on earth, these principalities and powers of darkness will still find themselves confused and powerless in the presence of the great King.

Perhaps for a very brief moment all these lost spirits, both human and demonic, will look to their master Satan for some desperately brilliant stroke of diabolical cunning which can deliver them all from the terrible fate which seems about to overwhelm them forever. If so, they will realize soon enough that they have been merely the willing dupes of the great deceiver, who had in turn deceived himself most of all.

Revelation 20:10.   And the devil that deceived them was cast into the lake of fire and brimstone, where the beast and the false prophet are, and shall be tormented day and night for ever and ever.

Here is the final end of the primeval cherub, the highest angel of all, the rebellious "son of the morning" who wanted to exalt his own throne above God's throne. The great blasphemer, the idol, the false god, the breaker of God's rest, the rebel against his father, the murderer from the beginning, the robber, the great adulterer, the father of lies, the coveter of divine worship, the one who is the very antithesis of the holy and gracious God, the Devil, will finally be cast forever into outer darkness.

The great deceiver is gone! He had deceived the whole world, beginning with Adam and Eve, and even after a thousand-year confinement in Hades he had still been able to deceive the vast Millennial-Age populations. He had deceived a third of God's innumerable company of angels into following him in his cosmic rebellion. But now he is gone.

And if he had never realized it before, he surely must have realized as he was hurtling toward the lake of fire, that he had deceived himself first and most of all. God indeed was all He had said—eternal and omnipotent, the Creator. The cosmos was not the ultimate reality after all; God, in Christ, had created space and time and all things, and therefore He was, and is, King forever.

For a thousand years Satan's two greatest human accomplices had already been tormented in the lake of fire and, as he himself plunges into the fiery lake, he no doubt will see them there. Hell is torment, not annihilation. It is the place where these evil men *are,* not were, even a thousand years later. Their bodies and souls had been "destroyed" in hell, but they are still there. And so will Satan, and so will his angels, and so will all unsaved men and women from every age, the antediluvians as well as the millennialites, continue in the lake of fire, in conscious torment, day and night, forever (Revelation 14:11).

The Great Judgment Day

Revelation 20:11.   And I saw a great white throne, and him that sat on it, from whose face the earth and the heaven fled away; and there was found no place for them.

Now, before the amazed John a vision is unfolded of an even grander scene than any he had ever witnessed before. In fact, the spectacle is so blindingly glorious that the very earth itself disintegrates before it.

The fire which had fallen from heaven to consume the multitudes following Gog and Magog seems to be nothing less than the unveiled glory, the pure, white-hot energy, of the Creator in all His ineffable brilliance. Now that same cosmic power penetrates the very atomic structure of the earth and its atmosphere, and they are vaporized in a gigantic holocaust that brings this present world to an end.

This is the cataclysmic fire foretold by the Apostle Peter: "But the heavens and the earth, which are now, by the same word are kept in store, reserved unto fire against the day of judgment and perdition of ungodly men. . . . But the day of the Lord will come as a thief in the night; in the which the heavens shall pass away with a great noise, and the elements shall melt with fervent heat, the earth also and the works that are therein shall be burned up. Seeing then that all these things shall be dissolved, what manner of persons ought ye to be in all holy conversation and godliness, looking for and hasting unto the coming of the day of God, wherein the heavens being on fire shall be dissolved, and the elements shall melt with fervent heat?'' (2 Peter 3:7, 10-12).

The very *elements* (Greek *stoicheion,* a word properly referring to the fundamental components of matter, the very ''dust of the earth'' out of which all things were made in the beginning) will be ''melted'' (Greek *luo,* translated ''melt'' in 3:10, with respect to the elements, but ''dissolved'' with respect to ''these things'' in 3:11 and with respect to ''the heavens on fire'' in 3:12).

The elements of the earth are to be dissolved in the intense heat of the divine fire and all of man's ''works'' on the earth will also be burned up (Greek *katakaio,* ''wholly consumed''). The agelong effects of God's great curse on the ground (Genesis 3:17) must be purged from the very elements before the earth can be renewed for its eternal purposes. The great beds of fossils and other testimonials of an agelong reign of sin and death must all be burned away.

The atmosphere likewise will ''pass away,'' because its structure is inseparably intertwined with that of the earth. This is the same word used by Jesus in Matthew 24:35: ''Heaven and earth shall pass away.'' An even more graphic term is used here in Revelation 20:11. ''The earth and the heaven fled away.'' It is as though the sin-cursed earth quails before the advancing glory cloud of the divine fire and runs away, disappearing in a great explosion of light and sound and fervent heat.

This should not be understood, however, as an actual annihilation of the earth and its atmosphere. By the principle of mass/energy conservation, nothing is ever actually annihilated, except by miraculous act of God, in God's completed creation (Hebrews 1:3; Colossians 1:17). The phenomenon may well be one of mass/energy conversion, with the ''matter'' of earth structure converted into ''energy'' (heat, sound, or light). This same energy will be available for reconversion into the materials of the renewed earth, with all the contaminating effects of sin and the curse purged out of it. On the other hand, it may be simply that the solids and liquids of the earth will be dissociated and vaporized by the intense heat.

In either case, the solid earth and its atmosphere will disappear and scatter their elements and energies out into space so that their former ''place'' in the cosmos is bare and empty. But then John sees the cause of their flight. The awful fire was merely a prologue, a field of divine energy advancing ahead of the mighty Creator of the universe ascending His great throne of judgment.

There is no rainbow above this throne (compare Revelation 4:3), speaking of grace in the midst of judgment. There is no sign of a Lamb on the throne, once slain in substitution for sinful men (contrast Revelation 5:6). Here is seen only the great throne of divine justice, blinding in its whiteness. No human figure can be discerned there, no incarnate Son of man. It is rather an awesome Presence, none other than the triune Godhead, the Creator and King and Judge of the universe, "who only hath immortality, dwelling in the light which no man can approach unto" (1 Timothy 6:16).

No explanation has been given concerning the inhabitants of the millennial earth, except for the rebels who were devoured in the fire. The camp of the saints and the beloved city with its occupants had surely been preserved through the conflagration that destroyed the Magogites, but then the earth itself had been burned up.

These saints do not appear at the great white throne, and nothing further is said concerning them until after the new Jerusalem descends to the new earth. Since at that time all the people of God will be in the heavenly city, it is quite likely that another great rapture will have taken place just before the dissolution of the earth. The godly Israelites in the beloved city as well as those from other nations who had remained true to the Lord during the last rebellion, thus demonstrating the genuineness of their faith in Christ, must have been "caught up to meet the Lord in the air," translated to the new Jerusalem still suspended high above the terrestrial atmosphere. Those saints who had already participated in the first resurrection and rapture, before the millennium, will already have shared in the blessings of the heavenly city, but now there will be a host of new inhabitants, coming out of the Millennial Age.

Before the blessings of the holy city are described, however, the tragic events at the great white throne must be revealed to John and recounted for our own admonition, for multitudes from our own age will assemble there.

Revelation 20:12.   And I saw the dead, small and great, stand before God; and the books were opened: and another book was opened, which is the book of life: and the dead were judged out of those things which were written in the books, according to their works.

The terms "dead" and "death" in these verses refer to the body rather than to the soul. The latter, of course, had continued its conscious existence in Hades during all the centuries when the body was dead.

As noted before, the term "resurrection" also applies only to the body. Those who were "dead in Christ" (1 Thessalonians 4:16) had all been resurrected from the dead before the millennium, but the "rest of the dead lived not again until the thousand years were finished" (Revelation 20:5). *That* was the first resurrection, *this* is the second resurrection. Over these will also prevail a second death (verses 6, 14).

But for one awful hour they must stand before God for judgment. This will be the "resurrection of damnation" spoken of by Christ (John 5:29). Actually the word "damnation" is a translation of the Greek word *krisis,* which is normally and properly translated "judgment" (see, for example, the next verse, John 5:30, "my judgment is just"). Thus this passage in John 5:29 says that the first resurrection will be unto life, the second unto judgment. Those who have believed on Christ unto salvation will not appear for judgment at the great white throne at all. "He that heareth my word, and believeth on him that sent me, hath everlasting life, and shall not come into condemnation [same Greek word, *krisis*]; but is passed from death unto life" (John 5:24).

God has books in heaven, so that no deed or word of any man or woman who ever lived has been lost. These books may be in the form of scrolls as used in John's day; or bound pages as in our day, or some other type of book about which we know nothing. Possibly they will consist of something analogous to modern videotapes. If man can use electronics to preserve sights and sounds, there is no question that God, who created all forms of electromagnetic energy in the first place, can certainly do it, and far more efficiently at that.

No unsaved man or woman should ever take comfort in the fact that certain of their ungodly words and deeds were performed in secret. "For nothing is secret, that shall not be made manifest; neither any thing hid, that shall not be known and come abroad" (Luke 8:17). Evidently the record of all these works of every individual will not only be shown to God, but also will be displayed to everyone else, so that all will know that God bases His judgment on the true facts. God would not need books of records Himself, of course, since He is omniscient, so that these books apparently are mainly for a testimony to all His creatures.

There is also another book, which is not a book of records of works but the book of life. In this book had once been inscribed the name of every child ever conceived and who, therefore, had been granted "life" by God. Sadly, however, multitudes during their lifetimes (whenever it became evident that they had irrevocably rejected God's provision of salvation for them through Jesus Christ) had had their names "blotted out of the book of life" (Revelation 3:5; Exodus 32:33; Psalm 69:28). This book will also be opened, as the resurrected dead stand before the awful Majesty on the shining throne.

Then judgments will be pronounced, one after another, as each stands before God for a review of his life. If each were to take an hour, the tribunal scene would last perhaps 5 million years, (assuming 45 billion people to be judged). But this is nothing in the scale of eternity. This judgment is to be based on works, so all of man's works must be reviewed, and reviewed fairly, in light of opportunity and motivation. "And that servant, which knew his lord's will, and prepared not himself, neither did according to his will, shall be beaten with many stripes. But he that knew not, and did commit things worthy of stripes, shall be beaten with few stripes. For unto whomsoever much is given, of him shall be much required: and to whom men have committed much, of him they will ask the more" (Luke 12:47, 48). God's punishment, in each case, will be carefully meted out in perfect justice.

428

Revelation 20:13.   And the sea gave up the dead which were in it; and death and hell delivered up the dead which were in them: and they were judged every man according to their works.

When "death" overtakes a man, his body decays and goes back to the dust. However, in most nations his body is first buried in some kind of tomb, and this was true of the nation of Israel in particular. Consequently, the terms "death" and "the grave" are often used essentially as synonyms in Scripture, as in 1 Corinthians 15:55, "O death, where is thy sting? O grave, where is thy victory?"

However, when the body dies, the soul descends into Hades (the word for "hell" here is *Hades;* see discussion on Revelation 1:18). In most cases, the body had been claimed by "death," that is, by a tomb in the ground. Many, however, have drowned in the sea, so their bodies were never in the ground. Many also have had their bodies cremated and their ashes scattered. But wherever they are, God is able to call the atoms all back into place, presumably in the same form as when they died. Bodies will emerge from both land and sea and, as they come, the great pit of Hades will also disgorge all its imprisoned souls, enabling them to reenter their former bodies.

One other reason for the initial reference to the sea here is probably the tremendous numbers of people who had been drowned long ago in the waters of the great Flood (Genesis 6:17). The Flood had destroyed the first cosmos (2 Peter 3:6); now the fire had destroyed the second cosmos (2 Peter 3:10) each slaying multitudes of sinners. It is possible that the souls of those who had perished in the final conflagration had never reached Hades proper, since the physical earth had been dissolved soon after their own destruction. This possibility is intimated by the reference to "the dead" in verse 12, right after the holocaust. Thus, first there may be a reference to those who died in the fire, then to those in the Flood, finally to all others buried in graves, with Hades then emptying out all its lost souls when the great fire dissolved its walls.

In any case, every unsaved man or woman through the ages, from every nation of every time, rich or poor, mighty or insignificant, educated or ignorant, all will be raised in their old bodies of flesh to stand before God in judgment. This resurrection will not, like the first, be a resurrection unto life, however—that is, the bodies will not be immortal, like those of the saints in the first resurrection, but will be the same old mortal bodies, still subject to pain and death. Paul says that "death is swallowed up in victory" at the time when "this mortal shall have put on immortality," but that God gives "us the victory through our Lord Jesus Christ" (1 Corinthians 15:54, 57). Those who refuse to follow Jesus Christ obviously will not share in His victory.

There, in an aching, trembling body of flesh, every man will have to watch his deeds in the flesh displayed to the whole creation so that both he and every other man must finally acknowledge that his condemnation is just. Some may protest, as their evil works are reviewed, that they have also done many good works, even many religious works. "Many will say to me in that day, Lord, Lord, have we not prophesied in thy name? and in thy name have cast out devils? and in thy name done many wonderful works? And then will I profess unto them, I never knew you: depart from me, ye that work iniquity" (Matthew 7:22, 23).

Since they have rejected God's grace and His offer of forgiveness and salvation through personal faith in Christ, and have chosen instead to offer their own meritorious works in payment for salvation, God will indeed judge them by their works. But it is "not by works of righteousness which we have done" that He can save us, since the measure of righteousness is Christ Himself, and "all have sinned, and come short of the glory of God" (Titus 3:5; Romans 3:23). None have attained God's standard, and therefore "they were condemned every man according to their works."

Revelation 20:14.   And death and hell were cast into the lake of fire. This is the second death.

The result of a judgment according to works can only be condemnation, so "death and Hades," that is, everyone whose body had been dead until the second resurrection and whose soul had been locked in Hades, are cast into the lake of fire. There they will remain forever, with the Devil and his angels (Matthew 25:41), as well as the beast and false prophet, who had already been judged and condemned a thousand years earlier (Revelation 19:20; 20:10).

The exact character and location of the lake of fire have not been revealed in the Scriptures, but there is no reason to question the physical reality of its fires. There are more than twenty references in the New Testament alone to these fires of hell, most of them in statements of the Lord Jesus Himself, with no indication in the context that they are figurative fires of some kind. If, indeed, they do symbolize something else, no explanation is given anywhere as to what they designate. The warnings are given with such urgency as to leave no doubt that they should be taken with all seriousness. At the very least, one would have to conclude that the reality, whatever it might be, is every bit as fearful and tormenting as actual fires would be, so that no one should take any comfort in the thought that they might not consist of real fire.

The location of this final and everlasting hell of fire cannot, of course, be on this present earth, since the present earth is to be dissolved (2 Peter 3:10). It also seems highly unlikely that it will be on the new earth, since that will be an earth "wherein dwelleth righteousness" (2 Peter 3:13), and a fiery cauldron tormenting billions of unrepentant sinners forever would surely seem out of character anywhere on such an earth. Furthermore the lake of fire had been in existence even before the millennium, in order to receive the beast and the false prophet and yet it obviously survives the vaporization of the earth at the end of the millennium.

There are Scriptures which at least intimate that it may be located in some far corner of the universe, almost infinitely removed from the new earth and its holy city. Jesus spoke of apostate "children of the kingdom" who would finally be "cast out into outer darkness: there shall be weeping and gnashing of teeth" (Matthew 8:12). He used similar terms with respect to the usurper without a wedding garment: "Bind him hand and foot, and take him away, and cast him into outer darkness; there shall be weeping and gnashing of teeth" (Matthew 22:13). The same judgment was meted to the "unprofitable servant" (Matthew 25:26-30).

In Jude's epistle, the false teachers are said to be "wandering stars, to whom is reserved the blackness of darkness for ever" (Jude 13). Peter says such people are those "to whom the mist of darkness is reserved for ever"(2 Peter 2:17). These two expressions ("blackness" and "mist") are translations of the same Greek word, both expressing the concept of an impenetrable cloud. The same word is translated "darkness" in 2 Peter 2:4 and Jude 6, both speaking of the chains now binding the fallen angels awaiting the judgment. This "outer darkness" in some way must correspond to the "everlasting fire" into which the Lord Jesus also indicated the unsaved would ultimately be cast (Matthew 25:41).

The Apostle Paul says that all those "that know not God, and that obey not the gospel of our Lord Jesus Christ . . . shall be punished with everlasting destruction from the presence of the Lord, and from the glory of his power" (2 Thessalonians 1:8, 9). The term "destruction" here does not connote "annihilation," but rather "death" in the sense of bodily death (compare 1 Corinthians 5:5) or "ruin." The word "from" (Greek *apo*) is significant, carrying a strong sense of "away from." That is, the ungodly will be sent into their condition of eternal ruin in some location far away from the location of God's personal presence, where His glorious power is specially manifested. Since this location is on the earth, in the new Jerusalem (Revelation 21:23), the conclusion must be that the unsaved are removed from there as far as possible.

All of these specifications seem to point to the likelihood (though we cannot be certain at this time) that "hell" (Greek *gehenna*), or "the lake of fire," will be located on some far-distant star. A star, after all, is precisely that, a lake of fire. There are indeed, stars and galaxies that, although "burning," do not give off light in the visible part of the spectrum, so that they consist of both "fire" and "cloudy darkness." One might even suggest a "black hole," if and when such objects are actually proven to exist, would fit the description.

Wherever the lake of fire may be, there is still the question as to whether resurrected physical bodies can burn forever in a cauldron of real physical fire. It is possible, of course, that the fire will immediately consume these bodies, so that they will actually go through a physical "second death" similar to their first death, leaving their disembodied souls to suffer forever in the lake of fire. That souls can actually suffer in some way in a fiery environment is indicated by the testimony of the rich man in Christ's parable. "And in [Hades] he lift up his eyes, being in torments.... And he cried and said, ... send Lazarus, that he may dip the tip of his finger in water, and cool my tongue; for I am tormented in this flame" (Luke 16:23, 24). It seems that the souls in Hades (as well as those in Paradise—note 2 Corinthians 5:1-4) retain a form of spirit body which resembles their respective earthly physical bodies. Even disembodied souls seem to be recognizable in terms of their earthly identities. Note the remarkable descriptions of the dead in Sheol in Ezekiel 31 and 32, as well as Isaiah 14. That being so, such spirit bodies also may possess spirit senses and are capable of experiencing feelings analogous to those they possessed in the flesh. We obviously have little understanding of such things, having no instrumentation with which to measure degrees of pain or pleasure experienced by persons who are without their physical bodies but who still retain the spirit/soul identities associated with those physical bodies. We can only infer that such things are real on the basis of these and other biblical intimations to that effect.

This is another possibility. Just as the resurrected physical bodies of the saints will be living forever, perhaps the resurrected bodies of the unsaved will be dying forever. That is, their physical bodies will not be consumed by the fire, but will eternally remain in a state of being consumed!

This seems almost unthinkable, except for the fact that the Lord Jesus Christ Himself seems to have issued this dire warning. Three times (Mark 9:43-48), He spoke of the awful danger of being "cast into hell, into the fire that never shall be quenched: Where their worm dieth not, and the fire is not quenched."

Gehenna, translated "hell" in the above and other passages, received its name in reference to the valley of Hinnom, outside Jerusalem. Into this valley in ancient times were cast the dead bodies of criminals, as well as all the city's refuse. The terrible contents of the valley were continually being eaten of worms and were also frequently set on fire, so that the valley indeed often had the appearance of a lake of fire. The Lord Jesus seemed plainly to be saying that in the ultimate gehenna, the bodies of its inhabitants would be unconsumable bodies, everlastingly being consumed by undying worms and burned by unquenchable fires.

We have no idea *how* such a thing could be possible. The Lord will see to it, however, that the glorified resurrection bodies of the saints will be fully physical bodies, no longer subject to pain or death, "according to the working whereby he is able even to subdue all things unto himself" (Philippians 3:21). If He can do the one, He can surely do the other, making the unglorified resurrection bodies of the ungodly *eternally* subject to pain and death. If this should prove to be the correct understanding of this dread prospect, it is indeed appropriate to equate the lake of fire explicitly with the second death!

Whatever the exact meaning of all these sobering warnings may be, it is obvious that those who die as lost sinners face a terrifying future. If these should all be mere symbols, the reality must be still worse. No wonder Jude urges that many should be saved "with fear, pulling them out of the fire" (Jude 23).

Revelation 20:15.   And whosoever was not found written in the book of life was cast into the lake of fire.

Not only are lost men and women condemned by the record of their works but also by the absence of their names in the Lamb's book of life. One can speculate that beside each person's name as entered in the book at time of conception will be recorded the time of his "age of accountability," the date of his conversion to Christ as His Savior, and evidence demonstrating the genuineness of that conversion. However, if there are no entries for the last two items by the time that person dies, the entire record will be blotted out (Revelation 3:5), and an awful blank will be left in the book at the place where his name would have been. Exhibiting this blank spot in the book will be the final and conclusive evidence that the person being judged must be consigned to the lake of fire.

As already pointed out, there will be degrees of punishment in hell, just as there are degrees of reward in heaven, both being based on works in light of opportunity and heart motivation. With all the unsaved alike being cast into the burning lake of fire and brimstone, it is not yet revealed as to the means by which the more wicked will be made to suffer there more than the less wicked. Exactly *what* is meant by the "many stripes" and the "few stripes" of Luke 12:47, 48, and how it will be "more tolerable" for Sodom and Tyre "in the day of judgment" than for Capernaum and Bethsaida, as Jesus warned in Matthew 11:20-24, are unanswered questions.

In one sense, wickedness generates its own suffering. Among the last words of the Bible are these: "He that is unjust, let him be unjust still: and he which is filthy, let him be filthy still" (see on Revelation 22:11). Men and women will have to live with themselves and their own sinful, yet unrequited, lusts and hatreds forever. After all, that is what they preferred to the love of Christ. This consuming evil will surely torment them in proportion to its intensity.

It may also be that the resurrection bodies designed for them by God at the "second resurrection" will be designed with individual nerve systems whose sensory responses are graduated in proportion to the degree of punishment appropriate to the individual, so that the actual pains of hell will be felt differently by each one. Or it may be that some other graded system of punishment will be used of which we have no inkling at this time. God is surely able to inflict His punishments in perfect justice, individually tailored. We do not have very much specific information on this subject in the Bible, but we do know this much: every unsaved man and woman will spend eternity in conscious suffering in the terrible lake of fire, the second death.

These same ungodly men and women today scoff at such a notion, even using it as an excuse for rejecting Christ. "How could a God of love," they say, "send someone to such a horrible fate in retaliation for a few years of sin and rebellion on earth?"

They forget, however, that God has already suffered all these pangs of hell Himself, in substitution for them, when Christ died on the cross. In fact, He suffered infinitely, as the sinless One made sin for us, the awful separation from God which is the essence of hell, to deliver them from suffering eternally that same separation. No matter how great or numerous the record of their sins in God's books may be, the mere record of their names in the book of life of the Lamb slain from the foundation of the world would be more than sufficient to save them from the lake of fire and reserve for them an undefiled inheritance in heaven in the presence of the Lord (1 Peter 1:3-5). God loved them and Christ died for them, to give them forgiveness and eternal life.

But they did not desire Him nor His love nor His presence. They preferred to continue in their sins, independent of God and His will. There is no punishment that could possibly balance such a crime as this. To despise the loving care of their Creator and the infinite suffering of their Savior for them is to strike at the very heart of God and the purpose of their creation. This infinite sin will continue forever in their hearts, so they will actually suffer less in hell than if they were forced against their will to spend eternity in the presence of the One whom they have spurned and hated.

Finally, we should remember that the authority for these fearful warnings is none other than the One who has the keys of Hades and death (Revelation 1:18). Whether we can fully understand the ways of God or not, there is no excuse for rejecting the clear teachings of Christ. He is not only the Creator of all things (Colossians 1:16) and the Judge of all men (John 5:22) but is the only man who has conquered death Himself. When He warns of everlasting fire and outer darkness and the undying worm, we can be sure He is telling us things as they really are. Furthermore, even the Book of Revelation has come from Him (Revelation 1:1, 11) and He is Himself the Judge who will send the unsaved to their second death in the lake of fire. The most tragic and foolish mistake that one could ever make would be to ignore His warnings and reject His Word. "For the wages of sin is death; but the gift of God is eternal life through Jesus Christ our Lord" (Romans 6:23).

21

Heaven on Earth

(Revelation 21)

For ages it has seemed that futility rules the world. Year after year, the new year of hope soon becomes the old year of frustration and defeat. Resolutions to do better are regularly promised, and then as regularly broken. If God has had a purpose for the world and for mankind, it would seem He has either failed or forgotten, and things keep getting worse every year.

And yet God is omnipotent and omniscient and cannot fail. He is long-suffering, but the day of the Lord will come. His purpose in creation involves a glorious future for His creatures, and sooner or later that purpose must be fulfilled.

Finally these ages of probation and testing and judgment are over. The dispensations have run their course and "the dispensation of the fulness of times" (Ephesians 1:10) is come. The grand climax of the Book of Revelation—indeed, the climax of God's entire revelation and of all His purposes in creation—is about to be unfolded. The most glorious chapters of the Bible are these last two chapters, opening up the wonders of the endless ages of eternity, and the fruition of all the great plans of a loving God.

The Tabernacle of God

Old things have passed away now, and all things are new. The earth is new and the heaven is new, there is a new Jerusalem and, in fact, all things are new (v. 5). God, who had created all things in the beginning, and then rested from His work of creating and making all things, has once again undertaken a great work of creation. "For, behold, I create new heavens and a new earth: and the former shall not be remembered, nor come into mind. But be ye glad and rejoice for ever in that which I create: for, behold, I create Jerusalem a rejoicing, and her people a joy'' (Isaiah 65:17, 18).

Revelation 21:1.   And I saw a new heaven and a new earth: for the first heaven and the first earth were passed away; and there was no more sea.

As Jesus long ago had predicted (Matthew 24:35), the original earth and its atmospheric heavens had finally passed away. A fiery cataclysm had melted the very elements of that first cosmos (2 Peter 3:10), but God had promised (2 Peter 3:13) that a new heavens and earth would come in which would dwell perfect righteousness. Furthermore *that* heavens and earth, which, like the first, would be "made" as well as "created" (compare Genesis 2:3 with Isaiah 65:17 and 66:22), would never pass away. "For as the new heavens and the new earth, which I will make, shall remain before me, saith the Lord, so shall your seed and your name remain" (Isaiah 66:22).

In both the Old and New Testament passages, the words for "new" mean "new in respect of freshness," rather than "new with respect to existence." That is, "a new heaven and a new earth" could be properly also translated "a fresh heaven and a fresh earth." The new cosmos is not a novel cosmos; it is a renewed cosmos. It is just like the first, except that all its agelong ravages of decay have been expunged and it is fresh and new again. This complete reversal of the universal decay process will require both the creative and formative powers of God for its accomplishment.

The first heavens and earth had been contaminated by sin, with the very elements in bondage to God's curse. The only way they could be completely cleansed was to be completely renewed. "All these things" had to be "dissolved," with the elements melting in fervent heat (2 Peter 3:10-12). By the principle of mass/energy conservation, however, nothing had been really lost, except the effects and evidences of sin. After terrestrial matter had been converted either into the vapor state or, more probably, into pure energy, God had once again exercised His mighty powers of creation and integration, and the new heavens and new earth had appeared out of the ashes, so to speak, of the old.

People often forget that God cannot fail in any of His purposes. He was not capricious in any aspect of His original creative work; each part was "very good" (Genesis 1:31), intended to fill a specific function in His economy. In spite of the long interruption occasioned by sin, we can be sure either that everything that was good in the first creation will be restored in the new creation, or else that something better will be provided in its place. The earth and its heaven once again will be very good in every way.

To some degree, however, the first earth was designed for man's probationary state, whereas the new earth is equipped for his perfected state. While there are numerous similarities, there are also some significant changes, the most obvious of which is that there is no more sea. On the present earth approximately 70 percent of the earth is covered by the sea. Even on the antediluvian and millennial earths the sea was a significant feature (Genesis 1:9, 10; Zechariah 14:8), though much smaller in extent than at present, but the whole world will consist of inhabitable land surfaces on the new earth.

No explanation is given for the striking absence of a sea on the new earth, and some commentators say that this statement refers only to the passing of the first sea, with no necessity for assuming there is not a new sea, to go with the new heavens and the new earth. However, the text reads much more naturally to say that, although there is indeed a new earth, there is no sea on that earth.

There will, in fact, be no need for a sea on the new earth. The present sea is needed, as was the original antediluvian sea, as a basic reservoir for the maintenance of the hydrologic cycle and the water-based ecology and physiology of the animal and human inhabitants of the earth. In the new earth, however, there will be no animals at all, and presumably all the men and women who live there will have glorified bodies with no more need of water. Their resurrected bodies will be composed, like that of the Lord Jesus, of flesh and bone (Luke 24:39; Philippians 3:21) but apparently with no need of blood (1 Corinthians 15:50) to serve as a cleanser and restorer of the body's flesh as at present. This, in turn, eliminates the major need for water on the earth (blood is about 90 percent water, and present-day human flesh about 65 percent water).

So far as we know, there is no other planet in the universe containing significant amounts of liquid water. Only the earth is a "water planet," suitable for biological life as we know it *now*. This is, probably, therefore, not the norm for God's cosmic economy, and the seas of the earth will be eliminated when the need for them no longer exists.

There *will* be *water,* however (see on Revelation 22:1, 2) on the new earth, of which the water of the present age is only a type and prophecy. That water is the water of everlasting life!

Revelation 21:2.   And I John saw the holy city, new Jerusalem, coming down from God out of heaven, prepared as a bride adorned for her husband.

Not since the very first chapter has John referred to himself by name. It is as though the event taking place before his amazed eyes was so glorious and incredible that he must stress that he himself, the last of the apostles, had actually seen it happen.

The new earth had been fully prepared, with its new heaven. Now descending from that heaven, John sees in all the beauties of its perfections the majestic city of God. The holy city is not "heaven," although the new Jerusalem is usually what is meant when people speak of "going to heaven." Rather, it comes down from heaven. In this context, heaven is merely the earth's atmosphere, which has just been made "new" by the same God who has also made the *new* Jerusalem.

Even the old Jerusalem had been called "the holy city" (Matthew 4:5; 27:53; Revelation 11:2; Nehemiah 11:1; Isaiah 52:1; Daniel 9:24). The term "holy" signified merely that God had set it apart as a city dedicated to His own great purposes, even though the behavior of its people often was unholy. In the new Jerusalem, of course, not only will the city be holy, but so will all its inhabitants (Revelation 20:6; 22:11).

Most writers on the Book of Revelation have, to one degree or another, tried to spiritualize this great vision of the new Jerusalem. There is no reason at all, however, why we should not accept it literally, as a real place prepared by Christ in the distant heavens (John 14:2, 3) and now finally brought with Him to the new earth. It is the city for which Abraham had looked, one "which hath foundations, whose builder and maker is God" (Hebrews 11:10). It is the city which God "hath prepared for them" which have the faith to believe His Word and follow His will (Hebrews 11:16). It is "the city of the living God, the heavenly Jerusalem," where one day will be gathered together "the general assembly and church of the first-born" with all the "just men" whose spirits have been "made perfect" in the great resurrection (Hebrews 12:22, 23). It is that "Jerusalem which is above . . . which is the mother of us all" (Galatians 4:26). "For here have we no continuing city, but we seek one to come" (Hebrews 13:14).

Difficult though it may be, in the sophistication of our modern scientism, to believe such a thing, the Scriptures taken literally as they were meant to be taken, do teach that there is even now a great city being built by Christ far out in space somewhere. To this city go the spirits of all who die in Christ, there to await His return to earth. When He comes back, He will bring the holy city with Him and set it up for a time somewhere in earth's atmospheric heavens, perhaps orbiting the earth. There will be established His judgment seat, as well as the heavenly temple and its altar, to which John frequently refers in Revelation. The resurrected and raptured saints will dwell in this city, though with occasional visits to the earth, during the tribulation and millennial periods. Finally, when the earth is made new again, never to undergo any of the effects of God's curse or His judgments any more, the Lord Jesus Christ will bring it down to the earth where it will remain forever.

To John's enraptured gaze, the city seemed like a radiant bride, beautiful in glistening white garments, ready for her wedding. Indeed in one sense, the city was the bride, personified thus in virtue of all the saints residing therein. These saints comprise the eternal wife of the Lamb (vv. 9, 10).

The city had been "prepared" (Greek *hetoimazo*) completely by God Himself. This is the same word used by the Lord Jesus when He told His disciples, "I go to prepare a place for you" (John 14:2). It is also recorded in Hebrews 11:16: "He hath prepared for them a city." Most beautifully, it is the word chosen by the Apostle Paul in the wonderful promise: "Eye hath not seen, nor ear heard, neither have entered into the heart of man, the things which God hath prepared for them that love him" (1 Corinthians 2:9).

Revelation 21:3.   And I heard a great voice out of heaven saying, Behold, the tabernacle of God is with men, and he will dwell with them, and they shall be his people, and God himself shall be with them, and be their God.

Once again a loud voice calls out from heaven, and the message is one of triumph and great benediction. The proclamation from the skies echoes a promise made to the children of Israel long ago: "I will set my tabernacle among you: and my soul shall not abhor you: And I will walk among you, and will be your God, and ye shall be my people" (Leviticus 26:11). The tabernacle in the wilderness, of course, was but a dim foreshadow of the glorious tabernacle which now has come down on earth. Similar promises were made at various times in different ways. For example: "Many nations shall be joined to the Lord in that day, and shall be my people: and I will dwell in the midst of thee, and thou shalt know that the Lord of hosts hath sent me unto thee" (Zechariah 2:11). In fact the great prophetic name of Christ, Immanuel (Isaiah 7:14) means "God with us" (Matthew 1:23).

There will be "many nations" there, but all will be "my people," and He will be "their God." Further, every nation will once again speak the same language. "For then [that is, after all the earth has been "devoured with the fire" of God's jealousy] will I turn to the people a pure language, that they may all call upon the name of the Lord, to serve him with one consent" (Zephaniah 3:8, 9).

There was another foreshadowing of this great coming union when God first became man. "And the Word was made flesh, and dwelt among us" (John 1:14). The word "dwelt" (Greek *skenoo*) is not the usual word for "dwell" but is the same word as used here in Revelation 21:2. It is a direct variant of the word for "tabernacle" (Greek *skene*), also used in this verse. In the days of His flesh, in other words, the eternal God temporarily "tabernacled" among men and then returned to heaven. In the eternal age to come, however, He will set up His dwelling place on earth and "tabernacle" here forever.

The word for "tabernacle" in the Old Testament (Hebrew *mishkan*) is a cognate to its Greek equivalent (*skene*). The well-known term for the glory-cloud that filled the tabernacle, the *Shekinah,* developed from a related word, *sheken,* meaning "habitation" (Deuteronomy 12:5). Thus did the idea of God tabernacling with His people lead on naturally to the concept of God's glory in their midst. "We beheld his glory," said John, when the Word "dwelt among us" (John 1:14).

Revelation 21:4.   And God shall wipe away all tears from their eyes; and there shall be no more death, neither sorrow, nor crying, neither shall there be any more pain: for the former things are passed away.

The great voice from heaven continues with one of the most blessed messages ever heard. From the time when Eve first sinned, sorrow has been multiplied to her children (Genesis 3:16), and "man is born unto trouble, as the sparks fly upward" (Job 5:7). But the tears have been for man's good, and God has promised from the beginning that He will someday restore joy and peace to the world. "He will swallow up death in victory; and the Lord God will wipe away tears from off all faces; and the rebuke of his people shall he take away from off all the earth: for the Lord hath spoken it. And it shall be said in that day, Lo, this is our God; we have waited for him, we will be glad and rejoice in his salvation" (Isaiah 25:8, 9).

That great day has finally come, and there will never be another tear shed. Especially to the suffering saints in the tribulation period has this promise proved of great consolation (Revelation 7:17).

This is nothing less than a removal of the great curse, pronounced by God on the earth and its inhabitants when Adam sinned (Genesis 3:17-19). Its physical effects on the "ground" had been cleansed when the elements melted and the new earth arose from the ashes. Now is pronounced also the deliverance of all mankind from its fourfold impact on human life. In Eden, God had announced that men would universally experience sorrow, pain, sweat, and death, but now He announces that these will be no more.

This great deliverance, of course, has been purchased dearly, at the cost of infinite sorrow, pain, sweating, and dying on the part of God Himself, through Jesus Christ, Son of God and Son of man.

Were men and women to endure sorrow throughout their lives? Therefore, He would become "a man of sorrows, and acquainted with grief" and thus "He hath borne our griefs, and carried our sorrows" (Isaiah 53:3, 4). Were they to suffer the physical pain of thorns and thistles and a multitude of other messengers of Satan sent to buffet them as they struggled through life (2 Corinthians 12:7)? Well, He would wear a very crown of thorns (John 19:2) and endure such wounds and bruises and stripes (Isaiah 53:5) as no other man would ever know. Would it require the sweat of bitter labor, the strong crying of never-ending toil for men to wrest a meager sustenance from a cursed and reluctant ground under the bondage of futility and decay (Romans 8:20-22)? But He was willing to sweat great drops of blood (Luke 22:44) and to pour out strong crying and tears (Hebrews 5:7) in order to give rest to all "who labour and are heavy laden" (Matthew 11:28). Then, after all their sorrow and pain and tear-stained labor, would their bodies finally die and return to the dust anyway? Yes, but He would experience the "dust of death" Himself (Psalm 22:15), make His soul an offering for sin (Isaiah 53:10), and pour out His soul unto death (Isaiah 53:12) as their substitute.

He not only bore the curse, He was made the curse for us (Galatians 3:13). Therefore, God in perfect justice can remove the curse forever (Revelation 22:3). In all the world and throughout all ages, no one will ever die again. No one will suffer pain or sorrow or tears ever again, and death is swallowed up in victory. Like the first heaven and the first earth, all these former things are passed away,

---

Revelation 21:5.   And he that sat upon the throne said, Behold, I make all things new. And he said unto me, Write: for these words are true and faithful.

"The times of reconstitution of all things [Greek *apokatastasis,* translated "restitution" in the King James Version], which God hath spoken by the mouth of all His holy prophets since the world began" (Acts 3:21) have finally come. Not only is there a new heaven, a new earth and a new Jerusalem, but there is a new song (Revelation 5:9) and a new name (Revelation 2:17; 3:12). In fact, all things are to be made new, and we have the assurance of God Himself that this promise is true and faithful.

Presumably this means not only that everything will be made new but also that everything will then stay new. The entropy law will be "repealed." Nothing will wear out or decay, and no one will age or atrophy anymore. Every tree will bear fruit abundantly and eternally (Revelation 22:2). There will be no need to use up limited energy resources to provide illumination or other services (Revelation 22:5). All things will be and remain eternally young and fresh and new, just as they were in the week of creation itself.

The authority for this wonderful promise is none other than the enthroned Christ, who has descended with His throne in the heavenly city to His permanent home on the new earth. With respect to the new bodies of the resurrected and glorified saints, these also will remain forever strong and healthy. The Scriptures are not explicit on this, but there is at least a possible implication that the "apparent age" of each person in the resurrection may be in, say, his or her early thirties. When Adam and Eve were created, they were mature adults, capable of raising children. Since aging and death were part of the results of their sin, they would presumably have remained at the same "age" as that at which they were created if they had not sinned. At the same time, however, they were commanded to have children (Genesis 1:28), and these would surely have grown to a similar maturity before their "age" would have stabilized, as it were.

It also seems significant that those who were to serve as priests or Levites in the service of the tabernacle had to be thirty years old and upward (Numbers 4:3). Joseph was thirty years old when he was made ruler over Egypt (Genesis 41:43, 46), and David, the man after God's own heart, became king over Israel at age thirty (2 Samuel 5:4). Since those who are in the resurrection are also to serve as priests and kings in the millennium (Revelation 20:6), it would be likely that their resurrection "age" would be of this same order.

Even the Lord Jesus Christ entered on His earthly public ministry at age thirty (Luke 3:23), and went to the cross only about three-and-a-half years later. It is significant that His own resurrection body was of this same apparent age, different in its glorified state but still easily recognizable. The Scriptures, of course, also teach that those who are Christ's will be "like Him" when He comes again (1 John 3:3), with bodies "fashioned like unto his glorious body" (Philippians 3:21).

Perhaps, therefore (although it is not explicitly taught in Scripture) those who die in old age will be young again, at the age of greatest vigor, and those who die in infancy or youth, will mature to the age of full growth and development, in the resurrection. In any case, all things will be made new, for the Lord's Word is true and faithful.

Revelation 21:6.   And he said unto me, It is done. I am Alpha and Omega, the beginning and the end. I will give unto him that is athirst of the fountain of the water of life freely.

That it is none other than the glorified Christ who is speaking to John is demonstrated by His renewed reference to Himself as Alpha and Omega (see Revelation 1:8, 11; 22:13), the Word of both creation and consummation, the first and the last. Just as the work of creation was finished (Genesis 2:1-3) and the work of redemption was finished (John 19:30), so now the work of consummation and restoration has been finished.

Then the Lord renews a promise made long ago. John himself had recorded the conversation at the well of Samaria: "Whosoever drinketh of the water that I shall give him shall never thirst; but the water that I shall give him shall be in him a well of water springing up into everlasting life" (John 4:14). Then, later, the Lord had said: "If any man thirst, let him come unto me, and drink. He that believeth on me, as the scripture hath said, out of his belly shall flow rivers of living water. (But this spake he of the Spirit, which they that believe on him should receive: for the Holy Ghost was not yet given; because that Jesus was not yet glorified)" (John 7:37-39).

This "water of life" is both symbolic of the Holy Spirit, with the eternal life He gives all who believe on Christ and also literal water, sparkling pure and abundant in the beautiful river flowing through the holy city (Revelation 22:1). Having made all things new, He will maintain the glorified bodies of the saints in eternal health and strength by the fruit of the tree of life and the river of the water of life (Revelation 22:1, 2) created anew by their providing Lord.

Revelation 21:7.   He that overcometh shall inherit all things; and I will be his God, and he shall be my son.

To each of the seven churches (Revelation 2 and 3) had previously been given a gracious promise for the "overcomers" in that church. Now an eighth and final promise is given to him "that overcometh." This is an implicit assurance that all the overcomers in all true churches everywhere have now, in the resurrection and the new earth, finally received the fulfillment of all the promises of God. They shall inherit all things. And, of course, this is because Christ Himself is "heir of all things" (Hebrews 1:2; Psalm 2:8), and those who are in Christ are "joint-heirs with Christ" (Romans 8:17), receiving "an inheritance incorruptible, and undefiled, and that fadeth not away, reserved in heaven for you, who are kept by the power of God through faith unto salvation ready to be revealed in the last time" (1 Peter 1:4, 5).

The heir relation is also a son relation. "The Spirit Himself beareth witness with our spirit, that we are the children of God: And if children, then heirs, heirs of God, and joint-heirs with Christ" (Romans 8:16, 17). The overcomer (that is, every true believer, redeemed through faith in Christ as Savior and Lord) becomes both son and heir of the mighty God of creation. Therefore, "all things are yours; Whether . . . the world, or life, or death, or things present, or things to come; all are yours; and ye are Christ's; and Christ is God's" (1 Corinthians 3:21-23).

What a glorious inheritance! The believer's future is neither limited in time nor restricted in space. The infinite resources of the space/time cosmos itself, limitless in space and unending in time, are his, in the ages to come.

Revelation 21:8.   But the fearful, and unbelieving, and the abominable, and murderers, and whoremongers, and sorcerers, and idolaters, and all liars, shall have their part in the lake which burneth with fire and brimstone: which is the second death.

In contrast to the glorious promises to the redeemed, the Lord inserts another warning to those who remain (by virtue of their fear and unbelief) unforgiven in their murders and fleshpeddling, unrepentant of their demonic idolatries, and committed to their falsehoods. They will spend eternity in the awful lake of fire, in eternal torments, the second death (Revelation 20:14, 15).

This is the last reference in the Bible to "fire," and it refers to the fiery lake of burning brimstone, which is the final and eternal hell. The first reference in the Bible to fire is found in Genesis 19:24, where "fire and brimstone" are seen

443

raining from the skies, turning the whole valley of Sodom and Gomorrah into a precursive lake of fire. Christ is first and last in judgment as well as grace.

The catalog here of sinners inhabiting hell is vivid and most instructive. At the head of the list are the "fearful." This is not primarily a reference to physical cowardice, but rather to lack of trusting faith in the Lord. Christ used it in Mark 4:40. "Why are ye so *fearful?* how is it that ye have no faith?" Closely related is the word used in John 14:27: "Let not your heart be troubled, neither let it be *afraid.*" Similarly in 2 Timothy 1:7, 8: "For God hath not given us the spirit of *fear;* but of power, and of love, and of a sound mind. Be not thou therefore ashamed of the testimony of our Lord." Those who are more fearful of the disapproval of men than of Christ are dangerously close to this kind of sin.

This kind of fearfulness is very similar to the sin of unbelief itself, the next in the list. It is only the sin of unbelief, with its outward manifestation of fearfulness, which actually sends people to hell. "He that believeth on him is not condemned: but he that believeth not is condemned already, because he hath not believed in the name of the only begotten Son of God" (John 3:18).

The seemingly more repugnant sins which are catalogued next are actually less serious than that of unbelief. Even murder can be forgiven if there is genuine repentance and faith, but there is no salvation for unbelievers, and no degree of moral righteousness, short of absolute perfection, can ever offset this. The greatest sin of all is rejecting the infinite love and suffering of Christ for us, in atonement for our sins.

The "abominable" are those who practice abomination—that is, the blasphemous and licentious practices associated with idol worship. The term "murderers" refers not to manslaughter but to criminal homicide. Next is the "whoremonger" (Greek *pornos),* translated in other passages "fornicator." In the context here, it refers to any who practice or promote sexual activity outside of marriage.

As noted before (Revelation 9:21), the "sorcerer" (Greek *pharmakeus)* is one who uses drugs to induce pseudoreligious fantasies and occult experiences. The term is appropriately associated with the "idolater," one whose religious worship is directed toward a material object which, in turn, represents to him some spiritual reality, either an actual demonic spirit or some religious or philosophical concept. A number of Scriptures (Ephesians 5:5; Colossians 3:5) make it plain that even covetousness (inordinate love of material possessions) is idolatry.

Finally, "all liars" are included in the roster of the condemned. Satan himself is the father of liars (John 8:44), and those who practice deception and falsehood, especially false teachers (note 2 Peter 2:1-3; Jude 4, 13) must finally join their diabolical "father" in his lake of fire.

Although few may wish to acknowledge themselves to be such flagrant sinners as those described here, it must be remembered that idolatry includes covetousness, fornication includes lustful thoughts (Matthew 5:28) and murder includes anger (Matthew 5:21, 22). Further, who is there who has never lied or never been fearful? This listing of sinners thus includes all, for "all have sinned and come short of the glory of God" (Romans 3:23).

The condemnation, however, is specifically for those who die in their sins, and who are thus still seen, not in Christ, but in the stark ugliness of sin. However, there is wonderful forgiveness in Christ for all such sinners who will come to Him. "Neither fornicators, nor idolaters, nor adulterers, nor effeminate, nor abusers of themselves with mankind, nor thieves, nor covetous, nor drunkards, nor revilers, nor extortioners, shall inherit the kingdom of God. And such were some of you: but ye are washed, but ye are sanctified, but ye are justified in the name of the Lord Jesus, and by the Spirit of our God" (1 Corinthians 6:9-11).

For the sin of unbelief in the true God and Redeemer, however, there can be no forgiveness. "He that hath the Son hath life: and he that hath not the Son of God hath not life" (1 John 5:12).

The City of God

These sinners, and the awful judgment overtaking them, will soon be forgotten amidst the glories of the holy city. The former things have passed away and "shall not be remembered, nor come into mind" (Isaiah 65:17). The most glorious aspect of the city of God, of course, will be the fact that Christ is there, and "that where I am, there ye may be also" (John 14:3). "And so shall we ever be with the Lord" (1 Thessalonians 4:17).

Revelation 21:9.   And there came unto me one of the seven angels which had the seven vials full of the seven last plagues, and talked with me, saying, Come hither, I will shew thee the bride, the Lamb's wife.

The last previous specific reference to an angel had been from a time a thousand years earlier, when John had seen one bind Satan for his millennial incarceration in the bottomless pit (Revelation 20:1). But now a mighty angel again approaches John to give him a marvelous introduction to the beautiful city where he, along with all saints, would one day dwell.

This is an angel who, though not identified by name, was recognized by John as one of the seven who had been chosen by God to administer the seven final plagues at the end of the tribulation period (Revelation 15:1). In addition to the actual sending of the seven final judgments, it may be significant that six later references to angelic activities are found, with this being the seventh (Revelation 17:1; 18:1, 21; 19:10, 17; 21:1). The first and last of these seven are said to be among the angels with the seven last plagues, so possibly the other five are as well.

The first had instructed John to "come hither" in order to see the "great whore." The last tells him also to "come hither," but this time to see "the bride, the Lamb's wife." In both cases, John was shown a great city, Babylon in the first instance, Jerusalem in the second. One he saw thrown down with violence, to disappear forever (Revelation 18:21); the other he saw coming down in glory, to endure forever. Babylon was both a monstrous system of spiritual and political wickedness and also the literal city which served as the center and capital of that system. Just so, the new Jerusalem is also both a glorious literal city as well as the universal tabernacle of God, an eternal and unbounded kingdom of righteousness.

Revelation 21:10.   And he carried me away in the spirit to a great and high mountain, and shewed me that great city, the holy Jerusalem, descending out of heaven from God.

The first of these seven angels had carried John away in the spirit into the wilderness, to see Babylon (Revelation 17:1); the last carries him to a great and high mountain to see Jerusalem. In the first case he had been translated far back in time to observe Babel from its very beginnings, in the global wilderness resulting presumably from the devastations of the great Flood. Now it seems that, in spirit, he is translated far up in space, as though on an exceedingly high mountain reaching up into heaven. His vantage point is not actually within the city. He had previously been privileged to "come up" into the very presence of God in the heavens (Revelation 4:1). He had also frequently observed events taking place in both heaven and earth from that exalted position, which presumably was somewhere in the heavenly city as it remained suspended in the upper atmosphere throughout the tribulation and millennial periods.

Now, however, he is somehow stationed outside the city, in order to observe its entire structure, and yet close enough to it so that he can record the details of its beautiful perfections. At the beginning of the chapter (v. 2) he had noted in a simple summary statement that the holy city was coming down to the new earth, but his perspective there seemed to have been from a great distance, where he had observed the actual creation of the whole new earth and its new atmosphere. Now the angel conveys him to a closer location, where he can watch in great wonder as the glorious city moves down past his reverent gaze.

Revelation 21:11.   Having the glory of God: and her light was like unto a stone most precious, even like a jasper stone, clear as crystal.

The holy city will be like no other city. The greatest of all human cities had been mighty Babylon, arrayed in purple and scarlet, decked with gold and precious stones (Revelation 17:4). The new Jerusalem, on the other hand, is arrayed in radiant light, shining with the glory of God. The "Shekinah glory" had filled the ancient tabernacle (Exodus 40:34) and the temple of Solomon (2 Chronicles 5:14). When the Lord Jesus had "tabernacled among us," the glory of God had been manifested in a different sense, "and we beheld his glory, the glory as of the only begotten of the Father, full of grace and truth" (John 1:14). Now, finally and forever, the tabernacle of God is with men (v. 3), and His glorious presence will illumine the new Jerusalem, both spiritually and physically, as long as God Himself endures.

The appearance of the city is, no doubt, more glorious than human language can describe. John can only compare it to a very precious jasper stone (Revelation 4:3). The radiant light was "clear as crystal." A little later, John would note that the river of water of life is also "clear as crystal" (Revelation 22:1). The Lord Jesus is the very "brightness of his glory" (Hebrews 1:3), the "light of the world" (John 8:12), and the "living water" (John 7:38). The city of God is the bride of the Lamb, and she must be arrayed in fitting apparel for the ages to come, properly "adorned for her husband" (v. 2). She must, in fact, "put on the Lord Jesus Christ" (Romans 13:14), sharing His glory, reflecting His light, and enjoying His presence forever.

Revelation 21:12.   And had a wall great and high, and had twelve gates, and at the gates twelve angels, and names written thereon, which are the names of the twelve tribes of the children of Israel.

As the city draws nearer to John's observation post on his lofty summit, he sees emerging through the clear crystal radiance a majestic wall surrounding the city, evidently extending as high as the great height of the city itself. Unlike earthly cities, however, the wall is not for protection from enemies, for its gates are always open, and there are no enemies to fear. No doubt it speaks of strength and eternal security, but perhaps most of all it is a structure of transcending beauty.

In the wall are twelve gates and, although their dimensions are not given, it is likely that each extends nearly to the top of the lofty wall, making access to the city easy at all levels. Most significant is the identification of the gates with the names of the children of Israel. This fact certainly assures us that the godly men and women of ancient Israel will be residents of the city and thus are included among those in the heavenly bride.

But also the names on the entry gates will be an eternal reminder that it was first of all through the patriarchal ministry of Abraham, Isaac, and Israel, with the twelve sons of Israel, that we Gentiles first entered into the great family and city of God. It was the Israelites "to whom pertaineth the adoption, and the glory, and the covenants, and the giving of the law, and the service of God, and the promises;

whose are the fathers, and of whom as concerning the flesh Christ came, who is over all, God blessed for ever. Amen." (Romans 9:4, 5).

Furthermore, attending perpetually at each gate will be one of God's holy angels. They will not be guarding angels, of course, since there is no longer any need for angelic protection, but will be ministering spirits, ministering as needed to all "the heirs of salvation" (Hebrews 1:14) entering or leaving the city. Since there is "an innumerable company of angels" attached to "the heavenly Jerusalem" (Hebrews 12:22), it seems likely, although this is only a deduction—not a specific teaching—that there will be a continual rotation of these heavenly ministers assigned to these gates of the beautiful city, each ready to go and serve whenever and wherever needed.

Revelation 21:13.   On the east three gates; on the north three gates; on the south three gates; and on the west three gates.

The gates were to be symmetrically situated, three in each of the four walls, possibly in commemoration of the wilderness tabernacle, with three tribes encamped outside each wall. Judah, Issachar, and Zebulun were "far off about the tabernacle," pitching "on the east side toward the rising of the sun" (Numbers 2:1-9). On the south side were Reuben, Simeon, and Gad (Numbers 2:10-16). Ephraim, Manasseh, and Benjamin encamped on the west side (Numbers 2:18-24), and Dan, Asher, and Naphtali (Numbers 2:25-31) on the north. The Levites, not numbered with the twelve, were immediately around the tabernacle, between the tabernacle and the other tribes, in order to do the service of the tabernacle. Moses and Aaron and his sons were on the east side (Numbers 3:38), the family of Gershon on the west (Numbers 3:23), Kohath on the south (Numbers 3:29) and Merari on the north (Numbers 3:35).

The order of enumeration is different from the order of the tribal names on the gates in the wall of Jerusalem during the millennium (Ezekiel 48:31-34). As far as the order of the gates in the wall of the new Jerusalem are concerned, there is therefore probably no particular significance to be attached to it, except that the east gate is here mentioned first, symbolic perhaps of the rising sun. At the wilderness tabernacle, Moses and the priests were on the east and, outside of them, the messianic tribe of Judah.

Revelation 21:14.   And the wall of the city had twelve foundations, and in them the names of the twelve apostles of the Lamb.

As the wall has twelve gates, so it also has twelve strong foundations, deep and secure, transmitting the weight of the great wall down to the solid bedrock of the new earth. One foundation at each corner, plus two in each wall (located between the wall's three gates), is no doubt the pattern employed. This, indeed, is the "city which hath foundations, whose builder and maker is God" (Hebrews 11:10), and its foundations are secure on the Rock of ages (Isaiah 26:4; Matthew 7:24, 25).

The names of the twelve apostles inscribed on the foundations surely give testimony that those redeemed by the Lamb reside in the city, as the names of Israel's sons on the gates likewise assure that the saved of ancient Israel are there, too. "For he is our peace, who hath made both one, and hath broken down the middle wall of partition between us" (Ephesians 2:14). "Now therefore ye are no more strangers and foreigners, but fellowcitizens with the saints, and of the household of God; and are built upon the foundation of the apostles and prophets, Jesus Christ himself being the chief corner stone; in whom all the building fitly framed together groweth unto an holy temple in the Lord" (Ephesians 2:19-21). The analogy between the spiritual temple of God now being erected by the Holy Spirit, composed of living believers, and the heavenly tabernacle pitched by God and now coming to earth, is clear and beautiful.

Revelation 21:15.   And he that talked with me had a golden reed to measure the city, and the gates thereof, and the wall thereof.

The one talking with John is, of course, the angel, who had carried him to the high mountain. In order to impress upon him the tremendous dimensions of the city, the angel actually measures it before his eyes, using a distinctive measuring rod which, like so much else in the city, was made of gold, but fine and thin like a reed. A similar reed, though evidently not of gold, had been used to measure the temple of the tribulation period (Revelation 11:1). In both cases, the measuring process speaks also of a standard of evaluation and judgment. In the case of apostate Jerusalem the temple and its worshipers failed to measure up to God's standard and their dimensions were not even recorded. Consequently, they were brought under God's chastening. With the new Jerusalem, however, all the dimensions are measured and carefully recorded, fully satisfying God's highest standards of perfection.

The new Jerusalem is composed of such beautiful materials, such unique construction and such amazing dimensions as to be almost beyond human comprehension. It would all be impossible to believe, except that its builder and maker is God and He has carefully had it recorded in His Word. The city is so huge, its wall so majestic, its gates so magnificent as to transcend all imagination, and God must even have a mighty angel carefully measure and delineate it, for John's benefit and for ours. Even so, with all its detailed measurement and description, most commentators still refuse to believe that the account means what it says, seeking by many and varied stratagems of interpretation to make it all an allegory or a parable of some kind. All such devices flounder, of course, upon these very details of measurement and description.

Revelation 21:16. **And the city lieth foursquare, and the length is as large as the breadth: and he measured the city with the reed, twelve thousand furlongs. The length and the breadth and the height of it are equal.**

As the angel proceeds to measure the city, John can see directly that the plan of the city is that of a square. The term "foursquare" is the Greek *tetragonos* (literally "fourangled," a term used to mean equal angles). Further, the measurements confirm that the sides are all equal, as well as the angles, with each dimension no less than 12,000 "furlongs" (that is, *stadia,* a Greek measure corresponding to 600 Greek feet, or approximately 607 English feet). In terms of miles, this would make the dimensions of the base of the city each 1,380 miles in length.

Never, of course, was there ever a city like this! If it were to be superimposed upon the United States, its area would cover all the way from Canada to the Gulf of Mexico, and from the Atlantic Ocean to Colorado.

Furthermore, its height is the same as its width and breadth, the whole comprising a gigantic cubical structure 1,380 miles on every side. A number of writers have interpreted the city to be like a pyramid in shape, with the height of the pyramid equal to the dimensions of its base. Such an interpretation is quite forced, however, the language of the passage being much more naturally understood to mean a cube, with the length and breadth and height all the same. Such a shape was long ago associated with the sacred presence of God, suggesting the attributes of tri-unity as it does. That is, the fundamental cosmic entity of space is a genuine trinity. Space must be composed of three dimensions, but each dimension pervades all space. Space is always referenced to the first dimension (length), but can only be seen in terms of two dimensions (area = length squared) and experienced in three dimensions (volume = length cubed). Similarly, the Godhead is referenced to the Father, seen in the Son, experienced in the Holy Spirit.

The pyramidal shape, on the other hand (whether as in Egypt, Mexico, or the stepped-towers of practically all ancient nations), seems always to have been associated with paganism, with the pyramid's apex being dedicated to the worship of the sun, or of the host of heaven. The first such structure was the Tower of Babel, and the Bible always later condemns worship carried out in high places (Leviticus 26:30) whether these were simply natural high hills or artificially constructed hills in the form of a pyramid or ziggurat.

The cube, on the other hand, was the shape specified by God for the holy place, or the oracle, in Solomon's temple (1 Kings 6:20), where God was to "dwell" between the cherubim. Both the language and the symbology thus favor the cubical, rather than the pyramidal, shape.

450

It should also be remembered that the new bodies of the resurrected saints will be like those of angels, no longer limited by gravitational or electromagnetic forces as at present. Thus it will be as easy for the inhabitants to travel vertically as horizontally, in the new Jerusalem. Consequently, the "streets" of the city (verse 21) may well include vertical passageways as well as horizontal avenues, and the "blocks" could be real cubical blocks, instead of square areas between streets as in a present-day earthly city.

This kind of geometry makes it easier to understand how all the redeemed of all the ages could be domiciled in a single city. Although there is no way to know precisely how many people will be there, one can make at least an order-of-magnitude estimate. It can be calculated that the total number of people who have lived between Adam's time and our time is about 40 billion (see *Biblical Cosmology and Modern Science,* by Henry M. Morris, Craig Press, 1969, pp. 72-83). Then, assuming that a similar number will be born during the millennium, and allowing another 20 billion for those who died before or soon after birth, it is reasonable that about 100 billion men, women, and children will be members of the human race—past, present or future.

Assume also that 20 percent of these will be saved, including those who die in infancy. This is obviously only a guess, but the Lord Jesus did make it plain that the large majority will never be saved (Matthew 7:13, 14). If this figure is used, then the new Jerusalem would have to accommodate 20 billion residents. Also, assume that 25 percent of the city is used for the "mansions" of these inhabitants (John 14:2), with the rest allocated to streets, parks, public buildings, etc. Then the average space assigned to each person would be:

$$\frac{1380\ (1380)\ (1380)}{4\ (20)\ (1,000,000,000)} = \frac{1}{30} \text{ cubic mile}$$

This would correspond to a cubical "block" with about seventy-five acres on each face. Obviously, there is adequate room in the holy city for all who will be there. Another way of measuring the size would be that the average length (or width, or height) of each person's block would be a little over a third of a mile in each direction. Some, no doubt, would have larger amounts, some smaller, but this would be about the average size.

Revelation 21:17.   And he measured the wall thereof, an hundred and forty and four cubits, according to the measure of a man, that is, of the angel.

The angel, assuming the appearance of a man, uses an ordinary measure of length based on the typical size of a man, in making his measurements. In the ancient world it was common practice to use a measure equal to the length of a man's forearm, from elbow to middle finger tip, and this was called a "cubit."

When standardized, this is believed by most authorities to have become recognized at about eighteen inches. Probably the golden reed used by the angel was about two cubits long, like a yardstick.

He had already measured the length and height of the city's walls, finding them to be each 12,000 stadia, or 1,380 miles. Now he also measures the wall itself, showing it to be 144 cubits, or about 216 feet in thickness. No other wall was ever so thick. However, this wall is also the highest wall ever built, and its great thickness seems almost miniscule in comparison to its height.

Most commentators have, for some reason, interpreted the 144 cubits to represent the height of the wall, but if this were the case, the stipulated height of the city itself is meaningless. The latter must at least represent the vertical dimensions of the structures at the outer edges of the city, in which case a wall 216 feet high surrounding structures 1,380 miles high would seem pointless, especially since the wall is not needed for protection. It is far more likely that the thickness is 144 cubits.

The recurrence of the number twelve in these verses is striking—twelve angels, twelve gates, twelve foundations, twelve thousand stadia, a wall of twelve squared cubits in thickness. Twelve, like seven, seems to represent completeness, but particularly completeness in terms of God's administrative subdivisions of a corporate whole.

Revelation 21:18.   And the building of the wall of it was of jasper: and the city was pure gold, like unto clear glass.

The dimensions of the wall are amazing, but the construction material is even more amazing. The entire building ("structure," the only occurrence in New Testament) of the immense wall is of beautiful jasper stone. The exact nature of the jasper stone is uncertain, but it was renowned in the ancient world. Its name has been essentially transliterated from both the Hebrew (*yashpeh*) and Greek (*iaspis*), as well as other languages, but it still is unidentified today. It was one of the stones in the breastplate of the high priest (Exodus 28:20; 39:13) and in the heavenly Eden (Ezekiel 28:13). Its association with the sardine stone (Revelation 4:3) and with the clear crystal (Revelation 21:11), together with extrabiblical references, suggests that it was a fine translucent stone, capable of different colors, primarily radiant white but also with flashing fiery red and purple tints. In any case, there can be little doubt that the majestic wall of the city will be brilliantly beautiful.

Even more glorious than the wall is the city itself. Both the buildings and the streets (v. 21) of the city are made of gold. In the present world, gold is the most precious of metals, the standard of all currencies and the greatest of all objects of human greed and conflict. In the new Jerusalem, however, the very streets are paved with gold and the buildings are plastered with gold. The most beautiful and valuable of metals is now the most abundant of metals! And, like the primeval Havilah (Genesis 2:11, 12), "the gold of that land is good." The gold of heaven is so good and so flawless that, like the jasper stone, it is crystal clear, reflecting golden beams of brilliance from every surface. The words "pure" and "clear" in this verse are the same Greek word *(katharos),* speaking of the flawless perfection of the materials of the city.

Revelation 21:19.   And the foundations of the wall of the city were garnished with all manner of precious stones. The first foundation was jasper; the second, sapphire; the third, a chalcedony; the fourth, an emerald.

Beneath the giant walls are interspersed twelve great foundations (v. 14), inserted between the twelve gates. Like the wall itself, these massive foundations are constructed of precious stones. Each foundation consists of one particular type of stone, but apparently that stone is itself trimmed with many other different kinds of precious stones, so that the whole scene is magnificently beautiful.

There are twelve different gemstones for the twelve foundations, with each stone inscribed, perhaps using other precious stones, with the name of one of the twelve apostles (v. 14). There seems no way, however, of identifying the stone that corresponds to each apostle. Similarly, there is no apparent correlation with the order of the precious stones in the priestly breastplate (Exodus 28:17-20) or the stones in the heavenly garden (Ezekiel 28:13), although a number of the stones are the same in both instances (the Ezekiel listing includes only nine precious stones, plus gold). Six stones are in all three lists (jasper, sapphire, emerald, sardius, beryl, and topaz). No particular patterns or reasons for the particular sequences seem discernible at this time.

The first foundation, like the wall which it supports, is of jasper, presumably reflecting a different hue than that of the wall. The beautiful and hard blue sapphire constitutes the second foundation, and the third is a chalcedony (only occurrence in Bible), a copper-colored stone. An emerald stone is the first foundation in the second wall, radiant in its shining green color, like the divine throne itself (Revelation 4:3).

Revelation 21:20.   The fifth, sardonyx; the sixth, sardius; the seventh, chrysolyte; the eighth, beryl; the ninth, a topaz; the tenth, a chrysoprasus; the eleventh, a jacinth; the twelfth, an amethyst.

The sardonyx is a variety of onyx, with deep red layers ("sard," derived from the Sardis region in ancient Lydia) interspersed with white. The sixth foundation, sardius, is probably the same as the sardine stone (Revelation 4:3), a brilliant red stone of chalcedony quartz.

On the next wall are three foundations of chrysolyte, beryl and topaz, respectively. The chrysolyte ("gold stone") is probably not the present stone of that name, but could have been any yellow-hued gem. The beryl is also a yellow stone, probably the same as our modern beryl. The topaz likewise is a yellow gem, though possibly different from the stone presently recognized by that name.

The fourth wall rests on foundations of chrysoprasus, jacinth and amethyst. The chrysoprase (mentioned only this once in the Bible) is probably a gold-tinted green gemstone. The jacinth (= "hyacinth") is believed to represent a blue stone, possibly aquamarine or turquoise. Finally, the amethyst is undoubtedly the same as the beautiful purple stone known by that name today.

There is considerable uncertainty about the exact identity of most of these foundation stones, but perhaps even this is intentional. The purpose of John's description is surely to impress upon us the indescribable glories and beauties of the holy city, reflecting its heavenly light in the translucent white and rainbow hues of its mighty jasper wall, resting upon great and brilliant foundations containing every imaginable color and variety of the most beautiful materials that an omnipotent God can manufacture.

Revelation 21:21.   And the twelve gates were twelve pearls; every several gate was of one pearl: and the street of the city was pure gold, as it were transparent glass.

Although the description is not specific enough for us to be sure, it seems probable that these twelve gates extend upward through the entire height of the great walls, thus permitting access at all levels. The gates are never closed (v. 25), so they really constitute merely great openings in the wall. But each doorway, framed along the sides and over the crest of each gate, is one magnificent shimmering pure body of flawless pearl!

Through these pearly gates, at many levels, will pass for endless ages streams of holy angels and glorified saints, going in and out on the business of the King. One can picture, for example, the delightful homecoming of one of the King's "servants" (Revelation 22:3) who has been dispatched on a mission of exploration and development in some distant galaxy. After a long absence, he begins the long journey earthward. Traveling through space at angelic speeds, far greater than the velocity of light, though still at some finite speed, he enters the Milky Way galaxy and soon approaches the solar system. Slowing down in order to better savor the beauty of the earth as he draws near to it, he soon sees the fair planet with its soft vistas of blue and green beckoning him.

And then he sees the City! One would have to view it from a great distance, of course, really to see it in its full grandeur. The city is far too large for one to see the whole of its beauty otherwise. From the outer reaches of the new heavens, however (that is, the new atmosphere), he will be able to revel in its magnificence.

The great jasper wall, clear and glowing white in its soft, yet shimmering, hues, with the jeweled foundations imparts unimaginably beautiful rainbow colorings along its lower reaches. The shining pearl entrances, traversing its height through the intervals between the foundations, all will display the most beautiful panorama to be found in the entire universe, welcoming home the trusted emissary of the mighty King.

Then, as he approaches the wall, he will probably direct his flight toward the gate and the level nearest his own "mansion" (John 14:2), there to dine and rest and prepare for his coming audience with the Lord, where he will eventually make his report and receive further instruction.

As he enters the gate, passing through the wide wall, the transcendent beauty of the city itself will meet his eyes. The "street" of the city, which undoubtedly is really a great, three-dimensional network of avenues, is everywhere lined with the most pure gold, so pure that it is as transparent as clear glass. How this can be, we do not understand, but John saw it and assures us that it is so. The street is strong and solid, with the beautiful sunshine color of the finest gold, but nevertheless is translucent to the radiant light which everywhere permeates the city.

There is far more to the city than golden streets, of course. There are waterways and trees (Revelation 22:1, 2) and therefore beautiful parks, with occasional clear vistas to the starry heavens above. There are magnificent public buildings, no doubt, as well as homes for all of the saints, and many more things than we can now imagine (1 Corinthians 2:9).

No Night There

With all the great structures and marvelous sights of the city, there does seem to be one surprising omission, surprising at first, that is. In the old Jerusalem, and even in the millennial Jerusalem, one great building had dominated both the landscape and the life of the city. Set high on the hill of Zion was the beautiful Temple of God. There served the priests and there were brought the sacrifices and offerings of the people. Most important of all, it was there where God met with His people.

But now, in the new Jerusalem, God dwells with His people! The Lamb of God, who is the one sacrifice for sins forever, reigns there on His throne, and every redeemed saint is a king and priest unto God. There is no longer need for a temple structure, and one would search the huge city in vain for such a building. Nevertheless, there is a temple there.

Revelation 21:22.   **And I saw no temple therein: for the Lord God Almighty and the Lamb are the temple of it.**

Since all the purposes of the earthly temple will have been fully accomplished, no temple will be erected as a physical structure in the new Jerusalem. Before Christ, the temple was a prophecy; in the Christian era, the temple was in the Holy Spirit; in the Millennial Age, it will be a memorial. In the ages of eternity, however, all prophecies will have been fulfilled, the immediate presence of the Lamb will obviate any need for memorial ceremony, and the indwelling testimony of the Holy Spirit will be forever united with the all-pervasive reality of the personal glory of the triune God.

Even the heavenly city, before its descent to earth, had possessed a temple (Revelation 11:19) and an altar (Revelation 8:3), but these will be removed forever once their purpose is served. The Lord God Almighty Himself constitutes the temple of the city. This exalted threefold title probably speaks of His tri-unity. It was the title used by the cherubim in their thrice-repeated ascription to Him of absolute holiness (Revelation 4:8), as they also identified His holy omnipotence with the eternal past, continuing present, and endless future, as the one which was, and is, and is to come (see also Revelation 11:17). The title is also used in Revelation 15:3 and 19:6, and surely testifies of the Godhead in all its fullness.

But then also the Lamb "is the temple of it." Both God in His infinite majesty and God in His suffering humanity are one, both together as God-man, comprising the holy temple in which He dwells eternally with His own people, His both by virtue of creation and by right of redemption.

His people—what an identification! Furthermore, precisely because we are "in Christ" (Ephesians 1:3), and Christ is in us as our "hope of glory" (Colossians 1:27), we ourselves are spiritually components of the true temple. "Ye are the temple of the living God; as God hath said, I will dwell in them, and walk in them; and I will be their God, and they shall be my people" (2 Corinthians 6:16). We "of the household of God . . . fitly framed together . . . an holy temple in the Lord . . . builded together for an habitation of God through the Spirit" (Ephesians 2:19-22). Thus, the very city itself becomes the temple, personifying and arraying both itself and its residents as "the bride, the Lamb's wife" (v. 10), beautifully "adorned for her husband" (v. 2).

Revelation 21:23.   And the city had no need of the sun, neither of the moon, to shine in it: for the glory of God did lighten it, and the Lamb is the light thereof.

Since "God is light" and "in him is no darkness at all" (1 John 1:5) and since Christ Himself is "the light of the world" (John 9:5), it would be unfitting for the city ever to be darkened or for night to fall there. In His essential nature, He dwells "in the light which no man can approach unto" (1 Timothy 6:16), at least not any man in his natural human body. In like manner as "the glory of God" filled the ancient temple with devastating radiance (1 Kings 8:10, 11), and then also the millennial temple (Haggai 2:7-9; Ezekiel 44:4), so the glory of God will pervasively illumine the new Jerusalem.

Neither the sun nor the moon will ever really be destroyed, of course, since God has promised that they, as well as all the starry heavens, will endure forever (Psalm 148:3, 6; Daniel 12:3). It is just that their light is no longer needed to illumine the holy city, for the city itself radiates light to all the surrounding regions (v. 24). However, the sun and moon will continue to serve their present functions with respect to the nether regions of the earth, serving there as lights by day and night, respectively.

There is nothing intrinsically evil in darkness, of course, since God created it (Isaiah 45:7). The primeval creation included both evening and morning, light and darkness, day and night, and God called it all "very good" (Genesis 1:31). Light did not have to be created, since it was intrinsic in the very self-existence of God; it merely had to be "formed" (Isaiah 45:7), whereas the darkness was an actual creation. God simply said: "Let there be light" (Genesis 1:3), and the created earth and its primeval darkness were then enlightened and energized. Superficial modern philosophers imagine a difficulty when the Scriptures thus speak of "light" before the formation of the "lights" to rule the day and night (Genesis 1:14-18), but it is obvious that God's provision of light for the earth is not dependent upon sun and moon. These are not needed at all for New Jerusalem.

It may well be that the ineffable glory of the omnipotent Creator would be too much for even the glorified bodies of the saints to endure, so that the light for the city is mediated, as it were, through the Lamb, the glorified Son of man. Even His countenance is as bright as the sun (Revelation 1:16; 10:1), but at least those whom He has redeemed can survive its presence.

There is a beautiful passage describing this wonderful situation back in Isaiah's prophecy. Isaiah first speaks of the beautiful walls and gates of the city: "Thou shalt call thy walls Salvation, and thy gates Praise" (Isaiah 60:18).

And then he sees into the glorious city itself. "The sun shall be no more thy light by day; neither for brightness shall the moon give light unto thee: but the Lord shall be unto thee an everlasting light, and thy God thy glory. Thy sun shall no more go down; neither shall thy moon withdraw itself: for the Lord shall be thine everlasting light, and the days of thy mourning shall be ended. Thy people also shall be all righteous: they shall inherit the land for ever, the branch of my planting, the work of my hands, that I may be glorified. . . . I the Lord will hasten it in his time" (Isaiah 60:19-22).

Revelation 21:24.   And the nations of them which are saved shall walk in the light of it: and the kings of the earth do bring their glory and honour into it.

This unexpected revelation at this point in the description has, not surprisingly, been the object of speculation and varied interpretation. If all the redeemed, both Jew and Gentile, make up the Lamb's bride and the new Jerusalem is their home (which we have already inferred from previous passages), then who are these other kings and nations? We do, at least, learn that there are still "nations," even in the eternal ages to come, and that they have their kings. Further, they do seem to be associated with "kingdoms of the earth," that is to say, those parts of the earth outside the holy city.

Nevertheless, all these kings and their nations are said to be people who are "saved," and indeed, all others have been banished to the lake of fire (Revelation 20:15; 21:8). Furthermore, all of the saved seemingly possess mansions in the city, consisting as they do of the redeemed saints of all past ages (see the discussion on Revelation 19:7-9; 20:4-6).

Is there any way, however, that these could be nations of people still in a natural state (say, like Adam and Eve before the fall) continuing over from the millennium? The earth itself had been burned up at the end of the millennium, and it seems probable, as discussed previously, that any who had possessed saving faith at that time would have been immediately raptured and glorified, like the saints living at the time of Christ's return before the tribulation.

Admittedly, however, the Scriptures do not deal with this particular subject directly, so some degree of speculation may be warranted. It is possible, though one must certainly be tentative on this point, that this particular group of saints, some from each millennial nation, may have been (like Enoch and Elijah long before) translated to the heavenly Jerusalem still in the flesh. In such a hypothetical situation, they would then still be in that state in the city when it descended to the earth.

In that event, they could then go forth to colonize and multiply in the new earth, reestablishing their nations as before. This time, however, the sad history of the millennial apostasy could never be repeated, for Satan and all his hosts are bound forever in the lake of fire. As children were then born to the citizens of these nations of the saved, they would all be so "taught of the Lord" (Isaiah 54:13) that none would ever again rebel even in his heart against the gracious, onmipotent God in the beautiful city.

This interpretation of this text, doubtful and fraught with difficulties though it may be, would help in answering certain other questions. For example, the divine promise that God's primeval covenant with the descendants of Noah would be "for perpetual generations" as an "everlasting covenant" (Genesis 9:12, 16) could be taken quite literally, as could His promise that Abraham's seed would be multiplied "as the stars of the heaven, and as the sand which is upon the sea shore" (Genesis 22:17). There is also the amazing messianic promise that "of the *increase* of his government and peace there shall be no end . . . to establish it with judgment and with justice from henceforth even for ever" (Isaiah 9:7). The doxology of Ephesians 3:21 could properly and better be translated: "Unto him be glory in the church by Christ Jesus throughout all generations, to the age of the ages."

If, indeed, these nations of the saved were to continue to multiply, as would have Adam and Eve, had they not sinned, God's primeval command to "fill the earth" and to "subdue it" unto His glory would finally, for the first time, really be accomplished. The millennial multiplication, which had seemed about to do this, had ended in apostasy. Then, perhaps, they would be send out to colonize and develop other terrestrial planets throughout God's infinite universe, worlds without end.

This is all admittedly highly speculative, but it does appear somewhat reasonable, both as a possible interpretation of Scripture and as a program consistent with the nature and program of an omniscient and loving and purposeful God. It does have problems as well and, though it is a fascinating speculation, it must be left for future determination.

The best, and perhaps more likely, alternative exposition of this passage seems to be that the "nations of the saved" are identical with the redeemed residents of the city, but that, in addition to their homes in the city, they will also be given national boundaries in the new earth, within which they can still function as distinct nations. Certainly the new earth, with its increased land areas and far more equable and fruitful environments, could well accommodate such terrestrial "homes away from home" for its 20 billion or so human inhabitants. The nation of Israel would, as during the millennium, be the chief of all such earthly nations if this is the case.

All such activity on the external earth must, of course, be carried out under the aegis of the great capital city and its divine regime. They will not "walk in darkness" (John 8:12) but in the glorious light of the Lamb and His city. None of the peoples, even their kings, will seek their own glory through such accomplishments, but will give all honor to the Lord.

Revelation 21:25.   **And the gates of it shall not be shut at all by day: for there shall be no night there.**

The beautiful gates framed in pearl are entrances, not barriers. Unlike earthly cities, whose walls and gates have been needed from ancient times as barricades against their enemies, new Jerusalem has no enemies, and all people are welcome. Like the Lord Jesus Himself, who said: "I am the door: by me if any man enter in, he shall be saved, and shall go in and out, and find pasture" (John 10:9), the gates are gracious invitations, not forbidding deterrents.

Nor will they only be opened in the daytime, as were the gates of ancient cities, but they will always be open. The city itself will radiate light as bright as daylight, so night will never come, even when the earth's rotation carries the city away from the sun.

The absence of night also symbolizes the absence of all sin and sorrow. Even though, as noted previously, there is nothing intrinsically evil about the night time, it does entail the absence of light and thus appropriately is often used in the Bible as a figure of speech for the absence of God's presence and His blessing (John 9:4; 12:35; Romans 14:12; Ephesians 4:11; 1 Thessalonians 5:2-8; 1 John 5:5-7).

In New Jerusalem, there will be no more night, and this also correlates with the assurance that there will be "no more death, neither sorrow, nor crying, neither shall there be any more pain" (v. 4). Nothing will be "old" any more (v. 5) and there is "no more sea" (v. 1). In fact, there is "no more curse" (Revelation 22:3), so that nothing at all hinders any more at all the full and continual outpouring of the blessings of a loving God on the men and women who love Him.

Revelation 21:26.   And they shall bring the glory and honour of the nations into it.

In verse 24 John observed that the kings of the earth were bringing all their glory and honor into the city; now he notes also that "they" (evidently all the citizens of the nations as well, following the example of their kings) are bringing their glory and honor into it.

All "glory and honor," as well as all "power and riches and wisdom and strength and blessing" (note Revelation 4:11; 5:12), rightfully belong to God, for we are His by right of both creation and redemption. Every ability we possess, and every blessing we enjoy, have come from Him. Yet there are few who acknowledge this fact. The rich man boasts of his riches, the educated man is proud of his intellectualism, the strong man revels in his might, the nobleman disdains the commoner, and God hates all such human pride. "Thus saith the Lord, Let not the wise man glory in his wisdom, neither let the mighty man glory in his might, let not the rich man glory in his riches: But let him that glorieth glory in this, that he understandeth and knoweth me, that I am the Lord which exercise lovingkindness, judgment, and righteousness, in the earth: for in these things I delight, saith the Lord" (Jeremiah 9:23, 24).

The nations and their kings will finally have learned this great truth. The earth will yield her riches, both in human understanding and material resources, to human research and development in incomparably greater degree than ever before. Much glory and honor could well accrue to the men and nations accomplishing these things. But this "subduing of the earth" is a ministry of stewardship, to the glory of God, and there will be a continuing procession into the city, where the people, small and great, will all lay their trophies of learning and wealth, glory and honor, at the feet of Him who alone deserves the praise.

Revelation 21:27.   And there shall in no wise enter into it any thing that defileth, neither whatsoever worketh abomination, or maketh a lie: but they which are written in the Lamb's book of life.

With all this coming and going through the always-open gates of the city, John emphasizes once again that there is no danger whatever entailed in this right of unlimited access. There is no possibility that the wholesomeness of the city will ever be defiled by the entry of some unclean thought or impure motive. All who traffic there have long since been conformed to the image of God's Son (Romans 8:29), and have purified themselves even as He is pure (1 John 3:3).

All those who work abomination, meaning especially those who practice or nurture idolatry in their hearts, and this includes both unbelief and covetousness, and all liars, whose deceitful hearts are controlled by the father of liars, the Devil, have been dispatched to the far-off lake of fire (v. 8), whence there is no escape forever, so there is no way such as these can enter the city.

In fact, all whose names have not been written and retained in the Lamb's book of life have been cast into the lake of fire (Revelation 20:15), so none such can ever even approach the pearly gates. Both the city and the new earth on which it rests, and indeed all of God's marvelous universe, save the infinitely-removed hidden corner which hides the terrible lake of fire, are for the exclusive and eternal utilization and enjoyment of those who have been redeemed by the Lamb and whose names are recorded in His book of life.

22

Eternal Life

(Revelation 22)

In this final chapter of the Holy Scriptures, John continues with his description of the holy city and then, as it were, ushers us on into the eternal ages to come. When he closes with a last postscript of invitation, warning, and prayer, the book of God is complete. This climactic revelation will terminate God's written Word to man. All we need to know will have been revealed and recorded, and now we must simply await the fulfillment.

Finally we can begin to comprehend in some small measure the Lord's "unspeakable gift" of eternal life (2 Corinthians 9:15) to sinners who had earned the wage of eternal death (Romans 6:23). Having heard and believed the "word of life" (Philippians 2:16), we have feasted on the "bread of life" (John 6:35) and drunk deeply of the "water of life" (Revelation 21:6), assured that our names are indelibly inscribed in the Lamb's "book of life" (Revelation 3:5). We no longer walk in darkness but have the "light of life" (John 8:12), knowing that soon we shall receive the "crown of life" (Revelation 2:10) and have access forever to the "tree of life" (Revelation 22:14).

No More Curse

The omniscient, omnipotent God had a great and holy, eternal, and unchangeable purpose for His creation, established in His heart before the world began. The temporary intrusion of sin and death can never thwart or deter that purpose. Finally, in the counsels of God, the time has come to renew and fulfill that purpose. The great curse has been removed from the creation, and the kingdom of God has come.

Revelation 22:1.   And he shewed me a pure river of water of life, clear as crystal, proceeding out of the throne of God and of the Lamb.

Thus far John had described only the external beauties of the holy city, with merely a glimpse of the golden streets, inside its walls. Now we enter into the city itself, acquiring at least an introductory insight into the splendors that have been prepared for our enjoyment there.

Most prominent of all is a mighty river of clear sparkling water, coursing down from the center and apex of the city. Although the text does not say so, we are probably justified in inferring that this river (like the river in Eden which was its typological forerunner) parts "into four heads" (Genesis 2:10), which in turn descend from level to level, providing abundant water for every need (aesthetic as well as physiological) of the residents of the city.

Eventually its four distributaries will, presumably, reach ground level and then flow out through the four walls of the city, north, south, east and west, whence it, like the eyes of the Lord, will "run to and fro throughout the whole earth" (1 Chronicles 16:9). Since there is "no more sea" (Revelation 21:1) the inexhaustible waters of this mighty river will supply whatever hydrologic needs the new earth may have. There surely will be an abundance of luxurious grasses and herbs and trees everywhere, as in the original "very good" created world (Genesis 1:11, 31), and the whole earth will be a well-watered paradise of abundant resources and fulfilling ministries for the servants of God.

It is noteworthy that the same phrase, "clear as crystal," is used to describe the water as was used for the previous jasper stone in the walls of the city (Revelation 21:11) and the light radiating from them. Similarly the "sea of glass" at the heavenly throne was "like unto crystal" (Revelation 4:6). The emphasis throughout is that these heavenly entities are free of all impurities, clear and sparkling in radiance, bespeaking the character and the glories of their divine Creator.

But most notable of all is the source of this mighty river of life and its living waters. There is no sea from which waters are raised by the sun, as in the present hydrologic cycle (Revelation 21:1) and thus no rainfall to supply the river with its flow. Rather, it proceeds "out of the throne of God and of the Lamb," high at the central pinnacle of the holy city. Evidently the mighty Creator is continually creating the waters, then sending them forth to give perpetual life and cleansing and beauty to the city and its inhabitants, and then on out into the uttermost parts of the new earth. It is water of life, and there is no more death.

This marvelous fountain of an infinitely great deep was, in type, first opened on another central pinnacle, the inner cross on Mount Calvary. "But one of the soldiers with a spear pierced his side, and forthwith came there out blood and water" (John 19:34). Medical men through the centuries have speculated as to the source and nature of this "water" which emerged with the shed blood from the side of the Savior; it seems to have been essentially a unique phenomenon. But whatever may be its precise physiological explanation, it surely speaks typologically of the great water of life which the Lord had promised Nicodemus (John 3:5), the woman at the well (John 4:10-14) and the multitudes at the feast of tabernacles (John 7:37-39). The blood of the Lamb must be poured out in order to take away the sin of the world (John 1:29), but simultaneously a fountain of cleansing and refreshing must be opened, that the Spirit betokened by the water (John 7:39) might evermore indwell and guide and energize all the redeemed of the Lamb.

"This is he that came by water and blood, even Jesus Christ; not by water only, but by water and blood. And it is the Spirit that beareth witness, because the Spirit is truth. . . . And there are three that bear witness in earth, the spirit, and the water, and the blood: and these three agree in one" (1 John 5:6, 8).

As water flowed from the side of the Lamb on the cross, so a pure river of water of life will flow from the Lamb on the throne, and all may drink freely of the water of life forever (Revelation 22:17). Even now, the waters of baptism symbolize, to those who enter them, the cleansing blood (1 Peter 3:21; 1 John 1:7) and the enveloping Spirit (1 Corinthians 12:13), participation in the atoning death and glorious resurrection of their Savior (Romans 6:3-11).

Revelation 22:2.   In the midst of the street of it, and on either side of the river, was there the tree of life, which bare twelve manner of fruits, and yielded her fruit every month: and the leaves of the tree were for the healing of the nations.

Not only the river with the water of life but also the tree with the fruit of life is there. This is apparently the same tree that God had planted in the garden of Eden (Genesis 2:9), whose fruit possessed such remarkable life-preserving properties that God had to withdraw it from man's use after Adam's sin (Genesis 3:22-25). Now, however, though it had been withheld from sinful men and women, it is made freely available in the new earth to "him that overcometh" (Revelation 2:7), a characterization of all who participate in the first resurrection and who, therefore, are not subject to the judgment of the second death (Revelation 2:11; 20:6, 14-15).

Surprisingly, the tree bears twelve different kinds of fruits, one for each month of the year. Whether this was true of the first tree of life in Eden the Scripture does not say, but the inference at least seems to be that the trees of the first garden and the last garden are the same. In any case, this tree is a most marvelous creation of a loving God, with its genetic instructions beautifully programed for this perpetual variety. Yet every variety of its fruit carries the same life-sustaining ingredient, whatever that may be, imparted to it by its Creator. Actually, the word "manner" is not in the original, the phrase merely reading "twelve fruits," so it is possible that it could be understood as "twelve crops of fruit," but the more natural implication seems to be that of "twelve kinds of fruits."

The biblical lands abounded in fruit trees, and frequent reference to them is made in the Scriptures. However, it is rather surprising to note how few different kinds of fruit are actually named in the Bible. There are grapes, figs, apples (some think the Hebrew word for "apple" may have referred actually to the apricot), pomegranates, melons, and olives (if olives are considered a fruit), and that is about all. Although dates are not mentioned as such, the palm tree is often mentioned, and these almost certainly were date palms. In any case, the tree of life will bear about twice as many different kinds of fruit as are recognized by name in the Bible. And all are healthful and, no doubt, delicious.

Note also the implicit teaching that the actual time cycles will continue on forever. The fact that months are identified as such in New Jerusalem indicates that the orbital and rotational motions of the earth will go on as God established in the very beginning and that the moon likewise will continue orbiting around the earth.

Still another noteworthy aside is that the leaves of the tree of life have great value also, serving to bring healing to the nations. Some translators feel it would be more appropriate to translate this word (Greek *therapeia*) as "health," since it seems unlikely that the immortal peoples of the new earth would actually need healing, either physical or spiritual. However, the word basically meant "cure" or "service" in its original usage, and is translated "household" in Luke 12:42 and Matthew 24:45, referring to the staff of servants. In this case, the passage might be read: "the leaves of the tree were for the service of the nations." The chemical ingredients of the rich foliage of the trees might be available for innumerable uses in the economies and industries of the nations of the ages. Possibly it is the economy of the nations which is to be kept healthy by the leaves of the tree.

Furthermore, the tree is not rare, but prolific, growing in profusion all over the world. In the new Jerusalem, it grows along the esplanade in the center of all the golden streets and lines both banks of the cascading river. Presumably outside the city it grows along the shores of all the multitudes of distributaries of the mighty river as they spread out through all the world.

The tree of life! No wonder it has been used through the ages to symbolize so much that is good and wholesome. This is especially seen in the Book of Proverbs. "[Wisdom] is a tree of life to them that lay hold on her: and happy is every one that retaineth her" (Proverbs 3:18). "The fruit of the righteous is a tree of life; and he that winneth souls is wise" (Proverbs 11:30). "Hope deferred maketh the heart sick: but when the desire cometh, it is a tree of life" (Proverbs 13:12). "A wholesome tongue is a tree of life" (Proverbs 15:4).

Wisdom, righteousness, happiness, helpfulness, hopefulness, wholesomeness —all brought to mind by the tree of life! It is not possible for us to comprehend now how such a tree and its fruit and leaves can really be and do all that the Scriptures imply; but God's promises are true.

Finally, the necessity to continually partake of the life-giving fruit from the tree and water from the river will be a continual testimony to the people of the new earth that their Creator and Savior is Himself the source of life and breath and all things. And this knowledge and this requirement will never become a burden but will always remain a joy and a delight.

Revelation 22:3.   And there shall be no more curse: but the throne of God and of the Lamb shall be in it; and his servants shall serve him.

What has been made evident before, and is obvious in the very nature of things, is here rehearsed again, as though such a glorious truth cannot be contained and must burst forth repeatedly in its wonder. The agelong curse is gone. There is no more death and no more sin. The earth and its inhabitants, indeed the entire creation, are henceforth to thrive in fullest vigor forever. None will ever age, nothing will ever be lost, all work will be productive and enduring. The entropy law, the so-called second law of thermodynamics, will be repealed. Information will nevermore become confused, ordered systems will not deteriorate into disorder, and no longer will energy have to be expended merely to overcome friction and dissipation into nonrecoverable heat. Entropy will from now on be conserved along with energy and mass and momentum. Though "time" will continue on forever, "time's arrow" will no longer be directed downward.

"The throne of God and of the Lamb" has already been mentioned (v. 1) as the source of the mighty river of life. Now it is noted again, this time as the displacement of the curse. How could the creation possibly continue under "the bondage of corruption" (Romans 8:21) when both the divine omnipotence and His redemptive grace are manifested at its very heart?

What a wonderful revelation also is the final declaration of this verse! "His servants shall serve him." There can be no higher privilege than the service of the King of creation; and in this very service we are thereby His kings and priests, exercising dominion for Him and conveying knowledge about Him throughout His creation.

Life in this future world will not be merely a life of rest and singing, but rather a life of productivity and teaching. No doubt, there will also be abundant occasion for fellowship and testimony, for singing and playing harps. Every redeemed believer will have abundant time to meet and learn to know every other believer. What a thrill it will be to listen to Noah describe his experiences on the ark, to share the passion and vision of John the Baptist, to hear the testimonies of the martyrs. Each of us will have his own story to tell, his defeats and victories, and finally his overcoming faith, despite all its weaknesses and failures, redeemed by the Lamb.

But there is also work to do. Eternity is before us, and infinity surrounds us. We shall have an eternity of time to explore and discover the secrets of an infinitely varied and limitless cosmos. Perhaps each of us will be assigned an entire galaxy to explore and develop for the glory of God. Then each will share with the others what he has found and what he has accomplished and all will rejoice together.

Or, perhaps more likely, each will develop and use more fully the particular talents entrusted to Him by the Lord in this world and also have opportunity to learn and develop those skills he desired but could never attain before. Obviously the nature of our future service for the Lord can only be the object of reverent wonder and speculation now, but we can be sure it will be joyful and satisfying service, whatever it is.

Space travel will be commonplace, of course, in that day, even though it will always be impossible in any significant degree in this present world. The nearest star is four light years from the earth and the idea that people could travel from the earth to a star in a space ship operating under the laws of the physical universe is simply a delusion. With the force systems of the known universe (it is a *uni*-verse, not a polyverse!) this idea will always be mere science fiction. The four basic types of forces are known to be the gravitational forces, electromagnetic forces, nuclear forces and "weak" subnuclear forces. All matter must operate in force fields of gravity and electromagnetic force, and these are such as to render it impossible for sizable bodies of matter to move from one body to another at velocities even remotely approaching the speed of light. It would certainly take many human generations for a space ship designed under the most advanced technology conceivable ever to travel even from the earth to the very nearest star.

But these limitations will not apply to spiritual bodies. They will not be constrained by gravitational or electromagnetic forces but as in the case of angels, can "fly swiftly" (Daniel 9:21). Our spiritual bodies will be somehow like those of angels (Matthew 22:30) and even like that of Christ's resurrection body (Philippians 3:21), so that we, like they, can move—not instantaneously, of course, but very rapidly—across the cosmos. Thus, our future service for the Lord of glory may well include assignments in any part of the vast universe.

But home will always be in the new Jerusalem, where Christ is. There also is where the mansions are, which He has prepared for us (John 14:2), and there is where we shall always return.

Revelation 22:4.   And they shall see his face; and his name shall be in their foreheads.

It is the Lamb whom we shall serve, and it is the Lamb to whom we shall report concerning that service. Though He is King of the universe, He will always be accessible to His servants, for He loved them and died to be their Redeemer. Never will He hide His face from them, nor will they ever fear to enter His presence. As the Lamb, He has taken away their sin and there is nothing between each soul and the Savior. Again and again will they "enter into his gates with thanksgiving, and into his courts with praise" (Psalm 100:4).

And as they go out to "serve the Lord with gladness" (Psalm 100:2), they will go in His name, clearly identified as His servants with His name in their foreheads. This may be in the form of the divine seal, as was the case with the 144,000 witnesses during the tribulation (Revelation 7:3), or it may be engraved upon a golden plate suspended from a kingly crown, similar to the mitre and the golden plate described in Exodus 28:38 as "upon Aaron's forehead," in his capacity as high priest during the days in the wilderness. It may be simply in the impartation of the very character and appearance of the Lord, for they will have been "conformed to the image of his Son" and "shall be like him" (Romans 8:29; 1 John 3:2). Whatever precise form this identification may take, it will be a high privilege finally to share perfectly "the mind of Christ" (1 Corinthians 2:16) and for this fact to be evidenced by His name on our foreheads forever! "I will write upon him my new name," the Lord had promised those who would overcome the world and not deny His name (Revelation 3:8, 10, 12). His name will thus become our name and we shall be joint-heirs with Him of the whole creation.

Revelation 22:5.   And there shall be no night there; and they need no candle, neither light of the sun; for the Lord God giveth them light: and they shall reign for ever and ever.

Still further commentary on the characteristics of life in the new Jerusalem is given by John here, although the same facts had been mentioned previously. In verses 23 and 25 of the previous chapter, the unceasing light from the city, emanating directly from the Lord Himself, had been noted. There, however, the viewpoint was from outside the city; here it is inside.

Those who are in the city will enjoy perpetual sunlight. Never will there be clouds or storms, and never will there be any darkness. In our new bodies, we shall presumably have no need for sleep, although there will be ample time and opportunity for rest and leisure activities. In fact, the very nature of life in that day is called rest. "There remaineth therefore a rest to the people of God. For he that is entered into his rest, he also hath ceased from his own works, as God did from his" (Hebrews 4:9, 10). In stark contrast is the existence of those in the lake of fire: "they have no rest day nor night" (Revelation 14:11).

Even inside the dwelling places, there will always be ample illumination. No lamp is needed for inside lighting, even as neither sun nor moon are needed for outside lighting. The glory of God's presence (Revelation 21:23) is the light of that new world, and no other light is ever needed there.

The dwelling places are called "mansions" in John 14:2, a word which is used only one other time in the New Testament, and in the same chapter, when

Jesus said, "If a man love me, he will keep my words: and my Father will love him, and we will come unto him, and make our abode with him" (John 14:23). Thus, in the new Jerusalem, the Father and the Son will dwell in the very mansion (Greek *mone*) which has been prepared by the Lord Jesus Christ for each believer. Not only will God and the Lamb be seated on the glorious throne, but they will also, in some sense, reside in the home of each of their servants.

Presumably every saint will have his or her own individual mansion. It would, of course, be impossible for us to live in the same family groupings we have shared in this life. All of us belong to the families of our respective parents but then we also have established families of our own, and so have our children. In one sense, it will be recognized by all that everyone in the city belongs to the family of Adam—who will himself also be a resident there as the patriarch of the whole human race. Mother Eve will be there too, the "mother of all living" (Genesis 3:2), and there will, indeed, be a great family reunion.

It may be possible that husbands and wives will, in some cases, continue to live together in the same heavenly abode, but this is uncertain. In answer to the tongue-in-cheek question of the Sadducees about the woman who had been married seven times, the Lord said: "In the resurrection they neither marry, nor are given in marriage, but are as the angels of God in heaven" (Matthew 22:30). There are many different marital situations in this life that would be impracticable to perpetuate in the future life. Many people have been married more than once, and many have never married at all. In many cases, one partner in a marriage may have been a believer, with the other dying unsaved. At various times, in the past, some godly women have been members even of polygamous households. There are probably at least some instances where Christian men and women have lived together without a marriage ceremony.

Although the divinely-ordained arrangement has always been that of a permanent union of one husband with one wife (Matthew 19:4-6), there have been so many and varied exceptions to this rule throughout the centuries that it would be impossible to establish a universal continuation in eternity of all the same marriage relationships that have existed on earth.

On the other hand, it seems at least possible that, in those husband/wife unions which have been established and maintained on earth in accordance with God's commandment, the Lord may well allow them to continue together in the same union and in the same mansion forever, serving Him in some capacity where such a relationship would be consistent with God's purposes for their future ministries. The Lord has blessed the institution of marriage (Genesis 1:29), Jesus performed his first miracle at a wedding (John 2:1, 2, 11), and the Lord has even chosen the human marriage relation to be a portrayal of the union of Christ with His own people (Revelation 21:9). Thus, it may well honor Him to have such an institution perpetuated forever, not for all those who are saved, but for those whose homes can continue to bear this same testimony and to serve Him effectually through this means. The Scriptures have apparently left this question unanswered in any direct way, however, so dogmatism is impossible.

Coming Soon

In any case, all human relationships which have been spiritually fruitful in this life will surely be even more blessed in that life. Husbands and wives, parents and children, relatives and in-laws, friends and colleagues—all will love more and understand better than they could ever have imagined here. The Lord God will give light to all in every area of life, not only physical illumination, but also personal guidance and insight sufficient to meet every need and sanctify every relationship.

And though we are His servants, that very privilege suffices also to make us kings. Each of us will have his or her assigned "dominion" to subdue, develop, and utilize for the good of all the redeemed and the glory of the Lamb, and over that dominion we shall reign forever.

Revelation 22:6.   And he said unto me, These sayings are faithful and true: and the Lord God of the holy prophets sent his angel to shew unto his servants the things which must shortly be done.

The one who speaks at this point is apparently the same one of the angels with the seven last plagues who had been showing John the wonders of the holy city (Revelation 21:9, 15; 22:1). The scene had been so magnificent and the promises so amazing that he felt it needful to interject again the assurance that all this was actually real and true. John was not merely dreaming, nor were these all simply allegories of unknown meaning. They are true. These events would surely come to pass, exactly as John had seen and heard them. We can be sure that He whose very name is "Faithful and True" (Revelation 19:11) will speak words that "are true and faithful" (Revelation 21:5) and will see that His angel likewise conveys sayings that are faithful and true.

Some translations render "the Lord God of the holy prophets" by some such phrase as "the Lord, the God of the spirits of the prophets," because of certain manuscript evidence. The King James Version, however, and the textual evidence supporting it, seems more appropriate and is probably correct. The Old Testament prophets are frequently elsewhere called "holy prophets" (Luke 1:70; Acts 3:21; 2 Peter 3:2; Revelation 18:20) whereas there is only one other reference (and this reference is irrelevant to this passage) to "the spirits of the prophets" (1 Corinthians 14:32). Furthermore, the divine name, "the Lord God" has just been used in the preceding verse, and it would be beautifully appropriate to note that, as "the Lord God giveth them light," so the same One is "the Lord God of the holy prophets." The One who called and blessed the ancient prophets, and wrote through them the great prophetic messages of the Old Testament is the same Lord

God who, through His angel is conveying this grand climactic prophecy of the New Testament.

The final declaration of this verse: "to shew unto his servants the things which must shortly be done," is exactly the same in the Greek as in Revelation 1:1: "to shew unto his servants things which must shortly come to pass." In both cases, the adverb "shortly" is two words in the Greek, *en tachos* (in haste). The emphasis, perhaps, is that the entire sequence of events outlined in Revelation, once begun, will be completed in a short period of time (say, 1,007 years, the tribulation plus the millennium). More likely, however, it is a reference to the brevity of human time in contrast with eternity. The events prophesied in Revelation began to be fulfilled immediately, in the lives of the seven churches to whom the book was initially addressed. The Church Age which they foreshadowed, followed by the tribulation and the millennium, may seem like a long span of time to us but, when we look back on them from eternity, will indeed seem to have "shortly been done."

Revelation 22:7. Behold, I come quickly: blessed is he that keepeth the sayings of the prophecy of this book.

The last portion of the Book of Revelation reiterates in some degree the promises of its introduction. In the opening verse (Revelation 1:1) the Lord Jesus Christ is seen as sending His revelation concerning things to come by way of His angel to His servant John. This statement has, in effect, just been repeated (v. 6). The fulfillment had been indicated in Revelation 1:3 to be "at hand." Here, the Lord Jesus, as it were, speaks to emphasize the angel's urgent message, promising to "come quickly." The word "quickly" is the adverbial form of the Greek noun used in the preceding verse, translated "shortly" but actually meaning "in haste."

Then the wonderful promise of Revelation 1:3 is repeated. "Blessed is he that readeth, and they that hear the words of this prophecy, and keep those things which are written therein." There is blessing merely in the reading and hearing of the book, and this is the sixth of the seven "beatitudes" of Revelation. Now that its reading and hearing are almost complete, the emphasis shifts especially toward the vital importance of keeping its sayings. The Lord had commanded John to write all he would see (Revelation 1:11) and now his "book" was almost complete.

The reader or hearer is thus urged to keep (that is, to "guard" or "hold fast") the prophecy (that is, the "predictions," or "foretellings") of John's book. Of all the divinely inspired writings of the Holy Scriptures, few if any are more in need of such guarding. Countless readers and interpreters of this book have allegorized, spiritualized, rejected, or ridiculed it. But to him who reads it, believes it, and holds fast its "sayings," that is, the actual "words" (Greek *logos*) of this final book from God, divine blessing is promised by the Lord Jesus Christ Himself.

Revelation 22:8.   And I John saw these things, and heard them. And when I had heard and seen, I fell down to worship before the feet of the angel which shewed me these things.

John now adds his own testimony for the benefit of his readers. Those first readers, in the seven churches of Asia, knew him personally and loved and honored him. He assures them again (note Revelation 1:9; 21:2) that he had actually seen and heard the tremendous events he was reporting.

Then once again he was suddenly overwhelmed with the grandeur of the scene, and impetuously fell to his knees, prostrating himself before the angel. He had made this same mistake (Revelation 19:10) before, and had received a rebuke from his angelic guide as a result. Again, however, as almost a reflexive response which he could not restrain, John felt he must express his grateful submission to God's will (as noted before, this is the essence of true worship) and the means immediately at hand was simply to bow down before the angel. No doubt John intended this only as an expression of reverence and submission to God. The text does not say that he worshiped the angel, but that he worshiped before the feet of the angel. Nevertheless, even this was inappropriate and must be corrected.

Revelation 22:9.   Then saith he unto me, See thou do it not: for I am thy fellow-servant, and of thy brethren the prophets, and of them which keep the sayings of this book: worship God.

Even though John already well knew that he was not to worship angels (note Colossians 2:18, and compare Revelation 19:10) and surely did not really intend in this case that his prostration before the feet of the angel should be taken as anything but an expression of worship toward God, nevertheless the angel had to rebuke him for it. Even the appearance of worship toward anything or anyone other than God must be avoided. The first two of God's ten commandments stress that neither any creature nor any likeness of any creatures may be worshiped. Furthermore, no creature (whether man or angel) must allow himself to be worshiped by others. Herod, for example, was struck dead because he accepted such adulation (Acts 12:21-23) and Nebuchadnezzar was driven mad (Daniel 4:28-37). The highest of all the angels, Lucifer (identical with Satan) was cast out of heaven, and ultimately into the lake of fire, because he aspired to be worshiped as God (Isaiah 14:12-15). Knowing all this, John's angelic messenger could not allow John even to seem to worship him, reminding him, as had the other angel, in Revelation 19:10, that he was a fellowservant and spiritual brother to John, concerned to do exactly what John had just been commanded, namely to keep the sayings of this book.

Here also is a sharp rebuke to all those who feel they must have aids, in order to worship God, such things as images, a solemn atmosphere, a musical hand-clapping atmosphere, prayer beads and talismans, a special building or prayer room, or anything else. If not even a mighty angel of God provides a suitable aid or atmosphere for worship, surely none of these manmade objects can do so. "God is a Spirit: and they that worship him must worship him in spirit and in truth" (John 4:24). Once again we need to be reminded that even the greatest prophet is merely a sinner saved by grace, and even the most eminent angel is merely a ministering spirit (Hebrews 1:14), and true worship is simply honoring and submitting to the revealed will and purposes of God.

Revelation 22:10.   And he saith unto me, Seal not the sayings of the prophecy of this book: for the time is at hand.

Not only are we to keep the sayings of the prophecy of this book, but we are also to unseal them. They are not to be guarded under lock and key, as it were, where no one would ever learn their message. Rather, they are to be opened and expounded and proclaimed. These sayings were directed to the churches, and they are urgently needed by the churches, all the more as the time draws near for their final and complete fulfillment.

Here for the third time in four verses (see vv. 7, 9) "the sayings" of "this book" are stressed. The same word (Greek *logos*) appears twice more at the end of the chapter, there translated "the words" of "this book" (vv. 18 and 19). God wants the actual words, not just the thoughts, or the interpretations, guarded and believed and preached.

In one sense, this commandment has itself become a prophecy, for probably as many books have been written and sermons preached from this Book of Revelation as from any other book ever written. Yet, in another sense, this multitude of expositions has contributed little to the unsealing of the book, for there is surely no other book that has been so variously interpreted and so fancifully spiritualized.

We are to guard the words of the book. God is surely capable of speaking plain words, through His angel and through John, to us, and we had better let Him say what He says. This is a book of revelation, not mystification, of apocalypse, not apocrypha. As the book of redemption had finally been completely unsealed (Revelation 5:5), so let the Book of revelation and consummation never become sealed, especially as the day approaches.

Revelation 22:11.   He that is unjust, let him be unjust still: and he which is filthy, let him be filthy still: and he that is righteous, let him be righteous still: and he that is holy, let him be holy still.

This surprising fiat is apparently spoken by the Lord Himself. Although the angel was the speaker in verse 9, it is clear that Christ is speaking in verses 12-16. The transition apparently occurs between verses 9 and 10, when the angel had exhorted John to worship God only. Verse 10 begins with: "And He saith... ," evidently telling us that it is that God-to-be-worshiped who is now speaking.

Thus the solemn declaration of this verse becomes all the more serious, and vitally important. It is inserted in context between two assertions of urgency and imminency, "the time is at hand"; and then, "behold, I come quickly" (vv. 10, 12). That is, in view of the certainty of the coming of the Lord and the uncertainty of the time, all men everywhere should evaluate their lives in light of the coming judgments that have just been revealed, as well as all the blessings that have been promised, and then behave accordingly.

It is an amazing paradox of human character that the preaching of the gospel of Christ draws and wins some while at the same time it repels and hardens others. "To the one we are the savour of death unto death; and to the other the savour of life unto life" (2 Corinthians 2:16). "For the preaching of the cross is to them that perish foolishness; but unto us which are saved it is the power of God" (1 Corinthians 1:18). Although a great multitude will be saved during the judgments of the great tribulation (Revelation 7:9, 14), there will be even more who determine to resist all the more stubbornly (Revelation 6:15-17; 8:20, 21; 16:9). Similarly today the preaching or reading of the Book of Revelation will bring great blessing to many but will repel others, eliciting from them only ridicule or anger. At the time of the end, "many shall be purified, and made white, and tried; but the wicked shall do wickedly: and none of the wicked shall understand; but the wise shall understand" (Daniel 12:10).

Thus an awesome principle is enunciated here. The greater the awareness of the full implications of the gospel, including its ultimate consummation, the more clearcut will be its divisive impacts. Nevertheless, it must still be proclaimed. The Lord is saying, in effect: "Whatever you do, guard and proclaim the words of this prophecy: some of the wicked, when they hear, will be all the more confirmed in their wickedness. So be it! There are also those godly men and women who will be greatly blessed and more firmly fixed in their godly disposition."

The adverb "still" could even be understood in the sense of "more." "Let him that is unjust, that is, 'unrighteous,' become more unrighteous." In contrast, "let the righteous man become still more righteous." Such indeed will often be the result of the study of this marvelous book of the unveiled future, a book which generates fright on the one hand, delight on the other.

The "filthy" ones of whom the Lord speaks are not merely those who are unwashed. Rather, they are the morally filthy, the depraved. The "holy" are those who are sanctified in both heart and life, consecrated to the will of God by the Holy Spirit.

This fixation and development of character will apparently continue throughout eternity. In the lake of fire, wicked and depraved men will continue in their wickedness and depravity forever, with the worm of corruption never dying and their tormented spirits never resting. Such a terrible environment is itself a "world of iniquity . . . set on fire of hell" (James 3:6).

But, in wonderful contrast, all who have been granted true righteousness and holiness, through faith in Christ, have the blessed prospect of eternal growth in that "righteousness and true holiness" (Ephesians 4:24) in which they were created.

Revelation 22:12.   And, behold, I come quickly; and my reward is with me, to give every man according as his work shall be.

No less than six times does the Lord promise in this book that He will "come quickly." Twice it is a warning (Revelation 2:5, 16), four times a promise (Revelation 3:11; 22:7, 12, 20). Twice He indicates He will "come as a thief" (Revelation 3:3; 16:15), again first as a threat, then as a promise. Twice He says that John is being shown "things which must shortly come to pass" (Revelation 1:1; 22:6).

Thus there is a real sense of urgency throughout the book, along with an air of expectancy, looking for the imminent return of Christ. Setting of an exact date is not warranted; rather, the believer should always be expecting Him at any moment, ordering his life in the light of that blessed hope. The entire sequence of events narrated in the Book of Revelation, at least from the fourth chapter on, will begin suddenly and then proceed quickly to their grand consummation.

Further, when the Lord does come, He will bring with Him rewards to present to His faithful servants, rewards to be apportioned in accordance with their works. This, of course, is the promise of many Scriptures: salvation is apart from works, but rewards are according to works. The wicked shall be judged ("condemned") according to their works (Revelation 20:13), but the righteous rewarded in accordance with their works. Such rewards will be granted at the judgment seat of Christ (2 Corinthians 5:10) and will be based, not on the quantity, but the "sort" or "quality" of the works (1 Corinthians 3:13-15). And all this will be accomplished when Christ returns and sets up His throne above the earth (Revelation 4:2).

Revelation 22:13.   I am Alpha and Omega, the beginning and the end, the first and the last.

For the fourth time (Revelation 1:8, 11; 21:6; 22:13) the Lord Jesus calls Himself by the remarkable name "Alpha and Omega." Twice near the beginning of the book, twice near the ending of the book, the Lord reminds us that He is the beginning and the ending. From everlasting to everlasting, He is God (Psalm

90:2). He was the Creator, and He is the Consummator. He was "before all things" (Colossians 1:17) and He is the "heir of all things" (Hebrews 1:2), the First and the Last. Three times He calls Himself "the beginning and the ending" (Revelation 1:8; 21:6; 22:13) and four times "the first and the last" (Revelation 1:11, 17; 2:8; 22:13).

The Apostle John, in fact, in his five New Testament books refers to "the beginning," in connection with Christ, referring to the creation, no less than twelve times, first of all in John 1:1: "In the beginning was the Word." The Lord Jesus is both Creator and Revelator. The very fact of creation by the Lord leads to the fact of revelation by the Lord, since He would not create without a purpose, nor would He leave that purpose unrevealed to those whom He had created in His own image. The living Word is revealed by the written Word, through human writings in human language, divinely inspired. In Genesis He is the Alpha; in Revelation, He is the Omega, with sixty-four other wonderful "letters" in the books between, all conveying to man the glorious plan and purpose of his Creator. It is foundational to know Him as Maker; it is salvational to know Him as Redeemer, Friend and Lord; it is motivational to know Him as coming King.

Revelation 22:14.   Blessed are they that do his commandments, that they may have right to the tree of life, and may enter in through the gates into the city.

This is the seventh and last of the great "beatitudes" of the Book of Revelation (see also Revelation 1:3; 14:13; 16:15; 19:9; 20:6; 22:7). The Lord once again emphasizes the twofold division of all mankind. These are the saved and the lost, those who can and cannot enter the holy city. The righteous will be eternally righteous and the unjust forever unjust (v. 11). The Holy Scriptures are now almost complete, and the Lord must convey a final urgent warning and one more gracious invitation and promise, before the last Amen.

The Lord's final promise of blessing is to them "that do his commandments," assuring them the right of entry to the holy city and to the tree of life. However, certain of the ancient manuscripts differ from the received text at this point, rendering the verse in some such fashion as: "Blessed are those who wash their robes, that they may have the right to the tree of life..." (New American Standard Version).

There is, of course, an earlier reference to the tribulation saints who "washed their robes, and made them white in the blood of the Lamb" (Revelation 7:14). Also, the Scriptures plainly teach that salvation is by God's grace, not by the keeping of commandments.

However, there are also two other references in Revelation to keeping God's commandments. " . . . the remnant of her seed, which keep the commandments of God, and have the testimony of Jesus Christ" (Revelation 12:17). "Here is the patience of the saints: here are they that keep the commandments of God, and the faith of Jesus" (Revelation 14:12).

Further, there are at least ten other references in John's writings to "keeping his commandments" (John 14:15, 21; 15:10 (2); 1 John 2:3, 4; 3:22, 24; 5:2, 3). Even though one is not saved through keeping commandments, it is surely true that those who are saved will love His commandments and sincerely try to keep them. The Lord Jesus said: "If you love me, keep my commandments" (John 14:15). "If ye keep my commandments, ye shall abide in my love" (John 15:10). In John's epistle, these strong words occur: "And hereby we do know that we know him, if we keep his commandments. He that saith, I know him, and keepeth not his commandments, is a liar, and the truth is not in him" (1 John 2:3, 4). There are many other references that say essentially the same thing.

Thus the weight of internal evidence, as in so many other disputed renderings, turns out to be strongly in favor of the King James translation after all. It is only those who keep His commandments who have right to the tree of life, not because they have obeyed the commandments, but because their saving faith in Christ has both impelled and enabled them to keep His commandments. Their faith cannot be seen outwardly, but their love of Christ's commandments has demonstrated to all the genuineness of their inward faith.

The first and greatest commandment, of course, is the love of God (Matthew 22:37), and "we love him, because he first loved us" (1 John 4:19). "And this is his commandment, that we should believe on the name of his Son Jesus Christ, and love one another, as he gave us commandment" (1 John 3:23). Those who go in and out of the holy city and who partake of the wonderful tree of life are surely those who love the Lord Jesus Christ and who, therefore, love His commandments and His perfect will.

Revelation 22:15.   For without are dogs, and sorcerers, and whoremongers, and murderers, and idolaters, and whosoever loveth and maketh a lie.

Those who love the Lord and keep His commandments can enter the city, for their names are in the Lamb's book of life, and they have been redeemed by His blood. But there is a far greater number (Matthew 7:13, 14) who will never enjoy the delights of the new earth. Their names are not in the book of life (Revelation 21:27) and they have been confined forever to the lake of fire (Revelation 20:15).

Here again are listed some of the prominent categories of sinners who must suffer eternally in hell (note also Revelation 21:8, 27). The first group listed here is given the harsh appellation of "dogs," evidently a pejorative describing a particularly obnoxious group of people. A similar metaphor occurs in Philippians 3:2: "Beware of dogs, beware of evil workers, beware of the concision." The term probably could be applied to various types of men whose character betakes in one way or another of certain doglike behaviors. Isaiah speaks of the unfaithful teachers in Israel as "dumb dogs, they cannot bark; sleeping, lying down, loving to slumber," and then as "greedy dogs which can never have enough" (Isaiah 56:10, 11).

An even more unsavory figure is used in Deuteronomy 23:17, 18: "There shall be no whore of the daughters of Israel, nor a sodomite of the sons of Israel. Thou shalt not bring the hire of a whore, or the price of a dog, into the house of the Lord thy God for any vow: for even both these are abomination unto the Lord thy God." The term "dog" is obviously used here as a synonym for "sodomite," and indeed the word was used in ancient Israel as a euphemism for a male prostitute in the licentious temple worship of the heathen In fact, Gentiles as a group were sometimes insultingly called "dogs" by the Israelites, probably because of their association with such practices. The prohibition here against bringing a whore or a sodomite into the house of the Lord is clearly a warning against turning the true temple of God into a heathen temple, and this answers to the barring of "dogs," or sodomites, from the new Jerusalem.

The sin of homosexuality, as well as prostitution of any kind, is "abomination unto the Lord," and "whatsoever worketh abomination" shall not enter into the city (Revelation 21:27). In this passage, these "dogs" are grouped with "sorcerers," also associated with pagan religious ceremonies and their use of drugs, as discussed before, and with "whoremongers" "and idolaters," all of which are associated together in terms of the wicked sexual practices associated with the religious worship of the heathen peoples in biblical days.

But note how modern all these sins are, as well. Consider the amazing revival of acceptability in modern "Christendom" of homosexuality as well as sexual permissiveness in general, associated so commonly today again with drugs and occult paganism, not to mention idolatrous covetousness and even blatant idol worship. All show that John was writing in the context of the last days as much as he was of apostolic times. "Murderers" are in the list as well, those who destroy bodies as well as those who destroy souls. And modern technological, intellectual civilization has experienced the greatest murder rates of any period of history. And once again, lest anyone feel self-righteous because of freedom from such gross sins, the Lord adds liars to the list as well (compare Revelation 21:8, 27). Unless forgiven and cleansed by the blood of Christ, those who practice lying will also be barred from the city and its tree of life.

Closing the Book of God

In this last section of the last chapter of the last book of the Holy Scriptures, the Lord Jesus Christ gives a final invitation to salvation, as well as a final warning not to change or to augment even a word of Scripture, and then a final promise of His imminent return. He has revealed to us all the great events of the future throughout the remainder of the Church Age, the tribulation, the millennium, and the last judgment. The new earth will come, and the new Jerusalem, and we have been given just a glimpse of the glories of the ages to come. But nothing in all this grand epic can be more urgent and more important than these final words with which the Lord Jesus terminates His written revelation to man.

Revelation 22:16.   I Jesus have sent mine angel to testify unto you these things in the churches. I am the root and the offspring of David, and the bright and morning star.

There has been no mention of the Church since the beginning of Revelation 4. After the letters to the seven churches, representing all the churches of the Church Age, and the events described in them, the institution of the local church seems to have vanished from the scene. No churches are seen in the Book of Revelation during the tribulation or the millennium, nor are they mentioned even in the new earth. In the latter, of course, all the resurrected inhabitants of the new Jerusalem seem to correspond to the Bride of Christ, which is the "church of the firstborn, assembled in heaven." In this present world, the "church" is an assembly "called out" from the world. The very word in the Greek *(ecclesia)* means "called-out ones." In the new world, on the other hand, all people will be the people of God, and all the ungodly will have been "cast out."

As far as the tribulation is concerned, there will probably still be many liberal religious organizations calling themselves churches, but all true churches will have been raptured at the coming of Christ to the earth's atmosphere, so these "liberal churches" are accordingly not even identified as churches. These will all be amalgamated in the syncretistic religious organization of the great harlot Babylon and will themselves be eliminated when the worldwide religious worship of the beast is ordained at the middle of the tribulation.

Now that the Book of Revelation is almost complete, however, the Lord again calls attention to the fact that it is intended primarily for instruction of the true churches, during our present age, concerning things to come. It was, indeed, John's letter to the churches (Revelation 1:4), but it also came from the angel (Revelation 1:1) and from the Holy Spirit to each church (Revelation 2:7). Preeminently it was from Christ Himself, who had purchased each church with His own blood (Acts 20:28) and who had sent the angel to convey through John all these wonderful revelations to it.

Then comes a final and unique identification of Himself, the last of the many distinctive names by which He is called in Scripture. Although the churches, including the seven churches of Asia, were by this time largely composed of Gentile believers, the Lord was still lovingly solicitous of His ancient people Israel, and so He would remind the churches once more that He was still a kinsman of King David, both His progenitor and His descendant.

He had already been called a "root of David" (see on Revelation 5:5); now

He also calls Himself David's "offspring" (Greek *genos,* a word which can carry a variety of meanings depending on the context, all the way from that of an immediate child to the much broader concept of "nation" or "kindred"). The claim is actually that of being the God/man. There is no other way that one could be both an ancestor and descendant of the same person. Jesus Christ is both David's Lord and David's son (Matthew 22:41-46). He is Creator of all nations, yet specially identified with His chosen nation, occupying forever both the throne of the universe and the throne of Israel.

The final title is "bright and morning star." This title is nowhere else applied to Christ, so it would seem that a special significance is intended in its use here at the very end of the Scriptures, relating the climactic end of the purposes and works of God. This is also the only occurrence of a unique word for "morning" (Greek *orthrinos,* a term applied by the Greeks primarily to Venus, in the brilliant rising of the planet in the early dawn). When Christ had promised the "morning star" to the overcomers (Revelation 2:28), He had used an entirely diferent word (Greek *proinos)* for "morning." Here he identifies Himself as the special and unique *bright* morning star.

The angels of God are frequently called "stars" in Scripture, and on one occasion were called "morning stars" (Job 38:7). There was one angel, however, identified as "Lucifer, son of the morning" (Isaiah 14:12), who had led the heavenly rebellion against God and who, undoubtedly, is identical with Satan, that old serpent. The name "Lucifer" is translated in many versions as "Day-star," referring again especially to Venus, the brilliant "star" of early dawn (Hebrew *heylel,* the bright star of the dawning).

These two words are used only once each in the Bible: *heylel* in the Old Testament, referring to Satan, and *orthrinos* in the New Testament referring to Christ, with both connecting symbolically with the bright rising dawn-star.

The conclusion seems inescapable that the Lord Jesus intended for this unique appellation to call final attention to the fact that *He,* not Satan, was the rising star whose coming would herald the dawn of eternal day. The entire history of the world and the entire Word of God had been occupied, directly or indirectly, with the great conflict of the ages between Christ and Satan, the seed of the woman and the great red dragon. Satan had claimed to be the rising star of the heavens, who would exalt his throne above the stars of God and ascend above the heights of the clouds (Isaiah 14:13, 14), but now his star had fallen from heaven, and he was entombed forever in the lake of fire.

The Lord Jesus Christ, on the other hand, was the true morning star, the "bright" morning star, the one whose light would never be dimmed and could never be cast out of the sky. This is, thus, a blessed reminder to all His people in the churches, that they should watch through the night for His coming, not being led astray by Lucifer, who had aspired to rise above God but whose rebellion would soon be put down. Satan would deceive many, in fact, the "whole world"

(Revelation 12:9), but we need not be "ignorant of his devices" (2 Corinthians 2:11). If he is faithfully "resisted" in proper knowledge of who he is and who Christ is, he will flee (James 4:7). Thus it is, whether or not they have understood the full significance of the term, the redeemed people of Christ have, through the ages, always loved and rejoiced in this glorious name of their Savior, "the bright and morning star."

Revelation 22:17.   And the Spirit and the bride say, Come. And let him that heareth say, Come. And let him that is athirst come. And whosoever will, let him take the water of life freely.

The immediate response to this gracious and triumphant word from the Lord Jesus is a mighty cry from the Holy Spirit of God and from the holy city, the bride (Revelation 21:2, 9, 10). It is as though the glorious city itself calls out its invitation for all the world to hear. But then, also, this cry is anticipated even in this present age as the Holy Spirit, indwelling each believer (whose home and citizenship positionally are already in the new Jerusalem) utters His invitation by way of the heartfelt emotion of the believer. Their souls and lips alike earnestly and continually call out, "Come!" The vision is of the future, but the future issues its plea even in the present. No doubt, it is first of all addressed to the Lord Jesus Himself. Three times in this chapter, He has promised to "come quickly" (verses 7, 12, 20) and the final exhortation is clearly directed to Him: "Even so, come, Lord Jesus" (v. 20). All through the centuries the Holy Spirit has wrought within each believer's heart an earnest desire for the Lord's return. In fact Christ Himself exhorted us to watch and long for His return (Luke 21:35-40). The Apostle Paul indicated we should "love his appearing" (2 Timothy 4:8).

This plea to Christ to come is evidently the only recorded prayer of the Holy Spirit. Possibly it is especially this prayer of which the apostle speaks in Romans 8:26: "Likewise the Spirit also helpeth our infirmities: for we know not what we should pray for as we ought: but the Spirit itself maketh intercession for us with groanings which cannot be uttered," while "we ourselves groan within ourselves, waiting for the adoption, to wit, the redemption of our body" (Romans 8:23). Furthermore, "he that hath an ear, let him hear" (Revelation 2:7) and, as he hears and receives the blessing promised to those who truly hear (with the heart) the words of this prophecy (Revelation 1:3), the one who hears also must surely join in the earnest plea for Christ to come.

But there is another side to this invitation. Not only do the Spirit and the Bride and the new hearer desire Christ to come back to the world: they also long for the world to come back to Christ. So the invitation is like the two sides of a coin. On the one hand, it is, "Come, Lord Jesus!" On the other, it is "Come to the Lord Jesus!"

The two invitations are certainly complementary. In the last days, men will scoff: "Where is the promise of his coming?" (2 Peter 3:4). But He has not forgotten. "The Lord is not slack concerning his promise, as some men count slackness; but is longsuffering to usward, not willing that any should perish, but that all should come to repentance" (2 Peter 3:9). If we are, indeed, "looking for and hasting unto the coming [or "hastening the coming"] of the day of God" (2 Peter 3:12), we should be seeking by all means to invite men to Christ. "Account that the longsuffering of our Lord is salvation" (2 Peter 3:15). When He returns, He will "reconcile all things unto himself" (Colossians 1:20) but, until then, He "hath committed unto us the word of reconciliation," so that "we pray you in Christ's stead, be ye reconciled to God" (2 Corinthians 5:19, 20).

Thus the invitation to "come," goes out also to all men who need Christ, going out through the Spirit, through the Bride, and through each hearer of this gracious word. Men and women need the pure water of everlasting life for their thirsty souls and the supply is abundant for the taking. "There is a river, the streams whereof shall make glad the city of God, the holy place of the tabernacles of the most High. God is in the midst of her; she shall not be moved" (Psalm 46:4, 5).

Furthermore, the invitation is to "whosoever will." The mystery of God's election ultimately can only be explained and revealed through the divine perspective of God Himself, who alone knows the end from the beginning and who, therefore, "worketh all things after the counsel of his own will" (Ephesians 1:11). Our minds are of mere creatures in space and time, but His Mind *created* space and time, and we therefore cannot at present fathom matters which relate to His own omniscience. Whether, and how He conditions and constrains our wills to conform to His will, we simply cannot know and it is presumptuous for us to try to explain divine prerogatives in human terms.

But we do know this, for He has said it! If any person has any least desire to taste the water of life, he can come. In fact, he is urged to come, to drink deeply, to plunge into the great river proceeding out of the throne of God and of the Lamb, and then never thirst again!

Revelation 22:18.   For I testify unto every man that heareth the words of the prophecy of this book, If any man shall add unto these things, God shall add unto him the plagues that are written in this book.

Now, as the book of prophecy is complete, the Lord Jesus gives a most sober and serious warning concerning what has been revealed and written. He has told us everything He intends to tell us; therefore, let no man or woman or angel presume ever to come with additional revelation from God. We have the actual words of the Lord (Greek *logos,* same word as translated "sayings" in v. 7), and He has promised to bless all who keep them. Precise words are needed to convey precise thoughts; we will think the thoughts He desires us to think if we believe the words He says, and no other words are needed or appropriate.

Therefore, He promises an extremely severe judgment on those who ignore this warning. If anyone presumes to come forward with some supposed new "revelation" and claims it to be from God, that very fact will demonstrate that he does not really know the Lord at all. Therefore, since he has not "kept the word of my patience," the Lord cannot apply to such a one His promise to "keep [them] from the hour of temptation, which shall come upon all the world, to try them that dwell upon the earth" (Revelation 3:10). Even though he or she may profess to be a Christian, he will not be raised to meet the Lord at the rapture of the Church, but will instead be "cast . . . into a bed . . . into great tribulation" (Revelation 2:22). The "plagues that are written in this book" are, of course, unique to this book and to the world in its coming time of great tribulation, so this can only mean that such false prophets will participate in that period of travail.

Some may suppose that the warning only applies to someone who would suggest adding, say, a chapter or two to the Book of Revelation, but not some completely new "book of Scripture." This interpretation, however, would only trivialize the whole matter. John was a very old man at the time he wrote and he was well known personally to all the seven churches of Asia. It is obvious that no one would ever venture to come forward with a new appendix supposed to be added to John's Book of Revelation. Such an imposter would immediately be branded a liar and a charlatan, even without this warning at the end of John's book. Consequently it is not such a trivial possibility as this about which the Lord was concerned.

However, the danger was indeed very real that false prophets would arise later and would come to the churches with epistles and gospels and apocalypses which they would claim had been received by divine inspiration. Such people might ask that their words be accepted as new Scriptures, thus leading people away from "the foundation of the apostles and prophets, Jesus Christ himself being the chief corner stone" (Ephesians 2:20). John was the last of the apostles, and the Apostle Paul had said that "prophecies, they shall fail [same word as "vanish away"] . . . when that which is perfect [that is, "complete"] is come" (1 Corinthians 13:8, 10). Now that all of Christ's revelation concerning all the ages to come had finally been delivered to the churches through His last living Apostle, the beloved John, the Scriptures had been completed. It would be the height of presumption, even blasphemy, for anyone to come along later and pretend to "add unto these things." The very act would prove him or her to be a false prophet.

If anyone questions this, let him say, then, how else would God ever be able to tell us when His revelation was complete. It would have to be open-ended, and the churches would have no way of ever distinguishing the false and the true. The New Testament contains many warnings of false prophets and false teachers who would arise, presuming to speak for God but actually undermining the foundational witness of His true prophets and apostles (Matthew 24:24; Galatians 1:8, 9; 2 Corinthians 11:13-15; 2 Peter 2:1-3). The danger was very real, and John himself had previously warned his readers concerning them (1 John 4:1). The entire history of the church, from apostolic days to these latter days, has been plagued with such false prophets and their supposed "revelations." Some, such as Mohammed, have led whole nations away from the truth, and the total effect of all of them has been incalculably tragic. No wonder, therefore, that the Lord appends such a sober warning and severe penalty concerning this deadly danger to the final revelation which He would give through His last apostle.

One question might be asked, however. How could such false prophets as Mohammed, Joseph Smith, Mary Baker Eddy and others go through the plagues of the great tribulation when they were dead long before the great tribulation began? The plethora of pseudoprophets plaguing Christendom in the last generation could go into the tribulation, but what about the false prophets of previous generations? This problem is probably resolved, however, in the fact that there are varieties and degrees of punishments reserved for all who enter the lake of fire. To the extent that individuals may not have "received the due reward of their deeds" in this life (Luke 23:41), there is an eternity of equalization still awaiting them.

In any case, there is surely a most grave punishment specified here by the Lord for anyone who would add anything to the final and complete written Word of God, as consummated here in the wonderful Book of Revelation, the final inspired record of the great future events that will transpire when the Lord returns. In view of the latter-day proliferation of all kinds of cults and winds of doctrine which are now sweeping the world, most of them based on some great charismatic personage and his claims to divine illumination and authority, the warning is more needed today than ever before.

Revelation 22:19.   And if any man shall take away from the words of the book of this prophecy, God shall take away his part out of the book of life, and out of the holy city, and from the things which are written in this book.

Now if it is a crime of deadly seriousness to add to the words of Scripture, it is even more wicked and dangerous to take away from them. Adding false scripture to true Scripture at least leaves the latter, with its saving gospel, intact. Trying to "cut off" (same Greek word as "take away") certain unwanted words of God from the Bible, on the other hand, will dilute or destroy its saving message and living truth. That is why the influences of the cults, with their pseudorevelations, as bad as they are, still are not as deadly as those of the so-called "liberals," who have specialized in cutting out or explaining away all those portions of the Holy Scriptures which offend their humanistic prejudices and evolutionary presuppositions. All of the Scriptures have been attacked by such people, but none so much as the books of Genesis and Revelation.

The cults add to the words of the book of this prophecy, the liberals take away from them, and both are regarded by the Lord as blasphemies deserving of the most serious punishment. "The Scripture cannot be broken," He said (John 10:35).

Moses had issued a like warning concerning his own divinely inspired writings in the Pentateuch. "Ye shall not add to the word which I command you, neither shall ye diminish ought from it" (Deuteronomy 4:2). That is, no later "editor" or "redactor" should ever presume to change or rearrange the words of Genesis, Exodus, Leviticus, Numbers, or Deuteronomy. In view of the high veneration in which Moses and the Law were held by ancient Israel, and the meticulous care with which the scribes copied the manuscripts of their Torah, we can be completely confident that these writings have been transmitted accurately to us since the time of Moses himself. If not, it is inconceivable that any such redactor would include Deuteronomy 4:2 in his edited version of Moses' writings. Yet, modern "higher critics" have arrogantly done to these writings exactly what Moses commanded not to be done, and they have presumed to ascribe their present form to a variety of later writers and editors, merely to suit their own evolutionary fancies.

Moses' warning, of course, applied strictly only to his own books, and did not preclude God's later use of other prophets to convey other scriptures to God's people. In fact, prophesying of Christ's coming, God said through Moses: "I will raise them up a Prophet from among their brethren, like unto thee, and will put my words in his mouth; and he shall speak unto them all that I shall command him. And it shall come to pass, that whosoever will not hearken unto my words which he shall speak in my name, I will require it of him" (Deuteronomy 18:18, 19). That this prophecy had been fulfilled in Christ was confirmed by the Apostle Peter, in his great sermon at the temple gate (Acts 3:20-26).

The Lord Jesus, in turn, had called His own apostles and prophets, had given them the words His Father commanded (John 17:8) and had promised these words would all be brought to their remembrance through the Holy Spirit (John 14:26), so that they in return could record them for others. He promised also that the Holy Spirit "will guide you into all truth" and that "he will shew you things to come" (John 16:13). "He shall receive of mine, and shall shew it unto you" (John 16:14).

This New Testament revelation was to be given through His chosen apostles and prophets, "Which in other ages was not made known unto the sons of men, as it is now revealed unto his holy apostles and prophets by the Spirit" (Ephesians 3:5). In fact, these apostles and prophets to whom were now being given the New Testament Scriptures were said to constitute the foundation of the great "building" of living believers which was to be erected by the Holy Spirit (Ephesians 2:19-22). Once the foundation is laid, of course, then it does not continue to be laid at intervals during the erection of the superstructure. The apostles, all of whom, as one condition of their apostleship, had seen the Lord after His resurrection (1 Corinthians 9:1), laid the foundation of the Church in the Scriptures they wrote, under the guidance of the Holy Spirit. John was the last of these, so his final book is the last block in the foundation. Nothing more is to be added, because it would be superfluous and distracting; nothing can be removed because it would undermine the structure and eventually cause the whole building to collapse.

The penalty for removing anything from the "book" (Greek *biblos,* the word from which we get "Bible," the *book)* is nothing less than removal of one's name from the Lamb's book of life. Those who add extraneous pseudorevelations to the completed revelation of God may be cast into the great tribulation, but there may still exist the possibility of repentance on their part before they die. Those, on the other hand, who presume to judge and reject any part of God's true revelation will, by that very attitude, demonstrate that they are irreconcilably antagonistic to the revealed will of God. They have read and understood the Word of God and then repudiated it. Therefore, their names, as with all other names, which had been entered in the book of life at the time of conception, sadly will be removed from the book (Revelation 3:5) by the Lord whose word they refused, and they must then be consigned forever to the lake of fire (Revelation 20:15).

This constitutes a most serious indictment and sober warning to any who would tamper with the Holy Scriptures. Lest anyone still object that it applies only to the Book of Revelation, it may be noted, historically, that the various atheists and humanists, as well as the motley array of modernists, liberals, higher critics, and other pseudointellectuals in Christendom who have rejected or questioned, ridiculed or allegorized away the books of Daniel, Isaiah, Jonah, Acts, Peter, or any other books of the Bible have also, invariably, done the same to the Book of Revelation, to the Book of Genesis, and the other books of the Pentateuch. The first and last books of the Bible have constituted a touchstone, as it were, so that the attitude of men and women toward these books always seems to determine their real attitude toward all the Scriptures. Therefore, the Lord had Moses stress the divine integrity of his writings (Deuteronomy 4:2) and John stress the inviolability of Revelation.

Not only will such people cut themselves off from the book of life but also, as the Lord reminds them, from all the blessings that He wanted them to have. He has "no pleasure in the death of him that dieth" (Ezekiel 18:32), and has prepared a beautiful eternal home with indescribable joys and satisfactions, as very sketchily reported in John's book, for "whosoever will." For those who "will not," however, He will not compel them to come. Since they have rejected His Word, thus rejecting Him as He is, perhaps professing all the while to believe in "another Jesus" of their own invention, they would be indescribably miserable if forced to abide in His presence. Sadly, therefore, He must separate their names from His book, and them from the blessings of His presence, forever, in the lake of fire.

Not only should humanists and religious liberals take warning from this serious pronouncement. There are many professing evangelical believers who consider it fashionable and intellectual to "dialogue" with unbelieving critics and often even to compromise Scripture in order to retain their favor. The Apostle Peter also warns against the real possibility of such pseudointellectuals becoming "they that are unlearned and unstable [who] wrest, as they do also the other scriptures, unto their own destruction" (2 Peter 3:16).

Only the Lord knows, when the line of irreconcilable unbelief has been crossed, and one's name has been erased from the book of life. But such a warning, at the very end of the Bible, surely should constrain each reader to examine his heart, and to be sure that he believes without question or distortion "every word of God" (Proverbs 30:5).

Revelation 22:20.   He which testifieth these things saith, Surely I come quickly. Amen. Even so, come, Lord Jesus.

One last promise to return quickly, and the great prophetic testimony of Jesus Christ (Revelation 1:2; 19:10) is ended. "These things" include all the events and promises and warnings of the Book of Revelation, culminating in the grave injunction not to change even a word of the completed Scriptures. Even though His promise to return was made almost 1,900 years ago, His coming is always imminent, and each passing year brings it nearer. From the standpoint of eternity, His coming will be very soon, even though on the scale of human time it may seem long delayed. In any case, His coming is sure. And when He does come, all the events prophesied to accompany His coming, as testified by Him in this book, will be fulfilled speedily and certainly.

To this wonderful promise, John can only reply with a deep-felt "So be it!" He had seen as no one before or since has ever seen, the glories of the world to come, and he could only henceforth long earnestly for the day of its reality to hasten. The final prayer of the Bible, beseeching the Lord to come quickly as He had promised, was John's prayer, but it has also been echoed on the lips of countless Christians through the centuries ever since. "I will come again," the Lord had promised, even before his death on Calvary (John 14:3), and believers will continue to utter this prayer until the very moment He returns.

And even though Christians in every generation have always, quite properly, anticipated His possible coming in their own lifetimes, it is surely true that believers of this present generation are expecting His imminent return with greater conviction and in greater numbers than ever before in history. More believers are praying for His return than ever, and perhaps this in itself may betoken His soon coming.

Revelation 22:21.   The grace of our Lord Jesus Christ be with you all. Amen.

In closing, John adds his personal greeting and prayer for his own friends in the seven churches, who will soon be reading and hearing his amazing record of things to come. The Holy Spirit, however, is also sending this same message to all churches everywhere, and He would convey the same greeting and exhortation to them, for there is no more fitting way to close the Book of Revelation, and the entire written Word of God, than this.

"The grace of our Lord Jesus Christ!" Paul begins his epistles (not including Hebrews) with a similar greeting (Romans 1:7; 1 Corinthians 1:3; 2 Corinthians 1:2; Galatians 1:3; Ephesians 1:2; Philippians 1:2; Colossians 1:2; 1 Thessalonians 1:1; 2 Thessalonians 1:2; 1 Timothy 1:2; 2 Timothy 1:2; Titus 1:4; and Philemon 3), and he ends each epistle (including Hebrews) with a similar farewell (Romans 16:24; 1 Corinthians 16:23; 2 Corinthians 13:14; Galatians 6:18; Ephesians 6:24; Philippians 4:23; Colossians 4:18; 1 Thessalonians 5:28; 2 Thessalonians 3:18; 1 Timothy 6:21; 2 Timothy 4:22; Titus 3:15; Philemon 25; Hebrews 13:25). Peter begins each of his two epistles with a similar salutation (1 Peter 1:2; 2 Peter 1:2) and so does John in one of his (2 John 3). And, of course, John begins his epistle of Revelation with the same testimony: "Grace be unto you, and peace" (Revelation 1:4). The grace of the Lord Jesus Christ illumines every page of the Holy Scriptures.

The Christian life begins by grace, is sustained by grace, and thus should always manifest grace. When we fail, as we often do, there is still forgiveness through grace, for He is "the God of all grace" (1 Peter 5:10), and His "grace is sufficient" (2 Corinthians 12:9). "God is able to make all grace abound" (2 Corinthians 9:8) to all who believe and obey His Word.

And in the ages to come, John's simple farewell prayer for his friends will become a magnificent prophecy fulfilled in all the redeemed. The "exceeding riches of his grace" will be manifest toward us in all "the ages to come" (Ephesians 2:7) through Christ Jesus; and "the grace of our Lord Jesus Christ" will, indeed be with us, and upon us, and in us, forever.

To which we can only answer, with John, and with deep thanksgiving: "Amen!"

Index of Subjects

Scripture Index

9:3-5	211, 289
9:4	59
9:7	289
9:15	177
9:23, 24	210
9:24	142
9:27	194, 334
9:27, 28	82
10:12	416
10:19, 20	210
10:19-22	290
10:22	258
10:25	82
10:26	300
10:26, 27	143
10:27	209, 379, 476
10:28, 29	144
10:29	177, 300
10:30-37	270
10:31	174
10:34, 35	246
10:37	33, 82
11:3	393
11:5	194
11:10	370, 438, 449
11:16	438
12:2	79, 220, 246
12:6	78
12:22	45, 104, 154, 166, 419, 448
12:22, 23	438
12:22-24	259
12:23	47
13:2	45
13:4	261
13:8	300
13:14	438
13:15	102, 104, 142
13:25	489

JAMES

1:12	55, 136
1:17	37
2:19	124
2:20	388, 416
3:2	262
3:6	476
4:7	482
5:1	367
5:1-3	354
5:1-8	82
5:6	367
5:7-9	367
5:17	198

1 PETER

1:1-5	87
1:2	489
1:3-5	434
1:3-7	82
1:4, 5	443
1:6, 7	270
1:7	77
1:12	45, 102, 125, 283
1:14-16	271
1:18-20	96
2:5	38, 74, 103
2:13	218
2:22	262
2:24	420
3:15	227
3:18-20	44
3:19	164
3:19, 20	159
3:20	286
3:21	286, 465
4:11	105
4:17	191, 264
5:8	155, 225, 408
5:10	86, 183, 489
5:13	323

2 PETER

1:2	489
1:19-21	20
2:1	52, 313
2:1-3	444
2:3	52
2:4	155, 164, 431
2:7, 8	202
2:15	58
2:17	431
2:18	52
3:2	471
3:3-13	82
3:4	483
3:5	29
3:5-7	287
3:6	29, 166, 429
3:7	29, 393, 426
3:8	206
3:9	152, 161, 183, 483
3:9, 10	381
3:10	29, 314, 429, 430, 436
3:10-12	426, 436
3:12	483
3:13	430, 436
3:15	483
3:16	488